ISBN 978-1-5281-3681-5
PIBN 10914306

PUBLICATIONS

of the

NEW YORK STATE

TEMPORARY EMERGENCY RELIEF ADMINISTRATION

1931 - 1937

VOLUME II

VOLUME II

STATE OF NEW YORK

Temporary Emergency Relief Administration

STATE OFFICE BUILDING, ALBANY, N. Y.

NEW YORK OFFICE, 79 MADISON AVENUE
Telephone—LExington 2-9480

THE STATE IN PUBLIC UNEMPLOYMENT RELIEF

Report of the New York State Temporary Emergency Relief Administration to the Governor and the Legislature on Public Unemployment Relief Expenditures from November 1, 1931 through October 31, 1933, with a Summary of Further Expenditures through January 31, 1934

March 1, 1934

MEMBERS

ALFRED H. SCHOELLKOPF OF BUFFALO, Chairman
SOLOMON LOWENSTEIN OF NEW YORK
CHARLES D. OSBORNE OF AUBURN
JOSEPH P. RYAN OF NEW YORK
HENRY ROOT STERN OF NASSAU COUNTY

FREDERICK I. DANIELS, Executive Director

J. B. LYON COMPANY, PRINTERS, ALBANY, N. Y.

To His Excellency, Herbert H. Lehman, Governor, and to the Honorable Members of the Senate and the Assembly of the State of New York:

In accordance with instructions in Section 21 of Chapter 798 of the Laws of 1931, which directs the Administration to "report to the Governor and the Legislature from time to time in such detail as may be required, the operations of the Administration together with the condition of unemployment and the relief afforded unemployed persons in the State," there is submitted herewith a report on the State's part in public unemployment relief, covering the period from November 1, 1931 through October 31, 1933, together with a summary and brief analysis of what has taken place under the Federal Civil Works program from its start on November 21, 1933 to February 1, 1934.

A detailed report on Relief Activities of City and County Welfare Districts in New York State from November 1, 1931 through December 31, 1933 is in process of preparation.

The present report for the two year period begins with the entrance of the State on a program of public unemployment relief and ends with the last full month of that program before the Federal Civil Works Administration was created. This report of the Administration's stewardship thus presents a history of the State's aid to the municipalities in their increasingly difficult problem of providing for the unemployed, from the beginning of such State aid up to the time that the Federal Civil Works program came into being. It presents, as well, certain trends in unemployment and in relief needs and is intended to offer Legislators and taxpayers a survey of the problems that have confronted the Administration and the manner in which they have been met.

As this report is sent to you the demobilization of the Federal Civil Works program has begun. As yet there has been no announced policy as to the extension of Federal assistance in direct unemployment relief to New York State, the Federal Government's aid in direct unemployment relief having practically ceased with the introduction of the Civil Works program. No prophecy is attempted in this report of the extent of the need that may develop in the coming year for the State to aid the local government units in the relief of those unemployed men and women who through no fault of their own can no longer sustain themselves in the great economic crisis against which we are struggling. The analysis of what has taken place under the Civil Works program, shows that, despite the material lessening of the burden of unemployment relief made possible by that program, the State's share of that burden has grown, and provides a factual picture of the situation as it exists today, on which any State action which may become necessary must be based.

ALFRED H. SCHOELLKOPF of Buffalo, *Chairman*
SOLOMON LOWENSTEIN of New York
CHARLES D. OSBORNE of Auburn
JOSEPH P. RYAN of New York
HENRY ROOT STERN of Nassau County

FOREWORD

State Aid in Relief

New York was the first State to provide substantial assistance to its local units of government in the relief made necessary by the prolonged duration of the economic depression, with its subsequent unemployment. By the Wicks Act, passed in Special Session called by the Honorable Franklin D. Roosevelt, Governor, and effective September 23, 1931, the State of New York declared an emergency existed in which "the public health and safety of the State and of each county, city and town therein was imperilled by the existing and threatened deprivation of a considerable number of their inhabitants of the necessaries of life."

Previous to the Wicks Act unemployment relief in New York State had been provided by the local governments in conjunction with private agencies. It was their inability to continue to meet this problem adequately in the face of a growing need that forced the State to supplement their efforts. The Legislature found State assistance "vitally necessary to supplement the relief work accomplished or to be accomplished locally and to encourage and stimulate local effort in the same direction," appropriated $20,000,000 to this end and created the Temporary Emergency Relief Administration, delegating to it the pioneer task of administering such assistance according to certain broad principles laid down in the Act.

On October 1, 1931 the Temporary Emergency Relief Administration was established and started organization for the gigantic task of administering the Wicks Act which began on November 1, of that year, and still continues. Under the Act local welfare districts were to be reimbursed from State funds for 40 per cent of their Home Relief expenditures and given similar direct assistance for Work Relief in amounts to be determined by the Administration. Provision was made for increasing the rate of Home Relief reimbursement to any municipality whose financial condition made adequate relief otherwise impossible. By Chapter 567 of the Laws of 1932, passed March 31, of that year, Work Relief was placed on an equal basis of reimbursement with Home Relief.

The emergency period was originally defined as extending from November 1, 1931 to June 1, 1932, but because of the continued need has been successively extended until now it includes the period up to February 15, 1935. In March, 1932, the Legislature appropriated an additional $5,000,000 for relief. In the general election in November of that year a $30,000,000 bond issue for relief purposes was voted by the people. In the November, 1933, general election the issuance of a second relief bond issue, of $60,000,000 was approved by the people.

In February, 1933, Federal funds became available through grants by the Reconstruction Finance Corporation and were allotted by the State Administration to local welfare districts that were incapable of financing adequate relief. The total grants from the Reconstruction Finance Corporation amounted to $26,400,000. Subsequently, under the terms of the Federal Emergency Relief Administration Act, until the start of the Federal Civil Works program on November 21, Federal funds were allocated to the State Administration on the basis of one-third of the total public relief expenditures. By this arrangement a total of $37,219,741 of Federal funds was received by the Temporary Emergency Relief Administration for the period ending October 31, 1933, to supplement State and local resources. Additional claims for approximately $4,000,000 are still pending.

Throughout the emergency period it became necessary for the State Administration to assume more and more of the relief burden of the municipalities, until, in October, 1933, to insure that every effort would be made to prevent suffering, the Honorable Herbert H. Lehman, Governor, in consultation with the Legislative leaders announced a uniform policy for the State, by which the State Relief Administration would reimburse local Home and Work Relief expenditures by 66⅔ per cent. This policy of two-thirds reimbursement by the State on relief expenditures has been continned since the institution of the Federal Civil Works program, with the proviso that the localities appropriate for materials under that program the amount of net saving made possible by the Federal Government's absorption of Work Relief into the Civil Works program.

The State Under the Civil Works Administration

From the beginning of the Federal Civil Works program, in November 1933, the State Temporary Emergency Relief Administration accepted the task of acting as the Federal Administration of Civil Works for New York State in order that the unemployed of the State might benefit as quickly as possible from the Federal program. As the State division of the Federal Civil Works

Administration it has acted as the agent of the Federal Government, and in execution of instructions from Washington it has planned and supervised local projects that have resulted in the employment of more than 340,000 men and women throughout the State, of whom about 155,000 were in New York City and 185,000 up-State. Approximately $41,250,000 in Federal wages were distributed up to February 1, 1934. No State funds were used.

The Civil Works Service program, instituted by the Federal Government under the Civil Works Administration, has operated as a relief division for professional and "white collar" groups, and of the figures quoted above accounted for employment of more than 40,000 men and women, who to February 1, were paid about $4,400,000 in salaries and wages by the Federal Government. All men and women employed on the Civil Works Service payroll were required to show need of public assistance.

The Civil Works program, however, which was on an entirely different basis than the Civil Works Service, was of far greater scope, employing nearly 300,000 men and women, who received in wages and salaries approximately $36,850,000 up to February 1. The Federal policy in regard to this major part of the program, made clear at the outset and frequently reiterated, was that the Civil Works Administration was conceived primarily as a recovery as well as a relief program, that wages were to be paid for work done, that ability to do the job was to be the criterion for employment and that need was not to be considered a factor in the placement of applicants. The State division of the Federal Civil Works Administration had no part in the formulation of this policy and in the execution of it has acted solely as the agent of the Federal Government. As a result of this Federal policy the effect of the Civil Works Administration program in reducing relief needs has necessarily been minimal, except at its inception, when it assumed almost the entire burden of Work Relief, which at the time had bulked somewhat larger than Home Relief in expenditures, though not in persons cared for. While it is impossible to estimate the number of families who may have been saved from reliance on public aid by the wages paid out under the Civil Works Administration, it is certain that as the final exhaustion of their resources has forced more and more families to seek public aid their potential wage earners, under the Federal policy, have had to take their mathematical chances with others not in need in the allocation of Civil Works Administration jobs. In the State as a whole the Federal Civil Works Administration has provided only about one job for every six who applied. Those in need who failed of employment necessarily have been forced to turn to the Home Relief rolls.

With the start of the Civil Works Administration program the Federal Government practically stopped its contribution to unemployment relief, the State continuing its two-thirds reimbursement to the local districts without Federal aid. In November, in New York State $12,084,223 was spent on public relief. A comparison of the figures for December, 1933, when the Civil Works Administration program was well under way, with October, 1933, the last complete month before the program began, shows that the drain on State funds for unemployment relief was greater than before. Although the total relief expenditure in December of $7,302,130 was about $4,575,000 less than was spent in October, a reduction made possible by the Civil Works Administration, the State's contribution of two-thirds was about $4,900,000 or approximately $1,800,000 more than it had been in the earlier month. Two-thirds of the smaller figure placed a greater burden on the State than one-third of the larger figure had done. In January, 1934, the total expenditure for public unemployment relief in New York State was $7,271,061, of which approximately $4,850,000 was the State's contribution to the municipalities. Under present conditions the additional load upon the State may be expected to continue.

At the same time the local units of government have not found their burden lighter as they have spent on materials for Civil Works projects approximately the amount they have saved on relief through the Civil Works program.

TWO YEARS OF STATE AID IN UNEMPLOYMENT RELIEF

Public Relief Expenditures of More Than $190,000,000

From November 1, 1931 through October 31, 1933 the local welfare districts reported spending $190,251,491, in public unemployment relief subject to partial reimbursement by the State Temporary Emergency Relief Administration from funds made available to it. During the first year of this period of State co-operation the total public relief expenditure thus reported was $59,701,197. In the second year it was 119 per cent higher, or $130,550,294.* These expenditures were for Home Relief, Work Relief and emergency work on State improvements. Beginning with June, 1933, pursuant to an amendment to the Law enacted by the Legislature, all public relief to unemployed veterans has been subject to reimbursement by the State. From June to October, inclusive, $7,522,981 of the above total provided Home Relief or Work Relief for an average of 44,417 veterans per month.

Home Relief is given through existing county and city public welfare departments as required by the Law, and Work Relief through emergency county and city work bureaus, with local nonpartisan, non-political chairmen and members from the districts. Home Relief is the furnishing of food, shelter, light, heat, clothing, medicine, medical attendance and necessary household supplies in the domicile. Work Relief was in the form of wages for emergency employment on county and municipal projects and on State improvements. With the hourly wage fixed at the local prevailing rate for the type of work done, the State Temporary Emergency Relief Administration ruled that sufficient Work Relief should be assigned to meet the budgetary needs of the family.

Of the total two-year public relief expenditure, approximately $92,600,000, or 48.7 per cent was spent by up-State cities and counties while approximately $97,600,000, or 51.3 per cent was spent by New York City. Of this same total, Work Relief wages paid in cash represented approximately $100,100,000 or 52.7 per cent of the total. Home Relief accounted for approximately $89,100,000, or 47.3 per cent of the total. Almost ten million dollars of the total Work Relief wages was earned on State improvement projects carried on by eighteen State Departments which received allocations from the Temporary Emergency Relief Administration.

* For monthly expenditures see Appendix, Table I.

[9]

Of the 115 welfare districts as defined by the Unemployment Relief Act, 114 have co-operated with the State Administration, the number having increased until January, 1933, since when only one county district comprising 0.3 per cent of the population has not been included.

In the original Unemployment Relief Act the Legislature declared the care of the unemployed to be fundamentally a local problem and at the same time found State aid a necessity because local resources were unable adequately to meet the need. As the relief requirements have mounted the municipalities have found their resources even more inadequate. While there has been a general trend toward making unemployment relief a purely public function instead of a joint responsibility in which private subscription aided, the local governments at the same time have found it more and more difficult to raise revenue from real estate, their chief source of taxation. State and Federal aid to municipalities administered through the Temporary Emergency Relief Adminis- tration in the two-year period have lightened the burden of local real estate by more than 50 per cent of the total cost of relief.

During the two-year period the State Temporary Emergency Relief Administration reimbursed the welfare districts for Home Relief and Work Relief by approximately $100,900,000. The remainder of the expenditure of $190,251,491, or about $89,300,000 has been borne by the cities, counties and towns. In the year ending October 31, 1932 the municipalities carried approximately 55 per cent of the total cost of relief and the State 45 per cent. In the year ending October 31, 1933, approximately 43 per cent of the total cost was met by local funds and 57 per cent by State and Federal funds.

The cities and counties of the State have not shirked their responsibilities in caring for their own unemployed. They have made a noteworthy record in carrying their part of the relief burden. Not only in the provision of relief funds have the local administrative units met the needs to the limit of their ability. Equally deserving of remark is the co-operation which they have given the State Administration in its efforts to raise the standards of relief and to secure efficient and economical administration of public funds.

2,500,000 Receive Relief in Two Years

Approximately 600,000 family groups or non-family persons have received public relief at some time in the two years from

November 1, 1931 through October 31, 1933. This number included a total of at least 2,520,000 individuals, or one out of every five of the population of the State. In the month of October, 1933, 329,572 families or non-family persons received public relief. The 1,342,000 different persons included in this total represent one out of every nine of the State's population. Of this number 625,000 were children under 16 years of age—one-fifth of the total number of children under 16 years in the State.*

These men and women who have been receiving relief are typical Americans from all walks of life. Skilled and unskilled, artisan and laborer, professional and layman have alike been deprived, by an economic cataclysm beyond their control, of work to which their strength and ability entitle them and which their self-respect demands. The assistance which has saved them from defeat and complete loss of morale has been an investment in the future of the community in which they will now be able, by virtue of the aid received, to resume their respected positions when normal conditions are re-established.

There can be no minimizing that the burden of this aid has been and continues to be heavy. During the year ending October 31, 1932, $4.77 was expended for public relief per capita of the population of the State. In the year ending October 31, 1933, the per capita expenditure was $10.40.

From June to October, 1932, inclusive, a monthly average of 147 families or non-family persons received relief per 10,000 of the population of the State. In the year ending October 31, 1933, there was an average of 263 relief cases per month to each 10,000 of the population. In the up-State welfare districts the relief load for the two-year period reached its peak in March, 1933, with an index number of 229 as compared with the basic 100 representing expenditures in January, 1932. In New York City, on the other hand, the highest point in relief expenditures, was reached in June, 1933, with an index figure of 308. Because of the greater stability of expenditures, the up-State figures may be assumed to reflect more accurately the actual relief needs than in New York City where relief expenditures have been affected more largely by variation in the funds available from month to month. For the State as a whole the relief index for October, 1933, shows an increase of 99 per cent over the index for the corresponding month of 1932. The index numbers show that the seasonal relief trends found in normal times have comparatively small influence

---

* For number of families receiving relief, by months, see Appendix, Table II.

in an extended period of general unemployment. Relief expenditures during the summer months of 1933 were higher than those of the preceding winter months. During the depression the main factor in relief expenditure has not been increase in unemployment, nor even the greater relief needs of winter months, but the unpredictable number of families whose resources have been exhausted during long periods of unemployment and who are forced to apply for public aid after perhaps two or three years of self-maintenance with the aid of savings, loans, mortgaging of homes, liquidation of insurance policies and other assets, and credit with merchants for the necessities of life.

The break in the steady rise of relief expenditures in the middle of 1933 lends encouragement to the hope that reemployment has definitely begun to reduce the number of families who reach the end of their resources before they can find some means of self-support.

Economy and Adequacy of Relief

From the inception of the program it has been the object of the Administration to see that the relief dollar was stretched as far as possible in caring for those who because of events beyond their control were unable to care for themselves. In the distribution of the approximately 100,900,000 which went to supplement the relief funds of the local welfare districts from November 1, 1931 through October 31, 1933, the Administration spent $707,543 or less than one per cent for its administrative expenses. These included the salaries of a trained social work staff to help relief bureaus organize and establish policies; of engineers to cooperate in planning valuable work projects suitable for local needs; of advisers on medical services, nutrition and garden activities for the unemployed; and of an auditing staff employed to insure sound business and accounting methods in the local relief bureaus to which the State contributes funds.

At the same time the Administration drew up certain rules to be observed by local relief authorities if they are to receive State aid. These rules require that relief be given the needy without discrimination on grounds of political adherence, religion, race. color, or non-citizenship.

The Administration can report that throughout this emergency, mayors, boards of supervisors and other local authorities have cooperated to an extraordinary degree.

To increase the adequacy of relief through economy the Administration has cooperated with the local relief authorities in problems of organization, purchase and investigation. Its trained field staff has assisted local officials in order that relief might be given the destitute promptly and efficiently and that competent workers might in their careful investigation of need, eliminate any applicants who did not actually require public assistance or no longer required it.

By preparation of schedules showing the estimated cost of food allowances for families of different sizes, by emphasis on the provision of the necessary quantities of foods of various types, with frequent change to include foods most plentiful and economical, the Administration has aided the local districts in the great improvement of relief standards that has taken place since the beginning of the emergency relief period. By calling attention to the possibility of reducing the cost of relief food through contract buying, cooperating with local committees on food costs wherever set up, and negotiating with distributors, it has helped effect these improved standards with a minimum increase in cost. In many up-State cities, for instance, agreements between relief officials and distributors have so materially cut milk prices that in some localities nearly twice as much milk can now be distributed at the same cost.

Subsistence gardens for the unemployed provided by local public welfare departments and industrial concerns with the cooperation of the Administration, aided the unemployed and lightened the relief burden by furnishing vegetables to 14,292 families in 1932 and to 41,149 families in 1933. The estimated value of the produce during the two seasons was $1,434,000. The total cost incurred in connection with these garden projects was approximately $282,000.

In furtherance of the policy of having relief work itself provide further relief wherever practicable, some of the gardens were operated as projects to grow and preserve food for distribution to other relief cases. Similarly relief workers have been employed in making and repairing clothes for relief distribution.

The visiting nurse service, giving work to unemployed nurses and established without overhead in almost sixty communities since February, 1933, by the Administration, has proved an important phase of the economical improvement of relief standards. Between thirty and forty thousand bedside visits a month have been made at an average cost of approximately forty cents, about a third of the figure common among private welfare organizations. Since home nursing has materially reduced the number of cases it has been necessary to hospitalize and has shortened the duration of hospitalization in other cases, the service has released for other relief purposes local welfare funds that would otherwise have had to go to this type of medical care, a charge under Sections 83 and 85 of the Public Welfare Law.

The average relief per family, Home Relief and Work Relief combined, was $30.85 a month in the year ending October 31, 1932. In the up-State welfare districts it was $27.25, and in New York City, $35.90. In the face of a general rise in prices and the necessity of including shelter allowances to more and more families as the depression continued, the average for the State for the year ending October 31, 1933 increased only to $32.68 per family per month; $29.65 in up-State districts and $35.82 in New York City.

Economic Dividends from Relief

When the State Unemployment Relief Act went into effect Work Relief was practically a new venture. New administrative agencies had to be created in each welfare district for this form of relief, since only Home Relief remained the function of the departments of public welfare. During the two years ending October 31, 1933, 110 of the 115 welfare districts in the State had Emergency Work Bureaus which furnished employment during all or part of this period, providing approximately $100,100,000 in Work Relief wages.

Work Relief wages represented approximately 52.7 per cent of the total relief expenditures during the two years. In twelve of the twenty-four months more than half of the relief expenditures were in the form of Work Relief wages. In the month of October, 1933, 150,747 different families received Work Relief aid.

It has been natural and proper that the welfare effect of the program has been paramount. To a great extent, however, this larger purpose has obscured the solid economic value of the work done, apart from the economic value of enabling this group to carry on so that they may again become the ultimate consumers that business so urgently needs today. Hundreds of miles of streets and highways have been built and other hundreds of miles of streets and highways repaired where construction and repair

were needed apart from relief, but where resources were lacking.
Necessary bridges have been constructed, necessary sewers have
been laid and water works improved, and maintenance and repairs
on public canals, docks, baths, hospitals, libraries, city halls,
court houses, police stations, fire houses, and schools have saved
the State and its local divisions millions of dollars in depreciation.

The new projects approved by the Temporary Emergency Relief
Administration from January to October 1933, are typical:

	Per cent of total new projects
Highways	43.1
Utilities and structures	12.8
Sanitation	12.0
Parks and playgrounds	7.6
Water supply	5.3
Clerical and professional	7.8
General public improvements	3.8
Miscellaneous	7.6

A survey for the period from September 1, 1932, to September
1, 1933, in the up-State communities shows that work on streets
and highways accounted for approximately 42 per cent of
expenditures on completed local Work Relief projects. Care and
improvement of parks and playgrounds came next with approximately 16 per cent and others in order: sanitation, 12 per cent;
clerical and professional work, 7 per cent; public works and
buildings, 7 per cent; water supply, 6 per cent; general public
improvements, 4 per cent; and home necessities, the making of
clothing, the growing and preserving of food, etc., for relief
purposes, 3 per cent.

In the same period in New York City improvement of parks
and playgrounds accounted for approximately 38 per cent of
expenditures on completed Work Relief projects; the five Borough
Presidents' projects, divided between streets, sanitation and public
buildings, 23 per cent; clerical and professional, 18 per cent; utili-
ties and public structures, 9 per cent; sanitation, 8 per cent; water
supply, 2 per cent and miscellaneous, 1 per cent.

In addition to these Work Relief projects, in which the
Administration aided the localities, other Work Relief projects
operated under eighteen State Departments that received allocations
from the Administration. Fifty-seven cities and fifty-four counties
supplied workers for these projects from their relief lists, a
monthly average of 25,114 persons being employed. The departments' expenditures in Work Relief wages and the average number
of persons receiving them, follows:

Department	Expenditure	Average number per month receiving work relief wages[a]
Total	$9,726,544.67	25.114
Agriculture and Markets	101,658.97	141
Audit and Control	18,501.33	40
Conservation	4,487,333.72	9,535
Correction	427,616.51	1,216
Education	1,196,020.32	2,615
Executive	248,879.17	889
George Washington Bicentennial Commission	985.69	[b]
Health	234,750.86	395
Insurance	6,814.60	11
Labor	94,250.45	161
Law	10,928.31	21
Mental Hygiene	548,392.37	1,218
National Reemployment Service	13,721.77	101
Public Works	1,602,349.32	7,351
Saratoga Springs Commission	49,021.20	92
Social Welfare	333,518.65	1,134
State	7,731.53	12
Taxation and Finance	254,069.90	310

[a] Based on reports beginning with February, 1933.
[b] Not reported.

Besides providing extra clerical help needed because of an increase of duties in the State Departments, for which no budget provision was made, Work Relief projects have included, construction of a milk house and cantonment at Auburn Prison; drainage of a quicksand area and grading at Attica Prison, eliminating the escape hazard; excavation of rocks offering escape hazard and conversion into parking space at Sing Sing; construction of concrete warehouses for Division of Canals and Waterways in Utica at a saving to the State of approximately $50,000, operation of a stone quarry for the same division, the stone being used to riprap the banks of the canal and the Mohawk River; construction of Perkins Memorial Drive at Bear Mountain and roads, buildings, drains and sewer lines throughout Palisades Interstate Park and similar works under the Long Island State Park Commission; and many others, including road work in more than 75 per cent of the counties.

The Home Relief Dollar

Expenditures for Home Relief accounted for approximately $89,125,000 in the two-year period ending October 31, 1933. In the last month 206,162 families* were on Home Relief rolls.

---

* Includes cases for which the Temporary Emergency Relief Administration does not reimburse costs.

Home Relief is provided in the form of orders for food, shelter, and other necessities as before enumerated and thus is to be distinguished from Work Relief which provides emergency wages. The law forbids cash allowances in Home Relief even for carfare.

Beginning with June, 1932, information has been obtained from the local Departments of Public Welfare administering Home Relief on the distribution of expenditures for the various necessaries reimbursable from State funds. In the State as a whole 74.2 cents out of each Home Relief dollar were spent for food during the five months, June through October, 1932, and 70.1 cents during the year November 1, 1932 through October 31, 1933. Next in importance was shelter for which 21.0 cents were spent of each dollar during the five month period and 19.2 cents during the year ending October 31, 1933.

Fuel and light accounted for 2.4 cents in the five-month period and 7.6 for the year; clothing for 1.3 cents and 1.5 cents, respectively; household necessities for 0.2 cents and 0.3 cents respectively, and medical services for 0.9 and 1.3, respectively.

During the first nine months medical service in the up-State districts accounted for from 1.5 cents to 2.7 cents of each dollar. Beginning with March, 1933, it cost from 3.0 cents to 3.6 cents, indicating a broadening of policies with reference to medical care in the home. In New York City the amount paid for medical service from Home Relief funds was very small during the first months. There have been no such expenditures from Home Relief funds since early in December, 1932 because the State Administration made available a special fund for medical, dental and nursing service and supplies for Home Relief and Work Relief families.

In most of the months New York City spent a larger proportion of each dollar for food than did the up-State districts. Variation in the proportionate amounts spent for each type of relief in up-State districts was due mainly to higher expenditures for fuel and light in the winter months; except for this fluctuation and increasing expenditures for medical service the relative expenditures for the various items remained fairly static.

Supplementary Federal Relief Activities

In addition to the Home Relief and Work Relief provided by local, State, and Federal funds, supplementary Federal relief activities were organized toward the close of the two-year period with the State Temporary Relief Administration acting as agent.

Approximately $3,000,000 was made available to families, most of whom were on relief rolls, through allotments from the monthly pay of $30, which was received in addition to maintenance, by more than 25,000 young men from New York State who were enrolled in the Civilian Conservation Corps from the end of April through October, 1933.

Distribution of Federal surplus food supplies, to be used to supplement regular relief orders, was begun late in October, 1933. The only commodity supplied during the month was salt pork of which 2,310,000 pounds were shipped to the welfare districts throughout the State. In the distribution the Temporary Emergency Relief Administration acted as intermediary between the Federal Government and the local welfare officers, chiefly in negotiations over allocation of amounts.

On the basis of plans worked out by the Transient Division of the Temporary Emergency Relief Administration in October, the Federal Relief Administration early in November approved a program for relief of persons domiciled in the State less than twelve months. The program combines operation of shelter and feeding stations and provision of medical and dental care with a constructive effort to solve the individual's problem.

Relief and the Future

In the Wicks Act the Legislature expressly declared that "the duty of providing for those in need or unemployed because of lack of employment is primarily an obligation of the municipalities." At the same time it found the public health and safety of the State as a whole as well as of its local units imperilled by the existing emergency and to meet this peril created the Temporary Emergency Relief Administration to supplement and stimulate local relief efforts.

The event proved, as the depression intensified following the summer of 1931, the reality of the peril and the wisdom of the Legislature in meeting it.

There can be no measuring the extent to which State aid to municipalities in emergency unemployment relief has improved morale and contributed to present prospects for recovery.

It is evident that the prompt action of the State Administration in instituting a State-wide program of relief, administered in the field by a trained staff without political affiliations. has been a bulwark against suffering. In spite of inadequate appropriations in some districts and the rapidity with which the program was organized, the State's relief program, carried on without any break-down through the worst years of the depression, has had an incalculable effect in not only preventing the starvation of hundreds of thousands but in preserving the home life of the unemployed families and their children.

Wide-spread unemployment in the State, reaching into the homes of hundreds of thousands of citizens who in normal times supported themselves and formed one of the strongest links in the economic chain of the State, threatened not only the security of the home but the future of the children—the citizens of tomorrow. Approximately 1,100,000 children under sixteen years of age, one-third of all under sixteen in the entire State, have been included in families receiving unemployment relief at some time during the two-year period. In a most practical sense the State's program of relief has been an investment in its own future.

Assuming their obligation to care for their unemployed, the State and municipalities have with scientific and modern relief measures helped the unemployed in helping themselves and saved for normal times those who will again be able to provide for themselves and contribute to the welfare and prosperity of the State.

TABLE I

PUBLIC UNEMPLOYMENT RELIEF EXPENDITURES SUBJECT TO REIMBURSEMENT FROM STATE AND FEDERAL FUNDS

(As Reported by the Welfare Districts)

NOVEMBER, 1931—OCTOBER, 1933

Month	Total	Home Relief	Work Relief
November, 1931	$994,648	$894,195	$100,453
December	2,134,339	1,380,932	753,406
January, 1932	5,360,393	1,864,841	3,495,551
February	6,503,978	2,671,566	3,832,412
March	7,740,043	3,431,558	4,308,486
April	5,606,500	2,608,246	2,998,254
May	5,318,395	2,497,723	2,820,651
June	4,715,490	2,459,099	2,256,391
July	4,797,167	2,552,748	2,244,420
August ..:....................	5,221,419	2,776,853	2,444,587
September	5,155,486	2,690,580	2,464,905
October	6,153,360	3,242,637	2,910,723
Total Year Ending October 31, 1932	$59,701,198	$29,070,958	$30,630,239
November, 1932	$6,498,965	$3,683,294	$2,815,671
December	8,369,240ᵃ	4,681,890	3,684,301
January, 1933	8,878,637	4,733,710	4,124,182
February	10,839,337	6,164,952	4,580,593
March	13,711,633	6,784,836	6,776,345
April	12,604,843	5,287,258	7,199,994
May	12,908,802	4,997,804	7,763,913
June	11,966,848	4,929,357	6,903,462
July	10,925,389ᵇ	4,562,149	6,298,609
August	11,315,682	4,526,122	6,707,602
September	10,715,227	4,395,692	6,222,384
October	11,815,692	5,307,218	6,405,490
Total Year Ending October 31, 1933	$130,550,295	$60,054,282	$69,482,546

ᵃ Beginning with December, 1932, includes expenditures for school lunches and medical service to Home Relief and Work Relief clients in New York City.

ᵇ Beginning with July, 1933, includes Home Relief to veterans.

TABLE II

NUMBER OF FAMILIES RECEIVING PUBLIC UNEMPLOY-MENT RELIEF [a]

(As Reported by the Welfare Districts)

NOVEMBER, 1931—OCTOBER, 1933

	Total [b]	Home Relief	Work Relief
November, 1931	[c]	38,074	[c]
December	[c]	56,636	[c]
January, 1932	-	95,284	
February	-	122,398	
March	-	145,608	
April	-	142,833	
May	[c]	129,251	[c]
June	171,302	117,036	60,251
July	169,256	116,398	60,078
August	183,323	124,742	67,434
September	186,607	126,183	70,054
October	199,664	132,828	77,746
November	212,600	145,453	78,154
December	247,037	168,525	92,234
January, 1933	279,523	194,877	107,516
February	328,040	219,110	138,676
March	368,938	243,439	163,220
April	397,077	245,885	189,767
May	380,854	231,123	186,008
June	359,891	221,962	168,669
July	365,915	236,538	161,644
August	360,781	222,191	164,255
September	332,710	205,894	153,770
October	329,572	203,112	150,747

[a] Includes family groups and single and unattached individuals.
[b] Duplications between Home Relief and Work Relief have been eliminated.
[c] Data on number of unduplicated families receiving Work Relief are not available until June, 1932.

TABLE III

TEMPORARY EMERGENCY RELIEF ADMINISTRATION OF NEW YORK STATE

Expenditure Statement

A TABLE showing the disbursements of the Temporary Emergency Relief Administration for Home Relief, Work Relief, and State Improvements, pertaining to the period of November 1, 1931 to November 1, 1933. Welfare district is defined as either a city or a county beyond the limits of a city, with the exception of Ontario County, which includes the cities of Geneva and Canandaigua.

Welfare District	Population per census of 1930	Home Relief		Work Relief		State Improvements	Total Nov. 1, 1933
		Total paid	Estimated commitments	Total paid	Estimated commitments		
Albany county	45,232	$53,053 03	$5,705 79	$40,610 89	$33,964 86	$22,188 50	$155,523 07
Albany	127,412	160,395 42	32,221 36	245,206 58	27,033 73	209,868 34	674,725 43
Cohoes	23,226	107,148 95	32,755 22	303,463 22	5,120 39	36,525 00	485,012 78
Watervliet	16,083 (county total 211,953)	31,489 11	8,646 97	27,219 68	3,058 44	5,627 50	76,041 70
Broome county	70,360	38,800 60	7,980 80	12,998 14	759 14	22,880 00	83,418 68
Binghamton	76,662	108,183 64	17,721 66	75,092 12	3,709 27	26,070 00	230,776 69
[illegible]	38,025 (county total 147,022)	153,696 87	37,243 86	216,482 83	5,672 87	76,575 21	489,671 64
Cattaraugus county	41,031	41,454 33	15,291 60	47,653 95	3,778 89	36,920 00	145,098 78
Olean	21,790	55,831 01	1,965 65	89,726 54	2,370 69	53,665 00	203,558 89
Salamanca	9,577 (county total 72,398)	39,803 93	4,337 57	15,036 06	1,852 93	55,914 00	116,944 49
Cayuga county	28,099	15,263 61	....	26,686 86	407 07	36,680 00	79,037 54
Auburn	36,652 (county total 64,751)	133,973 89	3,320 20	179,087 40	13,596 07	31,317 00	361,294 56
Chautauqua county	63,500	49,143 81	9,760 84	13,510 87	800 82	7,200 00	80,416 34
Dunkirk	17,802	102,830 40	4,255 51	133,294 67	....	73,513 00	313,893 58
Jamestown	45,155 (county total 126,457)	116,679 34	22,699 89	52,539 69	17,070 24	26,467 00	235,456 16
Chemung county	27,283	61,473 75	44,650 78	80,003 74	2,568 52	10,529 00	199,226 79
Elmira	47,397 (county total 74,680)	153,622 44	50,692 26	59,287 53	....	34,479 00	298,081 23

County / City	Population	Total						
Chenango county	26,287	34,665	8,348 46	1,549 52	63,129 29	1,524 26	23,100 00	97,651 53
Norwich	8,378		6,338 87	1,045 60	33,312 34	1,270 96	15,600 00	57,567 77
Clinton county	33,338	46,687	12,155 43	1,768 07	11,957 51	1,450 35		27,331 36
Plattsburg	13,349		8,614 00	1,578 31	5,958 01	1,115 74	9,800 00	27,066 06
Columbia county	29,280	41,617	11,881 04	1,239 78	16,555 85	10,656 23	11,877 50	52,210 40
Hudson	12,337		54,094 82		70,731 42	1,938 33	146,000 00	272,764 57
Cortland county	16,666	31,709	10,017 25	1,321 69	25,484 44	1,013 08	10,500 00	48,336 46
Cortland	15,043		38,764 73	2,058 16	23,264 12	1,377 54	1,890 00	67,354 55
Delaware county	41,163		12,047 63	2,396 48	2,659 60	948 43	800 00	18,852 14
Dutchess county	53,241	105,462	86,813 11	14,723 96	39,161 44		47,508 00	188,206 51
Beacon	11,933		16,648 83	4,082 22	42,528 43	952 05	4,400 00	68,611 53
Poughkeepsie	40,238		152,522 40	14,702 90	85,247 17	1,102 29	138,224 02	391,798 78
Erie county	152,703	762,408	612,212 27	91,700 02	746,160 60	91,340 87	479,488 00	2,020,901 76
Buffalo	573,076		4,367,160 43	384,321 97	1,679,655 95	245,557 67	211,372 19	6,888,068 21
Lackawanna	23,948		274,677 72		269,433 65	*30,268 37	20,615 00	594,994 74
Tonawanda	12,681		63,009 57		39,036 66	3,023 27	12,784 00	117,853 50
Essex county	33,959		66,651 10	15,563 35	87,143 32	18,814 75	66,085 50	254,258 02
Franklin county	45,694		88,314 33	1,132 40	59,793 56	12,485 33	26,000 00	193,725 62
Fulton county	12,660	46,560	10,257 84	1,279 03	3,993 04	2,788 97	2,149 00	20,467 88
Gloversville	23,099		16,675 40	1,285 60	24,558 51	1,026 20	3,549 00	47,094 71
Johnstown	10,801		7,706 04	553 80	5,130 20	156 84	1,449 00	14,995 88
Geneseo county	27,093	44,468	37,397 10	5,366 15				42,763 25
Batavia	17,375		57,668 75	5,260 77	22,521 55	2,189 16	63,930 40	151,570 63
Greene county	25,808		20,375 19	1,927 22	722 53		4,500 00	27,524 94
Hamilton county	3,929		2,831 61	454 06	5,309 84	2,502 80		11,098 31
Herkimer county	52,901	64,006	206,410 80	19,553 74	90,815 48	13,780 83	38,261 00	368,826 85
Little Falls	11,105		10,957 03	700 15	15,546 34	116 50		27,320 02
Jefferson county	51,369	83,574	61,849 64	14,537 16	21,077 86	7,809 70	10,500 00	115,774 36
Watertown	32,205		206,673 80	6,350 89	190,795 41	926 61	18,726 00	423,472 71
Lewis county	23,447		10,095 04	1,390 31	8,215 61			22,348 62
Livingston county	37,560		49,530 79	14,219 45	36,923 76	2,647 66	36,927 00	139,392 83
Madison county	29,232	39,790	19,250 19	2,439 48	22,144 76	1,791 83	7,000 00	50,834 43
Oneida	10,558		16,031 35	979 56	7,291 68		5,095 00	29,397 59
Monroe county	95,749	423,881	257,937 39	56,627 45	1,053,380 76		119,514 00	1,487,459 60
Rochester	328,132		1,790,490 33	356,861 15	884,317 00	226,562 57	121,359 50	3,379,590 55
Montgomery county	25,259	60,076	22,857 17		16,058 63		6,000 00	51,388 60
Amsterdam	34,817		179,119 75	3,860 32	176,671 72	2,612 48	115,881 00	471,672 47

* Subsequently charged to Erie county.

TABLE III—Concluded

WELFARE DISTRICT	Population per census of 1930	HOME RELIEF Total paid	HOME RELIEF Estimated commitments	WORK RELIEF Total paid	WORK RELIEF Estimated commitments	State Improvements	Total Nov. 1, 1933
Nassau county	285,806 (303,053)	$731,752 81	$263,830 07	$2,520,518 78	$467,717 61	$208,327 00	$4,192,146 27
Glen Cove	11,430	29,567 57		13,644 17		5,000 00	48,211 74
Long Beach	5,817	6,663 98		36,478 23		10,000 00	53,142 21
New York city	6,930,446	25,242,458 01	1,923,690 01	26,064,853 76		3,199,272 14	56,430,273 92
Niagara county	31,690 (149,329)	28,187 87	4,776 72	21,377 70	3,253 50	28,200 00	85,795 79
Lockport	23,160	72,467 15	5,905 03	59,982 36	6,157 84	32,410 00	176,922 38
Niagara Falls	75,460	98,233 75	37,653 31	315,298 75	25,354 89	114,331 00	590,871 70
North Tonawanda	19,019	172,021 79		140,119 12	10,322 43	62,082 00	384,545 34
Oneida county	62,535 (198,763)	51,571 61	7,558 66	80,859 38	830 99	30,030 40	170,851 04
Rome	32,338	53,300 03	6,965 19	91,064 78		52,311 00	203,641 00
Sherrill	2,150						
Utica	101,740	211,690 26	63,099 47	530,295 19	1,905 27	163,758 00	970,748 19
Onondaga county	82,280 (291,606)	198,897 45	33,397 14	561,053 67	255,625 13	21,330 00	1,070,303 39
Syracuse	209,326	802,907 99	148,573 11	1,120,312 17	217,995 84	518,689 00	2,808,478 11
Ontario county	54,276	87,095 60	7,381 81	61,261 66	9,325 20	26,816 00	191,880 27
Orange county	67,589 (130,383)	34,509 92	5,472 73	153,506 00		159,351 00	352,839 65
Middletown	21,276	9,373 58	615 63	27,053 40	510 39	31,800 00	69,353 00
Newburgh	31,275	113,259 10	8,284 50	111,854 95	10,398 70	16,465 00	260,262 25
Port Jervis	10,243	19,364 65	4,551 39	68,351 38	5,770 71	17,070 00	115,108 13
Orleans county	28,795	10,011 78	1,398 97	5,834 32	707 93		17,953 00
Oswego county	34,531 (69,645)	5,287 28					5,287 28
Fulton	12,462	108,960 68	5,655 05	223,958 95	230 09	83,125 00	421,929 77
Oswego	22,652	113,415 56	24,076 90	352,271 21	2,751 01	99,345 00	591,859 68
Otsego county	34,174 (46,710)	9,676 93	4,392 41	19,862 42	2,368 26	300 00	36,600 02
Oneonta	12,536	4,008 34	696 69	36,339 09	1,562 99	4,000 00	46,607 11
Putnam county	13,744	16,881 15	4,388 30	6,149 86		26,190 00	53,609 31
Rensselaer county	35,795 (119,781)	28,571 87	1,457 51	42,029 02	1,263 63	9,940 50	83,262 53
Rensselaer	11,223	21,315 61	3,877 38	31,203 19	202 84	17,198 00	73,797 02
Troy	72,763	241,744 63	32,656 79	250,448 31		56,783 00	581,632 73

	(1)	(2)	(3)	(4)	(5)	(6)	(7)	Total
Rockland county	74,045	59,599	52,304 22	10,130 65	56,179 53	621 62	87,291 25	206,527 27
St. Lawrence county	16,915	90,960	113,157 63	11,973 45	139,108 25	16,715 76	28,057 00	309,012 09
Ogdensburg			22,769 36		97,048 75	8,262 55	105 00	128,185 66
Saratoga county	42,221	63,314	58,280 63	21,389 62	21,550 64	3,514 52	12,000 00	116,735 41
Mechanicville	7,924		42,762 53	2,230 36	32,909 59	2,368 73	47,149 00	127,420 21
Saratoga Springs	13,169		18,893 58	8,196 42	10,025 55	1,747 43	33,149 00	72,011 98
Schenectady county	29,329	125,021	139,827 08	42,928 50	119,040 44	24,324 42	8,849 00	334,969 44
Schenectady	95,692		293,937 98	90,920 35	373,153 47	119,344 15	68,749 00	946,104 95
Schoharie county		19,667	2,034 67	763 79	7,255 29	2,354 12	6,600 00	19,010 87
Schuyler county		12,909	27,030 04	7,376 40	6,005 52	2,545 00	27,000 00	69,956 96
Seneca county		24,983	37,230 94	3,212 74	9,613 13	1,818 97	22,000 00	73,875 78
Steuben county	50,644	82,671	42,752 18	8,018 50	21,712 72	21,430 50	16,250 00	110,163 90
Corning	15,777		58,290 43	862 92	67,286 76	2,330 10	21,410 00	150,180 21
Hornell	16,250		11,368 20	4,493 83	84,297 38		58,431 00	158,590 41
Suffolk county		161,055	272,499 98	62,743 46	598,849 67	65,160 91	294,055 00	1,293,309 02
Sullivan county		35,272	11,248 37	949 36			70 00	12,267 73
Tioga county		25,480	23,864 47	3,011 31	6,478 90	1,274 09		34,628 77
Tompkins county	20,782*	41,490	16,413 27	1,729 14	17,084 57	817 45	10,000 00	46,044 43
Ithaca	20,708		33,925 18	3,617 34	73,461 27		55,898 00	166,901 79
Ulster county	52,067	80,155	41,800 71	4,918 24	27,669 37	18,076 92	19,800 00	112,265 24
Kingston	28,088		78,752 31		106,703 84	6,283 18	31,368 00	223,107 33
Warren county	15,643	34,174	18,480 02	2,690 93	7,998 48			35,469 43
Glens Falls	18,531		79,839 83	10,643 29	40,480 63	2,104 43	6,300 00	133,068 18
Washington county		46,482	142,351 45	17,559 23	80,856 10	878 10	51,149 00	292,793 88
Wayne county		49,995	33,745 86	17,000 97	4,054 03	948 10	8,000 00	63,752 96
Westchester county	234,972	520,947	442,302 58	181,943 56	1,538,653 31	29,051 15	400,354 00	2,592,304 61
Mt. Vernon	61,499		115,446 34	21,260 75	292,801 69		20,017 00	449,525 78
New Rochelle	54,000		213,754 35	41,292 23	210,706 33	22,068 02	5,517 00	493,337 93
White Plains	35,830		172,247 21	56,424 05	33,391 36	51,251 22	5,140 00	318,453 84
Yonkers	134,646		721,924 68	1,651 17	928,845 86	34,735 15	276,121 00	1,983,277 86
Wyoming county		28,764	24,972 50	2,410 70	18,541 94	2,997 00	8,500 00	57,422 14
Yates county		16,848	2,078 19	647 17				2,725 36
State Improvements allocated on a State wide basis							1,624,688 91	1,624,688 91
		12,588,066	*$42,486,714 55	*$4,581,435 89	*$45,482,338 00	*$32,278,814 95	*$10,795,425 86	*$105,624,729 25

* Figures given in this table include relief advances made to districts and State Departments not entirely spent in the period, and allowances by the State Administration to the localities for local administrative salaries, which have been excluded in the figures on Temporary Emergency Relief Administration disbursements in the body of the report.

OF

RULES AND REGULATIONS

GOVERNING

Medical Care Provided in the Home To Recipients of Home Relief

—————

Adopted March 3, 1934; amended from time to time; now completely
rewritten and revised to conform with F.E.R.A. Rules and
Regulations No. 7, issued September 8, 1933; adopted
in revised form, June 8, 1934, to take
effect on July 1, 1934

June, 1934

STATE OF NEW YORK

TEMPORARY EMERGENCY RELIEF ADMINISTRATION
79 MADISON AVENUE, NEW YORK, N. Y.

OF

RULES AND REGULATIONS

GOVERNING

Medical Care Provided in the Home To Recipients of Home Relief

———————

Adopted March 3, 1934; amended from time to time; now completely
rewritten and revised to conform with F.E.R.A. Rules and
Regulations No. 7, issued September 8, 1933; adopted
in revised form, June 8, 1934, to take
effect on July 1, 1934

June, 1934

STATE OF NEW YORK

TEMPORARY EMERGENCY RELIEF ADMINISTRATION
79 MADISON AVENUE, NEW YORK, N. Y.

T. E. R. A. MANUAL

of

RULES AND REGULATIONS

Governing

Medical Care Provided in the Home to Recipients of Home Relief

(Adopted in revised form, June 8, 1934, to take effect on July 1, 1934)

TABLE OF CONTENTS

STATE OF NEW YORK
Temporary Emergency Relief Administration
RULES AND REGULATIONS
Governing Medical Care Provided in the Home to Recipients of Home Relief

---

Adopted March 3, 1933; modified by official interpretations as issued in T. E. R. A. Official Bulletin Number 1, and in official letters from the Administration to Commissioners of Public Welfare; now completely rewritten and revised to conform with Federal Emergency Relief Administration Rules and Regulations Number 7, issued September 8, 1933; and adopted in the revised form, June 8, 1934, to take effect on July 1, 1934.

INTRODUCTION

The conservation and maintenance of the public health is a primary function of Government. In the present economic depression, the ingenuity of Federal, State, and local relief officials is being taxed to conserve available public funds and, at the same time, to give adequate relief to those in need.

For the purpose of facilitating the discharge of these obligations with regard to medical care, the following rules and regulations governing medical care provided in the home to recipients of home relief are hereby established.[1]

CHAPTER I

Statement of Policy

Section A.—**Definitions.** As used in these rules and regulations:

Item 1. "Medical care provided in the home" means medicine, medical supplies, and medical attendance furnished by a municipal corporation or a town, where home relief is a town charge, to persons or their dependents in their abode or habitation whenever possible and does not include hospital or institutional care.

a. It does not include medical, nursing and dental services, given either "in the home," in the office, or in a clinic, where such services are already established in the community and paid for, in whole or in part, from local and/or State funds in accordance with local

---

[1] Basic legislation, a summary of prior regulations, and quotations from the public welfare law, may be consulted in Chapter III.

[7]

statutes or charter provisions. Federal and State Emergency Relief Funds shall not be used in lieu of such local and/or State funds to pay for these established services.

b. The scope of "medical care" as above defined shall be construed to include: *Bedside nursing care,* as an adjunct to medical attendance; and *emergency dental care*—subject to the restrictions stated in the preceding paragraph.

c. "Medical care" as above defined shall be construed ordinarily to include only necessary care for conditions that cause acute suffering, interfere with earning capacity, endanger life, or threaten some permanent new handicap that is preventable when medical care is sought.

d. "Emergency dental care" shall in general be restricted to those extractions, fillings, treatments and repairs which are necessary for the relief of pain and other conditions referred to in the preceding paragraph.

e. "Medicine" and necessary drugs shall be restricted to a formulary which excludes expensive drugs where less expensive drugs can be used with the same therapeutic effect. Proprietary or patent medicines shall not be authorized.

f. "Medical supplies" shall be restricted to the simplest *emergency* needs of the patient consistent with good medical care.

g. The phrase "in the home" shall be interpreted to include medical and dental office service for ambulatory patients: Provided, that such medical and dental office service shall not supplant the services of clinics and/or salaried physicians and dentists already provided in the community.

Item 2. "Recipients of home relief" means all cases of home relief who have been duly investigated, as required by section 13 of chapter seven hundred and ninety-eight of the laws of nineteen hundred and thirty-one, and found to be eligible for home relief.

Section B.—**Objectives.** The common aim of the state-wide medical relief program is the provision of good medical care at a low cost—to the mutual benefit of the indigent patient, professional attendant and taxpayer. This program has the following objectives:

Item 1. Uniform policy. Medical care is to be provided to recipients of home relief, under these regulations, in accordance with a uniform policy formulated by the Temporary Emergency Relief Administration in consultation with representatives of the organized State medical, dental and other participating professions.

Item 2. Maintenance of professional standards. This policy recognizes, within legal and economic limitations,[2] the traditional relationships existing between the patient and physician or other professional attendant, and provides that authorized professional attendants shall furnish to recipients of home relief the same quality of service as would be rendered to a private patient, with the under-

---

[2] See Section D., Item I, on page 11.

standing that such authorized service shall be a minimum, consistent with good professional judgment, and shall be charged for at an agreed rate which makes due allowance for the conservation of relief funds.

Item 3. More adequate medical care. a. The policy adopted shall be to augment and render more adequate, facilities already existing in the community for the provision of medical care by medical, dental and nursing professions to indigent persons.

b. This policy and the scope of the program of medical care adopted locally, under the provisions of these regulations, shall be restriced to supplementation of local facilities and services, and shall imply continuance in the use of hospitals, clinics and medical, dental and nursing services already established in the community and paid for, in whole or in part, from local and/or State funds in accordance with local statutes or charter provisions or in accordance with provisions of the Public Welfare Law[3] which require or permit services not within the scope of the Emergency Relief Act of the State of New York.

Item 4. Uniform procedure. a. In the interest of simplified administration and accounting, as well as the provision of adequate medical care at a low cost, a uniform procedure for authorization of medical, dental, and nursing care in the home shall be established by each local department of public welfare. This procedure shall not be in conflict with the detailed requirements stated in Chapter II of these regulations.

b. The purpose of the uniform procedure adopted is to provide more adequate medical care to recipients of home relief and to provide an equitable distribution of authorization to professional attendants participating in the program. Hence, the Administration and the professional advisory committees are opposed to any undue stimulation of demands for medical care on the part of individual physicians, dentists and nurses. If such stimulation is discovered in any local welfare district, the local commissioner of public welfare shall report the facts in writing to the welfare advisory committee of the local county medical society or comparable professional advisory committee, and send a copy of the written complaint to the Director of Medical Care, T. E. R. A., 79 Madison Avenue, New York, N. Y. All authorizations for medical care are a responsibility of the local commissioner of public welfare and should not be unduly stimulated by the physician, dentist or nurse.

c. Recipients of home relief shall be notified by the local commissioner of public welfare that application for necessary medical care should be made to the welfare office from which orders for other forms of relief are issued. The welfare office is responsible for calling the physician, dentist or nurse instead of the medical attendant being responsible for initiating the call upon the welfare office. Hence, if authorization is desired, physicians and dentists should

---

[3] Chapter 565, Laws of 1929, with subsequent amendments; see Chapter III, Section C.

not encourage ambulatory patients to come to their offices in the first instance, but shall, during the hours when the local welfare office is open, refer patients requesting medical care to such welfare office. Exceptions to this rule are covered in Regulation I, Chapter II, below.[4]

Section C. **Professional supervision and advice.** The Administration has recognized the need for professional supervision and advice in the administration of medical care provided in the home to recipients of home relief. To meet this need the following steps have been taken.

Item 1. Division of medical care. a. The Administration, under the provisions of section 5 of the Emergency Relief Act,[5] has received advice and expert assistance from the state department of health, and has appointed a member of the staff of said department as director of medical care.

b. The Administration has further established a division of medical care to provide additional expert supervision over medical and related problems confronted in the administration of both home and work relief.

c. The duties of the staff of the division of medical care are to make surveys, formulate procedures, promote professional standards, and suggest policies for the more effective provision of adequate medical care to recipients of home relief.

d. The director of medical care also acts as liaison officer with respect to medical problems between the Administration, State and local professional organizations, and local Departments of Public Welfare and Health.

Item 2. Professional advisory committees. a. The Administration has requested the State medical, dental and nursing organizations, respectively, to designate an existing committee or appoint a special advisory committee, to assist in the formulation and adoption of an adequate program for medical, dental, and nursing care in the home for recipients of home relief. These advisory committees assist the Administration both in maintaining proper professional standards and in enlisting the co-operation of the constituent professional membership in the State and local programs for medical care.

b. The State medical and dental organizations have recommended that similar professional advisory committees be appointed locally to serve in each public welfare district. If such committees have not already been appointed, the local commissioner of public welfare should request such a committee from the appropriate local professional organization to advise with him both in the promotion of the State and local program of medical care and with regard to disputed problems of medical, dental and nursing policy and practice.

---

[4] See page 14, below.
[5] Chapter 798, Laws of 1931.

c. The local professional advisory committees may be asked by the local Commissioner of Public Welfare to assist in the formulation of a mutually satisfactory schedule of flat-rate charges which, in general, shall not exceed: two-thirds of the usual minimum local fees; nor the fees ordinarily charged indigent persons; nor, for the purpose of reimbursement by the Administration, shall the schedule exceed the charges specifically listed in Regulation 9, Chapter II, below.[6]

d. The local professional advisory committee may submit to the local commissioner of public welfare, a list of physicians or dentists who have agreed to co-operate under this program. To this list, may be added the names of other reputable local physicians or dentists, licensed to practice in the State of New York, who are not members of the local professional organizations. These additional practitioners may be cleared with the local professional advisory committees however, to insure that their licenses and professional standing are checked up, and that they are otherwise qualified.

e. Local professional advisory committees are recommended by the Administration, even in public welfare districts where professional participation is restricted.[7]

Section D. **Scope of participation.** The scope of participation in the state-wide program of medical care, provided in the home to recipients of home relief under the Emergency Relief Act[8] of the State of New York, is subject to statutory and/or charter limitations applying either, or both, to municipal corporations or/and to professional personnel.

Item 1. Municipal corporations (cities and counties) and towns, where home relief is a town charge, are eligible for participation in this state-wide program of medical care, subject to the following restrictions.

a. A municipal corporation or a town, where home relief is a town charge, with clinics and/or medical, dental and bedside nursing services already established in the community and paid for in whole or in part from local and/or State funds in accordance with local statutes or charter provisions requiring employment of city, county or town physicians and/or other professional personnel on a salary basis, is eligible for reimbursement, by the Administration, only for such items of medical care as can be accounted for on a unit basis (i. e., drugs, medical supplies, and prosthetic devices) and, in addition, only for such professional services as have been specifically authorized by the Administration to render more adequate, but not to supplant, existing local services.

b. A municipal corporation or a town, where home relief is a town charge, where there are no such established salaried services for providing medical care to recipients of home relief (i. e., communities where medical care is provided primarily on an individual

[6] See page 29.
[7] See Section D., Item 1, a, below.
[8] Chapter 798, Laws of 1931, with subsequent amendments.

fee basis), is eligible for reimbursement by the Administration, for all types of medical care covered by these rules.

Item 2. Professional personnel. a. Only physicians, dentists, nurses and other professional personnel who are licensed and/or registered to practice their respective professions in the State of New York, shall be authorized to participate, with a view to reimbursement from the Administration, in the provision of medical care in the home to recipients of home relief: Provided, that authorization of such professional personnel and services is restricted to welfare districts eligible [9] to provide professional services, on a fee basis.

b. The traditional relationships existing between patient and professional attendant shall be recognized in the authorization of medical care under this program, subject to the restrictions imposed by charter provisions, local statutory limitations, and the provisions of these Rules and Regulations.

c. In recognition of the principle of maintaining traditional relationships between patient and professional attendant, where a preference is expressed by the patient, midwives, licensed to practice in the State of New York, may be authorized to provide obstetrical care in the home to recipients of home relief, subject to restrictions imposed by law and the provisions of these Rules and Regulations.

d. In order to provide adequate medical care it is recommended that commissioners of public welfare maintain on a district basis, approved lists or files of physicians and other licensed professioual attendants who have agreed in writing to comply with these Rules and Regulations. In general, authorizations for medical care, in districts eligible to issue such authorizations with a view to reimbursement by the Administration, shall be restricted to those professional attendants who are already on such approved lists. When a patient does not choose a physician or other professional attendant at the time that medical care is requested, assignments should be made from the approved list by the local welfare office, alphabetically and in rotation. When a patient requests the services of a physician or other professional attendant who has not applied for inclusion on the approved list, as indicated above, such attendance may be authorized, provided that the written authorization is accompanied by a copy of these Rules and Regulations and a statement that acceptance of the order automatically implies compliance with these rules in giving professional care. No limited number of physicians or other professional attendants should secure an excessive amount of the work.

e. If a recipient of home relief, who requires continued care, under the care of a physician or other professional attendant who is not on the authorized list, because of unwillingness to conform to the provisions of these rules and regulations or because of legal ineligibility, the welfare officer should ask the attendant if he wishes to continue to care for the patient without compensation. If the physician or other attendant does not wish to continue such care,

[9] See Section D, *Item 1, a* and *b*, page 11.

the patient may be requested to select another physician or other attendant from the authorized list.

f. The Administration recommends that the local commissioners of public welfare require signature on the following statement as a prerequisite to being placed on the authorized list of physicians or other professional attendants:

"The undersigned, a regularly licensed and/or registered ——— ——— (physician, dentist, nurse, other) hereby certifies that he (or she) is desirous of participating in the officially adopted program for providing medical care in the home to recipients of home relief; that he (or she) has carefully read the Rules and Regulations adopted by the Temporary Emergency Relief Administration to govern such medical care; and that he (or she) hereby agrees to conform to the provisions of said Rules and Regulations and to co-operate fully with the (City or County) department of public welfare and the Temporary Emergency Relief Administration. My license is No. ———————, issued by the State of New York, and my current registration is No. ——————, date ———, 19—, County of ———.
Dated this ———, day of ——————— 193-.
Address ——————————————— (Signed) ———————"
(Street)   (City, Village, etc.)

Section E. Qualifications of recipients of medical care.

Item 1. Person eligible. Medical care, under the provisions of these Rules and Regulations, shall be restricted to persons who are recipients of home relief or who, upon investigation by the welfare officer, are found to be eligible for home relief.

Item 2. Other restrictions. Types of cases usually referred to physicians or other professional attendants who are paid on a salary basis from local and/or State funds, shall continue to be so referred: Provided, that adequacy of medical care can be maintained for these patients.

Item 3. Persons not eligible: procedure. Patients who request medical care from the welfare office, but who do not qualify under the above requirements, should be referred to their family physicians or other professional attendants for free treatment, or for credit given by such family physicians or attendants, provided the physicians or attendants agree to give the necessary care.

CHAPTER II

Regulations Governing Procedure

In welfare districts eligible to participate[10] in the state-wide program of medical care provided in the home to recipients of home relief, a uniform procedure for the authorization and provision of medical, dental and bedside nursing care shall be established, which shall not be in conflict with the following regulations.

---

[10] See Chapter I, Section D, *Item 1, a* and *b*, page 11.

Regulation 1. **Written order required.** *Item 1. General.* All authorizations for medical, dental and bedside nursing care shall be issued in writing by the proper authorizing officer of the local department of public welfare, on the regular relief order blank, prior to giving such care; except that telephone authorization shall immediately be followed by such a written order; and provided that in the case of an emergency call the physician or other professional attendant shall request authorization from the local department of public welfare within 48 hours after making such an emergency call.

Item 2. Retroactive. Any authorization for medical, dental or bedside nursing care issued more than 48 hours after the first call authorized shall be considered to be retroactive and payment for care rendered under such a retroactive authorization shall not be eligible for reimbursement by the Administration.

Item 3. Dental care. Authorizations for dental care may, in cases where extensive treatment seems indicated, be restricted to authorization for one visit only, for the purpose of examination and estimate of necessary treatment. In such cases, additional written authorization, based upon the dentist's estimate, shall be required, prior to starting extensive treatment. Authorized dental care shall be limited to such work as is specifically indicated in the written order, and such order shall not be valid for more than thirty days from the date of issue.

Item 4. Bedside nursing care. Authorization for bedside nursing care, in welfare districts eligible to provide such care on a fee basis, shall as a rule be based on a recommendation by the attending physician, who shall certify to the need for bedside nursing service as an adjunct to the medical care.

Item 5. Medicine, medical supplies, etc. Authorizations for medicine, medical supplies and prosthetic devices shall also be issued in writing, prior to the provision of such materials and supplies, and, in general, such authorizations shall not be issued except upon written request of the physician authorized to attend the person for whose use they are desired.

Item 6. Submission with bill. Written orders shall be submitted with the bill covering services performed under such orders, upon completion of the service.

Regulation 2. **Acute illness.** *Item 1. Medical care.* Authorizations for medical care for acute illness shall be limited to: not more than two weeks; not more than ten home and/or office visits; and an expenditure, as a basis for reimbursement by the Administration, of not more than twenty dollars ($20).

Item 2. Bedside nursing care. Authorizations for bedside nursing care for acute illness, in districts eligible to provide such care on a fee basis, shall be limited to: not more than two weeks; not more than ten home visits; and an expenditure, as a basis for reimbursement by the Administration, of not more than ten dollars ($10).

Item 3. Renewal of order. Medical and bedside nursing care in excess of this period or expenditure shall not be authorized until after a reinvestigation of the case in the home by an accredited representative of the local department of public welfare.

Item 4. Consultant or specialist. When in the course of an acute illness, the physician in attendance, the patient, or his family, desires the services of a consultant or a specialist, such services may be authorized in writing, subject to the restrictions imposed by Items 1 and 2 of Regulation 5, below.

Item 5. Emergency; first aid. When a physician makes an emergency call or gives first aid treatment to a recipient of home relief under circumstances which prevent him from obtaining prior authorization, a written authorization may be issued to him to cover such emergency call or first aid treatment provided it is requested within 48 hours. Subsequent care for the same patient shall be provided only after further written authorization, if reimbursement from the Administration is contemplated.

Item 6. Additional patients in household. When advice and/or care is given to other members of the same household by a physician or nurse in the course of an authorized home visit, an allowance for extra compensation for such additional care shall not be eligible for reimbursement; nor shall an allowance for more than one member of the same household, seen in the course of an authorized office visit, be eligible for reimbursement.

Regulation 3. **Chronic illness.** *Item 1. Medical care.* Medical care for prolonged illnesses, such as chronic asthma, chronic heart disease, chronic rheumatism, diabetes, etc., shall be subject to the restrictions imposed upon authorization for medical care for acute illness in Regulation 2, above; except that care for chronic illness shall be authorized only on an individual basis, and, in general, such written authorization shall be limited to: not more than one visit per week for not more than ten weeks or, not more than ten home and/or office visits made at longer intervals; and an expenditure, as a basis for reimbursement by the Administration, of not more than twenty dollars ($20).

Item 2. Bedside nursing care. a. Bedside nursing care for chronic illnesses shall be provided: through existing community services, such as visiting nurses associations, public health nurses, etc., paid for in whole or in part from local and/or State funds; through nurses employed, on work relief under the state-wide bedside nursing service; and by written authorization of registered nurses, only in communities where and to the extent which existing services are not adequate to carry the load, and then only in accordance with the need for such bedside nursing care as indicated by the attending physician.

b. Authorizations for bedside nursing care for chronic illnesses, in communities eligible to issue such authorizations as a basis for reimbursement shall be limited to not more than ten visits, and at intervals and for the period indicated by the attending physician. The purpose of authorized nursing visits shall be demonstration and instruction to some member of the household in the necessary care, in addition to giving such care.

Item 3. Acute attack. If necessary, more frequent visits, by the physician and/or nurse, for an acute attack occurring in the course or during the critical terminal phase, of a chronic illness, may be authorized: Provided, that a request is made, by the physician and/or nurse in attendance, for additional written authorization for more frequent visits, stating the need for such visits. Such additional written authorization shall be subject to the limitations placed upon medical and/or bedside nursing care for an acute illness under the provisions of Regulation 1, above.

Item 4. Care restricted. Care for chronic illness authorized under this regulation shall supplement and not supersede existing community services, such as visiting nursing service, salaried physicians, public clinics, or institutional care.

Regulation 4. **Obstetrical Care.** *Item 1. Scope.* Authorization for obstetrical service in the home shall include: prenatal care, delivery in the home, and postnatal care; and a requirement that, as far as possible, such obstetrical service shall conform, both in frequency of visits and in quality of care, at least to the standards of maternity care[11] adopted by the regional consultants in obstetrics of the New York State Department of Health.

Item 2. Not emergency service. Maternity care should not be considered an emergency service to be authorized late in pregnancy. Local welfare and health officials, public health nurses, social workers, family physicians, and families on home relief should cooperate to the end that continuous medical supervision should begin for every expectant mother as soon as pregnancy is suspected.

Item 3. Minimum standards. The following standards of maternity care shall be maintained.

a. Prenatal care shall, wherever possible, conform to the following minimum requirements: 1. First visit at or prior to the fifth month of pregnancy. This first visit should include: histories of previous pregnancies and labors; determination of expected date of confinement; and instruction in the hygiene of pregnancy. 2. A general physical examination as early in pregnancy as possible, with special attention directed to determination of blood pressure, urinalysis, heart, lungs and kidneys, general nutrition, and a blood

[11] For further details, write to the New York State Department of Health, Albany, N. Y.

Wasserman or comparable test. 3. Pelvic measurements and examination at or before the seventh month. 4. Visits at least monthly until the ninth month and weekly thereafter, with urinalysis, blood pressure determination, and abdominal examination made at each visit. 5. Treatment as needed for ordinary disturbances incident to pregnancy. 6. Social service or visiting nursing service adequate to insure the patient's cooperation with the attending physician and prenatal clinic.

b. *Delivery in the home* shall include, in addition to obstetrical attendance for the mother, treatment for the infant as needed, including the administration of prophylaxis, as required by law,[12] to prevent blindness.

c. *Postnatal or postpartum care* shall include care for both mother and infant as often as may be needed, and bedside visits should be made at least on the first, third and fifth days after delivery. Authorization for obstetrical care shall include provision for a final gynecologic examination of the mother about six weeks after delivery or before she resumes usual activities.

Item 4. Restrictions and precautions. Due caution shall be exercised that authorization for delivery in the home does not involve undue risk to a patient for whom hospital care may be imperative. The judgment of the attending physician shall be a decisive factor in issuing such an authorization. The physician authorized to attend the confinement in the home shall be responsible for certifying to the local commissioner of public welfare, that, in his professional judgment, delivery in the home will be safe. In those cases where it is the professional opinion of the attending physician, that confinement in the home will be hazardous he should notify the local commissioner of public welfare immediately, in order that hospitalization may be authorized in accordance with the provisions of Article X, sections 83 and 85 of the public welfare law.[13] However, expenditures for such authorized hospitalization and hospital care shall not be eligible for reimbursement by the Administration.

Item 5. Complications of pregnancy. Authorization for obstetrical care in the home shall include the items of maternity care specified in the preceding paragraphs. Where complications and/or intercurrent illnesses arise in the course of pregnancy and/or the puerperium and require medical care in addition to that outlined above, the attending physician may request, giving full reasons, additional written authorization for giving supplementary care. Reimbursement may be granted by the Administration on the basis of regular home and/or office visits for medical care given under such additional authorization. Some of the complications of pregnancy which may justify additional authorization and reimburse-

---

[12] See Penal Law, § 482, subd. 3, and the State Sanitary Code, Chapter II, Regulation 12. "Precautions to be observed for the prevention of opthalmia neonatorum."

[13] See Chapter III, Section C, Appendix.

ment are: any acute intercurrent infection; pernicious vomiting of pregnancy; uterine hemorrhage; eclampsia, pre-eclampsia and/or any toxemia of pregnancy; and threatened miscarriage.

Item 6. Miscarriage, etc. When pregnancy is terminated prior to the full term, a pro rata allowance may be reimbursable on the basis of the authorized home and/or office visits actually made: Provided that, in case of an early miscarriage (prior to the sixth month of gestation), where a dilatation and curettage is performed, or care is given for any miscarriage at or after the sixth month, an extra allowance may be granted for such service. The total allowance, as a basis for reimbursement, for all such authorized care where the pregnancy is terminated prior to the full term, shall not exceed the allowance made for authorized complete obstetrical care of a normal confinement in the home.

Item 7. Prenatal clinic. Prenatal care given in a local clinic by arrangements approved by the authorized attending physician shall count for regular prenatal home and office visits, and, if the dates of visits to the clinic are entered in the physician's bill, the regular flat obstetrical fee may be allowed, as the basis for reimbursement.

Item 8. Emergency hospitalization. a. When, in the course of a delivery in the home, complications arise, during the *second* stage of labor, which make transfer to a hospital imperative, and such delivery is subsequently performed by the authorized attending physician or by another physician, reimbursement may be allowed for payments to the physician originally authorized to attend the confinement in the home, on the basis of a sliding scale, up to 80 percent of the flat obstetrical fee, depending upon the adequacy of prenatal care given.

b. In certain cases, for whom delivery in the home was originally authorized, but for whom hospitalization was ordered prior to the onset of labor, allowance may be made for the prenatal and postpartum care actually given, on the basis of the regular home or office charges for each visit.

Item 9. Major obstetrical operations. To safeguard the lives of both mother and child major obstetrical operations shall not be undertaken in the home, except where there are no hospital facilities within a reasonable distance. Wherever possible, hospitalization should be authorized locally,[14] for such obstetrical operations as mid or high forceps application, internal podalic version with or without subsequent extraction, Caesarian operation, and the introduction of a Voorhees bag.

Item 10. Obstetrical nursing. Bedside nursing care, as an adjunct to the obstetrical service, is provided in many communities through local public health nurses employed on work relief. As a supplement to the existing community services, bedside nursing

[14] Under section 85 of the Public Welfare Law, see Chapter III, Section C.

care for expectant mothers and young infants, may be authorized on an individual basis, at the request of the attending physician.

Item 11. Care by midwife. Whenever an expectant mother eligible for home relief requests the attendance of a licensed midwife at her confinement, such service may be authorized, and arrangements should be made for adequate prenatal and postnatal care through existing community services. If there is doubt about the normal progress of pregnancy or delivery, the patient should be transferred immediately to a physician or to a hospital. Authorized obstetrical service provided by a licensed midwife may be eligible for reimbursement by the Administration on the basis of not to exceed one-half of the fee paid to a physician for the same type of service.

Regulation 5. **Special services.** Medical care not covered above shall be authorized only on an individual basis under the restrictions stated below and elsewhere[15] in these regulations. Such special medical care[16] shall not ordinarily be authorized by welfare officials for conditions that do not cause acute suffering, interfere with earning capacity, endanger life, or threaten some permanent new handicap that is preventable when such medical care is sought.

The types of special medical services which may be authorized under the provisions of this regulation are as follows:

Item 1. The usual services of a specialist. a. A specialist may be authorized to provide necessary care for those types of illness which are not amenable to treatment by the general practitioner: Provided, that such authorization shall not be issued in communities where specialized services are already provided in clinics or by salaried physicians supported or paid in whole or in part from public funds. As a rule, such special service shall only be authorized upon the written recommendation of the physician in attendance upon the case. Authorizations for the usual services of a specialist shall be subject to the limitations stated in Item 1 of Regulation 2 in this chapter.

b. A specialist is defined, under these rules, as a licensed practitioner of medicine who has had special training and experience in the treatment of a special disease or class of diseases, and who is restricting his practice in whole or in part to such specialty. The services of a specialist shall not be authorized, with a view to reimbursement by the Administration, except for cases and types of illness ordinarily referred to a specialist in that welfare district.

c. Reimbursement for expenditures made for the usual services of an authorized specialist shall be on the basis of an ordinary home or office visit: Provided, that in no instance shall that basis exceed the charge for a home visit.

---

[15] See Chapter I: Section A, *Item 1;* Section B, *Items 2* and *3;* and Section D, *Items 1* and *2,* above.

[16] Dental care is covered in Regulation 6, and bedside nursing care is covered in Regulation 7, of this Chapter.

Item 2. Consultations. The services of a consultant may be authorized when they are requested by the patient, his family, or the physician in attendance. Reimbursement may be granted for such authorized services, provided the charge does not exceed the charge for a home visit.

Item 3. First aid and/or emergency treatment. Authorized first aid and/or emergency treatment shall be eligible for reimbursement by the Administration: Provided, that such treatment is given in the patient's home, at the physician's office or at the place of accident, and provided further that the claim for such first aid treatment shall not exceed the charge for a home visit under these rules.

Item 4. X-ray diagnosis and treatment. a. Emergency and necessary x-ray examinations may be authorized, with a view to reimbursement from the Administration, only in those communities where x-ray examination and treatment service is not available[17] in clinics and hospitals supported in whole or in part from public funds. Under these rules, reimbursement may be obtained only on the basis of authorizations, issued for x-ray examinations and treatment provided in the office of a physician. The advisory committee of the New York State Medical Society at a conference on February 14, 1934, recommended that the basis of reimbursement for x-ray examinations authorized in physician's offices should be at a rate not to exceed fifty per cent more than the fee schedule adopted,[18] by the United States Employees Compensation Commission, after a conference with official representatives of the American, Catholic and Protestant Hospital Associations for use in hospitals, for injured Civil Works Administration Employees. This fee schedule, with the fifty per cent increase added is given in Regulation 9, below.

b. X-ray treatment shall be authorized on a limited basis, subject to the restrictions stated in the preceding paragraph, only when there is no satisfactory alternative treatment for the condition found. Full details of reasons for giving such treatment shall be submitted with the bill.

c. Dental x-rays may be authorized in accordance with the provisions of Regulations 6 and 9 below, for diagnostic purposes only.

Item 5. Minor surgery. a. Minor surgery, involving the less formidable manual and operative procedures for relieving traumatic and pathological conditions may be authorized, either on the basis of ordinary office calls or on an individual basis, in communities eligible to participate,[19] if it is to be performed in the patient's home, at the place of accident, or in the physician's office. The charge for such medical care shall be, for the purposes of reimbursement, either on the basis of a regular home or office visit, or

[17] Under provisions of §§ 83 and 85 of the Public Welfare Law; see Chapter III, Section C, *Item 1.*

[18] See Section 100, pages 5 and 6 of T.E.R.A. and F.C.W.A. Official Bulletin Number 18, issued January 16, 1934.

[19] See Chapter I, Section D, *Item 1,* page 11.

on a basis agreed upon by the attending physician and the local welfare official for the individual case, within the limits set by Regulation 9, below.

b. The charge for the minor operation shall include the administration of the necessary anaesthetic, if local in type, and necessary dressings and secondary services at the time of the operation. If a general anesthetic is given, a separate claim for reimbursement shall be submitted by the physician authorized to administer such general anesthetic.

c. Follow-up visits, when authorized, shall be eligible for reimbursement on the basis of regular office visits, and the written authorization shall be subject to the limitations imposed for attendance upon acute illness by Regulation 2, above. The name of the operation and description of the work done shall be entered in the physician's bill, if reimbursement is expected.

Item 6. Reduction of fractures. a. Authorizations may be issued for reduction, splinting, and after care of simple fractures, when such procedures are to be undertaken in the patient's home, at the place of accident, or in the physician's office. Such authorizations shall be issued only as a supplement to existing community services, where services supported locally in whole or in part from public funds, are available to provide this type of treatment.

b. Reimbursement for the reduction of fractures, may be allowed for charges not to exceed the schedule listed under Regulation 9, below. The charge should be dependent on the relative amount of work done, in relation to the maximum charge eligible for reimbursement.

c. When the fracture is compound, involving prolonged treatment in bed with the use of plaster casts and/or traction, such treatments shall be given in a hospital[20] whenever possible, and reimbursement shall not be allowed for treatment provided to such cases in the home, except on an individual basis, and following a review, by the authorizing official and the Administration, of the reasons for giving such treatment in the home.

d. After care and follow-up treatment of fractures shall be on the basis of regular home and/or office visits: Provided, that such treatment for fractures which do not impair the patient's ability to walk, shall be reimbursable only on the basis of regular office visits.

Item 7. Major surgery. a. Authorizations for major surgery on recipients of home relief shall not ordinarily be eligible for reimbursement. However, such authorizations may be issued on an emergency basis and in instances where it is not practicable to move the patient to a hospital for necessary care, and full reasons must be given in writing for performing the more important and dangerous operations in the home, at the site of the accident, or in the physician's office.

---

[20] In accordance with § 85 of the Public Welfare Law, See Chapter III, Section C.

22

b. Reimbursement for authorized major surgery may be allowed on the basis of charges not to exceed two-thirds of the minimum county fee schedule: Provided, that in no instance shall the basis for reimbursement exceed the limit set by Regulation 9, below.

Item 8. General anesthesia, surgical assistance and physiotherapy. a. When authorized, the physician giving the general anesthetic or acting as assistant at a major operation performed in the home, at the site of the accident, or in the physician's office under the restriction of Items 5 to 7 of this regulation, shall submit a separate claim for reimbursement, which may be allowed on the basis stipulated in Regulation 9, below.

b. Physiotherapy shall not ordinarily be authorized for recipients of home relief. Physiotherapy may be reimbursable on a limited scale, only when a special written authorization, following a review of the case by the advisory committee of the local medical society, is issued by the welfare official. Such special authorization shall be limited to five consecutive treatments. Reimbursement for further treatment shall be allowed only on authorization issued following submission of the request, and full details of the case, to the Division of Medical Care of the Administration[21] and after prior approval has been given by that division.

Item 9. Laboratory diagnostic service. a. The facilities of state, county and city laboratories and other laboratories approved by the state department of health for performing specified examinations and procedures shall continue to be used, by physicians authorized to provide medical care to recipients of home relief, for performing such diagnostic examinations under the existing procedures.

b. Laboratory diagnostic examinations authorized under the provisions of these Rules and Regulations shall be only as a necessary supplement[22] to the full use of existing facilities maintained under local statutes and/or charter provisions and paid for, in whole or in part, from local and/or state funds. Such authorized diagnostic examinations should be confined to making more adequate a program of medical care which is restricted to conditions that cause acute suffering, interfere with earning capacity, endanger life, or threaten some permanent new handicap that is preventable when medical care is sought.

c. Routine diagnostic examinations, such as urinalysis, made as part of an authorized office visit to a physician, shall be considered as part of such authorized office visit, and shall not be considered as a basis for additional reimbursement.

d. Reimbursement for authorized laboratory diagnostic examinations, provided under this regulation shall be on the basis of charges not to exceed two thirds of the minimum rate charged persons in the lowest income class by local state approved laboratories.

[21] T.E.R.A., 79 Madison Avenue, New York, N. Y.
[22] For which prior approval shall be obtained by the public welfare district, from the Administration, before it shall take effect.

e. Claims for reimbursement for such authorized sevice may be subject to review by a committee representing the New York State Association of Public Health Laboratories.

f. Authorization for a specified laboratory examination shall be restricted to laboratories approved, for making that examination, by the New York State Department of Health.

Item 10. Other special services. Other special services not covered above or in Regulations 6, 7, 8 and 9 of this chapter, shall be authorized only on an individual basis subject: to the restrictions, imposed by Chapter I; and to an expenditure, as a basis for reimbursement, which shall not exceed the maximum specified for each type of service in these Rules and Regulations.

Regulation 6. **Dental care.** *Introduction.* *a.* Emergency dental care in welfare districts eligible[23] to provide such care under these Rules and Regulations, shall be restricted to these extractions, fillings, treatments and repairs which are necessary for the relief of pain and for the correction of conditions that interfere with earning capacity, endanger life, or threaten some permanent future disability that is preventable when dental care is sought.

b. Such dental care shall be authorized only as a supplement to existing community services or to services provided on a work relief basis, except in welfare districts with no available dental services supported in whole or in part from local and/or State funds.

c. No dental program for school children shall be set up, under these regulations, which supplants a school dental service already supported by local and/or State funds.

Authorization and provision of dental care to recipients of home relief shall be subject to the following requirements:[24]

Item 1. Extractions. Dental extractions may be authorized when indicated: Provided that extractions of one or more permanent teeth, the loss of which would necessitate a denture which could not be provided from local funds, or which serve as key teeth for the retention of a denture, and extractions of one or more temporary teeth, the loss of which may result in the malocclusion of the permanent teeth in a child, shall not be authorized or undertaken, except in cases of infection.

Item 2. Fillings. *a.* Authorization of necessary dental fillings shall require that an approved method of pulp protection be a necessary preliminary procedure. All fillings shall be thoroughly polished after being properly contoured, constructed with correct contact points and with grooves and cusps carved to occlusion. Both work and material shall conform to the highest standards, except that gold shall be used only when prosthetic repairs are authorized.

[23] See Chapter I, Section D, page 11.
[24] See also Chapter I. Section B, Item 2, page 8.

b. Pit and fissure cavities shall not be considered as in need of "emergency dental care," and authorized expenditures for filling such cavities shall not be eligible for reimbursement by the Administration.

Item 3. Treatment.[25]   *a.* Emergency treatment may be authorized for the relief of pain and/or any acute oral pathological condition which endangers the health of the patient. Authorizations for emergency treatment shall be subject to the restrictions of Item 3 of Regulation 1 and of Item 8 of Regulation 6, of this chapter.

b. Emergency treatment shall include treatment for inflammation of the pulp and/or draining an alveolar abscess.

c. Bills submitted for authorized treatment of Vincent's stomatitis shall be accompanied by a report from a laboratory approved, by the State department of health, to make such an examination.

Item 4. Dental prophylaxis. *a.* The policy followed under these rules in the authorization of dental prophylaxis shall be restricted in scope.[26] Prophylaxis shall be authorized, with a view to reimbursement, only in cases where the patient suffers from diseases of the supporting tissues of the teeth, such as pyorrhea, Vincent's stomatitis, marked gingivitis, etc., or when heavy deposits of calculus endanger the health condition of the soft tissues of the oral cavity.

b. Dental prophylaxis, when authorized, shall consist of both thorough scaling and polishing of the teeth. When expenditures are made for cleaning and polishing of the teeth for purely aesthetic reasons, such expenditures shall not be eligible for reimbursement by the Administration.

c. Authorized prophylactic and other dental treatment should include detailed instructions in mouth hygiene and the proper use of the tooth brush.

Item 5. Dental x-ray examinations. *a.* Authorization of dental x-ray examinations shall be restricted to a minimum consistent with good dental care, and shall be for the purpose of diagnosis only.

b. X-ray films, taken under an authorization for dental care shall be the property of the department of public welfare, from which the authorization was obtained, and shall be given to it upon request without further charge.

Item 6. Special dental services. Special dental services not covered in the preceding items of this regulation, shall be authorized only on an individual basis, and then only when they cannot be provided through existing local agencies. The types of special dental service which are included in the scope of this program are as follows:

---

[25] See also Chapter I, Item 2, page 8.
[26] See Regulation 6, Dental care, *Introduction*, page 23.

a. Root canal therapy, which is to be authorized only when a key tooth, by such therapy, can be made to remain useful in the retention of a denture already present or, where the removal of an anterior tooth or teeth would necessitate a denture which could not be provided from local funds; and

b. Dental surgery, other than simple extractions, which may include such necessary operative procedures as removal of cysts, impacted teeth, or infected areas.

Item 7. Repair of dental prosthetic devices. a. The provision of dentures is not interpreted as within the scope of the Emergency Relief Act of New York State nor these Rules and Regulations. Paragraph six, of Item 1, *f*, section A, chapter I, of these regulations states[27] that "Medical" (dental and nursing) "supplies shall be restricted to the simplest *emergency* needs of the patient consistent with good medical" (dental and nursing) "care."

b. These *emergency* needs are interpreted to include the repair of vulcanite dentures and/or the replacement of teeth and clasps on such dentures. Work and material used in making such repairs shall conform to the highest standards and only 18.3 carat gold shall be used in making clasps.

c. Dentures may be authorized for recipients of home relief under the provisions of the Public Welfare Law[28] but such authorized expenditures shall not be eligible for reimbursement by the Administration.

Item 8. Maximum expenditure. To conserve Federal and/or State relief funds in the provision of adequate dental care to all recipients of home relief needing such care, the maximum charge for all dental care provided, under these Rules and Regulations, to one patient, shall not exceed twenty dollars ($20) as a basis for reimbursement.

Regulation 7. **Bedside nursing care.**[29] *Introduction. a.* Bedside nursing care to recipients of home relief shall be provided, whenever possible, by registered nurses employd by the Administration, on a work relief basis, under the state-wide bedside nursing service supervised by the New York State Department of Health in more than ninety public welfare districts in the State.

b. Bedside nursing care shall continue to be provided through existing community services, such as visiting nurses associations, public health nurses, etc., paid for in whole or in part from local and/or State funds, in accordance with local statutes and/or charter provisions.

---

[27] See also F.E.R.A. Rules and Regulations No. 7, page 6, paragraph 3.
[28] § 83, see Chapter III, Section C, Item 1.
[29] See Regulation 9, Section C.
(NOTE.—*Re dentures.*—For the guidance of local commissioners of public welfare authorizing dentures under § 83 of the Public Welfare Law, a schedule of charges for such dentures recommended by the Dental Society of the State of New York, is on file in the Division of Medical Care, T.E.R.A., 79 Madison Avenue, New York City. It will be sent to any commissioner of public welfare upon request.

Item 1. Bedside nursing, per visit. *a.* Bedside nursing care shall be authorized, on a per visit basis, only in communities where and to the extent to which work relief nurses are not available or where existing community services, mentioned above, are not adequate to carry the load, and then, as a rule, only in accordance with the need for such bedside nursing care as indicated by the attending physician. Authorizations for bedside nursing care shall be issued, subject to the restrictions imposed by Regulations 1, 2, 3, 4, 9 and 10 of this chapter.

b. Standards of accredited local nursing organizations shall be followed by nurses authorized to give bedside nursing care to recipients of home relief in their homes.

Item 2. Bedside nursing, per day. Bedside nursing care for acute and serious illnesses, when recommended by the physician in attendance on the case, may be authorized on a per diem basis where hospitalization is not possible or practicable and where such bedside nursing care is not available through work relief nurses or other existing local agencies.

Item 3. "Home helps," practical nursing. In isolated communities where the services of a registered graduate nurse are not available and for the care of chronic illnesses not requiring expert attention or institutional care, "home helps" or practical nurse housekeepers may be authorized to provide necessary service, on a per diem basis, provided that the employment of such "home helps" is recommended by the physician in attendance on the patient.

Regulation 8. **Medicine, drugs, sickroom supplies and prosthetic devices.** Such materials and supplies as are necessary to provide adequate medical care to recipients of home relief shall be authorized, subject to the following restrictions imposed on each type, if reimbursement from the Administration is contemplated for such authorized expenditures.

Item 1. Medicine and drugs. *a.* Physicians providing authorized medical care to recipients of home relief shall use a formulary which excludes expensive drugs where less expensive drugs can be used with the same therapeutic effect.

b. When expensive medication is considered essential by the attending physician, it may be authorized after consultation with the local medical advisory committee: Provided that, to be eligible for consideration with a view to reimbursement, the bill for such expensive medication, shall be accompanied by the written approval of the local medical advisory committee.

c. Certain special remedies[30] which are in general use for the treatment of specific maladies and which have been accepted as approved in "New and Non-official Remedies" by the Council of the

[30] Such as insulin, liver extract, digifolin and similar compounds of digitalis, ephedrin and its compounds, agarol, petrolagar and other mixtures containing only mineral oil and agar-agar.

American Medical Association may be authorized with a view to reimbursement, upon the prescription of the attending physician, without further consultation.

d. With the exceptions noted above, prescriptions for necessary drugs and medicine shall be restricted to the latest edition of the National Formulary and/or the United States Pharmacopeia; and proprietary or patent medicines, patent infant foods, and prescriptions containing proprietary remedies, shall not be eligible for reimbursement by the Administration. Substitutions should be made, from the National Formulary or the United States Pharmacopeia, for certain proprietary remedies, for example: phenobarbital should be substituted for luminal; hexamethylenamin for urotropin; silver nucleinate for argyrol; etc.

e. Arsphenamin or neo-arsphenamin may be eligible for reimbursement only for the treatment of other than venereal infections. These and other specific remedies for the treatment of venereal disease may be obtained by the attending physician, free of charge, from the state department of health, for the treatment of indigent patients. Expenditures for the treatment of venereal disease in recipients of home relief shall not be eligible for reimbursement by the Administration. Such treatment is by law[31] a responsibility of the local health department.

f. Certain approved sera, vaccines and biologicals, may be obtained free of charge from the Division of Laboratories and Research of the state department of health;[32] expenditures for such therapeutic or diagnostic materials shall not be eligible for reimbursement by the Administration.

g. Medicine dispensed directly by a physician in the course of an authorized home or office visit is ordinarily included in the flat charge for such a visit. In certain instances where an expensive drug is used or a large quantity of an ordinary medicine is required, the physician may submit an additional claim for the medicine he dispenses: Provided that, such a claim shall be eligible for reimbursement only if it is itemized to include the name and amount of each ingredient.

Item 2. Sickroom supplies. Authorization for medical and sickroom supplies shall be restricted to the simplest *emergency* needs of the patient consistent with good medical care. Such authorizations shall be issued only on the basis of a physician's prescription for an individual patient and shall be confined to such necessary items as gauze, adhesive tape, cotton, ear syringe, eye cup, ice bag, clinical thermometer, hot water bottle (not electric pad), and hypodermic syringe and needles (for diabetics).

Item 3. Prosthetic devices and surgical appliances. a. Authorizations for necessary prosthetic devices shall be issued to meet emergency needs only, and shall *not* include, with a view to reimburse-

---

[31] Article XVII, B, § 343m to 343t (added by Chapter 264, Laws of 1918) of the Public Health Law.
[32] Albany, N. Y.

ment, such expensive devices as artificial limbs, vulcanite dentures, etc. Such devices may be authorized by the local commissioner of public welfare,[33] but expenditures on the basis of such authorization shall not be eligible for reimbursement by the Administration.

b. Expenditures for authorized repairs for artificial limbs shall be eligible for reimbursement only on an individual basis and then only after approval has been secured from the Administration.[34] Expenditures for authorized repairs of dentures shall be eligible for reimbursement subject to the restriction imposed by these Rules and Regulations.[35]

c. Necessary surgical and orthopedic appliances, including simple braces and other devices, may be authorized under these Rules and Regulations, upon the written order of a competent physician, for the rehabilitation of recipients of home relief who are twenty-one or more years of age.

d. Claims for reimbursement for authorized orthopedic appliances may be subject to review by the Division of Orthopedics, or an orthopedic consultant of the state department of health.

e. Expenditures for such prosthetic devices for persons under twenty-one years of age shall not be eligible for reimbursement by the Administration. Care and necessary prosthetic devices for a "physically handicapped child" comes under the jurisdiction of the State Education Law.[36] Under subdivision seven-a of section two of the Children's Court Act:[37] "A 'physically handicapped child' is a person under twenty-one years of age who, by reason of a physical defect or infirmity, whether congenital or acquired by accident, injury or disease, is or may be expected to be totally or partially incapacitated for education or for remunerative occupation, but shall not include the deaf and the blind."

f. Optical supplies, including eye glasses, shall be authorized, with a view to reimbursement, only upon the written prescription of a licensed physician who, in his specialty as an oculist or opthalmologist, is permitted to use drugs in examining eyes. The reimbursable claim for such an examination and prescription shall be restricted by the provisions of Item 4 of Regulation 9, below.

Expenditures for eye glasses shall be eligible for reimbursement only when they are provided under the following conditions: 1. When glasses are necessary in order to enable a recipient of home relief to secure employment; 2. When, in the opinion of the examining physician-oculist eyesight is endangered because of lack of glasses; 3. When the patient cannot attend to usual household tasks, or a child cannot make proper progress in school, without glasses; and 4. When, according to the attending physician-oculist

---

[33] In accordance with § 83 of the Public Welfare Law, see Chapter III,
[34] Division of Medical Care, T.E.R.A., 79 Madison Avenue, New York, N. Y.
[35] See Regulation 6, Item 7, page 25, and Regulation 9, Section D, Item 3, b.
[36] For details write the Physically Handicapped Children's Bureau, State Education Department, Albany, N. Y.
[37] Chapter 547, Laws of 1922, with subsequent amendments.

or opthalmologist, the patient has a disease or defect of the eye which requires glasses for its cure or correction.

Regulation 9. **Schedule of reimbursable charges.** *Introduction.* *a.* It is realized by the Administration that with the funds available, it is impossible to compensate fully the physician, dentist or nurse for his or her professional services. The following schedule of charges, therefore, should not be considered as complete compensation for services rendered, but rather as a maximum basis for reimbursement, with due consideration for the conservation of relief funds to the mutual benefit of the patient, the professional attendant and the taxpayer.

The following schedule of reimburseable charges was prepared following a conference, in Albany, N. Y., on April 16, 1934, between authorized representatives of: the Medical and Dental Societies of the State of New York; the Administration and the State Commissioner of Health.

b. The charges listed are hereby established by the Administration as the maximum eligible for reimbursement, under these Rules and Regulations. However, no statement in these regulations shall be construed to prevent a local commissioner of public welfare: from making additional payments, for specified services, from local funds;[38] or from making payment at less that the maximum charges stated in these regulations, where the local professional organization has agreed to the authorization of specified services at a lower rate.

Section A. *Medical Care.* (Personal Services.) The services of a physician, authorized with a view to reimbursement by the Administration, shall be subject to the restrictions imposed by these Rules and Regulations, and expenditures for such services shall be eligible for reimbursement at not to exceed the following schedule of charges.

Item 1. Home visit. Authorized home visits, subject to the restrictions imposed by Section D, and Regulations 1, 2,[39] and 3, above, shall be reimbursable at a rate not to exceed $2.00

Item 2. Office visit. Authorized office visits, subject to the restrictions stated for Item 1, above, shall be reimbursable at a rate not to exceed................. 1.00

Item 3. Obstetrical care. Authorized obstetrical care in the home including necessary prenatal care, delivery in the home and postnatal care, subject to the general restrictions and requirements imposed by these Rules and Regulations and the specific requirements of Regulation 4, above, shall be eligible for reimbursement:

---

[38] Under § 83, of the Public Welfare Law, See Chapter III, Section C.
[39] Note especially Item 6, page 14.

a. For the services of a physician, on the basis of a flat rate which shall not exceed.. .... 25.00
or,

b. For the services of a physician, on the basis of a flat rate for delivery in the home and necessary post-natal and postpartum care at not to exceed......... 15.00
and, prenatal care at a rate not to exceed $1.00 per visit, with a maximum for such prenatal care at a rate not to exceed 10.00

c. For the services of a midwife, subject to the requirements of Item 2, c,[40] Section D and Item 11,[41] of Regulation 4, above, on the basis of a rate not to exceed 12.50

d. For other authorized obstetrical services not covered above, on the basis indicated in Regulation 4, above.

Special Services

Item 4. The usual services of a specialist. Authorized services of a specialist, shall be subject, for the purposes of reimbursement, to the general restrictions of these Rules and Regulations and the specific requirements of Item 1 of Regulation 5,[41] and shall be eligible for reimbursement at a rate not to exceed............ 2.00

Such services include: refraction; eye, ear, nose, throat and skin treatment; intravenous therapy; etc.

Item 5. Consultation. The services of a consultant, authorized under these Rules and Regulations,[42] shall be eligible for reimbursement at not to exceed........ 2.00

Item. 6. Emergency or first aid treatment. Authorized emergency or first aid treatment, including necessary dressings, to be provided in the home, at the place of accident or in the physician's office, shall be eligible for reimbursement at not to exceed.................. 2.00

Item 7. X-ray examinations and treatment. a. Diagnostic X-ray examinations authorized subject to the requirements of Item 4, Regulation 5, above, shall be eligible for reimbursement on the basis of a rate not to exceed 50 per cent more than the schedule of charges[43] adopted by the United States Employees Compensation Commission for use in the examination of injured Civil Works Administration employees. The 50 per cent additional charge was recommended for X-ray examinations restricted to physicians' offices, by the Advisory Committee of the Medical Society of the State of New York, at a conference on January 16, 1934.

[40] See page 12.
[41] See page 19.
[42] See Item 2, Regulation 5, on page 19.
[43] See Section 100, pages 5 and 6 of T.E.R.A. and F.C.W.A. Official Bulletin Number 18, issued January 16, 1934.

The following schedule of charges for specified X-ray examinations made in physicians' offices shall be the maximum basis for reimbursement by the Administration:

	No. of films	Maximum Reimbursable Charge[44]
Ankle joint, antero-posterior and lateral views...	2	$3.75
Arm, humerus, antero-posterior and lateral views.	2	3.75
Bladder, with injection, antero-posterior view...	1	7.50
Chest, for pulmonary or cardiac diagnosis, plain.	1	5.75
Chest, for pulmonary or cardiac diagnosis stereoscopic	2	7.50
Clavicle, postero-anterior view.................	1	3.75
Elbow, antero-posterior and lateral views.......	2	3.75
Fluoroscopy, when required, without film.......	1	1.50
Foot, antero-posterior and lateral views.........	2	3.75
Forearm, radius and ulna, antero-posterior and lateral views	2	3.75
Foreign body in eye, location of (the fragment charted in three planes and its dimensions ascertained by the method of Sweet or equivalent as needed).............................	..	18.75
Gall bladder, Graham technic, including cost of dye	1	15.00
Gastro-intestinal tract, complete X-ray study, including fluoroscopy, as needed..............	..	18.75
Hand, antero-posterior and lateral views........	2	3.75
Hip joint, plain, antero-posterior view..........	1	5.75
Hip joint, stereoscopic, antero-posterior view..	2	7.50
Intestine, barium clysma, 14 x 17 films for position and outline, as needed	..	11.25
Jaw, upper or lower.......................	1	3.75
Kidneys, right and left, for comparison, 11 x 14 films as needed...........................	..	7.50
Knee joint, antero-posterior and lateral views..	2	3.75
Leg, tibia and fibula, antero-posterior and lateral views	2	3.75
Lipoidol injection for bronchiectasis, etc. including Roentgenograms and interpretation, as needed	..	18.75
Pelvis, 14 x 17, single film, antero-posterior view	1	7.50
Pyelography, using uroselectan or similar preparation (including cost of drug)...........	4	15.00
Ribs, plain view over suspected area, 10 x 12 film	1	5.75
Scapula	1	3.75
Shoulder joint, plain, antero-posterior view....	1	3.75

[44] Only when taken in the office of a physician.

	Maximum No. of Reimbursable films	Charge[44]
Shoulder joint, stereoscopic, antero-posterior views	2	7.50
Sinuses, frontal and ethmoid, antero-posterior and lateral views.........................	2	7.50
Sinuses, mastoid, right and left sides for comparison	2	7.50
Sinuses, maxillary, antero-posterior and lateral views	2	7.50
Skull, ventriculogram — air injection — as needed ....:...............................	..	11.25
Skull, natero-posterior and lateral views........	2	7.50
Skull, stereoscopic	2	11.25
Spine, cervical, antero-posterior and lateral views	2	7.50
Spine, dorsal, antero-posterior and lateral views.	2	7.50
Spine, lumbo-sacral, with coccyx antero-posterior and lateral views	2	7.50
Stomach, barium or bismuth meal, 14 x 17 film, after ingestion, four 8 x 10 films for detection of duodenal cap; total of four 8 x 10 films, including fluoroscopy	4	18.75
Teeth, See Item 5, Section B, Regulation 9, below.		
Thigh, femur, antero-posterior and lateral views	2	5.75
Ureters, right and left, for comparison........ (1 or 2)		11.25
Wrist, antero-posterior and lateral views......	2	3.75

b. X-ray treatments authorized subject to the requirements of Item 4, Regulation 5, above, shall be eligible for reimbursement at a rate not to exceed:

for low voltage or superficial treatments.......... 2.00

for high voltage or deep X-ray therapy.......... 3.00

Item 8. Minor operations. a. Minor surgery, authorized to be performed in the home or in the physician's office, shall be subject to the general restrictions imposed by these Rules and Regulations and the specific requirements of Item 5, of Regulation 5, above, and shall be eligible for reimbursement on a sliding scale, dependent upon the services rendered,[46] at a rate not to exceed........................... 3.00

to 10.00

[45] Only when taken in the office of a physician.

[46] Examples of claims submitted for reimbursement which have been approved by the Administration are: circumcision of an infant—$5.00, for an older boy or adult—$10.00; blood transfusion—$5.00; myringotomy—$3.00; tonsillectomy and adenoidectomy—$6.00 to $10.00; minor incisions and excisions—$2.00 to $5.00; etc.—all performed in the home or in the physician's office.

Such reimbursable charges for minor surgery shall include necessary dressings at the time of the operation.

b. Authorized follow-up visits shall be eligible for reimbursement on the basis of a charge not to exceed that for an authorized office visit...................... 1.00

Item 9. Reduction of simple fractures. Reduction and splinting of simple fractures shall be authorized subject to the general restrictions imposed by these Rules and Regulations and the specific restrictions imposed by Item 6 of Regulation 5, above, and shall be eligible for reimbursement on a sliding scale, dependent on the relative amount of work involved, on the basis of (except for a fracture of the pelvis or the surgical neck of the femur) a charge not to exceed.... 10.00 Expenditures for authorized reduction (including cast) of a fracture of the pelvis or the surgical neck of the femur shall be on the basis of a charge not to exceed.. 25.00 Authorized after care and follow-up treatment of fractures shall be eligible for reimbursement subject to the restrictions imposed by Item 6, *d* of Regulation 5, above.

Item 10. Major operations. Authorizations for major surgery on recipients of home relief shall not generally be eligible for reimbursement by the Administration. However, subject to the general restrictions imposed by these Rules and Regulations and the specific restrictions imposed by Item 7 of Regulation 5, above, major surgery authorized in the home, at the site of the accident, or in the physician's office, shall be eligible for reimbursement on the basis of a charge not to exceed two-thirds of the minimum county fee schedule: Provided that, in no instance shall such basis of reimbursement exceed 25.00

Item 11. General anesthesia, surgical assistance, and physiotherapy. Subject to the general restrictions imposed by these Rules and Regulations and the specific restrictions imposed by Items 5 to 8, inclusive, of Regulation 5, above, separate claims for the above services, when authorized, shall be eligible for reimbursement on the basis of a charge not to exceed the following schedule of charges:

a. General anesthesia given by a physician in the home or at the physician's office, not to exceed........ 5.00

b. Surgical assistance given by a physician, not to exceed 5.00

c. Physiotherapy, restricted to a maximum of 5 visits, at not to exceed, per treatment................ 1.00

Item 12. Laboratory diagnostic services. Authorized laboratory diagnostic examinations, subject to the requirements and restrictions imposed by Item 9 of Regulation 5,[47] shall be eligible for reimbursement on the basis of a rate not to exceed two-thirds of the minimum rate charged by local State approved laboratories.

Item 13. Other special services.[48] Special services, not covered above shall be eligible for reimbursement, when authorized, only on the basis of a rate not to exceed two-thirds of the local minimum fee schedule: Provided that, in no instance shall the basis of reimbursement exceed 25.00

Section C. *Dental Care.* (Personal services.) The following schedule of charges for authorized dental care is hereby established, as the basis for reimbursement, by the Administration, after consultation[49] with authorized representatives of the Dental Society of the State of New York.

Item 1. Extractions. Authorized dental extractions subject to the restrictions imposed by Item 1 of Regulation 6, above, shall be reimbursable at not to exceed the following charges:

a. First tooth, including necessary anesthetic and postoperative treatment 1.50

b. Each additional tooth extracted from the same patient, not necessarily extracted at the same visit.... 1.00

c. Maximum charge for authorized extraction of teeth from any one patient shall not exceed................ 10.00

d. All gold crowns and bridge work removed by a dentist authorized to extract teeth, in the course of such extractions, shall be the property of the department of public welfare issuing the authorization and such gold crowns and bridge work shall be submitted to that department of public welfare at the same time that the bill is presented for performing such authorized extractions. Gold obtained under this provision may be disposed of and the money obtained therefore may be utilized by the department of public welfare as indicated in the last paragraph of Item 3, *b*, Section D, Regulation 9, below.

Item 2. Fillings, including an approved method of pulp protection, and subject to the requirements and restriction imposed by Item 2, Regulation 6, above, shall be reimbursable at charges not to exceed the following:

---

[47] See pages 22 and 23.

(Note.—Prophylaxis for purely aesthetic reasons shall not be eligible for reimbursement.)

[48] Dental services are covered in Regulation 6, above and Items 1 to 7, inclusive in Section B, of Regulation 9, below.

[49] In Albany, N. Y., April 16, 1934.

a. Silver amalgam meeting specifications approved by the American Dental Association: one surface........   2.00

two or more surfaces.............................   3.00

b. Silicious cement meeting specifications approved by the American Dental Association (Restricted to fillings in anterior teeth only)..........................   3.00

c. Other cements, meeting specifications approved by the American Dental Association, restricted to conditions for which a temporary filling is indicated: for a permanent tooth 1.00

temporary tooth 0.50

Item 3. Treatment. Emergency treatment for conditions listed under Item 3, Regulation 6, above, shall be reimbursable on a per visit basis not to exceed......   1.00

Item 4. Dental prophylaxis, subject to the general restrictions imposed by these Rules and Regulations and the specific restrictions and requirements of Item 4, Regulation 6, above, shall be reimbursable at a rate not to exceed 2.00

Item 5. Dental X-ray examinations, for diagnosis only and subject to other restrictions of Item 5, Regulation 6, above, shall be eligible for reimbursement at a rate no to exceed:

Single film 0.50

Each additional film for the same patient, not necessarily taken at the same visit, up to and including the tenth film 0.25

Full mouth X-ray series, not less than eleven films....   3.00

Item 6. Special dental services, authorized only on an individual basis, and subject to the restrictions imposed by Item 6, *a* and *b,* Regulation 6, above, shall be reimbursable at charges not to exceed the following:

a. Root canal therapy, including silicate filling and at least one extra X-ray when the therapeutic procedure and filling is completed, for the first root canal........   5.00

for the second root canal treated in the same tooth....   3.00

for the third root canal treated in the same tooth....   2.00

b. Dental surgery, other than simple extractions, to include such necessary operative procedures as removal of cysts, impacted teeth and/or infected areas, from....   5.00

to 10.00

depending upon the time spent and the skill required: Provided that, the total reimbursable charge for dental surgery, for any one patient shall not exceed.........   10.00

Item 7. Maximum expenditure, for all reimbursable dental care provided for any one person under these Rules and Regulations, shall be, for the persons stated in Item 8, Regulation 6, above, on the basis of total charges not to exceed 20.00

a. Should a patient fail to return for the completion of authorized treatment, the dentist may receive a pro rata share of remuneration for the authorized work actually completed.

Section D. *Bedside nursing care.* (Personal services.) The following schedule of charges for authorized bedside nursing care and authorized service of "home helps" is hereby established by the Administration as its basis for reimbursement.

Item 1. Registered nurses on a per visit basis. Subject to the general restrictions imposed by these Rules and Regulations,[50] and the specific restrictions imposed by Item 1, Regulation 7, above, bedside nursing care provided by registered nurses authorized on a per visit basis, shall be reimbursable at a rate not to exceed.....   1.00
per visit: Provided that, no additional allowance shall be reimbursable for advice and/or care given to other members of the same household by the nurse in the course of an authorized home visit.[51]

Item. 2. Registered nurses on a per diem basis. Subject to the general restrictions imposed by these Rules and Regulations, and the specific restrictions imposed by Item 2, Regulation 7, above, necessary bedside nursing care provided by registered nurses authorized on a per diem basis, shall be reimbursable at charges not to exceed the following:
a. For acute non-communicable diseases, per 12 hour day 4.00
b. For acute communicable diseases, per 12 hour day   5.00

Item 3. "Home helps" on a per diem basis. a. Subject to the general restrictions imposed by these Rules and Regulations, and the specific restrictions imposed by Item 3, Regulation 7, above, the necessary services provided by "home helps" or practical nurse housekeepers authorized on a per diem basis, shall be reimbursable at charges per day not to exceed............   1.50
to 2.00
b. When a "home help" or practical nurse housekeeper lives in the household of a family on home relief during her period of authorized service, an additional allowance for food added to the household home relief food budget shall be eligible for reimbursement by the Administration when specifically authorized by the local welfare official.

[50] See Chapter II; Regulations 1, 2, 3, 4, 8 and 10.
[51] See Chapter II, Regulation 2, Item 6, page 15.

Section E. *Materials and Supplies. Introduction. a.*
The scope of materials and supplies which may be
provided to recipients of home relief shall include necessary medicine, drugs, sickroom supplies and prosthetic
devices, subject to the restrictions imposed by these
Rules and Regulations.

b. Commissioners of public welfare are urged to make
trade agreements or request bids for the provision of
these materials and supplies, in order that available
relief funds may be conserved.

Item 1. Medicines and drugs. a. Physicians providing authorized medical care to recipients of home relief
shall use a formulary which excludes expensive drugs
where less expensive drugs can be used with the same
therapeutic effect. Medicine and drugs, ordered in writing by a physician, shall be authorized subject to the
general restrictions of these Rules and Regulations and
the specific requirements of Item 1 of Regulation 8,
above,[52] and shall be eligible for reimbursement at
charges not to exceed the following:

b. Compounded prescriptions containing no rare or
costly drugs 0.75

c. Uncompounded prescriptions for ordinary drugs.. 0.50

d. Uncompounded prescriptions for the more expensive drugs 0.75

e. Compounded or uncompounded prescriptions for
special and more costly medicines and preparations,
such as insulin, at prices not to exceed: 20 per cent more
than the wholesale price listed in the current "Druggists' Circular"
plus a service charge not in excess of................ 0.25
in cases where these drugs are compounded.

f. Simple drugs furnished by a physician in the course
of a home or office visit shall not ordinarily be eligible
for reimbursement except as part of the service provided
under an authorized visit. In certain instances where a
physician, in the more isolated communities, dispenses
large quantities or more expensive drugs, a claim may
be submitted for reimbursement at a rate not to exceed. 0.50
Provided, that the claim lists the name and quantity of
each drug, and complies with the restrictions imposed by
Item 1 of Regulation 8, above.

Item 2. Sickroom supplies. Necessary sickroom
supplies shall be authorized as a rule only on the order
of a physician, and expenditures for such materials,
subject to the restrictions imposed by Item 2 of Regula-

[52] See page 26.

tion 8, above, shall be eligible for reimbursement either:
a. On the basis of the price secured by competitive bids, or

b. In any case at a price not to exceed............. 20%
more than the standard current wholesale price for such materials.

c. Provided that, the name of the physician issuing the order for necessary sickroom supplies shall be made a part of the claim for reimbursement.

Item 3. Prosthetic devices and surgical appliances. Introduction. Subject to the general restrictions imposed by these Rules and Regulations and the specific requirements of Item 3 of Regulation 8, above, necessary prosthetic devices and appliances (including glasses, glass eyes, simple braces, repair of dentures, etc.) may be authorized for recipients of home relief, with a view to reimbursement by the Administration. Prosthetic devices shall be purchased, whenever possible, on the basis of the lowest bid submitted to the commissioner of public welfare for such devices.

a. Orthopedic and surgical appliances. Subject to the restrictions imposed by Item 3 of Regulation 8, above, authorized expenditures for orthopedic and surgical appliances shall be eligible for reimbursement at a charge obtained upon competitive bid and/or at an appreciable reduction from the current retail price.

b. Repair of dentures. The repair of dental prosthetic devices, including repairs of vulcanite dentures and/or the replacement of clasps on such dentures shall be subject to the requirements of Item 7, Regulation 6, above, and shall be reimbursable at a rate not to exceed:

1. Vulcanizing charge including repair of all cracks, fissures and/or fractures; replacement of one or more teeth; and attaching by vulcanization one or more clasps —in any one vulcanite denture................... 3.00
2. Additional charge for first tooth replaced in such a vulcanite denture 1.00
3. Additional charge for each additional tooth, after the first, replaced in any such vulcanite denture...... 0.50
4. Additional charge for making and fitting a clasp, only in cases where a new clasp is required, to replace a broken clasp or to change the point of retention due to loss of a key tooth, to insure an accurate fit of any such vulcanite denture 4.00;
Provided, that only 18.3 carat gold shall be used in making clasps, and provided further, that all clasps removed by the dentist and/or laboratory technician shall be the property of the department of public welfare authorizing dental care for the owner of the denture, and such

clasps be submitted to that department of public welfare authorizing dental care for the owner of the denture, and such clasps be submitted to that department of public welfare at the same time that the bill is presented for performing authorized services. Gold clasps obtained by a department of public welfare under this provision may, when a sufficient quantity is collected, be submitted by it to the Treasurer of the United States for reimbursement on the basis of gold content. Monies obtained by a department of public welfare from this source, or under the similar provisions of Item 1, Section B, Regulation 9, above, may be used by such department to provide more milk and hence better teeth for children in families receiving home relief.

c. Optical supplies. Subject to the general restrictions imposed by these Rules and Regulations and the specific requirements of Item 3, *f* of Regulation 8, above,[53] authorized expenditures for eye glasses shall be eligible for reimbursement preferably on the basis of prices obtained by competitive bids, at charges not to exceed the following:

1. Average lenses and frame, of standard quality, per pair ....2.25 to 3.50
2. Toric lenses and frame, of standard quality, per pair ....2.75 to 3.75
3. Bifocal lenses and frame, of standard quality, per pair .... 4.00 to 5.50

The above reimbursable charges do not include the charge, for the prescription for the glasses, which is subject to the restrictions imposed by Item 4 of this regulation.[54] In addition to the specifications for the lenses, the prescription shall also give measurements necessary to insure that frames will fit: namely, pupilary distance, size of nose piece, and temple length.

Regulation 10. **Bills.** The following procedure is hereby established for the submission of bills for services and materials authorized for the purpose of providing more adequate medical care to recipients of home relief.

Item 1. General requirements. a. Physicians, dentists, nurses, druggists and others who are providing authorized medical care, to recipients of home relief, under the requirements of these Rules and Regulations, shall submit to the local welfare official, monthly (within 10 days after the last day of the calendar month in which such medical care was provided), an itemized bill for each patient.

b. Each bill shall be chronologically arranged and shall contain full details as required in Items 2 to 4, below, to permit proper audit.

[53] See pages 28 and 29.
[54] See page. 30.

c. All vouchers for medical care (provided by physicians, dentists, nurses, druggists, others) shall be submitted to the Administration under a separate claim, not later than the last day of the calendar month next succeeding the month during which the provision of such care and/or medical supplies was authorized. Claims submitted later than such date may not be audited until after audit of current claims is completed with corresponding delay in reimbursement to local welfare districts. In order that proper evaluation may be made of medical care for individual patients, so far as possible, the claims for reimbursement for medicines, drugs and medical supplies shall be submitted with the claim for medical, dental and nursing care for the same patients.

Item 2. Specific requirements. a. Physicians, dentists, nurses and other professional personnel providing authorized personal services to recipients of home relief shall submit, in their bills, the following details: date and number of written order; name, age, and address of patient (also name of the head of the household receiving home relief, unless he or she is the patient); diagnosis, or specific indication of the nature of the illness (acute or chronic); whether treatment was given in the patient's home or in the office of the physician or dentist, with full details, if unusual services are given; a chronological list of the dates on which services were rendered; and the status of the case at the end of the month—"cured, needs further treatment, hospitalized (give date and name of hospital), dead (give date of death), etc."

b. Druggists or pharmacists authorized to provide drugs and/or medical supplies under the general and specific restrictions of these Rules and Regulations, to recipients of home relief shall submit, in their bill, the following details: date and number of written order; name, age and address of patient (and head of household if other than the patient), a copy of the prescription or, the name and amount of each drug and the name of the physician prescribing it. Bills for large amounts of medication or medical supplies, which involve unusual expenditures should give sufficient details on the case, or a reference to the bill of the attending physician, as a justification for such expenditure. For example, when insulin is given, the bill should include, the size of 'the vial the number of units per cubic centimeter, and the physician's estimate of the monthly needs of the patients.

c. Medical supply houses or other firms authorized to provide prosthetic devices shall submit bills with the data required above, including a specific description of the device or material provided under the authorization, and the written order and name and address of the physician prescribing it.

Item 3. Bill form. Bills shall, as a rule, be submitted on T.E.R.A. Form 211, adapted to present the details required in this regulation. Bills for medical care (including personal services of physician, dentist, nurse, etc., and materials and supplies) shall be accompanied by the original written order, except for cases in

which medical service under an authorization has not terminated
during the calendar month covered by the bill, in which cases the
bill shall show, in addition to the details required above, the date
and serial number of the outstanding order.

Item 4. Retroactive bills. Bill submitted for services or materials and supplies provided on the basis of retroactive authorizations as defined in Item 2 of Regulation 1, above,[55] shall not be
eligible for reimbursement by the Administration.

Regulation 11. **Professional audit and arbitration.** The Administration is desirous of maintaining professional standards in the
provision of medical care to recipients of home relief, and solicits
the cooperation of the organized profession in establishing arrangements for providing medical and other professional advice to commissioners of public welfare. Under the provisions of Section C[56]
of Chapter I of these Rules and Regulations, audit and arbitration
of bills for professional service may be conducted under professional supervision with regard to: reasonableness of any individual
bill for authorized service; failure to maintain professional standards; proposed changes in policy and procedure; and principles
to be followed in the allocation of cases to physicians.

Regulation 12. **Monthly report.** The local department of public
welfare, shall submit, at the end of each calendar month, a monthly
report of total medical, dental, nursing services and drugs and
medical supplies authorized and submitted for reimbursement
for the preceding month. This report should contain a summary
of relevant data for each physician, dentist, nurse and druggist,
including: the number of different patients for whom care was
authorized number of home visits; number of office visits; number
of confinements; number of special services;[57] and total charge on
all claims included in bills.

Regulation 13. **Authorization of change in scope of local program.** The local program of medical care adopted under these
Rules and Regulations shall be subject to the restrictions imposed
by Items 1 and 2 of Section D, above.[58] No change in the scope
of local services, provided under existing statutes from non-relief
funds, shall be made with a view to securing reimbursement from
the Administration for such services, without prior written
approval by the Administration. A request for approval in change
of scope of the local program of medical care shall be accompanied
by detailed monthly records of the services in question for a period
of not less than the two preceding years, as well as evidence that
these services are not adequate to give needed care to recipients
of home relief.

[55] See page 14.
[56] See pages 10 and 11.
[57] See Items 4 to 13, pages 30 to 34.
[58] See pages 10 and 11.

CHAPTER III

A Summary of Basic Legislation and
A Chronological Review of
Prior Regulations

With an Appendix of Quotations from the Public
Welfare Law

Sections and regulations, governing the policy and procedures of the Administration, as adopted in Chapters I and II, above, which conflict with analogous statements in the following regulations and/or official statements, shall supersede such conflicting statements.

Section A. Basic legislation

Item. 1. The Emergency Relief Act of the State of New York (Chapter 798 of the Laws of 1931) defines medical care as one of the necessaries of life to be provided to such of its inhabitants as are found to be imperilled by the existing and threatened deprivation of such necessaries of life, owing to the present economic depression. Paragraph 8 of Section 2 of this Act reads as follows:

"'Home Relief' means shelter, fuel, food, clothing, light, *medicine or medical attendance furnished* by a municipal corporation to persons or their dependents *in their abode or habitation* and does not include relief to veterans under existing laws, old age relief or allowance made to mothers for the care of dependent children." [59]

Item 2. The Emergency Relief Act was subsequently amended on May 1, 1933 by Chapter 646 of the Laws of 1933 to read as follows:

"'Home Relief' means shelter, fuel, food, clothing, light, necessary household supplies, *medicine, medical supplies,* relief to veterans under existing laws *and medical attendance furnished* by a municipal corporation or a town, where home relief is a town charge, to persons or their dependents *in their abode or habitation* whenever possible and does not include old age relief or allowances made to mothers for the care of dependent children or *hospital or institutional care.*" [59]

Item 3. The Act was further amended on April 27, 1934 [60] by Chapter 303 of the Laws of 1934 to read as follows:

"§ 16-a. *Work relief disability allowance.* 1. Persons employed on work relief projects under the provisions of this act as heretofore or hereafter amended and receiving "work relief" as defined

---

[59] Italics mine (Ed.) ; See Section C, *Item 1,* on page 46, below, for legal provisions for authorizing services, such as hospital or institutional care, excluded from the scope of the Emergency Relief Act.

[60] To take effect immediately and provisions thereof effective as of April 1, 1934.

herein shall not be deemed to come within the scope of the provisions or benefits provided by chapter six hundred fifteen of the laws of nineteen hundred twenty-two as amended. and known as the workmen's compensation law; but all persons receiving "work relief" who shall become temporarily disabled or injured by reason of any cause arising out of and in the course of their employment shall, during the period of said disability, so caused within the duration of the emergency period as defined herein, continue to receive" *(home)* "*relief* on the basis of the budgetary needs of the said person's family as determined under the standards and pursuant to the rules and regulations of the administration and in addition thereto shall be provided with such medical services as the administration may deem necessary.[61]

Section B. **Chronological review of prior regulations.**

Item 1. The first detailed instructions on medical care under the Emergency Relief Act of 1931 were sent "To Public Welfare Officials" on December 8, 1931. They are quoted below in full:

"Interpretation of 'Medicines or Medical Attendance
to Persons or Their Dependents in
Their Abode or Habitation.' "

"This shall include medical service in the home[62] as well as medicines, and such sickroom supplies as are necessary. Other expenditures for the care of the sick may be approved depending upon the circumstances."

"Condition of Approval

"The Administration reserves the right to refuse approval in whole or part of claims by Municipal Corporations in cases:

"1. Where necessary hospital or institutional care has not been provided or has been unduly delayed: and

"2. Where full use has not been made of all existing public and private facilities providing free medical services.

"Procedure: Orders for Medical Service.

"When public welfare officers authorize expenditures for medical relief, they shall fill out the usual home relief order forms, in duplicate, and note that medical care is authorized. The original should be sent to the physician or the authorized medical agent immediately and must be returned by him with his bill. This bill should contain the following items:

"1. Diagnosis or condition of patient.

"2. Duration of treatment.

"3. Nature of services rendered.

"*Note.*—The inclusion of the above data on the physician's bill will waive the usual requirement for the countersignature (on the Home Relief Order Form) of the person receiving relief.

---

[61] Italics mine. (Ed.)

[62] The attorney general has interpreted this in the interest of economy to included medical attendance at a physician's office in cases in which the patient is able to go there.

"The duplicate home relief order should be retained by the welfare officer as a memorandum for check against the bill, on receipt of which the total expenditure under this order should be noted.

"Procedure: Orders for Medicines and Sickroom Supplies

"1. A physician's prescription is required for all medicines and sickroom supplies. According to the local custom, it may be sent directly to the pharmacist or filed with the welfare officer who uses it as a basis for issuing an order to the pharmacist.

"2. The physician's prescription must show the date, patient's name and address, and specifically state the nature and quantity of medicines or supplies ordered.

"3. Countersignature of patient or a member of his family must be affixed on either the order or the prescription.

"4. Bills must indicate the nature and quality of medicines or supplies furnished. Separate bills need not be made for each relief order or physician's prescription filled; instead bill may cover a number of orders, or prescriptions filled.

"5. Either the welfare officer's order or the physician's prescription, as the case may be, should be attached to the pharmacist's bill.

"TEMPORARY EMERGENCY RELIEF ADMINISTRATION,

JESSE ISIDOR STRAUS,

Chairman."

Item 2. A detailed supplement of the above interpretation of the definition under Home Relief of "Medicine or medical attendance furnished by a municipal corporation to persons or their dependants in their abode or habitation . . ." was issued on January 7, 1932 as a "Memo for Field Workers."

Item 3. On March 3, 1933, the Administration adopted "Rules and Regulations Governing Medical Care to Home Relief Clients," in the form approved by the Special T.E.R.A. Advisory Committee, of the Medical Society of the State of New York, and the State Commissioner of Health. These rules included in their scope preceding statements of policy and procedure.

Item 4. On April 11, 1933, Harry L. Hopkins, then chairman of the Administration wrote to "Public Welfare Commissioners" as follows:

"The Administration would like you to know that the Rules and Regulations Governing Medical Care were established for the fundamental purpose of providing more adequate medical care, as well as establishing an official liaison between the public welfare officials and the local county medical societies. The Executive Committee of the State Medical Society has felt that the arrangement now established will result in the use of a great many more physicians in providing necessary medical care to home relief clients,

"For the reasons above stated, the Administration is considering the $2 fee for a home visit and the $1 fee for an office visit as its uniform basis for reimbursement. This does not preclude payment of an additional amount by welfare commissioners where unusual circumstances, such as large mileage, etc., seem to warrant such payment, but the Administration will not be able to assume this additional charge.

"Our present records indicate that in the course of a year, the number of calls for which more than the usual payment is authorized constitutes a relatively small percentage of the total expenditure, hence, payment of this additional expense in unusual instances would not seem to work any undue hardship on any welfare district."

Item 5. A request that all vouchers for medical care be submitted to the T.E.R.A. under a separate claim and detailed instructions with regard to filing of claims by physicians and other authorized professional personnel, were issued on May 26, 1933 (Effective June 1, 1933.)

Item 6. On July 11, 1933, T.E.R.A. Official Bulletin Number 1 was issued. Section B of this bulletin was an "Amendment to Rules and Regulations Governing Medical Care to Home Relief Clients." which stated " . . . the policy of the Administration with respect to reimbursement for the services of a consultant physician in the home, the usual authorized services of a specialist in his office and professional services given to additional patients in the course of an authorized home visit by a physician."

Item 7. Finally, on September 8, 1933, the Federal Emergency Relief Administration issued "Rules and Regulations No. 7 Governing Medical Care Provided in the Home to Recipients of Unemployment Relief."

These rules were based on experience under the Emergency Relief Act of 1931 in New York State and recognized, on a nation-wide scale, that "The conservation and maintenance of the public health is a primary function of our Government." It was further noted that "To assist State and local relief administrations in the achievement of these aims, with regard to medical care, two steps have been taken: First, to define the general scope of authorized medical care, where the expenditure of Federal Emergency Relief Funds is involved; and second, to establish general regulations governing the provision of such medical care to recipients of unemployment relief."

In a letter to the governors and state relief administrations transmitting the Federal Emergency Relief Administration Rules and Regulations No. 7, Harry L. Hopkins, Administrator, said:

"I particularly call to your attention the common aim of these regulations—the provision of good medical service at low cost—to the mutual benefit of indigent patient, physician and taxpayer."

Section C. **An appendix of quotations from the Pubic Welfare Law of the State of New York.**[63]

The public welfare law, to which the Emergency Relief Act of 1931 was a supplement to meet some of the additional needs occasioned by the "present economic depression," governs the basic procedures by which the State of New York and its component political subdivisions discharge their responsibility "to provide adequately for those unable to maintain themselves."

The quotations were selected to present general and special sections of the public welfare law which have both a direct and an indirect bearing on the provision of medical care "for those unable to maintain themselves."

These, and other, sections of the public welfare law allow methods of providing medical care in the home to recipients of home relief, which do not fall within the scope of the emergency relief act, and in addition make provision for such vitally essential services as hospitalization, dispensary and institutional care to recipients of home relief, and to "such persons otherwise able to maintain themselves, who are unable to secure necessary medical care   .   .   ."

Item 1. Sections of the public welfare law *directly* relating to medical care:

"ARTICLE X

" MEDICAL CARE[64]

"§ 83. *Responsibility for providing medical care.* The public welfare district shall be responsible for providing necessary medical care for all persons under its care, and for such persons otherwise able to maintain themselves, who are unable to secure necessary medical care, except insofar as, in cases of communicable disease, that duty may be imposed upon the health officer by law or the state sanitary code. Such care may be given in dispensaries, hospitals, the person's home or other suitable place.

§ 84. *Physicians in public welfare districts.* When a legislative body shall make an appropriation for the purpose, one or more physicians shall be appointed to care for sick persons in their homes. In a county public welfare district, such physician or physicians shall be appointed by the county commissioner. In a city, such physician or physicians shall be appointed in accordance with the provisions of the general or local law, relating to such city. In a town, such physician shall be appointed by the town board. Where no physician is so appointed, the public welfare official shall employ a physician or physicians to visit sick persons in their homes whenever necessary.

---

[63] Chapter 565, Laws of 1929, constituting chapter forty-two of the consolidated Laws.

[64] As amended by chapter 629, Laws of 1930.

"§ 85. *Care in hospitals.* A public welfare district shall provide needed care for sick and disabled persons in a hospital maintained by the municipality or in any other hospital visited, inspected and supervised by the state board of charities. It may contract with such other hospital to pay such sum for the care of sick persons as may be agreed upon.

"As far as practicable, no patient whose care is to be a charge on a public welfare district, or a subdivision thereof, shall be admitted to a hospital without the prior approval of the public welfare official responsible for his support. Acceptance of any patient as a public charge shall be in the discretion of the public welfare official. In any case where the patient is a public charge, the public welfare official may, when the condition of the patient permits, transfer such patient to another hospital or provide care in any other suitable place.

"If, in case of emergency, a patient is admitted without prior authorization of the public welfare official empowered to approve payment for such care, and the hospital wishes to receive payment from public funds for such patient, the hospital shall, within forty-eight hours of the admission, send to such official a report of the facts of the case, including a statement of the physician in attendance as to the necessity of the immediate admission of such patient to the hospital. If the settlement of the patient is not known by the hospital, such notice shall be sent to the commissioner of the public welfare district in which the hospital is located, and such commissioner shall be responsible for making an investigation to discover whether any public welfare district or the state is liable for payment for the care of such patient. The cost of the care of such a patient shall be a charge against the public welfare district only when authorized by the commissioner.

"§ 86. *Care of patients suffering from tuberculosis.* The public welfare district shall likewise provide suitable care for patients suffering from tuberculosis in a county or city tuberculosis hospital or in any other hospital or sanitarium approved by the state board of charities or in a boarding house approved in writing for this purpose by the health officer in charge of the locality where it is situated. . . ."

"(As amended by chapter 481, Laws of 1931.)"

Item 2. Sections of the public welfare law, *indirectly* relating to medical care, which outline responsibilities and standards for public relief and care:

"Public Welfare Districts and Their Responsibility for Public Relief and Care

"§ 17. *Public welfare districts.* For the purpose of administration of public relief and care the state shall be divided into county and city public welfare districts. . . ."

"§ 18. *Responsibility for public relief, care and support.* A person in need of relief and care which he is unable to provide for himself shall be relieved and cared for by and at the expense of a public welfare district or the state as follows:

"1· The state shall be responsible for:

"(a) The support of any person having no settlement in any public welfare district in the state, who shall not have resided in any public welfare district in the state for sixty days during the year prior to an application for public relief and care.

"(b) The support of any Indian who is eligible for relief from the state under the provisions of section sixty-five of this chapter.

"(c) The expense of transportation of any alien poor person who is returned to his own country and of any non-resident poor person who is returned to the state in which he has a settlement or in which he has friends or relatives willing to support him.

"2· Each public welfare district shall be responsible for:

"(a) The relief, care and support of any person who resides and has a settlement in its territory.

"(b) The relief, care and support of any person found in its territory not having a settlement in the state, for whose support the state is not responsible.

"(c) The relief and care of any person found in its territory who has a settlement elsewhere in the state, subject to reimbursement by the public welfare district of the person's settlement in accordance with the provisions of this chapter.

"(d) The relief and care of any person found in its territory for whose support the state is responsible, subject to reimbursement by the state in accordance with the provisions of this chapter.

"(e) The payment of the cost of the relief and care of a person having a settlement in its territory given by some other public welfare district."

"§ 25. *Responsibility for public relief and care in a county public welfare district.* The responsibility for the administration of public relief and care in a county public welfare district and the expense thereof may either be borne by the county public welfare district or be divided between such district and the towns and cities therein as hereinafter provided.

"1· Unless otherwise determined by the board of supervisors as hereinafter provided, each town shall be responsible for the expense of providing home relief and medical care given at home for persons having a settlement and residing in such town, except defective or physically handicapped children and children born out of wedlock. . . ."

"2. Unless otherwise determined by the board of supervisors as hereinafter provided, a city forming a part of a county public welfare district shall be responsible for the expense of providing home relief and medical care given at home or in a hospital for any person having a settlement and residing in its territory except defective or physically handicapped children and children born out of wedlock. . . ."

"3. A county public welfare district shall be responsible for the expense of providing all relief and care for persons having a settlement in a town or city in its territory for which such towns and cities may not be responsible under the provisions of subdivisions one and two of this section, and for the relief and care of any person found in its territory who has no settlement in any such town or city. . . ."

"The cost of relief and care of any or all of the following types administered by the county commissioner to a person having a settlement in a town or city in the county public welfare district may be charged back to such town or city if the regulations established by the board of supervisors so direct:

"(a) Institutional care of an adult.

"(b) Relief and care for any child who is cared for away from his parents, for defective or physically handicapped children, and for children born out of wedlock.

"(c) Hospital care.

"(d) Home relief and medical care of persons residing in the district but in a town or city other than that of their settlement.

"(e) Home relief and medical care of persons residing in another public welfare district.

"The county commissioner shall immediately notify the town or city public welfare officer of any person alleged to have a settlement in his town or city, the cost of whose relief and care is to be charged back to such town or city. Commitments to a county home may be made by town and city public welfare officers subject to the approval in writing of the county commissioner. All other commitments to hospitals or other institutions at the expense of the county public welfare district shall be made by the county commissioner."

"§ 31. *Powers and duties of city public welfare districts.* A city public welfare district shall be responsible in its territory for the administration of public relief and care and the expense incident thereto. . . ."

"ARTICLE IX

"RELIEF AND SERVICE

"§ 77. *Care to be given.* It shall be the duty of public welfare officials, insofar as funds are available for that purpose, to provide adequately for those unable to maintain themselves. They shall, whenever possible, administer such care and treatment as may restore such persons to a condition of self-support, and shall further give such service to those liable to become destitute as may prevent the necessity of their becoming public charges.

"As far as possible families shall be kept together, and they shall not be separated for reasons of poverty alone. Whenever practicable, relief and service shall be given a poor person in his own home; the commissioner of public welfare, may, however, in his discretion, provide relief and care in a boarding home, the home of a relative, a public or private home or institution, or in a hospital.

"§ 78. *Investigation.* Whenever a public welfare official receives an application for relief, or is informed that a. person is in need of care, an investigation and record shall be made of the circumstances of such person. . . . If it shall appear that such person is in immediate need, temporary relief shall be granted pending completion of the investigation.

"§ 79. *Supervision.* When relief is granted to a person in his own home, or in any place outside of an institution, such person shall be visited once a month, or as often as necessary, in order that any care or service tending to restore such person to a condition of self-support and to relieve his distress may be rendered and in order that relief may be given only as long as necessary for this purpose. . . ."

"§ 80. *Cooperation of public welfare officials.* It shall be the duty of every public welfare official to render assistance and cooperation within his jurisdictional powers to children's courts, boards of child welfare and all other governmental agencies concerned with the welfare of persons under his jurisdiction. Every public welfare official shall also cooperate whenever possible with any private agency whose object is the relief and care of persons in need or the improvement of social conditions in order that there may be no duplication of relief and that the work of agencies both public and private may be united in an effort to relieve distress and prevent dependency."

U. S. EMPLOYEES' COMPENSATION COMMISSION

WASHINGTON

April 17, 1934.

Pursuant to the provisions of the Act of Congress approved February 15, 1934 (Public No. 93, 73d Congress), the following special schedule of compensation for death and/or for the loss or loss of use of members or functions of the body, resulting from traumatic injury in the performance of duty sustained by employees of the Federal Civil Works Administration, is hereby established and the compensation specified therein shall be in lieu of all other compensation in such cases.

1. Compensation for death shall be payable only to or for the benefit of the following persons and at the following percentages of the deceased employee's monthly pay at time of injury:

(a) To the widow, if there is no child, 35 per centum. This compensation shall be paid until her death or marriage.

(b) To the widower, if there is no child, 35 per centum if wholly dependent for support upon the deceased employee at the time of her death. This compensation shall be paid until his death or marriage.

(c) To the widow or widower, if there is a child, the compensation payable under clause (a) or clause (b) and in addition thereto 10 per centum for each child, not to exceed a total of 66⅔ per centum for such widow or widower and children. If a child has a guardian other than the surviving widow or widower, the compensation payable an account of such child shall be paid to such guardian. The compensation payable on account of any child shall cease when he dies, marries, or reaches the age of eighteen, or, if over eighteen, and incapable of self-support, becomes capable of self-support.

(d) To the children, if there is no widow or widower, 25 per centum for one child and 10 per centum additional for each additional child, not to exceed a total of 66⅔ per centum, divided among such children share and share alike. The compensation of each child shall be paid until he dies, marries, or reaches the age of eighteen, or, if over eighteen and incapable of self-support, becomes capable of self-support. The compensation of a child under legal age shall be paid to its guardian.

(e) To the parents, if one is wholly dependent for support upon the deceased employee at the time of his death and the other is not dependent to any extent, 25 per centum; if both are wholly dependent, 20 per centum to each; if one is or both are partly dependent, a proportionate amount in the discretion of the Commission.

The above percentages shall be paid if there is no widow, widower, or child. If there is a widow, widower, or child, there shall be paid so much of the above percentages as, when added to the total percentages payable to the widow, widower, and children, will not exceed a total of 66⅔ per centum.

(f) To the brothers, sisters, grandparents, and grandchildren, if one is wholly dependent upon the deceased employee for support at the time of his death, 20 per centum to such dependent; if more than one are wholly dependent, 30 per centum, divided among such dependents share and share alike; if there is no one of them wholly dependent, but one or more partly dependent, 10 per centum divided among such dependents share and share alike.

The above percentages shall be paid if there is no widow, widower, child, or dependent parent. If there is a widow, widower, child, or dependent parent, there shall be paid so much of the above percentages as, when added to the total percentage payable to the widow, widower, children, and dependent parents, will not exceed a total of 66⅔ per centum.

(g) The compensation of each beneficiary under clauses (e) and (f) shall be paid for a period of eight years from the time of the death, unless before that time he, if a parent or grandparent, dies, marries, or ceases to be dependent, or, if a brother, sister, or grandchild, dies, marries, or reaches the age of eighteen, or, if over eighteen and incapable of self-support, becomes capable of self-support. The compensation of a brother, sister, or grandchild under legal age shall be paid to his or her guardian.

(h) As used in this schedule, the term "child" includes stepchildren, adopted children, and posthumous children, but does not include married children. The terms "brother" and "sister" include stepbrothers and stepsisters, half brothers and half sisters, and brothers and sisters by adoption, but do not include married brothers or married sisters. All of the above terms and the term "grandchild" include only persons who at the time of the death of the deceased employee are under eighteen years of age or over that age and incapable of self-support. The term "parent" includes stepparents and parents by adoption. The term "widow" includes only the decedent's wife living with or dependent for support upon him at the time of his death or living apart for reasonable cause or by reason of his desertion.

(i) Upon the cessation of compensation for death under this schedule to any person, the compensation of the remaining persons entitled to such compensation for the unexpired part of the period during which their compensation is payable shall be that which such persons would have received if they had been the only persons entitled to compensation at the time of the decedent's death.

(j) In case there are two or more classes of persons entitled to compensation for death under this schedule and the apportionment of such compensation as above provided, would result in injustice, the Commission may, in its discretion, modify the apportionment to meet the requirements of the case.

2. Compensation for disability shall be payable to the injured employees as follows:

(a) In case of permanent and total disability, 66⅔ per cent of the monthly wage received at the time of injury, to be paid during the continuance of such disability.

(b) In case of temporary total disability, 66⅔ per cent of the monthly wage received at the time of injury, to be paid during the continuance thereof.

(c) In case of permanent partial disability, 66⅔ per cent of the monthly wage received at the time of injury, to be paid for the following periods:

(1) Arm lost, two hundred and eighty weeks' compensation.

(2) Leg lost, two hundred and forty-eight weeks' compensation.

(3) Hand lost, two hundred and twelve weeks' compensation.

(4) Foot lost, one hundred and seventy-three weeks' compensation.

(5) Eye lost, one hundred and forty weeks' compensation.

(6) Thumb lost, fifty-one weeks' compensation.

(7) First finger lost, twenty-eight weeks' compensation.

(8) Great toe lost, twenty-six weeks' compensation.

(9) Second finger lost, eighteen weeks' compensation.

(10) Third finger lost, seventeen weeks' compensation.

(11) Toe other than great toe lost, eight weeks' compensation.

(12) Fourth finger lost, seven weeks' compensation.

(13) Loss of hearing: Compensation for loss of hearing of one ear, fifty-two weeks. Compensation for loss of hearing of both ears, two hundred weeks.

(14) Phlanges: Compensation for loss of more than one phlange of a digit shall be the same as for loss of the entire digit. Compensation for loss of the first phlange shall be one-half of the compensation for loss of the entire digit.

(15) Amputated arm or leg: Compensation for an arm or a leg, if amputated at or above the elbow or the knee, shall be the same as for a loss of the arm or leg; but, if amputated between the elbow and the wrist or the knee and the ankle, shall be the same as for loss of a hand or foot.

(16) Binocular vision or per centum of vision: Compensation for loss of binocular vision or for 80 per centum or more of the vision of an eye shall be the same as for loss of the eye.

(17) Two or more digits: Compensation for loss of two or more digits, or one or more phlanges of two or more digits, of a hand or foot may be proportioned to the loss of use of the hand or foot occasioned thereby, but shall not exceed the compensation for loss of a hand or foot.

(18) Total loss of use: Compensation for permanent total loss of use of a member shall be the same as for loss of the member.

(19) Partial loss or partial loss of use: Compensation for permanent partial loss or loss of use of a member may be for proportionate loss or loss of use of the member.

(20) In any case in which there shall be a loss or loss of use of more than one member or parts of more than one member set forth in subdivisions (1) to (19) of this paragraph, but not amounting to permanent total disability, the award of compensation shall be for the loss or loss of use of each such member or part thereof, which awards shall run consecutively, except that where the injury affects only two or more digits of the same hand or foot, subdivision (17) shall apply.

(21) Other cases: In all other cases in this class of disability the compensation shall be 66⅔ per cent of the monthly wage for a proportionate number of the weeks for which compensation would be payable for permanent total disability, to be determined by the percentage the degree of partial disability bears to total disability.

(22) Compensation under subdivisions (1) to (21) of this paragraph, for permanent partial disability, shall be in addition to compensation allowed for temporary total disability under paragraph (b), and the awards for temporary total and permanent partial disability shall run consecutively.

3. Compensation payable under this schedule shall not exceed the rate of $25 per month, and the total aggregate compensation in any individual case shall not exceed the sum of $3,500.

U. S. EMPLOYEES' COMPENSATION COMMISSION.

Approved
June 30, 1934.

J. B. LYON COMPANY, PRINTERS. ALBANY, N. Y.

Emergency Relief Act

of the

State of New York

and

Related Statutes as Amended to July 1, 1934

Emergency Relief Act

of the

State of New York

and

Related Statutes as Amended to July 1, 1934

THE TEMPORARY EMERGENCY RELIEF ADMINISTRATION

CONTENTS

FOREWORD

The emergency relief enactments of 1934 fall into three classes, (a) amendments of the Emergency Act, (b) amendments of the State Recovery Act, and (c) financial measures and special provisions.

Amendments of the Emergency Act

The Emergency Relief Act (Chapter 798 of the Laws of 1931, as amended by Chapter 567 of the Laws of 1932, and Chapters 2, 9, 34, 44, 69, 259 and 646 of the Laws of 1933) has been amended by Chapters 15, 65, 71 and 303 of the Laws of 1934.

Chapter 15 of the Laws of 1934 numbers the definitions in Section 2 of the Emergency Act, provides that work relief shall include wages paid by the State, extends the emergency period to February 15, 1935, and provides that the Governor shall designate the chairman of the Administration; that the Administration may, with the approval of the Governor, act as the designated agency of duly authorized federal or other relief within the State; that local work bureaus shall be subject to the approval of the Administration and shall serve at the Administration's pleasure, and such bureaus or members thereof may be designated by the Administration to act as local agencies of federal or other relief under the supervision and control of the Administration. Also that the State, as well as municipal corporations, may furnish work relief.

Chapter 65 of the Laws of 1934 amends Sections 2 and 16 of the Emergency Act to provide that home relief may be given in cash, until February 15, 1935, if and where approved by and under rules and regulations made and conditions specified by the Administration.

Chapter 71 of the Laws of 1934 amends Section 18 of the Emergency Act to raise the proportion of State improvement moneys which may be spent for materials, tools and supplies from 15 to 20 per cent.

Chapter 303 of the Laws of 1934 adds to the Emergency Act a new Section 16-a, taking persons employed on work relief projects out of the coverage of the Workmen's Compensation Law and making the Administration liable for all claims arising from the injury, disability or death of such persons.

[3]

Amendments of the State Recovery Act

The State Recovery Act (Chapter 782 of the Laws of 1933), authorizing cooperation by the State with the National Recovery Administration, has been amended by Chapters 39, 104 and 301 of the Laws of 1934.

Chapter 39 of the Laws of 1934 added to the Recovery Act a new Section 5-a, authorizing municipalities, by vote of their governing bodies, to borrow for materials, supplies and equipment for use on projects undertaken through the federal Civil Works Administration, notwithstanding the provisions of any general, special or local law.

This new Section 5-a was amended by Chapter 301 of the Laws of 1934 to extend the borrowing power to projects undertaken by the federal Emergency Relief Administration or any other work relief authority of the State and/or federal government.

Chapter 104 of the Laws of 1934 amends Sections 2, 3, 4 and 5 of the State Recovery Act and adds new Sections 4-a, 6-a and 6-b.

Section 2 is amended to clarify the definition of governing boards and to provide that "national industrial recovery act" shall include amendments and revisions thereof and any further federal act to encourage public works, reduce unemployment and thereby assist in national recovery and promote public welfare.

Section 3 is amended to extend the power of municipalities to accept direct grants from the federal Emergency Administration so as to allow them to accept grants from any federal agency for labor and materials on federal projects.

Section 4 is amended to extend the contracting power of municipalities in regard to federal projects to include contracts with any federal agency; to provide for a mandatory referendum whenever a federal project is for the construction or operation of a public utility or the supply of gas, electricity or water in competition with or substitution for a utility supplying the same in the same area; preserving the right of school district meetings to vote on all federal projects of whatever nature; allowing a permissive referendum whenever a governing board desires one, and authorizing the issuance of notes, temporary bonds, certificates of indebtedness, interim certificates or security receipts in anticipation of a bond issue duly authorized.

Section 5 is amended to make the bonds or obligations of a municipality, assumed for these purposes, saleable directly to the United States, instead of to an agency thereof.

The new section 4-a allows a public works project to be undertaken at the expense of the municipality at large, instead of wholly or partly at the expense of property benefited, and permits borrowing for the entire cost of a project in the first instance, prior to its completion or prior to any levy.

The new Section 6-a provides that, notwithstanding any general, special or local law, a public works project, contract or bond issue may be finally approved on the same day on which it is introduced, and such resolution need not be published before becoming effective.

The new Section 6-b provides that the act shall be liberally construed and the duties imposed by it are to be independent and severable, and if any section, clause, sentence or part thereof shall be adjudged unconstitutional or invalid, such judgment shall affect no other provision of the act.

Financial Measures and Special Provisions

Chapter 71 of the Laws of 1934 appropriated the balance of $48,000,000 remaining out of the proceeds of the sale of $60,000,000 bonds authorized by Chapter 260 of the Laws of 1933, $33,000,000 of which was allocated to the reimbursement fund, and $15,000,000 to the discretionary fund.

By Chapter 821 of the Laws of 1934 $1,500,000 of the said discretionary fund was reappropriated to supply fresh milk free to needy children through the schools or public or private milk stations, under rules and regulations of the Relief Administration.

By Chapter 718 of the Laws of 1934 there is submitted to the voters at the next general election a proposition to incur a further State debt of $40,000,000 for emergency relief purposes, and by Chapter 717 $10,000,000 of such moneys, if and when the indebtedness has been approved, are appropriated for emergency relief up to and including February 15, 1935, $7,000,000 of this sum to go to the reimbursement fund and $3,000,000 to the discretionary fund.

There have already been two other such bond issues, one of $30,000,000 and another of $60,000,000, and in addition there have been direct appropriations of $5,000,000 and $20,000,000, so that the proposed new $40,000,000 bond issue will bring the State's total unemployment relief contributions to $155,000,000. In recommending the $40,000,000 proposal to the Legislature, the Governor expressed the hope that it would be the last bond issue that would be necessary for relief purposes.

Chapter 716 of the Laws of 1934 amends Chapter 8 of the Laws of 1933, in regard to State participation in federal funds, so as to allow the Governor to transmit the same directly to the Relief Administration, acting as a federal agency.

Chapter 654 of the Laws of 1934 authorizes the State to receive federal moneys, for expenditure through the Department of Public Works, for the cost and expense of engineering, designing, supervision and inspection of the construction, repair and improvement of public highways, parkways, buildings, etc., as federal projects, and appropriates $100,000 to be advanced by the State in the first instance for such expense.

Chapter 769 of the Laws of 1934 amends Section 10 of Article 2 of the Workmen's Compensation Law, to provide that such law shall not apply to persons receiving work relief and employed on work relief projects. This is complementary to the new Section 16-a of the Emergency Act, noted above, under which the Relief Administration assumes all liability for work relief injuries or disability.

By Section 2 of Chapter 39 of the Laws of 1934, as amended by Chapter 301, all acts and proceedings heretofore taken by municipalities, their boards and officers, in raising money or using the same for the purchase of materials, supplies and equipment for work relief projects of the federal Civil Works Administration, or the work division of the federal Emergency Relief Administration, or any other work relief authority of the State and/or federal government, is legalized, validated, ratified and confirmed, notwithstanding any want of statutory authority therefor or any defect or irregularity therein.

The complete text of the Emergency Act as amended, the Recovery Act as amended, and the financial and special acts referred to in the foregoing, will be found in the following pages.

The Emergency Relief Act of the State of New York

CHAPTER 798 OF THE LAWS OF 1931 AS AMENDED TO THE END OF THE REGULAR LEGISLATIVE SESSION OF 1934

CHAPTER 798 OF THE LAWS OF 1931, AS AMENDED BY CHAPTER 567 OF THE LAWS OF 1932 AND CHAPTERS 2, 9, 34, 44, 69, 259 AND 646 OF THE LAWS OF 1933, AND CHAPTERS 15, 65, 71 AND 303 OF THE LAWS OF 1934

An Act to relieve the people of the state from the hardships and suffering caused by unemployment, creating and organizing for such purpose a temporary emergency relief administration, prescribing its powers and duties and making an appropriation for its work.

The People of the State of New York, represented in Senate and Assembly, do enact as follows:

SCHEDULE OF SECTIONS

Section   1. Declaration of emergency.
2. Definitions.
3. Administrative authority.
4. Preliminary studies.
5. Assistance of existing agencies.
6. Public welfare districts.
7. Local bureaus.
8. Administration agencies.
9. Relief by municipal corporations or by the state.
10. Local funds for relief.
11. City and county work relief.
12. Duties of the local bureaus.
13. Investigation of home relief.
14. Private contributions.
15. Records and accounts of relief.
16. State aid.
17. Private contributions to the administration.
18. Expenditures on state improvements.
19. Salaries of local staffs.
20. Reports of commissioners.
21. Reports by administration.

§ 1. **Declaration of emergency.** The public health and safety of the state and of each county, city and town therein being imperilled by the existing and threatened deprivation of a considerable number of their inhabitants of the necessaries of life, owing to the present economic depression, such condition is hereby declared to be a matter of public concern, state and local, and the correction thereof to be a state, county, city and town purpose, the consummation of which requires, as a necessary incident the furnishing of public aid to individuals. While the duty of providing aid for those in need or unemployed because of lack of employment is primarily an obligation of the municipalities, nevertheless, it is the finding of the state that in the existing emergency the relief and assistance provided for by this act are vitally necessary to supplement the relief work accomplished or to be accomplished locally and to encourage and stimulate local effort in the same direction. This act, therefore, is declared to be a measure for the public health and safety and occasioned by an existing emergency. The provisions of any general, special or local law which are inconsistent with the provisions of this act or which limit or forbid the furnishing of shelter, fuel, clothing, light, medicine and medical attendance to persons other than poor persons shall not apply to the relief authorized by this act.

§ 2. **Definitions.** As used in this act:

1. "Administration" means the temporary state agency created by this act, to be known as the temporary emergency relief administration.

2. "City commissioner" means the chief administrative public welfare officer or board of a city.

3. "County commissioner" means the chief administrative public welfare officer of territory of a county beyond the limits of a city.

4. "Municipal corporation" means a county or city except a county wholly within a city.

5. ''Public welfare district'' means one of such districts created by this act.

6. ''Local bureau'' means one of the temporary emergency work bureaus created by this act in cities and counties.

7. ''Work relief'' means wages paid by a municipal corporation or by the state to persons, who are unemployed or whose employment is inadequate to provide the necessaries of life, and/or their dependents, from money specifically appropriated or contributed for that purpose during the emergency period, for the performance of services or labor connected with work undertaken by such corporation independent of work under a contract or for which an annual appropriation has been made.

8. ''Home relief'' means shelter, fuel, food, clothing, light, necessary household supplies, relief to veterans under existing laws and medical attendance furnished by a municipal corporation or a town, where home relief is a town charge, to persons or their dependents in their abode or habitation whenever possible and does not include old age relief or allowances made to mothers' for the care of dependent children or hospital or institutional care. For the purposes of and in order to provide wholly or in part home relief as herein defined, until February fifteenth, nineteen hundred thirty-five, money may be given in cash if and where approved by and under rules and regulations made and conditions specified by the administration.

9. ''Emergency period'' means the period defined by chapter seven hundred and ninety-eight of the laws of nineteen hundred thirty-one, as extended and continued, by chapter five hundred and sixty-seven of the laws of nineteen hundred thirty-two, and further extended and continued by chapter two of the laws of nineteen hundred thirty-three, and such period is hereby further extended and continued to the fifteenth day of February, nineteen hundred thirty-five.

10. ''State aid'' means payments to a municipal corporation or town by the state for work relief and/or home relief furnished during the emergency period in accordance with this act.

Section 2 amended by Laws of 1932, chapter 567, Laws of 1933, chapter 646, and Laws of 1934, chapters 15 and 65.

§ 3. **Administrative authority.** The administration of the emergency relief provided by this act shall be vested in a temporary state agency, to be known as the temporary emergency relief administration, to consist of five persons to be appointed by the governor, one of whose number shall be designated by the governor as chairman and all of whom shall serve during his pleasure. Any vacancy in the membership of the administration, occurring from any cause whatsoever, shall be filled by the governor. The administration shall organize immediately upon the appointment of its complete membership. It may employ, and at pleasure remove, a secretary and such other clerks and assistants as may be deemed necessary by it to carry out the provisions of this act. The administration may fix the compensation of all such employees within the amounts available by appropriation. The administration may accept from any person or organization and avail itself of any and all offers of personal service or other aid or assistance in carrying out any of the provisions of this act made without expectation of compensation or other reward. Any persons or organizations so contributing such services and giving such other aid or assistance shall be entitled to receive only such expenses as are actually and necessarily incurred by them by reason of such services, aid or assistance. Employees and volunteers of the administration shall not be subject to the provisions of the civil service law. The principal office of the administration shall be in the city of Albany in suitable quarters set apart for its use by the superintendent of public buildings, but offices in other localities of the state may be maintained by it. Each of the members of the administration, before entering upon the duties of his office, shall take and subscribe the constitutional oath of office and file the same in the office of the department of state. The chairman of the administration shall be compensated at the rate of eleven thousand five hundred dollars per annum and actual and necessary traveling and other expenses incurred by him in the performance of his duties. The other members of the administration shall receive no compensation for their services hereunder but shall be allowed their actual and necessary traveling and other expenses incurred by them in the performance of their duties. The administration shall continue to function only during the emergency period, except that it may examine and certify, after the expiration of such period, claims for state aid under this act for expenditures for work and/or home relief furnished prior to the expiration of such period. The administration may, with the approval of the governor, accept a designation from and act as the agency of duly authorized federal relief or like bodies in the administration of relief and related activities within the state of New York.

'Section 3 amended by the Laws of 1933, chapter 44, and by Laws of 1934, chapter 15.

§ 4. **Preliminary** studies. The administration shall (a) make or cause to be made with the aid of such data as may be available a thorough and comprehensive study and survey of unemployment within the state, the occupations, industries, and trades most seriously affected thereby and the number of persons suffering or in want by reason thereof.

(b) Discover the extent and nature of public work required or useful to be done by the state or any political subdivision thereof.

(c) Ascertain the amount of resources made available by public appropriations or private contributions for the relief of unemployed persons throughout the state.

§ 5. **Assistance of existing agencies.** In making any of the surveys preliminary to the work of the administration and for the more effective consumption of any of its powers and duties, the administration may request and shall receive advice and expert assistance from the department of social welfare, the tax department, the department of public works, the department of public health, and any other state or local department or agency. It shall have access to the records of any state or local department, board or other agency pertaining to the functions of the department and the cooperation and assistance of each and every officer or employee thereof. It may, in its discretion cooperate with existing national, state or local unemployment relief commissions or agencies and, if deemed advisable or expedient by it, coordinate and correlate its work with the work or projects of any such commission or agency.

§ 6. **Public welfare districts.** For the purpose of facilitating the administration of the provisions of this act and the distribution of the state aid thereby provided, each city of the state and the territory of each county beyond the limits of cities is hereby constituted a separate public welfare district, which are hereby designated as city and county public welfare districts respectively, except that the cities of Geneva and Canandaigua shall be included in the county welfare district of the county of Ontario and the town of Newburgh shall be included in the city public welfare district of the city of Newburgh.

§ 7. **Local bureaus.** The mayor or chief administrative officer of a city may establish in a city public welfare district and the governing board of a county may establish in a county public welfare district, for the emergency period, an emergency work bureau, to consist of three or more persons to be appointed by such officers or governing boards respectively. City commissioners shall be members ex officio of the local bureau in their respective city public welfare districts and county commissioners shall be members ex officio of the local bureau in their respective county public welfare districts. Members of local bureaus heretofore or hereafter appointed shall continue in office for the duration of the emergency period unless removed as herein provided. Local bureaus shall serve at the pleasure of the administration and shall be responsible for the administration of work relief and may employ necessary clerks and assistants, whose compensation shall be fixed by the officer or governing board by which such bureau was created. Local bureaus may accept from any person or organization and avail itself of any and all offers of personal service or other aid or assistance in carrying out any of the provisions of this act made without expectation of compensation or other reward. Local bureaus or members thereof may, in the discretion of the administration, be designated by it to act as the local agency of federal relief or related bodies under the supervision and control of the administration.

Section 7 amended by the Laws of 1932, chapter 567, and Laws of 1934, chapter 15.

§ 8. **Administration agencies.** Under rules adopted by the administration, which shall not conflict or be inconsistent with the provisions of this act, the city commissioner shall represent the

administration in a city public welfare district as hereby constituted in providing home relief and administering the provisions
of this act therein in relation thereto and the county commissioner
shall represent the administration in a county public welfare district as hereby constituted in providing home relief and in
administering the provisions of this act therein in relation thereto.
Local bureaus shall represent the administration in their respective city and county welfare districts in providing work relief and
in administering the provisions of this act therein in relation
thereto. Local bureaus, city commissioners and county commissioners shall in all matters be subject to the supervision, direction
and control of the administration.

§ 9. **Relief by municipal corporations or by the state.** Subject
to the supervision and control of the administration by rules, a
municipal corporation or the state may furnish work relief, and a
municipal corporation or a town where home relief is a town
charge, notwithstanding any provision or limitation in any charter
or law, may furnish home relief, during the emergency period, to
needy persons, who are unemployed or, if employed, whose compensation therefrom is inadequate to provide the necessaries of
life and who have been resident of the state for at least two years
prior to the date of application for aid under this act and to the
dependents of such persons.

Section 9 amended by Laws of 1932, chapter 567, and Laws of 1934, chapter 15.

§ 10. **Local funds for relief.** The legislative body of a municipal
corporation or town may appropriate and make available sufficient
money to pay for work relief and/or home relief and also may raise
such money during the emergency period by interest bearing notes,
certificates of indebtedness, bond or other obligations of such
municipal corporation or town payable within a period not exceeding ten years, provided the money so raised shall not exceed the
constitutional or statutory debt limit of such municipal corporation, and provided further in the case of towns that such borrowing for relief purposes shall not exceed two per centum of the
assessed valuation of said town. Pending the issuance of the foregoing obligations temporary certificates of indebtedness may be
issued due and payable within six months from their date, and
paid either by raising the same by taxation or by refunding the
same by issuance of interest bearing notes, certificates of indebtedness, bonds or other obligations as aforesaid. In any county the
board of supervisors in making any appropriation for home and/or
work relief for the county welfare district may provide that such
appropriation or certificates issued therefor, together with interest
thereon shall be a charge against the county but the amount of
such appropriation or certificates issued therefor, together with
interest thereon shall be reimbursed to the county from the taxable
property within the county public welfare district for whose benefit
said appropriation was made or said certificates issued as provided by this act and the board of supervisors of said county shall

levy a tax upon the taxable property within the county public welfare district sufficient to provide such sums as may be necessary to meet such appropriation or certificates issued therefor, together with the interest thereon. The legislative body of a municipal corporation or town is also authorized and empowered during the emergency period to raise money for relief of veterans under existing laws by interest bearing notes, certificates of indebtedness, bonds or other obligations of such municipal corporation payable within a period not exceeding ten years, provided the constitutional or statutory debt limit of such municipal corporation or town shall not be exceeded thereby. Obligations heretofore incurred pursuant to section ten of chapter seven hundred and ninety-eight of the laws of nineteen hundred thirty-one and/or chapter five hundred and sixty-seven of the laws of nineteen hundred thirty-two may be refunded by the issuance of obligations herein authorized provided the maturity thereof does not exceed a period of ten years. The proceeds of all borrowings of municipal corporations or towns for the purposes set forth in chapter seven hundred and ninety-eight of the laws of nineteen hundred thirty-one as amended, except such as are needed for the refunding of prior obligations incurred under section ten of chapter seven hundred and ninety-eight of the laws of nineteen hundred thirty-one and/or chapter five hundred and sixty-seven of the laws of nineteen hundred thirty-two, shall not be credited or deposited in the general fund of the muunicipal corporation or town but shall be made available solely and exclusively for the relief purposes for which the said borrowings have been made. Such legislative body may authorize the performance of public work undertaken other than by contract by such municipal corporation or town, during the emergency period, through and under its local emergency work bureau or by its public works or other department under the supervision and control of its local emergency work bureau. These provisions shall be effective notwithstanding any provisions contained in any charter or in general, special or local laws to the contrary and notwithstanding any such provisions therein contained requiring such work as may be undertaken to be let by contract.

Section 10 amended by the Laws of 1932, chapter 567, and the Laws of 1933. chapters 9, 34, 69, and 259.

§ 11. **City and county work relief.** Before a city or county shall receive the state aid provided by this act for work relief, it shall establish an emergency work bureau as provided in this act which shall select the persons to be employed on the basis of their needs as determined by investigation.

§ 12. **Duties of the local bureaus.** 1. It shall be the duty of a local bureau to ascertain the extent of unemployment existing in its district and make investigations and surveys as to the need for public works and the amount and kind of public work available and not required to be let by contract. From such surveys and investigations it shall determine, from time to time, with the approval of the administration, whether the employment constitutes work relief; how the available employment useful to the public shall best and most equitably be apportioned among the needy unemployed; on what particular project or work they shall be engaged; the number of days in each week they shall be employed and the amount of compensation which they shall receive. It shall pay such compensation, so fixed daily or otherwise, as it may determine, and shall conduct the work in accordance with such rules of the administration as will best secure the proper and equitable administration of the relief sought to be provided by this act. If any city commissioner or county commissioner shall violate any rule of the administration or in the judgment of the administration, shall be inefficient or remiss in the performance of his duties, the administration may transfer all the powers, functions and duties of such city commissioner or county commissioner with respect to home relief under this act during the emergency period to the local bureau and thereafter the local bureau shall exercise all of the powers, functions and duties of the city or county commissioner with respect to home relief under this act.

2. Upon the written application of the mayor of a city in the case of a city welfare district or of the chairman of the board of supervisors of a county in the case of a county welfare district, the administration may in its discretion and subject to such regulations as it may provide, approve and authorize the consolidation of all relief activities within each public welfare district carried on under chapter seven hundred and ninety-eight of the laws of nineteen hundred and thirty-one, as amended, into an emergency relief bureau, consisting of not less than three nor more than five persons to be designated by the mayor of such city or the chairman of the board of supervisors of such county. The said emergency relief bureau so established shall have exclusive control of and be solely responsible for the administration in such public welfare district of home relief and/or work relief under chapter seven hundred and ninety-eight of the laws of nineteen hundred and thirty-one, as amended. Upon the appointment of said emergency relief bureau, the local bureau theretofore established pursuant to section seven, shall be terminated and all the powers and duties of the local bureau and of the commissioner of public welfare as to relief administered under chapter seven hundred ninety-eight of the laws of nineteen hundred and thirty-one, as amended, shall be forthwith vested in said emergency relief bureau. All records of the local bureau and all records of the commissioner of public welfare relating to recipients of relief under chapter seven hundred and ninety-eight of the laws of nineteen hundred and thirty-one as amended, shall be forthwith transferred to the emergency relief bureau so established. The commissioner of public welfare of the public welfare district in which such emergency relief bureau shall have been established shall be ex-officio a member of said bureau in addition to the members appointed as above provided, and shall perform such duties in respect to relief administered under chapter

seven hundred and ninety-eight of the laws of nineteen hundred and thirty-one, as amended, as may be directed by said bureau.

3. In any county upon written application of the chairman of the board of supervisors of the county and of the mayor of a city or the mayors of two or more cities located in such county, the administration may in its discretion and subject to such regulations as it may provide, approve and authorize the consolidation of all work relief in such county and city public welfare districts in a joint emergency work bureau consisting of not less than three nor more than five persons appointed jointly by the chairman of the board of supervisors and the mayor or mayors of such city or cities. Such joint emergency work bureau so established, shall have exclusive control of and be solely responsible for the administration of work relief in such welfare districts under chapter seven hundred ninety-eight of the laws of nineteen hundred and thirty-one, as amended. Upon the appointment of said joint emergency work bureau the local bureau or bureaus theretofore established pursuant to section seven shall be terminated and all the powers and duties of the local bureau or bureaus shall be forthwith vested in the joint emergency work bureau. All records of the local bureau or bureaus shall be forthwith transferred to the joint emergency work bureau. The commissioners of public welfare of such public welfare districts shall be ex-officio members of the joint emergency work bureau in addition to the members appointed as above provided.

4. In any county where home relief is a county charge and is administered by the county commissioner of public welfare, upon written application of the chairman of the board of supervisors of the county and of the mayor of a city or of the mayors of two or more cities located in such county, the administration may in its discretion approve and authorize the consolidation of all relief activities in such county and city public welfare districts carried on under chapter seven hundred and ninety-eight of the laws of nineteen hundred and thirty-one, as amended, into an emergency relief bureau consisting of not less than three nor more than five persons appointed jointly by the chairman of the board of supervisors of such county and by the mayor or mayors of such city or cities. The said emergency relief bureau so established shall have exclusive control of and be solely responsible for the administration in such public welfare districts of all home and/or work relief under chapter seven hundred and ninety-eight of the laws of nineteen hundred and thirty-one, as amended. Upon the appointment of said emergency relief bureau the local bureau or bureaus theretofore established under section seven shall be terminated and all the powers and duties of the local bureau or bureaus and of the commissioners of public welfare of such county and city or cities, as to relief under chapter seven hundred and ninety-eight of the laws of nineteen hundred and thirty-one, as amended, shall be forthwith vested in the emergency relief bureau. All records of the local bureaus and all records of the commissioners of public

welfare relating to recipients of relief under chapter seven hundred and ninety-eight of the laws of nineteen hundred and thirty-one as amended, shall be forthwith transferred to the emergency relief bureau so established. The commissioners of public welfare of such welfare districts in which such emergency relief bureau shall have been established shall be ex-officio members of the bureau in addition to the members appointed as above provided, and shall perform such duties in respect to relief administered under chapter seven hundred and ninety-eight of the laws of nineteen hundred and thirty-one, as amended, as may be directed by said bureau.

5. When such an emergency relief bureau has been established in a city or county public welfare district or by a consolidation of a county public welfare district and one or more city public welfare districts, any balances remaining unexpended of the funds appropriated for home and/or work relief and the administration thereof in such public welfare district or districts shall be transferred to the emergency relief bureau. When a joint emergency work bureau has been established in a county public welfare district and one or more city public welfare districts any balances remaining unexpended of the funds appropriated to the local bureau or bureaus for work relief and the administration thereof in such public welfare districts, shall be transferred to the joint emergency work bureau.

6. Appropriating bodies in county and/or city public welfare districts where an emergency relief bureau or a joint emergency work bureau shall have been established are hereby authorized to make appropriations for home and/or work relief and the administration thereof to an emergency relief bureau, and to make appropriations for work relief and the administration thereof to a joint emergency work bureau. Said appropriations shall be made in accordance with the provisions of chapter seven hundred and ninety-eight of the laws of nineteen hundred and thirty-one, as amended.

Section 12 amended by the Laws of 1933, chapter 259.

§ 13. **Investigation of home relief.** In a city public welfare district the city commissioner shall investigate all cases of home relief. In a county public welfare district where home relief is a county charge, the county commissioner shall investigate such cases. In a county public welfare district where home relief is a town charge, the town public welfare officers shall investigate such cases under the supervision and general direction of the county commissioner.

§ 14. **Private contributions.** In furtherance of the purposes of this act a municipal corporation may accept contributions in cash or otherwise, during the emergency period, from individuals and corporations for work relief and/or home relief which shall be disbursed in the same manner as money appropriated by such municipal corporation for such purposes, but any such contributions in cash for home relief made by a single individual or lawfully by a corporation which aggregate more than the sum of ten thousand dollars during the emergency period shall not be considered in payments to a municipal corporation under the provisions of this act. All expenditures of such contributions in cash under the provisions of this act by a municipal corporation to the extent of ten thousand dollars or less in the aggregate from a single individual or lawfully from a corporation for home relief shall be allowed in determining the amount of state aid to which such municipal corporation is entitled.

§ 15. **Records and accounts of relief.** A municipal corporation furnishing work relief and/or home relief under the provisions of this act shall keep such records and accounts in relation thereto as the administration shall prescribe.

§ 16. **State aid.** A municipal corporation or a town, where home relief is a town charge, furnishing home relief, and a municipal corporation furnishing work relief, under the provisions of this act shall be paid by the state from the money hereby appropriated in the manner and to the extent provided in this section and such money shall be credited by such corporation or town to its general funds. Payment by the state to a municipal corporation or town under this section shall be forty per centum of the amount of expenditures for such home relief and/or work relief as is approved by the administration during the emergency period.

The administration may in addition make direct grants to a municipal corporation or town for home relief and/or work relief on such conditions as it may prescribe from the funds hereinafter provided for such purpose. Money received by a municipal corporation or town as a direct grant for home relief and/or work relief shall not be paid into the general fund of such municipal corporation or town but shall be made available for home relief or work relief as designated by the administration. Moneys paid to a person in cash under the provisions of this act shall be in the form of day's wages for day's work or hour's wages for hour's work or for home relief as defined by subdivision eight of section two and the payment to any unemployed person of any part of such money in any form other than for wages or such home relief is hereby prohibited. All moneys paid to persons receiving the relief provided by and pursuant to this act shall be inalienable by any assignment or transfer and shall be exempt from levy and execution under the laws of the state. All payments by the state for home relief furnished in the public welfare district comprising the city of Newburgh and the town of Newburgh shall be made to the commissioners of the home of the city and town of Newburgh and for such purpose such public walfare district shall be deemed a municipal corporation.

Section 16 amended by the Laws of 1932, chapter 567, and Laws of 1934, chapter 65.

§ 16-a. **Work relief disability allowance.** 1. Persons employed on work relief projects under the provisions of this act as heretofore or hereafter amended and receiving "work relief" as defined herein shall not be deemed to come within the scope of the provisions or benefits provided by chapter six hundred fifteen of the laws of nineteen hundred twenty-two as amended and known as the workmen's compensation law; but all persons receiving "work relief" who shall become temporarily disabled or injured by reason of any cause arising out of and in the course of their employment shall, during the period of said disability so caused within the duration of the emergency period as defined herein, continue to receive relief on the basis of the budgetary needs of the said person's family as determined under the standards and pursuant to the rules and regulations of the administration and in addition thereto shall be provided with such medical services as the administration may deem necessary.

2. In the event that accidental injuries or occupational disease arising out of and in course of said relief employment result in (a) death, (b) permanent total disability, or (c) permanent partial disability, the administration may provide such allowance as it may deem proper, but not exceeding in any single case the sum of three thousand five hundred dollars, inclusive of funeral expenses. Said funeral expenses in no case shall exceed two hundred dollars. The industrial commissioner of the state shall, when requested by the administration, cause to be provided medical examinations of injured or disabled relief workers and shall render reports on such questions as may be certified by the administration in respect of such cases. Within the limit hereinabove set forth, the administration shall determine the amount and manner of payment of said disability allowance to be made. In respect of all of the foregoing and any and all questions arising thereunder, the determination of the administration shall in every case be final and not subject to appeal or review.

3. The allowances made for said disabilities and/or the relief furnished to the injured work relief employee during the period of said disability shall be exclusive and shall relieve the employing municipal corporation, town, or state from any and all further liability by reason thereof.

4. All claims for relief and/or any such disability allowance pursuant to the provisions of this section shall be made and filed with the administration or its duly authorized agency within thirty days after the occurrence of the accident, injury or illness causing or creating the said disability; and the administration may disallow and refuse to entertain any claim which shall have been filed more than one week after the completion of the project on which the claimant was employed as a work relief employee.

5. The comptroller of the state shall set aside from each allocation of relief funds for work relief wages, whether state or local projects, such proportion thereof as shall be determined by the comptroller and the chairman of the relief administration to be sufficient for the purposes hereof and which said funds when so set aside shall constitute a disability fund from which there shall be paid, upon the certification of the administration, such allow-

ances by reason of (a) death benefits, (b) permanent total disability, and/or (c) permanent partial disability, as shall have been made by the administration pursuant to the provisions hereinabove set forth.

Section 16-a added by Laws of 1934, chapter 303, effective as of April 1, 1934.

§ 17. **Private contributions to the administration.** The administration is authorized also to accept, without conditions, private contributions of moneys and expend them directly in any part of the state for relief of the kind described in the definitions of home relief and work relief, but the kind and location of work for which the administration may expend such moneys directly within a county, city or town, other than state work shall be such as the governing board thereof shall approve. Such direct expenditure may be made through employees of the administration, public welfare officials, local bureaus and municipal authorities, or any of them, as the administration may determine. The administration also may allocate any of such moneys to municipal corporations and towns, as reimbursement under this act, to apply on state aid and to the credit thereof.

Section 17 amended by the Laws of 1932, chapter 567.

§ 18. **Expenditures on state improvements.** The administration may expend of the moneys allocated to the discretionary fund such amount as it may deem necessary for temporary employment on public improvements undertaken or required by the state and not let or to be let by contract, of persons entitled to relief under this act and of such amount the administration may expend a sum not to exceed twenty per centum thereof for the purchase of materials, tools and other supplies needed for the proper performance of such work.

Section 18 amended by the Laws of 1932, chapter 567, Laws of 1933, chapter 9, and Laws of 1934, chapter 71.

§ 19. **Salaries of local staffs.** The administration may authorize city and county commissioners and emergency work bureaus to employ such additional clerical and other assistants or volunteers with qualifications satisfactory to the administration, as may be necessary for the administration of home and/or work relief in accordance with the rules of the administration and shall determine the number of such additional clerks and assistants and fix their salaries, such part, or all, of which salaries as the administration shall determine shall be paid from the money allocated to the discretionary fund. No person employed pursuant to this act, during the emergency period, shall be subject to the provisions of the civil service law.

Section 19 amended by the Laws of 1932, chapter 567, and the Laws of 1933, chapter 9.

§ 20. **Reports of commissioners.** Each city and county commissioner and each local bureau shall file with the administration at its office in the city of Albany as soon after the first day of the month as practicable a verified detailed statement of relief granted unemployed persons of the district during the preceding month. Such reports shall contain such information as the administration may from time to time require.

Section 20 amended by the Laws of 1932, chapter 567.

§ 21. **Reports by administration.** The administration shall report to the governor and the legislature from time to time, in such detail as may be required, the operations of the administration together with the condition of unemployment and the relief affored unemployed persons of the state.

§ 22. **General powers of administration.** In executing any of the provisions of this act, the administration, and any person duly authorized or designated by it, may conduct any investigation pertinent or material to the furtherance of its work. The administration and each person so authorized is hereby empowered to subpoena witnesses, administer oaths, take testimony and compel the production of such books, papers, records and documents as may be relevant to any such investigation. The administration shall have and may exercise such other powers as may be necessary to carry out the provisions of this act.

§ 23. **Claims for payments by the state.** Claims by a municipal corporation or a town for payments by the state for home relief and/or work relief under the provisions of this act shall be made to the administration through the agency representing it in such municipal corporation, which agency shall transmit to the administration forthwith all claims with recommendations in respect thereto.

Section 23 amended by the Laws of 1932, chapter 567.

§ 24. **Allowance of claims.** Upon receipt of claims for payment by the administration, it shall examine such claims and certify to the state comptroller the amount thereof approved by it, specifying the amount to which each municipal corporation is entitled.

§ 25. **Payment of claims.** The amount so certified by the administration as provided in the last section shall be paid from the state treasury upon the audit and warrant of the comptroller to the fiscal officer of the municipal corporation, when such municipal corporation is a city, and to the county treasurer, when such municipal corporation is a county. County treasurers shall distribute the amounts so received by them to the municipal corporations and towns therein entitled thereto.

§ 26. **Blank forms.** The administration shall prescribe and furnish such forms of records, accounts, reports and claims as it may deem advisable for the proper enforcement and administration of the provisions of this act.

§ 27. **Rules of the administration.** The administration shall make and enforce rules in accordance and consonance with the provisions of this act which will best promote the efficiency and effectiveness of the relief which this act is intended to furnish.

None of the money appropriated by this act shall be expended or allowed except in accordance with such rules. A certified copy of such rules shall be filed in the office of the department of state. The administration shall mail to each city and county commissioner and each local bureau, copies of such rules to be posted by them in not less than five public conspicuous places throughout the district.

§ 28. **Dissolution of administration on completion of work.** The administration shall be dissolved and cease to function at the time fixed by this act. At such time, all unexpended or unpledged moneys in the hands of the administration shall be returned forthwith to the state comptroller to be by him deposited into the state treasury to the credit of the general fund; all tools, materials and supplies remaining unconsumed and in the physical possession and control of the administration shall be turned over to the department of public works and all tools, materials and supplies remaining unconsumed and in the hands of the administrative heads shall become the property of and be turned over by them to the city or county in and for which they carried on their duties under this act. The administration shall require such final reports from each administrative head and local bureau under this act as it shall deem necessary and shall, after receipt and audit of such reports, make its own final report to the governor and to the legislature stating such other information or recommendations as it may deem helpful or conducive to promote the public welfare, health and safety of the people of the state. All office equipment purchased by or for the administration shall be turned over to the department of public works. All books, papers, files and records of the administration and all documents, including reports of proceedings, surveys or investigations made or caused to be made by the administration shall be transferred by the administration to the department of state.

§ 29. **Liberal construction.** This act shall be liberally construed to the end that the work of the administration shall be consummated as equitably and expeditiously as practicable.

§ 30. **Violations and penalties.** Rules adopted by the administration under this act shall have the force and effect of law. A violation of any of the provisions of this act or of any rule of the administration, subsequent to the certification, filing and posting of such rule as provided herein, shall constitute a misdemeanor and shall be punishable by a fine of not less than one hundred dollars or more than one thousand dollars or by imprisonment for not more than one year or by both such fine and imprisonment. The penalty prescribed by this section shall not be exclusive, and if a rule be not obeyed, the administration, by the exercise of any power, conferred by this act, may carry out its provisions.

§ 31. **Inconsistent statutory powers or duties.** If a statute, general or special, or any local law or ordinance confers a power, prescribes a duty, or imposes a restriction inconsistent with this act or with a rule of the administration made pursuant to this act, such power shall not be exercised, or such duty or restriction enforced during the emergency period.

§ 32. **Constitutionality.** If any clause, sentence, paragraph, or part of this act shall for any reason be adjudged by any court of competent jurisdiction to be invalid, such judgment shall not affect, impair, or invalidate the remainder of this act, but shall be confined in its operation to the clause, sentence, paragraph, or part thereof directly involved in the controversy in which such judgment shall have been rendered.

§ 33. **Appropriation for state aid.** *

§ 34. **State funds.** The comptroller is hereby authorized and directed to borrow on the faith and credit of the state, in anticipation of the receipt of taxes and revenues, direct or indirect, pursuant to the state finance law, sufficient money, within the appropriations herein made, to pay the legal demands authorized by this act.

§ 35. **Application.** This act shall apply to every county and city in the state and state aid, under the provisions of this act and the rules and regulations of the administration, shall hereafter be available for all counties and cities, whether or not their governing boards have adopted resolutions accepting the provisions of this act, but the governing board or body of a county or city may adopt a resolution that it does not intend to request or accept the state aid authorized by this act. A certified copy of such resolution shall be filed with the administration and, thereupon and thereafter, the provisions of this act shall not apply to such county or city.

Section 35 amended by the Laws of 1932, chapter 567.

§ 36. **Time of taking effect.** This act shall take effect immediately.

___
* Made obsolete by subsequent enactments.

THE STATE RECOVERY ACT

CHAPTER 782 OF THE LAWS OF 1933, AS AMENDED BY LAWS OF
1934, CHAPTERS 39, 104 AND 301

An Act declaring a public emergency and enabling municipalities
and public bodies to secure the benefits of and aid in carrying
out the provisions of the National Industrial Recovery Act.

Section 1. **Public emergency.** The legislature having declared
a public emergency to exist by chapter seven hundred and ninety-
eight of the laws of nineteen hundred thirty-one, it is hereby
declared that the said emergency still exists. The congress of
the United States having taken cognizance of the public emergency
and having enacted the National Industrial Recovery Act, approved
June sixteenth, nineteen hundred thirty-three, making funds available for the construction of public works, the public health and
safety require, and it is hereby provided, that all provisions of
any general, special or local law which tend to prevent, hamper or
delay municipalities, or to prevent, hamper or delay public bodies
to which this act applies from taking advantage of the provisions
of the National Industrial Recovery Act shall be inoperative; but
the above provision or any other provision of this act shall not operate to dispense with the approval by a state department, board,
officer or commission of a project where such approval is necessary under existing provisions of law.

§ 2. **Definitions.** For the purposes of this act, 1. "Municipality" means and includes any county, city, town, village, school
district, water, fire, sewer, lighting, sidewalk, sanitary, drainage,
improvement district, and any other district, having territorial
boundaries, organized for constructing and maintaining buildings,
improvements, works and instrumentalities for the use and benefit
of the public generally or the inhabitants of and/or property within
the district.

2. "Public body" means and includes any state or local officer,
board, trustees, commission or commissions, corporation or other
authority constituted by or pursuant to law to construct and
maintain buildings, improvements, works and instrumentalities for
the use and benefit of the public.

3. "Governing board" of a county, includes the board of supervisors; of a city, the local legislative body, as defined by the city
home rule law; of a town, the town board; of a village, the board
of trustees; or a school district, the board of education, the board

[23]

of trustees, or trustees or trustee; of any other district, the board, commission, commissioners, officer, officers, trustees or other authority empowered by law to authorize expenditures and projects by or for the district and/or the borrowing of money by it or for its purposes and to direct the levying of taxes on property within the district for district purposes. Where the separate concurrence or approval of two or more sets of authorities with respect to either or any of the above matters is now required by law, "governing board," to the extent so required, shall mean and include both or all of them; and the term "majority vote," when such a board consists of two or more sets of authorities, means majority vote of each, including the concurrence or approval of the officer constituting such an authority if it consists of but one person.

4. "National industrial recovery act," shall mean and include not only the act of the congress of the United States of America, approved June sixteenth, nineteen hundred and thirty-three, entitled "An act to encourage national industrial recovery, to foster fair competition, and to provide for the construction of certain useful public works, and for other purposes," but also any acts amendatory thereof and any acts supplemental thereto, and revisions thereof, and any further act of the congress of the United States to encourage public works, to reduce unemployment and thereby to assist in the national recovery and promote the public welfare.

Section 2 amended by Laws of 1934, chapter 104.

§ 3. Notwithstanding the provisions of any general, special or local law, any municipality, by majority vote of its governing board, and any public body of this state, having the power under existing law to borrow money are hereby authorized to accept from the United States through the federal emergency administrator of public works, or other federal agency, direct grants of moneys paid in defraying the cost of the labor and materials employed upon any project undertaken under the provisions of the national industrial recovery act. The funds received as such grants shall be expended on the project so undertaken in the same manner as other funds made available for such project whether as loans or otherwise.

Section 3 amended by Laws of 1934, chapter 104.

§ 4. Notwithstanding the provisions of any general, special or local law, any public body or the governing board of any municipality, by majority vote, may authorize the proper officers of such municipality or body to enter into contracts with the United States through the federal emergency administrator of public works, or such other federal agency as may be authorized so to act, to obtain funds pursuant to the provisions of the national industrial recovery act for public works projects under the supervision of said municipality or body, providing, however, that if under existing law such public works are to be paid for by direct assessment on real estate benefited where the area of the benefit is less than that of the municipality, any existing provisions for a permissive referendum shall remain in full force and effect and providing, further, that, if such public works project is for the construction or operation of a public utility or facility for the supply of gas, electricity or water in competition with or substitution for a public utility or facility supplying gas, electricity or water in the same area, any action of the public body or governing board of a municipality in relation thereto, pursuant to the provisions of this section, shall be subject to a mandatory referendum, notwithstanding any other provisions of this act. It shall not be necessary for any such board or body to hold hearings on or publish notices of such projects or for such projects to be initiated by petition of taxpayers or owners of property nor shall such project be subject to vote at any election (other than a school district meeting) or to referendum, mandatory or permissive, except as above provided, and except that this provision shall not operate to dispense with a hearing under the general district law and the constitution on the sole question of whether a proposed improvement benefits all the property in a district liable to taxation for defraying all or part of its cost. If before or after the execution of any such contract the governing board shall determine to submit the authorization of the project, or the issuance of bonds or the levying of a tax, to vote at a school district meeting or at an election or to referendum, whether or not required by law, it may, notwithstanding the provisions of any other law, provide for such vote or referendum on notice published at least once in a newspaper circulating in the municipality, and posted in at least ten conspicuous places on any day at least seven days prior to such meeting or election; and no other notice shall be required. Such contract may provide for the issuing of bonds of said municipalities and in anticipation thereof for the issuing of notes, temporary bonds, certificates of indebtedness, interim certificates, or security receipts, hereinafter generally referred to as "other obligations," and for the rights of the holders of such bonds and other obligations. The termination of the emergency prior to the completion of or ultimate liquidation of obligations incurred by reason of public works projects financed hereunder shall in no manner affect the validity of such contracts or other agreements. Nothing in this act contained, however, shall be construed to alter, modify or affect the provisions of existing laws of this state in such manner as to lower the standards therein provided with regard to labor, hours of labor, wages for labor and employment of females and children.

Section 4 amended by Laws of 1934, chapter 104.

§ 4-a. Notwithstanding the provisions of any general, special or local law, requiring a project to be undertaken under such law, wholly or partly at the expense of property specially benefited thereby, such project may in the discretion of the governing board or public body, be undertaken as a public works project wholly at the expense of the municipality at large. Notwithstanding the provisions of any general, special or local law requiring that the cost of a stated project or kind of project be borne in whole or in part by assessments on property specially benefited, bonds in an amount to pay the entire estimated cost or part thereof of such a project may be issued in the first instance and prior to the completion of the project or prior to the levy of any such assessments.

Section 4-a added by Laws of 1934, chapter 104.

§ 5. Notwithstanding the provisions of any general, special or local law, any municipality, by majority vote of its governing board, or public body, empowered by law to borrow money for a public works project is hereby expressly authorized to issue and sell its negotiable bonds or its other obligations to the United States through the federal emergency administrator of public works, or such other federal agency as may be authorized so to act, without advertisement, proposals or public or private bidding, in order to carry out any contract entered into as provided in section four of this act, and such bonds or other obligations may be in such form, and be subject to such terms and conditions, with such privileges as to registration, conversion, reconversion, redemption, interchangeability and exchange and such other provisions as may be provided by the contract; and it is hereby further expressly provided that the provisions of any general or special law of this state requiring bonds or other obligations of the municipality to be serial or payable in annual installments or fixing the maximum or minimum time or times when the debt contracted or any part of it shall be payable shall not be binding with respect to moneys borrowed from the United States. Such contract may provide for the establishment, investment and safekeeping of sinking funds to meet payments not accruing annually and for contributions of the municipality thereto.

§ 5-a. Notwithstanding the provisions of any general, special or local law, any municipality, by a majority vote of its governing body or public body empowered by law to borrow money for a public works project may issue its bonds to purchase materials, supplies and equipment and may purchase and furnish such materials, supplies and equipment for such projects as may have been or may be undertaken through or by authority of the civil works administration of the federal government or the work division of the federal emergency relief administration or any other work relief authority of the state and/or federal governments; the terms of such bonds shall not exceed the probable life of said improvements or the estimated average probable life of said improvements, and shall mature in annual installments, the first of which shall mature not more than two years from the date of the bonds and the last of which shall mature not more than ten years from the date of the bonds; provided, however, that in the event that the cost, or total cost, as estimated by such governing body or public body, is in excess of two hundred thousand dollars, the last installment of such bonds shall mature not more than twenty years from the date of the bonds, and no installment shall be more than fifty per centum in excess of the amount of the smallest prior installment. Pending the issuance of such bonds, such indebtedness may be temporarily financed by certificates of indebtedness or notes of the municipality running not more than six months, which certificates of indebtedness or notes may be renewed and any renewal thereof shall mature not more than one year from the date of the certificates of indebtedness or notes first issued, and such temporary obligations shall bear interest at a rate not exceeding six per centum per annum, and may be sold at private sale for not less than par value, and said temporary obligations shall be paid from the proceeds of such bonds. Said bonds shall be sold in the manner provided by law for not less than par and shall be general obligations of the municipality, and there shall be raised annually by tax upon the taxable property of the municipality a sum sufficient to pay the principal and interest of such bonds as the same became due. The making of such improvements or the purchase of such materials, supplies or equipment or the incurring of such indebtedness shall not be subject to any petition or notice or hearing or permissive or mandatory referendum or approval by any public board or any requirement of law requiring advertisement for bids.

Section 5-a added by Laws of 1934, chapter 39, as amended by chapter 301.

§ 6. All provisions of this act applicable to municipalities and public bodies may also be availed of by and shall be deemed to apply to the state itself in aid of any public works projects undertaken or to be undertaken by any of its departments, boards, commissions or other state agencies. It is expressly provided that if an appropriation shall have been made, or other state moneys shall have become available, for an authorized public works project prosecuted or to be prosecuted by or under the jurisdiction of a state department or division, commission, board or state agency therein, additional moneys provided for such project, by allotment under the National Industrial Recovery Act, may be used therefor, subject to such act and rules and regulations adopted pursuant thereto, and the facilities of such project enlarged accordingly. The head of the department and the state comptroller, by joint application, may request such federal aid, in behalf of the state; and the concurrence therein of the superintendent of public works shall be necessary as to any such work for which he is required by law to prepare or approve the plans. The comptroller may accept such moneys and deposit them with the commissioner of taxation and finance, and they shall be available therefor, as though appropriated. Notwithstanding any other provision of law, contracts may be let for such project within the amount appropriated together with any such additional moneys that have been so received and deposited or otherwise made immediately available pursuant to such act.

§ 6-a. Nothwithstanding the provisions of any general, special or local law other than this act, public work projects or any contract referred to in section four of this act, or the issuance of bonds or other obligations pursuant to such contract, or any other acts or proceedings in connection therewith, may be authorized by resolution which may be finally adopted on the same day on which it is introduced by a majority of all the members of the governing board, and such resolution need not be published before becoming effective.

§ 6-b. This act shall be liberally construed and the powers granted and the duties imposed by this act shall be construed to be independent and severable. If any one or more sections, clauses, sentences, or parts of this act shall for any reason be questioned in any court, and shall be adjudged unconstitutional or invalid, such judgment shall not affect, impair or invalidate the remaining provisions thereof, but shall be confined in its operation to the specific provisions so held unconstitutional or invalid.

Sections 6-a and 6-b added by Laws of 1934, chapter 104.

THE LEGALIZING AND VALIDATING ACT

SECTION 2 OF CHAPTER 39 OF THE LAWS OF 1934, AS AMENDED BY CHAPTER 301

§ 2. All acts and proceedings heretofore taken by municipalities, their boards and officers, in raising moneys by appropriation or otherwise and/or using such moneys or other moneys for the purchasing and furnishing of materials, supplies and equipment for use on such work or projects as have heretofore been undertaken through or by authority of the civil works administration of the federal government or the work divison of the federal emergency relief administration or any other work relief authoriity of the state and/or federal governments are hereby legalized, validated, ratified and confirmed, notwithstanding any want of statutory authority therefor or any defect or irregularity therein.

APPROPRIATION OF THE BALANCE OF THE 1933 BOND ISSUE .

CHAPTER 71 OF THE LAWS OF 1934, AS AMENDED BY CHAPTER 273

Section 1. The balance of forty-eight million dollars ($48,000,-000) remaining out of the proceeds of the sale of bonds authorized by chapter two hundred and sixty of the laws of nineteen hundred thirty-three, sixty million dollars ($60,000,000), not heretofore appropriated is hereby appropriated and made immediately available to the temporary emergency relief administration, created by chapter seven hundred and ninety-eight of the laws of nineteen hundred thirty-one, as amended for the purposes specified in chapter seven hundred and ninety-eight of the laws of nineteen hundred thirty-one, as amended, for the period from February fifteenth, nineteen hundred thirty-four to February fifteenth, nineteen hundred thirty-five.

Thirty-three million dollars ($33,000,000) of the moneys appropriated by this section shall be allocated to a reimbursement fund to be used and expended for payment to municipal corporations, as defined by chapter seven hundred and ninety-eight of the laws of nineteen hundred thirty-one, and towns of forty per centum of their expenditures for home relief and/or work relief from February fifteenth, nineteen hundred thirty-four to February fifteenth, nineteen hundred thirty-five, expenditures from the said reimbursement fund to be made as heretofore provided by section sixteen of chapter seven hundred and ninety-eight of the laws of nineteen hundred thirty-one, as amended.

Fifteen million dollars ($15,000,000) of the money appropriated by this section shall be allocated to the discretionary fund to be used and expended (a) for direct grants to municipal corporations, as provided for by section sixteen of chapter seven hundred and ninety-eight of the laws of nineteen hundred thirty-one as amended by chapter five hundred and sixty-seven of the laws of nineteen hundred thirty-two, for work relief and/or home relief and to towns for home relief, on such conditions as the administration may prescribe; (b) for salaries and expenses of the administration from February fifteenth, nineteen hundred thirty-four, to February fifteenth, nineteen hundred thirty-five; (c) for salaries of local bureaus as provided in section nineteen of chapter seven hundred and ninety-eight of the laws of nineteen hundred thirty-one as amended by chapter five hundred and sixty-seven of the laws of nineteen hundred thirty-two for the period from February fifteenth, nineteen hundred thirty-four to February fifteenth, nineteen hundred thirty-five; (d) for state improvements as provided for in section eighteen of chapter seven hundred and ninety-eight of the laws of nineteen hundred thirty-one as last amended by chapter nine of the laws of nineteen hundred thirty-three. The sum of two hundred thousand dollars ($200,000) or so much thereof as may be needed, is hereby appropriated from such discretionary fund and made available for the relief of sick and disabled veterans under article one-a of the military law. The money appropriated by this section shall be expended on the audit and warrant of the comptroller upon vouchers certified or approved by the chairman of the administration or a member of the administration duly authorized by him.

All sums remaining in the reimbursement, discretionary, state improvement or other funds from moneys heretofore appropriated thereto by chapter seven hundred and ninety-eight of the laws of nineteen hundred thirty-one as amended by chapter six of the laws of nineteen hundred thirty-three and by chapter two hundred fifty-nine of the laws of nineteen hundred thirty-three, which shall be unexpended and/or unpledged and/or unallocated as of February fifteenth, nineteen hundred thirty-four, are hereby reappropriated to the reimbursement, discretionary, state improvement or other funds herein created respectively and shall be in addition to the thirty-three million dollars ($33,000,000) heretofore set up as a reimbursement fund and the fifteen million dollars ($15,000,000) heretofore set up as a discretionary fund out of the unappropriated forty-eight million dollars ($48,000,000) remaining from the bond issue moneys authorized by chapter two hundred sixty of the laws of nineteen hundred thirty-three.

Section 1 amended as to veteran relief by chapter 273 of the Laws of 1934.

FRESH MILK

CHAPTER 821 OF THE LAWS OF 1934, REAPPROPRIATING FOR FRESH MILK FOR NEEDY CHILDREN $1,500,000 OF THE DISCRETIONARY FUND PROVIDED BY CHAPTER 71 OF THE LAWS OF 1934

Section 1. Of the sum of forty-eight million dollars appropriated by chapter seventy-one of the laws of nineteen hundred thirty-four, including amendments, from proceeds of the sale of bonds authorized by chapter two hundred and sixty of the laws of nineteen hundred thirty-three, the sum of one million five hundred thousand dollars ($1,500,000), is hereby re-appropriated to the temporary emergency relief administration and directed to be expended by it for supplying fresh milk free to needy children, through the agency of the public school system, other schools where the tuition is free and public or private milk stations maintained for the free distribution of milk, such service to be rendered under rules and regulations of the administration. The moneys so re-appropriated shall be paid out of the sum of fifteen million dollars allocated to the discretionary fund by such chapter seventy-one of the laws of nineteen hundred thirty-four, as enacted or amended, on the audit and warrant of the comptroller upon vouchers certified or approved by the chairman of the temporary emergency relief administration or by a member of the administration duly authorized by him.

§ 2. This act shall take effect immediately.

AUTHORIZING REFERENDUM ON NEW STATE DEBT OF $40,000,000 FOR RELIEF

CHAPTER 718 OF THE LAWS OF 1934

Section 1. The creation of a state debt to the amount of forty million dollars is hereby authorized to provide funds, to be available from November fifteenth, nineteen hundred thirty-four to February fifteenth, nineteen hundred thirty-six, to relieve the people of the state from the hardships and suffering caused by unemployment and the effects thereof on the public health and welfare, including the granting of aid to municipalities for such purpose. The legislature may continue existing agencies and provisions of law, or may create other agencies and/or other ways and means to administer and distribute temporary emergency relief for such purpose, and may provide for cost thereof, from the proceeds of the sale of the bonds authorized by this act, in such amounts as the legislature, from time to time, shall have appropriated or may appropriate and make available therefrom and the money so appropriated shall be paid from the treasury on the audit and warrant of the comptroller upon vouchers certified or approved pursuant to law.

§ 2. The state comptroller is hereby authorized and empowered to issue and sell bonds of the state to the amount of the debt hereby authorized to be created and for the purpose hereby authorized to be known as "emergency unemployment relief bonds." Such bonds shall bear interest at the rate of not to exceed five per centum, which interest shall be payable semi-annually in the city of New York. Such bonds, or the portion thereof at any time issued, shall be made payable in ten installments, the first of which shall be payable one year from date of issue and the last of which shall be payable within ten years after the date of issue and in no case to exceed the probable life of the work or object, to which the proceeds thereof are to be applied as determined by the state finance law. Such bonds or the portion thereof at any time sold, shall be of such denominations, subject to the foregoing provisions, as the comptroller may determine. Such bonds shall be sold in such lot or lots, from time to time, as may be required to carry out the provisions of laws making appropriations for the purposes for which such bonds were issued. Such bonds shall be sold at not less than par to the highest bidder after advertisement for a period of ten consecutive days, Sundays excepted, in at least two daily newspapers printed in the city of New York and one in the city of Albany. Advertisements shall contain a provision to the effect that the comptroller, in his discretion, may reject any or all bids made in pursuance of such advertisements and, in the event of such rejection, the comptroller is authorized to readvertise for bids in the form and manner above described as many times as, in his judgment, may be necessary to effect a satisfactory sale. The proceeds of bonds sold pursuant to this act shall be paid into the treasury and shall be available only for the work or object authorized by this act in accordance with appropriations therefrom made or to be made by the legislature for such work or object.

§ 3. The comptroller is hereby authorized and directed to borrow, on the faith and credit of the state, in anticipation of the receipt of proceeds of the sale of the bonds authorized by this act, pursuant to the state finance law, sufficient money to pay the legal demands authorized by appropriations theretofore or thereafter made by the legislature for the purpose for which a state debt is authorized to be created by this act.

§ 4. This law shall not take effect unless and until it shall have been submitted to the people at a general election, and have received a majority of all the votes cast for and against it at such election and such law shall be submitted to the people of this state at the general election to be held in November, nineteen hundred and thirty-four. The ballots to be furnished for the use of the voters upon the submission of this law shall be in the form prescribed by the election law and the proposition or question to be submitted shall be printed thereon in substantially the following form, namely, "Shall chapter (here insert the number of the chapter) of the laws of nineteen hundred thirty-four, entitled 'An act authorizing the creation of a state debt, to the amount of forty million dollars, to provide funds, to be available from November fifteenth, nineteen hundred thirty-four to February fifteenth, nineteen hundred thirty-six, to relieve the people of the state from the hardships and suffering, caused by unemployment, and the effects thereof on the public health and welfare, including the granting of aid to municipalities for such purpose, through such agencies and by such ways and means as the legislature shall have prescribed or hereafter may prescribe for the administration and distribution of temporary emergency relief and the cost thereof, and providing for the submission to the people of a proposition or question therefor to be voted upon at the general election to be held in the year nineteen hundred thirty-four, be approved?''

APPROPRIATION OF $10,000,000 FOR RELIEF IF 1934 REFERENDUM IS APPROVED

CHAPTER 717 OF THE LAWS OF 1934

Section 1. If and when an act, entitled "An act authorizing the creation of a state debt to the amount of forty million dollars to provide funds, to be available from November fifteenth, nineteen hundred thirty-four to February fifteenth, nineteen hundred thirty-six, to relieve the people of the state from the hardships and suffering, caused by unemployment, and the effects thereof on the public health and welfare, including the granting of aid to municipalities for such purpose through such agencies and by such ways and means as the legislature shall have prescribed or hereafter may prescribe for the administration and distribution of temporary emergency relief and the cost thereof, and providing for the submission to the people of a proposition or question therefor to be voted upon at the general election to be held in the year nineteen hundred thirty-four," shall have been approved, by the people at the general election to be held in the year nineteen hundred thirty-four, in the manner prescribed in the constitution, the sum of ten million dollars ($10,000,000) of the proceeds of the sale of bonds authorized by such referendum vote, is hereby appropriated and made immediately available for the purposes authorized by chapter seven hundred ninety-eight of the laws of nineteen hundred thirty-one, as amended, for the period of the emergency up to and including February fifteenth, nineteen hundred and thirty-five.

§ 2. Seven million dollars ($7,000,000) of the moneys appropriated by this act shall be allocated to a reimbursement fund to be used and expended for payment to municipal corporations, as defined by chapter seven hundred and ninety-eight of the laws of nineteen hundred thirty-one, and towns of forty per centum of their expenditures for home relief and/or work relief to February fifteenth, nineteen hundred thirty-five, expenditures from the said reimbursement fund to be made as heretofore provided by section sixteen of chapter seven hundred and ninety-eight of the laws of nineteen hundred thirty-one, as amended.

§ 3. Three million dollars ($3,000,000) of the money appropriated by this act shall be allocated to the discretionary fund to be used and expended (a) for direct grants to municipal corporations, as provided for by section sixteen of chapter seven hundred and ninety-eight of the laws of nineteen hundred thirty-one as amended by chapter five hundred and sixty-seven of the laws of nineteen hundred thirty-two, for work relief and/or home relief and to towns for home relief, on such conditions as the administration may prescribe; (b) for salaries and expenses of the administration to February fifteenth, nineteen hundred thirty-five; (c) for salaries of local bureaus as provided in section nineteen of chapter seven hundred and ninety-eight of the laws of nineteen hundred thirty-one as amended by chapter five hundred and sixty-seven of the laws of nineteen hundred thirty-two for the period of February fifteenth, nineteen hundred thirty-five; (d) for state improvements as provided for in section eighteen of chapter seven hundred and ninety-eight of the laws of nineteen hundred thirty-one as last amended by chapter seventy-one of the laws of nineteen hundred thirty-four. The money appropriated by this act shall be expended on the audit and warrant of the comptroller upon vouchers certified or approved by the chairman of the administration or a member of the administration duly authorized by him.

§ 4. This act shall take effect immediately.

STATE PARTICIPATION IN FEDERAL FUNDS

CHAPTER 8, LAWS OF 1933, AS AMENDED BY LAWS OF 1933, CHAPTER 258, LAWS OF 1934, CHAPTER 716

Section 1. On behalf of the state of New York the governor is hereby authorized from time to time to apply to the Reconstruction Finance Corporation or other similar federal agency pursuant to title I, section one, of the emergency relief and construction act of nineteen hundred thirty-two enacted by congress of the United States and approved July twenty-first, nineteen hundred thirty-two, or any acts amendatory thereof or supplemental thereto or any other acts hereafter enacted by the congress for the purpose of relieving unemployment distress, for funds for use in furnishing relief and work relief to needy and distressed people and in relieving hardship resulting from unemployment.

Any application by the governor shall be made upon the express understanding and condition that any funds paid by the Reconstruction Finance Corporation or other similar federal agency to the governor shall not constitute a loan to the state of New York.

§ 2. The governor is hereby authorized to receive such moneys from time to time and to transmit them to the commissioner of taxation and finance or to authorize the receipt and the expenditure of said funds by the temporary relief administration of the state of New York acting as a state or federal agency within the state of New York. Such moneys when so transmitted by the governor shall be held by such commissioner in a separate account in a depository or depositories designated by such commissioner and the comptroller, and shall be expended by the temporary emergency relief administration of the state of New York, created by chapter seven hundred ninety-eight of the laws of nineteen hundred thirty-one, on the audit and warrant of the comptroller upon vouchers approved by the chairman of the temporary emergency relief administration or a member thereof duly authorized by him.

Section 2 amended by Laws of 1934, chapter 716.

§ 3. Such monies from the reconstruction finance corporation or other federal agency may be expended by the temporary emergency relief administration for the purposes and in the manner provided by chapter seven hundred ninety-eight of the laws of nineteen hundred and thirty-one as now or hereafter amended and for such other relief or related purposes as may be authorized by the emergency relief and reconstruction act of nineteen hundred and thirty-two enacted by the congress of the United States and acts amendatory thereof or supplemental thereto and by any other acts enacted by the congress and pursuant to and under such conditions and in the manner specified by the reconstruction finance corporation or other federal agency, but nothing in this chapter or in any other law shall create a liability against the temporary emergency relief administration or the state of New York for, in respect of, in relation to or by reason of the administration or expenditure of such federal funds.

Section 3 amended by Laws of 1933, chapter 258, and Laws of 1934, chapter 716.

§ 4. It is the intention of the legislature that in so far as possible such moneys be not so expended by the temporary emergency relief administration as to relieve the municipal corporations of the state of their responsibility to furnish funds for the relief of unemployed distress within their respective jurisdiction.

§ 5. The temporary emergency relief administration is directed to keep complete records of the disbursement of all such moneys and to submit to the governor when requested by him a statement thereof. The governor shall file with the Reconstruction Finance Corporation or such other federal agency, if required, and with the comptroller of the state of New York, a statement of the disbursement of all such funds.

§ 6. The governor is hereby empowered to do, either acting directly or through the temporary emergency relief administration as his agent, all other acts relative to any application for funds, required of him to be performed by title I, section one, of the emergency relief and construction act of nineteen hundred thirty-two, any acts amendatory thereof or supplemental thereto and any other acts hereafter enacted by the congress of the United States for the purpose of relieving unemployment distress, or by the rules and regulations of the Reconstruction Finance Corporation or other similar federal agency.

§ 7. This act shall take effect immediately.

FEDERAL MONEY FOR STATE ENGINEERING

CHAPTER 654 OF THE LAWS OF 1934

Section 1. The comptroller is hereby authorized to receive from the federal government or its agents any moneys which the federal government, its agents or municipal beneficiaries of the federal government under the national industrial recovery act shall offer to the state of New York for expenditure through the department of public works for the cost and expense of engineering, designing, supervision and inspection of the construction, repair and improvement of public highways and parkways, public buildings and any publicly owned instrumentalities and facilities of municipalities or other public bodies wherein and whereby any of such construction, repair and improvements of such projects is financed in whole or in part by grants or loans from the federal government pursuant to and in accordance with the terms and provisions of the national industrial recovery act as passed by congress June thirteenth, nineteen hundred thirty-three.

§ 2. The superintendent of public works, upon request from the federal government, is hereby authorized to carry on such engineering, designing, supervision and inspection by and with the employees of the department of public works and to do and perform all necessary acts in connection therewith for the convenient and expeditious consummation thereof.

§ 3. The sum of one hundred thousand dollars ($100,000), or so much thereof as may be needed, is appropriated from any money in the state treasury not otherwise appropriated for payment in the first instance by the state of the cost and expense of such engineering, designing, supervision and inspection, all as above set forth. No part of the moneys hereby appropriated shall be available unless and until either an allotment of moneys for such engineering, designing, supervision and inspection shall have been made by the federal government to the state directly or satisfactory assurances, declarations or confirmations are made by the federal government or its agents to the comptroller and the department of public works that federal moneys will be placed with and made available to respective municipalities wherein such projects are financed as aforesaid for the paying over by such municipalities to the state comptroller sufficient sums for the reimbursement to the state of moneys so paid out by the state in the first instance in carrying out this act; nor shall moneys hereby appropriated be available to an amount in excess of any amount directly allotted to the state as aforesaid or in excess of any amount assured by the federal government to be paid over by municipalities which are beneficiaries under said national industrial recovery act. The comptroller is hereby authorized upon receipt of any such allotment or of any advancement thereof or of any moneys received from any such municipalities pursuant to any assurance, direction, declaration or confirmation by or from the federal government to deposit such moneys with the commissioner of taxation and finance and they shall be placed from time to time to the credit of the general fund in such amounts as will reimburse the state for expenditures made in the first instance for said engineering, designing, supervision and inspection.

§ 4. The moneys hereby appropriated shall be payable by the commissioner of taxation and finance on the audit and warrant of the comptroller on vouchers approved by the superintendent of public works.

§ 5. Notwithstanding any other general or special law to the contrary, if in the carrying out of the intent and purpose of this act any civil service employee of the department of public works is discontinued from state service by reason of being temporarily employed or is transferred to the federal government or to any municipality designated by it in furtherance of the aforesaid work, for which the government extends financial aid, he shall continue to be a member of the New York state employees' retirement system and shall not suffer any loss of rights or benefits now enjoyed under the civil service law and shall be entitled to all the rights granted under article four of the civil service law provided such member thereafter pay into the retirement fund and pension fund in monthly installments a proportion of the salary paid to him by the federal government or its agents or any such municipality as the case may be, computed upon his rate of contribution for all rights and benefits under said civil service law, and the comptroller is empowered to do all necessary and convenient acts to orderly effectuate such contribution.

§ 6. This act shall take effect immediately.

WORKMEN'S COMPENSATION

CHAPTER 769 OF THE LAWS OF 1934

Section 1. Section ten of article two of the workmen's compensation law is hereby amended by adding a sentence to read as follows:

The provisions of this chapter shall not apply to persons receiving "work relief" and employed on work relief projects under the provisions of chapter seven hundred ninety-eight of the laws of nineteen hundred thirty-one as amended, and the definition of the word "employee" as herein definde shall not include persons receiving "work relief" and employed on work relief projects under the provisions of chapter seven hundred ninety-eight of the laws of nineteen hundred thirty-one as amended.

§ 2. This act shall take effect immediately.

THREE YEARS OF PUBLIC UNEMPLOYMENT RELIEF IN NEW YORK STATE

THE NEED AND HOW IT HAS BEEN MET
1931–1934

TEMPORARY EMERGENCY RELIEF ADMINISTRATION
STATE OFFICE BUILDING, ALBANY, N. Y.
NEW YORK OFFICE, 79 MADISON AVENUE

October 15, 1934

MEMBERS
ALFRED H. SCHOELLKOPF OF BUFFALO, Chairman
SOLOMON LOWENSTEIN OF NEW YORK
CHARLES D. OSBORNE OF AUBURN
JOSEPH P. RYAN OF NEW YORK
HENRY ROOT STERN OF NASSAU COUNTY

FREDERICK I. DANIELS, Executive Director

THREE YEARS OF PUBLIC UNEMPLOYMENT RELIEF IN NEW YORK STATE

CONTENTS

THREE YEARS OF PUBLIC UNEMPLOYMENT RELIEF IN NEW YORK STATE

To His Excellency, Herbert H. Lehman, Governor, and to the Honorable Members of the Senate and the Assembly of the State of New York:

In accordance with instructions in Section 21 of Chapter 798 of the Laws of 1931, directing the Temporary Emergency Relief Administration of New York State to "report to the Governor and the Legislature from time to time in such detail as may be required, the operations of the Administration together with the condition of unemployment and the relief afforded unemployed persons in the State," there is submitted herewith a summary of State aid in public unemployment relief from its inception on November 1, 1931 to September 1, 1934, together with an estimate of relief needs this winter after the first three years of the "temporary emergency" have come to a close.

In the three-year period the relief need, passing all bounds of theory in its magnitude and persistence, has confirmed the necessity of State aid to everyone who has been familiar with the problem, whatever his party or social creed, and demonstrated the wisdom of the State of New York in its pioneer action to aid its communities in the alleviation of human suffering. Despite decrease in unemployment that has come with the improvement of business conditions from the depth of the depression, cumulative exhaustion of resources among those unemployed has forced more and more of our people to seek public relief. A peak in the number of relief cases was reached last April, since when there has been a slight recession in the percentage of the population forced to rely on public support.

Faced, in view of calculable trends, with the probable necessity of continuing State aid for at least several years to come, even if the most sanguine hopes for a continued business upturn should be realized, this Administration last June requested the Governor to undertake an impartial study of the present emergency machinery so that a vehicle for a more permanent administration of relief might be devised.

The Governor's Commission on Unemployment Relief, appointed by the Honorable Herbert H. Lehman, Governor, in response to that request is now at work. Meanwhile the relief must go on.

The Legislature, by Chapter 718 of the Laws of 1934, authorized the submission to the people at the coming November election of a $40,000,000 bond issue to provide for the State's continued part in the program. This bond issue, to be voted upon by the electorate, is the State's sole provision for continuing her share of relief costs, essential both to supplement local funds for relief and to assure receiving the State's share of Federal relief funds toward which her citizens pay taxes.

The attached report gives as simply as may be an accounting of the Administration's stewardship in the great effort to conserve for the State the human resources on which her wealth and well-being in the last analysis depend.

ALFRED H. SCHOELLKOPF of Buffalo, *Chairman*
SOLOMON LOWENSTEIN of New York
CHARLES D. OSBORNE of Auburn
JOSEPH P. RYAN of New York
HENRY ROOT STERN of Nassau County

THE NEED

Growth of the Emergency

Following the break in prosperity in 1929, public-spirited citizens undertook by private campaigns to supplement the efforts of local governments in providing relief for the growing army of those who, through no fault of their own, found themselves unemployed and destitute. As the problem grew to such proportions that their aid was obviously insufficient to enable the localities to meet the need, they were among the foremost in urging that the State, with its broader tax base, bear its share of the burden.

New York was the first state to face this situation with substantial assistance. The Wicks Act, passed in Special Session called by the Honorable Franklin D. Roosevelt, Governor, and effective September 23, 1931, declared the existence of an emergency in which "the public health and safety of the State and of each county, city and town therein was imperilled by the existing and threatened deprivation of a considerable number of their inhabitants of the necessaries of life," found State assistance "vitally necessary to supplement the relief work accomplished or to be accomplished locally and to encourage and stimulate local effort in the same direction," and created the Temporary Emergency Relief Administration, delegating to it the pioneer task of administering such assistance according to certain broad principles laid down in the Act.

On November 1 of that year the Administration began its colossal task, which still continues. The extent to which the growing human need made private benevolence inadequate to try to continue meeting the relief problem in conjunction with the local governments alone is apparent from certain significant figures. In New York City the energetic and public-spirited 1931–1932 drive of the private Emergency Unemployment Relief Committee raised approximately $19,635,000, or enough to carry the city's present relief load for scarcely more than a month.

But as time passed the very factors that threw more and more into the army of unemployed also made the private raising of money more difficult. The depression played few favorites. In the general exhaustion of individual resources that even now, with

[5]

unemployment on the wane, has forced a greater and greater percentage of those unemployed to seek relief if they were to continue to live, private means for benevolence have ineluctably dried up. Nor have the local units of Government been able to undertake heavier burdens.

Under the original Wicks Act local welfare districts were to be reimbursed from State funds for 40 per cent of their home relief expenditures and given similar direct assistance for work relief. The emergency period in the State was first defined to terminate June 1, 1932. Continuing need has forced the successive extension of the period until February 15, 1935. With the municipalities unable to find correspondingly larger funds to meet the growing need within their gates, the share of the burden undertaken by the State, and later by the State with Federal assistance, has increased to more than 75 per cent in the determination that the hungry be fed and the homeless have shelter.

The distribution of relief funds has remained in the hands of the localities, as provided for in the Wicks Act, which expressly declared that the "duty of providing for those in need or unemployed because of lack of employment is primarily an obligation of the municipalities." The Administration has consistently regarded relief as a local function to be worked out with such freedom as is compatible with adequate control and supervision to insure the most constructive as well as the most economical use of State and Federal relief funds. In the unforseeable expansion of its activities dictated by the circumstances, the Administration has made every effort to give force to its conviction that local effort is the heart of the relief problem and that the success of the whole program rests squarely upon the organization, imagination and efficiency of the local units.

There can be no minimizing the burden that has been borne by the State in the accomplishment of this great social good, a burden destructive in its weight, had not the Government of the United States, from the same necessity that led the State to contribute its aid, eventually stepped in to assume its own share of the load.

Previous experience in the present emergency has shown that in determining the need the cumulative exhaustion of the resources of the unemployed is a more important factor than normal seasonal trends. With both these factors operating for increase in the coming months, a rise over present levels is to be anticipated.

Sinews of State Aid

By the Wicks Act the Legislature appropriated $20,000,000 for the State's share in meeting the relief need, adding $5,000,000 in March, 1932, to carry on its aid until a $30,000,000 bond issue could be submitted to the people at the general election in November, 1932. That bond issue and a second relief bond issue of $60,000,000 in November, 1933, received the approval of the electorate and have been duly appropriated. Thus the State has so far made available for relief purposes $115,000,000.

At the present rate of State expenditure under the current policy of Federal moneys supplementing State aid to the communities, State relief funds now available will be exhausted by February 15 next.

Federal grants to the State for relief are dependent upon the State contributing its share, according to the frequently reiterated policy of the Federal Emergency Relief Administration. Consequently, State relief funds are necessary not only for their aid to the communities but to insure continued Federal aid for the relief programs of the communities.

At the coming general election in November, the people are to pass upon a further relief bond issue of $40,000,000 to be available for State aid to the municipalities up to February 15, 1936. Reduction in the amount asked for did not reflect any reliance upon a reduction in the anticipated need in the next year but followed the policy enunciated by the Honorable Herbert H. Lehman, Governor, in his special message, after consultation and agreement with the Legislative leaders, advising that the State should not "continue indefinitely to pay for its relief out of the proceeds of bond issues" but that "gradually the amount obtained from bond moneys should be reduced until within a reasonable time the entire cost of unemployment relief will be borne from current revenues."

Contingent upon approval of this $40,000,000 relief bond issue by the electorate, the Legislature has appropriated $10,000,000 of it to be available in case of emergency need until February 15 next, when the Legislature will have had an opportunity to act.

The future of State aid in relief rests with the people of New York State at the polls.

HOW THE NEED HAS BEEN MET

2,000,000 Receive Relief Monthly

The number of relief cases, which reached its peak in April after the demobilization of the Federal Civil Works Administration, with a total of 536,384 resident families and non-family persons on public relief rolls, dropped progressively to 496,931 in June, then rose to 497,906 in July and 509,927 in August, the last month of the period.

The 1,980,270 individuals benefitted in the month of August, including 800,600 children, represented almost one out of every six of the entire population. They were found to be in need after investigation of their resources had demonstrated their inability to support themselves.

Even the fluctuations in the totals from month to month give no picture of the human ebb and flow as mounting private employment takes thousands from the relief rolls while exhaustion of their resources forces others long unemployed to seek public support.

Typical Americans from all walks of life have made up the relief rolls, with increasing numbers from the higher income groups with cultural and educational advantages needing public aid as their backlog of savings and that of their friends and families have been consumed. Artisan and laborer, professional and layman, skilled and unskilled, all alike have been forced to seek public aid by economic forces beyond their control that deprived them of work to which their ability and strength entitle them and which their self-respect demands. Assistance which has saved them from starvation and physical and moral breakdown has been an investment in the future of the community in which they will now be able, by virtue of the aid received, to resume their places when normal conditions are re-established.

Public Relief Costs of Approximately $400,000,000*

From November 1, 1931 to September 1, 1934, more than $356,-000,000* has been given in direct public unemployment relief in New York State. In that same period the total cost, including materials for work relief projects and supervisory and administrative expense, was approximately $400,000,000.* In the early part

* Exclusive of Federal Civil Works Administration expenditures, for a discussion of which see pages 12–15.

of the period local expenditures for materials and supervisory expenses were outside the legal control of the Administration, not being reimbursable by it, and were not reported to it. They have been estimated conservatively in arriving at the total cost above. These figures exclude the Federal expenditure of approximately $88,700,000 on the Civil Works program in New York State in the winter of 1933-1934, of which approximately $81,250,000 was paid in wages.

In the first two years home relief and work relief accounted for practically the whole of direct relief expenditure. In November, 1933, with the start of the Federal Civil Works Administration program financed chiefly by Federal Public Works funds and discussed in a subsequent section, a new element was injected. Although the Federal Civil Works Administration at its inception took over the bulk of work relief, it did not subsequently give employment on the basis of need but on the basis of ability to do the job. The quasi-relief, quasi-recovery status of the Civil Works Administration makes it impossible to estimate how much of its expenditures were for relief, and this dual purpose of Civil Works, as well as the development of special Federal and State supplementary relief programs, has led in the last months to a changed emphasis so that home and work relief, while still paramount, can no longer be said to constitute practically the whole of public relief.

Beginning with April last the figures have been gathered for total relief expenditures, whether controlled by the policies of the Administration or not. A complete analysis of public relief expenditures from that month to August, 1934, inclusive, is given in the Appendix, Table I.

Work relief wages and home relief together accounted for expenditure of approximately $340,668,000 in the period from November 1, 1931 to September 1, 1934, of which approximately $3,750,000 was for local home relief not eligible for reimbursement by the Temporary Emergency Relief Administration while partial reimbursement was granted on a total of approximately $336,918,000. Supplementary programs, discussed in a subsequent section, provided direct relief and commodities valued at approximately $15,300,000 additional in the period.

Beginning with May, 1933, pursuant to an amendment to the law, all public relief to veterans has been subject to reimbursement by the State. Of the total home and work relief expenditure given above, approximately $11,673,000 provided relief to a monthly average of 27,000 veterans up to September 1, 1934.

Home relief is the furnishing of orders for food, shelter, light, heat, clothing, medicine, medical attendance and necessary household supplies in the domicile, or the cash equivalent. Work relief is in the form of cash wages for emergency employment on county and municipal projects and on State improvements. With the hourly wage fixed at the local prevailing rate for the type of work done, work relief is assigned to meet the budgetary needs of the family. At the start home relief was given through existing county and city public welfare departments, and work relief through emergency county and city work bureaus, with local non-partisan, non-political chairmen and members from the districts. A permissive amendment passed in April, 1933, has led to consolidation in the interest of economy and efficiency in about one-third of the districts so that the two forms of relief are administered from one central agency under the same safeguards of fairness and impartiality, without discrimination on grounds of non-citizenship, political adherence, religion, race or color.

Of the total work relief wages and home relief of approximately $336,918,000, on which partial reimbursement from State or Federal funds was given in the period covered by this report, approximately $143,637,000 or 43 per cent, was spent by up-State cities and counties while approximately $193,281,000, or 57 per cent, was spent by New York City. Of this same total, work relief wages paid in cash represented approximately $164,808,000, or 49 per cent. Home relief accounted for approximately $172,110,000, or 51 per cent of the total.

In the month of August, 1934, the last month of the period, public unemployment relief cost approximately $28,343,000, an expenditure of $2.26 per capita of the population. Of this total, home relief and work relief combined amounted to approximately $21,124,000, the difference representing supplementary relief programs and supervisory and administrative costs, as detailed in the Appendix, Table I. Of this home and work relief total, approximately $6,815,000 or 32 per cent was spent by up-State cities and counties while approximately $14,309,000, or 68 per cent was spent by New York City. Of this same total, work relief wages paid in cash represented approximately $11,042,000, or 52 per cent. Home relief accounted for approximately $10,082,000, or 48 per cent of the total.

$234,532,000* *in Aid to Local Communities*

Responsibility for the care of the needy in the State of New York has traditionally rested on the local governments,† and need in the present emergency for State and later through the State for Federal aid to the localities has involved no change in that sound and fundamental policy.

In the manner that has been described, the need became too great for local funds, dependent chiefly on taxes from real estate. But with the increase in State and Federal assistance the cities and counties of New York State have not shirked their responsibilities to their own. Their record in continuing to carry their heavy part of the relief burden has been noteworthy. With the mounting relief costs the twenty-five per cent that they now pay is at least as much as they paid in 1932 when they bore sixty per cent of the load. They are especially deserving of praise for the cooperation they have given the Administration in its efforts to raise relief standards and assure efficient and economical use of public funds.

Of the welfare districts as defined by the Unemployment Relief Act, all but one have cooperated with the State Administration since January, 1933, only one county district comprising 0.3 per cent of the population not being included.

During the thirty-four month period the State Temporary Emergency Relief Administration has reimbursed or committed itself to reimburse the local welfare districts for home relief and work relief by approximately $234,532,000 from State and Federal funds, exclusive of the Federal Civil Works expenditures. In addition State and Federal projects provided supplementary relief of approximately $15,300,000,** at a cost of approximately $8,440,000.†† The remainder of the total relief cost of approximately $400,000,000 (again exclusive of the Civil Works Administration), or approximately $157,000,000, has been borne by the cities, counties and towns.

State and Federal aid to municipalities administered through the Temporary Emergency Relief Administration up to September 1, 1934, thus lightened the burden on local real estate by more than sixty per cent of the total cost of relief.

---

* Exclusive of Federal Civil Works Administration disbursements.
† New York City cannot under its Charter accord home relief except under the Wicks Act.
** Including estimated retail value of Federal surplus foods distributed to the needy.
†† Including only the cost, not the retail value, of Federal surplus foods distributed to the needy.

A chief object of the Administration from its inception has been the stretching of the relief dollar to the end that adequate relief might be given economically. Of the total of approximately $211,-024,000* actually disbursed by it for reimbursement of local districts, financing supplementary relief activities and other purposes from November 1, 1931 to September 1, 1934, exclusive of the Civil Works Administration program, the Administration spent $1,661,-819.94, or less than one per cent of the total for its administrative expense. This has included the salaries of a trained social work staff to help relief bureaus organize and establish policies; of engineers to cooperate in planning valuable work projects suitable for local needs; of advisors on medical services, nutrition and garden activities for the unemployed; and of an auditing staff employed to insure sound business and accounting methods in the local relief bureaus to which the State contributes funds.

The Federal Government and Relief

In February 1933, Federal funds first became available for relief through grants by the Reconstruction Finance Corporation and were allotted by the State Administration to local welfare districts. The total grants from the Reconstruction Finance Corporation amounted to $26,400,000. Subsequently, under the terms of the Federal Emergency Relief Administration Act, until the start of the Federal Civil Works program on November 21, 1933, further Federal funds were allocated to the State Administration on the basis of one-third of the total public relief expenditures, making a total of $63,619,741 of Federal funds received by the Temporary Emergency Relief Administration to supplement State and local resources for the period up to that time.

At its start the Federal Civil Works Administration program in New York State absorbed all but a negligible amount of the work relief, which at that time represented more than half the total relief expenditure. At the same time the Federal Government virtually stopped its contribution to other relief.

Throughout the life of the program the State Temporary Emergency Relief Administration accepted the task of acting as the Federal Administration of Civil Works for New York State in order that the State might benefit as quickly as possible from the Federal program. As the State division of the Federal Civil Works Administration it acted as the agent of the Federal Government,

---

* This figure is exclusive of commitments for this period.

and in execution of instructions from Washington it planned and supervised local projects that resulted in the employment of more than 340,000 men and women throughout the State, of whom about 155,000 were in New York City and 185,000 up-State. Approximately $81,250,000 in Federal wages were paid through April 1, 1934, when the program was demobilized. The total cost of the program was approximately $88,700,000, of which the Administration spent $331,699, or less than half of one per cent, for administrative expenses. No State funds were used. Other special Federal programs brought the total of Federal expenditure during the Civil Works period to approximately $89,400,000.

As previously stated, the Civil Works Administration program was conceived by the Federal Government partly as an aid to recovery and only partly as a form of relief. It did take over the bulk of work relief at its start, but except in its Civil Works Service division, explained below, further labor was recruited, by Federal order, solely on ability to do the job without consideration of need as a factor.

The Civil Works Service division, merged with the Civil Works Administration itself in the last weeks, was a relief division for professional and "white collar" groups, and of the figures quoted above accounted for employment of more than 40,000 men and women, who up to the date of demobilization were paid more than $15,000,000 in salaries and wages by the Federal Government. All employed on the Civil Works Service payroll were required to show need of public assistance.

While the number of those who were saved from reliance on public relief by the Civil Works Administration wages cannot be estimated, it is certain that those who were forced by need to seek public aid, under the Federal policy were forced to take their mathematical chances with others not in need in the allocation of Civil Works Administration jobs. In the State as a whole the Federal Civil Works Administration was able to provide only about one job for every six who applied. Those in need who failed of employment necessarily were forced to turn to the home relief rolls, whose mounting expenditures were met one-third by the localities and two-thirds by the State.

The following charts illustrate, by the increase of home relief and the drop of work relief during the Civil Works Administration period, the extent of these trends. By showing what part of Civil Works Administration expenditures actually replaced relief ex-

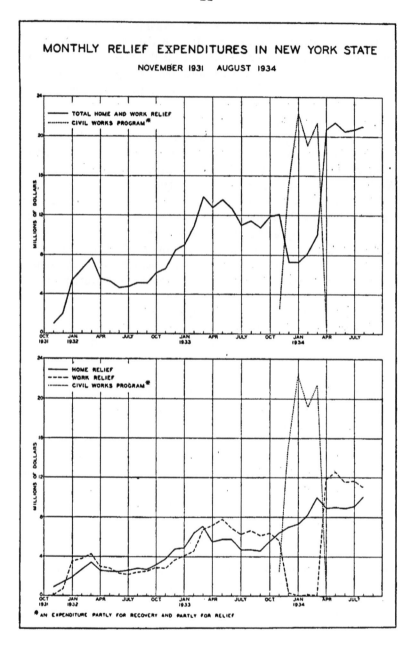

penditures, they give a rough picture of the ratio of the relief effect to the recovery effect of the program.

With the disbanding of the Civil Works Administration practically completed by April 1, 1934, the Federal Government resumed its contribution to direct relief, and committed itself to pay approximately $88,369,000 from April 1 to September 1, to supplement State and local funds. With the $63,619,741 contributed for the period previous to the start of the Civil Works Administration, the expenditure of approximately $700,000 on special programs during the Civil Works program, and a Federal contribution of approximately $4,500,000 for surplus foods,* the total Federal contribution to relief in New York State (as distinct from the Civil Works Administration) has been approximately $157,200,000. The total Federal contribution to relief in the State from February, 1933, when it began, to September 1, 1934, is thus approximately $245,900,000 if the Civil Works expenditure is included.

Economic Dividends from Relief

From November 1, 1931, to September 1, 1934, approximately $164,808,003† was spent in work relief wages reimbursable by the Temporary Emergency Relief Administration exclusive of Federal Civil Works. The period before the Civil Works Administration was covered in a previous report.†† Of the total just given, approximately $69,750,000 of the work relief wages were paid after the demobilization of the Civil Works Administration, from April 1, to September 1, 1934. In that period approximately 2,800 projects operated, employing more than 240,500 persons in the peak month.

While the chief purpose of work relief was to give to unemployed wages earned by work which would preserve their work habits and their morale, it has been planned with the economic view of producing useful service to the community.

Work relief has evolved in New York State, originally concentrating on improving the capital plant of the communities through such projects as painting of public buildings, repairs, other maintenance work, and minor improvements. This type of work was soon exhausted and a trend towards public works developed with

---

* See page 18.
† Exclusive of wages paid by the Federal Civil Works Administration amounting to $81,250,000.
†† The State in Unemployment Relief—Legislative Document (1934) No. 59, March 1, 1934.

the result that there is now in the State a substantial practical work relief program, with a relatively higher materials cost, constructing major projects that are needed in the community but could not be carried on in the ordinary city and county budgets.

Typical examples of this type of work are the extension of high pressure fire mains in the business section of Buffalo; the construction of a storm sewer in Utica; the construction of reservoirs; development of lake front areas and transformation of mosquito-breeding marshland and municipal dumps into attractive parks; extensive mosquito extermination projects; the restoration and repair of canals where important navigation was impaired; extending, repairing and renovating the water supply systems of the five boroughs of New York City; the conversion of an abandoned reservoir into a needed high school stadium; the conversion of an unused armory into a needed municipal auditorium; the building of hundreds of miles of highways and streets, and the construction of municipal golf courses, swimming pools, and other recreational facilities.

A picture of the relative employment on the different types of projects is given by the following:

Projects Operating April 1 to Aug. 31, 1934	Per Cent of Workers
Planning Projects	2.99
Public Property Projects	71.33
Projects to Provide Housing	.84
Production and Distribution of Goods Needed by Unemployed	1.80
Public Welfare, Health and Recreation	2.86
Public Education, Arts and Research	11.95
Administrative Projects	7.97
Tool and Sundry Equipment Projects	.26

The relief program has recognized the importance of placing the unemployed according to their previous training and occupational experience, in order to make their work most valuable not only to them but to the taxpayers who pay for their subsistence. In the typical month of August, 1934, more than 45,000 men and women of the "white collar" and professional class were given emergency work in performing services, such as teaching in 71 nursery schools for children in under-privileged families; making slum surveys in preparation for slum clearance and model housing; organizing recreational work in settlement houses and community centers; operating fifteen dental clinics for the unemployed;

teaching retarded and crippled children in public institutions; and playing in bands, orchestras and plays given in public buildings and institutions for those who could not afford paid recreation of this type.

Among the outstanding "white collar" projects in which the unemployed not only are receiving relief wages but in turn offer unusual services to other unemployed are the adult education classes in which an average of 2400 highly trained unemployed have taught classes which reached 55,000 students. During the winter more than 900 unemployed nurses supplemented existing public health facilities and aided in combating the menace to health that has grown with the ravages of the depression.

The Home Relief Dollar

Expenditures for home relief on which partial reimbursement was granted by the Temporary Emergency Relief Administration amounted to $172,110,000 in the thirty-four month period ending September 1, 1934, an average of approximately $5,062,000 a month. By August, 1934, the last month of the period, the figure had risen to $10,082,162.

An increase in the adequacy of the relief given, and greater budget deficits of the families benefitted operated to raise expenditures, as well as the increase in the number of families and non-family persons on relief, of whom there were 509,927 in August.

Many of those aided, both by home relief, in the form of orders for food, shelter, and other necessities, or in the form of cash allowances and by work relief, providing emergency wages, rely only partially on public support. The exhaustion of resources that has forced more and more families on relief has also increased the relief needs of those who receive assistance.

Beginning with June, 1932, information has been obtained from the local districts on the distribution of expenditures for the various necessaries reimbursable from State funds. In the State as a whole, 74.2 cents out of each home relief dollar were spent for food during the five months, June through October, 1932, and 70.1 cents during the year November 1, 1932, through October 31, 1933. In the ten months ended September 1, 1934 the figure was 61.1. The drop in the ratio of food allowances reflects a raising of home relief standards, with more adequate provision for shelter, clothing and medical care as well as provision for food.

The responsibility of providing medical care to her needy unemployed was expressly recognized by the State of New York in the Wicks Act. The necessity for adequate care of this type has been stressed by the State Temporary Emergency Relief Administration and in the thirty-four month period ended September 1, 1934 more than $2,500,000 of home relief expenditures were for this relief. In the final month of this report, August, 1934, $180,000 was spent for this type of aid.

The promptness of relief in New York State, almost as essential from a human standpoint as its adequacy, is revealed by a special study made in forty-one cities last summer. All applications for relief within the period were included. Of the total 1,602 cases reported on, 54 per cent were visited within three days of the application and an additional 29 per cent within a week. In 11 per cent of the cases from one to two weeks elapsed between the application and home visit and in 5 per cent more than two weeks.

Thirty cities furnished adequate data on the interval elapsing between the application and the first relief order. Of the total 1,026 families so reported on, 28 per cent received a relief order on the day aid was requested, and 8 per cent on the following day. Seventeen per cent were given a relief order two or three days after application, and an additional 23 per cent within a week. Fifteen per cent of the families did not receive a relief order until one or two weeks had elapsed, and 9 per cent waited more than two weeks.

In this great emergency the State of New York has progressed steadily toward the goal set for itself by the Temporary Emergency Relief Administration at the beginning of its stewardship, that relief must "actually function to the end that people should not be permitted to suffer from want when the organs of the government have supplied the machinery aimed to prevent such suffering."

Supplementary Relief Activities

The direct relief and commodities valued at $15,300,000 given in supplementary programs at a cost of approximately $8,400,000 were as follows:

FEDERAL SURPLUS FOODS

The estimated retail value of 89,760,000 pounds of Federal Surplus foods distributed up to September 1, 1934, was $11,400,-000. To finance purchase of these foods the Federal Government deposited approximately $4,500,000 to the credit of New York State.

These surplus foods, distribution of which began in November, 1933, are purchased for the most part by the Agricultural Adjustment Administration and turned over to the States for distribution. In New York State they are allocated to welfare districts by the Federal Surplus Division of the State Temporary Emergency Relief Administration, which acts as the agent of the Federal Government chiefly in the allocation of amounts of foods to the local public welfare commissioners in each district.

TRANSIENTS

In November, 1933, the Federally financed program for transients was organized in New York State with the purpose of housing, feeding, providing medical treatment and giving work, when possible, to that group of men and boys and whole families who were not residents of the State but who represented in this depression a migratory population moving, for the most part, in a vain search for work. A net-work of transient bureaus and centres were located in geographically strategic points to deal with this problem.

Seven camps are now open: Camp Roosevelt at Southfields; Camp Greenhaven at Stormville; St. Johnsville Camp at St. Johnsville; Camp Frontier at Langford; Saratoga Springs Camp at Saratoga Springs; Stony Brook Camp at Dansville and Elks Park Camp at Port Jervis. They were instituted so that the men could leave the road, live in healthy conditions, and work a limited number of hours for a cash allowance of $1.00 a week. Six of the seven camps will be valuable ultimately as supplementary housing to the State hospitals. The camps, situated near State property, made it possible for the men to bale hay and dig potatoes for the State hospitals, build a large dam with an artificial lake, help in the landscaping of State parks, improve the roads, and do other types of useful work.

Included in the transient program was the transporting back to their homes of individuals and families who could be assured of aid there.

From November, 1933 to September 1, 1934, the Transient Division of the Temporary Emergency Relief Administration aided about 75,000 transients. Approximately $1,177,000 was expended for this type of relief in that period.

REHABILITATION OF RURAL FAMILIES

The rehabilitation of unemployed rural families by helping them make a subsistence from the land and again become self-supporting has been begun according to a plan drawn up by a group of experts on farm and rural problems forming the Agricultural Advisory Committee of the Temporary Emergency Relief Administration. The program, inaugurated October 1, 1934, will be carried out in eighteen rural counties, the counties most in need of this type of relief, and is financed by the Federal Emergency Relief Administration.

Sixteen emergency rural rehabilitation agents and sixteen emergency agents in home economics have been employed to work in cooperation with the county agricultural and home economics agents. The rehabilitation agents will study, investigate and make specific proposals for the rehabilitation of rural families on relief and those who if not aided would soon need to apply for it. The home economics agents will have as their task the education of the homemaker to be able better to do her part in improving the economic health and social condition of her family.

In another step for the relief of farm and rural families Tompkins County was selected as a demonstration centre in rural relief development and a guide to future planning in this phase of relief work. The State Temporary Emergency Relief Administration has committed itself to pay 75 per cent of a work project improving farm-to-market roads in the County.

MILK DISTRIBUTION

Purchase of fresh milk for babies, children and nursing and expectant mothers from the special $1,500,000 milk appropriation made by the Legislature in July, 1934, from existing relief funds was begun the latter part of that month. Up to September 1 approximately $45,500 was spent to give 350,000 quarts to needy undernourished children in New York City with their school and playground lunches. The distribution of fresh milk from this fund was not begun in other parts of the State until September.

The Administration ruled that disbursements from this fund should pay for milk distributed by municipalities only to the extent that the milk was in excess of the normal distribution to the needy of the locality and pointed out that to permit the use of this special fund to purchase milk already being provided through public and private relief agencies for active relief cases would be to defeat the purpose of the fund which is to assure increased consumption of milk for the State as a whole.

School Lunches

Believing the prevention of undernourishment of children to be a chief concern of the State, the Temporary Emergency Relief Administration in February, 1933, began reimbursement of municipalities for school lunches, including milk, served to needy children to supplement other forms of relief. To September 1, 1934, approximately $1,750,000 was spent by the administration for this purpose.

Subsistence Gardens

As a part of its effort to stretch every dollar of relief to the utmost by having the unemployed, in so far as possible, serve their own needs and the needs of others on relief, the Temporary Emergency Relief Administration has developed its subsistence gardens program. Fresh vegetables with an estimated retail value of $2,500,000 were obtained from the 69,000 subsistence gardens planted by relief workers last spring under its supervision. This harvest was made available at a cost of about $500,000 to the 114 welfare districts participating in the program, which were reimbursed seventy-five per cent of their expenditure by the Administration. The surplus beyond the needs of the individual gardeners, estimated to have a retail value of $75,000, is being canned for consumption this winter exclusively by the needy unemployed. Between 400,000 and 500,000 cans will be preserved for use this winter. In 1932, the first season of operation, the gardens produced vegetables of an estimated retail value of $333,079, and in 1933, approximately 42,000 gardens produced vegetables with a retail value of about $1,100,864. The cost incurred in those two years was $282,038. These costs are included in home and work relief figures given in the body of the report.

Camp Tera

Camp TERA on Lake Tiorati, near Bear Mountain, was opened on June 10, 1933 for unemployed girls and women who are in need of rest and rehabilitation, mentally and physically, and has provided through August 1934 on an average a six weeks' vacation for a total of 767 girls and women. The camp is financed by the Federal Emergency Relief Administration and is directly under the supervision of the State Temporary Emergency Relief Administration. The cost of maintenance of the camp per girl is exceptionally low, being about fifty cents per day or $3.52 per week. This includes expenditures for food, ice, coal, electricity, laundry, medical supplies, office supplies, telephone, small equipment, transpor-

tation, rental of boats and housing. During the summer 150 girls
at a time are housed and cared for at the camp. Because of the
lack of adequate winter quarters, 80 girls at a time are accommodated in the winter.

PART-TIME EMPLOYMENT FOR COLLEGE STUDENTS

From February, 1934 when it was first inaugurated to the closing of the academic year in June the Federal Emergency Relief
Administration program of providing part-time employment for
college students who could not afford to pay their own education
costs provided $288,505 in wages to an average of 5,500 students in
55 non-profit-making colleges in New York State. A maximum of
$20.00 was given a month to each student.

CIVILIAN CONSERVATION CORPS

Since the institution of the Federal Civilian Conservation Corps
in May 1933, a total of 50,000 New York State boys, practically all
drawn from relief families, have been working at the camps for
a period of from six to fifteen months each. They have contributed
an estimated sum of more than $7,000,000 towards the support of
their families and thus a lightening of relief expenditures that
otherwise would have been made.

Winter, 1934

As New York State enters into her fourth winter of public
unemployment relief, the length and the deepening of the emergency make her relief problem at least as large as the maximum of
the winter of 1933. Those on the relief lists who have left public
support for work in private industry have had their places on
relief rolls taken by others who have been long unemployed but who
until now have been able to exist on their savings and other means
of maintenance now exhausted.

It is estimated that home and work relief from State, Federal
and local public funds will rise to at least $25,000,000 a month
during the winter. Total relief costs, including essential supplementary relief such as relief of transients and rehabilitation of
rural families, and also including work relief materials and supervisory and administrative costs will rise, it is estimated, to more
than $30,000,000 a month.

The need of the unemployed is a colossal reality penetrating
every city, town and village in the State, so widespread that its
size and devastating effects are difficult for the outside observer
to visualize.

From the point of view of public policy it is not only the need of the unemployed but the need of the State itself that makes adequate relief a necessity and not a choice. The chief resource of the State of New York is the initiative, capacities, strength and courage of her people, without which her other resources are worthless. The State's conservation and preservation of this human wealth is an act of simple economic self-preservation.

TABLE I

MUNICIPAL, STATE AND FEDERAL OBLIGATIONS INCURRED FOR RELIEF PURPOSES
APRIL—AUGUST, 1934

	April	May	June	July	August
*Controllable by T. E. R. A.					
Up-State welfare districts					
Home relief (a)	$2,765,581	$2,617,284	$2,316,952	$2,179,101	$2,394,453
Care of local homeless	16,735	15,400	17,513	17,074	16,861
School lunches	188		189	196	190
Free milk					
Work relief wages	4,461,140	4,571,377	4,476,450	4,399,402	4,368,070
Materials for work projects	758,116	676,374	1,053,718	1,275,534	1,388,466
†Administrative and supervisory salaries (b)	757,512	781,739	638,453	597,604	549,783
Total	$8,759,084	$8,662,362	$8,503,276	$8,468,912	$8,717,813
New York City					
Home relief	$5,929,002	$6,123,941	$6,357,484	$6,732,707	$7,544,925
Care of local homeless	59,898	57,927	44,224	43,676	43,516
School lunches	119,597	124,099	119,193	37,815	46,535
Free milk				21,127	24,461
Work relief wages	7,296,710	7,889,095	7,097,108	7,269,470	6,673,873
Materials for work projects	256,196	1,246,550	1,717,925	1,317,629	1,701,058
†Administrative and supervisory salaries (c)	1,215,697	2,002,830	2,250,062	1,982,791	1,996,433
Total	$14,877,100	$17,444,442	$17,585,996	$17,405,215	$18,030,801
State departments — materials for work projects	$128,073	$335,291	$290,163	$342,552	$300,597
Central State administration	161,979	159,406	155,113	145,739	175,451
Total	$23,926,236	$26,601,501	$26,534,548	$26,362,418	$27,224,661
Non-recurring expenditures					$38,085
Non-controllable (d)					
State transient program (care of Federal and State transients)	$144,005	$172,208	$182,456	$239,232	$288,785
National Re-employment Service		71,847	74,779	39,000	40,000

	1	2	3	4	5
College Students Aid	78,479	75,285	44,510	....	....
Cattle program	....	....	....	....	249,644
Cotton program	....	....	....	....	445,794
Other	22,729	42,625	26,253	69,012	55,590
Total	$245,213	$361,965	$327,998	$347,245	$1,079,813
Grand total	$24,171,449	$26,963,466	$26,862,546	$26,709,663	$28,342,561

* In which the policies were controlled by the State Temporary Emergency Relief Administration.

† Includes salaries of many in need of relief who do not local supervisory and administrative work.

(a) In addition to this amount the welfare districts reported expenditures classified as non-reimbursable as follows: April, $50,256; May, $46,134; June, $36,439; July, $41,741; August, $35,692.

(b) In addition to this amount the welfare districts reported non-reimbursable expenditures for local office rent, supplies, salaries, and miscellaneous administrative costs as follows: April, $43,737; May, $116,758; June, $131,993; July, $144,891; August, $162,298.

(c) In addition to this amount New York City reported non-reimbursable expenditures for salaries and other administrative costs as follows: April, not reported; May, $99,467; June, $140,540; July, $142,297; August, $153,429.

(d) Work relief wages resulting from these projects are included above.

TABLE II

TEMPORARY EMERGENCY RELIEF ADMINISTRATION OF NEW YORK STATE

Expenditure Statement

A TABLE showing the disbursements of the T. E. R. A. to welfare districts from the State and Federal unemployment relief funds for Home Relief and Work Relief pertaining to the period of November 1, 1931 to August 31, 1934, and including disbursements under the Federal Civil Works Administration from November 20, 1933 through its demobilization on April 1, 1934.

WELFARE DISTRICTS	HOME RELIEF		WORK RELIEF AND CIVIL WORKS		Total August 31, 1934
	Total paid	Estimated commitments	Total paid	Estimated commitments	
Albany county	$82,560 62	$9,312 38	$1,541,979 70	$58 00	$1,633,910 70
Albany	335,385 66	78,833 75	1,094,380 94	8,465 31	1,517,065 66
Cohoes	257,067 37	209,988 07	352,083 30	24,878 46	844,017 20
Watervliet	46,024 56	11,549 93	49,168 88	29,301 34	136,044 71
Allegany county	55,233 43	25,054 00	214,422 72	2,844 89	297,555 04
Broome county	189,200 37	45,174 30	458,749 67	5,447 50	698,571 84
Binghamton	283,428 54	68,244 87	752,616 80	16,277 62	1,120,567 83
Cattaraugus county	75,095 95	29,105 03	293,773 60	14,847 49	412,822 07
Olean	75,706 00	4,969 86	337,369 63	25,377 33	443,422 82
Salamanca	46,079 69	23,561 74	203,923 11	6,603 28	280,167 82
Cayuga county	35,566 38	7,414 05	225,535 42	5,233 49	273,749 34
Auburn	228,536 04	40,758 98	596,966 96	18,416 28	884,678 26
Chautauqua county	102,317 00	13,881 38	420,388 60	30,923 44	567,510 42
Dunkirk	142,252 93	24,736 61	442,305 96	868 86	610,164 36
Jamestown	222,400 09	78,414 89	413,551 40	19,385 69	733,752 07
Chemung county	172,328 30	93,451 2	299,230 74	9,170 63	574,180 89
Elmira	448,603 72	106,936 30	304,995 61	2,022 46	884,558 09
Chenango county	20,797 31	5,998 19	234,614 50	7,496 1	268,906 71
Norwich	14,095 23	5,235 77	115,085 16	60 28	134,476 44
Clinton county	81,122 59	7,740 25	167,149 84	4,188 57	210,201 25
Plattsburg	20,112 64	6,668 22	184,113 79	7,192 28	218,096 93
Columbia county	26,869 34	8,352 00	284,691 59	6,393 77	326,306 70
Hudson	77,733 79	16,525 13	410,477 06	6,626 08	511,362 06
Cortland county	20,766 68	2,226 10	208,208 89	200 04	231,401 71
Cortland	66,771 02	6,883 40	71,618 71	731 43	146,004 56
Delaware county	37,781 98	13,716 57	171,741 16	12,187 97	235,427 68

Dutchess county	191,062 11	32,699 80	849,913 95	16,069 44	1,089,745 30
Beacon	33,745 61	5,817 09	95,640 90	4,455 71	139,659 31
Poughkeepsie	317,518 71	69,671 93	280,204 09	19,418 91	686,813 64
Erie county	1,244,698 05	418,523 87	3,441,265 01	313,325 35	5,417,812 28
Buffalo	7,820,396 91	898,888 10	9,125,793 89	532,094 72	18,377,173 62
Lackawanna	268,694 69		269,155 45	8,476 86	546,725 48
Tonawanda	84,150 55	6,128 22	177,228 44	7,331 66	207,838 87
Essex county	124,313 36	32,191 21	576,045 29	7,863 54	740,413 40
Franklin county	161,922 12	21,695 13	566,015 26	1,648 64	751,281 15
Fulton county	27,237 28	11,723 04	84,524 97	640 08	124,125 37
Gloversville	34,930 44	5,787 85	187,726 38	3,484 99	231,929 66
Johnstown	13,508 27	2,500 59	54,543 02	535 57	71,087 45
Genesee county	70,806 23	14,926 05	247,421 71	7,292 26	340,446 25
Batavia	98,947 46	11,207 39	145,726 28	6,690 19	262,571 32
Genesee city	4,308 19	6,705 51	78,761 57	8,321 40	135,096 67
Hamilton county	6,449 62	6,723 07	80,960 72	111 99	88,245 40
Herkimer county	315,094 47	28,185 68	745,621 47	11,829 43	1,100,731 05
Little Falls	24,081 43	1,868 23	45,646 66	5,456 55	76,952 87
Jefferson county	177,064 52	36,660 69	402,359 93	7,077 85	623,162 99
Watertown	318,990 22	47,508 71	617,107 22	18,333 51	1,002,239 66
Lewis county	30,932 43	2,590 76	148,256 30	129 48	181,908 97
Livingston county	102,922 43	10,561 24	321,380 25	61 05	434,925 47
Madison county	41,840 75	6,651 12	152,978 12	1,160 56	202,630 04
Oneida	24,164 12	2,703 87	74,750 89	4,440 28	106,059 16
Monroe county	493,765 62	178,238 17	5,495,136 57	212,506 83	6,379,647 19
Rochester	3,394,272 23	623,900 96	2,322,078 94	261,816 48	6,602,068 61
Montgomery county	40,385 03	4,281 85	251,367 52	47 06	305,081 46
Amsterdam	236,755 44	40,448 70	541,742 00	14,629 45	833,575 59
Nassau county	29,567 57	1,038,446 87	6,910,113 17	39,029 86	9,328,181 10
Glen Cove	6,663 98		13,644 17		43,211 74
Long Beach			46,478 23		53,142 21
New York City	60,610,975 05	12,692,499 11	104,111,979 69	4,653,110 25	182,068,564 10
Niagara county	43,700 69	7,993 92	271,780 52	10,208 82	333,683 31
Lockport	109,750 87	10,392 53	378,264 37	7,006 50	505,414 27
Niagara Falls	561,207 90	35,478 77	1,527,739 31	60,800 27	2,185,226 25
North Tonawanda	212,471 06	18,544 24	461,979 55	16,608 88	709,603 73
Oneida county	142,345 96	20,042 08	389,368 36	6,818 84	558,575 24
Rome	100,554 73	39,461 37	509,303 55	13,499 11	662,818 76
Sherrill		20 13			20 13
Onondaga county	520,974 22	75,983 28	1,575,624 78	56,432 54	2,229,014 82
Syracuse	354,298 98	112,806 31	3,497,457 72	31,414 47	3,995,977 48
Ontario county	1,739,884 14	293,448 50	2,941,339 18	148,647 22	5,123,319 04
Orange county	202,245 91	46,489 21	369,787 90	7,430 69	625,953 71
Middletown	80,991 22	7,568 23	728,491 12	14,274 08	831,324 79
Newburgh	20,426 73	2,131 23	162,071 81	6,900 36	191,530 13
Port Jervis	179,464 78	16,731 05	552,562 43	17,964 35	766,712 61
	32,664 21	8,581 31	430,701 13	11,684 38	483,631 03

TEMPORARY EMERGENCY RELIEF ADMINISTRATION OF NEW YORK STATE—Concluded

WELFARE DISTRICTS	HOME RELIEF		WORK RELIEF AND CIVIL WORKS		Total August 31, 1934
	Total paid	Estimated commitments	Total paid	Estimated commitments	
Orleans county	$43,727 45	$971 65	$204,055 70	$8,317 47	$257,072 27
Oswego county	5,287 28		83,244 30		88,531 58
Fulton	154,363 82	5,724 87	691,519 60	9,168 15	860,776 44
Oswego	155,796 94	17,585 78	1,113,310 81	19,944 05	1,306,637 58
Otsego county	33,851 13	8,306 99	154,746 36	7,735 04	204,639 52
Oneonta	8,802 75	379 47	129,456 74	5,137 79	143,776 75
Putnam county	20,813 43	22,594 39	138,042 37	2,908 72	184,358 91
Rensselaer county	65,554 83	25,643 40	201,710 45	5,292 62	298,201 30
Rensselaer	38,360 29	1,1993 32	118,917 97	3,292 50	172,564 08
Troy	427,629 52	101,551 45	628,337 51	24,176 73	1,181,695 21
Rockland county	117,977 19	31,316 50	443,984 84	9,977 39	603,255 92
St. Lawrence county	220,681 36	50,635 36	640,123 90	35,194 75	946,635 37
Saratoga county	34,034 42	5,807 25	379,161 29	20,880 89	439,883 85
Mechanicville	98,070 52	36,930 50	431,687 96	10,236 86	576,925 84
Saratoga Springs	56,764 53	5,093 70	228,979 15	3,334 56	294,171 94
Schenectady county	33,383 96	22,929 28	230,638 35	5,431 64	292,383 23
Schenectady	234,083 76	41,986 36	888,594 75	4,792 49	1,169,457 36
Schoharie county	522,353 59	92,975 38	2,051,252 72	137,667 39	2,804,249 08
Schohare county	9,835 05	291 84	127,577 84	284 70	137,989 43
Schuyler county	64,443 66	16,634 07	87,881 45	8,032 75	176,991 93
Seneca county	75,490 38	16,074 62	172,448 75	9,916 20	273,929 95
Steuben county	91,070 51	15,127 05	478,129 94	16,867 54	601,195 04
Corning	83,070 49	5,074 16	227,761 77	8,705 43	324,611 85
Hornell	29,483 27	4,689 34	317,906 50	10,225 46	362,304 57
Suffolk county	614,724 74	132,873 46	1,979,086 52	102,495 43	2,829,180 15
Sullivan county	26,260 30	5,367 04	125,201 83		156,829 17
Tioga county	63,730 21	10,541 94	99,947 44	1,424 60	175,644 09
Tompkins county	35,455 15	880 77	198,285 62	5,126 23	239,747 77
Ithaca	60,704 25	4,435 85	430,393 65	39,939 30	535,473 05
Ulster county	88,629 88	3,721 26	363,201 55	4,683 13	460,235 82
Kingston	123,669 70	19,267 01	598,651 79	20,087 32	761,675 82
Warren county	38,587 80	9,061 30	95,273 49	1,216 78	144,139 37
Glens Falls	121,799 70	17,671 66	207,257 14	37,501 48	384,229 98

Washington county	257,842 52	27,026 13	430,667 30	12,229 11	727,765 06
Wayne county	85,736 02	47,425 07	264,001 39	10,019 03	407,181 51
Westchester county	847,324 92	515,191 62	5,359,420 94	84,833 11	6,806,770 59
Mt. Vernon	222,990 39	112,238 09	744,174 84	18,941 16	1,098,344 48
New Rochelle	498,091 48	41,741 27	554,201 59	52,924 77	1,146,959 11
Wite Plains	418,309 75	132,494 94	343,372 24	27,045 94	921,222 87
Yonkers	1,042,714 02	481,280 25	2,2 873 26	59,088 57	3,825,956 10
Wyoming county	53,701 57	14,855 23	226,221 45	10,918 98	305,697 23
Yates county	25,721 19	5,992 20	67,684 76	....	99,398 15
State Improvements allocated on a State-wide basis	....	....	16,146,956 34	....	16,146,956 34
	$92,402,497 79	$20,017,220 30	$202,753,417 69	$7,713,275 72	*$322,886,411 50

* Supplementary relief programs and administrative costs, detailed in the body of the report, bring the grand total of State and Federal relief expenditures to $332,988,690.11.

J. B. LYON COMPANY, PRINTERS, ALBANY, N. Y.

STATE OF NEW YORK

Temporary
Emergency Relief Administration

STATE OFFICE BUILDING, ALBANY, N. Y.

NEW YORK OFFICE
79 MADISON AVE.
Telephone—LExington 2-8901

RULES GOVERNING
HOME RELIEF AND WORK RELIEF

November, 1934

Rules Governing Home Relief and Work Relief

LAWS OF NEW YORK, 1931, CHAPTER 798, AS AMENDED

§ 27. Rules of the administration. The administration shall make and enforce rules in accordance and consonance with the provisions of this act which will best promote the efficiency and effectiveness of the relief which this act is intended to furnish. None of the money appropriated by this act shall be expended or allowed except in accordance with such rules. A certified copy of such rules shall be filed in the office of the department of state. The administration shall mail to each city and county commissioner and each local bureau, copies of such rules to be posted by them in not less than five public conspicuous places throughout the district.

RULES GOVERNING HOME AND WORK RELIEF

Municipal Corporations may make a claim on the State Administration for a refund to the extent (as hereinafter qualified) of forty per cent (*1) of monies expended for Home and/or Work Relief granted to persons who are unable to provide the necessaries of life for themselves and/or their dependents, and who have resided in the State two years prior to the date of application for aid, under the following conditions and restrictions:

GENERAL RULES GOVERNING HOME RELIEF

1. Relief to persons in need as defined above shall be in the form of food, shelter, clothing, light, fuel, water, necessary household supplies, medicine, medical supplies and medical attendance which is furnished in the home; or such relief may be furnished in cash (*2) for the purpose of providing any or all of the items herein listed.

2. Home Relief under the Act must have been given to meet needs existing on and after November 1, 1931, and not extending beyond February 15, 1935. Only claims for relief to meet needs existing during the specified emergency period will be allowed.

3. In calculating the expenditures of the Municipal Corporation for Home Relief in which the State is to share, the following items are to be excluded: old age relief, allowances made to mothers for the care of dependent children, and hospital or institutional care, where the obligation to furnish such relief is expressly imposed upon the Municipal Corporation by a law other than the Emergency Relief Act (Ch. 798, Laws of 1931 as amended).

(*1) Supplement No. 1, hereinafter presented, summarizes T.E.R.A. Official Bulletin No. 34, Item 167, issued under date of March 28, 1934, which fixed the present reimbursement policy at seventy-five per cent.

(*2) Chapter 65 of the Laws of 1934 amends the Wicks Act to permit the use of cash for home relief under the rules and regulations of the Administration.
For rules and regulations under which cash relief may be given, refer to Supplement No. 2.

4. The Administration reserves the right to refuse approval in whole or in part of claims by Municipal Corporations in cases:

   (a) Wherein it believes that a locality is not making bona fide efforts and appropriations adequately to relieve the emergency actually existing.

   (b) Where there is non-compliance with the rules and regulations laid down by the Administration.

   (c) Where there is discrimination in the giving or withholding of relief by reason of considerations of race, color, religion, non-citizenship or political connections or activities.

5. Administrative expenses incurred by Municipal Corporations in administering Home Relief as provided by the Act, other than certain salaries as approved by the Administration, may not be included in computing the gross amount otherwise subject to proportional reimbursement by the Administration.

Office Arrangements and Records

6. Every Public Welfare Official should be provided with sufficient office space:

   (a) To insure privacy in interviewing applicants for relief, satisfactory waiting room facilities, with proper heating, lighting, ventilation and sanitary facilities.

   (b) To provide satisfactory working conditions which will result in efficiency of operation, and the comfort of the employees.

7. The Administration will prescribe and furnish record, account, report, and claim forms for the proper enforcement and administration of the provisions of the Act. These forms must be used. Request is made that the forms be filled in by typewriter.

GENERAL RULES GOVERNING WORK RELIEF

1. A local Emergency Work Bureau, or a local Emergency Relief Bureau (*1) in making application to the Temporary Emergency Relief Administration for authority to operate work relief projects, shall submit information on project forms furnished by the Administration concerning specific public work projects which may be undertaken by its Municipal Corporation. Such projects may not be for work to be done under contract, nor for work for which an annual appropriation has been customary. Those projects which have lasting value to the Municipal Corporation are preferable. The rules and regulations of the Administration shall govern in the prosecution of all projects on which reimbursement is granted.

(*1) Chapter 259 of the Laws of 1933 provides for the consolidation of administrative authority for a home and work relief program under an Emergency Relief Bureau.

2. When a project has been approved, monies required to pay wages therefor shall be advanced by the Municipal Corporation. As the work progresses, reimbursement will be made by the Administration for forty per cent (*1) of the wages paid, unless its rules and regulations have been violated. Claims for reimbursement shall be submitted at stated intervals, as indicated on the forms provided by the Administration.

3. An approval of a project by the Administration implies no obligation on its part to provide reimbursement from relief funds, over and above the original approved estimate, should such original estimate prove inadequate to complete the project.

4. Each local Emergency Work Bureau or Emergency Relief Bureau shall have a Chairman, who, together with the members of the committee, shall be charged with responsibility for the operation of the Bureau and with maintaining contact with the Administration.

5. Work Relief shall be given only to needy persons who are employable. In respect to needy persons not fitted for employment on Work Relief projects, attention is called to the Home Relief provisions of the Act. Any discrimination on account of race, color, religion, non-citizenship or political connections or activities in granting relief through employment is prohibited. Local Work Bureaus or Emergency Relief Bureaus will be held strictly accountable in preventing any such discrimination.

6. Payment shall be by check for work performed; payment in any other form is prohibited. It shall cover day's wages for day's work or hour's wages for hour's work. The hourly or daily rate of wage shall be fixed by the local Emergency Work Bureau or the local Emergency Relief Bureau on the basis of the prevailing rate of wage in the locality for the type of work performed (*2).

Records

7. The Administration will prescribe and furnish record, account, report and claim forms for the proper enforcement and administration of the provisions of the Act. These forms must be used. Request is made that the forms be filled in by typewriter.

ADEQUACY OF AND BASIS FOR GRANTING HOME AND/OR WORK RELIEF

The Act provides that relief shall be given to needy persons. Those whose employment is inadequate to provide the necessaries

(*1) Present practice is seventy-five per cent. See Supplement No. 1, hereinafter presented.
(*2) Total allowable hours as fixed by the Federal Emergency Relief Administration for other than administrative projects are thirty hours per week or one hundred and twenty-eight hours per month. Administrative projects are limited to thirty-nine hours per week. For further details, see T.E.R.A. Official Bulletin No. 43, issued under date of April 18, 1934, Revision of this Bulletin, issued under date of May 3, 1934, and Departmental Letter, Works Division Series No. 3, issued under date of July 30, 1934.

of life for themselves and their dependents, are included. This imposes an obligation on the Administration and on all Municipal Corporations, insofar as lies in their power, to see to it that all such needy persons shall receive sufficient Home and/or Work Relief to prevent physical suffering and to maintain minimum living standards. At the same time an obligation exists to develop maximum efficiency and economy in furnishing relief.

The determination of the amount of relief which each applicant and his dependents should obtain weekly must be based on the following:

(a) An estimate of the weekly needs of the individual or family, including an allowance for food sufficient to maintain physical well-being, for shelter, clothing, medical care and other necessities.

(b) An estimate of the weekly income of the family, including wages and other cash income, produce of farm or garden, and other resources.

(c) The relief granted should be sufficient to provide the estimated weekly needs insofar as the family is unable to do so from its own resources.

Any or all of the following types of relief may be granted in either or both of the two following ways (See T.E.R.A. Bulletin No. 54, July 14, 1934):

1. In the form of an order for the commodity to be supplied.

2. Cash in the form of a check, to include an allowance for any or all of the types of relief specified below and authorized by the Administration in accordance with rules and regulations governing cash relief, as appearing in Supplement No. 2.

Home Relief

(a) Food, of sufficient quantity, determined by the number, ages and needs of the individual members of the family in general accordance with food schedules issued as the official standards of the Administration.

(b) Payment of current rent, or payment in lieu of rent, in an amount not in excess of the current rent, to be applied for taxes and interest on a home owned and occupied by the client.

(c) Light, gas, fuel and water, for current needs.

(d) Necessary household supplies.

(e) Clothing, sufficient for decent minimum standards.

(f) Medicine and/or medical attendance to be furnished in the home whenever possible.

Work Relief

(a) Payment by check for Work Relief wages for work performed. The amount of work shall be governed by the relief needs and may cover any or all of the types of relief listed above under Home Relief. The provisions of Paragraph 6, General Rules Governing Work Relief, also apply.

INVESTIGATION AND SERVICE FOR HOME AND WORK RELIEF RECIPIENTS

The following rules are hereby established for the investigation of all applications for Home and Work Relief:

(a) Each Municipal Corporation shall employ an adequate staff of supervisors and investigators and such other classifications of employees as are required to maintain the standards of investigation and service as required by the Administration. T.E.R.A. Official Bulletin No. 27, Item 129, issued under date of February 15, 1934, shall govern as to the qualifications of such supervisors, investigators and other employees.

(b) There shall be registration of all local applications in a local central index. Where no such central index now exists, one must be established by the Commissioner of Public Welfare.

(c) The minimum investigation shall include a prompt visit to the home; verification of residence requirements under the Act; inquiry as to real property, bank accounts, insurance and other financial resources of the family; an interview with at least one recent employer; and determination of the ability and agreement of family, relatives, friends and churches and other organizations to assist.

(d) There must be contact with each family through visits to the home at least once a month, or oftener if necessary. The local field worker should be in sufficiently close touch with the family situation to avoid the necessity of applicants reapplying to the office for each individual order.

(e) Adequate clerical staff and transportation facilities shall be provided for the investigators.

(f) For each local welfare administration, during this emergency, the standard shall be not more than one hundred cases per field worker for the investigation and supervision of relief cases. The Administration disapproves, as inefficient and uneconomical, the practice of loading more than one hundred cases on one investigator.

(g) All work relief persons employed by a local Emergency Work Bureau or Emergency Relief Bureau, on, or in connection with, work projects are covered by work relief disability allowance as provided for under Chapter 303 of the Laws of 1934.

T.E.R.A. Official Bulletins and Departmental Letters as issued from time to time from this office, may amend these rules and regulations.

PENALTY FOR VIOLATIONS

Any diversion of relief as defined in the Act from the family or person for whose needs said relief is intended shall constitute a violation of these rules and is punishable as a misdemeanor under Section 30 of the Relief Act.

The T.E.R.A. Official Bulletins and Departmental Letters as issued from time to time from this office may, in furtherance of these rules and regulations, set forth administrative details and directions to govern local action.

SUPPLEMENT NO. 1

(Summary of T.E.R.A. Official Bulletin No. 34, Item 167, issued under date of March 28, 1934)

Effective April 1, 1934, the Administration fixed the rate of reimbursement at seventy-five per cent to municipalities for approved relief expenditures including home relief, work relief, and approved materials for work relief projects.

The continuation of this policy is contingent upon the continued availability of funds from State and Federal sources, and is subject to change by the Administration at any time.

* * *

SUPPLEMENT NO. 2

CASH RELIEF

An amendment to the Wicks Act, chapter 65 of the Laws of 1934, amends paragraph 8 of chapter 798 of the Laws of 1931, including cash as a relief item in the definition of home relief.

The amendment provides that "For purposes of and in order to provide wholly or in part home relief as herein defined, until February 15, 1935, money may be given in cash if and where approved by and under rules and regulations made and conditions specified by the Administration."

Controls Required of Local Administration

The Administration is prepared to authorize the use of cash in lieu of orders in any districts where the staff is adequate to provide the necessary control required to properly dispense cash relief. In order to be adequate, the local administration must provide:

1. A proper disbursing and accounting system with persons handling the money properly qualified and bonded.

2. A sufficiently low case load per worker (not in excess of one hundred cases for any individual worker) to permit the worker enough time to gain a knowledge of the individual family situation so that he or she may exercise good judgment as to the family's ability to expend cash economically and intelligently.

3. Continuous, careful and sound supervision of the investigating staff by capable supervisors.

Those districts in which the local welfare administration does not measure up to the required standard will be denied the use of cash until requirements have been met.

Recommended Limitations

In order to prevent the improper use of cash, the following limitations are suggested which may be used in the transfer of the load from home relief orders to relief in cash. It is suggested that these limitations be used for individual cases only where necessary, and that limitations be removed from the total group when it is indicated that they are no longer necessary.

1. Cash Relief on Limited Number of Items.
   (a) Cash relief may be given for all items or for specific items only, such as food and incidentals. Rent, for example, may be paid by order in case experience shows that giving the client the amount of his rent in cash will result in the money being used for other purposes.
   (b) Local officials may prescribe that milk for children shall be delivered to the home in specified amounts as a means of preventing the use of cash given for milk being diverted to other purposes.
   (c) Local officials may make any selections which they deem most advantageous as to which items shall be given in cash and which in orders. Central or contract purchasing of milk and coal, for example, as well as the probable advantage which the municipality may gain through a collective policy with reference to such items as rentals, should be given careful consideration when determining budget items to be allowed in cash or in kind.
2. Cash Relief for all Items to Selected Families.
   (a) A selective system may be used as a means of dividing the case load between those families who will be given cash and those from whom cash will be withheld. In case the selective system is used, each individual case must be reviewed first by local officials, and shall be subject to review by the field representative of the Temporary Emergency Relief Administration.
   Under the selective system, when a decision is given to give or withhold cash it must be based on the case

record of the family, in which must be stated a specific reason why cash is given or withheld. In case sufficient reason is not given, the field representative may require additional information as a basis for a proper review.

(b) Cash relief may be given to individual families on a temporary basis. Cash may be withdrawn and relief in orders substituted upon evidence that the money is not properly spent, on the basis of the review as provided above.

(c) In general, it is felt that within the limitations under No. 1 above, that the decision to give cash should be clear cut, and that cash relief where decided upon as a policy, should be used for all families at the outset, and should be withheld only on definite evidence of its improper use.

Accounting

The basis for a claim for reimbursement for cash relief shall be a properly authorized voucher or receipt form signed by the client. Details of further accounting procedures will be available upon request.

Cash relief shall be disbursed by check only (currency may not be used), and shall be authorized by the Commissioner of Public Welfare, or his properly delegated staff members.

Applications for Permission to Use Cash Relief

Applications for permission to use cash relief must be signed by the Commissioner of Public Welfare and the Mayor in the case of cities, and the Commissioner of Public Welfare and the Chairman of the Board of Supervisors in the case of counties.

J. B. LYON COMPANY, PRINTERS, ALBANY, N. Y.

EMERGENCY RELIEF

IN THE

STATE OF NEW YORK

Statutes, Regulations, and Opinions
and Interpretations of Counsel

THE TEMPORARY EMERGENCY RELIEF
ADMINISTRATION

ALFRED H. SCHOELLKOPF OF BUFFALO, Chairman
SOLOMON LOWENSTEIN OF NEW YORK
CHARLES D. OSBORNE OF AUBURN
JOSEPH P. RYAN OF NEW YORK
HENRY ROOT STERN OF NASSAU COUNTY

FREDERICK I. DANIELS, Executive Director
CONRAD VAN HYNING, Assistant Executive Director

HENRY EPSTEIN, Solicitor General, Counsel

ALBANY OFFICE: Journal Building, Plaza.
NEW YORK OFFICE: 79 Madison Avenue.

ALBANY: NOVEMBER, 1934

EMERGENCY RELIEF

IN THE

STATE OF NEW YORK

Statutes, Regulations, and Opinions and Interpretations of Counsel

THE TEMPORARY EMERGENCY RELIEF ADMINISTRATION

ALFRED H. SCHOELLKOPF OF BUFFALO, Chairman
SOLOMON LOWENSTEIN OF NEW YORK
CHARLES D. OSBORNE OF AUBURN
JOSEPH P. RYAN OF NEW YORK
HENRY ROOT STERN OF NASSAU COUNTY

FREDERICK I. DANIELS, Executive Director
CONRAD VAN HYNING, Assistant Executive Director

HENRY EPSTEIN, Solicitor General, Counsel

ALBANY OFFICE: Journal Building, Plaza.
NEW YORK OFFICE: 79 Madison Avenue.

ALBANY: NOVEMBER, 1934

THE TEMPORARY EMERGENCY RELIEF ADMINISTRATION
Second Edition — Revised to November 1, 1934

CONTENTS

4

NOTE.—Inasmuch as the whole subject of Medical Relief is covered in a separate publication, no reference to it is included in this volume.

INTRODUCTORY STATEMENT

This is an inclusive second edition of the pamphlet dated October 1, 1932, entitled "Emergency Unemployment Relief Laws in the State of New York, 1931–1932," and contains all of the laws affecting that subject, to date, together with every pertinent legal ruling and interpretation which has been made in regard thereto.

Such modifications as have been made in prior rulings have been dictated either by statutory changes or changing needs. The original precepts under which the Emergency Relief Act has been interpreted from the beginning have, nevertheless, been continuously respected.

These enactments may be said to be acts sired out of dire need. Relief to those in distress in this economic crisis is assuredly not an experiment. On the contrary it has been and is still a social necessity, perhaps even a political necessity when viewed in the light of the preservation of our governmental institutions.

The Emergency Relief Acts were aimed to alleviate and prevent hunger and suffering. They were intended to work. The Temporary Emergency Relief Administration determined that they should work. When humans hunger laws intended to relieve them must not bar them food.

As counsel to the Temporary Emergency Relief Administration, and in construing these enactments of the Legislature, these tenets have been held to be fundamental:

> First, these laws must be made to function to accomplish the end for which they were designed, namely: the relief of suffering.
> Second, these laws, born in an economic crisis, must be interpreted in the framework and background of the social, economic and political stress which gave them birth.

Faced with numberless case problems arising almost instantly; with apparent inconsistencies between these and other existing statutes, it became the province of counsel and his problem, so far as humanly possible, to harmonize the execution of this with other existing laws; to have them dovetail in their operation; but above all else, to have this Act—the Emergency Relief measure, actually function to the end that people should not be permitted to suffer from want when the organs of the government had supplied the machinery aimed to prevent such suffering.

With the foregoing principles in mind, the cases which arose had to be determined quickly. Decisions had to be made and opinions rendered without extended research. Aided with the knowledge that precedents in such situations were not plentiful, we charted our course by the application of the elementary principles of common law, constitutional and statutory construction, maintaining where possible legal reasoning consistent with the human factors and the economic stress involved. If, in so doing, certain provisions of other statutes were done violence, it was not through thoughtless application of the statute but rather through force of necessity and in the conscientious recognition of the fact that millions in want had to be relieved.

The opinions and case determinations which embody the substance of the rulings hereinafter set forth, are to be read in the light of the foregoing.

In the preparation of the data and the opinions found herein, appreciation is expressed for the invaluable assistance of Mr. Amos D. Moscrip, Special Assistant Attorney-General.

HENRY EPSTEIN

Solicitor-General
Counsel to T.E.R.A.

November 1, 1934

Rules Governing Home Relief and Work Relief

LAWS OF NEW YORK, 1931, CHAPTER 798, AS AMENDED

§ 27. **Rules of the administration.** The administration shall make and enforce rules in accordance and consonance with the provisions of this act which will best promote the efficiency and effectiveness of the relief which this act is intended to furnish. None of the money appropriated by this act shall be expended or allowed except in accordance with such rules. A certified copy of such rules shall be filed in the office of the department of state. The administration shall mail to each city and county commissioner and each local bureau, copies of such rules to be posted by them in not less than five public conspicuous places throughout the district.

RULES GOVERNING HOME AND WORK RELIEF

Municipal Corporations may make a claim on the State Administration for a refund to the extent (as hereinafter qualified) of forty per cent (*1) of monies expended for Home and/or Work Relief granted to persons who are unable to provide the necessaries of life for themselves and/or their dependents, and who have resided in the State two years prior to the date of application for aid, under the following conditions and restrictions:

GENERAL RULES GOVERNING HOME RELIEF

1. Relief to persons in need as defined above shall be in the form of food, shelter, clothing, light, fuel, necessary household supplies, medicine, medical supplies and medical attendance which is furnished in the home; or such relief may be furnished in cash (*2) for the purpose of providing any or all of the items herein listed.

2. Home Relief under the Act must have been given to meet needs existing on and after November 1, 1931, and not extending beyond February 15, 1935. Only claims for relief to meet needs existing during the specified emergency period will be allowed.

3. In calculating the expenditures of the Municipal Corporation for Home Relief in which the State is to share, the following items are to be excluded: old age relief, allowances made to mothers for the care of dependent children, and hospital or institutional care, where the obligation to furnish such relief is expressly imposed upon the Municipal Corporation by a law other than the Emergency Relief Act (Ch. 798, Laws of 1931 as amended).

(*1) Supplement No. 1, hereinafter presented, summarizes T.E.R.A. Official Bulletin No. 34, Item 167, issued under date of May 28, 1934, which fixed the present reimbursement policy at seventy-five per cent. See p. 12.

(*2) Chapter 65 of the Laws of 1934 amends the Wicks Act to permit the use of cash for home relief under the rules and regulations of the Administration.
For rules and regulations under which cash relief may be given, refer to Supplement No. 2, *infra*, p. 12.

[7]

4. The Administration reserves the right to refuse approval in whole or in part of claims by Municipal Corporations in cases:

(a) Wherein it believes that a locality is not making bona fide efforts and appropriations adequately to relieve the emergency actually existing.

(b) Where there is non-compliance with the rules and regulations laid down by the Administration.

(c) Where there is discrimination in the giving or withholding of relief by reason of considerations of race, color, religion, non-citizenship or political connections or activities.

5. Administrative expenses incurred by Municipal Corporations in administering Home Relief as provided by the Act, other than certain salaries as approved by the Administration, may not be included in computing the gross amount otherwise subject to proportional reimbursement by the Administration.

Office Arrangements and Records

6. Every Public Welfare Official should be provided with sufficient office space:

(a) To insure privacy in interviewing applicants for relief, satisfactory waiting room facilities, with proper heating, lighting, ventilation and sanitary facilities.

(b) To provide satisfactory working conditions which will result in efficiency of operation, and the comfort of the employees.

7. The Administration will prescribe and furnish record, account, report, and claim forms for the proper enforcement and administration of the provisions of the Act. These forms must be used. Request is made that the forms be filled in by typewriter.

GENERAL RULES GOVERNING WORK RELIEF

1. A local Emergency Work Bureau, or a local Emergency Relief Bureau (*1) in making application to the Temporary Emergency Relief Administration for authority to operate work relief projects, shall submit information on project forms furnished by the Administration concerning specific public work projects which may be undertaken by its Municipal Corporation. Such projects may not be for work to be done under contract, nor for work for which an annual appropriation has been customary. Those projects which have lasting value to the Municipal Corporation are preferable. The rules and regulations of the Administration shall govern in the prosecution of all projects on which reimbursement is granted.

(*1) Chapter 259 of the Laws of 1933 provides for the consolidation of administrative authority for a home and work relief program under an Emergency Relief Bureau.

2. When a project has been approved, monies required to pay wages therefor shall be advanced by the Municipal Corporation. As the work progresses, reimbursement will be made by the Administration for forty per cent (*1) of the wages paid, unless its rules and regulations have been violated. Claims for reimbursement shall be submitted at stated intervals, as indicated on the forms provided by the Administration.

3. An approval of a project by the Administration implies no obligation on its part to provide reimbursement from relief funds, over and above the original approved estimate, should such original estimate prove inadequate to complete the project.

4. Each local Emergency Work Bureau or Emergency Relief Bureau shall have a Chairman, who, together with the members of the committee, shall be charged with responsibility for the operation of the Bureau and with maintaining contact with the Administration.

5. Work Relief shall be given only to needy persons who are employable. In respect to needy persons not fitted for employment on Work Relief projects, attention is called to the Home Relief provisions of the Act. Any discrimination on account of race, color, religion, non-citizenship or political connections or activities in granting relief through employment is prohibited. Local Work Bureaus or Emergency Relief Bureaus will be held strictly accountable in preventing any such discrimination.

6. Payment shall be by check for work performed; payment in any other form is prohibited. It shall cover day's wages for day's work or hour's wages for hour's work. The hourly or daily rate of wage shall be fixed by the local Emergency Work Bureau or the local Emergency Relief Bureau on the basis of the prevailing rate of wage in the locality for the type of work performed. (*2).

Records

7. The Administration will prescribe and furnish record, account, report and claim forms for the proper enforcement and administration of the provisions of the Act. These forms must be used. Request is made that the forms be filled in by typewriter.

ADEQUACY OF AND BASIS FOR GRANTING HOME AND/OR WORK RELIEF

The Act provides that relief shall be given to needy persons. Those whose employment is inadequate to provide the necessaries

(*1) Present practice is seventy-five per cent. See Supplement No. 1, hereinafter presented.
(*2) Total allowable hours as fixed by the Federal Emergency Relief Administration for other than administrative projects are thirty hours per week or one hundred and twenty-eight hours per month. Administrative projects are limited to thirty-nine hours per week. For further details, see T.E.R.A. Official Bulletin No. 43, issued under date of April 18, 1934. Revision of this Bulletin, issued under date of May 3, 1934, and Departmental Letter, Works Division Series No. 3, issued under date of July 30, 1934.

of life for themselves and their dependents, are included. This
imposes an obligation on the Administration and on all Municipal
Corporations, insofar as lies in their power, to see to it that all
such needy persons shall receive sufficient Home and/or Work
Relief to prevent physical suffering and to maintain minimum living standards. At the same time an obligation exists to develope
maximum efficiency and economy in furnishing relief.

The determination of the amount of relief which each applicant
and his dependents should obtain weekly must be based on the
following:

   (a) An estimate of the weekly needs of the individual or
family, including an allowance for food sufficient to
maintain physical well-being, for shelter, clothing, medical care and other necessities.

   (b) An estimate of the weekly income of the family, including wages and other cash income, produce of farm or
garden, and other resources.

   (c) The relief granted should be sufficient to provide the
estimated weekly needs insofar as the family is unable to .
do so from its own resources.

Any or all of the following types of relief may be granted in
either or both of the two following ways (See T.E.R.A. Bulletin
No. 54, July 14, 1934):

1. In the form of an order for the commodity to be supplied.

2. Cash in the form of a check, to include an allowance for any or
all of the types of relief specified below and authorized by the
Administration in accordance with rules and regulations governing cash relief, as appearing in Supplement No. 2, on page
12 of this publication.

Home Relief

   (a) Food, of sufficient quantity, determined by the number,
ages and needs of the individual members of the family
in general accordance with food schedules issued as the
official standards of the Administration. (*1)

   (b) Payment of current rent, or payment in lieu of rent, in
an amount not in excess of the current rent, to be
applied for taxes and interest on a home owned and
occupied by the client.

   (c) Light, gas, fuel and water, for current needs.

   (d) Necessary household supplies.

   (e) Clothing, sufficient for decent minimum standards.

   (f) Medicine and/or medical attendance to be furnished in
the home whenever possible.

Work Relief

   (a) Payment by check for Work Relief wages for work performed. The amount of work shall be governed by the

(*1) Pamphlet entitled "Budget Allowances" issued August 15, 1934.

relief needs and may cover any or all of the types of relief listed above under Home Relief. The provisions of Paragraph 6, General Rules Governing Work Relief, also apply.

INVESTIGATION AND SERVICE FOR HOME AND WORK RELIEF RECIPIENTS

The following rules are hereby established for the investigation of all applications for Home and Work Relief:

(a) Each Municipal Corporation shall employ an adequate staff of supervisors and investigators and such other classifications of employees as are required to maintain the standards of investigation and service as required by the Administration. T.E.R.A. Official Bulletin No. 27, Item 129, issued under date of February 15, 1934, shall govern as to the qualifications of such supervisors, investigators and other employees.

(b) There shall be registration of all local applications in a local central index. Where no such central index now exists, one must be established by the Commissioner of Public Welfare.

(c) The minimum investigation shall include a prompt visit to the home; verification of residence requirements under the Act; inquiry as to real property, bank accounts, insurance and other financial resources of the family; an interview with at least one recent employer; and determination of the ability and agreement of family, relatives, friends and churches and other organizations to assist.

(d) There must be contact with each family through visits to the home at least once a month, or oftener if necessary. The local field worker should be in sufficiently close touch with the family situation to avoid the necessity of applicants reapplying to the office for each individual order.

(e) Adequate clerical staff and transportation facilities shall be provided for the investigators.

f) For each local welfare administration, during this emergency, the standard shall be not more than one hundred cases per field worker for the investigation and supervision of relief cases. The Administration disapproves, as inefficient and uneconomical, the practice of loading more than one hundred cases on one investigator.

g) All work relief persons employed by a local Emergency Work Bureau or Emergency Relief Bureau, on, or in connection with, work projects are covered by work relief disability allowance as provided for under Chapter 303 of the Laws of 1934,

T.E.R.A. Official Bulletins and Departmental Letters as issued from time to time from this office, may amend these rules and regulations.

PENALTY FOR VIOLATIONS

Any diversion of relief as defined in the Act from the family or person for whose needs said relief is intended shall constitute a violation of these rules and is punishable as a misdemeanor under Section 30 of the Relief Act.

The T.E.R.A. Official Bulletins and Departmental Letters as issued from time to time from this office may, in furtherance of these rules and regulations, set forth administrative details and directions to govern local action.

SUPPLEMENT NO. 1

(Summary of T.E.R.A. Official Bulletin No. 34, Item 167, issued under date of March 28, 1934)

Effective April 1, 1934, the Administration fixed the rate of reimbursement at seventy-five per cent to municipalities for approved relief expenditures including home relief, work relief, and approved materials for work relief projects.

The continuation of this policy is contingent upon the continued availability of funds from State and Federal sources, and is subject to change by the Administration at any time.

SUPPLEMENT NO. 2

CASH RELIEF

An amendment to the Wicks Act, chapter 65 of the Laws of 1934, amends paragraph 8 of chapter 798 of the Laws of 1931, including cash as a relief item in the definition of home relief.

The amendment provides that "For purposes of and in order to provide wholly or in part home relief as herein defined, until February 15, 1935, money may be given in cash if and where approved by and under rules and regulations made and conditions specified by the Administration."

Controls Required of Local Administration

The Administration is prepared to authorize the use of cash in lieu of orders in any districts where the staff is adequate to provide the necessary control required to properly dispense cash relief. In order to be adequate, the local administration must provide:

1. A proper disbursing and accounting system with persons handling the money properly qualified and bonded.

2. A sufficiently low case load per worker (not in excess of one hundred cases for any individual worker) to permit the worker enough time to gain a knowledge of the individual family situation so that he or she may exercise good judgment as to the family's ability to expend cash economically and intelligently.

3. Continuous, careful and sound supervision of the investigating staff by capable supervisors.

Those districts in which the local welfare administration does not measure up to the required standard will be denied the use of cash until requirements have been met.

Recommended Limitations

In order to prevent the improper use of cash, the following limitations are suggested which may be used in the transfer of the load from home relief orders to relief in cash. It is suggested that these limitations be used for individual cases only where necessary, and that limitations be removed from the total group when it is indicated that they are no longer necessary.

1. Cash Relief on Limited Number of Items.
   (a) Cash relief may be given for all items or for specific items only, such as food and incidentals. Rent, for example, may be paid by order in case experience shows that giving the client the amount of his rent in cash will result in the money being used for other purposes.
   (b) Local officials may prescribe that milk for children shall be delivered to the home in specified amounts as a means of preventing the use of cash given for milk being diverted to other purposes.
   (c) Local officials may make any selections which they deem most advantageous as to which items shall be given in cash and which in orders. Central or contract purchasing of milk and coal, for example, as well as the probable advantage which the municipality may gain through a collective policy with reference to such items as rentals, should be given careful consideration when determining budget items to be allowed in cash or in kind.

2. Cash Relief for all Items to Selected Families.
   (a) A selective system may be used as a means of dividing the case load between those families who will be given cash and those from whom cash will be withheld. In case the selective system is used, each individual case must be reviewed first by local officials, and shall be subject to review by the field representative of the Temporary Emergency Relief Administration.
   Under the selective system, when a decision is given to give or withhold cash it must be based on the case

record of the family, in which must be stated a specific reason why cash is given or withheld. In case sufficient reason is not given, the field representative may require additional information as a basis for a proper review.

(b) Cash relief may be given to individual families on a temporary basis. Cash may be withdrawn and relief in orders substituted upon evidence that the money is not properly spent, on the basis of the review as provided above.

(c) In general, it is felt that within the limitations under No. 1 above, that the decision to give cash should be clear cut, and that cash relief where decided upon as a policy, should be used for all families at the outset, and should be withheld only on definite evidence of its improper use.

Accounting

The basis for a claim for reimbursement for cash relief shall be a properly authorized voucher or receipt form signed by the client. Details of further accounting procedures will be available upon request.

Cash relief shall be disbursed by check only (currency may not be used), and shall be authorized by the Commissioner of Public Welfare, or his properly delegated staff members.

Applications for Permission to Use Cash Relief

Applications for permission to use cash relief must be signed by the Commissioner of Public Welfare and the Mayor in the case of cities, and the Commissioner of Public Welfare and the Chairman of the Board of Supervisors in the case of counties.

A Brief Digest of the More Important General Rulings, Opinions, and Interpretations of the Emergency Act, Adopted by the Relief Administration to November 1, 1934

(An Index to these Rulings begins on page 229.)

I. ADMINISTRATIVE PROBLEMS

Political Activities of Relief Recipients or Persons Administering Relief

See T.E.R.A. Bulletins 60 (August 31, 1934) and 61 (September 26, 1934).

The Administration finds it necessary to define its policy with definiteness in respect to alleged political activities on the part of those who are in some manner connected with the administration of relief, as well as those who are recipients thereof. Some confusion has apparently arisen in the minds of many by reason of the statements issued pertaining to political activities of those concerned with the administration of relief who may at the same time be seeking elective political office.

In the first place, a clear distinction must be drawn between those who are the recipients of relief, whether it be work relief or home relief, on the one hand, and those who may be concerned with the administration of relief, on the other. *Under no circumstances should any work relief recipient or home relief recipient be in any manner discriminated against by reason of his political activities.*

The right to participate in the affairs of government, freely to voice his political views, the right to be a candidate for any office political or otherwise, is an incident to citizenship which cannot be denied to an unemployed person or one in need, simply because he is so unfortunate as to be unemployed or in need. This is the first clear distinction which the Administration desires to have understood.

With relation to those who may be members of local bureaus, administrative relief staffs, investigators, employees, or others concerned more or less directly with the administration of relief itself the question becomes vital because of the possibility of their activities conflicting with the performance of their duties in administering relief. Thus far there has been no statement of policy from the Federal Relief Administration which goes further than to bar the participation in political activities which may interfere with the duties of the person engaged in the administration of relief. This Administration has adopted the policy and here reiterates it, that those who may be members of local bureaus or engaged more directly in the administration of relief as investi-

[15]

gators or employees of administrative staffs, may not continue to hold such positions and be also active candidates for elective public office, or for the nomination for such in a primary election. There are three possible situations which may arise:

(1) Candidacy for elective Public Office in an election.
(2) Candidacy for the nomination for Public Office in a primary election.
(3) Candidacy for a party position, such as local, County or State Committee, which is not a public office.

In cases (1) and (2), no person may hold membership in a relief administration, local bureau, or employment as a member of a relief administration staff, who is a candidate either for an elective public office or who seeks, in a primary election, the nomination for such public office. The distinction must here be observed between candidacy for an elective public office and a candidacy for a party position within a party itself, which is not, within the contemplation of the Election Law, a public office.

Unless and until such activities within a party furnish evidence of an interference with his or her duties as a relief officer or employee, the Administration does not now place any barriers to such participation in primary or pre-election *intra-party activities*. This distinction between candidacy for elective public office and intra-party positions is here repeated for emphasis. The extent to which the Administration at present desires to bar political activities is solely to hold that members of bureaus or relief staff employees may not actively seek or be candidates for elective public office either in primary or general election. When such activities, political in their nature, interfere with the proper performance of duties of the individual as a relief employee or staff member, the Administration may take further action and modify or alter this policy.

Federal Policy on Political Affiliations

The following official communication from the Federal Emergency Relief Administration is self-explanatory:

"The President has repeatedly stated that partisan politics shall have no place in Federal Emergency Relief activities. Notwithstanding the publicity given this policy, there arises from time to time cases where there is every indication that partisan politics do enter into the administration of relief in the States.

"Continued employment of personnel must be on the basis of qualification and in the case of relief recipients, actual need is the only factor to be considered.

"Political and religious beliefs are of no concern to relief agencies and must not enter into relief activities.

"Employes of Relief Administrations shall in no way use their official positions in attempts to control political movements and shall not engage in political activities that in any way interfere with the effectiveness and integrity of relief operations.

"Any relief employe who may run for political office, whether National, State, or local, must resign, and any employe found to be engaging in activities in conflict with the clear intent of this order will be summarily dismissed."

This communication conforms with the policy of the Temporary Emergency Relief Administration of New York State, which has always been that political or religious affiliations or activities shall not be injected into the administration of relief, or in any manner be made a part of or be used in the activities of individuals who are members or employes of relief administrations or staff.

Work Relief Must Be Supplemental

The General Rules provide that work relief projects "may not be for work to be done under contract, *nor for work for which an annual appropriation has been customary.*"

This rule, at the outset of the Relief Administration's activities in 1931, set forth the guiding principle that regular budgetary appropriations were not to be permitted to be eliminated by reason of emergency relief projects and relief workers. Work relief in its essence is supplemental, additional to the normal budget items in a city's planning. It aims at future planning brought forward several years in accomplishment through the use of relief workers and funds. It was never the intention that cities and counties might effect budget economies at the expense of regular civil service workers through the subterfuge of substituting relief workers and projects. The work being the same, the economy is a false one; temporary in its nature, deceiving in its effect, and destructive of the morale of the regular governmental civil service. It is one thing to supplement the service with additional relief workers, to expand certain phases of public work, or to assist in bringing them up to date. It is quite another—to permit regular employees to be replaced by temporary relief workers at lower pay under the guise of an economy budget reduction. The practice should be condemned; the evils remedied by replacing ousted workers whose places were so abolished (in work only); reimbursements refused in all such projects until the wrongs done have been remedied.

No matter how extensive the practice has become; no matter how burdensome the restoration may be to the municipality, it should be compelled—and promptly. Emergency work relief must not be permitted to be used as a weapon with which to destroy the civil service under the false guise of a budgetary economy, and transferring the burden to the State and Federal Governments. It is a temporary, a short-sighted, a censurable expedient, and steps should be taken promptly to enforce the Administration's stated policy.

Payment of Work Relief Projects Out of Regular Annual Appropriations for Municipalities

The attention of the Administration has been called to instances where municipal corporations are financing work relief projects out of the regular annual appropriations and departmental activities, and not out of monies specifically appropriated for that purpose. For example, wages for work relief projects are taken from the annual appropriations for a department of public works and the reimbursement is then credited to that departmental account.

This procedure is contrary to the basis for work relief and the definition of work relief, which is provided for in section 2 of the Relief Law. Work relief is therein defined as "wages paid by a municipal corporation . . . from money *specifically appropriated* or contributed *for that purpose* during the emergency period, for the performance of services or labor connected with work undertaken by such corporation independent of work under a contract or *for which an annual appropriation has been made.*"

This definition makes it absolutely essential that work relief projects be financed from specific work appropriations for relief projects.

The Administration desires once more to draw attention to the fact that normal public work programs of a municipal corporation are not intended to be financed by the State, under the guise of relief projects. Relief projects are those additional public improvements which would not normally be undertaken and which are only put forward because of the unemployment situation, and in order to provide lasting improvements for which the municipal corporation would probably have to await the future.

More Than One Person in a Family; Part-Time Jobs

Previous rulings to the effect that not more than one person in a family may be employed on work relief have been rescinded. In the future, the budget deficit shall be the controlling basis, and if the budget deficit requires, the employment of more than one person in a family is permissible.

The employment of persons on work relief who have other part-time employment is also permissible, provided the amount of employment is limited to the budget deficit.

Cost of Transient Relief

The Federal government through its Relief Administration has provided camps for what it chooses to term "interstate transients." The latter are a public welfare charge and some are eligible for emergency relief under the two-year residence in the State act. All are eligible for relief when needed under the Federal Relief and Reconstruction Act of 1933. The fact is that separate funds are supplied by the Federal Relief Administration for the *interstate transients* whereas, the *intrastate* transients are charged to the state's own allocation of F.E.R.A. funds.

Under these circumstances I cannot see where the difficulty lies in paying for the cost of maintenance of State transients in the Federal interstate camps within the State. When cared for by the Salvation Army or others (municipal lodging houses, etc.), the cost is met from such relief funds. What difference does it make that they are to be cared for in Federal transient camps instead of by other agencies? The only required change is an entry in the accounting records which will mark the amount chargeable to State transients as distinct from the Federal. Since the cost is borne by the F.E.R.A. funds, the replenishing of the Federal Transient funds to the extent of expenditures on State transients is simple and unobjectionable. There is no misuse of State Relief moneys here. Both funds are supplied by the Federal Relief Administration. They require a separate accounting for these two types of transients. The method of meeting the initial expense from one fund and charging a part to the proper State share of Federal Relief funds should furnish no basis for refusing to meet this proper expense in administering relief to State transients.

Liability of Municipality in Accident Cases of Transients

Section 16-a covers only those who are employed on work relief projects under the Wicks Act. A transient does not come within that category, even though working out his bed and board.

If a Federal transient is injured, ascertain what, if any provision, the Federal E.R.A. has made for such cases.

If a State case, no liability is incurred unless actual negligence can be established in the municipality or State responsible for said case.

The only relief possible is continued care of such transient, i. e., home relief.

Hospital Care for Transients

State transients would be covered as to hospital care by our own laws of settlement and charged back under the Public Welfare law and Wicks Act regulations. They do not furnish any problem in respect of such cases. The real problem is Federal transients, who are not normal local or State burdens. Since this program is of Federal initiation, it behooves the F.E.R.A. to provide the means of and take responsibility for such costs.

Federal Transients' Burial Expenses

Federal transients find no definition nor place in our Public
Welfare set up. They are creations of Federal initiation with our
consent in aid of a relief program. Under our law the burden of
such a charge cannot be placed upon the welfare district where
the death occurs when it was not responsible for his entry. Such
a charge would be equivalent to a tax upon the political subdivision of the State imposed by the Federal government's activity
(F.E.R.A.), which is contrary to the well-established constitutional
immunity of State and municipal governmental units and agencies
from Federal taxing powers.

Such charges should be borne by the F.E.R.A. Transient fund
and the F.E.R.A. should make some provision for these, as for
Federal transients' hospital charges.

Transients Selling Clothing, etc.

Where it is presumed that transients are selling clothing, etc.,
given them at camp, everyone is innocent until proved guilty. It
would be next to impossible to establish that the buyer knew the
source of the clothing, etc.

It would appear unlikely that the transient would have funds
left so that recovery could be had from him. He should be barred
further relief. If he is a Federal transient, a possible violation of
law is involved. Local courts are available. The case should be
referred to District Attorney.

Transient Camp Easement

There is no provision in the State Relief Acts which will permit
the State to be bound by contract for a transient camp site, nor
to assume any such liability.

Transient Camps are a Federal project financed by F.E.R.A.
funds and the amendment to Chapter 8, Laws of 1933, specifically
bars any such use of Federal funds so as to bind the T.E.R.A. or
the State:

"Section 3. Such moneys from the reconstruction finance
corporation or other federal agency may be expended by the
temporary emergency relief administration for the purposes
and in the manner provided by chapter seven hundred ninety-
eight of the laws of nineteen hundred and thirty-one as now
or hereafter amended and for such other relief or related
purposes as may be authorized by the emergency relief and
reconstruction act of nineteen hundred and thirty-two enacted
by the congress of the United States and acts amendatory

thereof or supplemental thereto and by any other acts enacted by the congress and pursuant to and under such conditions and in the manner specified by the reconstruction finance corporation or other federal agency, but nothing in this chapter or in any other law shall create a liability against the temporary emergency relief administration or the state of New York for, in respect of, in relation to or by reason of the administration or expenditure of such federal funds.

"This act shall take effect immediately."

This contract, if made, must be made with the Federal Emergency Relief Administration, an agency of the United States, through the Transient Division for New York State, not with the State of New York nor with the State T.E.R.A. As to the approval of the contract, therefore, it should be referred for such approval to the Federal Administration since the liability, if any, is Federal, not State.

Civil Service Exemptions

Workers on emergency relief staffs are not within the scope of the Civil Service Rules or Law.

Chapter 567 of the Laws of 1932, as amending chapter 798 of the Laws of 1931 (Temporary Emergency Relief measure or Wicks Act), specifically provides as follows:

"No person employed pursuant to this act, during the emergency period, shall be subject to the provisions of the Civil Service Law."

This sets at rest once and for all the entire question. No attention need be paid to the rules of the local civil service commissions. These workers are not subject to their approval or their direction in any manner whatsoever. They are merely emergency relief employees, and all that is necessary for their continued employment is the approval of the Temporary Emergency Relief Administration.

Work Relief Projects for National Reemployment Service

The Temporary Emergency Relief Administration has allocated a sum of money to the National Reemployment Service for the State of New York, to be used for the payment of work relief wages to clients of local work bureaus assigned as clerical assistants to local offices of the National Reemployment Service.

The wages of such employees will be paid one hundred per cent by the Temporary Emergency Relief Administration.

The project will be carried out as other State Department projects.

The usual rules and regulations of the Temporary Emergency Relief Administration apply. The rate of wages paid shall conform with the rate of wages paid on other white collar projects in the local work bureau. Such personnel is to be taken from the present relief lists.

Payroll Check Against Relief Rolls

The Federal Emergency Relief Administration urges careful check in each community between employers of labor and the local relief offices on a regular weekly, bi-weekly or monthly basis in order that all persons who have returned to normal labor and are earning sufficient to meet their needs will be taken from relief rolls.

This check-up is particularly important, in order that those genuinely in need receive adequate assistance.

The Federal Emergency Relief Administration further urges that each community make a careful study of the adequacy of relief allowances with a view to making definite plans to carry the unemployed without suffering or damage to health.

Several districts have already arranged for regular check with local employers to secure information as to persons returned to local employment. The system requires full cooperation of local employers, and an understanding with them as to the purposes for which the information is to be used.

The Administration has available an experienced person who will assist you in setting up this checking system upon request.

N.R.A. Work Relief Projects

The Administration wishes to cooperate in every way possible with the National Recovery Administration.

Accordingly, work relief projects for the purpose of assigning qualified workers on a work relief basis for clerical and stenographic assistance to local N.R.A. offices will be approved if in keeping with local needs and submitted in proper form.

The usual rules and regulations must be complied with.

Hours of Work on Work Projects

(See Department Letter, WD series No. 3, July 30, 1934)

In accordance with a new ruling received from the Federal Emergency Relief Administration, the restriction of twenty-four hours per week on manual labor projects is removed from all districts, and the maximum number of hours increased to thirty.

The maximum of 128 hours in any calendar month remains in

force. This ruling does not affect the requirement that hours of employment must be controlled so that earnings will conform to the budget deficit.

* * *

Solicitation of Funds

The following resolution has been passed by the Administration:

"The solicitation of funds for any purpose whatsoever from employees of home or work relief bureaus in the payment of whose wages or salaries this Administration is participating is strictly prohibited. All home and work relief bureaus shall be required to bring this resolution to the attention of all employees."

Misuse of Initials "T.E.R.A."

The initials "T.E.R.A." have been widely misused throughout the State by officials and workers and by the press and other publications. Emergency work bureaus have been called T.E.R.A. work bureaus. Strict care should be shown to use the initials T.E.R.A. only in connection with the Temporary Emergency Relief Administration. Work bureaus should be called the Emergency Work Bureau of the district concerned and a consolidated bureau should be called the Emergency Relief Bureau of the district in which it belongs.

Federal Grants to Colleges to Aid Needy Students

The Federal Emergency Relief Administration has set up a program of granting funds to colleges so that they may give part-time employment to needy students. The allotment to each college will be based upon 12 per cent of that college's full-time enrollment in October, 1933. A college, in order to be eligible, must be a non-profit making institution exempt from State and local taxation. Each college that participates in this scheme will set up its own work program. The college must pay the students not less than 30 cents an hour, and no student shall work more than 30 hours in any week, or 8 hours in any day. The maximum amount which may be paid to any student will be $20 a month.

At the request of the Federal Emergency Relief Administration, the National Re-employment Service and the New York State Employment Service are co-operating in this program. They will refer to colleges any high school graduates whom they may find who are qualified for and interested in attending college on this basis. The local offices of these organizations will be furnished with full information about the program, including the list of colleges in New York State which are participating.

In case you come in contact with any person who might be eligible to attend college and to apply for this part-time employment, we suggest that you communicate with the local office of the N.R.S., or the N.Y.S.E.S. It is to be noted that persons in order to be eligible for this employment do not necessarily have to be on relief, or eligible for relief. In order to be eligible for this employment, a student's financial status must be such as to make impossible his or her attendance at college without this aid. The particular college concerned is to be the sole judge as to any student's need and qualifications for this aid.

* * *

Relief Employees in the State Retirement System

The State Retirement System and the provisions of law applicable thereto were never intended to apply to temporary employees of an emergency nature. Surely it cannot apply to relief recipients whose wages are the estimated family needs. Whether these are working on projects of a manual or "white collar" nature does not alter the true picture. No more can it be made to apply so as to compel membership of those who are staff workers of the temporary Relief Bureau.

To one group, or individuals thereof, it might apply—namely—those regular county (or municipal) employees whose duties have been merely transferred to the relief work and who now are members of the Relief Bureau staff. They may be said to continue in their Civil Service of a permanent character.

The Wicks Act in express words exempts all employees thereunder from the provisions of the Civil Service Law. The same reasoning is clearly applicable to compulsory membership in the Retirement System.

Employees of the Relief Bureaus, and those of the Temporary Emergency Relief Administration, whether on a relief basis or not, are not subject to compulsory membership in the State Retirement System by reason of the entry into said system of the county or municipality in which they work. T.E.R.A. employees in general are exempted from the State Retirement System, except that present T.E.R.A employees who were formerly members of the Retirement System may continue to retain their membership by payment of the usual fee.

Deductions from Salaries of Local Staffs

In view of the changed language of Section 13 of Chapter 826, Laws of 1934, from that theretofore used therein, it becomes necessary to ascertain the extent to which it can be applied. The question has been placed before me to determine if such deductions as are therein provided are applicable to salaries of those on the local Relief Bureau staffs, paid from local funds and reimbursable by the State under the Relief Act as amended, either in whole or part.

The section as amended now reads:

"This section applies to all compensation for personal service payable from an appropriation or authorization for such purpose for the fiscal year ending June thirtieth, nineteen hundred thirty-five, except those made by chapter sixteen of the laws of nineteen hundred thirty-four where the scale of salary reductions therein is applicable. The certified payrolls including approved individual vouchers in cases where such are used, for personal service in the fiscal year beginning July first, nineteen hundred thirty-four, of each department, board, commission, and office in the state government, shall state the full compensation and the maintenance value, if any, which for the purposes of this section also shall be deemed compensation, of each officer or employee named therein, for the payroll or voucher period."

The local staff members, Home Relief or Work Relief Bureaus, are paid out of local funds. They are not and have never been regarded as State employees. They are municipal employees of the city or county as the case may be. The fact that they act on behalf of the State Relief body does not alter that conclusion. The appropriation by the legislature for relief in aid of the municipalities does not come within the language or intention of the legislative expression in said section which relates solely to personal service appropriations from State funds.

In some instances, local employees are themselves subject to salary deductions which cover these local bureau workers. In other instances the salaries paid are in consideration of other conditions. Work Division payrolls (Project workers) are of course not so considered because of the very nature of the task and employment. Yet the relative status of the local staff worker and the project worker are parallel. The reimbursable factor, instead of rendering them subject to the State's deduction, has quite the contrary effect,—i. e., of taking them outside of that field or scope, whether reimbursed in whole or in part.

*   *   *

Health Projects, etc., on Private Property

Health projects are of course for a public purpose and may properly be so construed as public work. The benefits are widespread and general. Among such are mosquito extermination, ragweed extermination, agricultural pest extermination, drainage districts, etc.

In carrying out these projects, entry upon private property is necessary at time; work upon such property in draining, oiling, cutting, etc., may be necessary. True, the property may itself be benefited thereby. Rotting timber harbor pests, swampy pools are breeding grounds for mosquitoes and disease carriers; fields of ragweed, etc., are sources of pollenation carrying suffering to thousands. Under proper circumstances, in aid of such health projects, with a waiver of claim and a release to the State by reason of incidental trespass or entry upon such property from the owners, such work is purely incidental to the major purpose and this does not violate the public work provision in the relief act, pertinent to such project.

Improvements to Relief Recipients' Homes

In regard to improvements on relief recipients' homes, there is no way of doing this. It would be a matter for public health authorities. However, a loan might be sought from the Federal Home Owners' Loan Corporation.

Payroll Certification by Local Work Bureaus on State Projects

Local work bureaus must check and approve all work relief payrolls on State department projects before the payroll has been passed for payment.

The policy of retroactive approval of payrolls on a routine basis is not permissible. State department projects must be checked weekly. The responsibility on the part of the local work bureau for the correctness of the payroll for workers assigned to State projects is the same as for workers employed on local projects.

Deductions from disallowed claims on State department projects will be made to local work bureaus the same as from claims presented by local work bureaus.

* * *

Payment of Manufacturer's Processing Tax

The question of exemption from the Federal processing tax on goods sold to welfare departments, or to relief recipients, has caused considerable difficulty in various welfare districts.

Because of the amount of detail involved, the difficulties of securing exemption, and the impossible task of requiring retailers to adjust prices by a small fraction of a cent on individual articles, the Administration, on advice of its legal counsel, rules that as to Federal processing taxes, the certification that taxes have been eliminated from claims need not apply to the retailers' price on relief orders. The Administration will honor claims for reimbursement without regard to the payment of the Federal processing tax where purchases are at retail.

Certain Tax Claims Not Payable

The State and the political subdivisions thereof are exempt from payment of taxes of the character covered by the recently established State sales tax and the Federal tax on certain types of expenditures. Furthermore, the State will not reimburse a public welfare district for any claim based on bills which include such tax.

This ruling, however, has no relation to the Federal processing tax, as to which the Administration's policy is expressed in the preceding paragraph.

The State Comptroller requires that all bills upon the basis of which a claim is made against the State shall have a certificate placed on the face thereof directly above the receipt, as follows:

"The claimant hereby certifies that there are no Federal or New York State taxes included in this bill."

This certification may be made without reference to the Federal processing tax.

In making purchases or incurring expenditures for any service it should be ascertained that the amount to be paid does not include any tax, and it would be well to advise claimants that the public welfare district is exempt therefrom. It is, therefore, desirable that the above statement be stamped or typed in the required position before the bills are prepared.

The bills submitted in substantiation of home relief claims will be returned unless they bear such certification.

Theory of the Processing Tax

Where a town has contracted with a baker to furnish bread to certain welfare clients at seven cents a loaf, and it is stated that the Federal processing tax has made it "impossible" for the baker to supply bread at that price, we are asked whether such tax is to be absorbed by the processor or dealer, and not passed on to the consumer, and whether the dealer is exempt from the tax if the commodity is sold to a municipal corporation, in which event, it is stated, much clerical work would be involved in claiming refunds, etc.

The statute involved is Part 2 of the Federal Agricultural Adjustment Act of May 12, 1933 (c. 25, 48 Stat.) in which it is provided, in section 18, that as to contracts with private persons, under circumstances like these, the tax shall be paid by the purchaser (unless the contract prohibits such addition). But as this contract is with a political subdivision of the State of New York, such provision, or any provision for passing the tax to the vendee, would be inoperative. (Indian Motocycle Co. v. United States, 283 U. S. 570, 575, and cases cited.)

In this situation the vendor must fulfill his contract as written and take up with the Secretary of Agriculture the method by which he shall be reimbursed, that official being authorized (section 10, subd. (c)) to make all necessary regulations in this respect.

It may be noted that in section 15, subd. (c), it is provided that "any person delivering any product to any organization for charitable distribution or use shall, if such product or the commodity from which processed, is under this title subject to tax, be entitled to a refund of the amount of any tax paid under this title with respect to such product so delivered." The means of specific exemption thus expressly provided for sales to private charities must be easily extensible to sales to municipal corporations.

Exemption from Tax on Checks

All checks drawn by emergency work bureaus or home relief offices are drawn on public funds, and such checks are accordingly exempt from the tax on checks imposed by the Federal Revenue Act of 1932.

Article 36 of the regulations promulgated by the United States Bureau of Internal Revenue provides:

"The checks, drafts, or orders drawn by officers of the United States or of a State, county or municipality, or of a foreign government, in their official capacities, against public funds standing to their official credit and in furtherance of duties imposed upon them by law, are not subject to the tax."

If, therefore, electricity bills, for example, are paid by city checks, there should be deducted therefrom the amount of the Federal tax, notwithstanding that the bills are rendered in the names of private persons.

The Motor Fuel Tax

Private contractors furnishing trucks to a work bureau are not exempt from the State motor fuel tax. The exemption does not extend to contractors even indirectly. It might be possible for the bureau to arrange to furnish gasoline and give orders on the oil company to the drivers. The payment to the oil company to be by the bureau or county (or city) as the case might be, so that the payment will be that of the municipal corporation.

Milk Prices Not Fixed

The Milk Control Board holds that it has no control over the price of milk sold to municipal corporations. It permits the sale of milk to private charities at the dealers' or store price; but where there is door to door delivery it believes the door to door price should be paid, even though the delivery is on the order of a public welfare official and paid for out of public funds. See Section 3, "Free Milk," page 60 of this pamphlet.

Construction of the Act

Where a corporation counsel has raised constitutional objections to the work of the Relief Administration, it appears that he has mistaken the purposes of the statute authorizing relief and has misconstrued the constitutional provisions, which are sought to be interposed as barriers.

The Constitution prevents a county from lending its credit to a town, village or person, etc. (Article VIII, section 10.) A similar section bars the State from lending its credit "in aid of any individual, association or corporation." (Article VII, section 1.) This constitutional limitation does not bar the State from advancing funds to aid the unemployed. It is the fundamental purpose, the ultmate goal that governs, and it is this which the corporation counsel fails to grasp. Relief to the unemployed—wages to the unemployed—not the incidental benefit of the public work project to the municipality—governs the construction of the Act and its operations.

The State is not lending its credit to the unemployed; it is granting relief. The county, or city, or town or village, as the case may be, is not lending its credit. It is granting relief to the needy, an obligation imposed by the Public Welfare Law. The obligation is one that antedates all organic or statutory law; it is the basic obligation of communal existence.

The incidental machinery which involves spending county money for wages or for "home relief" on local cases or local projects is not in violation of any constitutional provision. Nor is the law authorizing such relief in any sense unconstitutional.

Project Approvals

A number of work relief projects have been received lately with a request for approval, on which "the date to be started" is prior to the date the project is received in our office.

The Administration cannot grant retroactive approvals. Projects should be submitted in sufficient time prior to starting date, so that our Project Department can give full consideration to the details before the date on which it is planned to start the project.

This policy applies also to retroactive approvals on resubmissions or additions to projects.

Budget for "White Collar" Workers

The setting up of a different budgetary standard for white collar workers, above that of manual laborers, is open to serious attack:

(a) It represents a radical departure from previous policies. It should have the approval of Harry L. Hopkins, federal relief administrator, since otherwise it might jeopardize Federal refunds. It constitutes what appears to me to be a violation of Federal Regulation No. 3, paragraph 6, under work relief rules, which bars discrimination in work relief because of membership in any special or selected group. For this reason, any exception to that rule should have Mr. Hopkins' express written approval.

(b) There is created by this separate budget standard, a social stratification as a basis for relief.

(c) If the nature of the particular task demands continuity, a possible exception might be made because of the peculiar nature of the task involved. The basis for the budget, however, cannot be made the difference in the social strata or a selected group in which the recipients happen to be. The reason for this is that such a discrimination or preference may not be socially defensible.

(d) There is, however, within our published rules and regulations, no bar (nor in the Wicks Law), to the administration of relief on such a basis. The Administration has previously I believe, in a communication, established the same policy which appears in the Federal rules on work relief. It is a question of policy which the Administration should seriously consider before adoption, and then only in the light of the Federal relation referred to.

Household Supplies

The Administration feels that in many instances the purchase of household supplies as a part of a food relief order causes an unnecessary hardship to clients.

It is recommended that food relief orders include a small weekly allowance for such necessary supplies as may be required weekly, but that large household supplies, costing 20 cents or more, be purchased as a separate household relief item, on separate order, and not be deducted from a food relief order which has made no allowance for such expenses.

Limiting Use of Wages

Where a county work bureau is following the plan of stipulating the exact amount of money that shall be used for different items, for instance, so much for food, so much for clothing, light, heat, etc., this defeats the purpose of work relief. While recommendations in way of budgetary diet may be appropriate and conceivably helpful, it must not be mandatory—else you return to the essence of "home" as against "work" relief, and destroy independence.

Expenses of Bureau Members

There is nothing in the Emergency Relief statutes which forbids counties defraying actual and necessary expenses incurred by Work Bureau members. Of course, this does not permit of a salary or payment of a stated sum "in lieu" of expenses, but refers to actual expenses. Nor does this imply any reimbursement from the State.

Expenses of Work Bureau

Income from bonds or certificates of indebtedness sold under the Emergency Act may be used to pay the administrative expenses of a work bureau in a reasonable proportion, without prejudice to the application to the Administration for assistance in meeting that part of the project's cost which is chargeable to wages, in the thought that those expenses are allowable without which it would be impossible to accomplish the work relief intended and to enable those who are to be paid the wages to perform the work contemplated under the project.

Traveling Expenses for Education Department

The Administration has set aside $2,400 to cover traveling expenses for those in charge of the supervision of the educational program undertaken as part of the Emergency Relief Administration, under the Education Department of the State. Regular employees and officials of the State Education Department have volunteered their services and have been assigned to supervise this work. They are not work relief employees and it becomes uecessary, because of the extraordinary nature of their activities, to bear their actual traveling expenses while engaged in carrying out these projects.

The Comptroller raises the question as to whether or not these traveling expenses may properly be chargeable to such projects and calls attention to section 18 of the law as amended by chapter 9 of the Laws of 1933. That provision merely permits the allocation out of the discretionary fund of sums for State projects. It does not in any manner diminish the effect of the provisions of section 3 of chapter 798 as amended, or of the provisions of chapter 6 of the Laws of 1933, making an appropriation of fifteen million dollars.

Section 3 reads as follows:

"The Administration may accept from any person or organization and avail itself of any and all offers of personal service or other aid or assistance in carrying out any of the provisions of this act made without expectation of compensation or other reward. Any persons or organizations so contributing such services and giving such other aid or assistance shall be entitled to receive only such expenses as are actually and necessarily incurred by them by reason of such services, aid or assistance."

Chapter 6 of 1933 appropriates three million dollars for a discretionary fund:

"(a) for direct grants to municipal corporations as provided for by section 16 of chapter 798 of the Laws of 1931 as amended by chapter 567 of the Laws of 1932, for work relief and/or home relief, and to towns for home relief, on such conditions as the administration may prescribe;

"(b) for salaries and expenses of the administration from February 1, 1933 to February 15, 1934;

"(c) for salaries of local bureaus as provided in section 19 of chapter 798 of the Laws of 1931 as amended by chapter 567 of the Laws of 1932 for the period from November 15, 1933, to February 15, 1934."

It would seem quite appropriate that the allocation of this amount for traveling expenses would come within the clear scope of section 3 as quoted above, and also within the appropriation under subdivision "(b)" of the four groups of purposes for which the discretionary fund might be used.

In other words, it could clearly be classed as an expense of the administration chargeable to the discretionary fund, even if under a strict construction of section 18 as amended, it did not cover the necessary expenses as a charge against the State project appropriation itself. The propriety of the charge against the discretionary fund, however, cannot in the light of the foregoing provisions be questioned.

Municipality in Private Business

(a) Cord wood produced on a work relief project carried on by the town of Wilna, Jefferson county, has been sold by the town to private customers at $2 a cord, a price lower than that at which dealers in wood can purchase the same. The Administration has been reimbursing 50 per cent of the wages of men employed in this work. Objection is made by local fuel dealers.

It is also stated that men employed on this job are paid by the cord, so that one cutting four cords in 12 days would receive the same compensation as one cutting four cords in two days.

In a war-time case (Howard v. City of New York, 199 App. Div. 56, reversed on other grounds 236 N. Y. 91), it was held that within constitutional limitations the Legislature may authorize a municipal corporation to engage in the business of the purchase and sale of food and fuel in cases of emergency or extraordinary conditions. Whether even the Legislature could authorize such procedure on a permanent basis is doubtful. "The Constitution does not contemplate this as one of the ends for which government was established, or as a public service for which cities and towns may tax their inhabitants." (In re Opinion of Justices, 155 Mass. 598, 30 N. E. 1142). But in any event, no municipal corporation may carry on private business of this nature without specific statutory authority, and the Legislature has granted no such authority. The practice referred to is, therefore, subject to injunction, actions for restitution, etc., and should not be countenanced by the Administration in any way.

As to payment, the Relief Act (L. 1932, ch. 567, section 16) and the Work Relief Rules (section 6) both require that moneys paid to a person in cash under the provisions of this act shall be in the form of day's wages for day's work or hour's wages for hour's work. Piece work payments are, therefore, prohibited.

(b) The foregoing is equally applicable to a contract entered into by the town with a private construction company to supply crushed stone, produced by relief workers, to be used on a State highway. A town may buy or condemn the right to remove stone from a quarry and may buy, lease or hire machinery therefor (Highway Law, sections 49–51), but only for its own use, except that it may rent the machinery to a village constituting a separate road district wholly or partly within the town (section 49) or to the county (section 329-b). A town may not lawfully sell stone for a State highway, in competition with private stone companies.

Unification of Investigations

Dutchess County is comprised of 20 towns and the city of Poughkeepsie and the city of Beacon, with the following relief and welfare organizations:

County Welfare Commissioner. This department takes care of hospitalization, welfare relief, both indoor and outdoor, and old age relief in the 20 towns and the city of Beacon. It also operates the County Alms House or County Home.

City of Poughkeepsie, Welfare Department. This department takes care of old age relief, public welfare relief, indoor and outdoor and hospital cases within the city of Poughkeepsie. It also operates the City Alms House or City Home.

Board of Child Welfare, Dutchess County. This department is set up under a special act and takes care of indoor and outdoor relief for children under sixteen years of age and investigates all families who need relief, having children in the home under sixteen years of age. It also cares for widows' pensions where there are children under sixteen years of age needing relief, not only in the 20 towns of the county, but also in the cities of Poughkeepsie and Beacon.

As a result, each of these departments has a staff of clerical workers and investigators doing the same kind of work in three separate offices and it is nothing unusual for an investigator from the Child Welfare Department to travel 75 or 80 miles to investigate one case in Millertown while on the same day an investigator from the County Welfare Department may investigate a case next door in Millertown and travel the same number of miles. The same thing applies in the city. Application will be made for relief to the City Welfare Department and the investigator will find that there is a child or children under sixteen years of age and then the County Child Welfare Commission will be notified and they will investigate. If they think it is a case for them, they will take it over and if not, the Welfare Department of the city then takes it back on and then resumes control of the case.

All of these investigators and their expenses are paid from taxation and it is believed there is no good reason why the work would not be performed as efficiently if the heads of the County and City Welfare Departments and the Child Welfare Department coordinated their forces and assigned an investigator from one department or the other to cover a certain territory and make reports to the department which the investigator finds should assume responsibility for each case. In this way, a great amount of time now consumed in traveling would be eliminated and closer contact could be maintained with each individual case, without duplication of time in traveling and cross investigations.

The conclusion from the foregoing is that there is no legal obstacle to such unification of service. In fact, it is desirable. While the divisional lines in these specialized phases could not be eliminated without legislation, workers could be assigned part time on one job and part time on another.

School Funds Not Available

A central high school district has a surplus of $400 which it would like to spend in grading the school grounds, etc., with reimbursement by the State.

Being a public improvement, this work is eligible for a work project. However, in so far as the school funds are derived from State contributions, they could not be used for any purpose not within the scope of the Education Law. If not so derived, the money would have to be turned over to the county emergency work bureau (or to the village, if the village is acting as an authorized agency of the county) and administered by that body, as a board of education is not recognized by the Relief Act.

Use of Scrip Money

In regard to the use of scrip money as payment for work relief, no such possibility is authorized under the Emergency Act and therefore there could be no reimbursement of work relief wages which are not paid in cash or by check which would be the equivalent of cash in this instance. No other form of wages would be valid under the act.

Checks Must be Cashed

Work relief wages will, it is assumed under the law, be paid in cash but that normally would mean a check which is readily redeemable.

There is no question but that every work relief employee should have an opportunity promptly to cash his or her pay check— or have it cashed. To do otherwise is to impose undue hardship on a relief case.

Private Funds

Private funds raised by a work bureau must be turned in to the city treasurer, but may be earmarked for the relief bureau work expressly so that it may not be necessary to reappropriate them. This practice is outlined in section 14 of the Relief Act. If, however, it is not to be reimbursed by the State, then it may be turned over to the bureau as an agency of the T.E.R.A., as provided in section 17.

Citizenship Papers

We have no means of paying for citizens' papers, but an alien may be eligible for relief—the requirements being residence and need.

Insurance of Relief Cars

Work relief recipients who drive their own cars on the bureau's business should not be required to provide insurance for themselves at their own expense. It amounts to an arbitrary reduction of compensation which presumably has been calculated upon their absolute and actual subsistence needs.

Wages of Deceased Recipients

We are asked as to the payment of work relief wages after the death of the worker. It is noted that "the amounts due these individuals are so small that it does not really pay to have an administrator appointed where they have nothing except the few dollars pay due them for work on the road."

It is by no means necessary in all cases to administer upon an estate through the Surrogate's Court. "Letters should be withheld unless there is some substantial reason for their issuance" (Heaton's Surrogates, 5th ed., vol. 2, p. 25). Where there are no debts and the property is already distributed, and there are no suits to be brought, there can be no necessity for the granting of letters. (Matter of Lossee, 119 App. Div. 107.) Workmen's compensation due a deceased person is payable to surviving spouse or children without an administrator (Workmen's Compensation Law, sec. 33), and under Banking Law, section 248, subd. 4, as amended, it is no longer necessary to have an administrator appointed to obtain payment to spouse, next of kin, etc., of a savings account up to $500. Even where an administrator is named, money or other personal property up to $150 in value is no part of the estate but is the property of surviving spouse or children. (Surrogate's Court Act, section 200.)

It would seem to me, therefore, to be proper to pay work relief wages due a deceased worker to his wife, children or other dependents, for their support, without any formality other than proof of their status. In the case of *non-dependent* relatives, creditors, undertakers, etc., I would let them go to the Surrogate for letters if they claim such work relief wages, which they could not touch during decedent's lifetime, to be due them from his "estate." I think such claim would not be sustained. See, for procedure, Departmental Letter, October 3, 1934, accounting series No. 9.

In regard to undertakers, in particular, note that the cost of burial of a relief recipient is a charge on the welfare district under section 154 of the Public Welfare Law.

Projects Within City Scope

Property in a school district which is entirely within the city limits but which is not a part of the city school system would nevertheless be liable for its share of the cost of a work project on the city school grounds, paid for from city tax funds levied upon the entire taxable area of the city, as such charge is not for school purposes but is a city purpose. A relief project on a recreation field left in trust for the use and enjoyment of all the people of the city, free of charge, and under the supervision and management of city authorities, would be lawful under the Emergency Act, although title to the property is not actually in the city's name.

Administration of Oaths

Certain claims have been rejected on the ground that the affidavits were not sworn to before a notary public. It is stated that "the State Comptroller's office will not recognize the signature of a deputy commissioner or a town clerk."

It is provided, however, in section 147 of the Public Welfare Law that "Public Welfare officials shall have power to administer oaths and take affidavits in all matters pertaining to their office," which, in my opinion, constitutes such officials and their authorized deputies ex-officio notaries public in so far as the matters with which they deal are public welfare matters. They could not, of course, attest their own signatures, but the oath in such case could be administered by another deputy.

As to town clerks it is provided in section 88 of the Town Law that "Any town officer may administer any necessary oath in any matter or proceeding lawfully before him, or to any paper to be filed with him as such officer," and this has been held to authorize a town clerk to administer oaths (People v. Watts, 73 Hun 404). But welfare matters are not before a town clerk or to be filed with him, and his authority as a notary ex-officio would not extend thereto.

* *

Forest Work Not Compulsory

Refusal to volunteer for Reforestation work in encampments should not be made a basis for refusal of relief. There is no provision in either the Public Welfare Law or Emergency Relief Act to warrant such attitude. The Federal Act makes no such condition even for Federal aid. There can be no justification for the State doing so. It bears the imprint of a draft. The moral effect may be decidedly harmful, if enforced. The Reforestation plan is purely voluntary and local officials have no legal right to make it mandatory by indirection through the use of State Relief as a weapon.

* * *

Must Follow Federal Statute

It is desired to place in a forest corps a young man, born abroad 22 years ago, who has been resident in this country for 21 years but whose parents, who are now public charges whom the youth desires to support, were never naturalized, we cannot undertake to stretch the Federal law. The young man is not eligible.

State Projects for Indians

The Administration asks whether a work project may be initiated for relief to needy Indians on the Reservations. It is proposed that the project be a State project and so operated, with workers chosen from needy Indians who apparently are not receiving an opportunity on other work relief programs of cities and counties:

The Indians in this State are the wards of the State and the Department of Social Welfare audits their relief claims to the whole extent thereof, payable of the State Treasury. (Public Welfare Law, §§ 60–70.)

This would make a project for work relief by the Department of Social Welfare or some other Department, i.e. a State Project, admirably suited to relief for the Indians in the form of work relief, since the State in any event is bound to the entire extent of their "home relief" when on Reservations.

Such a project may be approved by the Administration.

Thomas Indian School Project

A county project embodying work at the Thomas Indian School in Erie County was submitted and approved by the State Relief Administration, on the basis of a reimbursement of 100 per cent. It appears that the County Attorney now objects that the county cannot so expend its funds, even though it be reimbursed to the full extent.

It is unquestioned that the work is on a public institution. The Indians are Erie County residents, even though also State charges in the sense that the Public Welfare Department exercises supervision, etc. It has often been the case that State work in a county has been utilized as county projects to employ county relief workers. The Indians are also entitled to share in the work relief program of the county and if the State reimburses the county to the full amount, I cannot understand the objection to payment in the first instance out of county funds.

Status of Indians

It is not the fact that Indians of New York State are not in welfare districts, as each reservation is included in the "territory of a county beyond the limits of a city" which constitutes a county public welfare district under the Emergency Relief Act, and in every case the counties in which Indian reservations are situated have accepted the provisions of the act. But notwithstanding this, an Indian who has resided upon a reservation at least six months prior to an application for public relief and care, or who has within one year prior to such application received relief from the State for himself or any member of his family, is already a State charge to the whole extent of any relief which is furnished to him, the same being administered by the county commissioner and paid for out of the State treasury on the approval and audit of the Department of Social Welfare (Public Welfare Law, sections 65–70). Moneys so expended are not subject to reimbursement or contribution from the Emergency Relief funds.

On the other hand, an Indian who is not a State charge under the Public Welfare Law, as indicated in the foregoing paragraph, is to be given care and relief at the expense of the county or town, as the case may be, and if such person has been a resident of the State for two years prior to November 1, 1931, claim may be made upon the administration for reimbursement of the cost of any home relief so provided, to the extent of 40 per cent thereof. The initiative in such case, however, lies with the local commissioners of public welfare, and not with the administration.

So, as to work relief, the emergency work bureaus of the various counties in which reservations are situated are the ones to whom application should be made.

Discretion of Independent Town

In the town of Minetto, Oswego county, it is the practice that the head of a family requiring home relief shall (if he is able to work) first do a certain amount of work on the town roads under the direction of the town superintendent of highways, being then recompensed in grocery orders to the value of his earnings. This town states that *it claims no reimbursement* from the State for such relief, also that this plan is *not* applied to persons receiving aid which is *charged back* to other welfare districts. It asks the Attorney-General if it has a legal right to handle the matter in this manner.

If reimbursement were involved the answer would certainly be no, as work relief must be paid for in cash and we have ruled that under no circumstances will we reimburse for home relief when there is any evidence that work has been required in exchange therefor. However, if it is true that no reimbursement is claimed, the Emergency Act and rulings thereunder do not apply, and I can see no reason why a town paying the whole cost of its own relief may not impose such labor requirements as it pleases. This it is entitled to do under the common law.

Assignment of Relief Orders

It is asked whether merchants honoring home relief orders may assign said orders to wholesalers, and if such assignment, when properly audited, is subject to payment against home relief administered. The answer to this is unquestionably, yes. Retailers who furnish food for home relief on the basis of orders from the bureau may assign these to their wholesalers, and if they are properly audited and checked they are payable against such assignment to the wholesalers.

* * *

Payments for Central Index

There is no legal obstacle to the payment of public funds in compensation for the services of a central index which is privately conducted. As essential to the proper administration of public relief, the cost of the services of such an index is unquestionably a public purpose (L. 1931, ch. 798, as amended, section 1). Further-more, the rule of the Administration that "there shall be registration of all local applications in a local central index" has the force and effect of law (L. 1931, ch. 798, as amended, sections 27, 30, 31), and there is no requirement that such index be publicly conducted. Indeed, public authorities are not instructed to establish such an index unless none now exists. (Home Relief Rule.)

Compare section 80 of the Public Welfare Law, requiring public officials to cooperate whenever possible with any private agency whose object is the improvement of social conditions "in order that there may be no duplication of relief," and the specific sanction given in section 155 to "a central index or social service exchange for the purpose of preventing duplication and of coordinating the work of public and private agencies."

Reimbursement for Farm Labor

The current value of a day's work on a farm being stated at $1 and meals, certain farmers offer to pay 50 cents a day and meals for farm labor if the public authorities will pay an additional 50 cents a day to the farm laborers thus employed. We are asked what reimbursement the Administration could make on such a basis.

The Administration can reimburse only (a) for work relief, that is, wages paid by a municipal corporation for services on a public project, or (b) for home relief, that is, shelter, fuel, food, etc., furnished by a municipal corporation to persons or their dependents in their abode or habitation whenever possible, etc.

The employment of day labor by farmers on the ordinary farm work of the season could not possibly be a work relief project under the law. No cash payment by a municipal corporation to farm laborers would be home relief within the law. A municipal corporation could, however, pay, as home relief, the cost of any beneficiary's meals, and this would be reimbursable, and if good faith were observed all the way around the instant problem might be worked out on this basis, namely, that the farmer should pay in cash to the laborer the full value of a day's work, in addition to his board, and should receive in return from the local welfare officer the value of the laborer's board, on vouchers in due form, which would be reimbursable by the Administration. While I think this might be done, I cannot recommend it.

Use of Town Truck

While a town superintendent of highways may not carry out a program or buy or dispose of road machinery, equipment, etc., without the approval of the town board, it is provided, nevertheless, in section 49 of the Highway Law that, when purchased, "all road machines, stone crushers, power rollers, motor trucks, scarifiers, concrete mixers, or traction engines, tools and other implements owned either by the town or the highway districts therein, shall be used by the town superintendent in such manner and at such places in such towns as he shall deem best. They shall be under the control of the superintendent and be cared for by him at the expense of the town," and it would seem, therefore, that it is prima facie within the discretion of the town superintendent to refuse to allow the town truck to be used to transport work relief project employees.

On the other hand, it is provided in section 5 of the Emergency Act that the administration (and so, its agencies) "shall have the cooperation and assistance of each and every officer or employee of any State or local department, board or other agency," and in section 31 of the Emergency Act that a power, duty or restriction conferred, prescribed or imposed by any other law shall not be exercised or enforced during the emergency relief period if it is inconsistent with the Emergency Act. The attitude, therefore, of a town superintendent, who refuses to carry work project employees in a town truck, is unwarranted and contrary to the statute.

Use of Highway Machinery for County Projects

Where a county superintendent of highways refuses permission for the use of machinery in his custody for work upon county work relief projects, stating that he is not permitted by the State to use his equipment on any besides county highways, the answer is that highway machinery is the property of the county. The State Commissioner of Highways has made no rule affecting its use as suggested here and it is not one which would fall within his scope. The County Superintendent's power over highway machinery is purely one of custody, the ownership remaining in the county (Highway Law, sections 329-b, 16 and 17). The direction of the board of supervisors will be sufficient for the availability of the machinery in question. Attention is invited to section 5 of the

Emergency Relief Act which provides that the Administration (and also its agencies) ''shall have the cooperation and assistance of each and every officer or employee of any State or local department, board of other agency.'' Section 31 of the Emergency Relief Act places a restriction upon the exercise of any function which is inconsistent with the purposes of the act.

Fishing Licenses

The question of fishing licenses has again been raised, and the Administration wishes to repeat its previous ruling that fishing licenses may be issued as a relief allowance, thus making it possible, in some sections of the State, for welfare clients to supplement their food allowances.

The Administration will reimburse expenditures for fishing license fees issued to relief clients. It is, of course, necessary that those applying for such licenses be registered and properly investigated persons on relief lists. The county, village and town clerks, who act as agents for the Conservation Department, will, we are certain, cooperate in the issuance of these licenses.

Property Owner in Need

In regard to the right of a property owner, who is in need, to have relief, it was held in Albany v. McNamara, 117 N. Y. 168, that ''the possession of some property by a person does not always and necessarily preclude such person from a just claim for relief,'' and we have held repeatedly that, while the decision in such cases is within the discretion of the local welfare officers, such officers ought not to refuse relief to one who is in actual need, and is otherwise qualified, merely because such person is the owner of property which, perhaps, is non-productive.

Local Workers Not State Employees

In several instances it has come to the attention of the Administration that local employees whose salaries are reimbursed partially or in full by the Temporary Emergency Relief Administration are representing themselves as State employees.

The Administration wishes to inform you, and requests that you inform any person on your staff in the payment of whose salaries the Temporary Emergency Relief Administration is participating, that they are local employes and should not represent themselves as State employees.

Reimbursement on Community Store

In regard to a claim for reimbursement on bags and twine used in a community grocery store conducted by a public welfare commissioner, so long as this overhead charge is not raising the cost of groceries to the clients over and above what clients would normally have to pay, the claim would be warranted as part of the cost of furnishing the food, etc., as "home relief." The command to interpret the act "liberally" (section 29) would assuredly warrant this construction. It would only be where the cost of such items bears an unreasonable proportion relative to the cost of the merchandise furnished that any question might be raised. But that would also be true of the food itself.

On the other hand, salaries of employees in community stores must not be charged against overhead. The only way in which the State can reimburse on such salaries would be for the employees to qualify for work relief and be placed under a work project.

Borrowing Powers Unrestricted

Section 31 of the Emergency Act was meant to operate only where some provision of substantive law conflicted grossly with the Emergency Act, and it would have no bearing upon a city's general power of borrowing. Indeed, the borrowing powers conferred in section 10 of the Emergency Act are additional to and supplementary of all existing powers of borrowing, and there is nothing in the Emergency Act in derogation of such existing powers.

Garnishment

The provision in the Emergency Relief Law (section 16, as amended by L. 1932, ch. 567) that "all moneys paid to persons receiving the relief provided for and pursuant to this act shall be exempt from levy and execution under the laws of this State" protects from garnishment the entire relief allowance to relief cases, but does not apply to staff workers or administrative employees whose employment is not as to them a relief measure or whose compensation, if they are on a relief basis, is in excess of the relief standard.

Wages of workers on a relief status are not subject to attachment. (Section 16 of the Wicks Act as amended.)

Wages of workers on a non-relief status are, however, subject to attachment, as the C.W.A. provisions as to Federal checks are no longer applicable.

Amounts due vendors for materials, supplies and equipment are subject to liens and assignments. There are no legal provisions or regulations which make these different from any other vendors to a city.

A person employed under the T.E.R.A. at a salary of $19.50 a week is in the course of his employment forced to make certain disbursements in the regular order of his business. Thereafter he receives checks from the county reimbursing him for his disbursements made for the county. The question is are these expense checks attachable or are they to be treated in the same light as salary under the T.E.R.A. If the case is a relief case, reimbursement for expenses would be the same as a relief salary and so not attachable.

Town Lighting Bills

Where three towns have a municipal light commission which buys electric current at a low wholesale rate and retails the same to private consumers at a considerable profit to the commission and, in due course, to the towns, and the lighting bills of relief recipients are paid by the towns, and reimbursement thereof requested from the Relief Administration, I cannot advise that the T.E.R.A. is liable in such circumstances to refund any more than the electric current has actually cost the town, as otherwise we should be making reimbursement upon a profit which the town has pocketed. I can see, however, that with one commission operating in and for three towns it might be difficult to fix the exact cost to a particular town for a particular bill of lighting, and for this reason it would be permissible, on grounds of convenience, to make the reimbursement to a town upon the retail rate for current, provided the same is reasonable. But if in any case it is possible to fix the actual cost, the reimbursement should be based upon the sum found to have been actually spent.

Claims of Creditors

It is not evident how relief recipients can be brought into court for relief wages. "Work relief" wages are exempt from legal execution or garnishment. The case of "home relief" does not appear to enter into the problem. Nor can back bills representing debts incurred before the relief recipient became a relief case be charged to the municipality. We can't prevent creditors from procuring judgments for past debts. They may not execute these judgments against relief wages.

Restitution on State Projects

Money improperly paid out as wages on a State project should, if refunded, be returned to the State Comptroller for redeposit in the State funds available for State projects. Where instances of this character have appeared on claims reimbursed to city or county welfare districts, the practice, as indicated, of making a deduction on the next claim passed for such account has been correct. But where a State project is involved the rule is not the same.

Restitution of Local Relief

There are cases in welfare districts where excessive or improper relief has been furnished and/or where relief has been procured through imposition and misrepresentation. In such cases, welfare officials and local bureaus have often succeeded in forcing a refund from the recipients who were guilty of misrepresentation or those responsible legally for their support. In some cases these refunds represent 40 per cent reimbursement and in some 100 per cent reimbursement. Obviously, it should not be possible for the local community to have the full benefit. Hence, where such refunds have been procured, report should be made to the Temporary Emergency Relief Administration, and such amounts as represent Temporary Emergency Relief Administration funds may be deducted from future claims within the discretion of the Temporary Emergency Relief Administration.

Verification by Commissioner

The act provides (section 23) that "claims by a municipal corporation for payments by the State for home relief shall be made to the Administration through the agency representing it in such municipal corporation, which agency shall transmit to the Administration forthwith all claims with recommendations in respect thereto."

The agency representing the Administration for home relief in a county is the county commissioner of public welfare (section 8), unless such duties have been assumed by a joint bureau under Chapter 259 of the Laws of 1933. The county treasurer does not come into the legal picture except as receiving moneys from the State, for distribution (section 25).

Where, therefore, the county treasurer draws a warrant for a lump sum in favor of the welfare department, and all disbursements are made by the commissioner of public welfare, it would seem that the affidavit that claims have been paid might properly be made by the commissioner instead of by the county treasurer.

Audit by Local Bureau

Section 12 of the Relief Act provides that work relief compensation shall be paid in the manner fixed by the work bureau, whether it be daily or otherwise. The matter of audit is one which normally would be taken care of by each bureau of the municipal corporation for which the work bureau is acting. In view of the fact that section 23 of the Act provides that claims for reimbursement for home relief by a municipal corporation shall be made to the administration through the agency representing it in such municipal corporation, I do not see why the audit of the local bureau, if acceptable to the municipal audit officer, is not sufficient to warrant the payment of the bills so audited and so presented.

With regard to home relief claims presented to the State for reimbursement, the audit by the local bureau and/or the commissioner of welfare is subject to re-audit and approval by the Administration and thereupon is presented to the Comptroller of the State for his payment. It would seem that an arrangement might be worked out satisfactorily with the Comptroller and the city chamberlain to permit of payment at such times as may be provided for by the local work bureau.

Facilitating Wage Payments

There is no objection to permitting the New York City emergency work bureau to keep the time sheets of workers employed on work relief projects for the Department of Social Welfare, in New York City, paying such workers weekly in cash, and being reimbursed for the same by the department's check upon the sum allotted to it by the Relief Administration for that purpose, the reason for the arrangement being that it is difficult for persons in New York City, who have no bank accounts of their own, to cash checks for small amounts.

Advances by Citizens

The situation is unobjectionable in which two citizens lend their credit to a city by note, on the basis of which the city would be able to borrow from a bank in anticipation of a refund by the State to match the local funds, the purpose of the loan from the bank being to expedite the city's obtaining the money, the understanding being that the sum received from the State Comptroller on the basis of the State's appropriation should repay the loan made by the bank on the endorsement and credit of these two citizens.

Payment of City Salaries

We are asked as to the city of Lackawanna advancing moneys from relief funds to the city employees who are unpaid because of lack of city funds; the employees endorsing their checks to the relief bureau to be reimbursed if and when the city pays.

If the city should never pay, or if the pay should be unduly delayed, the relief funds would be used to pay the salaries of city employees and not relief workers. The question specifically raised is whether this privilege may be extended to policemen, firemen and, if need be, to school teachers.

It cannot be doubted that these unpaid city workers may be in need, but there is grave uncertainty that the Relief Administration is authorized to assist them. We can give only home relief, or work relief, or wages to clerks and assistants of public welfare commissioners and emergency work bureaus. Paying the salaries of city employees in the circumstances presented fits the definitions of none of these. It is a hard case, but one in which the remedy, I think, must be found elsewhere than in Relief Administration funds.

If, however, the difficulty is to be overlooked, I can see no reason why policemen and firemen, and school teachers also, should not be taken care of the same as any other city workers.

Attention, however, is invited to the fact that other cities, in such instances, have provided promises to pay which the employees may discount or use with merchants in the city in lieu of their own pay. I have no doubt that the checks, because of their being endorsed to the Relief Bureau, would be purchased or taken at discounts by merchants in the cities. The question is whether under such circumstances relief funds may be used when otherwise they could be utilized for families who are in dire need and cannot even obtain such promissory paper as the city itself might issue to its employees.

* * *

Withdrawal of County Appropriation

The power to appropriate money includes the power to repeal the appropriation except as such power is limited by contract rights which have come into existence upon the faith of the appropriation. Such rights are protected by Article I, section 10, paragraph 1, of the Federal Constitution.

The employment of public officers is not a contract. Leases or other agreements, involving property, would, however, have to be fulfilled in the absence of such a provision as protects the State in such circumstances, i. e., that the same shall be valid only to the extent that appropriations for the purpose exist.

Where the Relief Administration has advanced State moneys on the basis of local appropriations, such advances must be refunded if the appropriation fails. If a refund is impossible the local appropriation must continue in force to the agreed extent, and cannot, to that extent, be rescinded or withdrawn.

Salary Aid for Employees Only

The Administration's authority to contribute to the salaries of relief workers in local employ is limited to employees of commissioners (Emergency Act, section 19) and would not cover a contribution to the salary of a city or county commissioner as such.

＊　·

Repayment of Bank Loan

Where a loan is contemplated from the banks of the city of Fulton in order to provide for relief which will be reimbursed by the State on the basis of 100 per cent, in the form of 40 per cent reimbursement and 60 per cent out of the free funds as a direct grant, the bank raises the question that under section 16 the direct grant is to be made available for home relief and not to go into the general fund of the municipal corporation, into which said general fund the 40 per cent reimbursement goes. It would seem that what we are attempting to accomplish here is a definite amount of relief, and the State is willing to pay 100 per cent thereof, 40 per cent of which goes into the general fund and 60 per cent to be available for relief. As the relief has already been furnished by reason of the advance which the bank has made available in the form of a loan to the city, I am not so hypercritical of the actual technique or machinery involved as to believe that it is not feasible for this to be accomplished and for the bank to be repaid out of the reimbursement from the State. It would seem that the goal to be achieved well warrants the sweeping aside of such technical objections, and we may well say that the direct grant is made available for home relief when the bank is repaid for the money which the bank has made available, and which has been administered from home relief. If the bank is willing to trust the good faith of the municipal authorities to repay them, the Administration, I am quite sure, will find no objection to this machinery, and I feel, upon consideration, the State Comptroller's office will also agree.

＊　＊　＊

Labor on City Project

The Rotary club of a city has organized a plan of collecting, cleaning and repairing clothing, which is stored and distributed on orders of accredited relief agencies. Two workers are needed in addition to those supplied by the Rotary club. It is asked if the labor of these additional persons may be included as one of the city's work projects. If the city undertakes, as a city, by ordinance or official order, to supply these additional workers, which I think it may do, there being no question of aid to a private institution involved, their labor would be a valid charge under our law.

Home Relief All-Inclusive

Reimbursement by the Administration for home relief administration during the emergency period has been determined by the Administration to be all-inclusive. In other words, it is not limited to the relief only of those whose need is dictated by the unemployment of the employable members of the household. It may be noted, however, that section 2, defining home relief, specifically exempts widows' allowances, there defined as "allowances made to mothers for the care of dependent children."

Inclusive Language

Where a county work project resolution refers to "public buildings, lands, etc., of the county," its operation is not limited to buildings, lands, etc., which are owned by the county, but may extend to any public buildings, lands, etc., within the county.

Reimbursement for New Garments

In the operation of a work relief project for the collection, cleaning, repairing and distribution of used clothing, by means of which some 30,000 garments have been made available and large sums have been saved to the Bureau of Charities, it is necessary to buy certain new materials and in some cases new garments. It is asked by what method these purchases may be made a proper charge under home relief, in order that some reimbursement may be received from the Administration for the cost thereof.

If these garments go to regular home relief cases, registered as such, in accordance with indicated needs, the expense of the purchases referred to is clearly a legitimate charge upon home relief, and to obtain the usual reimbursement thereon would be only a matter of proper auditing, for which, in my opinion, it would be sufficient to produce vouchers for the purchases themselves and receipts from the recipients of the garments.

Partial Appropriations

It is asked if, in a case where a city contemplates starting work which will cost $40,000, it may appropriate $10,000 at a time, or if it must appropriate the full amount for all projects at the beginning. This is a matter for the Administration to determine, on the merits of each case. Before any project will be approved, the Administration must be satisfied with the financial arrangements proposed.

Automobile License Plates

In response to an inquiry as to the refusal of relief by a public welfare officer to persons who refuse to leave their automobile license plates with him, I may say that the discretion of a public welfare officer as to whether or not relief shall be granted is very nearly absolute under the law. "The circumstances which control the exercise of the power to grant relief to poor persons are so various in the case of different persons, and are so incapable of being defined by strict rules, that much must be left to the judgment and discretion of the officers." (Albany v. McNamara, 117 N. Y. 168.) "The question of the propriety of giving relief is confined to the discretion of the poor authorities." (Matter of Chamberlain, 73 Misc. 256.)

I think, moreover, the view is correct that there may be cases in which it would be a hardship amounting to confiscation to deprive of his car a man who could not make a living without it. For this reason I think it is wise not to commit the Administration to any rule in the premises. Local welfare officers, acquainted with all the circumstances, must be required to make the decisions in such instances. Where, however, they decide adversely to the applicant, there is no doubt of their legal and constitutional right to do so, and, short of a showing of discrimination or prejudice on their part, their judgment would be conclusive.

Use of Social Agencies

There can be no objection to sending cases from the office of a public welfare commissioner to local social agencies better equipped for case work and follow up, provided the work is under the supervision of the commissioner, the forms are kept in his office, and T. E. R. A. requirements are fully understood and met. Reimbursement may be claimed on public moneys expended for home relief through these agencies in this manner.

Teachers' Contributions

Teachers of a certain city are giving 1 per cent of their salaries toward unemployment relief. They would like to turn it in to the city commissioner's fund in order to receive the State reimbursement. The fund will amount to some $150 a month and will be spent for shoes, gloves, clothing, etc., for children in families known to the commissioner. If this contribution is made available to the city commissioner, and is expended, as indicated, for items which come within the definition of home relief, the contributing employee is entitled to reimbursement.

Employability

Employability is a question purely of fact which must be determined in each instance by the bureau to whom the individual applies for work relief. If it is deemed that he is incapable of performing the task which is available for work relief, then adequate relief should be furnished him through home relief.

*   *

Living in Adultery

A woman living in adultery with a married man cannot be considered "family" in the relief sense.

*   *

Divorced Men

There is no legal ruling to the effect that divorced or separated men must be treated as "single" and denied relief, to the hardship of their families. The said "ruling" probably refers to a general practice, warranted from experience, that such men do not support their families and hence family men should be preferred in work relief.

We have ruled however, that where such men voluntarily assign a proper portion of their wages to their dependent families and so authorize the Work Bureau to pay it—and where also a court order may so direct—this may be done.

*   *   *

Refusal of Single Men

With the approval of the Relief Administration, a rule may be adopted that the applications for work relief of single men without dependents will be refused, such cases to be referred to home relief instead. It would, however, be a matter for the Administration's determination as to policy.

Persons Without Dependents

It is asked whether or not individuals without dependents should be approved for work relief under the Emergency Relief Act, when they can obtain food and sleeping places through other agencies.

The act was intended to supply those who are unemployed and in need. The only requirements laid down are need and a two-year residence in the State. The extent to which the need exists and the question as to whether or not preference should be given to those with dependents, not otherwise provided for, is one which the individual bureau must in each case determine for itself. If the individuals are otherwise cared for and work relief can be furnished to others who are more in need, that is obviously a determination which calls for the exercise of the bureau's discretion. There is no prohibition, however, under the terms of the act which rules such individuals out of the work relief phase. They are entitled to apply for work relief and their applications must, of course, be considered together with the circumstances in each individual case.

Improper Local Expenditures

We are asked what responsibility the Administration has for the audit and expenditure of work relief funds that are not concerned with wages. The law defines work relief as wages. However, boards of supervisors and city councils make appropriations for work relief in two ways: either in appropriating money that is for wages, while the materials are provided by the city or county direct through other departments; or they make an appropriation to the work bureau for materials and wages. A case in point, for instance, is one in which expenses in the city of Ogdensburg for persons not members of the work bureau were charged to the material account of the work relief bureau, without the approval of the work bureau. Other expenditures, such as the repair of trucks, amounting to several hundreds of dollars, were authorized by the mayor without the approval of the work bureau.

In reply to the foregoing:

1. With regard to wage items, the power and responsibility of the proper audit of such expenditures resides absolutely within the T. E. R. A. by virtue of the fact that the wage items are the very essence of work relief as defined in the act.

2. With regard to the audit of the municipal accounts on materials furnished by the municipal corporation: in so far as such expenditures are not charged to the actual funds appropriated to the work relief bureau by the municipal corporation, no actual obligation rests upon the T. E. R. A. to ascertain the propriety of the expenditures of such materials furnished to the emergency work bureau by the municipal corporation. To place such an obligation of accounting responsibility upon the T. E. R. A. would be to impose upon the T. E. R. A. the practical responsibility for supervision of the auditing and accounting practices of the municipality, and would place an impossible accounting burden upon the Relief Administration.

3. With regard to expenditures for materials out of funds specifically appropriated for work relief project by the municipal corporation, and allocated to the work relief bureau, or allocated to the project and made available to the work relief bureau, and with regard to such expenditures as are not called for by the particular project or authorized by the work relief bureau, any such charged to the work relief funds are improperly so charged.

It should be the responsibility of the local work relief bureau to see to it that no such improper charges are made against the funds specifically appropriated to a work relief project. When called to the attention of the T. E. R. A., or when discovered by the T. E. R. A. through its field auditors, it becomes the duty of the T. E. R. A., which is responsible to the citizens of the State to see that their funds are not wasted when appropriated for work relief projects, to call the attention first, of the State Comptroller, Department of Municipal Audit and Control, to the said improper charges, so that cognizance may be taken thereof by the State Comptroller's office, which has the supervision of municipal accounts. Secondly, the attention of the municipal administration, to wit: the mayor or town board or city council or county board of supervisors, should be called to the alleged improper accounting practice, or improper charges made. The Administration may exercise its power to withhold approval of reimbursement to such municipal corporation in order that pressure might be brought to bear in the nature of an economic boycott until such practices are righted, and the proper steps taken to remedy that which was theretofore improperly done.

The Administration should not hesitate to use the power which it has by virtue of the funds which it is enabled to allow municipal corporations in order to see that the local funds are properly expended. Of course, where the work relief bureau itself has made such charges, the responsibility becomes centralized within its power to control at once.

Work Bureau a Fixture

A work bureau is intended to be a fixture for the duration of the emergency, with a membership not to be arbitrarily removed or added to. The only manner in which the bureau may be increased in size, therefore, would seem to be through the resignation or removal of its members and the appointment of a new body. In general, it has been the Administration's experience that small bureaus are best, with, of course, sufficient supervisory and clerical assistance to carry the burdens.

Subsistence Gardens

The Administration has established a policy of reimbursing on approved Subsistence Gardens projects for the express purpose of encouraging the development of individual gardens for relief clients, to help provide employment, supplement the food allowances and build up morale.

The Administration will reimburse public welfare districts at the regular rate (75%) on approved claims for seeds, fertilizers and some small garden tools. The Administration will make a similar reimbursement on approved work relief projects, involving such labor as may be necessary in the preparation of food subsistence gardens.

The entire garden promotion plan prepared by the municipality should be submitted to the Administration for its approval, and will be subject to the general supervision of our Agricultural Director.

* * *

Public Announcement of Local Committee Memberships

At its meeting on Monday, October 8th, the Administration ruled that nominations of persons to Emergency Work Bureau or Emergency Relief Bureau Committees as defined under Chapter 798 of the Laws of 1931 as amended shall be submitted to the State Administration for approval before public announcement is made locally by the Mayor or the Chairman of the Board of Supervisors who are the nominating officials.

This ruling is made for the purpose of preventing embarrassment to local officials and to persons who are nominated, in case the State Administration does not approve nominations as submitted.

\- \- \-

Reappointments Unnecessary

Considering the repeated extensions of the emergency period, no new appointment need be made of any person duly appointed for the duration of that period.

* * \-

2. RELATIONS OF COUNTIES AND CITIES

Under section 12 of the Emergency Act, as amended by L. 1933, ch. 259, a county and a city or cities within such county may merge all work relief (subd. 3) or all relief (subd. 4) within such county and city or cities. This enactment renders obsolete much that was previously written in interpretation of the relationships between city and county welfare districts under the Emergency Act.

Joint Relief Responsibilities, Consolidation of Agencies

Facts: Erie County has combined its relief activities under one Emergency Relief Bureau pursuant to §12 of Chapter 798 of the Laws of 1931, as amended by Chapter 259 of the Laws of 1933. The City of Lackawanna has joined this unit.

The County of Erie has also adopted a resolution under § 27 of the Public Welfare Law and operates on a county relief basis thereunder. Naturally this relief is governed by the consolidated committee under §12 of the Relief Act above cited.

The City of Tonawanda desires to join the County unit under

§27 of the Public Welfare Law and has so resolved. The Board of Supervisors of Erie County are doubtful of the operation of §27 of the Public Welfare Law in view of the provisions of the Relief Act.

Questions: 1: Is §27 of the Public Welfare Law operative during the period of the Relief Act's enforcement?

2: Is it necessary to establish a new bureau because Tonawanda desires to join the unit?

3: May Tonawanda thereafter withdraw under §27 of the Welfare Law and resume under the provisions of the Wicks (Relief) Act?

4: Does the present Board of the County Unit under §12 (Chapter 259) continue?

5: How are the expenditures chargeable?

Opinion: 1: The Emergency Relief Act (Chapter 798 L./1931 as amended) is not a permanent measure. Insofar as it may be applied consistent with the Public Welfare Law, it should be done. Only where patent conflicts appear should one give way to the other. The Relief Act by §12 as amended by Chapter 259 of the Laws of 1933 permits the consolidation of relief activities within the County. That has taken place. Erie County also has adopted the County Unit system under §27 of the Public Welfare Law. The provisions of §27 may continue to operate alongside of the provisions of §12 of Chapter 798 and the two should be read together and dovetail where such construction is reasonably possible.

2: It is unnecessary to establish a new bureau because Tonawanda seeks to become a part of the County unit under §27 of the Public Welfare Law. There is nothing inconsistent or improper in the County unit operating under §27 even though it be the creation of the Wicks Act. The same bureau operates whether Tonawanda joins under §27 of the Public Welfare Law or not.

3: Tonawanda's subsequent withdrawal under §27 by a repeal resolution presents another problem, perhaps not necessary to be presently answered. Under §27 of the Public Welfare Law it might be perfectly proper. A question of policy arises under the Wicks Act if in force when such a contingency arises. The consolidated unit might well be held by the Administration, and with good reason, to have been assented to by the City, and that the efficient administration of relief in the County as well as in the City called for such continued joint administration. There is no present need for anticipating that trouble.

4: The present Board under §12 as amended by Chapter 259 of the Laws of 1933 would, in view of the foregoing, continue to operate. There is no need for its interruption by the adoption of Tonawanda under §27 of the Public Welfare Law.

5: Under §10 of the Relief Act (Chapter 798 L. 1931) as amended by Chapter 567 of the Laws of 1932 and Chapter 259 of the Laws of 1933, the County in a County Welfare District may provide that the cost of relief may be reimbursed to the County out of the taxable property in the locality for whose benefit said appropriation was made. This was intended to enable the larger credit unit, the County, to bear the initial burden where circumstances made it imposible for smaller governmental units to borrow for relief. The provision for adding the expenditure to the tax burden of the place benefited is to safeguard against the argument made that one community might be shirking its duty and passing its load on to the neighboring units of government.

The operation of §10 as above construed is not affected by the joinder of Tonawanda to the County unit for relief purposes under §27 of the Public Welfare Law. The two provisions supplement one another and both may be jointly operative.

Rochester-Monroe County Problems

As a result of the consolidation of the Rochester and Monroe County Work Bureaus, pursuant to ch. 259, L. 1933, problems arose calling for prompt solution:

(1) *Joint Accounts:* Two governmental units, two public welfare districts, are here joining forces more effectually to meet the unemployment problem. Administrative payrolls, as well as other expenses of the joint bureau, must be met to which both are to contribute. Certain charter restrictions and accounting difficulties are raised which might encumber this desirable achievement which the Legislature intended to be accomplished by ch. 259, L. 1933.

Two possible solutions are visible, either one of which would seem to come within the permissive scope of the act and consistent with local financial autonomy—

(a) A joint account in the name of the Joint Relief Bureau, contributed to by both city and county units and disbursed by the bureau on its own vouchers; or

(b) An account in the county or city treasury to the extent of the share of each in the relief set-up, and to be drawn against by the Relief Bureau whose vouchers shall be recognized by the proper fiscal officers.

It would seem desirable and feasible for the entire account to be in one depository or fiscal control and subject to the withdrawal on vouchers of the new bureau. The accounts and expenditures are subject to audit, and the responsibility is clear. To compel the bureau to draw upon each fiscal agent in varying sums in the proportion each unit bears each item of expense would entail such difficulties as to defeat the whole purpose of the consolidation.

The funds should be made as readily available through consolidation as the relief is to be promoted by consolidation. There is no legal obstacle to the city appropriating and making available its share, through deposit with the county or in a joint account for the specific availability of the new work bureau.

(2) *Labor Costs:* There is nothing in the new set-up authorized by ch. 259, L. 1933, which prevents the payment of labor costs on city projects from welfare funds of the city. The internal accounting for labor and material costs between county and city fiscal departments may be readily adjusted to meet the problem which is here to be solved.

(c) *Material Purchasing Power—Local Restrictions:* Difficulties confront the joint work bureau in the matter of purchases, essential for the conduct of their tasks. The provisions of ch. 230, L. 1918, with respect to the purchasing control by the purchasing agent of the county and the commissioners of public buildings of the county board of supervisors, together with the city purchasing agent's powers over city purchases, render it next to impossible for the joint work bureau to accomplish speed and effective purchasing of materials. Their projects; administrative expense, etc.—all concern, or may concern, city, county or joint projects. Advertising, bids, conflicting authority of city and county purchase control officers would render uniform and smooth work impracticable. Delay, expense, shut down, confusion —all are readily foreseeable, if this be the legal procedure.

Ch. 259, L 1933, sec. 12, par. 3 reads:

> "Such joint emergency work bureau so established, shall have exclusive control of and be solely responsible for the administration of work relief in such welfare districts, etc."

To be effective such "exclusive control" must necessarily carry with it the power to make necessary purchases of materials, tools, etc., for the work projects. Local laws and/or ordinances conflicting, must give way and the Joint Emergency Work Bureau have the power to make such purchases without the need of the approval of the local purchasing agents. The accounts are audited and the bureau responsible for its actions.

(4) *Escrow Funds of Workers:* A plan is suggested whereby work relief wage earners work for a continuous period, earning sufficient for longer periods, including contemplated enforced unemployment and assign a portion of such earnings to the work bureau to be drawn by said wage earner during periods of enforced lay-off. Such arrangement is one voluntary between worker and work bureau. The plan has certain merits. When the worker has earned his wages, the State and city in paying said amounts have completed the government's obligation to pay. The work bureau assumes a voluntary and serious obligation in accepting the responsibility of administering the funds, undrawn though earned, for the remaining period of unemployment on the family budget allowance of the wage earner. Both city and county fiscal officers should pay the vouchers for the full amounts earned. The further operations, voluntary on part of worker and bureau, are subject to audit, etc., but when earned, there is no further need for fiscal control of disbursement by the municipal officer. The worker assigns an earned amount to the bureau which holds it

for his future withdrawal. These subsequent withdrawals need not have the fiscal officer's signature, etc. The bureau officials are responsible for their final disbursement.

The questions of signature on checks and signature machine control, etc., are for the bureau to determine.

Nature of Combination

It is asked if the Administration should make separate direct grants to Rochester and to Monroe county, addressing both to the Chairman of the Joint Work Bureau, or should Rochester and Monroe county be considered together, and the direct grant be made to cover both; that is, does chapter 259 make one public welfare district out of two, or does it simply combine them for purposes of administration?

The combination is for administrative purposes, although its consequences may be more extensive. The Administration could continue to allocate to the welfare districts, which are both administered by the joint bureau, or to both in one sum to be utilized as the joint bureau should direct. The problem should solve itself in the course of a short time under the new set-up.

Ontario County Situation

Since the statute provides that the cities of Geneva and Canandaigua shall be included in the county welfare district of Ontario county for the purposes of the Emergency Relief Act, it would be impossible for the board of supervisors of Ontario county to take any action which would throw back upon those cities the administration of emergency relief, without an enabling act of the Legislature.

City Workers on County Projects

A county work bureau may authorize city workers to be used on county projects. The administrative set-up should not become so confined to the geographic boundary of the city as to prevent the problem of the county as a whole being effectively worked out.

The share is a matter for them to work out locally.

Necessity of County Work Bureau

Where the town of Greenport, Columbia county, wishes to have its work relief administered by the work bureau of the city of Hudson, which it surrounds on three sides, the town contributing funds for the purpose, and there being no work bureau in and for the county because only in the town of Greenport is there any need for work relief in the county (outside of the city of Hudson), to the extent that the town of Greenport provides the funds for work relief within its limits, I can see no objection to the administration of the same by the work bureau of the city of Hudson. Yet such relief would not be reimbursable, and I can see no reason why, if there is relief needed in one town in the county, there should not be a county relief bureau to attend to it.

* * *

Joint City and County Project

The Administration has approved as a reimbursable work project the improvement of Sweeney street, North Tonawanda, at the joint expense of the city of North Tonawanda and the county of Niagara. It seems that section 320-m of the Highway Law authorizes the county to appropriate for this purpose, and under that section State aid pursuant to section 320-b is not available, thus eliminating the question of a reimbursement upon contributions already made by the State.

* *

3. FREE MILK

(See T.E.R.A. Bulletin 63, Sept. 26, 1934)

Provision of ''fresh milk free to undernourished and needy children, babies and nursing mothers'' under Chapter 874 of the Laws of 1934, amending Chapter 821 of the Laws of 1934. The following regulations governing the provision of ''fresh milk free to undernourished and needy children, babies and nursing mothers'' are hereby adopted.

A. *General Rules and Regulations*

1. *Scope*

   (a) Under section one of the Act as amended monies reappropriated by it shall be expended by the Administration for supplying fresh milk to undernourished and needy children, babies and nursing mothers ''through the agency of the public school system, other schools where the tuition is free, and public or private milk stations, maintained for the free disposition of milk, by direct purchase from dealers, by welfare commissioners, or local relief bureaus and delivery to the home where necessary, or through such other agency and in such other manner as may be approved by the relief administration, such service to be rendered under rules and regulations of the administration.''

(b) It is the purpose of the Act to provide an increased supply of fresh milk to needy persons. The Administration therefore rules that 100 per cent reimbursement for milk distributed under the rules and regulations as given below shall be paid only when the milk so distributed is in excess of the normal amount distributed by the district through the public and private relief agencies, and only to the extent that it is in excess of that amount.

The quantity of milk distributed by welfare commissioners and/or local relief bureaus in July, 1934, will be used as the first basis for computation. Such monthly reports on distribution and consumption are now being obtained. Milk supplied to a family listed as active on home or work relief lists shall not be charged to this fund. Only cases in which milk is the only item of relief and which are not active relief cases may be so charged. This does not exclude the provision of milk to children in a public school or clinic, and such children may include members of families on the active relief rolls.

To permit the use of this fund to purchase milk now provided through public and private relief agencies for active relief cases would be to defeat the purpose of the Act which is to provide an increased supply of milk to families in need, and therefore an increased consumption of milk for the State as a whole.

An ample supply of milk should be provided to all families on the active relief rolls through regular channels. The Administration reserves the right to withhold part or all of the free milk allowance where it is convinced adequate provision of milk for relief purposes has not been made.

2. *Procedure.* The following requirements shall govern the procedure to be followed in the distribution of fresh milk free to undernourished and needy children, babies and nursing mothers.

(a) *General.* Any existing milk station, clinic, free public or private school, free summer camp or recognized public health clinic equipped to distribute fresh milk and desiring to distribute milk shall make application to the Commissioner of Public Welfare in the district in which the station is located, or in the case of a summer camp, in the district in which the children reside. The agency making application shall present a written approval by the local Department of Public Health showing that all the State and local sanitary codes are being complied with, particularly regarding distribution of loose milk.

(b) *Certification.* The agency approved by the Commissioner of Public Welfare for the purpose shall agree to distribute milk only to children, babies, nursing and expectant mothers whose need is certified to them by some responsible person or organization, such as a public agency, an accredited private relief agency, hospital or clinic, an official of the Public Health Department, either a nurse or a doctor, a principal of a public or private school where the tuition is free, or other relief agency presenting information satisfactory to the Commissioner of Public Welfare, to the effect that the proposed recipients are in need of milk and are from families whose financial status is so near the borderline that they are unable to provide the extra milk required. In case children, babies or nursing mothers are given milk without referral by an accredited agency their need shall be passed on by a nurse or doctor assigned to the local Public Health Department, or certified to directly by the Commissioner of Public Welfare having jurisdiction.

(c) *Distribution.*

(1) *Local.* The distribution shall be in orderly fashion. The distribution center shall be inspected regularly by the Health Department to insure compliance with the local and State sanitary codes.
In case milk is to be supplied to children who are unable to consume it at the school or clinic, or in case the milk is to be supplied to babies and nursing mothers, delivery to the home may be authorized by the Commissioner of Public Welfare, upon recommendation to him from competent sources.

(2) *Summer Camps.* Milk may be issued to children at summer camps, provided the camps are entirely free, and that no charges are made for tuition, board, room, etc., where children come from homes which would qualify as a family in need of relief.

(d) *Source of Milk.* All milk purchased for distribution under the Act shall have been produced in dairies located on dairy farms within the State of New York and as to all or any part of that milk purchased for distribution in the City of New York, the Commissioner of Agriculture and Markets of the State of New York may specify to the Administration the persons, firms or corporations from whom same shall be purchased, in order to comply with the above provisions.

(e) *Identification*

(1) Children receiving milk at a distribution center shall be certified either by an identification card or by checking their names against a list which has

been approved by one of the persons or agencies listed under 2-(b) "Certification" of these rules and regulations. This identification is necessary for the proper accounting of claims presented to the municipality or State.

(2) For babies and nursing mothers for whom delivery of milk is made to the home, regular relief orders shall be issued, which order shall be the basis of claim for reimbursement and shall serve as sufficient identification.

(f) *Records.* The agency making application for distribution of free milk shall keep the following records if reimbursement is desired.

(1) Name, age and address of each recipient.

(2) Name and official title of the authorized agency and/or individual issuing the certification.

(3) Quantities of milk delivered to each child shall be based on the standard of one quart per day from this and other sources. In the case of a baby or nursing mother, the quantity supplied should be the amount recommended by the physician or nurse in charge of the case.

The above information shall be the basis for claim for reimbursement of 100 per cent for milk distributed to undernourished and needy children, babies and nursing mothers.

(g) *Claims.* Claims shall be presented in the form of a list of names of recipients, certifying agency and quantity of milk distributed and consumed during the calendar month; the total amount of milk distributed and reported as consumed shall check with the bills for milk as presented by the agency.

The municipal corporation, or town where home relief is a town charge, may submit such claims to the Temporary Emergency Relief Administration for reimbursement at 100 per cent. Such claims must be presented in separate forms apart from other claims.

(h) *Agencies not eligible.* Agencies which distribute free milk conditional upon membership in a club, settlement house or private agency shall not be eligible for participation in the T.E.R.A. milk fund established by this Act. (Chapter 874, Laws of 1934.)

* * *

246. *RULES GOVERNING THE PURCHASE OF MILK BY LOCAL DEPARTMENTS OF PUBLIC WELFARE*

The State Department of Agriculture and Markets, through its Division of Milk Control has established certain rules governing the purchase of milk and/or cream in New York State. There has been some confusion in the minds of both Commissioners of Public Welfare and the milk dealers as to the exact intent of some of these rules. For the above reason an official interpretation of the relevant rules was requested from the Division of Milk Control.

Under date of September 11, 1934, Mr. Kenneth F. Fee, Director of the Division of Milk Control of the State Department of Agriculture and Markets, sent the following communication to the Administration:

"I am writing to inform you of the interpretation placed by this office upon Paragraphs 11 and 12 of Official Order No. 80, promulgated by the Commissioner pursuant to the authority conferred upon him in Chapter 126 of the Laws of 1934, relating to milk control. This interpretation is as follows:"

(Re Paragraph 12 of Official Order No. 80 which reads:

"12. The prices fixed by this order shall not apply to milk or cream sold to hospitals using 40 quarts or more per day or to milk or cream purchased by the state or to any municipality; provided that the price charged for such milk or cream is not less than the appropriate class price required to be paid producers for such milk.")

"No fixed retail price has been established to be charged for milk and cream sold to the State or any municipal agency purchasing milk and/or cream for use in institutions or for distribution among the needy, provided no charge is made for such milk and/or cream either directly or indirectly.

"However, for all milk and/or cream so utilized, producers must be paid the Class 1 and Class 2-A price respectively, and the dealer must charge the agency purchasing the milk at least these respective prices. It is also expected that the dealer will make an additional charge to defray costs of transporting and processing.

(Re Paragraph 11 of Official Order No. 80 which reads as follows:

"11. In case of milk sold to or on account of welfare and charitable agencies and eleemosynary institutions, the minimum prices shall be the prices required to be charged by milk dealers to stores." Note: This does not apply to Departments of Public Welfare.)

"Milk and/or cream sold to *private* welfare and charitable agencies and eleemosynary institutions may not be sold at prices lower than the minimum dealer to store prices prescribed by the official orders promulgated by the Commissioner, and in the case of such milk also, the appropriate class price must be returned to producers."

4. VETERAN RELIEF; CHILD WELFARE; OLD AGE RELIEF

Relief to Sick and Disabled Veterans

(See Department Letter No. 4)

The Legislature in its 1934 session set aside $200,000 from State monies appropriated for the use of the Temporary Emergency Relief Administration to be spent for the relief of sick and disabled veterans under the direction of the Bureau for Relief of Sick and Disabled New York Veterans.

This organization operates under Article 1-A of the Military Law under the following general limitations and requirements:

The Bureau is under the supervision of the Adjutant General of the Division of Miliary and Naval Affairs and subject to the control and direction of the government. The Adjutant General appoints such employees as he deems necessary, giving preference to those persons who served honorably in the Army, Navy, or Marine Corps of the United States during the World War, and who at the time of their entry into such service were residents of the State of New York.

The Adjutant General is also authorized to appoint, and may at pleasure remove, Veterans' Relief Commissioners in each assembly district. Such Commissioners are given the responsibility of investigating all applicants for relief under this article, and of determining the amount of relief to be given within the limits prescribed. Relief is granted by the Veterans' Commissioners in cash from sums of money which are deposited with him from time to time by the Adjutant General.

All veterans of the Military or Naval Service of the United States, except those dishonorably discharged, discharged without honor, or discharged for the good of the service, may file an application for relief, provided they actually resided in the State of New York on May 2, 1933, as well as at the time of making the application, and were in service at least sixty days during the period of the World War. To be eligible, such Veterans must further show that they are suffering from a sickness or disability of at least ten per cent, incurred during the war period or prior to their first discharge thereafter. Applicants must also show that at the time of seeking relief they have been out of regular employment for a period of fourteen days, and that they are actually in need of such assistance.

Each veteran whose claim is allowed by the Veterans' Relief Commissioner shall receive, in the case of a person without dependents, the sum of $30 per month, and, in the case of a person having dependents, the additional sum of $10 per month for a dependent wife or widowed mother, and $5 per month for each other dependent, the total amount allowed for dependency in no case to exceed $30 per month. Should an applicant, however, be receiving aid from the United States Government, amounting to the total sum allowable under this act, he shall not be entitled to receive relief from this bureau. Should the amount paid an applicant by the Government be less than the sum herein allowable, he shall receive the difference between the amount paid him by the Government and that to which he would be entitled under this article.

In the event that a veteran, entitled to receive aid from this bureau shall be maintained in a hospital, other than at his own expense, his dependents shall receive the dependent allowance herein provided.

For the purpose of this article, wives, children and widowed mothers, with whom the veteran is living, are presumed to be dependents.

An applicant whose claim is rejected by a Commissioner, or who is not satisfied with the amount allowed, may appeal to the Adjutant General, who shall then have power to determine the matter and fix the amount, if any, to be paid.

The relief allowances granted by the Relief Commissioners are limited by the funds available. The policy followed is to spread the relief over a large number of cases in small amounts, rather than to give the maximum permitted by the law in fewer number of cases.

In consultation with the Bureau for Relief of Sick and Disabled New York Veterans, the Temporary Emergency Relief Administration has agreed to make available to the Bureau and to its Veterans' Relief Commissioners the services of local home relief offices in assisting with investigation of veterans requesting aid from the bureau; to make available to the Veterans' Relief Commissioners any records in home and work relief bureaus of veterans making such application; to clear all applicants to the Veterans' Relief Commissioner through the local central index or social service exchange; and to cooperate with the Veterans' Relief Commissioners in every way possible.

The Bureau has agreed to request its Relief Commissioners to use the facilities so provided, and not to grant relief to a veteran without first clearing the name through the central index and determining the extent of such other relief as the veteran may be securing from other public or private agencies.

The Administration requests that Commissioners of Public Welfare get in touch immediately with the Veterans' Relief Commissioners in their districts and arrange conferences to set up a cooperative procedure for the benefit of both.

A thorough understanding between both organizations should result in a more effective use of the money made available to the Bureau for Relief of Sick and Disabled New York Veterans, and should be of great assistance to local home and work bureaus in the use of the money on those cases which for certain specific reasons are better cared for in this way than through regular home or work relief.

Veteran Relief in General

Under chapter 646 of the Laws of 1933, amending the Wicks Act, Veterans' Relief was made reimbursable. This was effective as of May 1, 1933, and the Act now reads as follows:

"Home Relief means shelter, fuel, food, clothing, light, necessary household supplies, medicine, medical supplies, relief to veterans under existing laws, and medical attendance furnished by a municipal corporation or a town, where home relief is a town charge, to persons or their dependents in their abode or habitation whenever possible, and does not include old age relief or allowances made to mothers for the care of dependent children or hospital or institutional care."

Pursuant to the above section, the Administration will allow reimbursement on Veterans' Relief Claims if submitted according to the following rules and regulations:

1. The Administration will deal directly with and hold the commissioner of public welfare responsible for the proper administration of Veterans' Relief under the terms of the Wicks Act and the rules and regulations pursuant thereto.

a. However, since it was not the intention of the Legislature, nor is it of this Administration, to abolish the administration of relief as provided for under sections 117 and 118 of the Public Welfare Law, the commissioner of public welfare may permit the continuance of the administration of Veterans' Relief as provided for in sections 117–118, subject to conformity with T.E.R.A. rules and regulations.

[Note: Relief granted to veterans in the form of cash as permitted under sections 117–118 of the Public Welfare Law was not originally reimbursable under our Act. Chapter 65 of the Laws of 1934, however, has added to the definition of home relief the provision that until February 15, 1935, home relief may be given wholly or partly in cash, subject to rules and conditions specified by the Administration.]

The rules and regulations of the Administration are to be interpreted according to the above ruling.

2. The commissioner of public welfare will be responsible for proper investigations, administration and submission of claims to T.E.R.A. whether relief to veterans in the given public welfare districts is administered through veterans' organizations or through the office of the commissioner of public welfare.

3. Close coordination between veterans' relief and other home relief administered through Public Welfare Departments will therefore be required. The following rules should be carefully followed:

a. Equalization of family budgets and uniformity in systems of accounting is required within each welfare district for all relief administered under T.E.R.A. It will therefore be necessary to revise family budgets and accounting systems in veterans' relief organizations to conform to local policies and to T.E.R.A. requirements.

b. Forms now in use in the home relief department must be used in veterans' relief. Veterans' orders and claims must be stamped with a large stamp indicating "Veterans' Relief." Claim Sheets Form No. 7, Town Sheets Form No. 6, Intermediate Sheets No. 5, and all vouchers must therefore indicate "Veterans' Relief." Present relief order forms, if made out in duplicate, or other forms now in use, may be used if stamped "T.E.R.A.," in addition to "Veterans' Relief," subject to the approval of T.E.R.A.

c. Veterans' relief cases must be numbered serially. However cases which have been included in the serial numbers of home relief cases must be marked "Veterans' Relief." All veterans' relief cases must be kept together in a separate file.

d. Claims for reimbursement for veterans' relief must be made separately.

e. Separate reports will be required for veterans' relief including information as to numbers of individuals and families and amounts of relief granted. Forms for these reports will be mailed to you immediately.

4. Approved claims for veterans' relief will receive the statutory 40 per cent reimbursement under the Act. Reimbursement will be paid to the city or county fiscal officer, and must be credited by him to the General Fund.

5. Further information will be sent out from the Administration as is necessary. The Field Representative of the T.E.R.A. for your district is available to you for assistance in any questions arising concerning administration of veterans' relief under T.E.R.A.

⊦ * *

Veteran Relief by Welfare Commissioner

It is asked whether the Relief Administration may continue to reimburse veteran relief administered by the welfare commissioner when a joint veterans' committee exists and has no funds.

The answer to this is that where the said relief is being administered as a temporary measure, the Administration may reimburse, but the administration of veteran relief by a joint committee, when duly established under the provisions of Article 14 of the Public Welfare Law, should be insisted upon by the Administration as its duty under the definition of relief to veterans, now part of the law.

The public welfare commissioner may not justifiably continue to administer relief to veterans through his sole agency, where a joint veterans' committee is established for that purpose pursuant to law. The administration of veteran relief under T. E. R. A. rules and regulations may be insisted upon but there is no necessity, now that veteran relief is reimbursable, for the segregation of specific applications for veteran relief as such. The administration of veteran relief, however, should be by the agency created by law for that specific purpose.

Whether or not there should be given to a representative of a State veterans' organization certain facts or statistics with relation to veteran relief in a particular locality is a question which the Administration should determine as a matter of policy. There is no compulsion that such facts be disclosed to such an individual.

Explanatory Statement

The Administration ruled that beginning July 1, 1933, home relief to veterans would be reimbursed at the same percentage as other home relief claims. This includes gardens for veterans.

The percentage of reimbursement granted for a given public welfare district will be based on the total needs of the district including veterans' relief, and the total resources of the district, including veterans' funds available.

Claims for reimbursement for veterans' relief, both home and work, should be submitted separately according to instructions heretofore given. Veterans' cases must be separated from other home and work relief cases, so that the Administration may have an accurate picture of the total cost of veterans' relief in each welfare district. This applies regardless of the local form of administration of veterans' relief.

The Administration takes this opportunity to call your attention to reports that have been received to the effect that in certain instances Commissioners of Public Welfare have interpreted their authority to approve claims for reimbursement of veterans' relief as implying the eradication of the administration of veterans' relief by veterans' organizations.

The amendment to the Wicks Act permitting reimbursement of veterans' relief specifically states that it is veterans' relief "under existing laws," meaning section 117–118 of the Public Welfare Law. The authority of the welfare commissioner to check the compliance with the Temporary Emergency Relief Administration's standards and rules on the part of the veterans' organizations, does not contemplate the denial of the function of administering veterans' relief by veterans' organizations.

Welfare commissioners and veterans' agencies should work out an harmonious plan for administering veterans' relief in compliance with the Temporary Emergency Relief Administration's regulations and in conjunction with the provisions of the Public Welfare Law. The field representative of the Temporary Emergency Relief Administration is available to assist in setting up workable machinery.

No Differentiation Permitted

It has come to the attention of the Administration that in some districts there is a differentiation between veterans' relief and other relief.

Under the Wicks Act and the rules and regulations pursuant thereto there can be no differentiation because of race, religion, creed, color, non-citizenship, political connections or activities or membership in a special group.

There can be no reason for a difference in the standard of relief granted to one group as compared with another group. Where such differences exist, immediate steps must be taken to create uniformity.

Undertaking to Be Filed

Under the statute (Public Welfare Law, section 118), the filing of an undertaking is mandatory before veteran relief can be granted. In a town, the undertaking must be in an amount considered sufficient by the supervisor of the town, and is to be filed with the town clerk, along with the notice of intention.

* * *

Single Committee Required

There must be a single joint relief committee for veteran relief in the city of Rochester, and the two or more veteran agencies now administering such relief must get together and conform to the law.

* * *

Mothers' Allowances

The following statement of the Administration's policy on the inclusion, in request for reimbursement, of cases which are probably eligible to receive mother's allowance, has been mutually agreed upon by the Department of Social Welfare and the Temporary Emergency Relief Administration:

"There has been considerable misinterpretation regarding the status of potential mothers' allowance cases and of those receiving allowances from the board of child welfare.

"Under the Wicks Act, home relief does not include allowances made to mothers for the care of dependent children, and by inference does not include cases eligible for mothers' allowances. The type of relief afforded to mothers with dependent children under this law is in accordance with the best principles of social policy, and should be encouraged throughout the State. Should the Administration permit reimbursement of claims for relief given to cases eligible for mothers' allowance, it might seriously affect the operation of the Mothers' Allowance Law, and result in making this law less effective.

"The Administration feels that its policy should be to encourage the granting of relief under the Mothers' Allowance Law. It is recommended that possible eligible cases be referred to the board of child welfare for determination of eligibility.

"However, under the Mothers' Allowance Law, assistance is not provided for older children who, under normal conditions, would be employed, but who at the present time represent an extra burden which the family cannot care for by means of the allowances granted by the board of child welfare. The Administration wishes, therefore, to inform local home and work bureaus that it is to grant permissible additional assistance for the support of such older children where the total income is not sufficient to provide for them. Additional assistance for support of older children in mothers' allowance families is therefore reimbursable from or by the Administration.

"In auditing of home and work relief claims, the Administration's auditors are instructed to pay particular attention to the cases which formerly have been or are now eligible to receive mothers' allowance. The Administration will question allowing reimbursement for cases eligible for mothers' allowance in counties where the board of supervisors has not provided funds for this purpose, or where drastic reductions have been made in these appropriations."

— — —

Public Welfare Law and T. E. R. A.

In respect of veteran relief and allowances made to mothers for the care of dependent children, we are asked (a) how to find out if persons are entitled to such relief, and if so, if they are receiving it; (b) the duty of commissioners of public welfare in the premises; (c) can the furnishing of such relief be compelled; and (d) if such relief is granted from emergency funds, will such emergency relief be reimbursable under the Emergency Act.

I. Veteran relief. Veteran relief is governed by Article 14 (sections 117–121) of the Public Welfare Law. It is essentially the same as ordinary poor relief, except that it is administered through veteran organizations, with the purpose that indigent veterans and their families shall not be placed on a level with common paupers and shall be kept out of and away from the ordinary poor relief system. Boards of supervisors, town boards and the appropriating bodies of cities have the same obligation to make appropriations and raise money for veteran relief in the same manner as for the care and relief of other persons in need of public relief and care (Public Welfare Law, sections 43, 117), and such legislative bodies shall determine the method by which the veteran relief fund shall be drawn upon by the organizations authorized to dispense veteran relief (section 117). These organizations are certain well known societies of veterans, specified in the statute, operating through their relief committees or the commander and quartermaster or treasurer of each post, garrison or camp.

In the city of New York the commissioner of public welfare includes in his annual estimate the amount necessary for veteran relief, which is then to be placed in the budget, and relief may be paid directly to the beneficiaries by the commissioner, on written recommendations signed by the relief committee, the commander and the quartermaster or treasurer of a post, garrison or camp, out of a cash fund to be placed by the comptroller under the commissioner's control, such fund to be replenished upon presentation of properly receipted recommendations for amounts paid out. Or the comptroller may, in his discretion, authorize a post commander to furnish such relief, and may pay the amount by warrant to such commander, taking this receipt in duplicate therefor and forwarding one of the receipts to the commissioner of public welfare. (Section 119.)

In the city of Buffalo there may be three joint relief committees, representing respectively the civil war, the Spanish war and the world war veteran posts. In all other cities, except New York, where there is more than one post, there is one joint relief committee representing all the posts and including one member from the auditing board of the city. Elsewhere relief is to be applied for or recommended by a veteran organization located in the town, city or county where the person in need of relief resides, or, if there is none where he resides, by such organization in the nearest town, city or county. Except in cities of more than 100,000 inhabitants, the commander of any post undertaking to administer veteran relief must file with the clerk of the town, city or county a notice of such intention, with an undertaking approved by the city or county treasurer or town supervisor. Annually, during October, such commander must file a similar notice with the city, town or county clerk, with a detailed statement of relief requested and granted during the preceding year. This information is not to be divulged, except as provided by law. In cities of more than 100,000 inhabitants the notice and statements are to be filed with the city comptroller and the undertaking is to be approved by him. In such cities the public welfare official shall include in his annual estimate the amount necessary for veteran relief and the same shall be included in the budget. Monthly, in such cities, post authorities or relief committees submit to the public welfare official vouchers in duplicate, on blanks supplied by the comptroller, for all relief granted, with the recipients' receipts, and if the welfare official finds that the money has actually been expended he approves the vouchers and forwards one copy to the comptroller for payment. (Section 118.) Elsewhere the officers of a town, city or county having jurisdiction to raise and appropriate money for the relief of the poor have the duty to provide money for veteran relief, to be administered by veteran organizations, exercising, however, their judgment and discretion as to the amount. The money is to be granted on written application, and by such method as the legislative body shall determine. (Sections 117, 118.)

Veteran relief is available for the families of veterans, including dependent widowed daughters and for the families of deceased veterans. No person eligible to veteran relief shall be committed to a public home. (Section 117; Penal Law, section 1866.)

Similar relief for women nurses is provided for in section 121, and will be paid for by the State. The burial of veterans and nurses and their families, and the provision of headstones for their graves, is a county charge under section 120, and must not be in a plot used exclusively for the burial of poor persons. (Penal Law, section 1866.)

In answer to the specific questions presented: (a) veteran post commanders or relief committees will furnish information as to relief granted to veterans; (b) in New York City the commissioner of public welfare estimates the need for veteran relief and grants relief out of funds provided by the comptroller, accounting to the comptroller therefor; in other cities of more than 100,000 inhabitants he likewise estimates the need, and audits the claims of veteran organizations for reimbursement when presented to him; elsewhere he has no duty except as it is imposed upon him by the legislative body which provides the money; (c) the duty to make adequate appropriations for veteran relief is fixed by law (Public Welfare Law, sections 43, 117), and action in regard thereto may be compelled by mandamus, but the judgment and discretion of the local authorities as to the amount is final, and mandamus will not be sustained to compel them to appropriate any amount which a veteran organization may apply for (People v. Rome, 136 N. Y. 489; People v. Meyers, 161 App. Div. 315); (d) under L. 1933, ch. 646, veteran relief under existing laws is brought within the definition of home relief, and is therefore reimbursable.

II. Child welfare allowances. The granting of allowances to mothers for the care of dependent children is governed in most of the counties of the State by Article 7-A (sections 148 to 154) of the General Municipal Law, first enacted in 1915 (ch. 228) and considerably strengthened in 1920 (ch. 700). Dutchess county (L. 1917, ch. 354) and Suffolk county (L. 1921, ch. 696), have special acts of the same general purport, providing, however, for responsibility for the care of all dependent children in these counties, in addition to mothers' allowance work, and in Westchester county a special set-up authorizes mothers' allowances through a bureau of the commissioner of public welfare, instead of through a board of six appointed by the county judge with the county commissioner of public welfare a member ex-officio. In New York City the board is appointed by the mayor and has ten members, not including the commissioner of public welfare. Boards appointed in Clinton, Orange, Schenectady, and Sullivan counties are unable to grant allowances for lack of appropriations, and no boards have been appointed in Delaware, Fulton, Hamilton, Otsego and Schoharie counties. A supplementary plan, with additional jurisdiction, and somewhat better conceived than the original act, was made available in Article 7-B in 1922 (ch. 546) for counties outside of New York City, except Dutchess and Suffolk, which cared to adopt it, but it has been utilized only by Cayuga county.

Under Article 7-A a county board of child welfare is authorized to grant an allowance to any mother of dependent children, under circumstances and conditions specified in the statute. It is expressly provided in Article 7-B that all the powers and duties of public welfare officers exercising like functions with respect to dependent children are vested solely in the board of child welfare. (Section 156, subd. j.)

Allowances granted by the board under Article 7-A "shall be paid out of moneys appropriated by the local authorities for such purpose, or otherwise available by the board for such purpose; such local authorities shall appropriate and make available for the board of child welfare and include in the tax levy such sum or sums, as in their judgment, may be necessary to carry out the provisions of this article" (section 153, subd. 5), and this language is repeated in section 154, with an additional provision for emergency appropriations and for borrowing when there is insufficient money in the treasury to meet appropriations. Originally such appropriations were merely authorized, and the money was to be available "if any" were deemed needed, but the duty was made mandatory in 1920 (ch. 700), the statute nevertheless retaining the provision that "no board of child welfare shall expend or contract to expend under the provisions of this article or otherwise, any public moneys not specifically appropriated as herein provided."

In response to the specific inquiries, (a) emergency relief authorities will be able to learn from the county board of child welfare whether the mother of any child under the age of 16 years is receiving a child welfare allowance or is entitled to the same; (b) in New York City the commissioner of public welfare has no specific duty in connection with such allowances; elsewhere in the State that officer is ex-officio a member of the child welfare board and has one vote on all questions coming before it; (c) consideration and action by a board of supervisors upon the question of appropriating money for child welfare allowances can be compelled by mandamus, but should the board of supervisors, in its discretion and judgment, determine that no sum of money is needed to carry out the provisions of the statute, such determination is final; (d) in the counties where child welfare appropriations have been refused by the board of supervisors, and child welfare boards duly appointed are therefore inoperative for lack of funds, there is evident a purpose to nullify the plain intent of the Legislature, by continuing to support dependent children of widowed mothers through the processes of ordinary poor relief. We have held, therefore, in General Ruling No. 41, under date of December 30, 1931, that, notwithstanding that relief administered in such form was not technically an "allowance made to mothers for the care of dependent children," the Administration would make no reimbursement out of emergency funds for moneys expended in such palpable evasion of the statute. Counties which have fulfilled their duties in this respect can have no reimbursement, and delinquent counties should not profit by their own fault. This rule should be adhered to. Moreover, since the statute provides especially (section 154) for emergency appropriations for child welfare purposes and for borrowing child welfare funds when the treasury is unable to supply the same, there is no reason why reimbursement should ever be asked of the Administration in respect of expenditures for purposes falling within the mothers' allowance laws.

Additional Child Welfare Payments

Child welfare boards are governed by Article 7-A, sections 148–155, of the General Municipal Law, except in Cayuga county (Article 7-B), Dutchess county (L. 1917, ch. 354), and Suffolk county (L. 1921, ch. 696). The purpose of this statute was to take the persons entitled to relief thereunder entirely out of the operation of the Poor Law, in the administration of the funds available thereunder. An allowance, however, is not in any case to exceed the amount it would be necessary to pay to an institutional home for the care of the child or children involved (section 153, subd. 5), and where relief is required beyond such sum it would seem that it would have to come through the public welfare officer, and in such case, not being an allowance under the Child Welfare Law, such relief might be reimbursable. In this view medical care for child welfare families, over and above the child welfare allowance, would be reimbursable when paid by public welfare officers.

Counties Not Cooperating

The county of Schenectady does not operate under the Child Welfare Law, and widows, etc., with dependent children, are provided for in that city and county in the same way as ordinary cases of poor relief. The local authorities have been under the impression that relief thus granted to such widows, etc., was not reimbursable under the Emergency Relief Act and therefore omitted such cases from their first claims for reimbursement. Later, however, they asked if they were not entitled to such reimbursement.

The statute (section 2) provides that home relief, for which reimbursement may be made, "does not include old age relief or allowances made to mothers for the care of dependent children."

The Administration's Rules Concerning Home Relief amplify this language (Rule 5) to exclude "old age relief and allowances to mothers for the care of dependent children where the obligation to furnish such relief is expressly imposed by law upon the municipal corporation."

It was evidently the purpose of both the statute and the rule that there should be no reimbursement for relief of those special kinds which are provided for by statute, apart from ordinary poor relief. The language employed, however, seems to afford an opportunity to quibble, as care given in the form of ordinary poor relief is not an "allowance made to mothers for the care of dependent children," nor is it the fact that a county, under Article 7-A of the General Municipal Law, must perforce support its widows, etc., with dependent children, in the manner set forth in that statute. On the contrary, although Child Welfare Boards have been appointed in Clinton, Orange, Schenectady, and Sullivan counties, they are unable to function because the supervisors will not grant them any money, and no board has been appointed in Delaware, Fulton, Hamilton, Otsego and Schoharie counties.

Nevertheless, the situation appearing to be that Schenectady county has failed to take advantage of an exceptionally humane and well considered statute, a main purpose of which was to take the support of dependent children entirely outside of the operation of the Poor Law, it would seem to me to be a great injustice to the other counties which have not neglected their opportunities in this respect to hold that, by reason of such inaction, Schenectady county could become entitled to a reimbursement which the Legislature never meant to have and which the other counties cannot get.

In my opinion the first impression of the Schenectady authorities, that relief granted to widows, etc., with dependent children, is not reimbursable out of the emergency funds, ought to be confirmed by the Administration.

) *

Attempted Evasions

We are informed that certain counties are seeking to economize by forcing child welfare cases into the welfare commissioners' relief program. The effect of this is to abolish the child welfare boards and destroy the effective working of this specialized form of normal relief to dependent children in the form of mothers' allowances.

One can understand the natural desire of supervisors to obtain a reimbursement for home relief by throwing the mothers' allowance cases into the home relief program. This however, contravenes the spirit and the letter of chapter 798, Laws of 1931, as amended. Mothers' allowances for dependent children are specifically excepted from the relief act by virtue of the fact that it is not the type of need which is created by the unemployment emergency. It is a normal burden to be borne by the local community which should be met in its fullest extent in accordance with the Child Welfare Law, which has been passed for that specific purpose. It would not be proper for the Emergency Relief Act to be utilized as a medium for destroying the specialized work of the child welfare boards and the salutary effect of the administration of a specialized relief to those cases in order that counties should obtain a reimbursement for those cases.

Consistent with the policy of the Administration therefore, if it is determined that normal mothers' allowance cases are being thrown into the home relief program of the welfare commissioners, those cases should be eliminated from the reimbursable claims made. Counties must be impressed with the necessity of taking care of the particular needs of those types of relief not called for by the emergency and a false economy should not be invoked to avoid the effective administration of a salutary form of relief.

It would seem in this instance that the Department of Social Welfare and the T. E. R. A. could cooperate and that by their combined influence departments of public welfare throughout the State should be able to see to it that counties meet the burden of mothers' allowances as intended by the Child Welfare Law. They must also not be permitted to misinterpret this view and misconstrue it as a discrimination of the T. E. R. A. against the dependent children. It is merely a statement of the policy of the law as expressed by the Legislature to impress upon the counties the seriousness of their undertaking the permanent burden of mothers' allowances as entirely distinct from relief made necessary by the unemployment emergency.

Discretion of Board

It is asked whether the city of Beacon can force the Dutchess county board of child welfare to accept all eligible cases, it appearing that the board, which is authorized by special law and by regulation of the T. E. R. A. to administer relief to adults in a destitute family which contains a child under the age of 16 years, has adopted a policy of not giving allowances in families in which there is only one eligible child.

The Dutchess county board of child welfare operates under chapter 354 of the Laws of 1917, section 5 of which statute provides that the board shall have the powers and duties specified therein as to destitute, neglected, delinquent and defective children under 16 years of age "where the welfare of such children requires," and it is further provided (section 5, subd. 5, paragraph (f)), that the board is only to administer relief in their homes to the destitute parents of children under 16 years of age "when such relief is required to insure such care to the children as the board deems necessary."

I think these provisions leave it to the discretion of the board whether in any case the welfare of a child requires it to exercise its powers and also whether it would be necessary to grant relief to adults in order to insure the care deemed necessary for children. In this view the board could make a rule which could hardly be successfully attacked unless it could be demonstrated to be unreasonable, unjust and discriminatory.

Waiving Jurisdiction

The provision in chapter 354 of the Laws of 1917, which is the special statute under which the Dutchess county board of child welfare operates, that such board may administer relief in their homes to the destitute parents of children under 16 years of age when such relief is required to insure such care to the children as the board deems necessary, is permissive, in my opinion, and not mandatory. The provision is unique, conferring a power not shared by any other board of child welfare in the State, and to the extent that it is operative it divests the public welfare authorities of jurisdiction conferred upon them by every other statute relating to the subject matter. If, then, the Dutchess county board of child welfare wishes to waive this power, the relief of the destitute adults involved will merely fall back where it normally belongs, namely, upon the public welfare authorities, with several consequent advantages in administration. I see no objection to the plan.

Families in Need of Relief, of Which a Person Seventy Years of Age is a Member

(The following memorandum, referring particularly to cases of temporary need which might come under both home relief and old age relief, is endorsed jointly by the State Department of Social Welfare and by this Administration.)

When relief is needed in a family, one member of which is past seventy years of age, the question naturally arises as to the eligibility of the aged person for old age relief separately from relief given to other members of the family.

The requirements for eligibility for old age relief are contained in section 123 of the Public Welfare Law which, in its relationship to the entire article (Article XIV-A), is intended to provide for aged persons who are eligible and *permanently* in need of public aid.

If the aged person has continued to be a member of the family, and the family as a whole is considered to be only temporarily in need, it may be good social planning to give home relief upon the basis of the temporary need of the entire family without considering the aged person separately.

If, on the other hand, the need of the aged person appears to be a continuing or permanent need which under ordinary conditions could not be provided for by the family, even though the family itself were no longer in need of relief, a separate application for old age relief may properly be made. This should be done with the understanding that the need of the remainder of the family will be provided for in the same manner as if the aged member were not present—provided, of course, that old age relief is actually given to such aged person.

The budgeting of the family in this situation should be arranged so as to take into consideration those items which, if included in the budget of the person on old age relief, are a part of the total household costs—for example, rent, light and heat.

* * *

5. REIMBURSEMENTS

Local Homeless*

Regulations covering reimbursement of expenditures on behalf of local homeless.

Definition

Local homeless are unattached, undomiciled, individuals not having a recognized place of abode, as, for example, a room or other dwelling for which rent is paid, who do not classify as Federal or State Transients.

Standards of Care in Public Shelters

Lodging houses must be approved in the same manner as shelters used for transients, namely by the T.E.R.A. Safety Division, with the concurrence of the local Health Department, Fire Department and Building Department.

Three meals of reasonable quality and quantity must be served each person each day.

A work program must be instituted requiring from twenty to thirty hours work each week from each person in care so far as is required within the shelter to reduce the cost of operation, and in addition so far as is practicable outside of the shelter with relation to public projects. Such works program does not imply wages. Cash relief may be paid as in the case of transients (Transient Division Manual, *111*–1).

A medical program must be instituted and must provide medical inspection of each person admitted to care in the shelter sufficient to avoid the spread of contagious disease, and medical treatment of illness in accordance with the manual of rules and regulations covering medical care provided in the home to recipients of home relief. Special care should be exercised in reference to the treatment of and segregation of those suffering from contagious venereal disease and tuberculosis.

A social service program must be instituted in relation to all persons in care emphasizing the return of the individual to a condition of self-support, securing old age security benefits for those qualified to receive them, return of individuals to relatives and transfer of appropriate individuals to the County almshouse.

Insofar as the staff of the lodging house is composed of recognized city employees, salaries of employees are not available for reimbursement. Insofar as it is necessary to supplement the services of recognized city employees with the services of others, staff may be furnished by the Home Relief Department, subject to the same conditions of selection and reimbursement as applied to the home relief staff.

Claims for reimbursement may be submitted as follows:

> Expenditures for staff furnished by home relief, as per home relief claims.

---

* Ruling as of date of Departmental letter No. 7, Sept. 7, 1934.

For expenditures for all commodities necessary in the operation, exclusive of equipment, in accordance with the T.E.R.A. accounting procedure, and to be accompanied by a statistical summary showing the number of nights lodging and the number of meals served, together with the total number of individuals served. Reimbursement to be made upon expenditures which do not exceed in total a standard of 20 cents per lodging and 10 cents per meal.

Contract Shelters

Expenditures for care, under contracts with institutions operated by private agencies or individuals may also be reimbursed provided regulations which apply in the Transient Division for such contract care are carried out (Transient Division Manual, *111*-3) except that claims should be marked Local Homeless, not Transient, and provided such cost does not exceed 50 cents per day for each individual (one day's care to represent night's lodging and three meals).

Equipment Purchases by Municipalities

On rentals of equipment by municipalities for use in relief projects, reimbursement from Federal Relief funds has been authorized and is the policy. It has been established to the Administration's satisfaction that such rental policy is expensive, that through purchase agreements with partial payments in sums reasonably approximating such rentals the equipment can be purchased outright by the municipalities; that such equipment can be used more extensively and over a far greater period of time through such purchase plan.

There is no reason, nor any legal obstacle observed in the relief law, nor in the Federal regulations governing such reimbursement, why such partial payment installment or rental purchase plan should not be approved. Since the municipality itself purchases and contributes to the said purchase; and since the Administration's reimbursement from Federal funds is the same as if a rental were made, the property on payment being completed, belongs to the municipality.

Canning Equipment

On the question of reimbursing on the purchase of equipment for local canning units, such as steam cookers, this cannot be charged to Home Relief or to Work Relief funds of the State, unless it is purchased as "materials" for a State project for a State department, in this case the Department of Agriculture and Markets, for such canning projects as are under its general supervision.

Non-Relief Skilled Labor

Effective July 31, 1934, no reimbursement will be made on non-relief personnel other than supervisory and administrative.

Permission was granted for exception on skilled labor in order that C.W.A. projects requiring a certain amount of skilled labor might be completed promptly. These exceptions were granted only in particular instances, and no further exceptions will be made.

This policy was adopted by the Administration at its meeting on July 10th, 1934.

Payroll Irregularities

Many payrolls are being submitted for audit on which appear errors and irregularities of a serious nature. In the future, deductions will be made from any abstracts and reimbursement refused on any payment for payroll or other purposes which has not been made according to the prescribed regulations. Responsibility for payments which are in violation of existing regulations is upon the municipality whose bureau has contracted the irregular pay-payment.

Among the outstanding irregularities are:

(a) Budget deficiency waived payrolls showing payment in excess of $35.00 per week, and budget deficiency waived payrolls showing workers other than technical, supervisory and administrative.

(b) Relief payrolls showing payments in excess of budget deficiencies for several consecutive weeks.

(c) Labor rates in excess of those authorized in the project as originally submitted and approved, and in excess of the prevailing district rates submitted by the Rates Committees of the districts involved.

The T.E.R.A. Official Bulletins and Departmental Letters issued regularly by the Administration give full information covering all rules concerning proper presentation of payrolls, and limitations on payments for the various classifications. It is essential that the members of local emergency work bureaus, emergency relief bureaus, and staff members responsible for the presentation of claims be thoroughly familiar with the regulations as referred to above.

New Policy on Reimbursements

Under date of October 16, 1933, notification was made to the effect that the Administration, beginning November 1, would reimburse municipalities 66⅔ per cent of total approved home or work relief expenditures.

In connection with this statement, the following additional explanation is made:

1. The reimbursement of 66⅔ per cent is an inclusive percentage and in those districts where State Department Projects are assigned which are reimbursed 100 per cent, the reimbursement on local claims will be reduced accordingly. Educational work relief projects are excepted for the present.

(Thus if a given public welfare district estimates a total expenditure of $100,000 and the Administration makes an allocation of $10,000 through a State department, the percentage of reimbursement on the $90,000 of local claims would be at the rate of 62.9 per cent. The method of computation is as follows:

(66⅔ per cent of $100,000 equals $66,666.67, or the reimbursement in money to the local districts.

($66,666.67 minus $10,000 which will be paid out directly by this Administration, either through State departments or through local bureaus, in wages to work relief clients, leaves a balance of $56,666.67 to be reimbursed on local claims.

($56,666.67 divided by the $90,000 representing the total of local claims equals 62.9 per cent which will be reimbursed on local claims.)

The Administration reserves the right to decide on the question of whether a State department project should be assigned to a given district as a part of the total reimbursement.

2. The additional per cent above the statutory 40 per cent reimbursement is a direct grant, and as such shall be credited to a revolving fund for relief purposes, and may not be placed in the general fund. Effective November 1, the State Comptroller will issue two checks on reimbursement to municipalities—one for the statutory 40 per cent, and one for the additional percentage which is a direct grant.

3. Effective November 1, the Administration will reimburse on administrative payrolls at 66⅔ per cent. This new policy cancels all previous approvals on rate of reimbursement of local administrative personnel whether the former rate was 33⅓, 50 or 100 per cent.

All persons now on any administration payroll reimbursed by the Temporary Emergency Relief Administration will be automatically transferred to the 66⅔ per cent reimbursement, subject to review at a subsequent date. The continuation of administrative personnel at the 66⅔ per cent rate of reimbursement will be required by the Administration wherever their continuance is necessary to the proper supervision of the local staff.

Concurrent with this new policy on administrative payrolls, the Administration will no longer approve the employment of white collar workers in local relief administrations for an amount greater than their actual budget needs as was permitted in the past on the basis of the need of continuity in these particular positions.

Wherever persons are employed on a work relief payroll and are receiving compensation in excess of their budget needs, such persons must either be transferred to the administrative payroll subject to individual approval of the field representative and this Administration or must be reduced to the amount of their budget deficit.

In the future Administration will not reimburse on work relief in excess of the budget deficit.

[Note: The above applies to the policy of 75 per cent reimbursement subsequently adopted.]

Reimbursement Policy Effective April 1, 1934

Reimbursement to municipalities in New York State at the rate of 75 per cent of total approved relief expenditures including home relief, work relief and approved materials for work relief projects, was established as the policy of the Temporary Emergency Relief Administration for the next ten months at a conference between Governor Herbert H. Lehman, Legislative Leaders and the Administration held Monday, March 26th, in Albany.

The Temporary Emergency Relief Administration estimates that it will be able to reimburse at the above stated rate of 75 per cent for the period of ten months by an approximate matching of State and local funds with Federal funds. This includes in the total estimate a substantial allowance for materials. Approximately $45,000,000, the balance of the $60,000,000 bond issue voted by the people of New York State in November, 1933, is still available and represents the contribution from State funds.

At the conference on Monday, March 26th, Governor Lehman, Legislative Leaders and the Administration budgeted the available funds over the ten months' period, limiting State and Federal participation to the total available from these two sources. This total monthly budget must be strictly adhered to.

As it will require some time to reduce the total numbers on home relief and on Civil Works to the number of cases necessary to stay within the money available, the total estimate for April has been fixed at $25,000,000 for the whole State. The Administration will reimburse municipalities up to 75 per cent of this figure. This amount is in excess of the monthly budgeted amount, and therefore savings will have to be made in the succeeding months to bring the total within the reimbursable figure.

The amount which will be subject to reimbursement in May is $23,500,000 in June, $22,000,000, in July, $21,000,000, and in August, September and October, $19,500,000.

It will therefore be essential for municipalities to reduce their loads immediately by means of thorough investigation, so that only those who are absolutely in need of relief will remain on either home or work relief rolls.

The policy of reimbursing 75 per cent is contingent upon continued Federal participation as agreed to between the State Administration, the Governor, Legislative Leaders and the Federal Emergency Relief Administration.

Inasmuch as municipalities will not be able in many instances to advance sufficient monies from their own funds to meet work relief payrolls, the Temporary Emergency Relief Administration will arrange to advance, where necessary, monies for payroll purposes only to the extent of the State and Federal participation in the program.

* * *

Reimbursement For Non-Resident Cases

Inasmuch as the two year limitation regarding residence, as provided under the Wicks Law, does not apply on reimbursement received from the Federal Relief Administration, the New York State Temporary Emergency Relief Administration will accept claims for reimbursement for non-residents, regardless of the period of time which they have been in the State or in a given locality.

Reimbursement on this group of cases will be at the rate of 75 per cent. Home relief claims must be prepared separately, together with the usual supporting vouchers, and for work relief both separate payrolls and separate claim sheets must be made out. The same forms now in use are to be used, except that claims for these cases must be stamped "Non-Resident Cases."

The breakdown in these claims between veterans and non-veterans, and the separation of claims for medical service from other claims, need not be made for this group. All claims under the classification of "Non-Resident Cases" can be submitted on one claim sheet for either home relief or work relief.

This ruling was effective August 1, 1934.

* *

Reimbursement on Families Eligible for Relief Under the Welfare Law

The Administration has previously stated its policy in regard to reimbursement of claims for relief granted to children and families who are eligible for relief under the law governing Boards of Child Welfare.

It has been brought to our attention that in a number of instances local officials are granting home or work relief to persons who are eligible for relief under the Child Welfare Law, and whose relief is non-reimbursable under the provisions of the Wicks Act. The Administration is therefore re-stating its policy to the effect that in the future its auditors are instructed to eliminate as non-reimbursable claims all cases which, from the information available on local home and work relief records, indicates that the family is eligible for relief under the Child Welfare Law. Burden of proof as to whether the case is properly reimbursable under the Wicks Act is placed upon the local Commissioner of Public Welfare.

Claims for all cases eligible under the Child Welfare Law will be eliminated as non-reimbursable regardless of whether or not the appropriations made by the municipality are sufficient to provide relief as required by the Child Welfare Law.

The Administration makes this ruling because it believes that any policy of permitting reimbursement for relief granted to cases eligible under the Child Welfare Law would serve to nullify the provisions of this Law.

The Administration will continue to authorize reimbursement for home and/or work relief granted to individuals who are members of families which are receiving Child Welfare allowance, when such members are ineligible for the Child Welfare allowance, and to the extent of the individual's need of relief.

Reimbursement on supplemental relief granted to Child Welfare cases will not be granted even though the maximum allowance under the Child Welfare Law is being given, and even though need exists for additional relief. It is the opinion of the Administration that supplementation by one State agency in excess of the maximum allowed by law to be granted by another State agency is improper.

Purchases From Exempted Stores

According to the retail code, local retailers in towns of 2,500 or less, employing fewer than five persons, and retail merchants operating their stores without employing any additional persons besides themselves, are exempt from the regulatory provisions of the code.

Therefore in submitting claims for reimbursement for supplies purchased from such stores, the commissioner of public welfare may stamp such claims as having complied with the President's Re-employment Agreement, according to instructions in Official Bulletin No. 4, Item No. 18 (A).

The commissioner of public welfare must ascertain from the local branch of the N.R.A. whether or not a given supplier is complying with or is exempt from the provisions of the code, and if the supplier comes within either of these classifications, these claims may bear the required stamp. No claims will be honored for reimbursement which are not so stamped.

New Policy on State Funds

The Legislature, by chapter 430, Laws of 1933, made the county's share of motor fuel taxes available for relief purposes, as well as for current expenses. By so doing, such funds were made, if availed of for relief, reimbursable as other local funds so appropriated and used.

In line with this policy, and after due deliberation, the Administration has determined that it will hereafter approve for reimbursement, in addition to local funds appropriated and expended for relief projects, those special funds to which the State may have contributed, such as highway funds, etc.

Said reimbursement applies to local funds and does not include, as a basis, advances and direct grants by T.E.R.A.

Public Works Under Federal Bill

Public works prosecuted under the provisions of the Public Works and Construction Bill, of which the Federal government may bear 30 per cent of the cost, are not reimbursable by the Temporary Emergency Relief Administration as work relief projects.

Public works projects are for the purpose of stimulating normal employment, and should not be identified with relief as such. This is evident from the spirit and language of the Federal Act.

Work for Home Relief

Any home relief claim on which there is any evidence that regular work is required will not be subject to reimbursement.

School Books

Reimbursement cannot be made on school books furnished to children in families under the care of welfare officers. This does not come under any reasonable definition of shelter, fuel, food, clothing, light, necessary household supplies, etc. The school authorities or parent-teachers associations might assist in this. A work relief wage may nevertheless be made to cover the necessities of life, of which schooling is one, and it should also be borne in mind that the provision of school books is a regular and normal duty of the local welfare officer.

Milk to Children

There may be a regular reimbursement for the cost of milk given to undernourished school children, on order of the commissioner of public welfare, this being home relief within the meaning of the Emergency Act, though not actually administered within the abode. See Section 3, "Free Milk," page 209 of this pamphlet.

See Section 3, "Free Milk," page 209 of this pamphlet.

* * *

Reimbursement for Ice

The question has arisen as to whether or not expenditures for ice for the purpose of food preservation are reimbursable. It has been decided that ice may be purchased, and reimbursement claimed therefor, for those families having children under six years of age, or those families in which there are cases of illness.

It is necessary that the purchase of ice shall be strictly limited to that amount necessary for food preservation. A maximum of 25 pounds per family every other day should suffice for the preservation of milk and fats. It will be necessary to ascertain that those families to whom ice is supplied, where they do not have refrigerators, are instructed in the proper means of insolating in order to prevent too rapid consumption. The United States Department of Agriculture has available bulletins on the subject of methods of construction of home ice boxes which may be valuable in this connection.

It is advised that each district arrive at price agreements with the local distributors, which should result in an appreciable reduction in the price of ice delivered to relief clients.

School Lunches

The furnishing of lunches to school children in the schools where the families of such school children are proper subjects for home relief and/or work relief, may properly be included as a part of the home relief expenditures of the city, and even though they may be furnished in schools, the propriety of their inclusion in the home relief expenditures presents more a problem of auditing than one of actual legality of relief.

The schools should furnish the number of children who will receive the lunches; the actual expenditure vouchers, etc., so that an audit may be made of the said home relief expenditures as evidenced by the school lunches furnished. This is an accounting problem to be settled between the city and the Administration.

Injury to Relief Recipient

Where a recipient of emergency relief suffered a broken back, while on an automobile ride, and will be an incurable invalid, reimbursement upon the medical and nursing expenses is proper, but only for and during the emergency period.

- - -

"White Collars" on N. R. A. Project

It is impossible to understand how the utilization of the N.R.A. activities as a project and the payment of wages of workers thereon as work relief, when taken from local relief lists, can be deemed a violation of Article VIII, section 10 of the State Constitution. Article VIII, section 10, insofar as applicable hereto, reads

"No county, city, town or village shall hereafter give any money or property, or loan its money or credit to or in aid of any individual, association or corporation, or become directly or indirectly the owner of stock in, or bonds of, any association or corporation; nor shall any such county, city, town or village be allowed to incur any indebtedness except for county, city, town or village purposes. *This section shall not prevent such county, city, town or village from making such provision for the aid or support of its poor as may be authorized by law.*"

Certainly paying a work relief wage to a local relief recipient is not giving money or lending credit to any "individual, association or corporation," nor can it be doubted that the N.R.A. Compliance Board and other N.R.A. activities are "public" activities and therefore proper field for relief projects.

But we find definite provision in the last sentence quoted above, for "aid and support" of the poor in such manner as may be provided "by law." And such relief is specifically therein exempt from the limitation of said section 10 of Article VIII.

In paying salaries of relief workers, the municipality is bearing its due burden. In furnishing the worker to the N.R.A. local unit, it is aiding a "public" activity. In neither is the money being spent contrary to law or for any purpose unauthorized by law.

The project is proper, and the relief salaries, if approved, and within T. E. R. A. rules and regulations, are subject to local expenditure and apropriate reimbursement.

Private Roads

If public money is used on roads in a private park, there can be no reimbursement from the State. If, however, the roads are public town roads there will be a reimbursement.

Barbers' Charges

A charge by barbers for cutting the hair of relief applicants and their families is rejected, since it does not qualify under the definition of home relief.

Social Diseases

In regard to the reimbursement by the T. E. R. A. of physicians who are treating patients for social diseases, it is provided in section 343-p of Article 17-B of the Public Health Law, as last amended by L. 1931, ch. 481, that

> "any person who is suffering from a venereal disease who is unable to pay for treatment may make application for care and treatment to the board of health or health officer of the health district in which such person resides and such board or health officer shall promptly institute treatment. It shall be the duty of each county and city board of health to provide facilities adequate for the diagnosis, care and treatment of such persons suffering from venereal disease, who are unable to pay for the treatment by a private physician, which facilities shall meet such standards as may be prescribed by the State commissioner of health."

Inasmuch as the treatment of ailments of this nature at public expense is already provided for by law, it seems that reimbursement therefor should not be allowed by the T. E. R. A. out of its funds.

Morphine

Morphine prescribed by a physician becomes as medicinal as any treatment within home relief, and the cost thereof is reimbursable.

County-Town Lawsuit as Work Project

It is asked whether there may be properly approved by the Relief Administration, as a reimbursable work project, the employment of clerical and stenographic help to assist in the preparation of the case of Monroe county in a litigation in which that county is concerned and is a party.

The answer must certainly be in the affirmative. A county (or a town) has under the Constitution (Art. VIII, section 3), and the General Corporation Law, where its corporate rights are concerned, the same right to sue or defend a suit as has a private corporation or an individual. It is immaterial to us that one municipal corporation is arrayed against another or that a taxpayer in a town will have to pay his share of the town's legal expenses on one side of the argument and also his share of the county's legal expenses on the other side. We are asked only if we may contribute to the cost of clerical help, which we may, indeed, do, for one side or the other, or both.

It is, of course, important that the results of the project itself be made the subject of public knowledge in the event that the towns involved in the litigation may desire to avail themselves of the same information. In other words, a project of this nature, while apparently proper from the relief point of view in giving employment to unemployed clerks and stenographers, should not be availed of by one branch of the government against another. The facts ascertained and collated should be made available to all. I assume that these facts are not necessarily controversial but are merely to ascertain certain information which it is necessary to present upon the trial.

⊦ *

Status of Volunteer Committee Funds

The Gibson committee was a group of private individuals raising funds for the administration of relief in the city of New York, and was in every respect a non-public agency. Section 14 of the Emergency Relief Act covers the manner in which contributions from private individuals aggregating less than $10,000 may be reimbursable. A contribution may be reimbursable except as to such parts thereof as are contributed by a single individual in excess of $10,000. In order to be reimbursable, however, these funds must be turned over to the municipal corporation to be disbursed in the same manner as funds appropriated by the municipal corporation. The Gibson committee, therefore, could not receive reimbursement nor may the city receive reimbursement on the relief administered by the Gibson committee, even though it be to legitimate relief cases, unless these funds were administered by the city and were turned over to the city for such administration.

Municipal Stores

It is asked if, in a case where a city buys food supplies at wholesale and then gives relief by orders on its storehouse (as merchant) signed by recipient, the city would be entitled to claim reimbursement.

The reimbursement provision applies to the cost of all home relief furnished by a municipal corporation and approved by the Administration. It is not required that such relief be furnished in any particular manner. If furnished by order upon a private business concern, the right to claim reimbursement would be unquestioned. It may also be claimed if the relief is furnished by order of the city upon itself. The essential fact in either instance is that the city pays the bill. Note, however, that the reimbursement would be based upon the cost of the commodities to the city, and not upon the retail prices, and that the question of policy involved in the maintenance of such a storehouse is one for the Administration to consider.

Reimbursement for Coal, New York City

It appears that civil service employees of the city of New York, in order to assist in the carrying on of relief activities, have contributed to a fund which has been used in the purchase of coal, and this has been administered through the police to home relief recipients upon coal orders received from families upon the regular list of the home relief bureau.

The mayor's official committee, which has utilized this fund for administering this coal, has been able to make purchases at a considerable saving below the retailer's price, and, at cost, has billed the said cost of the coal to the Department of Public Welfare. The question has been raised as to whether this is reimbursable. The saving has been $7.60 per ton.

The fact that the employees of the city through a fund, have contributed their salaries for the purchase of this coal, in substance renders them contributors under section 14 of chapter 798, and their gifts, if made to the municipal corporation, would be reimbursable and by the means here provided the funds are at the disposal of the municipal corporation through the mayor's committee. The city actually expends the money for this fuel relief, which would otherwise be purchased directly from retailers and the reimbursement goes into the treasury of the city of New York on the basis of its own expenditure. There is therefore a dual basis upon which reimbursement may be made in the instant case.

Caution should be exercised, however, in cases such as this to avoid the possibility of all private agencies saddling the State with a reimbursement upon their relief. It should not be done unless it can be directly tied up to the administration of home relief by the municipal corporations and the funds administered as part of the municipal corporations' funds in the form of contributions thereto. These are cases wihch might be determined upon the basis of their individual status, and, where the facts vary considerably, a different determination might necessarily result.

Boarding Out

Where a county has no county home, and therefore, one who is in need of relief and has no home of his own has to be boarded in a private home, such cases may be considered home relief, for the reimbursable cost of which reimbursement may be claimed from the State.

A county, however, may not claim reimbursement for persons boarding in a public institution, nor for a child that is boarding out, providing the child has another legal home. In cases where the person has no other home, his home is in the place in which he is being boarded, and if this is in a locality within the county, and the person is otherwise eligible, reimbursement may be claimed, but it is not intended to reimburse for dependent or neglected children placed in foster homes, where the obligation for the support of such children is now provided by law.

Reimbursements Go to General Fund

By virtue of section 16 of chapter 567, Laws of 1932, entitled "State Aid," the reimbursement of part of the expenditures for "home relief" or "work relief" or both, from the State must be credited to the "general fund." The statute reads: "such money shall be credited by such corporation or town to its general fund."

It is only in the case of "direct grants" in addition to the normal reimbursement, that such money is to be made available for home or work relief as designated by the Administration.

This procedure is set forth with absolute clarity in the statute and should be followed.

When deposited in the "general fund," such money may, of course, be reappropriated to relief or other purposes.

Reimbursement to Welfare Society

Where a person was compelled, as the condition of a suspended sentence in a criminal prosecution, to remove from Schenectady to Albany, and was then in receipt of relief through the Albany Family Welfare Society, the validity of such a sentence is open to grave doubt, but in any event there can be no reimbursement to such society.

I also question whether the Administration should concern itself with the arrangements whereby Schenectady administers relief through an Albany agency in the city of Albany. Sanctioning such a procedure as this might lead to considerable confusion, and a number of possible cases might arise in which this would act as a questionable precedent.

The only basis upon which reimbursement could be made would be if the city of Schenectady administered the relief even though in Albany, and the Administration approved the relief as though it had been administered in Schenectady, upon the claim filed by the city of Schenectady for such relief, evidencing the actual expenditures.

6. RECOVERY FROM RECIPIENTS; OBLIGATION TO SUPPORT

Policy in Regard to the Authority Given in Chapter 60 of the Laws of 1934 in Relation to Authorizing Filing of Notice of Lien in Lieu of Executing Deed or Mortgage of Property

In view of the amendment to Section 130 of the Public Welfare Law, passed by the Legislature as Chapter 60 of the Laws of 1934, the Administration feels that a re-statement of its policy in regard to judgments in the form of liens, mortgages or other attachments to the property of recipients of relief is necessary.

The opinions of Counsel for the Administration, as previously rendered, entitled "Judgments for Relief" and "Liens for Relief," as reprinted immediately hereinafter, state clearly the policy of the Administration.

As further explanation of this policy, the Administration feels that, when judgments are taken against the property of a relief client for relief granted, the welfare district taking such judgment has, in effect, made a loan to such relief recipient in the amount of his relief, and that the welfare district has secured its recovery of the amount of money granted as relief. The Administration believes, therefore, that reimbursement in such cases is improper, as it could not be properly granted under the philosophy of the Emergency Relief Act.

Judgments for Relief

We are asked in regard to the practice of obtaining judgments for relief administered to those in need, such judgments becoming liens on property owned by the recipients of relief.

In the absence of contract, or of some express statutory provision, where public authorities relieve a poor person pursuant to their statutory obligation, neither the poor person, nor his estate, is under any obligation to make reimbursement; and this is the rule, even though the poor person owned property at the time the relief was furnished, in the absence of fraud or deception on his part as to his ability to support himself. (Albany v. McNamara, 117 N. Y. 168; Matter of Carroll, 55 Misc. 496, affirmed 127 App. Div. 932 mem.)

In Albany v. McNamara, Chief Judge Ruger said:

"The possession of some property by a person does not always and necessarily preclude such person from a just claim for relief. The question of the propriety of relief is confided to the discretion of the poor authorities, and if they grant the relief asked, it is to be presumed that they have made such investigations as they deemed necessary, and have determined the question as to the right of the party examined to such relief. There is no provision made in the law for a review of that determination, and such aid, once furnished, must thereafter be regarded as a charity extended by the city to the object of their benevolence without expectation of reimbursement. (Deer Isle v. Eaton, 12 Mass. 320; Medford v. Learned, 16 id. 215.) The misjudgment of the officers of the poor as to the necessities of the person relieved raises no implied promise on the part of such person that he will repay moneys expended in his behalf.

"It is urged by the respondent that every person is, in law, primarily liable to support himself. It is quite probable that most persons who do not support themselves are likely to get little or very poor support from any one; yet it is not true, as a legal proposition, that every person is liable to support himself. Every person has a natural right to choose the mode and manner of his life, and, so long as he does not violate any positive provision of law, to follow it, and if aid and assistance are voluntarily furnished by the charitable and credulous without deception to such person, we know of no rule that enables the persons giving to recover back from the object of their benevolence the money so advanced to him. (Deer Isle v. Eaton, supra.)"

It is not against public policy for a poor person voluntarily to indemnify the public authorities against expenses incurred on his account (Church v. Fannin, 44 Hun 302), but unless he agrees to do so, or there is some statute so requiring, the relief afforded to a poor person is in the nature of a charitable gift, made a legal duty by statute, and no promise can be implied to make reimbursement, and no reimbursement can be enforced. (Bremer County v. Curtis, 54 Iowa 72, 6 N. W. 135; Charlestown v. Hubbard, 9 N. H. 195; Bennington v. McGennes, 1 D. Chipmn. [Vt.] 44.)

Under the Public Welfare Law a public welfare commissioner may seize the property of a person who absents himself, leaving anyone for whose support he is liable dependent upon public support or liable to become so dependent (Section 127), or a public welfare official may sue a person discovered to have real or personal property, or his estate, if such person, or anyone for whose support he is or was liable, received relief or care during the preceding ten years, and may recover up to the value of such property the cost of such relief (Section 128), and the cost of relief shall be a preferred claim upon insurance (Section 129), and a public welfare official may accept a deed of real property or a mortgage thereon on behalf of the public welfare district for the care and maintenance of a person at public expense (Section 130).

The giving of a deed or mortgage, under Section 130, is purely voluntary and cannot be compelled. Section 128, authorizing an action to recover the cost of relief where the recipient is "Discovered" to have property, is the only statutory provision which would even tenuously support the practice of requiring one in need to confess judgment in order to obtain aid. But this, I think, would not apply where the person was known to have property at the time the relief was given, for then there could be no discovery. This thought is sustained by cases interpreting the cognate Section 57 of the former Poor Law as not warranting any recovery unless there had been an affirmative concealment of assets. (Matter of Humphries, 125 Misc. 62; Matter of Thomas, 132 Misc. 842.)

Even so, these provisions relate solely to relief under the Public Welfare Law, and have no operation as to relief under the Emergency Act. All relief for which reimbursement is sought from the State is under the Emergency Act, and there is in regard thereto no statutory provision whatever along the lines indicated. On the contrary, moneys paid under the Emergency Act are expressly inalienable by any assignment or transfer and are exempt from levy and execution. (L. 1932, ch. 567, Section 16), indicating a policy quite the reverse. The practice referred to appears to me to be most reprehensible, and it should be forbidden by the T.E.R.A. rules. You must not mortgage the recipient's future recovery in exchange for relief which is the government's obligation voluntarily assumed.

Liens for Relief

The Administration wishes to call the attention of all commissioners of public welfare in the State, to the following excerpt from a ruling by the Attorney-General's office regarding the practice of obtaining judgments and placing them as liens on property for relief administered under the Emergency Relief Act.

"Moneys paid under the Emergency Relief Act are expressly, by the provisions thereof (Laws 1932, chapter 567, section 16), made inalienable by any assignment, transfer or otherwise and are exempt from levy and execution. This is a definite direct expression of legislative intent quite contrary to and the reverse of the policy of obtaining by judgments or otherwise repayment from the person who is the recipient of relief. The practice of obtaining judgments for relief administered pursuant to the T. E. R. A. provisions and under the Emergency Relief Act should be forthwith forbidden by the Administration. It contravenes sound public policy in an emergency and is destructive to the morale and stability of those who are in need by forcing them to mortgage their future recovery for relief which the State has in this emergency undertaken as its own responsibility and the responsibility of the local governments.''

In accordance with this opinion, the Administration is hereby notifying all commissioners of public welfare that insofar as their expenditures are presented to the State for reimbursement under chapter 798 of the Laws of 1931 and chapter 567 of the Laws of 1932, the Administration declines to reimburse on relief orders for clients in cases in which liens have been placed on the property of such clients.

The Administration has been in consultation with the State Department of Social Welfare regarding this matter, and wishes to emphasize the fact that the above ruling has no bearing on any other forms of relief which commissioners of public welfare may be dispensing and which do not come under the provisions of the Emergency Relief Act.

The Administration reiterates its desire to in no way interfere with the normal, permanent functioning of the other aspects of the responsibilities of the commissioners of public welfare such as relief through the Public Welfare Law, old age security, and boards of child welfare.

Relief to Persons in Possession of Resources in Cash

It has been brought to our attention that several districts are extending work relief to persons who have cash resources in the way of bank accounts or unadjusted insurance policies with substantial loan values. In two instances we found districts operating on the policy that a maximum bank account of $75 would be permitted to work relief clients. A number of districts have disregarded entirely the loan value on unadjusted insurance policies.

The Commissioner of Public Welfare is accountable for certification of persons for relief on the basis of their actual need for relief. This certification must be based on an investigation of the family's income and resources.

The disbursement of relief monies to persons in possession of cash resources which makes it unnecessary for them to receive relief is illegal. The fact that the exhaustion of these resources will make the persons eligible for relief within a short period of time does not make it proper to grant relief so that these resources may be conserved. The only exception permissible would be the budgeting of known resources for particular purposes in conjunction with a partial relief allowance.

The Administration will refuse reimbursement and will demand an accounting from any public official violating this fundamental rule. No authority has ever been granted to extend relief to persons with resources in cash.

Misuse of Earnings by Relief Workers

Work Relief constitutes wages of unemployed to an extent sufficient to supply the necessaries of life to them and/or their dependents. The definition, Section 2 of Chapter 798, Laws of 1931, as amended, states that it is "wages paid to persons, who are unemployed or whose employment is inadequate to provide the necessaries of life, and/or their dependents, from money specifically appropriated," etc.

The very language of the statute authorized the payment of said wages to the worker "or their dependents." It is quite proper that it should be so construed and applied. The very basis of relief employment is the need of the worker's family and dependents. If he deserts and shirks his social and legal duties to them, the wages earned for their support may be paid directly to the family for their maintenance.

The reasoning is fully as applicable to those who abuse the privilege of work relief by misusing earnings intended for their family's support. The wages in such cases of *proved waste of earnings* may be paid to the dependent worker's family and, if necessary, at the expense of his losing his relief position, he may be required to authorize the local bureau so to deliver his wage check. It is necessary in such instances to inquire into the family status to ascertain the accuracy or falsity of the charges. Caution is necessary in such cases. The authority, however, is present.

Court Orders in Relief Work Cases

It is asked what should be the policy of the work relief bureau in regard to men living apart from their families, who are under court order to pay for the support of children.

1. When the children are in the home with the mother.
2. When the children are boarded with relatives.
3. When they are in institutions.

Reply:

1. See that the mother and children are properly provided for, or refuse him work and give family "home relief."
2. If court order provides for children who are with relatives, see that they get it as ordered.
3. If institutional support is free, don't give work to cover children. If order of court covers such sums, see that it is carried out.

In each case the problem can be solved by having an assignment directing proper apportioning of sums needed signed by the man. If he doesn't do it, you don't have to give him work relief. These cases call for discretion and tact properly used.

Problems:

1. Report is made that domestic relations courts are bringing pressure to force welfare departments or local bureaus to give work relief to men separated from families who are ordered to pay

specified amounts each week to the family under threat of jail. The Bureau is informed that the man will be jailed if no job is given.

2. Should a family budget prevail for a man separated from his family and who is ordered to pay stated sum each week, or should he have a single man status?

3. What should be done when the sum directed to be paid is out of line with the family budget and/or the work relief wage?

———

1. Relief bodies are not subject to any control by the domestic relations courts in the matter of deciding who shall be put to work. Nor should any such threats as are alleged be given heed. I doubt if any reasonable court would bring such pressure or make such demands. Since every person with dependent family cannot be given work relief, it would seem far more appropriate to pay more attention to those living with their families than the deserting husband or non-provider. At any rate, no such person should be put on work relief if he would not otherwise qualify and no such reason should permit such person to be employed. The relief administration is not the adjunct of the family court for such purposes.

2. The amount to be paid to the dependent family of a person on work relief should not be the result of a court order, but the result of the budgetary basis determined. It would seem highly improbable that you could set up a separate status for the family and the worker who did not live with them. Wisdom might dictate that the worker be limited to a share of the earnings based on the family's need as a whole or seek single relief on a home relief basis.

3. If the sum directed to be paid by the court or judge is out of line with the relief wage on a family relief budget basis, the Bureau investigator or supervisor should confer with the court and explain the situation. A sensible judge will readily observe the impossibility of paying on another basis when the earnings are solely based on relief needs. In any event, the court's order cannot determine how much a man will earn on work relief. That is determined solely by the family's needs.

Immediate Relief

Where a woman and her children are in immediate need, temporary relief should be granted at once, pending determination of the responsibility therefor. (Public Welfare Law, sections 77, 78.) If the husband is able to support the family, wholly or in part, he may be compelled to do so in proceedings brought by the town public welfare officer, in which proceedings past expenditures may be recovered and a bond required for future support (idem, sections 125–133).

- * *

Reimbursement from Clientele

(a) Where a recipient of relief has funds, but they are tied up or unavailable temporarily—as in a closed bank—there is no legal obstacle to subsequent repayment by such recipient when funds become available. Such understanding should be made clear to said applicant if facts be known.

(b) Where recipient is later found to have had resources, repayment is proper—see Public Welfare Law provisions. This is a stronger case than (a).

(c) Where no such funds are available or in possession—where there is no concealment—where relief is given to bona fide case, then subsequent good fortune, when relief recipient's "ship comes in," is no basis for requiring repayment. The law doesn't expect or permit it. You can not mortgage the recipient's recovery. It would defeat the purpose of the Relief Act.

Private Resources

Case I. Man, wife, infant child of three years. Sole resources a bank account of $150 in the name of the child and its mother; created out of savings for an educational fund for infant.

In this case, there is some color to the claim that the monies represent the child's own funds, deposited to its account and with the mother's name added, in nature of a joint control until child becomes of age—or old enough to make use of it. Further, the sum is not very substantial. The case presents a situation calling for a sensible and realistic decision. In these circumstances, there could be no criticism of a decision offering relief and maintaining the child's account in its present state. Were the sum much larger, another conclusion might be warranted. Much also would depend on when the account was opened—before or after the time when relief became a necessity. Good faith would be thereby disclosed.

Case II. Man, wife, three children. Two of latter are of working age, but in school. Bank account of $500 in father's name and not in trust.

This clearly calls for use of the fund before relief can be extended. It is not even a border-line case. To allow relief here, and maintain the bank account, would be obviously unfair to thousands in need who have no funds whatsoever.

Case III. Man, wife, adult epileptic son. Bank account in father's name of $550. No trust account.

Same decision as in Case II, above. No relief should be granted until funds are exhausted.

Comment. It should not be necessary to present such cases. The local officials and T. E. R. A. representative should make decisions, and as here, their determination would have been readily sustained. Even in Case I, it is a close and debatable issue.

Obligation to Support

Section 125 of the Public Welfare Law reads:

"Liability of relatives to support. The husband, wife, father mother, grandparent, child or grandchild of a recipient of public relief or of a person liable to become in need of public relief shall, if of sufficient ability, be responsible for the support of such person. Step-parents shall in like manner be responsible for the support of minor step-children."

Section 126 reads:

"Powers of public welfare officials to bring and defend suits. A public welfare official is empowered to bring proceedings in a court of competent jurisdiction to compel any person liable by law for support to contribute to the support of any person cared for at public expense, or person liable to become so dependent. A bond may be required of such person liable for support to indemnify the public welfare district against the cost of the support of such person. A public welfare official is also empowered to bring proceedings to recover penalties and prosecute any bonds, undertakings and recognizances and to sue and defend in any court all matters relating to the support of persons at public expense. All suits shall be instituted and defended in the name of the public welfare official."

It will be noted that the obligation for support only in "minority" applies to step-parents. Natural parents are obligated to support a *child* without limitation—the only requirement being that the child, parent, grandparent, etc., either be a "recipient of relief or a person liable to become in need of public relief" (section 125). The age-old obligation of parents to support children has in the progress of human relations been made a mutual obligation by the law. Children must support indigent elders in the direct line of relationship and vice versa. The law thus meets the exigency of the times.

Insurance Premiums

The practice of including an item for the payment of premiums on insurance policies in the budget of home or work relief clients is contrary to the rules and regulations of the Administration, and to the terms of the Emergency Relief Act, Chapter 798 of the Laws of 1931 as amended.

The only condition under which insurance premiums are allowed, and then not as a part of the budgetary item, is at the time of adjustment of a policy when loan values are paid, or other changes in policies are made which result in a cash payment. It is approved practice to permit the use of a portion of the cash secured from the adjustment of policies to pay premiums in advance for a reasonable period of time.

Insurance Policies

Regarding the cash surrender value of insurance policies, the question is closely akin to the savings account problem. The size of the policy and actual cash value must have some bearing upon the decisions. You cannot furnish money to pay premiums; neither can you support a family with funds in the bank while others are in need and have no such reserves. Fundamentally, all must share and share alike the woes of the times. The cash surrender value must therefore be utilized if of sufficient amount to carry the family or individual owning it until exhausted. There is no other determination possible in the light of those cases where no such reserves are available.

* * *

Children's Savings Accounts

In regard to children's savings accounts as an asset in a family situation, it would seem that in many cases of this kind a wise discretion would dictate permitting the children's deposits to remain, unless circumstances were such that local finances were becoming desperate. This type of case should never come to plague the Administration. Local officials and field representatives should have enough intelligence, tact and initiative to decide them. There is no law involved.

Improper Questions

An application blank for public relief should not include a question whether the applicant is an American citizen, nor require a statement that the applicant agrees to repay the sum advanced to him.

Trust Fund as Barrier

In regard to relief for a family in which there is $1,000 held in trust for an eighteen-year-old son, which the family does not desire to touch, I may say that while section 125 of the Public Welfare Law imposes a clear liability upon a child, who has means, to support a parent who is in need, Justice Close is of course correct in his statement that this money held in trust can not be touched without an order of the court, and then only for the support of the infant or his destitute parent.

If these parties make due application to the court, in good faith, to have this money applied to their support, and the court refuses to allow it, I should think they would then become entitled to emergency relief. Short of that, however, it is my view that they would not be so entitled.

Support of Prisoner's Family

The case is presented of a man imprisoned in a county penitentiary, whose family is being supported by the town and who refuses to sign an order permitting the relief authorities to turn over to his wife certain work relief wages which are due him. This man's work relief employment was as much, if not more, in consideration of the needs of his wife and family, as of his own. Equitably, therefore, a payment of the wages to his wife for the family's support would leave him without any remedy which he could enforce. He would simply not be heard. If, however, it is desired to be technically correct, the county commissioner should bring a proceeding and obtain an order under section 126 of the Public Welfare Law.

Work for Support of Children

Where no court order is involved, and the children are living in foster homes, with relatives, or in institutions (not free) it is permissible to place the father on work relief for the support of his children.

Uncertain Contributions

The following case is presented:

Applicant, 54 years; wife 48; sons 24, 22, 14, 12 and 3; daughters 17 and 13.

Applicant owns own home, which is not mortgaged. He has rental income of $3 a week. Son 24 earns $21 a week. Daughter 17 earns $9 a week. Total present income of family $33 a week. The son earning $21 a week refuses to give the family anything beyond $10 a month for his room. He feeds himself. The needs of the family figure to $27.20 a week.

As to this it is asked what legal obligations this, or any, son owes to the father and family, and if legal steps could be taken to compel the son to make more adequate provision. Also, if it is correct to assume that the work bureau is only to give aid beyond the pooled resources of a family living together.

It is provided in section 125 of the Public Welfare Law that "the husband, wife, father, mother, grandparent, child or grandchild of a recipient of public relief or of a person liable to become in need of public relief shall, if of sufficient ability, be responsible for the support of such person." This young man, therefore, has no responsibility for the support of his brothers and sisters, but he can be compelled, in a proceeding brought by the commissioner of public welfare, to contribute to the support of his father and mother such sum as the court may deem just and equitable.

As to the second inquiry, it is indeed the theory of the act that work relief shall only make up, but not exceed, "the difference between the resources of the family and the sum needed to provide the necessaries of life," and in calculating the resources of the family there should ordinarily be included its total weekly income from all sources. But in a case like this, as a practical matter, where it is uncertain as yet what contribution can be forced from the wage-earning son and there are six brothers and sisters for whose support he is not liable in any event, it would seem that in allotting work relief to the father the bureau should not figure on any more of the son's income than the family can count upon getting.

* * *

Family Earnings

A situation has been presented, concerning the liability of brothers and sisters for the support of younger members of their family during emergency. Three specific questions are asked with regard to what attitude the Public Welfare Department may take, and likewise the obligation involved. The answers to these questions are:

(1) The earnings of children may be counted in computing a budget for the family only so far as

(a) The support of a parent may be concerned and the child contributes either voluntarily or under compulsion of court, or

(b) A parent or guardian who is supporting or maintaining a minor child gives notice to the employer of said minor child that the wages are claimed for family support.

(2) There is no legal obligation by which children can be forced to support brothers and sisters.

(3) The Emergency Relief Administration has no power to extend the liability of individuals for support beyond that provided for by law. Such liability is already fixed by the terms of section 125 of the Public Welfare Law and does not extend to the inquiry here.

Notice to an employer of a minor that the wages are claimed by the parent or guardian is sufficient to warrant turning over such wages, but the parent or guardian must of course support and maintain the minor, and furthermore the rule is not applicable where the minor has become emancipated either by marriage, specific act or conduct of the parent, or circumstances indicating that the minor should maintain himself and support himself by his own wages. (Domestic Relations Law, section 72; Langan v. Kaufman, 94 Misc. 216.)

Where no legal guardian has been appointed, as in the instant case, a virtual emancipation has taken place and there is no legal obligation or basis for assuming that the children's earnings should go for common support. The Department of Public Welfare may not therefore rely upon the earnings of said children in computing budget requirements, other than their voluntary contribution. Of course legal proceedings might possibly be brought to seize the home of the family and apply the proceeds to the needs, provided the said home is in the name of either of the parents. (Public Welfare Law, section 127.)

- - -

7. RENTS, TAXES, ETC.

The Administration has been requested for a statement of its policy for reimbursement of allowable payments for taxes and interest to property owners in lieu of rent.

The Administration will reimburse welfare districts on amounts granted to active relief cases as payment on taxes or interest in lieu of rent, providing:

1. That the amounted grants in lieu of rent are in accordance with, and not greater than, the maximum rental allowance permitted by the local welfare department.

2. That the cases on which such allowable grants are made are not accepted as relief cases entirely on the basis of their inability to pay such taxes or interest. In other words, such taxes and interest must be a part of a relief budget granted to an active relief case. This policy applies to both home and work relief.

* * *

Interest on Federal Home Loan

An allowance in lieu of rent may be made for the payment of interest due on a Federal Home Loan. Such allowance is permissible in the same manner as allowances for payment of any interest charges on a mortgage.

* * *

Rent Payment Refused

The payment of rent is a legitimate charge upon home relief. Inasmuch, however, as the father of a person who is receiving public relief may be compelled to supply the whole cost thereof, if he is of sufficient ability to do so (Public Welfare Law, section 125), it would seem to be distinctly out of order for the town to pay rent to a person for three houses owned by him which are occupied by his two sons and his daughter, all of whom are being aided by the town.

Payment Approved

Certain tenants living in a village have presented bills for rent since November 1, 1931, which rent bills have not been accepted for payment by the home relief bureau, even though a town charge. The landlords are reluctant to evict tenants, and it would seem to be unfair discrimination to refuse to pay the rent of needy tenants of landlords who are humane, when they would obviously have to be paid were the landlords to insist upon an eviction. In other words, if these tenants are in need and their rent unpaid, and home relief, as in this instance, is a town charge, it would be proper for the rentals during the emergency period to be made the subject of home relief, and, if paid by the town, they would be subject to reimbursement by the State, under the Emergency Relief Act.

Work Bureau Not Liable

We are asked in regard to the payment of rents by a work relief bureau. It appears that the work relief granted includes allowances to cover rent in accordance with budget requirements noted on the case cards, but that the recipients do not pay their landlords, nor do the latter attempt to collect from them, preferring rather to rely upon an alleged verbal agreement with a former commissioner of public welfare, now deceased, that the city would pay the rents.

No such agreement as that referred to, if it was ever made, is binding upon the Emergency Relief Funds, which are to be administered in accordance with the Relief Administration Act (L. 1931, ch. 798) and the rulings of the administration pursuant thereto. Under that statute rents may be paid by the commissioner of public welfare as part of home relief (section 2, paragraph 8) where necessary and approved and not otherwise, regardless of any prior agreement, and there is no authority in the law for the payment of rents, as such, by the work relief bureau. The work relief bureau is limited to the payment of wages (section 17). Where it has included in the wages an allowance for rent its function in that respect is performed, and the landlords must look to the persons receiving the wages for the moneys due them. At any rate they have no claim upon the work bureau.

Saving Furniture

The payment of $10 to save a family's furniture may properly be allowed as reimbursable home relief. It becomes as essential as rent. The fact of its being part payment on a purchase is a secondary consideration, not vitiating it as home relief.

Payment of Taxes

In the case of a man who will be able to keep his home if he pays taxes and current interest thereon, which, combined, would amount to much less than the normal relief allowance for rent in his community, I see no objection to the issuance of T. E. R. A. home relief orders for such taxes and interest, on the theory that they are in place of rent orders, provided always, however, that there is not an equity in the property large enough to warrant refusing the case.

Pursuant to the rulings heretofore made, where a family is on the relief list and entitled to rental allowance, the use of the rental allowance for the payment of taxes assessed and payable, without which the family might be subject to the loss of homestead and eviction, is properly reimbursable in the same manner as the payment of interest on a mortgage, to the extent that the Relief Administration would approve of rental for such family. It is of course necessary that care be exercised in the investigation to ascertain the actual need of such family, in view of the ownership of the homestead. The fact that the reimbursement of taxes goes back into the possession of the municipal corporation should not militate against the effectual aid rendered to the family in the way of indirect rent.

Taxes in Lieu of Rent

In reply to a memorandum, asking (a) whether an actual bill for taxes may be passed by the Administration and reimbursement made to the welfare district, and (b) whether items of taxes may be included in the family budget in arriving at the budget deficiency of the family, and relief granted to the family for the amount of the deficiency, even though no tax bill has been rendered to the Administration as an item of relief, it may be said that where monthly payments on taxes, and even interest on a mortgage, do not exceed the normal allowance for rent in a welfare district, the same may be passed, audited as in lieu of rent, and reimbursed as home relief, provided there is not such an equity in the property as would warrant rejection of the case. In this view it would not seem to be necessary that the tax bill should be rendered to the Administration, but of course the welfare officer issuing the T. E. R. A. order on which reimbursement is sought would have to have actual knowledge of the amount of the taxes in order to complete his proof of claim.

* * *

Where Equity Has Vanished

The Rochester-Monroe county work bureau has been paying allowances for housing to home owners whose equity in the property has virtually disappeared, the mortgage holders allowing the families to remain in possession as long as these payments are kept up.

The fact that the equity has disappeared does not mitigate the necessity for shelter. Such payments, under the circumstances, are in fact payments of rent, and are unobjectionable if no greater than the normal rent allowance for relief cases in the vicinity.

Taxpayers Not on Relief

Projects by which taxpayers who are not on relief are to be allowed to obtain work through the welfare bureau for the purpose of paying their taxes have not been found by the Administration to be authorized by law, and hence are not approved.

Waiting for Eviction

It would appear as an unwise policy not to pay any rents until eviction notices are served.

In this instance, it appears that there is an interest of minors in the property which may be lost by reason of foreclosure if an amount is not permitted which might cover their taxes. Rentals are certainly allowable home relief, and there is no condition provided in the law that it must be allowed only upon threat of eviction. To wait until such time would be to defeat the purpose of the relief itself, and however wise it may be regarded by the local authorities, it is at best a short sighted economy and one which it would be well to discontinue.

Eviction of a Daughter by Father

Where it was sought to evict a woman and her husband, for non-payment of rent, from a room owned by the woman's father, the question of the father's responsibility to support his daughter was raised in bar, and the court held that the father's responsibility was not a good argument against dispossession, but that after the eviction action could be taken to compel the father to support his daughter.

The court's conclusion was undoubtedly correct. There are two aspects to a father's liability to support his daughter. The first, arising while she is a dependent minor, ceases upon her marriage and consequent emancipation, being then transferred to her husband. The second, under the Public Welfare Law, does not arise as to a married woman until her husband is no longer able to support her. In this case, eviction of the husband for non-payment of rent might be considered a condition precedent to an attempt to make the father liable.

Set-Off Against Landlords

While there may be no statutory authority for the comptroller of a city to deduct for back taxes the presently payable relief rents, there is some basis for a set-off by a city against a taxpayer owing taxes to the city.

The situation is not comparable to the dealings of the Administration so far as the city's payments to gas or electric companies are concerned,. If it reaches such proportions that it results in landlords refusing to accept rent orders, there might be some basis upon which the question should be brought before the city authorities. Without such problem being presented, however, the matter should be left between the city and the landlords against whose back taxes the city is seeking to set off these amounts.

* * *

Wages Not Tax Payments

Regarding a plan under which private persons will provide employment for the unemployed on condition that 60 per cent of the wages paid by them will be credited to them as paid upon their taxes, while similar projects have several times been presented to us in an extremely favorable light, we have not been able to find that the law would authorize such procedure. Taxation calls for the strictest adherence to statutory provisions, on pain of being void altogether.

* * ..

Wages in Form of Tax Notes

The city of New Rochelle proposes to issue a form of tax note covering that part of the work relief budget not concerned with rent. Under the Wicks Act work relief wages must be paid in cash.

The city is not a collector of rents for the landlord. The proposed plan would be a serious departure from the principle involved in paying cash wages and allowing the recipient his complete feeling of independence. Were the worker to be given the suggested slip or tax note it would differ little, if any, from a rent order in "home relief."

8. COERCION; ACCESS TO RECORDS, ETC.

Withdrawal from T. E. R. A.

Where a city asks as to its power to withdraw from the Emergency Relief System it may be said that the Administration does not intend, and has no power, to exert any compulsion over the department of public welfare in a city or county to force its cooperation. We have certain rules which, if met, permit the departments of public welfare to receive certain reimbursement on their expenditures for home relief. Moreover, we are equipped with field workers whose business it is to help departments of public welfare set up their offices, in order to meet our requirements. If at any time a department does not desire to continue to receive reimbursement of its expenditures from us, a simple method of handling the situation is not to send us the vouchers.

The law assumes that all departments of public welfare are cooperating with the State, to wit:

> "This act shall apply to every county and city in the State and State aid, under the provision of this act and the rules and regulations of the Administration, shall hereafter be available for all counties and cities, whether or not their governing boards have adopted resolutions accepting the provisions of this act, but a governing board or body of a county or city may adopt a resolution that it does not intend to request or accept State aid authorized by this act. A certified copy of such resolution shall be filed with the Administration, and thereupon and thereafter, the provisions of this act shall not apply to such county or city."

* *

Authority Over Town Welfare Officer

We are asked in regard to the authority of a county commissioner of public welfare over a town public welfare officer who is not granting adequate relief to a family, or no relief at all to some families. Under the Emergency Act, the county commissioner may refuse to certify for reimbursement the claims of a town welfare officer who fails to obey the rules and regulations of the Administration, which rules include adequacy of relief to all persons in real need. There is, in addition, a remedy under the Public Welfare Law.

It is the duty of all public welfare officials, in so far as funds are available for that purpose, to provide adequately for those unable to maintain themselves (Public Welfare Law, section 77), and it is the duty of a town board to make adequate appropriations for relief purposes and to take such action as may be necessary to provide public relief and care (id. section 43). Though the town public welfare officer is primarily responsible for the administration of such relief and care as is a town charge (section 25, subd. 1) and the county commissioner's primary responsibility is only for the relief and care for which the county public welfare district is responsible (section 22), the town welfare officer must report to the county commissioner as required (section 36, subds. 2 and 5), and the county commissioner has "general supervision and care" of all persons in need in the territory over which he has jurisdiction (section 22), and the town welfare officer is therefore subject to the county commissioner, just as both of them are subject to the State Department of Social Welfare (sections 36 and 138, subd. 4). When, therefore, a town welfare officer fails to provide necessary relief, mandamus will lie, on behalf of the needy person, to compel the officer to consider the case and act in regard thereto (Minklaer v. Rockefeller, 6 Cow. 276), and this proceeding may be brought by the county commissioner, the count attorne t' for him.

Furthermore, under the Public Welfare Law the county commissioner may order institutional care for any case, which care shall be a charge upon the town, and it is surmised that a stubborn town welfare officer would rather give necessary relief himself than to have the case taken out of his jurisdiction in this manner.

Bank Records

We are asked whether banks are required to give to a county work bureau information concerning the accounts of men who have applied for work. The Rules of the Administration, which have the force and effect of law (L. 1931, ch. 798, as amended, sections 27, 30, 31), require the investigation of all applications for work relief, which investigation must disclose, among other things, "the property and other resources of the family" and "the total income of the individual or family from all sources," and section 22 of the Emergency Act provides as follows:

> In executing any of the provisions of this act, the Administration and any person duly authorized or designated by it, may conduct any investigation pertinent or material to the furtherance of its work. The Administration and each person so authorized is hereby empowered to subpoena witnesses, administer oaths, take testimony and compel the production of such books, papers, records and documents as may be relevant to any such investigation. The administration shall have and may exercise such other powers as may be necessary to carry out the provisions of this act.

If, therefore, access to such bank records as the duty of a work bureau requires it to examine is refused, it should apply to the Administration for authority to compel the same. This power is separate and distinct from the similar powers of a public welfare official under a Public Welfare Law (section 78), but the provision of that statute (section 155) that information thus obtained shall be considered confidential is applicable thereto.

Fraud in Relief

Where a man was guilty of a fraud upon the Administration in attempting to obtain funds without working, and by selling his credentials, and a second man was guilty of the perpetration of a misrepresentation upon the Administration in obtaining work under false pretenses, neither one should be paid. They are both guilty of most reprehensible conduct, and such practices should be carefully guarded against. It may in some instances be advisable to recommend to the District Attorney the prosecution of such cases under the law, in order that such practices should be rooted out in the administration of emergency relief.

Penalty for False Statements

Referring to an inquiry as to what may be done to discipline persons who swear falsely in their applications for home relief, section 147 of the Public Welfare Law gives public welfare officials power to administer oaths and take affidavits in all matters pertaining to their office and to elicit, by examination under oath, statements of facts from applicants for relief, and section 148 provides that

"any fraud or false representation made by an applicant for relief, or by any person to secure relief for another person, or any wilful act designed to interfere with the proper administration of public relief and care, shall be deemed a misdemeanor."

Such misdemeanor is triable by any justice of the peace of the town (Code Crim. Proc., section 56, subd. 35), the procedure, punishment, probation, restitution, etc., being the same as in any other case in which a court of special sessions has jurisdiction (Code Crim. Proc., sections 483, 717.)

9. WORKMEN'S COMPENSATION

Chapter 769 of the Laws of 1934 has excluded persons receiving work relief from the operation of the Workmen's Compensation Law, and Section 16-a of the Emergency Relief Act, as added by Chapter 303 of the Laws of 1934, has placed upon the Relief Administration responsibility for care and relief of all such persons who may be disabled or injured, under terms therein provided. There is no further liability in such cases upon an employing municipal corporation or town, or upon the State.

These enactments render obsolete all that has previously been written upon this subject.

10. LABOR QUESTIONS

Administrative Policy on Labor Organization

The question is raised whether laws dealing with labor organizations and the right to "collective bargaining" with employers are applicable to relief workers and the State Administration, or between workers and the local governmental units representing the State Temporary Emergency Relief Administration.

There is nothing in the relief laws which has any bearing on this problem, and quite properly so. Relief employment is a form of public welfare aid and not the normal accepted form of employer, employee relationship. There is no reason why the workers, if they so desire, should not formulate organizations among themselves for such purposes as they may believe helpful to themselves.

It would be a short-sighted policy to deny them that privilege. Such organization has been attempted in other localities in some form or other and the Administration has no objection.

Certain safeguards to continuance of work should, however, be observed. In effecting such organization, there should be no interruption of work for that purpose, nor any form of activity which may interfere with the progressing of the work relief projects or the working without interruption or annoyance of others. There is no question of "bargaining" here, because the basis of earning is the relief need, and of that the Administration is the final judge.

So, too, of the duration of the employment and the approval of the project on which they may work. There may be matters, helpful in some way, in which the workers might be able to assist the local bureaus and the Administration. In such matters, they should be handled with sympathetic understanding and their suggestions given consideration. There should be no matter of "*demands*" because they are not properly in a position fairly or reasonably to make demands. It is the State they are dealing with. In matters of this kind we have found that the workers can be made to understand the true nature of the relationship with the government.

Such questions should be discussed with the Administration's field representative so that there may be a wholesome understanding of the problem and the manner of handling it.

Relief Workers' Organization

It would appear that the organization of emergency relief workers known as the A.O.P.E.E. seeks and in fact demands that the relationship between the State and the municipal governments and the relief workers be acknowledged as the existence of a normal employer-employee relationship as it exists in private industries conducted for profit. For example, they demand that the collective bargaining feature of the National Recovery Act should apply to an organization such as theirs and therefore they should be accorded the right to be heard upon the complaints either by or against relief workers, and the privilege of cross-examination of the employer who may have dismissed a relief worker in order to ascertain at a public hearing the causes for such dismissal.

On the other hand, the Administration's policy, as an agency of the State government, is thus expressed:

The administration of relief, whether it be work relief or home relief, is the administration and distribution of public relief by the State or local governments. It is a part of the public welfare program of the State. The relationship is not that of the normal private industrial employer who conducts his industry for profit with his employees, to which said relationship the collective bargaining features of the Recovery Act were specifically made applicable. The State government as such, through its agency the

Relief Administration, does not accept the features of the collective bargaining phase of the Recovery Act as applicable to the relief of the State, for those who are receiving relief, whether it be home relief or work relief.

It may well be that this difference in point of view has been an irritant to the members of the organization of relief workers which asserts its right to examine those who dismiss and to meet with and bargain with the Relief Administration in respect of the terms and conditions of their employment.

The same situation would prevail for home relief recipients if the policy urged by the relief workers organization were to be adopted. The Administration feels that such a policy is inconsistent with governmental efficiency and also inconsistent with sound public policy in the administration of relief.

It would be a misnomer to classify those who seek to impose this view on the Administration with the classification of "radicals" or "agitators." On the other hand, it may also be that attempts by organizations of relief workers to force acceptance of their views upon the public authorities and to take active steps may cause an interference with the effective administration of relief. It is probably this eventuality which has motivated certain welfare officials to place such employees or representatives of a workers organization in the category of "radicals," whether they in fact be such or not.

Prevailing Rate to Be Paid

A complaint has come in from several parts of the State that work bureau chairmen are not paying the current rate of wage for skilled workers. Where work bureaus are undertaking projects requiring skilled labor, it is understood that Rule 6 of the Administration, requiring the payment of the current rate of wage for the type of work performed should be carried out.

This rule has been neglected to such an extent by certain work bureau chairmen that the Administration feels it necessary to caution work bureau chairmen that continued negligence with regard to this matter will result in the elimination of reimbursement in cases where such negligence is established.

Labor Department to Be Consulted

The question of prevailing rates of wages is raised frequently by local work bureaus. The Administration has ruled that the final decision as to what is the actual prevailing rate of wage in a given locality rests with the local work bureau. (See Rule 6 of the Rules and Regulations governing work relief.)

For your information, Elmer F. Andrews, Industrial Commissioner of the State of New York, has fixed the minimum wage which must be paid (outside of cities) to laborers on contract highway construction and repair work, at 50 cents an hour in the counties of Nassau, Suffolk, Westchester and Rockland, and at 40 cents an hour in other counties of the State. A determination of the wage rate was made mandatory by the Canney Bill (chapter 733 of the Laws of 1933), which provides that:

> "The advertised specifications for every contract for the construction, reconstruction, maintenance and/or repair of highways to which the state, county, town and/or village is a party shall contain a provision stating the minimum hourly rate of wage which can be paid, as shall be designated by the industrial commissioner, to the laborers employed in the performance of the contract, either by the contractor, subcontractor or other person doing or contracting to do the whole or a part of the work contemplated by the contract, and the contract shall contain a stipulation that such laborers shall be paid not less than such hourly minimum rate of wage."

Rates paid for public works in the cities are determined by municipal officials, and not by the Industrial Commissioner.

The Industrial Commissioner's rates should be taken into consideration by the local bureau in establishing its own prevailing rate, but the provisions of the Canney Bill do not include work relief, and therefore final judgment in the matter rests with the local work bureaus.

May we suggest that wherever the local work bureau finds it difficult to decide what should be the prevailing rate for a given type of work, it request the advice of the State Department of Labor, which has information on file concerning wage rates for common and skilled labor.

Responsibility of Local Bureau

The determination of what constitutes the "prevailing rate" of wage for a kind of work is a question of fact and must be decided by the local work bureau. The Administration will not and cannot be expected to pass on the local situation in each case. The policy of the State Labor Department where union wages predominate, has been to accept them as "prevailing" rate for public work in general. Union rates, however, may not necessarily be the "prevailing rate." Care should be exercised not to permit the effects of the economic crisis to depress wage rates unduly so as to destroy an actual reasonable basis for skilled work. The local bureau should consider the extent of union employment in the locality as a vital factor in determining the "prevailing rate" as well as other factors. The mere fact that you can hire unemployed at a lower rate doesn't fairly establish that lower rate as the "prevailing" rate in the true labor sense. Unemployed men will work for what they can get. It should be the aim of the bureau to set a standard consonant with conditions as nearly normal as possible—and with due regard to the facts. Further than outlining the basis as above, the T.E.R.A. cannot undertake to decide the local bureau's problem nor assume the responsibility for fixing the local rate.

Duress by Contractor

Where a highway contractor on a Federal aid relief project, employing men furnished by a county work bureau, has requested employees to sign an agreement to work ten hours a day, in violation of the State and Federal regulations, this is a form of duress without legal or moral authority or propriety and it should be promptly and summarily stamped out.

Laborer and Technician

It has been brought to the attention of the administration that certain welfare districts in the State are empoying on work relief projects, highly trained technical workers (i. e. steam shovel, steam roller, compressor operators, etc.) who are being paid the prevailing rate of wage for the type of work performed, in accordance with Rule 6 of the Rules and Regulations governing work relief, but whose weekly earnings are far in excess of the requirements defined in Rule 9. In explanation, it is said that these individuals of necessity must work full time to insure efficiency of operation of the project, and that if employed on the so-called "stagger system" the resulting job might be poorly done.

It is not the intention of the Administration to discourage the employment of persons necessary for such projects, but it cannot reimburse any municipal corporation for wages paid which are not in accordance with the Rules and Regulations.

We believe that as far as possible all such skilled personnel should be taken from the work relief lists and should be staggered. If this skilled personnel, however, is required on full time, the total cost of it should be borne by the municipal corporation. If, on the other hand, the personnel can be employed in accordance with Rule 9, the Temporary Emergency Relief Administration will then reimburse on wages paid.

Union Labor

The question is presented of a union worker, entitled to assistance from the city under the Public Walfare Law, who refused to accept employment offered by the emergency work bureau, on the ground that skilled tradesmen who are not union members are employed on the same job. It is asked if, under these circum-

stances, and disregarding for the moment the necessity of supporting his family, this man is entitled to home relief.

The Administration has been desirous at all times to satisfy the
requirements of union labor, so far as it has been feasible to do
so. In respects of the prevailing rate of wage, for example, the
payment of which is specified as a State policy in the Labor Law,
the Administration has authorized the employment of union members on work relief projects at union (prevailing rate) wages,
provided the total paid to each man in any week did not exceed
his budgetary needs as determined under the work relief rules.
There is, however, nothing in the statutes requiring that relief be
limited to union men, and it would seem that where union rules
prevent the acceptance of work relief wages by a union member the
support of such union member becomes an obligation of the union,
rather than of the public.

In response to the specific inquiry relief under the Emergency
Act is for "needy persons who are unemployed, or, if employed,
whose compensation therefrom is inadequate to provide the necessaries of life" (section 9) and under the Public Welfare Law
it is for "those unable to maintain themselves" (section 77), and
in my opinion one who is able to work but who refuses to accept
work relief, for whatever reason, is not "needy" in the sense of
the Emergency Act or "unable to maintain himself" in the sense
of the Public Welfare Law, and such person is, therefore, not
entitled to home relief.

Relief in Labor Disputes

The following question has been submitted for determination
to ascertain the attitude of the Administration on relief to families
whose distress may temporarily be caused by the fact that the wage
earners of the family are engaged in a labor strike in opposition
to a proposed reduction of wages in the plant where formerly
employed. The case is put as follows by the field representative:

"A situation has developed which has certain potentiali-
ties. The local silk mill is out on a strike. About 125 previously
employed are involved. The resources of this group are questionable, and therefore we can assume that a fair proportion of these
individuals may ultimately apply, particularly if the strike is not
settled. What should be the thinking of the Public Welfare
Department re this? The individuals may become in need of relief
(they are protesting the cut in wages) and the city is put in the
position of saying whether or not it will support strikers. The mill
claims to have secured an order which can be handled only if wages
are cut."

It is not and should not be the province of the T. E. R. A., as an
agency of the State, to inject itself in or become party to a controversy between capital and labor. The T. E. R. A., as an agency
of the State and supported by State funds, should not permit its

resources, or the withholding of such resources, to be used as a possible determining factor in a dispute between labor and capital, in which labor is attempting to use its collective bargaining power in an endeavor to avoid a reduction in wages.

Each case applying for relief during the emergency under the T. E. R. A. rules and regulations, should be treated upon its merits, entirely irrespective of, and without regard to any labor controversy in which the applicant, or a member of the applicant's family may be involved. To hold otherwise might be interpreted as lending the aid of the State to the forces of industry in utilizing the denial of the State's resources to those in need as a means of breaking down the collective bargaining power of labor in a dispute with capital.

This should not be interpreted as the assumption by the T. E. R. A. of an attitude favorable to labor in such dispute, or to industry. It is merely the expression of an attitude of "hands off" in regard to such disputes, and the expression of a policy that the needs of those in distress will be met without regard to the cause of such need in an individual case, whether it results from a labor controversy or whether it results from unemployment otherwise created.

It is not the purpose or province of the Temporary Emergency Relief Administration to participate in a labor dispute on one side or other. The need of relief is the governing factor, not the origin of the strike or dispute.

The adjustment of a strike is a question in which the N. R. A. agencies are primarily concerned. Until the Federal authorities have indicated a definite attitude on the dispute in question, the State Relief Administration will not deviate from the policy above outlined. Relief should be furnished where the need exists. The fact that an honest labor dispute may have become a contributing factor in bringing the family to a relief level should not militate against the granting of relief.

11. MUNICIPAL PROBLEMS; CHARTER PROVISIONS

Buffalo Consolidation Problems

Under the consolidation of all relief work in the city of Buffalo, pursuant to subd 2, of section 12 of the Emergency Act, as amended by L. 1933, ch. 259, certain questions have arisen.

(1) The entire responsibility under this form of consolidation passes to the new committee. It is subject to such conditions and regulations as the Relief Administration may prescribe. Under the circumstances, the chairman of the new relief bureau would be the proper person to sign both home and work relief claims. How-

ever the Administration may alter such precedure by permiting them to designate the commissioner of public welfare for home relief and the chairman of the new bureau for work relief. The action, however, should be the action of the new bureau as a body and the said bureau bears full responsibility for both home and/or work relief.

The forms now in use offer no real obstacle, for a stamp with proper title of chairman could be used on the forms presented with claims and the affidavit attached thereto.

When the new bureau is allowed to function, they have the right to reduce the powers of the commissioner of public welfare insofar as relief under the act is administered. He is subject to their direction as though as to such extent superseded and must render services as directed.

The Administration with its power of conditional approval of such consolidation may prescribe as a condition that the Public Welfare Council in cases shall act for *"home relief"*— but as a matter of policy, I wonder whether it is advisable to intervene to such extent.

All these problems should be thoroughly considered before the approval is given to the proposed consolidation under paragraph 2 of section 12.

(2) Query as to what the administration should assume as to the policies of new joint Bureaus when established.

These are local problems which should be faced locally, with the Administration as *"parens patriae."*

* * *

Buffalo Board of Social Welfare

Under the Buffalo charter approved at a home rule referendum in 1927 and effective January 1, 1928, a board of social welfare of five members appointed by the mayor (section 291) "shall be the head of the department of social welfare" of the city (section 290), and shall administer all care and relief which is chargeable to the city under State law and have all the duties and powers of the overseer of the poor of a city in relation thereto, including veteran relief (section 293). The board of social welfare may appoint and at pleasure remove a director of social welfare (section 294), who shall be the board's chief executive officer and, subject to the board's direction, shall have supervision and management of relief, including the duty to make investigations and bring prosecutions in its name (section 295).

The Public Welfare Law (section 6) confirms all there powers of the city board, while giving the county commissioner general jurisdiction outside of Buffalo.

(1) With regard to an application for consolidation of city and county agencies, the foregoing would seem to be immaterial, as the statute provides (section 12, as amended by L. 1933, ch. 259) that such application shall be made, for a city, by the mayor thereof.

(2) This set-up does not give Buffalo any special right to remain out of a county unit system. If the legislative body of the city should confirm a resolution of the county board of supervisors establishing such unit, thereafter, pursuant to section 27 of the Public Welfare Law, all the powers and duties of the board of social welfare (which is the "city public welfare officer") would become inoperative. The Public Welfare Law, where applicable in terms and in effect alike to all cities, supersedes a home rule charter.

(3) The board of social welfare is the responsible relief author-ity for the city of Buffalo. Its chairman counts only one vote thereon, and the director of public welfare, while he is the chief executive officer of the board, is its creature, serving at its pleasure and subject to its directions in all things.

Erie County Work Bureau

The Erie county work bureau was appointed in December, 1931, by the chairman of the board of supervisors. There is no record in the minutes of the board, showing that the appointment of the bureau was confirmed. The county attorney has therefore ruled that the work bureau is not legally constituted, and the chairman is said to have so declared and to have appointed another bureau, which has been confirmed by the board.

The statute (section 7) then provided, and still provides, that "the governing board of a county may establish in a county public welfare district, for the emergency period, an emergency work bureau, to consist of three or more persons to be appointed by such governing board." Such appointment by the chairman, whether ratified by the board or not, would therefore be prima facie unlawful, and in fact the correct procedure, adopted in every other case, so far as I know, has been for the appointments to be made in a resolution adopted by the board.

On the other hand it was provided in L. 1932, ch. 567, that "Members of local bureaus heretofore or hereafter appointed shall continue in office for the duration of the emergency unless removed as herein provided." The board first appointed in Erie county, being a de facto body, functioning without question, appropriated to, and consented to and accepted by all, was, therefore, confirmed as de jure by this enactment, and can not be superseded unless removed on charges after a hearing.

Status of Mayor of Rochester

The mayor of the city of Rochester is no more than an appurte-nance of the city council, which appoints him. If not a member of the council he "shall have all the rights and privileges of a councilman except the right to vote in council.'' What he can do is to ''preside over the meetings of the council, appoint commissioners of deeds, and have such powers as are conferred upon him by law or ordinance.'' (1925 chapter, section 66.)

The city manager, on the other hand, is the chief administrative officer of the city, with power, among other things, to ''appoint and remove the heads of all departments, the members of all boards, and all subordinate officers and employees except as otherwise provided in this local law.'' (id., section 91.)

If L. 1933, ch. 259, did not confer the power to appoint work bureau members for a city solely upon the mayor thereof, instead of placing it in the hands of ''the Mayor or chief administrative officer'' as does section 7 of the Emergency Act, there would be no question that, in Rochester, the city manager has that power. Even so, I think he has it anyway, and that when the charter provides that the ''mayor'' shall ''have such powers as are conferred upon him by law,'' it means such powers as are conferred upon *him*, i. e., the mayor of Rochester, and not such powers as are conferred generally upon those mayors who are in fact the chief administrative officers of their cities with summary powers of appointment.

City Work on State Property

The city of Hornell has raised some objection to paying workers for work upon State property as a city project, on the ground that the city's funds may not be utilized for any but a city purpose, and that work on a State project is not a city purpose. The support of its poor or of those who are likely to become public charges, is a burden imposed on the city by the Public Welfare Law. Even if the burden were not imposed statutorily, it would still be the legal obligation of the city to support those who are unable to provide the means of sustenance for themselves. This is the city's burden and it is met by the city's providing them with the means of sustenance whether by work relief or otherwise, no matter where the work is carried out. In the instant case, it happens that it is carried out in a public manner and for a public purpose on State property. This conclusion that it is a proper city purpose would be so even if the State were not, as in the present instance, refunding the entire disbursement to the city. The objection, to say the least, is highly technical, and I feel even technically is completely overcome by the city's obligation to support its poor.

City Charters Superseded

The Public Welfare Law supersedes the inconsistent provisions of any city charter enacted prior thereto. This is a general principle. Whether the particular provisions referred to are in fact inconsistent, we could not say without knowledge of what they are.

Creating Additional Jobs

The right of a local work bureau or a welfare council to create positions under the Wicks Act is found in section 19. Where salaries are paid in part or all by the State funds or out of discretionary funds the Administration may, of course, dictate the conditions of approval.

The power to add necessary personnel to work or home relief bureaus, which is paid by the State, should rest with the local bureaus with the Administration's approval. Local government authorization (charter provisions, etc.) need not be a necessity, but perhaps would be wise, and the Administration should consider making it such.

However, often the local government might not wish to add an essential employee and the Administration and local bureau might deem it advisable. Under the Wicks Act as amended, I believe such power to exist. The local bureau alone, however, without Administration or government authority, cannot create such positions and charge them to the local treasury and/or State treasury.

The Administration should not flaunt its powers before local governmental bodies, but should cooperate and enable such bodies to function with proper control. They should not be placed under the heel of local bureaus.

In final analysis the pocketbook is the ultimate power to control. If local government refuses to appropriate, the local bureau is helpless and the State would have to bear the total burden. If it is desired to charged any of the cost of the position created to the local government, that body should approve, because they may refuse to appropriate the sum in question and thereby effectually defeat what would otherwise be approved. The power of the Administration through State funds is the greater, and should therefore be most judiciously exercised.

Charter Restriction Lifted

The common council of the city of Hornell raises money upon the budget plan, which includes the moneys needed by the city commissioner of public welfare "for public charity" (City Charter, sections 70, 58). The council may raise $70,000 more each year, outside the budget, for any purposes specified in the charter (section 71). It may raise $15,000 more for such purpose if authorized by a majority vote of the taxpayers (section 72). It is prohibited by section 73 from incurring any further liability. Under section 10 of the Emergency Relief Act the legislative body of a municipal corporation is authorized to incur the indebtedness therein provided for. It is my opinion that section 31 of the Emergency Act removes the restriction contained in section 73 of the charter, and that the common council may raise the money without referendum.

Funds Interchangeable

Where a city charter permits the raising of funds for "the temporary relief and support of the poor in the city for the ensuing fiscal year," there is nothing either in the interpretation of this charter provision or in the provisions of the Emergency Relief Act which prevents the use of either part or all of the funds so raised pursuant to said charter provision for work relief or home relief or part for one and part for the other so long as the funds themselves go to relieve those who are in need of temporary relief and support, in other words, those who are, strictly speaking, poor. The provisions of section 10 of the Emergency Relief Act provide additional means of raising revenues by municipal corporations for home or work relief but do not in any way provide the sole means of raising such funds. The said provisions are merely supplemental to and additional to those means which already are provided for by the local government or city charter. I do not see any provisions in the charter or in the Emergency Relief Act which necessitate the tagging of the funds raised for work relief or home relief; in other words, work relief and home relief are thrown together in the same category by section 10 of the Emergency Relief Act, and since both are for the support of the poor within the meaning of the act it is not necessary that funds raised be specified as for work relief or home relief by the municipality so raising those funds.

Welfare Law Controls

We are asked whether section 45, subd. 2, of the Public Welfare Law, providing that the legislative body of a city, forming part of a county public welfare district, shall appropriate money for public relief and care in the city and cause taxes to be levied for the same, superseded section 304 of the Lockport charter (L. 1911, ch. 807), which provided that such poor relief moneys shall be levied and collected in the city by the board of supervisors of Niagara county.

There can be no doubt, I think, that the provision of the Public Welfare Law, which is a general statute designed to prescribe a uniform system and practice throughout the State, supersedes a conflicting provision of a local or special act, particularly since the special provision is one of detail only. Property in the city of Lockport pays this tax in any event. The common council ought to amend the charter, to make it conform with the statute in this respect, but in the meantime the Public Welfare Law is to be considered controlling.

Borrowing Power Not Involved

There is no connection between the borrowing power of a city and reimbursement for home relief. If the city submits its vouchers for expenditure in proper form it is entitled to the reimbursement so long as there remain moneys available for that purpose. The city may avoid reimbursement simply by not claiming it but I fail to find anything in the Emergency Relief Act that would indicate that such a sacrifice was expected of a municipal corporation. Of course it enables the relief to go so much further if a city can handle 100 per cent of its own relief. The city of Ogdensburg is entitled to borrow for relief purposes under section 10 of the Emergency Relief Act without reference to the provisions of its charter concerning the anticipation of uncollected taxes. It may borrow upon the credit of the city alone, inasmuch as the powers set forth in section 10 are new, additional and supplemental to the powers already existing. The funds, of course, will have to be provided for in future budgets so that the indebtedness may be retired in the period set by section 10 of the statute.

Valid Obligations

In response to an inquiry with reference to the sale of certain notes of the city of Oswego issued under the Emergency Act, wherein certain banks desire the opinion of the Attorney-General as to the validity of said statute, it may be said that we have held repeatedly that the notes, certificates of indebtedness or other obligations of municipal corporations issued under section 10 of the Emergency Act are valid obligations of the municipal corporations.

Status of New York City

Notwithstanding the provision in section 662 of the Greater New York Charter that the city commissioner of public welfare "shall not have power to dispense any form of outdoor relief except as expressly provided in this chapter," it is provided in section 9 of the Emergency Relief Act that "a municipal corporation which has accepted the provisions of this act may furnish home relief." Therefore, when the city of New York duly accepted the provisions of the Emergency Relief Act, it became entitled to furnish outdoor relief during the emergency period, pursuant to the rules and requirements of the Temporary Emergency Relief Administration.

New York City Exempted

"Outdoor relief," except as in the charter provided, was forbidden to the Welfare Commisisoner of New York City by section 662 of the city charter. To that extent the State Public Welfare Law was, of course, inapplicable.

It .has always been a moot question, however, whether the city was responsible for the mutual obligations of the said Public Welfare Law arising out of '/settlement,'' etc.

We have continued to administer the Wicks Act, however, on the theory that by section 9, the ·city was permitted to share in the benefits of the Act. For the purposes of chapter 798, Laws of 1931 (Wicks Act) as amended, we have confined New York City's authority to the terms and provisions of that Act alone and will continue so to do, reading into the charter the Wicks Act exemption for the period of the emergency.

Agreements to Pay

The city of Fulton, having no money with which to pay certain relief bills and being unable to borrow, proposes to issue certified "agreements" to pay the same, which the banks have agreed to accept from the suppliers. It is asked if the Relief Administration will reimburse upon claims paid by such "agreements."

An agreement of this nature is a liquidated claim against the city, equivalent to a judgment or any other obligation assumed by the city, voluntarily or otherwise. Value has been received by the city, and the obligation is fully as binding as though a note had been issued and cash received for it and the bills thus paid. The net result is the same; i. e., the city owes someone the amount of the bills.

Always assuming that the obligations fall within the debt limit, I see no reason why "agreements" thus issued, if accepted by the merchants as full payment, as evidenced by vouchers properly audited and receipted by the merchants as "paid," may not be considered as "expenditures" by the city and be reimbursed as such.

Warrants as Payment

Where the city chamberlain of Elmira issues interest-bearing warrants, negotiable at the banks, which warrants, due March 1, are practically all outstanding, and it is asked if one may consider these warrants in lieu of checks and may deem the vouchers paid, I may say that if, as seems indicated, these warrants are being accepted by merchants and others in settlement of current transactions, I can see no reason why they should not be regarded as payments by the city for the considerations which they cover.

Private Business

A county work bureau proposes as a work project the opening of a mill manufacturing a cheap line of sweaters, underwear, etc., the product not to be put on the open market but to be disposed of in some fashion not disclosed in the plan. The use of the mill has been donated free of cost. It was always operated successfully until the death of the owner. The project would provide full time employment for a time for 125 men and women, 75 per cent of whom would be skilled workers, and the cost would be $20,000 for wages and $20,000 for materials, the funds to be raised by an appropriation by the board of supervisors. There is a long line of cases holding that a municipal corporation is not entitled to engage in business in competition with private interests. To be sure, the State, possessing every power not expressly forbidden to it by its Constitution, or reserved to the United States or forbidden to the States by the Federal Constitution, is not bound by the decisions referred to, and it could assuredly engage in manufacturing and merchandising, and so might a city or county if the Legislature said it could. But it does not appear that the Legislature has made such authorization. The project should not be approved without full consideration of probable consequences socially.

Land Under Lease

If certain land in the village of Cape Vincent, which is owned by the New York Central Railroad, is taken under lease by the village, there can be no question that it would be the property of the municipal corporation so as to make valid its use as the site of a work project under the Emergency Act.

All Relief Purposes Included

Where the city of Lackawanna borrowed $200,000 for work relief, pursuant to the Emergency Relief Act (L. 1931, ch. 708), but there was a much heavier demand for home relief than for work relief, and the city's home relief budget was about exhausted, the question arose whether a portion of the funds raised by the sale of work relief bonds might lawfully be transferred to the fund established for home relief. In this connection there were cited several decisions and opinions to the effect that money borrowed by a municipal corporation for a specific purpose may be used only for that purpose.

The rule of law referred to is, of course, well established. Section 10 of the Emergency Act, under which this loan was made, however, does not limit the city to a borrowing for work relief, but provides that the loan might be "for work relief and/or home relief," and despite the effort of the Relief Administration, and of the Attorney-General, in construing this statute, having been to interpret the same as liberally as possible (see Emergency Act, section 29), it would hardly seem to me to be permissible to use funds borrowed for work relief under the Emergency Act for any other kind of relief which the Emergency Act has authorized. Relief borrowing should cover "all relief purposes."

Barred by Charter Provision

The question is asked whether a member of a firm engaged in contracts with the city may be appointed to the work bureau. The answer would seem to be found in the clear provisions of the Rochester City Charter. Whether a city officer or mere employee, no member of the Rochester work bureau can do business directly or indirectly with the city, due to the unusual provisions of section 25 of the Rochester Charter (Laws of 1907, ch. 755), which reads as follows:

"Every officer and employee of the city is prohibited from being interested, directly or indirectly, in any contract to which the city is a party, either as principal, surety or otherwise; or in any purchase from or sale to the city, its boards or officers, of any real or personal property, or in any work performed for or services rendered to the city, its board or officers, other than the work or services imposed upon them by their office or position. Any contract made in violation of these provisions is void. This section does not apply to financial transactions between financial institutions and the city, its boards or officers, and does not include a commissioner of deeds."

*

Compliance With General Municipal Law

It is asked on behalf of the city of Rensselaer whether certificates of indebtedness, as provided for by section 10 of chapter 798 of the Laws of 1931, must be advertised and sold at public auction rather than at private sale. Section 9 of the General Municipal Law (amended 1917, ch. 534) provides that all bonds of a city in which Rensselaer would be classed shall be sold "at public sale not less than five or more than thirty days after a notice of such sale." This is a reasonable provision which would not unduly delay the sale of such certificates and I fail to see wherein it is inconsistent with the provisions of the Emergency Relief Act. It may perhaps cause some period of time to elapse in the raising of the funds but it is not inconsistent to such an extent as to warrant its being superseded by the provisions of the Emergency Relief Act. Certificates of indebtedness are classified as bonds (General

Municipal Law, section 21; Denver v. Home Savings Bank, 235 U. S. 101). I am constrained, therefore, to advise that the sale of certificates of indebtedness must follow the same procedure as the sale of bonds under the General Municipal Law. This is in conformity with sound public policy as well.

Supplementary Borrowing Powers

We have held that the power of a municipal corporation to borrow for work relief and/or home relief, as defined in the Emergency Relief Act (L. 1931, ch. 798, as amended by L. 1932, ch. 567), pursuant to section 10 thereof, is supplementary and additional to powers of borrowing possessed by such corporation under prior acts or charters. It would seem, therefore, that when the borrowing is for such purpose and pursuant to said act, restrictions upon ordinary borrowing, contained in a charter or other statute, would not be applicable thereto.

Assessment Provisions Inapplicable

In regard to the building and paving and grading of streets, normally a charter provision requiring 75 per cent of the cost to be provided by the property owners benefited would be carried out. In the instant situation, however, such streets might never have been built were it not for the necessity of providing work relief and the incidental benefit that such streets afford to the city. The primary consideration here is the emergency of the relief which the building of said streets offers to the workers. A portion of the funds in this instance is supplied by the State. All factors being considered, it would perhaps not be feasible to allocate that proportion of the cost which should be paid by the property owners themselves. There is the further consideration that the streets might never have been constructed in the normal course of municipal operations. Therefore it is not necesary, under the circumstances, that 75 per cent of the cost of building such new streets, undertaken as work relief projects pursuant to chapter 798 of the Laws of 1931, be assessed against the property owners supposedly benefited thereby.

The charter of the city of New Rochelle provides that paving improvements carried on by the city must be assessed against the abutting property owners. The city of New Rochelle, however, has adopted as an emergency work project a program of remedying defects in streets, curbing, gutters, sidewalks, etc., and has sent to the abutting owners a letter advising them that the cost of such work will not be assessed against them, at the same time expressing the hope that they will contribute voluntarily to the work relief fund. Men are already at work under this program. The work thus undertaken is not of a type which the city would attempt in the ordinary course. In these circumstances the exemption of abutting owners from assessments for repairing small defects in curbs, pavements, sidewalks, gutters, etc., not normally undertaken, is a local issue, not pertinent to the Administration's decision. This work may not be considered as paving improvements within the meaning of the charter provision, susceptible of equitable assessments thereunder. It may well be approved by the Administration as a work relief project.

The question has arisen whether a city can use any of the funds appropriated under the provisions of section 10 for carrying out projects such as the construction of sewers, curbs or sidewalks which are ordinarily paid for by assessments on properties benefited. (1) If the city is not otherwise able to finance said improvements, funds raised under section 10 are available. If the improvements would not otherwise be undertaken, they are eligible as work project. (2) Use of such funds for labor, etc., is not unconstitutional or invalid. It is not essential that the costs be charged back to property when the improvement could not normally be undertaken but as a relief measure. In any event, the labor costs reimbursable by the State could not be properly charged against property owners.

12. MUNICIPAL OFFICIALS

Supervisors as Work Bureau Members

A member of a board of supervisors is not eligible to membership on an emergency work bureau.

1. The emergency work bureau is not a committee of the board of supervisors. Though that board is authorized to establish it (L. 1931, ch. 798, as amended, section 7), such bureau is an agency of the Temporary Emergency Relief Administration and subject in all matters to the supervision, direction and control of the Administration (id., section 8). The chairman of a work bureau is not, as such, engaged in executing any of the duties or powers of a supervisor or a board of supervisors (County Law, section 12; Town Law, section 98).

2. No public board may lawfully appoint one of its own members to a public position. (People v. Pearson, 121 Misc. 26; affirmed 207 App. Div. 888 mem.; Wood v. Whithall, 120 Misc. 124; affirmed 206 App. Div. 768 mem.)

3. No member of a board of supervisors is eligible for any position the compensation of which is to be audited by the board, of which he is a member, for there would then arise an incompatibility, making it improper for both places to be held by the same person (People ex rel. Ryan v. Green, 58 N.Y. 295, 304; Attorney-General v. Henry (Mass.) 159 N.E. 539).

4. The established principle is too well founded to make it possible for us, under the authorities, to advise that it could be varied, or that it would be safe to attempt to do so. The dangers inherent in any such power to audit one's own accounts and to have control of one's own salary and employment have been recognized by the courts again and again, and ought, it would seem, to be readily apparent.

Incompatibility between two offices is an inconsistency in the functions of the two; as judge and clerk of the same court, officer who present his personal account subject to audit, and officer whose duty it is to audit it (People ex rel. Ryan v. Green, 58 N.Y. 295, 304). It lies in a conflict of interest. (Attorney-General v. Henry, Mass., 159 N.E. 539.) See also notes, 5 L.R.A. 853; 11 L.R.A. 613, 13 L.R.A. N.S. 240, L.R.A. 1917 A-216. And the courts have viewed the question with such sternness as to hold that where an office-holder is appointed to a second office which is incompatible, his first office is ipso facto vacated immediately upon his qualifying for the second (People v. Carrique, 2 Hill 93; People v. Dillon, 38 App. Div. 539).

* * *

City Chairman as County Chairman

We are asked whether the chairman of the emergency work bureau in Poughkeepsie may also be chairman of the Dutchess county work bureau.

The same person may hold any number of public positions unless there is some constitutional or statutory bar, or unless there is an incompatibility and inconsistency between the positions. Where one place is subservient to the other, or one audits or approves the other's accounts, or the relationship is otherwise one of chief and subordinate to a degree that it could not in good conscience be occupied by the same person, incompatibiilty and inconsistency are sufficiently indicated. These conditions do not appear to be present in the circumstances offered. On the contrary, cooperation between city and county bureaus would be highly desirable.

If, however, subsequent developments should make it appear that the duties of city and county chairmen were in conflict, the view herein expressed might be subject to revision.

Common Council Member

A member of the common council holds the same relative position as a member of the board of supervisors. He is a member of the appropriating and auditing body, which controls the finances available for the expenditures which as a member of the bureau he would disburse. The inconsistency has repeatedly been made the basis of judicial decision invalidating such appointment. We have held that common council members are not eligible for bureau appointment.

* *

When Town Clerk May Act

A town clerk, authorized by the town board to administer work relief in the town, has the right to approve applications and sign payroll checks, provided also he has the approval of the county work bureau, since work relief in a town can only be carried on as such by an agency of such county bureau.

* *

Bureau Chairman in Home Relief

The chairman of the Newburgh emergency work bureau, who appointed himself to that position upon his retirement as mayor, was appointed by the city commissioners to fill a vacancy on the board of commissioners of the City and Town Home, which is the local home relief authority.

A mayor's appointment of himself to a public position is of doubtful legality, but that point appears to have been waived: I see no objection to the work bureau chairman being also on the board of commissioners of the home. There is no incompatibility between home relief and work relief, and no subservience of one position to the other.

* *

Ex-Officio Members

An ex-officio officer is such "by virtue of the office" he already holds, without any other warrant or appointment than that resulting from the holding of such office. As such he has every power of one duly appointed. (Foote v. Lake County, 206 Ill. 185, 69 N.E. 97; Drennan v. People, 222 Ill. 592, 78 N.E. 937.) He counts to make a quorum (King v. Physicians Casualty Assn. (Neb.) 150 N.W. 1010) and has one vote on any question arising (Opinions, Attorney-General, 1930, p. 406).

Commissioner as Ex-Officio Member

Paragraph 2, section 12, of chapter 259 of the Laws of 1933 states that "The commissioner of public welfare of the public welfare district in which such emergency relief bureau shall have been established shall be ex-officio a member of said bureau in addition to the members appointed as above provided, and shall perform such duties in respect to relief administered under chapter

798 of the Laws of 1931, as amended, as may be directed by said bureau.''

* * *

Official Financially Interested

Although a town welfare officer offers to supply tomato plants at less than cost, it is forbidden by the Penal Law and by the Public Welfare Law (section 150) that such official should furnish to the town any article in which he is financially interested. There can be no exception to so salutary a rule.

Stockholder Not Barred

It is asked if a local Work Bureau official is disqualified from furnishing work relief materials if he is a stockholder of a firm. If the man is only a stockholder in a corporation the answer would be "No," but the same objections to other public officers would apply to him if he is a member of a partnership or an officer of the corporation, public policy being involved.

Liability for Predecessor's Acts

It is asked if a Town Commissioner of Public Welfare is responsible for the payment of bills incurred in irregular manner by the previous town welfare officer.

The town welfare officer may consult the town attorney, if any, as to his legal duties and obligations. It is my view that he has no duty to and should refuse to accept or approve claims for supplies where no relief order or signed voucher can be furnished for corroboration.

These claims are, of course, not reimbursable. The suppliers may sue either the city or the former welfare officer (if delivered on his oral order) as they see fit.

In respect of rent payments in a continuous period for a relief case, if the fact reveals the bona fides of the claim, it may be approved without any individual liability of the present welfare officer.

In respect of claims properly supported by vouchers, the fact of their being incurred under a previous incumbent of the same office does not create any personal liability, if no local law or other regulation prevents such approval.

County Probation Officer

A county probation officer is eligible to serve on a Works Division Committee.

Official as Bidder on Materials

A question has arisen regarding purchasing procedure under the new regulations. A member of a Works Division Committee is an executive in one of the local building supply houses. His services to the committee have been exemplary and it is asked if he is barred from participating in bids for material purchases, assuming that' such committee member engages in the regular bidding procedure and conforms to all regulations.

This is bad policy. It conflicts with well established municipal finance procedure and law. (Section 3 of Public Officers Law and section 1868 of the Penal Law.) While there is no question of the official's honesty, certainly there would be trouble if a member of the committee happened to be low bidder more than once, and certainly it would be bad policy to risk it, outside of the fact that it conflicts with a section of the municipal laws.

Supervisor as Welfare Officer

Under section 24 of the Public Welfare Law "each town board shall appoint a public welfare officer or authorize a supervisor of the town to act as such official." A supervisor, therefore, cannot appoint himself as town welfare officer, nor, if he is appointed to act as such by the town board, is he entitled to the compensation of a welfare officer, as there is no provision for the compensation of an acting welfare official, and the Department of Social Welfare has so ruled.

The new Town Law provides (section 20, subd. 4) that "No person shall be eligible to hold more than one town office." But this may not affect the situation, as when a supervisor is acting as welfare officer he is not holding the office.

Presumably if the supervisors find they cannot have the extra compensation, this practice will tend to diminish. It would be an argument for a county unit.

Fees for Non-Settled Cases

The practice of paying by a county or a city of a monthly fee to town welfare officers for handling non-settled cases is irregular. Such cases are to be handled by the county commissioner. (Public Welfare Law, section 58.)

Drawing Warrants for Funds

It is asked whether the town welfare officer or the town clerk should draw warrants on the supervisor for relief moneys. If the moneys have been raised by taxation, or by borrowing under section 10 of the Emergency Act as amended, the welfare officer draws the warrants. If, however, they are made available under section 141 of the Town Law, which requires an audit by the town board, the town clerk is the one to draw the orders in payment of claims so audited.

* * *

No Fee for Supervisor

A supervisor who keeps the books, manages the funds, and makes reports, etc., for a work relief bureau and performs much labor in the premises, while he claims nothing for his services to the work bureau, asks if he is entitled to 1 per cent of the money handled, in his capacity as supervisor. Work relief is not a town function in any sense, and a supervisor, as supervisor, has no legal contact with work relief moneys. Since he does not pay them out as supervisor, the case does not fall within section 85 of the Town Law, allowing the 1 per cent fee. His function is rather that of an agent of the work relief bureau of the welfare district, in which capacity a supervisor could not serve for pay.

* *

No Deductions by Supervisor from State Funds

The question arises by what legal authority supervisors retain 1 per cent of relief moneys in towns, and particularly the application of this rule, if such exists, to moneys contributed by the T. E. R. A. from State appropriations in aid of local relief.

Subd. 3 of section 85 of the Town Law, as added by L. 1905, ch. 642, provided as follows:

> "The supervisor of each town shall be allowed and paid, in the same manner as other town charges are allowed and paid, a fee of one per centum on all moneys paid out by him as such supervisor, including school moneys disbursed by him as provided in the Education Law, moneys paid out by him for damages arising from dogs killing or injuring as provided in Article 7 of the County Law, moneys in his hands paid out by him for the relief of the poor, and all other town moneys paid out by him for defraying town charges, except moneys expended under the Highway Law. But no such fee shall be allowed or paid upon moneys paid over by him to his successor in office. Such fees shall be in full compensation

for all services rendered by him in respect to moneys received and paid out by him as such supervisor as provided by law except the compensation provided in section 110 of the Highway Law.''

Under section 24 of the Public Welfare Law ''each town board shall appoint a public welfare officer or authorize a supervisor of the town to act as such official,'' and under section 41 of the same act ''the taxes levied for public relief and care in a town shall be paid to the town supervisor, who shall disburse them on written order of the town public welfare officer for the payment of verified bills and claims.''

The moneys, therefore, which may be considered to be in a supervisor's hands to be paid out by him for the relief of the poor, within the meaning of section 85 of the Town Law, are those which have been raised by taxation levied for public relief and care in the town. Moneys contributed by the T. E. R. A. out of State appropriations in aid of local relief are not such local moneys raised by town taxes, and, even if properly in the supervisor's hands, which is subject to some doubt, are not paid out by him as supervisor, but as an indirect agency of the T. E. R. A.

Under section 98 of the Town Law ''the supervisor of each town shall receive and pay over all moneys raised therein for defraying town charges, except those raised for the support of the poor, in towns where the poor is not a town charge; in counties where each town maintains the poor thereof, the town board of said town may by resolution direct that the money raised by said town for the outdoor relief of said town be held and retained by the supervisor and disbursed by him upon the orders of the respective overseers of the poor,'' etc. Under section 149-c, applicable only to certain towns, ''the supervisor of any such town shall demand, collect, receive and have the care and custody of, and shall disburse all moneys belonging to or due the town from every source, except as otherwise provided by law.'' But under this special act the supervisor may be salaried, in lieu of fees (section 143-a), and under the new Town Law, in effect January 1, 1934, while the supervisor is to have the same powers as those stated in the former section 149-c (section 29), he is to be salaried in lieu of fees except in such towns of the second class as have not adopted a budget system (section 27), in which towns he may still be allowed a fee of 1 per cent ''on all moneys paid out by him as such supervisor.''

These provisions are in every respect relative to town moneys, raised by the town or due to it as a town, and have no application to State moneys. Claims of towns for refunds under the Emergency Act are made by the county commissioner of public welfare, as the authorized agency of the T. E. R. A. (Emergency Act, sections 8 and 23), and payment of such claims is to the county treasurer for distribution to the towns (section 25). If such moneys come into the supervisor's possession, it is not by force of law, and they are certainly not in his hands as supervisor, nor paid out by him as such. Where the Administration is paying 100 per cent of the cost of relief in a town, the claim of a supervisor to a fee thereon ceases even to be debatable and becomes preposterous.

Fees to Welfare Officials

It is stated that in some counties the practice has existed of paying town welfare officers or their assistants on a fee basis; i.e., so much for each order granted or other official action taken.

This is not authorized by the Public Welfare Law, which expressly provides (section 24, amended by L. 1930, ch. 319, as to assistant welfare officers and other employees) that "the town board shall fix a salary to be paid a town public welfare officer, his assistant or other employees or fix the amount per hour to be paid them when they are performing any duty connected with their office," and contains nothing authorizing the payment of fees.

Fees are only collectible when expressly authorized by law, and an officer demanding or receiving a fee, from the public or from a governmental agency, must point to a particular statute authorizing the fee. This is a penal matter, and civil remedies, for restitution and damages, also exist against both the members of the town board authorizing the illegal payment and the recipients thereof.

There is an inherent right of action in a town the property of which has been wrongfully taken or received, to recover any compensation paid by the town not authorized by law or in excess of the compensation authorized by law, with damages, and this notwithstanding that the payment was made under a mistake of law and without fraud (46 C. J., p. 1030). By statute (Civ. Pr. Act, section 1222) the State, through the Attorney-General, is authorized to enforce this right of action on behalf of the town and (General Municipal Law, section 51) any taxpayer may pursue the same remedy.

* * *

Sales by City Officers

Referring to an inquiry whether members of the common council or other city officers, who are carrying on business of such kind that orders for relief issued by the city commissioner of public welfare may be presented to them, may lawfully accept such orders and claim payment therefor from the city, I am of the opinion that they may do so where there is no contract or arrangement between such officers and the city for the presentation and honoring of such orders.

It is true that under section 133 of the Town Law a member of a town board may not present to the town any claim or demand in which he has an interest (except his per diem compensation and official fees) or which is based wholly or partly on services or material rendered or furnished by him. But this does not appear to be the case as to city officials, who, in the absence of charter prohibitions, are governed by section 1868 of the Penal Law, making it a misdemeanor for a public officer who is authorized to make a contract in his official capacity, or to take part in making such contract, voluntarily to become interested in such contract, and by section 3 of the General City Law, forbidding any public officer of a city to be directly or indirectly interested in any contract the expense or consideration whereof is payable out of the city treasury.

Clearly, if the commissioner of public welfare should give cash to an applicant for relief, it would be lawful for a city official, who was also a merchant, to sell goods to such applicant and accept the cash in payment, and the contract relationship in such case would be between the merchant and the applicant, with the city no party thereto. I cannot see that the case is different where the applicant presents an order for merchandise, as, although the order is payable out of the city treasury, there is no contract between the merchant and the city. But, as I have indicated, it would be improper for a city official to enter into an arrangement with the city that such orders should be presented to him, and for this reason the issuance of orders good only at a store owned by a city official would probably be illegal.

▸ ＊

Officer as Relief Recipient

Where a foreman in charge of construction on a work relief project, which project is reimbursed 100 per cent by the State, is also a village trustee, and is out of work, and the village charter provides that "No member of the board of trustees or other officer having power or authority to contract, either individually or as a member of any board or body, shall be interested in any contract to which the village shall be a party," etc., I may say that the relationship between the recipient of relief and the municipal corporation I would not consider to be a contractual relationship, and hence the interest in such relationship is not the interest in a contract with the municipal corporation which would come within the prohibition of such provision of the charter.

The relationship rather is one of a person in need receiving relief from the government, and one whose welfare it is to the interest of the government to promote. Even though an individual, as the prospective recipient of relief, did work on a work relief project and violated the rules of the Administration and his work was improperly done, I question whether such an individual could recover from the State or the municipal corporation on the basis of a *quantum meruit*. In other words, for the value of such services as he rendered.

The relationship is one which has been created by circumstances, and the very fact that the relief in the form of home relief may be accepted without consideration inferentially leads to the conclusion that even though the relief is given in the form of work relief wages, it does not necessarily import a contractual relationship as contemplated by the charter and statutory provisions against such an interest by an office holder.

This would mean that a village trustee or other official actually in need of relief and who fulfilled all the other requirements of a recipient of relief might be the beneficiary of such relief, without necessarily being compelled to resign from his office.

*

13. WORK UNDER CONTRACT; PURCHASE OF MATERIALS

Relief projects under the Emergency statute must be for work undertaken by a municipal corporation "independent of work under a contract or for which an annual appropriation has been made" (section 2), and must be, in general, apart from normal governmental enterprises and not such as would have been carried out in due course regardless of an emergency. It would seem that the building of a public school would not fall within these limitations.

Non-Compliance With N.R.A. Codes

Where complaints are made, on the part of unsuccessful bidders or N.R.A. code authorities, of non-compliance by successful bidders with N.R.A. code requirements, the Administration has ruled that the question of code violations is for judicial decision and is not for determination by a purchasing officer. This is in accordance with the ruling of the Comptroller General of the United States, and applies not only to orders placed by the Administration but to orders placed by local emergency work bureaus.

Errors in Bids

The State policy in respect of such errors in bids as are obviously bona fide mistakes in transcription of figures, etc., and where insistence on the actual enforcement of the bid would be unconscionable, is to permit the withdrawal of bid before final award. The courts have consistently compelled a return of bid check where such a clear mistake has been shown and have excused performance. New bids may be asked or award made to next lowest bidder.

The Federal policy is therefore sound and may be followed, but exceptional care should be used to ascertain if the claim is in good faith or merely an excuse to escape a bad bargain.

Purchases of Materials Without Competitive Bids

Bulletin 44, Item 3, provided that purchases in the amount of $25 or less may be exempt from competitive bid requirements.

This has been amended to provide that purchases in the amount of $100 or less may be made without competitive bids, when in the judgment of the Purchasing Agent, such purchase may be efficiently made.

The amount of business awarded to any one vendor, without regularly advertised competitive bids, shall not exceed $300 in any one month.

This does not apply to rentals of trucks, teams and construction equipment, as competitive bids are required in every case.

＊　＊　＊

Purchasing Procedure

It is asked under what statute the Relief Administration is setting up the Purchasing Department Procedure.

The procedure, or the regulations governing purchasing, specifically provides that where local purchasing agents are provided for by law, the purchases should be made by them. The conditions governing such purchases and the procedure in respect to bids, etc., are made by the Temporary Emergency Relief Administration by virtue of the authority which is vested in them to name the conditions and the provisions, on the basis of which additional grants beyond the statutory reimbursement are permitted under sections 16 of the Emergency Relief Act.

The regulations which were set forth were, after conference with the Federal Relief Administration, adopted, and follow the procedure provided for by the Federal Relief Administration, after due consideration of the provisions of the State Finance Law and conference with Mr. Mullens of the Comptroller's Office.

Since 75 per cent of the expenditures for relief are reimbursed, it is reasonable that under the power to make the conditions under which the additional reimbursement is given, the Relief Administration may specify regulations governing the purchase of materials to be used on the relief project, which is also subject to its approval.

Buying Against Contracts

Early this year certain county authorities entered into contracts covering their entire requirements for 1934 of gravel and sewer pipe. No definite quantity was specified. Contracts were made on the basis of competitive bids, publicly advertised and publicly opened. Local people now ask permission to buy against these contracts and to present for reimbursement. This should be done where possible. So also where a city has contracts for 1934 covering cement, sand, gravel, road oil, crushed stone and sewer pipe, and asks permission to buy against these contracts. In such case a certificate of conformance with the President's executive order of March 14, 1934 should be required.

* * *

Rentals of Trucks, Teams and Construction Equipment

(a) The following instructions relating to the rental of motor trucks, teams, and other items of construction equipment were effective August 31, 1934.

(b) The practice of employing on a payroll basis, without contract, Owner-Operated Trucks, Teams, and other equipment will be discontinued after the payroll week ending August 30, 1934.

(c) On and after August 31st, the rental of motor trucks, teams and construction equipment will be handled on the basis of competitive bids, the procedure for which is detailed in Official Bulletin No. 44.

(d) Awards must be made to the lowest qualified bidder. In the case of "tie" bids, awards shall be made by lot in accordance with Paragraph No. 19, T.E.R.A. Official Bulletin No. 44. When a division of the award can be effected, preference should be given to individual owners rather than fleet owners, and further preference should be given to owners who may be on relief or who employ relief operators.

(e) No bid may be accepted unless the certificate of Code compliance on Form 207 is properly signed. Invitations to bid may not be restricted to members of associations, nor shall any bidder be required to join an association as a prerequisite to bidding.

(f) There is outlined in another Bulletin the official policy of this Administration in connection with N.R.A. Codes of Fair Competition. This policy applies to all rentals as well as to material purchases.

(g) Rented Trucks, Teams and Construction equipment may be worked as many hours as the job requires, but individual operators thereof may not work more than thirty (30) hours in any one week.

(h) Rental Contracts shall be numbered and copies routed as per Pp. No. 8, Bulletin No. 44. Purchase Order Form 209 must be issued to cover each contract and should bear the contract number. It is recommended that Invitation to Bid and Contract be based on "not to exceed" a specified number of hours per month; that the privilege be reserved to cancel at any time without notice; also the privilege of renewing for one, two or three months at the same rate, and for the same maximum hours. When cancellation or renewal is desired, it should be covered by Memorandum of Change, Form 210.

(i) The regulation contained in Par. 11, Bulletin No. 44 requiring the issuance of purchase orders each month to cover the rental of equipment is revised as follows:

"Should circumstances arise which prevent a vendor from furnishing all of the service called for by his contract during the month in which the purchase order is issued, he may, at the discretion of the local Administration, be permitted to finish out his contract during the following month. The entire cost of such contract will be chargeable to the material allotment for the month in which the purchase order is issued."

(j) Teams, Trucks and other equipment may be contracted for on the basis of complete service with operator, complete service without operator, or "bare," with gas, oil and operator furnished by the Work Bureau. In all cases the lessor must provide insurance protection as required in Bulletin No. 44, item 15.

(k) When Trucks, Teams and other equipment are operated by other than the actual owner, compensation insurance on operators must be provided by owners in accordance with the laws of New York State, and certificate of this coverage must be filed with the Work Bureau together with certificates of liability and property damage insurance provided for above (j).

(l) When practicable, contracts will be made for trucks with gas, oil, insurance and maintenance, with drivers acceptable to the owners to be supplied by the Work Bureau from the list of certified relief workers of the local Department of Public Welfare. When this procedure is followed, the wages of the operators become payable on regular relief payrolls while the equipment rental remains a charge against the materials allotment. When this procedure cannot be effected, and trucks with drivers are obtained on contract, the entire cost is chargeable to the materials allotment.

(o) With respect to trucks, teams and other equipment owned by municipalities, counties or towns: The rental of such equipment is not a reimbursable expense; operating supplies, service, repairs and wages of operators in the employ of municipalities, counties or towns are not reimbursable.

(p) In determining the capacity of a truck, the Work Bureau shall determine that the tonnage rating and/or capacity, as listed on the bid form, is in conformity with the rating upon which the State registration of the truck was based. No appurtenances or devices which may increase the tonnage or capacity of the truck beyond the registered rating may be permitted, as the resulting overloading may constitute a violation of existing State laws and other ordinances.

Official Interest Barred

There can be no direct or indirect interest on the part of a municipal official in the hiring or purchase of trucks or machinery. Whether such interest exists is a question for the local law officers.

Contracts for Materials

Where a special sewer and public works commission is required by law to provide for the construction of sewers and other public works "by letting the necessary contracts therefor," and by the same law is authorized, in its discretion, to require the use of work relief labor supplied under the Emergency Act, any reimbursements therefor to go into the sinking fund to pay the commission's debts, it is asked whether this commission may permit the construction under this act to be carried on by the county work bureau; or if the work can only be let by contract to a contractor, the contract requiring the contractor to employ men from the work bureau's lists; or if the element of contract would prevent reimbursement.

I think it may be held that the "necessary contracts" are to cover no labor items. Such contracts, it seems, might include, ought, in fact, to include, materials and supplies, labor being taken wholly from the work relief rolls.

It does not seem that the work bureau itself could properly assume a contract. The county, however, or in this case the sewer commission, could very well arrange for the furnishing of tools, apparatus, materials, supervision, etc., on a contract basis, while taking the labor from the work bureau, the furnishing of the labor to be submitted to the Relief Administration as a work project, and the wages of such labor would in such case be subject to reimbursement by the State upon approval of the project by the Administration.

Purchase of Materials

Under a liberal interpretation of sections 2 and 10 of the Emergency Relief Measure, having in view the purposes for which the measure was passed and the ends to be accomplished, the appropriation of funds for work relief may contemplate the purchase of materials without which it would be impossible to accomplish the work relief intended and to enable those who are to be paid the wages to perform the work contemplated under each project. The municipal corporation, however, should bear in mind that it is intended that by far the major portion of all appropriations for relief purposes should be for wages paid and this will be kept in mind in the submission of projects to the Administration for approval under the Act.

Only Contract Labor Barred

The question arises, whether it would be permissible to buy materials, not labor, under contract, such materials to be paid for out of the funds of the municipal corporation exclusively, without prejudice to the municipal corporation's application to the Administration for assistance in paying wages to the workers.

In my view it is only contract labor that is frowned on by the statute. The purpose was undoubtedly to see that none of the relief funds went into contractors' profits, but that labor got all that was spent for wages. There is no similar reason for forbidding the purchase of materials by contract. On the contrary, contract purchasing is the surest way of cutting down private profits on the purchase of materials, and not to buy materials by contract might easily be extremely wasteful.

We have already held that "the appropriation of funds for work relief may contemplate the purchase of materials without which it would be impossible to accomplish the work relief intended and to enable those who are to be paid the wages to perform the work contemplated.'' I can see no reason why such materials should not be bought by contract; in fact, I think they ought to be so purchased, and there would appear to me to be no difficulty in segregating the cost of materials from the cost of labor so completely as to make it possible for the Administration to take only the latter into consideration in its application of the statute.

Materials on State Projects

It is asked if 20 per cent of the whole amount available for State improvements may be used for the purchase of materials, tools and other supplies; that is, specifically, if a certain project calls for no expenditure for materials, tools, etc., if the amount thus saved may be applied to another project so as to make the expenditure for materials, tools, etc., on such other project in excess of 20 per cent of the cost thereof, the total expenditure for materials, tools, etc., being kept, nevertheless, within 20 per cent of the total sum available. In my opinion this question may be answered in the affirmative. There is no provision in the statute that the sum available for materials, tools, etc., shall be equalized or spread proportionately among the various projects. The Legislature must have foreseen that some State projects would require little or no expense for tools and materials. It has therefore placed no limitation upon the sound judgment of the Administration in that respect except to provide that the total expenditure for tools and materials shall not exceed 20 per centum of the total amount available, leaving methods and details to be carried out in any manner deemed by the Administration to be just and equitable.

* * *

Bond Issues for Relief and for Materials

It has always been our opinion, based on the language as well as in the spirit of the Wicks Act, that municipalities authorized therein to borrow for "work relief,'' must perforce include in said borrowing funds to permit work relief projects to be undertaken. Since work relief could only be furnished by providing projects and since projects are impossible without materials and supplies, it would seem to follow that the act which authorizes borrowing to supply work relief, would of necessity permit the same transaction to supply funds for the vitally necessary wherewithal. It would indeed be a strained construction to hold otherwise. Section 29 calls for a "liberal" construction to enable the aim of the statute to be accomplished.

Some "bonding attorneys," however, have continued to exercise an over-zealous leaning to words without meaning, and hesitate to approved an issue for materials under the authority of section 10. Hence, to satisfy all doubters of such authority, chapter 39 of the Laws of 1934 was passed and again amended to provide ample authority to borrow for materials for such projects.

It is indeed captious to interpose an objection to one bond issue for work relief and materials when we have statutes ample for both. The fact that there are supplementary statutes does not indicate the borrowing must be piecemeal. One issue may of course cover both phases of relief work, just as one could cover home and/or work relief. There is no rule of statutory construction which bars such borrowing for all purposes encompassed in both these acts. It has always been our belief, that materials could be included in a "work relief" borrowing. Chapter 39 Laws of 1934 was enacted to cover the C.W.A. borrowings under chapter 782 Laws of 1933, as not in the scope of the Wicks Act. Now all are covered by the most recent statutory provisions.

* * *

14. COUNTIES, TOWNS; BORROWING

Under the 1933 amendments to section 10 of the Emergency Act, a county in making an appropriation for home and/or work work relief may provide that the amount thereof shall be reimbursed to the county "from the taxable property for whose benefit" the appropriation was made (ch. 259), and towns are now allowed to borrow for home and/or work relief up to 2 per cent of their assessed valuation (ch. 9) and for veteran relief (ch. 34). These amendments render obsolete many prior rulings on these subjects.

* * *

Control by Governing Body

Where it is asked whether particular projects must be named for the purpose of borrowing or sale of bonds, the answer is "no." No such detailed allocation is necessary.

If, however, the question is whether a relief bureau may draw upon such funds without enumerating the approved project upon which the funds are to be expended, the obvious answer, it seems, is also "no." There should be no trouble in advancing approved projects. Since the local municipal body is the appropriating unit, it is quite appropriate that it should be apprized of the particular project to be financed and for which funds are to be advanced.

It must always be remembered that the local appropriating body holds the purse strings and therefore should properly know the end to which its funds are being used. Good sense would indicate that a bureau, before undertaking projects, would procure approval of the local council, which, as the governing body, has the control over appropriations. The fact that money has been borrowed does not constitute a mandate to appropriate it.

* *

Work in New Improvement District

In regard to a work relief project in a local improvement district it is pointed out that the district does not come into being as a functioning governmental agency or public unit until the work here projected shall have been completed and approved; that the work of surveying must be done on private property (involving possible trespass), and that there is doubt in your mind as to the authority to spend the money without some established agency, etc. The expenditure is also questioned by reason of the stricture upon county expenditures in Article VIII, Section 10 of the State Constitution.

1. It must be kept in mind that the expenditure of the county herein is primarily for a public welfare object, to wit: The wages paid for relief to distressed unemployed. This is a proper purpose, precisely as if the expense were in the form of home relief. The fact that the work done is not yet upon public property in a tangible manner does not argue that the project is not a proper public purpose or in aid of a public work. The survey is a necessary preliminary to the creation of the district. It has been approved as a State measure. The project has for its aim the creation of a public corporate or governmental agency. It may properly be classified, therefore, as a public project. The work does not necessarily have to be done on county property to be so classified. The fact that surveys may involve entry upon private property is an incident not going to the heart of the question. In the matter of possible claims for trespass, etc. (Conservation Law, § 485), I am not sure where the true responsibility lies. However, I doubt there exists any real danger of substantial damage due to the surveys. And at any rate I don't apprehend that the county assumes any obligation when the statute (Conservation Law) prescribes the machinery for such claims to be presented.

2. The first part of the foregoing furnishes the answer to your second inquiry. Since the money is spent in wages for the unemployed, a proper public welfare purpose, the constitutional barrier is not raised. There is no gift of county funds in any sense,— the money is spent in wages to the needy, merely another form of public relief designed the better to accomplish the end of meeting

the emergency. The fact that such expenditures may by virtue of another statute be chargeable to the property of the owners in the district does not change the nature of the original expenditure as a relief measure. It would appear that the project (survey) could not otherwise be undertaken, and I assume that the county favors the project and its being progressed. Otherwise I cannot understand why it should have been presented for approval.

Towns and Villages

The Administration cannot deal directly with towns or villages, which must function under the statute, if at all, as agencies of the county bureau. Therefore, where there is no county bureau there can be no reimbursement to a town. Town or village relief committees must act under the supervision and control of the county bureau, as agencies thereof, and their claims must be submitted through the county bureau, which will receive reimbursement from the Administration through the State Comptroller and county treasurer; and will distribute the same. If the county bureau is satisfied with the manner in which contributions to town and village relief committees are being handled, that is sufficient. Such a committee may be in one aspect in the employ of the town or village, but it is actually an agency of the county.

* * *

No Referendum Necessary

In chapter 782 of the Laws of 1933 it is expressly provided that, in borrowing for a public works project, it shall not be necessary for a village board to hold hearings, "nor shall any such project be subject to referendum, mandatory or permissive," the purpose of the enactment being to facilitate the promotion of such projects without the necessity of complying with local or general laws requiring a vote of taxpayers.

Apportioning Expense to Towns

Where there is involved the restoration of the town unit system of home relief and welfare work, the return to the town unit must be due to a misconstruction of the law, since the same results, from the point of financial burden, can be achieved under chapter 259, Laws of 1933.

It is provided by section 10 of the Emergency Relief Law as amended by said chapter 259 that:

"In any county the board of supervisors in making any appropriation for home and for work relief for the county welfare district may provide that such appropriation or certificates issued therefor, together with interest thereon shall be a charge against the county but *the amount of such appropriation or certificates issued therefor, together with interest thereon shall be reimbursed to the county from the taxable property within the county public welfare district for whose benefit said appropriation was made or said certificates issued as provided by this act and the board of supervisors of said county shall levy a tax upon the taxable property within the county public welfare district sufficient to provide such sums as may be necessary to meet such appropriation or certificates issued therefor*, together with the interest thereon."

The foregoing permits the county to borrow and/or appropriate for relief and charge the amounts so appropriated to the various localities for whose benefit the funds were expended. Thus the taxable property of a town or village is bearing the burden of the relief expenditures in said town or village even though the money is raised and spent by the county. The reason for this is that it permits the credit of the county to be utilized for the full benefit of the relief problem. Yet it still makes the local unit bear the taxable cost of such relief burden.

So also do we find in section 12, paragraph 2, of the Emergency Law as amended by chapter 259 of the Laws of 1933, the following:

"2. Upon the written application of the mayor of a city in the case of a city welfare district or of the chairman of the board of supervisors of a county in the case of a county welfare district, the administration may in its discretion and subject to such regulations as it may provide, approve and authorize the consolidation of all relief activities within each public welfare district carried on under chapter seven hundred and ninety-eight of the laws of nineteen hundred and thirty-one, as amended, into an emergency relief bureau, consisting of not less than three nor more than five persons to be designated by the mayor of such city or the chairman of the board of supervisors of such county. The said emergency relief bureau so established shall have exclusive control of and be solely responsible for the administration in such public welfare district of home relief and/or work relief under chapter seven hundred and ninety-eight of the laws of nineteen hundred and thirty-one, as amended. Upon the appointment of said emergency relief bureau, the local bureau theretofore established pursuant to section seven shall be terminated and all the powers and duties of the local bureau and of the commissioner of public welfare as to relief administered under chapter seven hundred ninety-eight of the laws of nineteen hundred and thirty-one, as amended, shall be forthwith vested in said emergency relief bureau. All records of the local bureau and all records of the commissioner of public welfare relating to recipients of relief under chapter seven hundred and ninety-eight of the laws of nineteen hundred and thirty-one as amended, shall be forthwith transferred to the emergency relief bureau so established. The commissioner of public welfare of the public welfare district in which such emergency relief bureau shall have been established shall be ex-officio a member of said bureau in addition to the members appointed as above provided, and shall perform such duties in respect to relief administered under chapter seven hundred and ninety-eight of the laws of nineteen hundred and thirty-one, as amended, as may be directed by said bureau.''

This provision enables the county to adopt the county unit for all relief activities in the welfare district. Concentration of relief, efficient supervision, uniformity of standards, central control of funds, economies of direction and execution—all are promoted by this provision. Combining the two provisions above quoted, there may be secured all the local fixation of costs ultimately to be borne and all the benefits of centralized control. It would seem needlessly cumbersome and expensive to return to the town unit system of haphazard relief control, when the sole purpose of such return can be attained by utilizing these provisions of law designed for the very purpose in mind.

Village Powers Limited

A village may not borrow under the terms of the Emergency Relief Act. Amendments to the Wicks Act have enabled towns to borrow up to 2 per cent of their assessed valuation, but no such privilege has been afforded villages. The term ''municipal corporation'' within the Relief Act is expressly limited to cities and counties.

Under the circumstances it would appear to be the relief duty of the town and the county to meet the situation unless the village can find other means of obtaining the necessary funds. We must keep in mind the fact that the Relief Act does not deal with villages at any time. In view of the law, the village and other small units are the rightful charge of the larger unit of government, which has such borrowing powers under the Act.

Dealing Through County Bureau

Although villages are not recognized under the Emergency Relief Act, if the village is able to cooperate with the county emergency work bureau a village relief committee may, if deputized as agents of the county bureau, carry on work relief within the village, presenting its projects, making its claims for reimbursement, and receiving the same from the State, through the county bureau, with which alone the Relief Administration can deal.

As to raising money for relief purposes, the village may do so in the emergency, under its welfare powers (Village Law, section 89, subd. 59), by resolution of the board of trustees (id., section 128), and unless the bonds or certificates of indebtedness are to be payable more than five years from the date of issue no referendum thereon will be necessary (id., section 139).

Village Sewer Project

If the extension of a village sewer system is presented by a county work bureau as a county work project, and is approved and accepted by the Administration as such, reimbursement may be made upon all "wages paid by the municipal corporation from moneys specifically appropriated or contributed for that purpose" (see definition of work relief, Emergency Act, section 2). This would not include moneys raised by assessment upon the property benefited. It is assumed that the status of the project as extra or made work, which would not have been undertaken in due and normal course, has been satisfactorily determined, and that none of the labor is to be on work under contract. It may be noted also that, while the village board has the power, subject to a permissive referendum, to assess any part of the cost of the project upon the property benefited (Village Law, section 263), it would not be required to do so.

Columbia County Borrowing

By chapter 182 of the laws of 1932 the county of Columbia, "any provision in any general or special law to the contrary notwithstanding," was authorized to issue notes or certificates of indebtedness for five years at 4½ per cent, in an amount not exceeding $157,921.20, to pay certain claims for rights of way, the funds for which were provided but diverted to pay other county obligations.

While such notes or certificates are outstanding, taxes for county purposes, over and above principal and interest on indebtedness, shall not exceed in one year $700,000, and during such time the county shall not borrow for any purpose other than for the construction or reconstruction of bridges, rights of way, or current expenses in anticipation of the collection of taxes, or for the renewal or funding of obligations or loans for any of said purposes, "except by authority of any special act passed at the present session of the Legislature." (Section 3.)

"The powers herein conferred shall be deemed to be in addition to all other powers conferred by law and except as herein expressly otherwise provided, the limitation of any power contained in any other law." (Section 5.)

By chapter 184 of the Laws of 1932 the county of Columbia was also authorized to issue $350,000 of five-year 6 per cent bonds to fund outstanding indebtedness, and to borrow on notes in anticipation thereof. Section 3 of this chapter, limiting taxes and loans while the bonds are outstanding, is identical with section 3 of chapter 182, cited above. But section 6 of this act, defining the county's powers, is singularly discrepant from the like section 5 of chapter 182, the underlined words in section 6, as here presented, *not appearing* in said section 5:

"The powers herein conferred shall be deemed to be in addition to all other powers conferred by law, and except as herein expressly otherwise provided the *limitations of this act are not to be construed in* limitation of any power contained in any other law."

In other words, chapter 184 does not pretend to cut off a power granted in another statute, but chapter 182, if it is to be literally construed as printed, might be thought to do so. In my opinion the omission of the words in question from chapter 182 was inadvertent, one of the commonest errors committed by transcribers being, where two nearly identical words appear in proximity, in this case "limitations" and "limitation", to omit the intervening text. The wording resultant is not even good English, though it might pass if there were not at hand the parallel provision of chapter 184, which is obviously correct in form and sense and must be taken as expressing the Legislature's meaning.

In this view the express authority in section 10 of the Emergency Act, enacted in 1931 and amended and re-enacted in 1932 and 1933, for a county to borrow "sufficient money to pay for work relief and/or home relief," is in no way affected by chapters 182 or 184 of the Laws of 1932, as such statutes confer powers "in addition to all other powers," in order to meet a special situation, and do *not* limit any powers which are contained in any other law.

If this were not so, I think that section 31 of the Emergency Act, adopted in 1931 and repeatedly re-enacted by implication, would govern nevertheless, and that chapters 182 and 184 of the Laws of 1932 would be held to be ineffective in so far as and to the extent that they could be interpreted as interfering with borrowing powers for relief purposes.

Charging Back to Towns

We are asked whether, if a board of supervisors makes a certain amount of money available for work relief, the wages paid therefrom may be charged back to the towns in which the recipients have settlement.

Work relief wages cannot be charged back to the town of settlement, as the cost of home relief might under section 26 of the Public Welfare Law. However, under section 10 of the Emergency Act, as amended by Laws of 1933, chapter 259, the board of supervisors, in making an appropriation for home and/or work relief, may provide that the amount thereof shall be reimbursed to the county from the taxable property for the benefit of which the appropriation was made, and may levy a tax upon such benefited property for the purpose of such reimbursement.

⊦ ＊

How Towns May Combine

Three towns in Herkimer county desire to unite and work under a co-ordinated relief bureau. There is no provision, in the new law regarding consolidations, for such procedure. However, if the persons acceptable to the towns as a central committee are duly delegated by the county authorities (work bureau and commissioner of public welfare) as their deputies, and their work is carried out as that of an agency of the county in all respects, the desired result may be obtained.

⊦ ＊

No Appropriations to Towns

Towns have never been eligible for direct State appropriations but through the commissioner of public welfare the statutory reimbursement has been made as a routine matter.

Under the Wicks Act, the commissioner of public welfare, and not the town, is responsible to the Administration. The Administration may grant a larger percentage of reimbursement to the given county, but only in unusual situations has there ever been any allocation designated for the use of certain towns within a county exclusive of others. In no case has the Administration ever made a direct appropriation to a town.

＊ ＊

County Appropriations

It is asked if it would be lawful for a board of supervisors, in appropriating money for work relief purposes, to raise such funds in accordance with the assessed valuations of the cities and towns in the county, and to allocate them upon the same basis, giving to the towns in each instance the option whether the funds will be utilized for work or home relief. There is the question whether in some cases work relief will be practicable during the winter and therefore the funds unavailable for work relief might be used for home relief, and also that the appropriation may not pass the board unless this flexibility is available. The plan is permissible, but it is suggested that the appropriation be not specifically for work relief as such, but be made in the terms of section 10 of the statute for "work relief and/or home relief."

It has been the uniform policy of the Administration that counties should be encouraged to provide funds for relief of one sort as well as the other, and while work relief is unquestionably the preferred policy stressed by the Administration, home relief naturally can not be refused for lack of funds when the money is available and it is not feasible to use the same for work relief. Caution, however, should be exercised.

It is suggested further that the board embody in the resolution a provision that the allocation of these funds to the localities in the county be made on the basis of need of the locality rather than on the basis of the assessed valuation, because it might well be that the need of the locality with a small valuation would actually be greater than the need of one with a greater valuation.

.   * * *

Town Equipment of Employment Bureau

We are asked as to the legality of an appropriation by the town board of the town of Hempstead for the purpose of equipping quarters in Hempstead village for an employment agency established for the emergency by the State Labor Department in conjunction with Federal agencies.

Section 170, subd. 2, of the Town Law provided that "town charges" shall include "the contingent expenses necessarily incurred for the use and benefit of the town." (In the new law, effective January 1, 1934, this language [section 100, subd. 2], is: "all expenses necessarily incurred for the use and benefit of the town.")

It is said in Daly v. Haight, 87 Misc. 425, that any charge against a town that is not authorized by statute is illegal. But I think the proposed expenditure, besides being clearly for the use and benefit of the town, is within the scope of town government in the emergency, the correction of the economic depression being expressly declared in the Emergency Act (section 1) to be a town purpose and "primarily an obligation of the municipalities."

County Relief for Towns

There is no provision in the Emergency Relief measure which forbids a county work bureau from furnishing relief to workers who perform work for the towns, provided, however, such work is administered pursuant to the rules and regulations of the Administration and under the supervision of the county work bureau. The county work bureau is, however, the only unit with which the State Administration deals. There is nothing in the law to prevent towns from appropriating funds for work relief and turning such funds for administration over to the county work relief bureau, in a manner deemed most expedient, which may involve the allocating by the said county work bureau of proportionate sums to towns which have so contributed.

: *. *

Town and County Co-operation

It is asked if a county work bureau may establish branch offices in towns, in its discretion, and if town boards in such towns may appropriate funds for work projects and limit the expenditure thereof to persons belonging in the town.

A county work bureau undoubtedly has power to establish branch offices where it pleases, within its jurisdiction, and so long as town boards in appropriating funds for work projects, act under the supervision, direction and control of the county bureau, it would seem that they may be authorized to make such contributions to the county bureau, and that, if the limitation is agreeable to the county bureau, the contribution may be conditioned upon its expenditure within the town. These are matters for the county bureaus to determine. The administration will deal with them only on the basis of county results, which they may arrive at by such methods as local situations indicate to be convenient or advantageous.

* ┝ *

Projects and Financing

The Emergency Relief Act defines work relief in section 2, as follows:

> "Work relief means wages paid by a *municipal corporation* to persons who are unemployed * * * from *money specifically appropriated or contributed for that purpose* during the emergency period, for the performance of services or labor connected with work undertaken by such corporation independent of work under a contract or for which an annual appropriation has been made."

From that definition the conclusion is impelled that the following is *definitely not* subject to approval as work projects:

(a) Work under contract, and

(b) Work for which an annual appropriation has been made and/or for which local funds are available in regular course. (Possible exception to (b) is work for which an annual appropriation might usually be made, for which funds are found to be inadequate or unavailable.)

Rejection of projects on any other ground would thus be a matter of policy with the Administration under section 16 of the amended act.

From the experience of the T. E. R. A. thus far, the foregoing has been generally followed by the cities, and their projects have been subject to other objections due to possible confusion of undertakings.

Considerable confusion has, however, arisen in regard to projects offered by counties, and projects now being submitted by county work bureaus for approval under section 16 and for wage reimbursement by the State. A number of town and village work projects have been submitted, calling for substantial outlays, where it is indicated that the funds with which to carry out the said projects are to be raised by bond issues by the said villages and towns, in some instances expressly stated to be under section 10 of the Wicks Act. Towns, under the 1933 legislation, may now borrow for home and/or work relief, but villages gain no borrowing power under the Emergency legislation.

This does not, however, bar villages from raising funds for "poor relief," whether administered in the form of work relief or home relief, provided such borrowing for poor relief is authorized by other laws governing the power of said villages. Appropriations out of funds properly raised but not the subject of normal annual budgetary requirements, may be turned over to the county work bureau for relief projects in such localities.

- - -

County's Duty to Provide

Where the public welfare appropriations of a town are exhausted and the town has absolutely no legal borrowing capacity remaining, it is without any doubt the duty of the county, under the Emergency Act, to provide for public relief within the town, not only work relief, which is altogether a county charge (L. 1931, ch. 798, as amended, sections 2, 7, 8, 9, 10, 16), except as the towns may voluntarily assist therein according to their ability, but also home relief, notwithstanding that the county is one in which home relief is, under the Public Welfare Law, a town charge.

We have constantly interpreted these statutes to allow towns to carry their own burdens so far as they can be made to do so, but where their funds are exhausted and they cannot possibly borrow, and the alternative would be the abandonment of relief within the town, the legislative intent that the county should shoulder the load seems unmistakable. This policy and arrangement may represent a new theory, superseding prior relationships, but they are nevertheless to be found in the statute, and there appears to be no constitutional bar. (Village of Kenmore v. County of Erie, 252 N. Y. 437, 442 et seq.)

Work Relief in Water District

A work relief project in Columbia county involved the laying of additional water mains in Water District No. 1, town of Greenport. The district commissioners wished to have the work done as a work relief project under the Columbia county work bureau, and the district had enough funds on hand to pay the cost of labor. It was necessary, however, to borrow for materials.

This borrowing was to be under sections 288 and 299 of the former Town Law, action under which was predicated upon section 287, which required such work to be done under contract. It was not clear to the attorneys for the bond buyers that the provisions of section 10 of the Emergency Act, dispensing with the letting of contracts, applied to work to be performed in a water district. We were asked, therefore, if a water district may lawfully extend its water mains as a work relief project, paying for the labor out of funds on hand and raising the money for materials from the sale of bonds.

It would be unfortunate if the somewhat anomalous status of a water district should be allowed to confuse this issue. Such a district is not a municipal corporation, nor are a town and a special district of the town identical. (People v. Stoll, 242 N. Y. 453; People ex rel. Farley v. Winkler, 203 N. Y. 445; Holroyd v. Indian Lake, 180 N. Y. 318.)

But, under the Emergency Act, neither is a town or a village a municipal corporation, and yet we have held that towns and villages may lawfully put through work relief projects so long as they act in such respect as agencies of the emergency work bureau of the county public welfare district, and I can see no reason why a water district may not do as much. Thus, in so far as the water district has funds at hand for that purpose, it may, in my opinion, carry on a work project under the direction of the county work bureau without letting contracts for the same. Within the meaning of section 10 of the Emergency Act, as amended, this work will be done, not by the water district, but by the *county work bureau*, the operations of which are authenticated, "notwithstanding any provisions contained in any charter or in general, special or local laws to the contrary, and notwithstanding any such provisions therein contained requiring such work as may be undertaken to be let by contract."

When we come to borrowing the situation was not quite the same, for the borrowing was not to be on the credit of the county work bureau. Neither, however, was it on the credit of the water district, but the town itself would be primarily liable, for, notwithstanding that the cost is to be collected from the real property within the water district, "the bonds shall be a charge upon the town" (Town Law, section 288), and the whole property of the town is pledged to the payment thereof. Since the administrative district is authorized by law to bind the whole town in this manner I have little difficulty, upon very careful consideration, in concluding that the indebtedness is sufficiently a town indebtedness to fall within the scope of section 10 of the Emergency Act, validating the same notwithstanding any provisions contained in any general, special or local laws requiring such work as may be undertaken thereunder to be let by contract. I am the more convinced of the correctness of this conclusion by examination of the provisions of the new Town Law (L. 1932, ch. 634), in effect January 1 last, and designed to consolidate the best present practice, under which the authority of the towns themselves over their administrative districts is made in all respects inclusive. (Sections 190–202.)

It is my view, therefore, that a water district, without letting contracts, may lawfully lay water mains as a work relief project, paying for the labor out of funds on hand and raising the money for materials from the sale of bonds.

＊

15. TOWN HIGHWAY MONEYS

Following the enactment of L. 1933, ch. 430, authorizing boards of supervisors to use money received from the motor fuel tax and motor vehicle registration fees, prior to March 1, 1934, for emergency relief or current expenses, the Relief Administration determined that if such moneys were used for relief purposes, they would be reimbursable by the Administration, although contributed by the State, and this ruling has been extended to other moneys provided by the State, including highway funds (but not advances and direct grants by the Relief Administration.)

This ruling affected not only county road systems under section 320-b of the Highway Law, but town road work to which the State contributes a proportion based on mileage, etc., under article 5 of the Highway Law, and various prior rulings were superseded thereby. However, such moneys must continue to be expended subject to the agreement approved by the State Commissioner of Highways, pursuant to section 105 of the Highway Law, and the work must still be under the direction of the town superintendent. The rule against contract work, moreover, is still in force, and where the expenditure is a normal one that would have been carried out in due course in any event, regardless of the emergency, the Administration may decline to approve it as a reimbursable work project.

Explanation as to Highway Work

Those town superintendents and local officials who are not careful in their construing of the language may believe that they are not able to use any highway funds to pay for relief workers' wages on highway projects under the superintendent's direction and supervision.

The statute and the make-up of the funds under sections 105–106 and 320-b of the Highway Law prevent the diversion of such funds from the highway fund to the county treasurer or to the general fund for relief payrolls. They do not, however, prevent the county superintendent from paying directly out of such funds relief workers on highway projects undertaken by him, pursuant to the said provisions of the Highway Law and conducted under his supervision as a proper highway project under the said provisions of the law; the only exception being that he is using relief workers and paying them on a relief basis. The fact that there results from this a reimbursement to the town, by reason of the relief nature of the relief payrolls, is merely an added benefit to the municipality.

These relief payrolls are of course on relief projects which happen to be under the direct supervision of the town superintendent and in the course of his proper work under these provisions of the Highway Law. The reason why these projects are undertaken is that additional labor is provided for the unemployed, and unless undertaken as relief projects, the said moneys may not otherwise be so expended.

So long as the projects are carried out in accordance with the agreements specified in sections 101 and 103 of the Highway Law, there would seem to be no objection to utilizing unemployed workers as a project on these highway improvements.

Classification of Highways

Highways are divided into four classes (Highway Law, section 3), as follows:

1. State highways, constructed or improved at the sole expense of the State.

2. County highways, constructed or improved at the joint expense of State, county and town, or State and county. (In 1929 the State took over all future construction costs of these. L. 1929, ch. 362.)

3. County roads, designated as such under a general or special law, constructed, improved, maintained and repaired by the county as such, in counties in which the county road system has been or may be adopted. (This refers to section 320-b, under which the State goes 50-50 with the counties on construction costs, and also contributes from the motor vehicle registration and gas tax receipts.)

4. Town highways, which are those constructed, improved or maintained by the town with the aid of the State, including all highways in towns, outside of incorporated villages constituting separate road districts, which do not belong to any of the three preceding classes.

This last refers primarily to highways built by the towns under article 5 of the Highway Law (sections 90–111) out of moneys raised by tax in the towns, with State aid on a mileage basis (section 101), and pursuant to the "highway agreement" called for in section 105, but it includes also joint county and town highways build under contract under section 320, and town highways with county aid under section 320-a, the county and towns in each of these cases sharing the cost in proportions determined by the board of supervisors. There is also a special provision (article 8-A) for towns in Westchester county, which may borrow without authorization of the board of supervisors and may provide that only a portion of the town shall be liable for the improvement.

Highways built under sections 320 and 320-a are not subject to the "highway agreement" called for in section 105, and receive no State aid. Neither is there any "highway agreement" or State aid for highways in Westchester county constructed under article 8-A. (The supervisor, however, is accountable to the State Comptroller for all moneys in connection therewith which pass through his hands). With these exceptions it seems that State money is involved in all highway construction.

* * *

Town Highway Moneys

Town highway moneys are governed by article 5 (sections 90 et seq.) of the Highway Law.

Under section 90 the town superintendent annually estimates the amount to be raised by taxation in the town for the ensuing year, Item No. 1 of which is for repairs and improvements. Under sections 101 and 103 the State makes an annual contribution to the towns, from State funds, for town highways, on a mileage basis. All town highway moneys, including State contributions, are payable to the supervisor, "who shall be the custodian thereof and accountable therefor." (Section 104.) "Such moneys shall be paid out by the supervisor on the written order of the town superintendent." (Section 105.) The State Comptroller has active supervision over these accounts. (Section 108.)

At the beginning of our work it was questioned whether such town moneys could be availed of for relief, and, having already been appropriated for a purpose which would have been carried out in any event, whether in such case the Administration would reimburse thereon.

We held that there was no illegality or impropriety in using town highways moneys for relief, "provided that the work is such as was described and agreed upon the agreement entered into by the county superintendent, the town board and the town superintendent, or was covered in the annual estimate or otherwise legally authorized. In either case the town superintendent should have charge of the work and his written order would be necessary to obtain the money from the supervisor. What it would amount to is, simply, that the town superintendent would put to work on the town roads the men supplied by the emergency work bureau. With a reasonable amount of co-operation such a plan should be operable, there being, as I have said, no legal bar."

This conclusion had the concurrence of the State Comptroller, and has since been the basis of numerous rulings from his office and ours. But the Comptroller has felt, and still feels, that it would not be lawful to turn this money over in a lump sum to the work relief bureau, nor can he see any good reason why it should be so turned over, since the men can be taken from work relief lists, given employment and duly paid, without interfering with his bookkeeping and accounting arrangements, covering every town in the State, and without attempting any procedure different from that laid down in the statute.

Town Financing

The town of Rotterdam being able to obtain a loan of money for bridge and highway purposes, pursuant to section 97 of the Highway Law, sufficient to take care of its relief situation for the winter, it appears (a) that money raised by borrowing under section 97 of the Highway Law is distinct from money raised by immediate taxation under prior sections of article 5 (Birge v. Berling Iron Bridge Co., 133 N. Y. 477), and does not enter into the State aid paid under section 101 on the basis of taxes levied, and is outside the scope of the "highway agreement" provided for in section 105. The work involved is, therefore, not normal highway work. (b) It may be said that the town is hereby fulfilling the requirement of section 43 of the Public Welfare Law that "It shall be the duty of the town board to take such action as may be necessary to provide public relief and care." All statutes in so far as they can be made to meet the situation, must be interpreted with a sufficient degree of elasticity and be made to harmonize for the salutary purpose which we are endeavoring to accomplish.

⊦　＊

16. NON-PROFIT INSTITUTIONS; DISPENSARIES, ETC.

Work projects for private hospitals, libraries, churches, etc., should not be authorized where there is no public contribution by the municipal corporation to such institution for its maintenance and support. The Constitution prevents it and the Emergency Act does not seek to authorize it. Section 2 of the act defines work relief as "labor connected with work undertaken by a corporation independent of work under a contract or for which an annual appropriation has been made." In the case of municipalities, the meaning of this definition is extended by the language used in connection with State work projects in section 18, that is, "temporary employment on public improvements undertaken or required by the State and not let or to be let by contract."

Hospital Grounds

In response to an inquiry concerning the use of State funds on hospital grounds, State funds are not available for the benefit of a private institution unless it is one to the support of which public moneys are regularly contributed. If the hospital is a private institution it is not eligible for a work relief project supported by State funds.

* * *

Dispensaries

The question is asked whether reimbursement can be permitted under the Emergency Act for care in dispensaries of private hospitals, for which the city is charged at the rate of 25 cents per visit. In the definition of medical attendance and medical supplies which has been approved, this has been taken care of, and I doubt therefore whether a further ruling is necessary. I might add, however, that the State Charities Law, section 290, defines a dispensary, and that while medical attention of the kind provided may be given privately, it would seem that such relief administered by a dispensary attached to a hospital would be in the nature of public relief, even though the institution itself is principally maintained by private endowment. The dispensary attention, however, is not given in the hospital but is given at the dispensary of a hospital, and there is no confinement of the patient in the hospital, which was made the basis of the determination of the Attorney-General in an opinion rendered in 1923; see page 248. The distinction is a valid one and may be pursued to the point of holding that, where a patient proceeds to a dispensary from his home for treatment, and then returns home, and has not been confined to the hospital or had treatment rendered in the hospital, he may very well be said to have received medical attendance which may be chargeable as Home Relief. Where the dispensary, however, is maintained and operated by the municipal corporation itself or a direct agency thereof, such as a public hospital, there should be no reimbursement for fees paid, since such fees constitute paying from one pocket of the municipality into another.

Private Dispensaries

It is asked if the Administration may reimburse a city on account of the city's contribution to the support of a free dispensary, which dispensary is privately owned but receives regular contributions from the city for its support based on needy cases treated. We have held that where a dispensary is not maintained and operated by the municipal corporation itself there may be reimbursement to the municipal corporation upon fees paid by it for the treatment of public patients thereat, relief administered at a dispensary being in the nature of "home relief" within the meaning of the Emergency Act. In this case there is a public contribution to the institution, but it is not publicly maintained. In my opinion the municipal contribution is for home relief and is reimbursable under the statute, where the patients treated would otherwise have to be privately treated and subject to public charge.

Public Lands

It is asked if a local emergency work bureau may include in its projects work upon property owned by the State. Such work being public work, and for the public use and benefit, I can find nothing in the law to prevent its inclusion as a local work project. It should be borne in mind, however, that an improvement of State property, though carried out by a city or county, will become the property of the State.

Fort Niagara

Inquiry is had as to whether or not the restoration of Old Fort Niagara may be lawfully made a county work project for Niagara county. The matter of the appropriation of funds and the general nature of the restoration of Old Fort Niagara has been made the subject of opinions by the Attorney-General under dates of May 21, 1931, and October 20, 1931. Despite the fact that the fort and the ground upon which the restoration is made are Federal property, the restoration itself is a form of public work which may well come within the provisions of the County Law, conferring the power upon the board of supervisors of the county to appropriate moneys for public monuments or memorials. The restoration of Old Fort Niagara is therefore a public county purpose, for which public moneys may lawfully be devoted, and may properly be made the subject of a work relief project under section 17 of the Emergency Relief Act, to which the Administration may, at its discretion, lawfully contribute if it desires to do so.

Airport

Where an airport is a private enterprise, even though operated at a loss, it cannot be termed a municipal project. If the airport were leased to the city so that it became to that extent municipal property, the project might then be approved as public work. I find nothing in article 14 of the General Municipal Law concerning airports and landing fields which prevents the leasing of such an airport except the restriction as to towns which is contained in subdivision 1 of section 350, and the further restriction in subdivision 2 upon trustees of villages. The lease might be made without cost to the municipality with the exception of the development project, since it is alleged that it is conducted at a loss and not intended to be operated for profit and is open for general public use. There might even be, in the event that the foregoing is not feasible under the circumstances, a general grant of the municipal airport for public purposes and such use consonant with the airport as the city might see fit to develop, without charge to the city. In each case by an acceptance thereof the city might utilize such a grant of the uses of the airport as a public project and develop it for general municipal purposes.

Westchester County S. P. C. C.

While the Westchester county S. P. C. C. presents a border line case, it does nevertheless perform a brief public function in connection with the work of the Childrens' Court and the district attorney's office. Public funds to a fairly substantial sum are appropriated to its support as an aid to regular governmental functions. A work project correlating its work with the public authorities would therefore be appropriate for reimbursement. I assume that the salaries or expenditures thus reimbursed are paid from public funds, other than the regular appropriation.

Albright Art Gallery

It would appear that the Albright Art Gallery in Buffalo is not of a sufficiently clear public need to qualify for a work project. Under L. 1909, ch. 97, it seems that while the Albright Art Gallery stands on city lands (it was built by the State as the New York State Building for the Pan-American exposition in 1901) and is supported by the city, the institution is, legally, in private hands.

Its power to bar the public if it should choose to do so (at the sacrifice of city aid) appears decisive on that point. Since it is on public lands, and in order to exercise this last-mentioned power it would have to move the buildings, this, perhaps, is not so substantial an objection that it might not otherwise be obviated. However, the subject matter is one which should be given consideration.

Hamilton Grange

On the question of an allotment by the Administration to the American Scenic and Historic Preservation Society of $10,000 for reconditioning Hamilton Grange, at 287 Convent Avenue, New York City, the society is not entitled to this money unless the title to the property is in the name of the State.

Various properties of historic interest are in fact owned by the State but are under the immediate control and jurisdiction of the American Scenic and Historic Preservation Society; notably Battle Island Park (Conservation Law, section 790), Fort Brewerton (id., section 800), Letchworth Park (id., sections 701-702), all parks in the third park region (id., sections 672, 700), Philipse Manor House (id., section 836), John Boyd Thacher Park (id., section 820), and Stony Point Peninsula (id., section 853), and as to these the Comptroller's criticism in this matter would not apply.

However, the division of parks in the Conservation Department has no record of the ownership by the State of the Hamilton Grange referred to, and it seems that such property must have been acquired by the society in its own name, in pursuance of the general powers granted to it by the Legislature, in which case the Hamilton Grange could not lawfully be the subject of an allotment by the Administration for a State improvement under section 18 of the Emergency Act.

While it is unlikely that the records of the Conservation Department are in error in this matter, it is suggested that the secretary of the society, Mr. Raymond H. Torrey, 475 Fifth Avenue, New York City, be asked for information as to the ownership of the Hamilton Grange.

17. THE WAR READJUSTMENT ACT*

It is asked if L. 1919, ch. 404 (the original War Emergency Act) is still in force, and if so, if work relief administered under it can be certified to the Administration to the extent that the moneys

---

* NOTE: It is now questionable if this statute is still available, in view of the further amendments to Ch. 798, L. 1931.

so expended have been paid to persons who would be qualified to receive work relief under the Relief Administration Act (cognizance being taken of the two-year residence requirement in the latter law).

The Attorney-General has ruled (Opinion March 23, 1931) that L. 1919, ch. 404, has not been repealed, nor has it been declared unconstitutional, and that the use of the phrase "during the war readjustment period," in the title thereof, did not deprive it of present force and effect. It would seem, therefore, that a municipality which desires to establish a relief bureau under its provisions may do so, and no doubt expenditures made through such a bureau could be considered, under section 17, in the apportionment of moneys to a municipal corporation for work relief, as "public contributions or appropriations for expenditure for the public welfare" (see clause (2) of the second sentence of that section). But it would be necessary, after all, in order to share in the Emergency Fund, to come in under the Emergency Relief Act and establish an emergency work bureau, for "before a city or county shall receive the State aid provided by this act for work relief, it shall establish an emergency work bureau as provided in this act, which shall select the persons to be employed." (Section 11.) The Administration, moreover, could not deal with towns in any event.

Where a municipal corporation is administering home relief through an industrial aid bureau, appointed by the mayor, pursuant to a local ordinance authorized by chapter 404 of the Laws of 1919, the so-called Lusk Act, which bureau furnishes home relief out of funds especially appropriated, in addition to the annual budget of the Department of Charity, the Administration cannot deal with such local industrial aid bureau as such, for it is not "the city commissioner," which officer under section 8 of the Relief Administration Act is the one to represent the Administration in providing home relief and administering the provisions of the Emergency Act in relation thereto. But, on the other hand, there can be no objection to dealing with the local industrial aid bureau as an agency of the public welfare commissioner, providing it is duly established as such agency.

* * *

Use of War Readjustment Act

Where a town has exhausted its poor funds and it is impossible to raise additional moneys in such town, the so-called War Readjustment Act, chapter 404 of the Laws of 1919, may fit the case, as it provides for the establishment of an industrial aid bureau in a town, which bureau shall assist unemployed persons in obtaining employment and shall have power to furnish home relief to such unemployed persons as are destitute, and their dependents, and provides further that the town board of a town in which such bureau has been established may borrow for the bureau's purposes "in addition to all other sums authorized by any general or special law, and no limitation or restriction contained in any such law as to the amount of money that may be raised by taxation in such municipal corporation shall apply to such sums."

In this situation, if the town should organize an industrial aid bureau, and borrow for the purposes thereof, and then make the bureau an agency of the town public welfare officer for home relief, and of the county work bureau for work relief, so that claims for reimbursement could be made to the Administration through those agencies, as the Emergency Act requires, I believe there would be little or no difficulty in obtaining the repayment which the law provides.

18. SETTLEMENT AND RESIDENCE

Collecting for Non-Settled Cases

When relief is furnished to a person having no settlement in the district where the relief is granted, the commissioner of public welfare of such district may claim from the Administration 75 per cent of the amount expended and reimbursable. The commissioner should then, following the procedure laid down in the Public Welfare Law, endeavor to collect the remaining amount from the public welfare district in which the person has a settlement.

The Administration will not determine questions of settlement and of responsibility arising from them, but will, as stated, reimburse the district making the original expenditure.

City commissioners of public welfare may either refer non-settled cases to the county commissioner for relief, as provided by the Public Welfare Law, which makes such cases a county responsibility, in which event the Administration will deal as to reimbursement with the county commissioner, or they may grant the relief themselves under the Emergency Relief Act, claim reimbursement as indicated above, and then proceed under the Public Welfare Law to collect the balance from the place of settlement through the county commissioner.

No claim will be audited by the Administration for expenditures for the relief of persons having settlement in a Public Welfare District which does not participate in the emergency relief system.

Between City and County

The problem is presented as to whether or not in the matter of non-settled cases in cities when relief is administered by the county welfare commissioner, reimbursement should be made.

Under the emergency relief measure, the city is a unit and the county is a unit. The simplest solution to the problem presented in each case would be that the cases to whom relief has been administered should be included in the city's claim for reimbursement—especially is this true since the cities and counties are both operating under the identical rules of the Temporary Emergency Relief Administration.

By this means the working of the Emergency Relief Act continues to be uniform and it would appear to be a simple matter for the county and city welfare departments to arrange for a balancing of accounts between the city and the county for the refunding of such sums as are due to these non-settled cases.

District Not Under T.E.R.A.

A district not working under the Relief Administration, but administering relief to a non-settled case under the Public Welfare Law, is entitled to a full 100 per cent reimbursement from the district of settlement, pursuant to the Public Welfare Law. In such case the Wicks Act does not apply. The reason is clear. A district which can care for itself 100 per cent is entitled to full support. The district receiving aid from the State should not be enabled to place said district at a disadvantage so as to penalize it to the extent of 40 per cent or more of the outlay for the benefit of the place of settlement.

- - -

"Residence" and "Settlement"

"Residence" and "settlement" must be kept distinct. They are subject to different legal and statutory definition. "Settlement" for welfare purposes cannot be obtained while a recipient of "public relief" unless the term of habitation be independently acquired. "Residence" is a legal term dependent upon intent to make a place one's *home* with all factors taken into consideration. One might conceivably acquire a "residence" for voting and other purposes and yet not a "settlement" under the Public Welfare Law. If a recipient of relief and a two year "residence" is acquired including the period of public support, the person is eligible for T.E.R.A. relief.

Settlement vs. Residence

A native of Pennsylvania who enlisted in the United States army from that State and has since remained in the army has a legal settlement continuing in Pennsylvania, as army service counts neither for nor against such settlement. However, having been more than two years resident in the State of New York, though as an enlisted man in the army, this man and his family are eligible for relief under the Emergency Act, which takes no cognizance of settlements.

County Commissioners to Act

The county commissioner should handle relief cases where the settlement is in another town in the same county, claiming reimbursement thereon from the Relief Administration and charging the balance back to the town of settlement, pursuant to section 25, subd. 3, of the Public Welfare Law.

Residence Under Emergency Act

The statute (section 9) limits the furnishing of relief under the Relief Administration Act to persons "who have been residents of the State for at least two years prior to the date of application for aid under this act, and to the dependents of such persons."

In construing this provision, we must throw out all ideas derived from the law of settlement, as set forth in the old Poor Law (sections 40-41) and the Public Welfare Law (sections 53-55) and the decisions based thereon. If we do this, the questions arising will probably not be found very intricate.

Thus, where the wife and children of a man who has the required two years' residence are dependent upon him they are eligible to relief under the act, whether they have the required residence or not. If the husband of a woman who has the required residence has not such residence himself, he is not entitled to relief under the act unless he is dependent upon his wife. And if the father and mother of a man who has the required residence are dependent upon him, they are eligible under the act; otherwise, not, unless they themselves have the residence.

Of course, in all these cases, the dependent person ought to be actually in the district from which relief is sought, and in need there. Where relief is sought on the ground of dependence upon some person who has the required residence, and the application is made in a district other than that in which the person is who has the residence, the law of settlement will apply, and the cost of such relief will be chargeable to the district in which the person possessing the residence is settled, or if he has no settlement and is a State poor person the relief will be a State charge. Further refinements may await specific cases.

* * *

New York City Not Chargeable

The Public Welfare Law (section 58) provides for charging back to the place of his settlement the cost of relief and care furnished in any public welfare district to any person having a settlement elsewhere in the State. If the bill is disputed, the question of responsibility may be referred to the State Department of Social Welfare, and the department's decision may be contested in the Supreme Court.

No exception is made for New York City in the statute. Since, however, the Greater New York Charter forbids the use of city moneys for the furnishing of home relief, I doubt seriously if, prior to this time, a community up-State would have been able to collect from New York city the cost of home relief furnished to a person having a settlement in the city. Two statutes covering the same subject must be read together and full force and effect given to both, so far as possible. New York does not come under home-relief provisions of the Public Welfare Law. It should not be chargeable merely by reason of the Emergency Act in the period of its operation.

* * *

New York City's Position

Where the city of Buffalo seeks to charge the city of New York with the cost of maintaining relief recipients with a settlement in the latter city, and the city of New York offers to bear the expense of returning such persons to New York but refuses to reimburse for their support in Buffalo, New York's offer is an evidence of its willingness to bear the burden, and it cannot be compelled to make such reimbursement. If this conclusion is questioned the courts are open to adjudicate the matter, which is not properly before the Relief Administration. We will reimburse, whenever the relief is given, and ought not to be troubled with such disputes.

Soldiers as Residents

With regard to the question of soldiers or others residing on government property either in military garrisons or otherwise, where the residence has been within the confines of New York State, even though it has been on government property and the individual is now an applicant for relief within the State, relief should be furnished and the two years residence should be deemed to be met.

* *

Merchant Marine Service

One who had a residence in this State to begin with does not lose the same by reason of service in the merchant marine or the United States army, but on the other hand time spent in such service does not count toward a residence here unless it was spent within the State.

The person involved appears to have had an actual residence in the State since March, 1932. If his prior residences in the State, interrupted by merchant marine voyages and army enlistment, which do not count for or against him, add up, together with this, to two years in all, I should deem him entitled to relief under the Emergency Act.

* * *

Non-Resident Work Relief

Men who have a legal settlement in a welfare district are eligible for work relief in that district, although not now actually resident there, if the local work bureau desires to give it to them.

Eligibility as Resident

A resident of a town is eligible for work relief on application to the county relief bureau. If he is a resident of a city he is entitled to apply to the city work relief bureau.

From Date of Application

The two-year residence makes a case eligible under the Relief Act. The recipient can apply for work or home relief and the two-year period operates from date of application. Many a residence of less than two years may ripen into a two-year residence within the period of the emergency and thus come within the scope of the Act.

No Settlement While on Relief

Settlement for welfare purposes cannot be obtained while a person is a recipient of public relief unless term of habitation be independently acquired. It would seem that this would have considerable bearing on the status of individuals who have not acquired settlement and are applying for work relief. According to our rules, work relief should be given to these persons, but they do not acquire a settlement while on work relief.

No One-Year Requirement

Applicants for work relief in a city should be furnished work relief by the city bureau and the only requirement of residence necessary is a State residence of two years. There is no provision in the law which will permit a city to refuse to furnish work relief to a resident of the city because of any one year requirement. No such limitation is recognized. Under the circumstances, therefore, with regard to work relief, there should be no question of charging back to the county, nor should such applicants be sent to the county bureau.

With regard to home relief, where it is a town charge or a city charge, the relief should be administered where it is needed and the question of charging back is a matter which must be worked out locally in accordance with the provisions of the Public Welfare Law and the practices of the particular county. The two should not be confused.

No Compulsory Provision

Where "home" relief is granted and enough local residents are available for "work" relief, there is no compulsion in the law that "work" relief *must* be furnished at all—or if furnished, then to non-residents.

Absence From State

An applicant's settlement in the town of Yorktown continued valid until he had been absent from that town for one year, and as he returned within that period, though he went to another State, he still has such settlement.

He would not, however, be entitled to emergency relief until he could show two years residence in the State prior to his application therefor, and this would bar him from work relief until he has been back for two years.

As a veteran, nevertheless, this man is entitled to home relief, and if the town cannot provide the same the county must. This is a matter to be handled through the nearest post or camp of a recognized veterans' organization.

Then there is the ruling of the Relief Administration that persons not eligible to relief under the State law may nevertheless have the same under the Federal law, which contains no residential limitation, and it will be reimbursed by the T.E.R.A.

Work Accepted in Error

Adult persons of sound mind cannot be made paupers against their will, and to constitute the "receipt of public relief", within the meaning of the Public Welfare Law the relief must have been *applied for* by the applicant, or received, with a full knowledge of its nature. (Bucksport v. Cushing, 69 Maine 214; Sheboygan County v. Sheboygan Falls, 130 Wis. 93, 109 N. W. 1030.)

It would seem, therefore, that persons who did not apply for relief, or understand that the work given them was relief work, did not forfeit their settlement by accepting it. In response to a further question, since these men had not been two years resident in the State at the time the work was given to them, they were not in any event eligible for the same under the Emergency Act, and there should be no reimbursement therefor. In short, work relief given illegally would not affect the settlement of the recipients, but the opinion that work relief does destroy a prior settlement is applicable to relief given at any given time during the emergency period and is not limited by the date of the opinion.

Settlement Not Acquired

We are asked if a family which has not a legal residence in the city of Fulton acquires such residence, so that the city may subsequently be held responsible for their support, by maintaining itself in said city for a full year by means of work relief, without recourse to the department of public welfare, and if work relief should be refused to men, otherwise qualified, whose settlement is in another county.

We have held work relief to be public relief, so that recipients thereof can gain no settlement while receiving it. Their settlement remains where it was. Nor need work relief be refused to a resident because of non-settlement. The cost of work relief, however, cannot be charged back to the town of settlement, because work relief arises solely under the Emergency Act and is not known to the Public Welfare Law, in which are contained the provisions for charging back.

Relief at Former Residence

One who has a settlement in a city continues to be entitled to relief from such city for one year, after he has removed therefrom, and while he is receiving relief from the city of his settlement he cannot acquire a settlement elsewhere. (Onondaga County v. Amsterdam, 139 App. Div. 877.) Thus a man with a settlement in Rome, who removed on May 1, 1931, to the town of Lee and on January 18, 1932, applied for and received relief in Rome, and has since been receiving such relief, is still settled in Rome, notwithstanding his residence in the town of Lee for more than two years. It is not the form of relief that constitutes the bar to obtaining settlement; it is the *fact* of receiving such relief.

Matter of Intent

We are asked in regard to the eligibility for work relief in Rome of a man who has lived in Constantia, Oswego county, all his life prior to January 31, 1933, when he came to Rome to join his wife, who left Constantia May 30, 1931, to live in Rome. This person makes affidavit that it was his intention in 1931, and since has been, to establish his home in Rome; that he has gone to Rome every week-end to be with his wife, has sent her money for her support whenever possible, and that he did not move to Rome with her in May, 1931, because he could get work in Constantia and could get no work in Rome.

Since residence is so very largely a matter of intent, I have little hesitation upon this record in advising that in my opinion this man's legal settlement is in Rome, where his wife has been for almost two years and from which place he has at no time been absent with the intention of making his home elsewhere. However, eligibility for work relief in no way involves settlement, two years' residence within the State being sufficient to establish it (Emergency Relief Act, section 9, as amended). Settlement arises under the Public Welfare Law, and thus is important in determining who shall pay for home relief, but it has no application to work relief.

Facts Must Determine

In determining the status of a person who has not been in the State continuously for the past two years, her eligibility would depend on whether her absence was merely intended to be temporary and not to establish a permanent home out of the State. The support of her mother is no evidence of her continuing residence. It would depend on the nature of her residence elsewhere, the purpose thereof, etc. The question of fact will need to be determined locally. All the facts must be inquired into. The question of residence is one of fact, depending on intent and circumstances. If an absence was never intended to be permanent, as evidenced by facts to be ascertained; if the person voted (for example) in New York, his residence might be said to have been here. The fact of one and a half years away with his family counts heavily on the other side. If not a resident for two years, he must be regarded as not reimbursable but a local charge. If the local bureau, on the facts, feels that all the time he was a New York resident *in good faith*, they may consider him eligible. This should be carefully considered because such cases may be used as precedent, and the facts in each must determine.

Two-Year Residence Essential

A family in question consists of an able-bodied man and a sickly wife. Their former residence was in Ohio. They now have a New York State residence of 20 months, having resided throughout this time in the city of Auburn. Due to unemployment and exhaustion of funds the family had to apply for relief three months ago. The woman's poor health now prevents her return to the State of Ohio (medically verified). Auburn's work relief bureau is willing to give work to the man, because it is felt that the previous residence for seventeen months without relief is a sound indication of the intended permanence of the residence of the family. The point is now raised whether work relief should be given to this man and will his wages be subject to the State refund. This is a truly unfortunate borderline case which must fall by the statutory axe. We cannot change the demarcation line set by the law. The relief cannot be reimbursed until he shall have been two years in the State. A public welfare settlement has apparently been achieved, but not for emergency relief under the definition of chapter 567, Laws of 1932. There are some times when a dividing line must be maintained.

Under the later federal enactments, this case, which arose early in the emergency, might have been duly cared for as a federal case.

* *

Settlement of Dependent Mother

A woman who has no independent means of support, lives with her son as a member of his family and moves about with the family, acquires any settlement which the son acquires while she is a member of his family. (Public Welfare Law, section 53.) She still has her son's settlement as long as she is a member of his family. Whether or not she has shared in contributions made to the son by the town of his settlement might be a corroborative point, but would not be vital.

Work Relief as Public Relief

Where a man, coming into the town of Veteran in September, 1932, was not a poor person under the Public Welfare Law at the time, but having applied for and accepted work relief in that town in June, 1932, he has since removed therefrom after a year's residence there, and into the town of Horseheads, we are asked whether the acceptance of work relief in the town of Veteran prevented him from gaining a settlement in that town. On this point we have held that work relief is public relief. Therefore, though one resides in a town for one year, he gains no settlement in such town by reason of such residence, if, during the year, he receives work relief there. But such person, if he had a settlement somewhere else in the State would still have it until he has lived elsewhere for one year continuously without applying for and receiving public relief, and the cost of his home relief in any town to which he might remove could in such case be charged back to such place of settlement under the Public Welfare Law.

Sentence to Penitentiary

The case is presented of a home relief case having three months' residence in North Tonawanda, who was sentenced to nine months in the penitentiary of another county. The law (Public Welfare Law, section 56) is plain that "no settlement shall be gained by residence as an inmate of any public institution." This man's time in a penitentiary is, therefore, perfectly blank for any purpose of acquiring a Poor Law settlement. And unless he has been two years in the State his case is not one for the Relief Administration to consider.

In answer to the specific questions, this man's settlement remains in the last public welfare district of the State, if there is such, where he has resided for one year without receiving support from public funds in any guise.

Transporting Alien Families

It is not evident how the State can under its Relief Act supply money for transporting aliens out of State funds. Under section 3 of chapter 8 as amended by chapter 258, Laws of 1933, only Federal funds may be used for Federal purposes.

ⱶ ✱ ː

No Aid for Removal

In response to an inquiry as to whether a family long resident in this State may be assisted out of New York State funds to locate on a farm in another State, in which State there are friends or relatives who would assist in putting the family on a subsistence basis, I may say that the use of New York State moneys for such purpose would be out of the question. Our statute allows us to assist only those who are bona fide residents of New York, with the presumption that they are intending or attempting to continue to be such. As to those who propose to take up residence in another jurisdiction, the presumption must be that they will be cared for by that other jurisdiction if they need it. We cannot, at any rate, be responsible in any manner for persons who are not actually within our borders.

Application at Former Home

We are asked for a general ruling as to those families applying for work relief which have not as yet established a Poor Law settlement, the specific instance being cited of a family resident for thirty-six years in Mount Vernon, which has removed for good reasons just over the boundary into the Bronx, and has been resident there for eight months, but which is now applying for work relief in Mount Vernon.

This family had a settlement in Mount Vernon, under the Public Welfare Law (section 53), which they could not lose until they had resided elsewhere for one whole year continuously without receiving public relief or care in such other place (id., section 56). Should they apply for home relief in the Bronx and receive it there, the cost of the same could be charged back to Mount Vernon (id., section 58). They are therefore still eligible for home relief in Mount Vernon under the Public Welfare Law, and in fact may have it in either place, as relief under the Emergency

Act takes no account of settlements under the Public Welfare Law, the only requirement of the Emergency Act being that the recipients be ''needy persons, who are unemployed or, if employed, whose compensation therefrom is inadequate to provide the necessaries of life and who have been *residents of the State* for at least two years prior to the date of application under this act and the dependents of such persons.'' (L. 1931, ch. 798, section 9, as amended by L. 1932, ch. 567.)

In regard to work relief the situation is the same, with the important exception that there is no charging back of the cost thereof to the place of the person's settlement, as work relief arises solely under the Emergency Act and is not known to the Public Welfare Law, and the question of settlement is therefore of no importance in connection therewith. Work relief ought ordinarily, therefore, to be given in the place where the family now resides, without regard to the place of settlement. But the place of a family's settlement may, if it chooses to do so, provide work relief for the family, though such family's actual residence is at the moment elsewhere. Whether this should be done would be a matter of policy to be determined on the facts of each case. In the particular instance presented such solution might be desirable, but should not be regarded as a binding precedent.

Residence in Another State

The Emergency Relief Act requires a two-year residence in the State, prior to applying for relief. An absence from the United States in Europe does not deprive the absentee of his legal residence. However, where such person, on his return from Europe, maintained an actual residence for nine months in New Jersey, within the two-year period, he is not eligible for relief under the act.

* * *

Dependents Outside State

It is asked whether an allowance may be made for dependents residing outside of the State of New York, the specific case being that of a widower, boarding in a city in this State, who has three minor children who are with their grandfather in Massachusetts, the grandfather being out of work. These children, if in need of relief, are no doubt receiving it at the place in Massachusetts where they are residing. We cannot, in any event, undertake to grant allowances for persons who are not within the state.

* * *

Settlement Not Acquired

The case is presented of the settlement of a family which, having a settlement in the city of Syracuse, has lived for nine months in the city of Cortland and then due to unemployment and exhaustion of funds has had to apply for relief. For three months this family has been the recipient of relief. It is asked whether a settlement for purposes of "poor relief" has been acquired in the city of Cortland. It has not, but strictly speaking, this is not a question to be determined by the Temporary Emergency Relief Administration, nor does it involve the administration of relief by the Temporary Emergency Relief Administration. "Poor relief" and relief under the Emergency Act should be clearly distinguished. Two years residence, regardless of settlement, creates eligibility under the Emergency Act.

* * *

Procedure in Extreme Cases

An inquiry presents the case of a supervisor who acts also as town public welfare officer, who owns the only grocery for miles about, and who is charged with the care and relief in the first instance of several families whose settlement is in other towns or even in another county. In regard to local relief, although much inconvenience is involved, this official has given up any idea of providing groceries from his store, by reason of the provisions of law forbidding either a supervisor or a welfare officer to be financially interested in any claim presented by him to his town for payment, but as to the families with settlement elsewhere the practice heretofore has been for him to send the bills directly to the town or city of the settlement, which in turn would pay him directly.

Now, in order to obtain State reimbursement, it is insisted that the procedure set forth in the Public Welfare Law be followed, which requires the county commissioner to provide relief and care and then to notify the commissioner of the other county of the charge. In practice, under the Emergency Act, the county commissioner issues the relief order, claims the reimbursement from the State, and bills the other county for the balance. Now the commissioner of one such county insists, in regard to a case handled in July last, that the county granting the relief shall collect the

State reimbursement before billing him for the balance, and as only paid bills can be submitted for reimbursement, this would require our subject either to write himself a check for the groceries or to accept a check drawn to his order by his county commissioner, either of which he is reluctant to do. It still is the fact that no funds of the supervisor's town or county are involved in the transaction, as that part of the cost which is not reimbursed by the State will be reimbursed by another county, and it is also to be considered that there are times in the winter when the roads are not open and it is practically impossible to reach the needy families from any other store. The question is whether this back bill may properly be paid to this supervisor by himself, or by the commissioner of his county, and whether, in view of the emergency aspects, this practice may be continued.

I think the difficulties here are mainly in the form of the procedure, and that there would be no impropriety in the payment by the county commissioner of the cost of groceries furnished for a family with a settlement in another county, in accordance with section 58 of the Public Welfare Law, though such payment has to be made, or happens to be made, to one who is a supervisor or welfare officer of his own town. None of the reasons why a public officer cannot collect a bill from the district which he serves would seem to be operative in such case.

It is not clear to me on what grounds the commissioner of the other county declines to pay his share of the cost until the refund has been collected from the State, as the Public Welfare Law takes no cognizance of such reimbursement and I do not recall that the Administration has adopted such a regulation. But that is not material, as the refund will have to be paid, in theory, out of the county's funds, in order to get the reimbursement, whether before or after the other county contributes its proportion.

Non-Resident of State

A man came to Schenectady from Detroit at some date unstated, and in November, 1931, applied to the Schenectady city authorities for home relief. He was referred to the county welfare department, which refused to assist him and suggested his return to Detroit. He refused to go, and later applied for city work relief, which, by error, as it is stated, he was given. Now he again asks for city home relief, and the question arises whether he can now be sent back to Detroit, it being assumed that he has gained a residence in Schenectady, this assumption seeming to rest upon his receipt of public relief in the form of work relief wages, as to which we are asked if work relief wages do constitute public relief so as to establish the residence of the recipient thereof.

There seems to be a little confusion here. Work relief wages assuredly constitute public relief, but no amount of public relief gives the recipient thereof a settlement in this State, as a settlement can only be acquired by living in a town or city in this State for one year continuously without receiving public relief or care (Public Welfare Law, section 56). So far as the State, county and city are concerned, this person is still a resident of Detroit and chargeable thereto, unless he lived in this State one full year without applying for and receiving public aid. His removal to Detroit, if it can be effected, is a State charge, and should be taken up with Mr. Harry M. Hirsch, assistant commissioner, Division of State Aid, State Department of Social Welfare (Public Welfare Law, section 73). His case is not, in any event, a T.E.R.A. question unless he has been in this State two years (Emergency Act, section 9). It seems, therefore, that it should be referred in its entirety to the county public welfare department, except as affected by federal relief regulations.

Loss of Residence

We are asked whether, inasmuch as under the Public Welfare Law one does not lose his residence in New York State until he acquires a residence elsewhere, the same interpretation should be accepted for work relief residence, so that one who had been out of the State for less than one year, during the two years' required residence period, would still be eligible for work relief, and if not, on what basis should be judged the many cases of men who have been residents of this State for the past several years, but during the two years prior to registering were in another State or another county for anywhere from two to ten months.

There seems to be some slight confusion here, as settlement under the Public Welfare Law (section 53) is not the same as the residence called for under the provision of the Emergency Act (section 9) limiting emergency relief, both work relief and home relief, to persons "who have been residents of the State for at least

two years prior to the date of application for aid under this act"
and their dependents.

One who has gained a settlement in a town or city in this State
by residing therein continuously for one year without receiving
public relief or care for himself or herself or for his wife or minor
child (Public Welfare Law, section 56) does not lose such settlement except by gaining a like settlement in some other town or
city of this State or by removing from this State and remaining
therefrom for one year (section 53), and such person may claim
relief under the Public Welfare Law from such place of his settlement, and such place of settlement will be responsible for such
relief, until he has lived a whole year elsewhere without receiving
relief, or, if he has removed from the State, a year has elapsed
since such removal. But under the Emergency Act no cognizance
is taken of settlements, the simple requirement being two years'
residence in the State. This means actual residence and bars
those who have, in the ordinary and non-technical sense of the
word, "lived" elsewhere during that period, except where such
absence has been shown to be temporary, with no intention of
making his or her "home" elsewhere than in the State. The facts in
each case must determine the result.

One who still has a settlement in this State may, of course, claim
relief under the Public Welfare Law, though by reason of absence
he would not be eligible for Emergency Relief, and as the Administration reimburses for all home relief, the effect would be that,
where the application is made in the place of the applicant's settlement, the distinction drawn above is inoperative as to home relief,
but such person would not be eligible for work relief, which arises
solely under the Emergency Act. And where such person, with a
settlement in this State but not eligible for work relief by reason
of absence, is given home relief in a place where he is not settled,
the Administration, while it will determine no questions of settlement or of responsibility arising therefrom, will reimburse such
district granting aid to the legal extent and such district may
then endeavor under the Public Welfare Law to collect the balance
from the district where the person has a settlement.

Conversely, one who has resided two years in the State prior to
his application is eligible to emergency relief, both work relief and
home relief, under the Emergency Act, whether he has a settlement in the State or not. If he has none, no question of charging
back the cost will arise, and the whole burden will therefore fall
upon the place where he is found, but the Administration will make
reimbursement in any event.

Work Relief in Non-Settled Case

An inquirer stated that he has eight dependents, and has lived in the town and county of his present residence for two years, paying taxes and making payments on a home, and has never lived outside of the State of New York. He has, however, received aid from the town in which he formerly resided, during each year in which he has had his present residence. Such aid, however, consists only of food and medical attention, and he needs money in addition to this to make payments on his home and pay taxes, but he cannot find employment. His question is, therefore, whether he is entitled to work relief under the Emergency Act at the place of his present residence, his contention being that if he has to return to the place of his settlement in order to obtain work relief he will have to give up the place he has been making payments on.

There is a distinction between home relief and the work relief which is granted under the Emergency Act. It appears that the former is being received by this applicant under the provision of law that the settlement which he had acquired in the place of his former residence is retained by him until he has gained a settlement elsewhere by residing in such other place for one year continuously without receiving public relief or care for himself or his dependents (Public Welfare Law, sections 53, 56), and the place of his settlement must support him, upon due notice, either directly, as it appears is being done, or by defraying the cost of such support when duly charged back (id., section 58). Whether later charged back or not, and regardless of his settlement, every needy person whose income is inadequate for his support and that of his dependents, and who has been a resident of the State for two years, is entitled to home relief under the Emergency Act, in the first instance, at the place where he is found. (L. 1931, ch. 798, section 9.)

As to work relief, involving the payment of wages, it is not a town purpose under the Emergency Act, but is under the direction of an emergency work bureau appointed for the whole county (id., sections 2, 7, 9), nor is there any provision for charging it back to the place of settlement. Whether it shall be granted in any particular circumstances is within the discretion of the work bureau of the county in which the person is. In the case presented it is stated that the necessaries of life are being provided (with, it seems, the exception of shelter, which is an important ingredient thereof), but the question is rather one of enabling the man to save the home on which he has been making payments. This is a close point, as to which I may say there is no authority for refusing the aid requested, but neither is the granting thereof compulsory. If the person's support were a charge upon the welfare district in which he now resides, the matter would be about as broad as it is long, for work relief wages may properly include allowances for rent, in accordance with budget requirements, and buying a home on a contract for a deed is closely akin to renting, and if the man loses his home and is forced to move elsewhere his rent would then be a charge on home relief in any event. But in the latter case the cost thereof could be collected from the town from which he came and where his settlement remains, and this thought may be controlling.

The proper person to be consulted in the matter, however, is the chairman of the county emergency work bureau, together with the county commissioner of public welfare.

Residence for Highway Work

The residence required to make one eligible for work on State highways under the Emergency Relief Act is two years in the State prior to the date of application for relief.

A temporary absence during this period will not destroy the residence, provided some place in the State was at all times the person's "home" and there was no intention to abandon the same and acquire a residence elsewhere. Whether there was such intent is a question of fact, to be determined upon the circumstances of each case, and it will in some instances be necessary for the local work bureau, when such questions arise, to pass judgment upon the *good faith* of the applicant.

It should be noted that this residence need not be at any particular place in the State, provided it was within the State. Also that it has nothing to do with "settlement" under the Public Welfare Law, which is acquired by residence for one year in a certain place without applying for or receiving public relief or care during that period. It should also be noted that where *federal* highway moneys are involved, the statute provides that only *American citizens,* or those who have declared intentions to become citizens, may be given employment, which is a distinction not drawn by the Emergency Act.

Divorced Woman

A woman, divorced from her husband, who lives in Chicago, is unemployed and will need assistance for several months. By June 10 she will have gained a settlement in the place where she now resides. It is asked if emergency relief provided for her is subject to reimbursement; if so, will this change her status as to settlement after the emergency period is over, and will her settlement still be in Chicago or will she have gained a settlement in this State in the meantime.

The inquiry does not reveal whether the individual has a two-year residence within the State of New York prior to November 1, 1931 (or, under the act just signed, prior to her application for relief). This is a primary prerequisite for the reimbursable relief provided for under the act. Under the Public Welfare Law a settlement may be obtained which would warrant the administration of home relief under that law, entirely separate and apart from the possibility of reimbursement under the Emergency Relief Act. The question of reimbursement, therefore, is not based upon settlement under the Public Welfare Law but upon the two-year residence laid down by the emergency statute. This is not affected by her divorced husband's residence in Chicago. Nor does the said divorce prevent her from obtaining an individual settlement in New York for all purposes. In fact, the divorce itself established that right, since the Emergency Relief Act does not in any manner affect the question of settlement so obtained under the Public Welfare Law.

SUPPLEMENT A—EMERGENCY RELIEF ACT OF THE STATE OF NEW YORK AND RELATED STATUTES AS AMENDED TO OCTOBER 15, 1934

FOREWORD

The emergency relief enactments of 1934 fall into three classes, (a) amendments of the Emergency Act, (b) amendments of the State Recovery Act, and (c) financial measures and special provisions.

Amendments of the Emergency Act

The Emergency Relief Act (Chapter 798 of the Laws of 1931, as amended by Chapter 567 of the Laws of 1932, and Chapters 2, 9, 34, 44, 69, 259 and 646 of the Laws of 1933) has been amended by Chapters 15, 65, 71 and 303 of the Laws of 1934.

Chapter 15 of the Laws of 1934 numbers the definitions in Section 2 of the Emergency Act, provides that work relief shall include wages paid by the State, extends the emergency period to February 15, 1935, and provides that the Governor shall designate the chairman of the Administration; that the Administration may, with the approval of the Governor, act as the designated agency of duly authorized federal or other relief within the State; that local work bureaus shall be subject to the approval of the Administration and shall serve at the Administration's pleasure, and such bureaus or members thereof may be designated by the Administration to act as local agencies of federal or other relief under the supervision and control of the Administration. Also that the State, as well as municipal corporations, may furnish work relief.

Chapter 65 of the Laws of 1934 amends Sections 2 and 16 of the Emergency Act to provide that home relief may be given in cash, until February 15, 1935, if and where approved by and under rules and regulations made and conditions specified by the Administration.

Chapter 71 of the Laws of 1934 amends Section 18 of the Emergency Act to raise the proportion of State improvement moneys which may be spent for materials, tools and supplies from 15 to 20 per cent.

Chapter 303 of the Laws of 1934 adds to the Emergency Act a new Section 16-a, taking persons employed on work relief projects out of the coverage of the Workmen's Compensation Law and making the Administration liable for all claims arising from the injury, disability or death of such persons.

Amendments of the State Recovery Act

The State Recovery Act (Chapter 782 of the Laws of 1933), authorizing cooperation by the State with the National Recovery Administration, has been amended by Chapters 39, 104 and 301 of the Laws of 1934.

Chapter 39 of the Laws of 1934 added to the Recovery Act a new Section 5-a, authorizing municipalities, by vote of their governing bodies, to borrow for materials, supplies and equipment for use on projects undertaken through the federal Civil Works Administration, notwithstanding the provisions of any general, special or local law.

This new Section 5-a was amended by Chapter 301 of the Laws of 1934 to extend the borrowing power to projects undertaken by the federal Emergency Relief Administration or any other work relief authority of the State and/or federal government.

Chapter 104 of the Laws of 1934 amends Sections 2, 3, 4 and 5 of the State Recovery Act and adds new Sections 4-a, 6-a and 6-b.

Section 2 is amended to clarify the definition of governing boards and to provide that "national industrial recovery act" shall include amendments and revisions thereof and any further federal act to encourage public works, reduce unemployment and thereby assist in national recovery and promote public welfare.

Section 3 is amended to extend the power of municipalities to accept direct grants from the federal Emergency Administration so as to allow them to accept grants from any federal agency for labor and materials on federal projects.

Section 4 is amended to extend the contracting power of municipalities in regard to federal projects to include contracts with any federal agency; to provide for a mandatory referendum whenever a federal project is for the construction or operation of a public utility or the supply of gas, electricity or water in competition with or substitution for a utility supplying the same in the same area; preserving the right of school district meetings to vote on all federal projects of whatever nature; allowing a permissive referendum whenever a governing board desires one, and authorizing the issuance of notes, temporary bonds, certificates of indebtedness, interim certificates or security receipts in anticipation of a bond issue duly authorized.

Section 5 is amended to make the bonds or obligations of a municipality, assumed for these purposes, saleable directly to the United States, instead of to an agency thereof.

The new section 4-a allows a public works project to be undertaken at the expense of the municipality at large, instead of wholly or partly at the expense of property benefited, and permits borrowing for the entire cost of a project in the first instance, prior to its completion or prior to any levy.

The new Section 6-a provides that, notwithstanding any general, special or local law, a public works project, contract or bond issue may be finally approved on the same day on which it is introduced, and such resolution need not be published before becoming effective.

The new Section 6-b provides that the act shall be liberally construed and the duties imposed by it are to be independent and severable, and if any section, clause, sentence or part thereof shall be adjudged unconstitutional or invalid, such judgment shall affect no other provision of the act.

Financial Measures and Special Provisions

Chapter 71 of the Laws of 1934 appropriated the balance of $48,000,000 remaining out of the proceeds of the sale of $60,000,000 bonds authorized by Chapter 260 of the Laws of 1933, $33,000,000 of which was allocated to the reimbursement fund, and $15,000,000 to the discretionary fund.

By Chapter 821 of the Laws of 1934 $1,500,000 of the said discretionary fund was reappropriated to supply fresh milk free to needy children through the schools or public or private milk stations, under rules and regulations of the Relief Administration.

By Chapter 718 of the Laws of 1934 there is submitted to the voters at the next general election a proposition to incur a further State debt of $40,000,000 for emergency relief purposes, and by Chapter 717 $10,000,000 of such moneys, if and when the indebtedness has been approved, are appropriated for emergency relief up to and including February 15, 1935, $7,000,000 of this sum to go to the reimbursement fund and $3,000,000 to the discretionary fund.

There have already been two other such bond issues, one of $30,000,000 and another of $60,000,000, and in addition there have been direct appropriations of $5,000,000 and $20,000,000, so that the proposed new $40,000,000 bond issue will bring the State's total unemployment relief contributions to $155,000,000. In recommending the $40,000,000 proposal to the Legislature, the Governor expressed the hope that it would be the last bond issue that would be necessary for relief purposes.

Chapter 716 of the Laws of 1934 amends Chapter 8 of the Laws of 1933, in regard to State participation in federal funds, so as to allow the Governor to transmit the same directly to the Relief Administration, acting as a federal agency.

Chapter 654 of the Laws of 1934 authorizes the State to receive federal moneys, for expenditure through the Department of Public Works, for the cost and expense of engineering, designing, supervision and inspection of the construction, repair and improvement of public highways, parkways, buildings, etc., as federal projects, and appropriates $100,000 to be advanced by the State in the first instance for such expense.

Chapter 769 of the Laws of 1934 amends Section 10 of Article 2 of the Workmen's Compensation Law, to provide that such law shall not apply to persons receiving work relief and employed on work relief projects. This is complementary to the new Section 16-a of the Emergency Act, noted above, under which the Relief Administration assumes all liability for work relief injuries or disability.

By Section 2 of Chapter 39 of the Laws of 1934, as amended by Chapter 301, all acts and proceedings heretofore taken by municipalities, their boards and officers, in raising money or using the same for the purchase of materials, supplies and equipment for work relief projects of the federal Civil Works Administration, or the work division of the federal Emergency Relief Administration, or any other work relief authority of the State and/or federal government, is legalized, validated, ratified and confirmed, notwithstanding any want of statutory authority therefor or any defect or irregularity therein.

The complete text of the Emergency Act as amended, the Recovery Act as amended, and the financial and special acts referred to in the foregoing, will be found in the following pages.

The Emergency Relief Act of the State of New York

CHAPTER 798 OF THE LAWS OF 1931 AS AMENDED TO THE END OF THE REGULAR LEGISLATIVE SESSION OF 1934

CHAPTER 798 OF THE LAWS OF 1931; AS AMENDED BY CHAPTER 567 OF THE LAWS OF 1932 AND CHAPTERS 2, 9, 34, 44, 69, 259 AND 646 OF THE LAWS OF 1933, AND CHAPTERS 15, 65, 71 AND 303 OF THE LAWS OF 1934

An Act to relieve the people of the state from the hardships and suffering caused by unemployment, creating and organizing for such purpose a temporary emergency relief administration, prescribing its powers and duties and making an appropriation for its work.

The People of the State of New York, represented in Senate and Assembly, do enact as follows:

SCHEDULE OF SECTIONS

§ 1. **Declaration of emergency.** The public health and safety of the state and of each county, city and town therein being imperilled by the existing and threatened deprivation of a considerable number of their inhabitants of the necessaries of life, owing to the present economic depression, such condition is hereby declared to be a matter of public concern, state and local, and the correction thereof to be a state, county, city and town purpose, the consummation of which requires, as a necessary incident the furnishing of public aid to individuals. While the duty of providing aid for those in need or unemployed because of lack of employment is primarily an obligation of the municipalities, nevertheless, it is the finding of the state that in the existing emergency the relief and assistance provided for by this act are vitally necessary to supplement the relief work accomplished or to be accomplished locally and to encourage and stimulate local effort in the same direction. This act, therefore, is declared to be a measure for the public health and safety and occasioned by an existing emergency. The provisions of any general, special or local law which are inconsistent with the provisions of this act or which limit or forbid the furnishing of shelter, fuel, clothing, light, medicine and medical attendance to persons other than poor persons shall not apply to the relief authorized by this act.

§ 2. **Definitions.** As used in this act:

1. "Administration" means the temporary state agency created by this act, to be known as the temporary emergency relief administration.

2. "City commissioner" means the chief administrative public welfare officer or board of a city.

3. "County commissioner" means the chief administrative public welfare officer of territory of a county beyond the limits of a city.

4. "Municipal corporation" means a county or city except a county wholly within a city.

5. "Public welfare district" means one of such districts created by this act.

6. "Local bureau" means one of the temporary emergency work bureaus created by this act in cities and counties.

7. "Work relief" means wages paid by a municipal corporation or by the state to persons, who are unemployed or whose employment is inadequate to provide the necessaries of life, and/or their dependents, from money specifically appropriated or contributed for that purpose during the emergency period, for the performance of services or labor connected with work undertaken by such corporation independent of work under a contract or for which an annual appropriation has been made.

8. "Home relief" means shelter, fuel, food, clothing, light, necessary household supplies, medicine, medical supplies, relief to veterans under existing laws and medical attendance furnished by a municipal corporation or a town, where home relief is a town charge, to persons or their dependents in their abode or habitation whenever possible and does not include old age relief or allowances made to mothers for the care of dependent children or hospital or institutional care. For the purposes of and in order to provide wholly or in part home relief as herein defined, until February fifteenth, nineteen hundred thirty-five, money may be given in cash if and where approved by and under rules and regulations made and conditions specified by the administration.

9. "Emergency period" means the period defined by chapter seven hundred and ninety-eight of the laws of nineteen hundred thirty-one, as extended and continued, by chapter five hundred and sixty-seven of the laws of nineteen hundred thirty-two, and further extended and continued by chapter two of the laws of nineteen hundred thirty-three, and such period is hereby further extended and continued to the fifteenth day of February, nineteen hundred thirty-five.

10. "State aid" means payments to a municipal corporation or town by the state for work relief and/or home relief furnished during the emergency period in accordance with this act.

Section 2 amended by Laws of 1932, chapter 567, Laws of 1933, chapter 646, and Laws of 1934, chapters 15 and 65.

§ 3. **Administrative authority.** The administration of the emergency relief provided by this act shall be vested in a temporary state agency, to be known as the temporary emergency relief administration, to consist of five persons to be appointed by the governor, one of whose number shall be designated by the governor as chairman and all of whom shall serve during his pleasure. Any vacancy in the membership of the administration, occurring from any cause whatsoever, shall be filled by the governor. The administration shall organize immediately upon the appointment of its complete membership. It may employ, and at pleasure remove, a secretary and such other clerks and assistants as may be deemed necessary by it to carry out the provisions of this act. The administration may fix the compensation of all such employees within the amounts available by appropriation. The administration may accept from any person or organization and avail itself of any and all offers of personal service or other aid or assistance in carrying out any of the provisions of this act made without expectation of compensation or other reward. Any persons or organizations so contributing such services and giving such other aid or assistance shall be entitled to receive only such expenses as are actually and necessarily incurred by them by reason of such services, aid or assistance. Employees and volunteers of the administration shall not be subject to the provisions of the civil service law. The principal office of the administration shall be in the city of Albany in suitable quarters set apart for its use by the superintendent of public buildings, but offices in other localities of the state may be maintained by it. Each of the members of the administration, before entering upon the duties of his office, shall take and subscribe the constitutional oath of office and file the same in the office of the department of state. The chairman of the administration shall be compensated at the rate of eleven thousand five hundred dollars per annum and actual and necessary traveling and other expenses incurred by him in the performance of his duties. The other members of the administration shall receive no compensation for their services hereunder but shall be allowed their actual and necessary traveling and other expenses incurred by them in the performance of their duties. The administration shall continue to function only during the emergency period, except that it may examine and certify, after the expiration of such period, claims for state aid under this act for expenditures for work and/or home relief furnished prior to the expiration of such period. The administration may, with the approval of the governor, accept a designation from and act as the agency of duly authorized federal relief or like bodies in the administration of relief and related activities within the state of New York.

Section 3 amended by the Laws of 1933, chapter 44, and by Laws of 1934, chapter 15.

§ 4. **Preliminary studies.** The administration shall (a) make or cause to be made with the aid of such data as may be available a thorough and comprehensive study and survey of unemployment within the state, the occupations, industries, and trades most seriously affected thereby and the number of persons suffering or in want by reason thereof.

(b) Discover the extent and nature of public work required or useful to be done by the state or any political subdivision thereof.

(c) Ascertain the amount of resources made available by public appropriations or private contributions for the relief of unemployed persons throughout the state.

§ 5. **Assistance of existing agencies.** In making any of the surveys preliminary to the work of the administration and for the more effective consumption of any of its powers and duties, the administration may request and shall receive advice and expert assistance from the department of social welfare, the tax department, the department of public works, the department of public health, and any other state or local department or agency. It shall have access to the records of any state or local department, board or other agency pertaining to the functions of the department and the cooperation and assistance of each and every officer or employee thereof. It may, in its discretion cooperate with existing national, state or local unemployment relief commissions or agencies and, if deemed advisable or expedient by it, coordinate and correlate its work with the work or projects of any such commission or agency.

§ 6. **Public welfare districts.** For the purpose of facilitating the administration of the provisions of this act and the distribution of the state aid thereby provided, each city of the state and the territory of each county beyond the limits of cities is hereby constituted a separate public welfare district, which are hereby designated as city and county public welfare districts respectively, except that the cities of Geneva and Canandaigua shall be included in the county welfare district of the county of Ontario and the town of Newburgh shall be included in the city public welfare district of the city of Newburgh.

§ 7. **Local bureaus.** The mayor or chief administrative officer of a city may establish in a city public welfare district and the governing board of a county may establish in a county public welfare district, for the emergency period, an emergency work bureau, to consist of three or more persons to be appointed by such officers or governing boards respectively. City commissioners shall be members ex officio of the local bureau in their respective city public welfare districts and county commissioners shall be members ex officio of the local bureau in their respective county public welfare districts. Members of local bureaus heretofore or hereafter appointed shall continue in office for the duration of the emergency period unless removed as herein provided. Local bureaus shall serve at the pleasure of the administration and shall be responsible for the administration of work relief and may employ necessary clerks and assistants, whose compensation shall be fixed by the officer or governing board by which such bureau was created. Local bureaus may accept from any person or organization and avail itself of any and all offers of personal service or other aid or assistance in carrying out any of the provisions of this act made without expectation of compensation or other reward. Local bureaus or members thereof may, in the discretion of the administration, be designated by it to act as the local agency of federal relief or related bodies under the supervision and control of the administration.

Section 7 amended by the Laws of 1932, chapter 567, and Laws of 1934, chapter 15.

§ 8. **Administration agencies.** Under rules adopted by the administration, which shall not conflict or be inconsistent with the provisions of this act, the city commissioner shall represent the

administration in a city public welfare district as hereby constituted in providing home relief and administering the provisions
of this act therein in relation thereto and the county commissioner
shall represent the administration in a county public welfare district as hereby constituted in providing home relief and in
administering the provisions of this act therein in relation thereto.
Local bureaus shall represent the administration in their respective city and county welfare districts in providing work relief and
in administering the provisions of this act therein in relation
thereto. Local bureaus, city commissioners and county commissioners shall in all matters be subject to the supervision, direction
and control of the administration.

§ 9. Relief by municipal corporations or by the state. Subject
to the supervision and control of the administration by rules, a
municipal corporation or the state may furnish work relief, and a
municipal corporation or a town where home relief is a town
charge, notwithstanding any provision or limitation in any charter
or law, may furnish home relief, during the emergency period, to
needy persons, who are unemployed or, if employed, whose compensation therefrom is inadequate to provide the necessaries of
life and who have been resident of the state for at least two years
prior to the date of application for aid under this act and to the
dependents of such persons.

Section 9 amended by Laws of 1932, chapter 567, and Laws of 1934, chapter
15.

§ 10. Local funds for relief. The legislative body of a municipal
corporation or town may appropriate and make available sufficient
money to pay for work relief and/or home relief and also may raise
such money during the emergency period by interest bearing notes,
certificates of indebtedness, bond or other obligations of such
municipal corporation or town payable within a period not exceeding ten years, provided the money so raised shall not exceed the
constitutional or statutory debt limit of such municipal corporation, and provided further in the case of towns that such borrowing for relief purposes shall not exceed two per centum of the
assessed valuation of said town. Pending the issuance of the foregoing obligations temporary certificates of indebtedness may be
issued due and payable within six months from their date, and
paid either by raising the same by taxation or by refunding the
same by issuance of interest bearing notes, certificates of indebtedness, bonds or other obligations as aforesaid. In any county the
board of supervisors in making any appropriation for home and/or
work relief for the county welfare district may provide that such
appropriation or certificates issued therefor, together with interest
thereon shall be a charge against the county but the amount of
such appropriation or certificates issued therefor, together with
interest thereon shall be reimbursed to the county from the taxable
property within the county public welfare district for whose benefit
said appropriation was made or said certificates issued as provided by this act and the board of supervisors of said county shall

levy a tax upon the taxable property within the county public welfare district sufficient to provide such sums as may be necessary to meet such appropriation or certificates issued therefor, together with the interest thereon. The legislative body of a municipal corporation or town is also authorized and empowered during the emergency period to raise money for relief of veterans under existing laws by interest bearing notes, certificates of indebtedness, bonds or other obligations of such municipal corporation payable within a period not exceeding ten years, provided the constitutional or statutory debt limit of such municipal corporation or town shall not be exceeded thereby. Obligations heretofore incurred pursuant to section ten of chapter seven hundred and ninety-eight of the laws of nineteen hundred thirty-one and/or chapter five hundred and sixty-seven of the laws of nineteen hundred thirty-two may be refunded by the issuance of obligations herein authorized provided the maturity thereof does not exceed a period of ten years. The proceeds of all borrowings of municipal corporations or towns for the purposes set forth in chapter seven hundred and ninety-eight of the laws of nineteen hundred thirty-one as amended, except such as are needed for the refunding of prior obligations incurred under section ten of chapter seven hundred and ninety-eight of the laws of nineteen hundred thirty-one and/or chapter five hundred and sixty-seven of the laws of nineteen hundred thirty-two, shall not be credited or deposited in the general fund of the municipal corporation or town but shall be made available solely and exclusively for the relief purposes for which the said borrowings have been made. Such legislative body may authorize the performance of public work undertaken other than by contract by such municipal corporation or town, during the emergency period, through and under its local emergency work bureau or by its public works or other department under the supervision and control of its local emergency work bureau. These provisions shall be effective notwithstanding any provisions contained in any charter or in general, special or local laws to the contrary and notwithstanding any such provisions therein contained requiring such work as may be undertaken to be let by contract.

Section 10 amended by the Laws of 1932, chapter 567, and the Laws of 1933, chapters 9, 34, 69, and 259.

§ 11. City and county work relief. Before a city or county shall receive the state aid provided by this act for work relief, it shall establish an emergency work bureau as provided in this act which shall select the persons to be employed on the basis of their needs as determined by investigation.

§ 12. Duties of the local bureaus. 1. It shall be the duty of a local bureau to ascertain the extent of unemployment existing in its district and make investigations and surveys as to the need for public works and the amount and kind of public work available and not required to be let by contract. From such surveys and investigations it shall determine, from time to time, with the approval of the administration, whether the employment constitutes work relief; how the available employment useful to the public shall best and most equitably be apportioned among the needy unemployed; on what particular project or work they shall be engaged; the number of days in each week they shall be employed and the amount of compensation which they shall receive. It shall pay such compensation, so fixed daily or otherwise, as it may determine, and shall conduct the work in accordance with such rules of the administration as will best secure the proper and equitable administration of the relief sought to be provided by this act. If any city commissioner or county commissioner shall violate any rule of the administration or in the judgment of the administration, shall be inefficient or remiss in the performance of his duties, the administration may transfer all the powers, functions and duties of such city commissioner or county commissioner with respect to home relief under this act during the emergency period to the local bureau and thereafter the local bureau shall exercise all of the powers, functions and duties of the city or county commissioner with respect to home relief under this act.

2. Upon the written application of the mayor of a city in the case of a city welfare district or of the chairman of the board of supervisors of a county in the case of a county welfare district, the administration may in its discretion and subject to such regulations as it may provide, approve and authorize the consolidation of all relief activities within each public welfare district carried on under chapter seven hundred and ninety-eight of the laws of nineteen hundred and thirty-one, as amended, into an emergency relief bureau, consisting of not less than three nor more than five persons to be designated by the mayor of such city or the chairman of the board of supervisors of such county. The said emergency relief bureau so established shall have exclusive control of and be solely responsible for the administration in such public welfare district of home relief and/or work relief under chapter seven hundred and ninety-eight of the laws of nineteen hundred and thirty-one, as amended. Upon the appointment of said emergency relief bureau, the local bureau theretofore established pursuant to section seven, shall be terminated and all the powers and duties of the local bureau and of the commissioner of public welfare as to relief administered under chapter seven hundred ninety-eight of the laws of nineteen hundred and thirty-one, as amended, shall be forthwith vested in said emergency relief bureau. All records of the local bureau and all records of the commissioner of public welfare relating to recipients of relief under chapter seven hundred and ninety-eight of the laws of nineteen hundred and thirty-one as amended, shall be forthwith transferred to the emergency relief bureau so established. The commissioner of public welfare of the public welfare district in which such emergency relief bureau shall have been established shall be ex-officio a member of said bureau in addition to the members appointed as above provided, and shall perform such duties in respect to relief administered under chapter

seven hundred and ninety-eight of the laws of nineteen hundred and thirty-one, as amended, as may be directed by said bureau.

3. In any county upon written application of the chairman of the board of supervisors of the county and of the mayor of a city or the mayors of two or more cities located in such county, the administration may in its discretion and subject to such regulations as it may provide, approve and authorize the consolidation of all work relief in such county and city public welfare districts in a joint emergency work bureau consisting of not less than three nor more than five persons appointed jointly by the chairman of the board of supervisors and the mayor or mayors of such city or cities. Such joint emergency work bureau so established, shall have exclusive control of and be solely responsible for the administration of work relief in such welfare districts under chapter seven hundred ninety-eight of the laws of nineteen hundred and thirty-one, as amended. Upon the appointment of said joint emergency work bureau the local bureau or bureaus theretofore established pursuant to section seven shall be terminated and all the powers and duties of the local bureau or bureaus shall be forthwith vested in the joint emergency work bureau. All records of the local bureau or bureaus shall be forthwith transferred to the joint emergency work bureau. The commissioners of public welfare of such public welfare districts shall be ex-officio members of the joint emergency work bureau in addition to the members appointed as above provided.

4. In any county where home relief is a county charge and is administered by the county commissioner of public welfare, upon written application of the chairman of the board of supervisors of the county and of the mayor of a city or of the mayors of two or more cities located in such county, the administration may in its discretion approve and authorize the consolidation of all relief activities in such county and city public welfare districts carried on under chapter seven hundred and ninety-eight of the laws of nineteen hundred and thirty-one, as amended, into an emergency relief bureau consisting of not less than three nor more than five persons appointed jointly by the chairman of the board of supervisors of such county and by the mayor or mayors of such city or cities. The said emergency relief bureau so established shall have exclusive control of and be solely responsible for the administration in such public welfare districts of all home and/or work relief under chapter seven hundred and ninety-eight of the laws of nineteen hundred and thirty-one, as amended. Upon the appointment of said emergency relief bureau the local bureau or bureaus theretofore established under section seven shall be terminated and all the powers and duties of the local bureau or bureaus and of the commissioners of public welfare of such county and city or cities, as to relief under chapter seven hundred and ninety-eight of the laws of nineteen hundred and thirty-one, as amended, shall be forthwith vested in the emergency relief bureau. All records of the local bureaus and all records of the commissioners of public

welfare relating to recipients of relief under chapter seven hundred and ninety-eight of the laws of nineteen hundred and thirty-one as amended, shall be forthwith transferred to the emergency relief bureau so established. The commissioners of public welfare of such welfare districts in which such emergency relief bureau shall have been established shall be ex-officio members of the bureau in addition to the members appointed as above provided, and shall perform such duties in respect to relief administered under chapter seven hundred and ninety-eight of the laws of nineteen hundred and thirty-one, as amended, as may be directed by said bureau.

5. When such an emergency relief bureau has been established in a city or county public welfare district or by a consolidation of a county public welfare district and one or more city public welfare districts, any balances remaining unexpended of the funds appropriated for home and/or work relief and the administration thereof in such public welfare district or districts shall be transferred to the emergency relief bureau. When a joint emergency work bureau has been established in a county public welfare district and one or more city public welfare districts any balances remaining unexpended of the funds appropriated to the local bureau or bureaus for work relief and the administration thereof in such public welfare districts, shall be transferred to the joint emergency work bureau.

6. Appropriating bodies in county and/or city public welfare districts where an emergency relief bureau or a joint emergency work bureau shall have been established are hereby authorized to make apPropriations for home and/or work relief and the administration thereof to an emergency relief bureau, and to make appropriations for work relief and the administration thereof to a joint emergency work bureau. Said appropriations shall be made in accordance with the provisions of chapter seven hundred and ninety-eight of the laws of nineteen hundred and thirty-one, as amended.

Section 12 amended by the Laws of 1933, chapter 259.

§ 13. **Investigation of home relief.** In a city public welfare district the city commissioner shall investigate all cases of home relief. In a county public welfare district where home relief is a county charge, the county commissioner shall investigate such cases. In a county public welfare district where home relief is a town charge, the town public welfare officers shall investigate such cases under the supervision and general direction of the county commissioner.

§ 14. **Private contributions.** In furtherance of the purposes of this act a municipal corporation may accept contributions in cash or otherwise, during the emergency period, from individuals and corporations for work relief and/or home relief which shall be disbursed in the same manner as money appropriated by such municipal corporation for such purposes, but any such contributions in cash for home relief made by a single individual or lawfully by a corporation which aggregate more than the sum of ten thousand dollars during the emergency period shall not be considered in payments to a municipal corporation under the provisions of this act. All expenditures of such contributions in cash under the provisions of this act by a municipal corporation to the extent of ten thousand dollars or less in the aggregate from a single individual or lawfully from a corporation for home relief shall be allowed in determining the amount of state aid to which such municipal corporation is entitled.

§ 15. **Records and accounts of relief.** A municipal corporation furnishing work relief and/or home relief under the provisions of this act shall keep such records and accounts in relation thereto as the administration shall prescribe.

§ 16. **State aid.** A municipal corporation or a town, where home relief is a town charge, furnishing home relief, and a municipal corporation furnishing work relief, under the provisions of this act shall be paid by the state from the money hereby appropriated in the manner and to the extent provided in this section and such money shall be credited by such corporation or town to its general funds. Payment by the state to a municipal corporation or town under this section shall be forty per centum of the amount of expenditures for such home relief and/or work relief as is approved by the administration during the emergency period.

The administration may in addition make direct grants to a municipal corporation or town for home relief and/or work relief on such conditions as it may prescribe from the funds hereinafter provided for such purpose. Money received by a municipal corporation or town as a direct grant for home relief and/or work relief shall not be paid into the general fund of such municipal corporation or town but shall be made available for home relief or work relief as designated by the administration. Moneys paid to a person in cash under the provisions of this act shall be in the form of day's wages for day's work or hour's wages for hour's work or for home relief as defined by subdivision eight of section two and the payment to any unemployed person of any part of such money in any form other than for wages or such home relief is hereby prohibited. All moneys paid to persons receiving the relief provided by and pursuant to this act shall be inalienable by any assignment or transfer and shall be exempt from levy and execution under the laws of the state. All payments by the state for home relief furnished in the public welfare district comprising the city of Newburgh and the town of Newburgh shall be made to the commissioners of the home of the city and town of Newburgh and for such purpose such public welfare district shall be deemed a municipal corporation.

Section 16 amended by the Laws of 1932, chapter 567, and Laws of 1934, chapter 65.

§ 16-a. **Work relief disability allowance.** 1. Persons employed on work relief projects under the provisions of this act as heretofore or hereafter amended and receiving "work relief" as defined herein shall not be deemed to come within the scope of the provisions or benefits provided by chapter six hundred fifteen of the laws of nineteen hundred twenty-two as amended and known as the workmen's compensation law; but all persons receiving "work relief" who shall become temporarily disabled or injured by reason of any cause arising out of and in the course of their employment shall, during the period of said disability so caused within the duration of the emergency period as defined herein, continue to receive relief on the basis of the budgetary needs of the said person's family as determined under the standards and pursuant to the rules and regulations of the administration and in addition thereto shall be provided with such medical services as the administration may deem necessary.

2. In the event that accidental injuries or occupational disease arising out of and in course of said relief employment result in (a) death, (b) permanent total disability, or (c) permanent partial disability, the administration may provide such allowance as it may deem proper, but not exceeding in any single case the sum of three thousand five hundred dollars, inclusive of funeral expenses. Said funeral expenses in no case shall exceed two hundred dollars. The industrial commissioner of the state shall, when requested by the administration, cause to be provided medical examinations of injured or disabled relief workers and shall render reports on such questions as may be certified by the administration in respect of such cases. Within the limit hereinabove set forth, the administration shall determine the amount and manner of payment of said disability allowance to be made. In respect of all of the foregoing and any and all questions arising thereunder, the determination of the administration shall in every case be final and not subject to appeal or review.

3. The allowances made for said disabilities and/or the relief furnished to the injured work relief employee during the period of said disability shall be exclusive and shall relieve the employing municipal corporation, town, or state from any and all further liability by reason thereof.

4. All claims for relief and/or any such disability allowance pursuant to the provisions of this section shall be made and filed with the administration or its duly authorized agency within thirty days after the occurrence of the accident, injury or illness causing or creating the said disability; and the administration may disallow and refuse to entertain any claim which shall have been filed more than one week after the completion of the project on which the claimant was employed as a work relief employee.

5. The comptroller of the state shall set aside from each allocation of relief funds for work relief wages, whether state or local projects, such proportion thereof as shall be determined by the comptroller and the chairman of the relief administration to be sufficient for the purposes hereof and which said funds when so set aside shall constitute a disability fund from which there shall be paid, upon the certification of the administration, such allow-

ances by reason of (a) death benefits, (b) permanent total disability, and/or (c) permanent partial disability, as shall have been made by the administration pursuant to the provisions hereinabove set forth.

Section 16-a added by Laws of 1934, chapter 303, effective as of April 1, 1934.

§ 17. **Private contributions to the administration.** The administration is authorized also to accept, without conditions, private contributions of moneys and expend them directly in any part of the state for relief of the kind described in the definitions of home relief and work relief, but the kind and location of work for which the administration may expend such moneys directly within a county, city or town, other than state work shall be such as the governing board thereof shall approve. Such direct expenditure may be made through employees of the administration, public welfare officials, local bureaus and municipal authorities, or any of them, as the administration may determine. The administration also may allocate any of such moneys to municipal corporations and towns, as reimbursement under this act, to apply on state aid and to the credit thereof.

Section 17 amended by the Laws of 1932, chapter 567.

§ 18. **Expenditures on state improvements.** The administration may expend of the moneys allocated to the discretionary fund such amount as it may deem necessary for temporary employment on public improvements undertaken or required by the state and not let or to be let by contract, of persons entitled to relief under this act and of such amount the administration may expend a sum not to exceed twenty per centum thereof for the purchase of materials, tools and other supplies needed for the proper performance of such work.

Section 18 amended by the Laws of 1932, chapter 567, Laws of 1933, chapter 9, and Laws of 1934, chapter 71.

§ 19. **Salaries of local staffs.** The administration may authorize city and county commissioners and emergency work bureaus to employ such additional clerical and other assistants or volunteers with qualifications satisfactory to the administration, as may be necessary for the administration of home and/or work relief in accordance with the rules of the administration and shall determine the number of such additional clerks and assistants and fix their salaries, such part, or all, of which salaries as the administration shall determine shall be paid from the money allocated to the discretionary fund. No person employed pursuant to this act, during the emergency period, shall be subject to the provisions of the civil service law.

Section 19 amended by the Laws of 1932, chapter 567, and the Laws of 1933, chapter 9.

§ 20. **Reports of commissioners.** Each city and county commissioner and each local bureau shall file with the administration at its office in the city of Albany as soon after the first day of the month as practicable a verified detailed statement of relief granted unemployed persons of the district during the preceding month. Such reports shall contain such information as the administration may from time to time require.

Section 20 amended by the Laws of 1932, chapter 567.

§ 21. **Reports by administration.** The administration shall report to the governor and the legislature from time to time, in such detail as may be required, the operations of the administration together with the condition of unemployment and the relief affored unemployed persons of the state.

§ 22. **General powers of administration.** In executing any of the provisions of this act, the administration, and any person duly authorized or designated by it, may conduct any investigation pertinent or material to the furtherance of its work. The administration and each person so authorized is hereby empowered to subpoena witnesses, administer oaths, take testimony and compel the production of such books, papers, records and documents as may be relevant to any such investigation. The administration shall have and may exercise such other powers as may be necessary to carry out the provisions of this act.

§ 23. **Claims for payments by the state.** Claims by a municipal corporation or a town for payments by the state for home relief and/or work relief under the provisions of this act shall be made to the administration through the agency representing it in such municipal corporation, which agency shall transmit to the administration forthwith all claims with recommendations in respect thereto.

Section 23 amended by the Laws of 1932, chapter 567.

§ 24. **Allowance of claims.** Upon receipt of claims for payment by the administration, it shall examine such claims and certify to the state comptroller the amount thereof approved by it, specifying the amount to which each municipal corporation is entitled.

§ 25. **Payment of claims.** The amount so certified by the administration as provided in the last section shall be paid from the state treasury upon the audit and warrant of the comptroller to the fiscal officer of the municipal corporation, when such municipal corporation is a city, and to the county treasurer, when such municipal corporation is a county. County treasurers shall distribute the amounts so received by them to the municipal corporations and towns therein entitled thereto.

§ 26. **Blank forms.** The administration shall prescribe and furnish such forms of records, accounts, reports and claims as it may deem advisable for the proper enforcement and administration of the provisions of this act.

§ 27. **Rules of the administration.** The administration shall make and enforce rules in accordance and consonance with the provisions of this act which will best promote the efficiency and effectiveness of the relief which this act is intended to furnish.

None of the money appropriated by this act shall be expended or allowed except in accordance with such rules. A certified copy of such rules shall be filed in the office of the department of state. The administration shall mail to each city and county commissioner and each local bureau, copies of such rules to be posted by them in not less than five public conspicuous places throughout the district.

§ 28. **Dissolution of administration on completion of work.** The administration shall be dissolved and cease to function at the time fixed by this act. At such time, all unexpended or unpledged moneys in the hands of the administration shall be returned forthwith to the state comptroller to be by him deposited into the state treasury to the credit of the general fund; all tools, materials and supplies remaining unconsumed and in the physical possession and control of the administration shall be turned over to the department of public works and all tools, materials and supplies remaining unconsumed and in the hands of the administrative heads shall become the property of and be turned over by them to the city or county in and for which they carried on their duties under this act. The administration shall require such final reports from each administrative head and local bureau under this act as it shall deem necessary and shall, after receipt and audit of such reports, make its own final report to the governor and to the legislature stating such other information or recommendations as it may deem helpful or conducive to promote the public welfare, health and safety of the people of the state. All office equipment purchased by or for the administration shall be turned over to the department of public works. All books, papers, files and records of the administration and all documents, including reports of proceedings, surveys or investigations made or caused to be made by the administration shall be transferred by the administration to the department of state.

§ 29. **Liberal construction.** This act shall be liberally construed to the end that the work of the administration shall be consummated as equitably and expeditiously as practicable.

§ 30. **Violations and penalties.** Rules adopted by the administration under this act shall have the force and effect of law. A violation of any of the provisions of this act or of any rule of the administration, subsequent to the certification, filing and posting of such rule as provided herein, shall constitute a misdemeanor and shall be punishable by a fine of not less than one hundred dollars or more than one thousand dollars or by imprisonment for not more than one year or by both such fine and imprisonment. The penalty prescribed by this section shall not be exclusive, and if a rule be not obeyed, the administration, by the exercise of any power, conferred by this act, may carry out its provisions.

§ 31. **Inconsistent statutory powers or duties.** If a statute, general or special, or any local law or ordinance confers a power, prescribes a duty, or imposes a restriction inconsistent with this act or with a rule of the administration made pursuant to this act, such power shall not be exercised, or such duty or restriction enforced during the emergency period.

§ 32. **Constitutionality.** If any clause, sentence, paragraph, or part of this act shall for any reason be adjudged by any court of competent jurisdiction to be invalid, such judgment shall not affect, impair, or invalidate the remainder of this act, but shall be confined in its operation to the clause, sentence, paragraph, or part thereof directly involved in the controversy in which such judgment shall have been rendered.

§ 33. **Appropriation for state aid.***

§ 34. **State funds.** The comptroller is hereby authorized and directed to borrow on the faith and credit of the state, in anticipation of the receipt of taxes and revenues, direct or indirect, pursuant to the state finance law, sufficient money, within the appropriations herein made, to pay the legal demands authorized by this act.

§ 35. **Application.** This act shall apply to every county and city in the state and state aid, under the provisions of this act and the rules and regulations of the administration, shall hereafter be available for all counties and cities, whether or not their governing boards have adopted resolutions accepting the provisions of this act, but the governing board or body of a county or city may adopt a resolution that it does not intend to request or accept the state aid authorized by this act. A certified copy of such resolution shall be filed with the administration and, thereupon and thereafter, the provisions of this act shall not apply to such county or city.

Section 35 amended by the Laws of 1932, chapter 567.

§ 36. **Time of taking effect.** This act shall take effect immediately.

---

* Made obsolete by subsequent enactments.

THE STATE RECOVERY ACT

CHAPTER 782 OF THE LAWS OF 1933, AS AMENDED BY LAWS OF
1934, CHAPTERS 39, 104 AND 301

An Act declaring a public emergency and enabling municipalities
and public bodies to secure the benefits of and aid in carrying
out the provisions of the National Industrial Recovery Act.

Section 1. **Public emergency.** The legislature having declared
a public emergency to exist by chapter seven hundred and ninety-
eight of the laws of nineteen hundred thirty-one, it is hereby
declared that the said emergency still exists. The congress of
the United States having taken cognizance of the public emergency
and having enacted the National Industrial Recovery Act, approved
June sixteenth, nineteen hundred thirty-three, making funds available for the construction of public works, the public health and
safety require, and it is hereby provided, that all provisions of
any general, special or local law which tend to prevent, hamper or
delay municipalities, or to prevent, hamper or delay public bodies
to which this act applies from taking advantage of the provisions
of the National Industrial Recovery Act shall be inoperative; but
the above provision or any other provision of this act shall not operate to dispense with the approval by a state department, board,
officer or commission of a project where such approval is necessary under existing provisions of law.

§ 2. **Definitions.** For the purposes of this act, 1. "Municipality" means and includes any county, city, town, village, school
district, water, fire, sewer, lighting, sidewalk, sanitary, drainage,
improvement district, and any other district, having territorial
boundaries, organized for constructing and maintaining buildings,
improvements, works and instrumentalities for the use and benefit
of the public generally or the inhabitants of and/or property within
the district.

2. "Public body" means and includes any state or local officer,
board, trustees, commission or commissions, corporation or other
authority constituted by or pursuant to law to construct and
maintain buildings, improvements, works and instrumentalities for
the use and benefit of the public.

3. "Governing board" of a county, includes the board of supervisors; of a city, the local legislative body, as defined by the city
home rule law; of a town, the town board; of a village, the board
of trustees; or a school district, the board of education, the board
of trustees, or trustees or trustee; of any other district, the

board, commission, commissioners, officer, officers, trustees or other authority empowered by law to authorize expenditures and projects by or for the district and/or the borrowing of money by it or for its purposes and to direct the levying of taxes on property within the district for district purposes. Where the separate concurrence or approval of two or more sets of authorities with respect to either or any of the above matters is now required by law, "governing board," to the extent so required, shall mean and include both or all of them; and the term "majority vote," when such a board consists of two or more sets of authorities, means majority vote of each, including the concurrence or approval of the officer constituting such an authority if it consists of but one person.

4. "National industrial recovery act," shall mean and include not only the act of the congress of the United States of America, approved June sixteenth, nineteen hundred and thirty-three, entitled "An act to encourage national industrial recovery, to foster fair competition, and to provide for the construction of certain useful public works, and for other purposes," but also any acts amendatory thereof and any acts supplemental thereto, and revisions thereof, and any further act of the congress of the United States to encourage public works, to reduce unemployment and thereby to assist in the national recovery and promote the public welfare.

Section 2 amended by Laws of 1934, chapter 104.

§ 3. Notwithstanding the provisions of any general, special or local law, any municipality, by majority vote of its governing board, and any public body of this state, having the power under existing law to borrow money are hereby authorized to accept from the United States through the federal emergency administrator of public works, or other federal agency, direct grants of moneys paid in defraying the cost of the labor and materials employed upon any project undertaken under the provisions of the national industrial recovery act. The funds received as such grants shall be expended on the project so undertaken in the same manner as other funds made available for such project whether as loans or otherwise.

Section 3 amended by Laws of 1934, chapter 104.

§ 4. Notwithstanding the provisions of any general, special or local law, any public body or the governing board of any municipality, by majority vote, may authorize the proper officers of such municipality or body to enter into contracts with the United States through the federal emergency administrator of public works, or such other federal agency as may be authorized so to act, to obtain funds pursuant to the provisions of the national industrial recovery act for public works projects under the supervision of said municipality or body, providing, however, that if under existing law such public works are to be paid for by

direct assessment on real estate benefited where the area of the
benefit is less than that of the municipality, any existing provisions for a permissive, referendum shall remain in full force and
effect and providing, further, that, if such public works project
is for the construction or operation of a public utility or facility
for the supply of gas, electricity or water in competition with or
substitution for a public utility or facility supplying gas, electricity or water in the same area, any action of the public body
or governing board of a municipality in relation thereto, pursuant
to the provisions of this section, shall be subject to a mandatory
referendum, notwithstanding any other provisions of this act. It
shall not be necessary for any such board or body to hold hearings on or publish notices of such projects or for such projects
to be initiated by petition of taxpayers or owners of property
nor shall such project be subject to vote at any election (other
than a school district meeting) or to referendum, mandatory or
permissive, except as above provided, and except that this provision shall not operate to dispense with a hearing under the
general district law and the constitution on the sole question
of whether a proposed improvement benefits all the property
in a district liable to taxation for defraying all or part of its
cost. If before or after the execution of any such contract the
governing board shall determine to submit the authorization of
the project, or the issuance of bonds or the levying of a tax, to
vote at a school district meeting or at an election or to referendum,
whether or not required by law, it may, notwithstanding the
provisions of any other law, provide for such vote or referendum
on notice published at least once in a newspaper circulating
in the municipality, and posted in at least ten conspicuous places
on any day at least seven days prior to such meeting or election; and no other notice shall be required. Such contract may
provide for the issuing of bonds of said municipalities and in
anticipation thereof for the issuing of notes, temporary bonds,
certificates of indebtedness, interim certificates, or security
receipts, hereinafter generally referred to as "other obligations,"
and for the rights of the holders of such bonds and other obligations. The termination of the emergency prior to the completion
of or ultimate liquidation of obligations incurred by reason of
public works projects financed hereunder shall in no manner affect
the validity of such contracts or other agreements. Nothing in
this act contained, however, shall be construed to alter, modify
or affect the provisions of existing laws of this state in such
manner as to lower the standards therein provided with regard
to labor, hours of labor, wages for labor and employment of
females and children.

Section 4 amended by Laws of 1934, chapter 104.

§ 4-a. Notwithstanding the provisions of any general, special or
local law, requiring a project to be undertaken under such law,
wholly or partly at the expense of property specially benefited

thereby, such project may in the discretion of the governing board or public body, be undertaken as a public works project wholly at the expense of the municipality at large. Notwithstanding the provisions of any general, special or local law requiring that the cost of a stated project or kind of project be borne in whole or in part by assessments on property specially benefited, bonds in an amount to pay the entire estimated cost or part thereof of such a project may be issued in the first instance and prior to the completion of the project or prior to the levy of any such assessments.

Section 4-a added by Laws of 1934, chapter 104.

§ 5. Notwithstanding the provisions of any general, special or local law, any municipality, by majority vote of its governing board, or public body, empowered by law to borrow money for a public works project is hereby expressly authorized to issue and sell its negotiable bonds or its other obligations to the United States through the federal emergency administrator of public works, or such other federal agency as may be authorized so to act, without advertisement, proposals or public or private bidding, in order to carry out any contract entered into as provided in section four of this act, and such bonds or other obligations may be in such form, and be subject to such terms and conditions, with such privileges as to registration, conversion, reconversion, redemption, interchangeability and exchange and such other provisions as may be provided by the contract; and it is hereby further expressly provided that the provisions of any general or special law of this state requiring bonds or other obligations of the municipality to be serial or payable in annual installments or fixing the maximum or minimum time or times when the debt contracted or any part of it shall be payable shall not be binding with respect to moneys borrowed from the United States. Such contract may provide for the establishment, investment and safekeeping of sinking funds to meet payments not accruing annually and for contributions of the municipality thereto.

§ 5-a. Notwithstanding the provisions of any general, special or local law, any municipality, by a majority vote of its governing body or public body empowered by law to borrow money for a public works project may issue its bonds to purchase materials, supplies and equipment and may purchase and furnish such materials, supplies and equipment for such projects as may have been or may be undertaken through or by authority of the civil works administration of the federal government or the work division of the federal emergency relief administration or any other work relief authority of the state and/or federal governments; the terms of such bonds shall not exceed the probable life of said improvements or the estimated average probable life of said improvements, and shall mature in annual installments, the first of which shall mature not more than two years from the date of the bonds and the last of which shall mature not more than ten years from the date of the bonds; provided, however, that in the event that the cost, or total cost, as estimated by such governing body or public body, is in excess of two hundred thousand dollars, the last installment of such bonds shall mature not more than twenty years from the date of the bonds, and no installment shall be more than fifty per centum in excess of the amount of the smallest prior installment. Pending the issuance of such bonds, such indebtedness may be temporarily financed by certificates of indebtedness or notes of the municipality running not more than six months, which certificates of indebtedness or notes may be renewed and any renewal thereof shall mature not more than one year from the date of the certificates of indebtedness or notes first issued, and such temporary obligations shall bear interest at a rate not exceeding six per centum per annum, and may be sold at private sale for not less than par value, and said temporary obligations shall be paid from the proceeds of such bonds. Said bonds shall be sold in the manner provided by law for not less than par and shall be general obligations of the municipality, and there shall be raised annually by tax upon the taxable property of the municipality a sum sufficient to pay the principal and interest of such bonds as the same became due. The making of such improvements or the purchase of such materials, supplies or equipment or the incurring of such indebtedness shall not be subject to any petition or notice or hearing or permissive or mandatory referendum or approval by any public board or any requirement of law requiring advertisement for bids.

Section 5-a added by Laws of 1934, chapter 39, as amended by chapter 301.

§ 6. All provisions of this act applicable to municipalities and public bodies may also be availed of by and shall be deemed to apply to the state itself in aid of any public works projects undertaken or to be undertaken by any of its departments, boards, commissions or other state agencies. It is expressly provided that if an appropriation shall have been made, or other state moneys shall have become available, for an authorized public works project prosecuted or to be prosecuted by or under the jurisdiction of a state department or division, commission, board or state agency therein, additional moneys provided for such project, by allotment under the National Industrial Recovery Act, may be used therefor, subject to such act and rules and regulations adopted pursuant thereto, and the facilities of such project enlarged accordingly. The head of the department and the state comptroller, by joint application, may request such federal aid, in behalf of the state; and the concurrence therein of the superintendent of public works shall be necessary as to any such work for which he is required by law to prepare or approve the plans. The comptroller may accept such moneys and deposit them with the commissioner of taxation and finance, and they shall be available therefor, as though appropriated. Notwithstanding any other provision of law, contracts may be let for such project within the amount appropriated together with any such additional moneys that have been so received and deposited or otherwise made immediately available pursuant to such act.

§ 6-a. Nothwithstanding the provisions of any general, special or local law other than this act, public work projects or any contract referred to in section four of this act, or the issuance of bonds or other obligations pursuant to such contract, or any other acts or proceedings in connection therewith, may be authorized by resolution which may be finally adopted on the same day on which it is introduced by a majority of all the members of the governing board, and such resolution need not be published before becoming effective.

§ 6-b. This act shall be liberally construed and the powers granted and the duties imposed by this act shall be construed to be independent and severable. If any one or more sections, clauses, sentences, or parts of this act shall for any reason be questioned in any court, and shall be adjudged unconstitutional or invalid, such judgment shall not affect, impair or invalidate the remaining provisions thereof, but shall be confined in its operation to the specific provisions so held unconstitutional or invalid.

Sections 6-a and 6-b added by Laws of 1934, chapter 104.

THE LEGALIZING AND VALIDATING ACT

SECTION 2 OF CHAPTER 39 OF THE LAWS OF 1934, AS AMENDED BY CHAPTER 301

§ 2. All acts and proceedings heretofore taken by municipalities, their boards and officers, in raising moneys by appropriation or otherwise and/or using such moneys or other moneys for the purchasing and furnishing of materials, supplies and equipment for use on such work or projects as have heretofore been undertaken through or by authority of the civil works administration of the federal government or the work divison of the federal emergency relief administration or any other work relief authoriity of the state and/or federal governments are hereby legalized, validated, ratified and confirmed, notwithstanding any want of statutory authority therefor or any defect or irregularity therein.

APPROPRIATION OF THE BALANCE OF THE 1933 BOND ISSUE

CHAPTER 71 OF THE LAWS OF 1934, AS AMENDED BY CHAPTER 273

Section 1. The balance of forty-eight million dollars ($48,000,-000) remaining out of the proceeds of the sale of bonds authorized by chapter two hundred and sixty of the laws of nineteen hundred thirty-three, sixty million dollars ($60,000,000), not heretofore appropriated is hereby appropriated and made immediately available to the temporary emergency relief administration, created by chapter seven hundred and ninety-eight of the laws of nineteen hundred thirty-one, as amended for the purposes specified in chapter seven hundred and ninety-eight of the laws of nineteen hundred thirty-one, as amended, for the period from February fifteenth, nineteen hundred thirty-four to February fifteenth, nineteen hundred thirty-five.

Thirty-three million dollars ($33,000,000) of the moneys appropriated by this section shall be allocated to a reimbursement fund to be used and expended for payment to municipal corporations, as defined by chapter seven hundred and ninety-eight of the laws of nineteen hundred thirty-one, and towns of forty per centum of their expenditures for home relief and/or work relief from February fifteenth, nineteen hundred thirty-four to February fifteenth, nineteen hundred thirty-five, expenditures from the said reimbursement fund to be made as heretofore provided by section sixteen of chapter seven hundred and ninety-eight of the laws of nineteen hundred thirty-one, as amended.

Fifteen million dollars ($15,000,000) of the money appropriated by this section shall be allocated to the discretionary fund to be used and expended (a) for direct grants to municipal corporations, as provided for by section sixteen of chapter seven hundred and ninety-eight of the laws of nineteen hundred thirty-one as amended by chapter five hundred and sixty-seven of the laws of nineteen hundred thirty-two, for work relief and/or home relief and to towns for home relief, on such conditions as the administration may prescribe; (b) for salaries and expenses of the administration from February fifteenth, nineteen hundred thirty-four, to February fifteenth, nineteen hundred thirty-five; (c) for salaries of local bureaus as provided in section nineteen of chapter seven hundred and ninety-eight of the laws of nineteen hundred thirty-one as amended by chapter five hundred and sixty-seven of the laws of nineteen hundred thirty-two for the period from February fifteenth, nineteen hundred thirty-four to February fifteenth, nineteen hundred thirty-five; (d) for state improvements as provided for in section eighteen of chapter seven hundred and ninety-eight of the laws of nineteen hundred thirty-one as last amended by chapter nine of the laws of nineteen hundred thirty-three. The sum of two hundred thousand dollars ($200,000) or so much thereof as may be needed, is hereby appropriated from such discretionary fund and made available for the relief of sick and disabled veterans under article one-a of the military law. The money appropriated by this section shall be expended on the audit and warrant of the comptroller upon vouchers certified or approved by the chairman of the administretion or a member of the administration duly authorized by him.

All sums remaining in the reimbursement, discretionary, state improvement or other funds from moneys heretofore appropriated thereto by chapter seven hundred and ninety-eight of the laws of nineteen hundred thirty-one as amended by chapter six of the laws of nineteen hundred thirty-three and by chapter two hundred fifty-nine of the laws of nineteen hundred thirty-three, which shall be unexpended and/or unpledged and/or unallocated as of February fifteenth, nineteen hundred thirty-four, are hereby reappropriated to the reimbursement, discretionary, state improvement or other funds herein created respectively and shall be in addition to the thirty-three million dollars ($33,000,000) heretofore set up as a reimbursement fund and the fifteen million dollars ($15,000,000) heretofore set up as a discretionary fund out of the unappropriated forty-eight million dollars ($48,000,000) remaining from the bond issue moneys authorized by chapter two hundred sixty of the laws of nineteen hundred thirty-three.

Section 1 amended as to veteran relief by chapter 273 of the Laws of 1934.

FRESH MILK

CHAPTER 821 OF THE LAWS OF 1934, REAPPROPRIATING FOR FRESH MILK FOR NEEDY CHILDREN $1,500,000 OF THE DISCRETIONARY FUND PROVIDED BY CHAPTER 71 OF THE LAWS OF 1934

Section 1. Of the sum of forty-eight million dollars appropriated by chapter seventy-one of the laws of nineteen hundred thirty-four, including amendments, from proceeds of the sale of bonds authorized by chapter two hundred and sixty of the laws of nineteen hundred thirty-three, the sum of one million five hundred thousand dollars ($1,500,000), is hereby re-appropriated to the temporary emergency relief administration and directed to be expended by it for supplying fresh milk free to needy children, through the agency of the public school system, other schools where the tuition is free and public or private milk stations maintained for the free distribution of milk, such service to be rendered under rules and regulations of the administration. The moneys so re-appropriated shall be paid out of the sum of fifteen million dollars allocated to the discretionary fund by such chapter seventy-one of the laws of nineteen hundred thirty-four, as enacted or amended, on the audit and warrant of the comptroller upon vouchers certified or approved by the chairman of the temporary emergency relief administration or by a member of the administration duly authorized by him.

§ 2. This act shall take effect immediately.

AUTHORIZING REFERENDUM ON NEW STATE DEBT OF $40,000,000 FOR RELIEF

CHAPTER 718 OF THE LAWS OF 1934

Section 1. The creation of a state debt to the amount of forty million dollars is hereby authorized to provide funds, to be available from November fifteenth, nineteen hundred thirty-four to February fifteenth, nineteen hundred thirty-six, to relieve the people of the state from the hardships and suffering caused by unemployment and the effects thereof on the public health and welfare, including the granting of aid to municipalities for such purpose. The legislature may continue existing agencies and provisions of law, or may create other agencies and/or other ways and means to administer and distribute temporary emergency relief for such purpose, and may provide for cost thereof, from the proceeds of the sale of the bonds authorized by this act, in such amounts as the legislature, from time to time, shall have appropriated or may appropriate and make available therefrom and the money so appropriated shall be paid from the treasury on the audit and warrant of the comptroller upon vouchers certified or approved pursuant to law.

§ 2. The state comptroller is hereby authorized and empowered to issue and sell bonds of the state to the amount of the debt hereby authorized to be created and for the purpose hereby authorized to be known as "emergency unemployment relief bonds." Such bonds shall bear interest at the rate of not to exceed five per centum, which interest shall be payable semi-annually in the city of New York. Such bonds, or the portion thereof at any time issued, shall be made payable in ten installments, the first of which shall be payable one year from date of issue and the last of which shall be payable within ten years after the date of issue and in no case to exceed the probable life of the work or object, to which the proceeds thereof are to be applied as determined by the state finance law. Such bonds or the portion thereof at any time sold, shall be of such denominations, subject to the foregoing provisions, as the comptroller may determine. Such bonds shall be sold in such lot or lots, from time to time, as may be required to carry out the provisions of laws making appropriations for the purposes for which such bonds were issued. Such bonds shall be sold at not less than par to the highest bidder after advertisement for a period of ten consecutive days, Sundays excepted, in at least two daily newspapers printed in the city of New York and one in the city of Albany. Advertisements shall contain a provision to the effect that the comptroller, in his discretion, may reject any or all bids made in pursuance of such advertisements and, in the event of such rejection, the comptroller is authorized to readvertise for bids in the form and manner above described as many times as, in his judgment, may be necessary to effect a satisfactory sale. The proceeds of bonds sold pursuant to this act shall be paid into the treasury and shall be available only for the work or object authorized by this act in accordance with appropriations therefrom made or to be made by the legislature for such work or object.

§ 3. The comptroller is hereby authorized and directed to borrow, on the faith and credit of the state, in anticipation of the receipt of proceeds of the sale of the bonds authorized by this act, pursuant to the state finance law, sufficient money to pay the legal demands authorized by appropriations theretofore or thereafter made by the legislature for the purpose for which a state debt is authorized to be created by this act.

§ 4. This law shall not take effect unless and until it shall have been submitted to the people at a general election, and have received a majority of all the votes cast for and against it at such election and such law shall be submitted to the people of this state at the general election to be held in November, nineteen hundred and thirty-four. The ballots to be furnished for the use of the voters upon the submission of this law shall be in the form prescribed by the election law and the proposition or question to be submitted shall be printed thereon in substantially the following form, namely, "Shall chapter (here insert the number of the chapter) of the laws of nineteen hundred thirty-four, entitled 'An act authorizing the creation of a state debt, to the amount of forty million dollars, to provide funds, to be available from November fifteenth, nineteen hundred thirty-four to February fifteenth, nineteen hundred thirty-six, to relieve the people of the state from the hardships and suffering, caused by unemployment, and the effects thereof on the public health and welfare, including the granting of aid to municipalities for such purpose, through such agencies and by such ways and means as the legislature shall have prescribed or hereafter may prescribe for the administration and distribution of temporary emergency relief and the cost thereof, and providing for the submission to the people of a proposition or question therefor to be voted upon at the general election to be held in the year nineteen hundred thirty-four, be approved?"

APPROPRIATION OF $10,000,000 FOR RELIEF IF 1934 REFERENDUM IS APPROVED

Chapter 717 of the Laws of 1934

Section 1. If and when an act, entitled "An act authorizing the creation of a state debt to the amount of forty million dollars to provide funds, to be available from November fifteenth, nineteen hundred thirty-four to February fifteenth, nineteen hundred thirty-six, to relieve the people of the state from the hardships and suffering, caused by unemployment, and the effects thereof on the public health and welfare, including the granting of aid to municipalities for such purpose through such agencies and by such ways and means as the legislature shall have prescribed or hereafter may prescribe for the administration and distribution of temporary emergency relief and the cost thereof, and providing for the submission to the people of a proposition or question therefor to be voted upon at the general election to be held in the year nineteen hundred thirty-four," shall have been approved, by the people at the general election to be held in the year nineteen hundred thirty-four, in the manner prescribed in the constitution, the sum of ten million dollars ($10,000,000) of the proceeds of the sale of bonds authorized by such referendum vote, is hereby appropriated and made immediately available for the purposes authorized by chapter seven hundred ninety-eight of the laws of nineteen hundred thirty-one, as amended, for the period of the emergency up to and including February fifteenth, nineteen hundred and thirty-five.

§ 2. Seven million dollars ($7,000,000) of the moneys appropriated by this act shall be allocated to a reimbursement fund to be used and expended for payment to municipal corporations, as defined by chapter seven hundred and ninety-eight of the laws of nineteen hundred thirty-one, and towns of forty per centum of their expenditures for home relief and/or work relief to February fifteenth, nineteen hundred thirty-five, expenditures from the said reimbursement fund to be made as heretofore provided by section sixteen of chapter seven hundred and ninety-eight of the laws of nineteen hundred thirty-one, as amended.

§ 3. Three million dollars ($3,000,000) of the money appropriated by this act shall be allocated to the discretionary fund to be used and expended (a) for direct grants to municipal corporations, as provided for by section sixteen of chapter seven hundred and ninety-eight of the laws of nineteen hundred thirty-one as amended by chapter five hundred and sixty-seven of the laws of nineteen hundred thirty-two, for work relief and/or home relief and to towns for home relief, on such conditions as the administration may prescribe; (b) for salaries and expenses of the administration to February fifteenth, nineteen hundred thirty-five; (c) for salaries of local bureaus as provided in section nineteen of chapter seven hundred and ninety-eight of the laws of nineteen hundred thirty-one as amended by chapter five hundred and sixty-seven of the laws of nineteen hundred thirty-two for the period of February fifteenth, nineteen hundred thirty-five; (d) for state improvements as provided for in section eighteen of chapter seven hundred and ninety-eight of the laws of nineteen hundred thirty-one as last amended by chapter seventy-one of the laws of nineteen hundred thirty-four. The money appropriated by this act shall be expended on the audit and warrant of the comptroller upon vouchers certified or approved by the chairman of the administration or a member of the administration duly authorized by him.

§ 4. This act shall take effect immediately.

STATE PARTICIPATION IN FEDERAL FUNDS

CHAPTER 8, LAWS OF 1933, AS AMENDED BY LAWS OF 1933, CHAPTER 258, LAWS OF 1934, CHAPTER 716

Section 1. On behalf of the state of New York the governor is hereby authorized from time to time to apply to the Reconstruction Finance Corporation or other similar federal agency pursuant to title I, section one, of the emergency relief and construction act of nineteen hundred thirty-two enacted by congress of the United States and approved July twenty-first, nineteen hundred thirty-two, or any acts amendatory thereof or supplemental thereto or any other acts hereafter enacted by the congress for

213

the purpose of relieving unemployment distress, for funds for use in furnishing relief and work relief to needy and distressed people and in relieving hardship resulting from unemployment.

Any application by the governor shall be made upon the express understanding and condition that any funds paid by the Reconstruction Finance Corporation or other similar federal agency to the governor shall not constitute a loan to the state of New York.

§ 2. The governor is hereby authorized to receive such moneys from time to time and to transmit them to the commissioner of taxation and finance or to authorize the receipt and the expenditure of said funds by the temporary relief administration of the state of New York acting as a state or federal agency within the state of New York. Such moneys when so transmitted by the governor shall be held by such commissioner in a separate account in a depository or depositories designated by such commissioner and the comptroller, and shall be expended by the temporary emergency relief administration of the state of New York, created by chapter seven hundred ninety-eight of the laws of nineteen hundred thirty-one, on the audit and warrant of the comptroller upon vouchers approved by the chairman of the temporary emergency relief administration or a member thereof duly authorized by him.

Section 2 amended by Laws of 1934, chapter 716.

§ 3. Such monies from the reconstruction finance corporation or other federal agency may be expended by the temporary emergency relief administration for the purposes and in the manner provided by chapter seven hundred ninety-eight of the laws of nineteen hundred and thirty-one as now or hereafter amended and for such other relief or related purposes as may be authorized by the emergency relief and reconstruction act of nineteen hundred and thirty-two enacted by the congress of the United States and acts amendatory thereof or supplemental thereto and by any other acts enacted by the congress and pursuant to and under such conditions and in the manner specified by the reconstruction finance corporation or other federal agency, but nothing in this chapter or in any other law shall create a liability against the temporary emergency relief administration or the state of New York for, in respect of, in relation to or by reason of the administration or expenditure of such federal funds.

Section 3 amended by Laws of 1933, chapter 258, and Laws of 1934, chapter 716.

§ 4. It is the intention of the legislature that in so far as possible such moneys be not so expended by the temporary emergency relief administration as to relieve the municipal corporations of the state of their responsibility to furnish funds for the relief of unemployed distress within their respective jurisdiction.

§ 5. The temporary emergency relief administration is directed to keep complete records of the disbursement of all such moneys and to submit to the governor when requested by him a statement thereof. The governor shall file with the Reconstruction Finance Corporation or such other federal agency, if required, and with the comptroller of the state of New York, a statement of the disbursement of all such funds.

§ 6. The governor is hereby empowered to do, either acting directly or through the temporary emergency relief administration as his agent, all other acts relative to any application for funds, required of him to be performed by title I, section one, of the emergency relief and construction act of nineteen hundred thirty-two, any acts amendatory thereof or supplemental thereto and any other acts hereafter enacted by the congress of the United States for the purpose of relieving unemployment distress, or by the rules and regulations of the Reconstruction Finance Corporation or other similar federal agency.

§ 7. This act shall take effect immediately.

FEDERAL MONEY FOR STATE ENGINEERING

CHAPTER 654 OF THE LAWS OF 1934

Section 1. The comptroller is hereby authorized to receive from the federal government or its agents any moneys which the federal government, its agents or municipal beneficiaries of the federal government under the national industrial recovery act shall offer to the state of New York for expenditure through the department of public works for the cost and expense of engineering, designing, supervision and inspection of the construction, repair and improvement of public highways and parkways, public buildings and any publicly owned instrumentalities and facilities of municipalities or other public bodies wherein and whereby any of such construction, repair and improvements of such projects is financed in whole or in part by grants or loans from the federal government pursuant to and in accordance with the terms and provisions of the national industrial recovery act as passed by congress June thirteenth, nineteen hundred thirty-three.

§ 2. The superintendent of public works, upon request from the federal government, is hereby authorized to carry on such engineering, designing, supervision and inspection by and with the employees of the department of public works and to do and perform all necessary acts in connection therewith for the convenient and expeditious consummation thereof.

§ 3. The sum of one hundred thousand dollars ($100,000), or so much thereof as may be needed, is appropriated from any money in the state treasury not otherwise appropriated for payment in the first instance by the state of the cost and expense of such engineering, designing, supervision and inspection, all as above set forth. No part of the moneys hereby appropriated shall be available unless and until either an allotment of moneys for such engineering, designing, supervision and inspection shall have been made by the federal government to the state directly or satisfactory assurances, declarations or confirmations are made by the federal government, or its agents to the comptroller and the department of public works that federal moneys will be placed with and made available to respective municipalities wherein such projects are financed as aforesaid for the paying over by such municipalities to the state comptroller sufficient sums for the reimbursement to the state of moneys so paid out by the state in the first instance in carrying out this act; nor shall moneys hereby appropriated be available to an amount in excess of any amount directly allotted to the state as aforesaid or in excess of any amount assured by the federal government to be paid over by municipalities which are beneficiaries under said national industrial recovery act. The comptroller is hereby authorized upon receipt of any such allotment or of any advancement thereof or of any moneys received from any such municipalities pursuant to any assurance, direction, declaration or confirmation by or from the federal government to deposit such moneys with the commissioner of taxation and finance and they shall be placed from time to time to the credit of the general fund in such amounts as will reimburse the state for expenditures made in the first instance for said engineering, designing, supervision and inspection.

§ 4. The moneys hereby appropriated shall be payable by the commissioner of taxation and finance on the audit and warrant of the comptroller on vouchers approved by the superintendent of public works.

§ 5. Notwithstanding any other general or special law to the contrary, if in the carrying out of the intent and purpose of this act any civil service employee of the department of public works is discontinued from state service by reason of being temporarily employed or is transferred to the federal government or to any municipality designated by it in furtherance of the aforesaid work, for which the government extends financial aid, he shall continue to be a member of the New York state employees' retirement system and shall not suffer any loss of rights or benefits now enjoyed under the civil service law and shall be entitled to all the rights granted under article four of the civil service law provided such member thereafter pay into the retirement fund and pension fund in monthly installments a proportion of the salary paid to him by the federal government or its agents or any such municipality as the case may be, computed upon his rate of contribution for all rights and benefits under said civil service law, and the comptroller is empowered to do all necessary and convenient acts to orderly effectuate such contribution.

§ 6. This act shall take effect immediately.

WORKMEN'S COMPENSATION

CHAPTER 769 OF THE LAWS OF 1934

Section 1. Section ten of article two of the workmen's compensation law is hereby amended by adding a sentence to read as follows:

The provisions of this chapter shall not apply to persons receiving "work relief" and employed on work relief projects under the provisions of chapter seven hundred ninety-eight of the laws of nineteen hundred thirty-one as amended, and the definition of the word "employee" as herein definde shall not include persons receiving "work relief" and employed on work relief projects under the provisions of chapter seven hundred ninety-eight of the laws of nineteen hundred thirty-one as amended.

§ 2. This act shall take effect immediately.

SUPPLEMENT B—FEDERAL RELIEF AND COMPLEMENTARY LEGISLATION

THE FEDERAL EMERGENCY RELIEF ACT OF 1933 (Public
No. 15, 73d Congress [H.R. 4606].)

An Act to provide for cooperation by the Federal Government with
the several States and Territories and the District of Columbia
in relieving the hardship and suffering caused by unemployment, and for other purposes.

*Be it enacted by the Senate and House of Representatives of the
United States of America in Congress assembled,* That the Congress
hereby declares that the present economic depression has created a
serious emergency, due to widespread unemployment and increasing
inadequacy of State and local relief funds, resulting in the existing
or threatened deprivation of a considerable number of families and
individuals of the necessities of life, and making it imperative that
the Federal Government cooperate more effectively with the several
States and Territories and the District of Columbia in furnishing
belief to their needy and distressed people.

* SEC. 2. (a) The Reconstruction Finance Corporation is authorized and directed to make available out of the funds of the Corporation not to exceed $500,000,000, in addition to the funds
authorized under title I of the Emergency Relief and Construction
Act of 1932, for expenditure under the provisions of this Act upon
certification by the Federal Emergency Relief Administrator provided for in section 3.

(b) The amount of notes, debentures, bonds, or other such obligations which the Reconstruction Finance Corporation is authorized
and empowered under section 9 of the Reconstruction Finance Corporation Act, as amended, to have outstanding at any one time is
increased by $500,000,000: *Provided,* That no such additional
notes, debentures, bonds, or other such obligations authorized by
this subsection shall be issued except at such times and in such
amounts as the President shall approve.

(c) After the expiration of ten days after the date upon which
the Federal Emergency Relief Administrator has qualified and has
taken office, no application shall be approved by the Reconstruction
Finance Corporation under the provisions of title I of the Emergency Relief and Construction Act of 1932, and the Federal Emergency Relief Administrator shall have access to all files and records
of the Reconstruction Finance Corporation relating to the administration of funds under title I of such Act. At the expiration of
such ten-day period, the unexpended and unobligated balance of

* Additional appropriation (also for C.W.A program) $950,000,000 to June 30,
1935.—Act of February 13, 1934.

the funds authorized under title I of such Act shall be available for the purposes of this Act.

SEC. 3. (a) There is hereby created a Federal Emergency Relief Administration, all the powers of which shall be exercised by a Federal Emergency Relief Administrator (referred to in this Act as the "Administrator") to be appointed by the President, by and with the advice and consent of the Senate. The Administrator shall receive a salary to be fixed by the President at not to exceed $10,000, and necessary traveling and subsistence expenses within the limitations prescribed by law for civilian employees in the executive branch of the Government. The Federal Emergency Relief Administration and the office of Federal Emergency Relief Administrator shall cease to exist upon the expiration of two years after the date of enactment of this Act, and the unexpended balance on such date of any funds made available under the provisions of this Act shall be disposed of as the Congress may by law provide.

(b) The Administrator may appoint and fix the compensation of such experts and their appointment may be made and compensation fixed without regard to the civil service laws, or the Classification Act of 1923, as amended, and the Administrator may, in the same manner, appoint and fix the compensation of such other officers and employees as are necessary to carry out the provisions of this Act, but such compensation shall not exceed in any case the sum of $8,000; and may make such expenditures (including expenditures for personal services and rent at the seat of government and elsewhere and for printing and binding), not to exceed $350,000, as are necessary to carry out the provisions of this Act, to be paid by the Reconstruction Finance Corporation out of funds made available by this Act upon presentation of vouchers approved by the Administrator or by an officer of the Administration designated by him for that purpose. The Administrator may, under rules and regulations prescribed by the President, assume control of the administration in any State or States where, in his judgment, more effective and efficient cooperation between the State and Federal authorities may thereby be secured in carrying out the purposes of this Act.

(c) In executing any of the provisions of this Act, the Administrator, and any person duly authorized or designated by him, may conduct any investigation pertinent or material to the furtherance of the purposes of this Act and, at the request of the President, shall make such further investigations and studies as the President may deem necessary in dealing with problems of unemployment relief.

(d) The Administrator shall print monthly, and shall submit to the President and to the Senate and the House of Representatives (or to the Secretary of the Senate and the Clerk of the House of Representatives, if those bodies are not in session), a report of his activities and expenditures under this Act. Such reports shall, when submitted, be printed as public documents.

SEC. 4. (a) Out of the funds of the Reconstruction Finance Corporation made available by this Act, the Administrator is authorized to make grants to the several States to aid in meeting the costs of furnishing relief and work relief and in relieving the hardship and suffering caused by unemployment in the form of money, service, materials, and/or commodities to provide the necessities of life to persons in need as a result of the present emergency, and/or to their dependents, whether resident, transient, or homeless.

(b) Of the amounts made available by this Act not to exceed $250,000,000 shall be granted to the several States applying therefor, in the following manner: Each State shall be entitled to receive grants equal to one third of the amount expended by such State, including the civil subdivisions thereof, out of public moneys from all sources for the purposes set forth in subsection (a) of this section; and such grants shall be made quarterly, beginning with the second quarter in the calendar year 1933, and shall be made during any quarter upon the basis of such expenditures certified by the States to have been made during the preceding quarter.

(c) The balance of the amounts made available by this Act, except the amount required for administrative expenditures under section 3 shall be used for grants to be made whenever, from an application presented by a State, the Administrator finds that the combined moneys which can be made available within the State from all sources, supplemented by any moneys, available under subsection (b) of this section, will fall below the estimated needs within the State for the purposes specified in subsection (a) of this section: *Provided,* That the Administrator may certify out of the funds made available by this subsection additional grants to States applying therefor to aid needy persons who have no legal settlement in any one State or community, and to aid in assisting cooperative and self-help associations for the barter of goods and services.

(d) After October 1, 1933, notwithstanding the provisions of subsection (b), the unexpended balance of the amounts available for the purposes of subsection (b) may, in the discretion of the Administrator and with the approval of the President, be available for grants under subsection (c).

(e) The decision of the Administrator as to the purpose of any expenditure shall be final.

(f) The amount available to any one State under subsections (b) and (c) of this section shall not exceed 15 per centum of the total amount made available by such subsections.

SEC. 5. Any State desiring to obtain funds under this Act shall through its Governor make application therefor from time to time to the Administrator. Each application so made shall present in the manner requested by the Administrator information showing (1) the amounts necessary to meet relief needs in the State during the period covered by such application and the amounts available from public or private sources within the State, its political subdivisions, and private agencies, to meet the relief needs of the State, (2) the provision made to assure adequate administrative supervision, (3) the provision made for suitable standards of relief, and (4) the purposes for which the funds requested will be used.

SEC. 6. The Administrator upon approving a grant to any State shall so certify to the Reconstruction Finance Corporation which shall, except upon revocation of a certificate by the Administrator, make payments without delay to the State in such amounts and at such times as may be prescribed in the certificate. The Governor of each State receiving grants under this Act shall file monthly with the Administrator, and in the form required by him, a report of the disbursements made under such grants.

SEC. 7. As used in the foregoing provisions of this Act, the term "State" shall include the District of Columbia, Alaska, Hawaii, the Virgin Islands, and Puerto Rico; and the term "Governor" shall include the Commissioners of the District of Columbia.

SEC. 8. This Act may be cited as the "Federal Emergency Relief Act of 1933."

Approved May 12, 1933.

SUMMARY OF THE NATIONAL INDUSTRIAL RECOVERY ACT (Public No. 67, 73d Congress [H.R. 5755].) Approved June 16, 1933

Title I—Industrial Recovery

Section 1 of this act provides as follows:

"A national emergency productive of widespread unemployment and disorganization of industry, which burdens interstate and foreign commerce, affects the public welfare, and undermines the standards of living of the American people, is hereby declared to exist. It is hereby declared to be the policy of Congress to remove obstructions to the free flow of interstate and foreign commerce which tend to diminish the amount thereof; and to provide for the general welfare by promoting the organization of industry for the purpose of cooperative action among trade groups, to induce and maintain united action of labor and management under adequate governmental sanctions and supervision, to eliminate unfair competitive practices, to promote the fullest possible utilization of the present productive capacity of industries, to avoid undue restriction of production (except as may be temporarily required), to increase the consumption of industrial and agricultural products by increasing purchasing power, to reduce and relieve unemployment, to improve standards of labor, and otherwise to rehabilitate industry and to conserve natural resources."

To these ends the President is authorized to establish an industrial planning and research agency to aid in carrying out his functions under this title, the same to cease to exist at the expiration of two years from the date of this enactment. (Section 2.)

With conditions and provisions acceptable to him in the interest of fairness, the President is authorized to approve codes of fair competition submitted by trade or industrial associations or groups, where such groups impose no inequitable restrictions of membership and are truly representative and such codes permit no monopolies or monopolistic practices. Upon approval, such a code shall be the standard of fair competition for the trade or industry involved. Violation thereof shall be deemed unfair competition within the meaning of the Federal Trade Commission Act, the United States courts are given jurisdiction to prevent and restrain the same, and it shall be the duty of Federal district attorneys to institute proceedings in equity to that end. (Section 3, (a), (b) and (c).)

On his own motion, or on complaint, the President may himself prescribe and approve a code for a trade or industry which has submitted none. (Id. (d).)

On his own motion, or on complaint, where it appears that articles are being imported into the United States on such terms or under such conditions as to endanger the maintenance of any such code, the President may order an investigation by the Tariff Commission, and if he finds the existence of such facts he may direct the admission of such articles only subject to such fees and in such quantities as shall not tend to render ineffective any such code. Importers may be licensed, in 'order to enforce this provision. The decision of the President as to facts shall be conclusive. Violation of any provision of a code shall be a misdemeanor, punishable by a $500 fine for each day such violation continues. (Id. (e) and (f).)

The President may enter into agreements with and approve agreements among persons or groups in trade or industry, to effectuate the policy of this title. (Section 4 (a).) If he finds that destructive wage or price cutting or other activities contrary to the policy of this title are being practiced in any trade or industry, the President may forbid any person to carry on any such business without a Federal license, revocable by the President. Violation is punishable by a $500 fine or six months' imprisonment, or o , and each day is to be deemed a separate offense. (Id. (b).)ḃ th

While this title is in 'effect, and for 60 days thereafter, any action complying with the same shall be exempt from the provisions of the anti-trust laws. Nothing in the act shall prevent a person from pursuing the vocation of manual labor and selling or trading the products thereof, nor prevent anyone from marketing or trading the produce of his farm. (Section 5.)

Every code shall contain provisions protecting collective bargaining, leaving employees free to join any labor organization they choose, requiring compliance with maximum hours of labor, minimum rates of pay and other conditions of employment prescribed or approved by the President. The President shall afford every opportunity for employers and employees to agree on these matters, but if they fail to do so he may fix maximum hours of labor, minimum rates of pay and other conditions of employment in any trade or industry, avoiding nevertheless any classification which might tend to set a maximum as well as a minimum wage. (Section 7.)

Title II—Public Works and Construction Projects

The President is authorized to create a Federal Emergency Administration of Public Works, which shall cease to exist two years after the enactment of this act, or sooner if the President shall proclaim or the Congress shall by joint resolution declare that the emergency recognized by section 1 has ended. (Section 201.) For the purposes of this act $3,300,000,000 is appropriated, of which the President may allocate not more than $100,000,000 to carry out the Agricultural Adjustment Act and for the purposes of the Farm Credit Administration. (Section 220.)

The public works administrator shall prepare a comprehensive program of public works, which shall include among other things the following:

Construction, repair and improvement of public highways and parkways, public buildings, and any publicly owned instrumentalities and facilities.

Conservation and development of natural resources, including control, utilization and purification of waters, prevention of soil or coastal erosion, development of water power, transmission of electrical energy, construction of river and harbor improvements adopted by Congress or recommended by the chief of army engineers and flood control.

Projects of the character heretofore constructed or carried on either directly by public authority or with public aid to serve public interests.

Construction, reconstruction, alteration or repair under public regulation or control of low-cost housing and slum-clearance projects.

Any other project heretofore eligible for loans under subsection (a) of section 201 of the Emergency Relief and Construction Act of 1932, including hospitals the operation of which is partly financed from public funds and reservoirs, pumping plants and dry docks. Also, if it seems desirable to the President, the construction of naval vessels, aircraft, heavier-than-air-craft, army housing, and the motorization of army units. (Section 202.)

The President is authorized, with a view to increasing employment quickly:

1. To construct, finance or aid in the construction or financing of any public works project included in the program prepared pursuant to section 202.

2. To make grants to States, municipalities, or other public bodies for such purposes, not to exceed 30 per cent of the cost of labor and materials required.

3. To acquire by purchase or condemnation any real or personal property required, and to sell or lease the same.

4. To aid in the financing of such railroad maintenance and equipment as may be approved by the Interstate Commerce Commission.

In deciding to grant aid to any State, county or municipality, the President may consider whether action is in process or in good faith assured therein reasonably designed to bring ordinary current expenditures within prudently estimated revenues. He may, however, extend the benefits of the act to any State, county or municipality, notwithstanding any constitutional or legal restriction or limitation on the right or power of such State, county or municipality to borrow money or incur indebtedness. (Section 203.)

Not less than $400,000,000 is to be granted to the highway departments of the several States to be expended in accordance with the Federal Highway Act of November 9, 1921, as amended:

1. For emergency construction on the Federal aid highway system and extensions thereof into and through municipalities, including elimination of hazards, such as grade crossings, narrow and unsafe bridges, etc., and routes to avoid congested areas.

2. For secondary or feeder roads agreed upon by the State highway departments and the Secretary of Agriculture, provided the State or locality will provide for proper maintenance.

No part of these funds need be matched by the States, and such funds may also be used in lieu of State funds to match unobligated balances of previous apportionments of regular Federal-aid appropriations. All contracts must include minimum wage rates. (Section 204.)

All contracts for construction projects and all loans and grants pursuant to this title shall contain such provisions as are necessary to insure (1) no convict labor, (2) the 30-hour week except for executive, administrative and supervisory positions, (3) just and reasonable wages sufficient to provide a standard of living in decency and comfort, (4) preference in employment to ex-service men with dependents, and then in the following order (a) citizens of the United States and aliens who have declared their intention of becoming citizens, who are bona fide residents of the political subdivision and/or county in which the work is to be performed, and (b) citizens of the United States and aliens who have declared their intention of becoming citizens, who are bona fide residents of the State, territory or district, provided these preferences shall apply only where such labor is available and qualified; (5) that the maximum of human labor shall be used in lieu of machinery wherever practicable and consistent with sound economy and public advantage. (Section 206.)

For work in national forests and on Indian reservations $50,000,000 is provided (section 205), and $25,000,000 to be used by the President for making loans for and otherwise aiding in the purchase of subsistence homesteads, moneys collected as repayment to constitute a revolving fund. (Section 208.)

SUMMARY OF THE NATIONAL EMPLOYMENT SYSTEM ACT (Public No. 30, 73d Congress [S. 510].) Approved June 6, 1933

This bill abolishes (September 6, 1933) the existing employment service in the Department of Labor and creates a United States Employment Service, a bureau in the Department of Labor, with a director appointed by the President at $8,500 a year, and officers, employees and assistants to be appointed by the Secretary of Labor without regard to civil service laws. (Section 2.)

This bureau is to promote and develop a national system of employment offices, including a veterans service and a farm placement service, assisting States and their subdivisions to this end and coordinating public employment offices throughout the county. (Section 3.) The director is to establish a Federal Advisory Council, representing employers and employees in equal numbers and the public, to serve without pay except for expenses, and to formulate policies and discuss problems with a view to impartiality, neutrality and freedom from political influence. (Section 11.)

For the fiscal year ending June 30, 1934, $1,500,000 is appropriated, and for each of the next four fiscal years $4,000,000.

Within 60 days after any appropriation has been made (section 6) 75 per cent of the amounts appropriated is to be apportioned according to population (section 5) among the States accepting the act and providing a cooperating agency (section 8), to establish and maintain public employment offices. No payment will be made to the State unless an equal sum has been made available for the year by the State and its political subdivisions, nor unless the State's contribution is at least equal to 25 per cent of its apportionment according to population and in no event less than $5,000. (Section 5.) Moneys unawarded under this plan will be reapportioned among the States which qualify.

During the current and the two succeeding fiscal years the unapportioned balances of the appropriation may be used by the director in his discretion in establishing and maintaining public employment offices in States which have no State system of public employment, or which, having such system, are not cooperating with the Federal plan. Thereafter no assistance will be given a non-cooperating State. (Section 10.)

Applicants for employment are to be given notice of strikes and lockouts. (Section 11.) The service and all State systems receiving Federal funds are to have free mailing privileges. (Section 13.)

EMERGENCY RELIEF FOR HOME MORTGAGES (Public No. 43, 73d Congress [H.R. 5240].) Approved June 13, 1933

This act authorizes the creation by the Federal Home Loan Bank Board of a Home Owners' Loan Corporation, an instrumentality of the United States, the directors of which shall be the members of the Board, serving without additional compensation. (Section 4 (a).)

The capital stock of this Corporation shall not exceed $200,000,000, which shall be subscribed for by the Secretary of the Treasury, for which purpose the resources of the Reconstruction Finance Corporation are increased by $200,000,000. (Id. (b).)

The Corporation is authorized to issue not to exceed $2,000,000,000 of 18-year, 4 per cent bonds, guaranteed as to interest only by the United States, the interest payable when due out of the United States treasury and if so paid to be an interest-bearing debt of the Corporation to the United States. The bonds shall be exempt, as to principal and interest, from all Federal, State or local taxes (except surtaxes, estate, inheritance, and gift taxes), and the Corporation's franchise, capital, reserves and surplus, and its loans and income, shall likewise be tax-exempt, but its real property shall be taxable as other real property is taxed. (Id. (c).)

The Corporation is authorized, for three years from date of the act's enactment:

1. (a) (id. (d).) To acquire in exchange for its bonds home mortgages and other obligations and liens secured by real estate (including the interest of a vendor under a purchase money mortgage or contract), and (b) in connection with any such exchange to make advances in cash to pay taxes and assessments and provide for maintenance and repairs, and to pay not exceeding $50 to the holder of the mortgage where there is a difference between the face value of the bonds plus accrued interest and the purchase price of the mortgage.

The face value of bonds exchanged and cash advanced shall in no case exceed $14,000 or 80 per cent of the appraised value of the real estate, whichever is the smaller.

Where the face value of bonds and cash advanced is less than the home owner owes, the Corporation shall credit the difference to the home owner and reduce his indebtedness to the Corporation to that extent.

Each mortgage acquired shall be carried as a first lien or refinanced as a home mortgage by the Corporation on the basis of the price paid therefor, and shall be amortized by monthly payments sufficient to retire interest and principle within not less than 15 years, but the amortization payments may be made quarterly, semi-annually, or annually, in the Corporation's judgment.

Interest on unpaid balances shall not exceed 5 per cent per annum.

Extensions of time for the payment of any installment may be granted at any time, and no payment of principal shall be required within three years from the date of the act, if the home owner is not otherwise in default.

"Real estate," as used in the act, means real estate held in fee simple or on a leasehold under a lease renewable for not less than 99 years upon which there is located a dwelling for not more than four families used by the owner as a home or held by him as a homestead and having a value not exceeding $20,000.

There shall be no discrimination by reason of the location of real estate in a tax district which is in default on any of its obligations.

2. (Id. (e).) To make loans in cash under the same limitations, up to 50 per cent of appraised values, where the property is not otherwise encumbered, to be secured by mortgage.

3. (Id. (f).) Where the mortgage holder will not accept the Corporation's bonds, to make cash advances up to 40 per cent of value to the home owner, for the purposes specified in (d), above, to be secured by mortgage at not to exceed 6 per cent.

4. (Id. (g).) To exchange bonds and advance cash as above to redeem or recover homes lost by foreclosure or forced sale or voluntary surrender within two years prior to such exchange or advance.

The Corporation's employees are exempt from civil service laws. It has the franking privilege. It shall be liquidated when its purposes have been accomplished, its surplus or accumulated funds to be paid into the treasury. It may declare and pay dividends to the United States.

The Corporation shall also provide for Federal Savings and Loan Associations, to lend not more than $20,000 each on first liens on homes, or combined home and business property, within 50 miles of their home office, except that not more than 15 per cent of their assets may be loaned without regard to such limitations except as to the first liens. Each such association shall become automatically a member of a Federal Home Loan Bank. On request of the Board, where such assistance is needed, the Secretary of the Treasury shall subscribe for not more than $100,000 of the preferred shares of such an association. For this purpose $100,000,000 is appropriated. All such associations and their shares as to value and income shall be free from every Federal tax (except surtaxes, estate, inheritance, and gift taxes) and shall not be taxed locally to an extent greater than other similar local institutions. (Section 5.)

Penalties: For false statements to obtain a loan, $5,000 fine or two years imprisonment, or both.

Forgery, embezzlement or false entry, or making of unauthorized charges, $10,000 fine or five years imprisonment, or both.

INDEX TO GENERAL RULINGS, OPINIONS, AND INTERPRETATIONS OF COUNSEL

236

239

ADMINISTRATION OF PUBLIC UNEMPLOYMENT RELIEF IN NEW YORK STATE

ITS SCOPE, ACCOMPLISHMENTS AND COST
April 1, 1934—March 31, 1935

TEMPORARY EMERGENCY RELIEF ADMINISTRATION
STATE OFFICE BUILDING, ALBANY, N. Y.
NEW YORK OFFICE, 79 MADISON AVENUE

May 1, 1935

ADMINISTRATION OF PUBLIC UNEMPLOYMENT RELIEF IN NEW YORK STATE

CONTENTS

ADMINISTRATION OF PUBLIC UNEMPLOYMENT RELIEF IN NEW YORK STATE

To His Excellency, Herbert H. Lehman, Governor, and to the Honorable Members of the Senate and the Assembly of the State of New York:

With the imminence of a new Federal work program it is fitting at this time to make an accounting to the people of the State of New York and to you, their representatives, of the costs of administering relief in the period which began with the demobilization of the CWA and is now to come to a close.

In view of the character of the new Federal program, it is particularly desirable also that the relative costs and advantages of home and work relief in actual operation be set forth impartially, with a relation of what that part of the relief dollar that goes for administrative expense actually buys for the taxpayer.

In accordance with instructions in Section 21 of Chapter 798 of the Laws of 1931, directing the Temporary Emergency Relief Administration of New York State to "report to the Governor and the Legislature from time to time in such detail as may be required, the operations of the Administration, together with the condition of unemployment and the relief afforded unemployed persons in the State," there is submitted herewith a report on the cost of administration of public unemployment relief in New York State in the year following the demobilization of the CWA on April 1, 1934, summarizing local relief costs and services and giving in detail the administrative costs and services of the Temporary Emergency Relief Administration in its stewardship of State and Federal funds, together with an analysis of the relative costs of home relief and work relief.

> ALFRED H. SCHOELLKOPF of Buffalo, *Chairman*
> ROBERT J. CUDDIHY of New York
> SOLOMON LOWENSTEIN of New York
> CHARLES D. OSBORNE of Auburn
> VICTOR F. RIDDER of New York
> JOSEPH P. RYAN of New York

May 1, 1935

FOREWORD: MAGNITUDE OF THE RELIEF TASK

In the month of March, 1935, approximately 2,200,000 men, women and children, more than one person in every six of the population of the State of New York, were dependent on public unemployment relief in all its forms, with the State still operating under an emergency relief law because of the grave problem of unemployment and consequent suffering. Of this number, 850,000 were children under sixteen years of age, one child out of every four of the State's future citizens. The total number of persons on relief had increased approximately 10 per cent since the previous April, when the Federal Civil Works program was demobilized, but the increase, huge of itself, was small in comparison with the turnover week by week and month by month that in the period led to the dropping from the rolls of hundreds of thousands of people, the heads of whose families became able to support them temporarily or permanently, while still larger numbers of unemployed, their resources exhausted by the years of the depression, were forced upon public aid.

Caring on an emergency basis for more than two million people, providing them with food and shelter and clothing and fuel, with necessary medical and nursing services, distributing to them the Federal surplus foods that became available through the national farm relief program, and providing them with other aid, such as school lunches and free milk, essential to avert wide-spread malnutrition and disease, if not starvation itself, has been a task unprecedented in its size and inherent problems.

"The existing and threatened deprivation of the necessaries of life" to such large numbers of the people was declared by the State of New York in 1931 to imperil "the public health and safety of the State and of each county, city and town therein." To see that these needy received food and clothing and shelter has been of the first importance throughout the present emergency. But this mechanical side of the operation has been only the beginning of the task.

Second, it has been necessary not only to care for the needy but to keep in constant touch with each family and individual, despite the growth of the widespread want, to make sure the relief is being given only to those in need, in the amounts to which need exists.

Third, because the administration of relief has been a public function, it has properly and of necessity been carried on through orderly governmental procedures, both for the spending of money and the accounting for it, to conserve and safeguard public funds.

Fourth, because the problem has been legislatively considered a temporary one since the beginning of the emergency, both by the State of New York which has extended the life of the Temporary Emergency Relief Administration by periods of six months or a year and by the Federal Government, whose funds have been available month by month or but for short periods, long-range planning has been exceedingly difficult.

Fifth, because relief administration has cut across all normal lines of political jurisdiction, involving Federal, State and a multitude of local monies and responsibilities, it has been subject to further necessary complications, rooted in our very form of government.

Above all, it has been proper, desirable and necessary that relief be not only prompt and adequate, but that it be also humane, that it help where possible to prevent the destruction of the initiative, self-respect and capabilities of the millions destitute because of unemployment in a period when there have not been enough jobs for those who wanted work.

It was particularly toward the accomplishment of this end that work relief was conceived in the first days of the depression when relief was still being handled in large part by private agencies. It sprang up in so many different places throughout the State and country without conscious knowledge of its existence elsewhere, that work relief may be considered as expressing the American choice for meeting the need.

When, as the need for relief grew, the State of New York, and later the Federal Government found it necessary to come to the aid of the localities in meeting the burden of relief, they carried forward the public and private work relief programs which had thus started as a characteristic American effort to give jobs instead of charity to those in need through unemployment. The Wicks Act, creating the State Temporary Emergency Relief Administration to administer State funds to assist the localities in caring for their needy unemployed, specifically provided for work relief as a form in which aid should be given.

In the following account of the costs of giving relief in the period from April 1, 1934 to March 31, 1935, and of the services and physical improvements provided, there must be kept ever in mind that relief has been given without break throughout the period and that the peril to the public health and safety recognized by the Legislature has been averted. The hungry have been fed.

RELIEF ADMINISTRATION: LOCAL, STATE AND FEDERAL

The Wicks Act reaffirmed the traditional policy of the State that "the duty of providing aid for those in need or unemployed because of lack of employment is primarily an obligation of the municipalities" and created city and county Welfare Districts for the local administration of relief. Although the percentage of State and later of State and Federal funds by which the Temporary Emergency Relief Administration has reimbursed the localities has increased, with the increase in the need, from the 40 per cent stipulated in the original Act to 75 per cent, the actual amount of relief expenditures borne by the localities has increased year by year. In the State of New York relief remains today a local responsibility heavier than ever before in history.

It is through local agencies that relief is administered. It is to local bureaus that the destitute appeal. Thousands of them every month, after five years of depression, find their resources at last exhausted and are forced to apply for public aid although with the upturn in private employment other thousands from relief rolls find themselves once more capable of self-support and return to normal economic life.

It is the local agencies that carry through the function of relief from the first interview to the investigation of the genuineness and extent of the need, and continue the job of actually giving needed aid. The local insurance adjusters help convert the savings in insurance into cash to help people keep off relief, leaving a reasonable minimum coverage of actual insurance. The experienced local workers determine the need, and help where they can to steer the breadwinner toward employment. The local paymasters draw the checks and the local accountants and auditors perform their necessary function. The local governments—town councils, county boards of supervisors, municipal councils or boards of aldermen—in the first instance appropriate and scrutinize all the money spent locally for relief even though the Temporary Emergency Relief Administration reimburses the localities from State and Federal funds by 75 per cent of these approved expenditures.

It is the local agencies, as well, that study the possibilities for work relief projects useful to the community in relation to the capacities of their needy unemployed. They draw plans and specifications, select from those in need the persons most suited to the job, and supervise the prosecution of the work once it is under way. Again it is the local paymasters who pay the wages in cash.

Such is the actual administration in New York State of home relief and work relief—by far the greatest part of all relief given —as stipulated in the Emergency Act, by which the State of New York pioneered in substantial assistance to its communities in this emergency and on which the original Federal relief statutes were based.

Your Relief Administration has found in actual practice that such a plan, chosen by the Legislature despite the overlapping accounting inherently involved, corresponding to the overlapping units of Government, is a chief means by which the sense of local responsibility for relief—essential to its economy and adequacy— has been kept alive despite the necessarily growing proportion of State and Federal relief funds. The alternatives, in view of the actual sources of funds, have been the direct Federal Administration of relief, with complete state and local abdication, or direct State administration under Federal supervision, with grave danger of atrophy of local responsibility.

The function of the Temporary Emergency Relief Administration has been to aid in the organization, encourage the initiative and stimulate the efficiency of the local relief units. In conformity with the mandate and stipulations of the Wicks Act, it has reimbursed the localities, helped them in their planning, and seen that State monies were expended according to law. A detailed account of the services and expenditures of the Administration in the period will be found in the next section. It has been concerned—in accordance with the provisions of the statute—chiefly with this supervision of the giving of relief by the localities, and with their reimbursement, not with the actual giving of relief itself.

Still more the Federal Government, in its relations with New York State has been a supervisory agency, helping gather for the Nation, as the Temporary Emergency Relief Administration has helped to spread within the State, the fruits of the best experience in other localities.

The expenditures for administration, local, State and Federal, for the period from April 1, 1934 to March 31, 1935 reflect these differences of function.

Total relief given in all forms to support a monthly average of more than 2,000,000 people amounted in the period to $284,829,953, or 79.8 per cent of the total amount of the relief operation as reported by the administrative units. Work relief materials which were converted into roads, sewers, buildings and other public works of benefit to the respective communities, accounted for a further $32,417,061, or 9.1 per cent of the total.

Administrative and supervisory costs are necessarily highest in the local districts where the actual work of investigation is performed and the relief given. Total administrative and supervisory costs in the period—local, State and Federal—were approximately $39,822,625, or 11.1 per cent of the whole. Of this last, local administrative costs for the actual giving of relief, were $37,074,701, or 10.4 per cent of the total amount of the relief operation. State supervisory costs, together with the administration of the State and Federal transient and other supplementary relief programs, were seven-tenths of one per cent. Federal central administrative costs for disbursement of funds to the State and supervision of the whole operation, estimated on a pro rata basis, were reported from Washington to be about one-twentieth of one per cent.

By far the largest part of the workers employed on a non-relief or continuous salary basis in relief administration in New York State came themselves from relief rolls and would be in need of relief were it not for these jobs.

TABLE I

Relief, Administrative Costs and Work Relief Materials
New York State—April 1, 1934 to March 31, 1935

(Compiled from reports of the administrative units)

RELIEF GIVEN	Amount	Per cent
Home Relief	$132,021,208	
Work Relief Wages	130,278,435	
Retail Value Surplus Foods	14,964,196	
Transients	3,280,685	
Milk	1,124,521	
College Students' Aid	1,063,286	
School Lunches	1,042,030	
Care of Local Homeless	1,030,002	
Death and Disability Benefits	25,690	
TOTAL	$284,829,953	79.8

SUPERVISORY AND ADMINISTRATIVE EXPENSE

Local:

	Amount	Per cent
Salaries for supervisory, planning, administrative staff, and other workers employed on a continuous basis as opposed to those paid on a part time relief budget basis	$33,743,685	
Other administrative and supervisory expenses	3,331,016	
TOTAL	$37,074,701	10.4

State:

	Amount	Per cent
Central State Administration	$2,069,578	
State and Federal Transient	352,007	
Other special programs	146,339	
Total	$2,567,924	0.7
Federal Supervisory and Administrative Expense	180,000*	*
Total	$39,822,625	11.1
WORK RELIEF MATERIALS	$32,417,061	9.1
GRAND TOTAL	$357,069,637†	100.0

* The figure for Federal Administrative expense is estimated pro rata, there being no way to segregate the actual amount applicable to New York State. Federal administrative costs have averaged about one-tenth of one per cent of disbursements; since the Federal Government pays approximately half of relief expenditures in New York State, its administrative expense would thus be roughly one-twentieth of one per cent of New York's total disbursement.

† Exclusive of $4,301,253 expended in the period on special Federal programs whose policies were not controlled by the Temporary Emergency Relief Administration as follows: $611,128 for the National Reemployment Service, a placement service, not relief; $2,527,519 for the cattle and $106,805 for the cabbage programs, already included above in the total of Federal surplus foods distributed and in the administrative costs of other special programs; $464,967 for the cotton program and $590,834 for other programs.

11

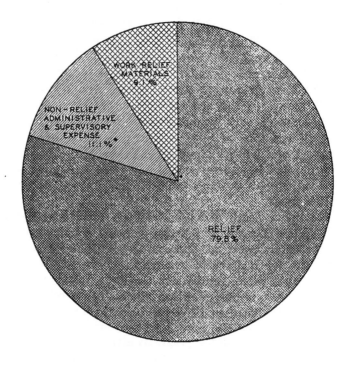

*LOCAL, STATE AND FEDERAL

THE STATE OF NEW YORK AND RELIEF

As the agency to allocate and protect from misuse State relief funds and Federal grants to the State, the State Temporary Emergency Relief Administration has felt the pressure from the Federal Government on the one hand for uniform practice and records and from the localities on the other for autonomy. It has felt the strain of competent individuals meeting day by day one of the most difficult administrative tasks ever attempted and as yet undisciplined to the inherent complications of the way it must be done, and occasionally, the attempted thrusts of local political opportunism.

The State Administration in its supervision of the local administration of relief has divided the State administratively into nine districts, each with a district director and staff. With the staff of the central administration itself these have provided experienced workers to help local relief bureaus organize, establish policies and systematize their records and to aid bureaus in selection of personnel; social statisticians to determine what data are of value and interpret them after they are obtained; engineers to cooperate in planning valuable work projects suitable for local needs; advisers on medical and nursing services, nutrition and gardens for the unemployed, and a multitude of other phases of the problem; and an auditing staff to insure sound business and accounting methods in the local bureaus to which the State and Federal Governments contribute funds.

In the twelve-month period from April 1, 1934 to March 31, 1935, the State Temporary Emergency Relief Administration disbursed a monthly average of approximately $19,664,000 to reimburse the localities for their relief expenditures. In this same period its total central administrative expense for providing the services that assured the continuity and coordination of this relief averaged $172,465,* or less than one per cent of the funds so disbursed. In this figure is included also rent, light, telephone and other general office overhead for all special programs given below. The total of $172,465 was divided into an average of $106,435 per month for salaries, $17,387 per month for travel, $10,003 per month for printing, $7,020 per month for expenses in connection with the sale of relief bonds, $5,294 per month for rent and light in the New York

---

* In arriving at this average, approximately $30,225, by which the Temporary Emergency Relief Administration defrayed expenses of the Governor's Commission on Unemployment Relief in the period, and $8,000, a non-recurring expense for an impartial industrial engineering survey of relief machinery to draft suggestions for greater efficiency in organization, have been excluded, as they were in Table I.

City office and in the district offices throughout the State, and the remainder for the other items detailed in Table II.

In addition, in the State and Federal transient programs, necessary under State and Federal laws to aid those in need who have no local settlement and therefore are in no way a local charge, the State Temporary Emergency Relief Administration not only supervised the giving of relief but itself actually distributed a monthly average of $273,390 in relief to a monthly average of 27,552 persons during the period, no other agency intervening between it and the needy who were helped. Since in regard to transient relief the Transient Division of the Temporary Emergency Relief Administration thus financed the whole job, the administrative costs here may be fairly compared to the total of State supervisory plus local service administrative costs of home relief and work relief. The administrative costs of the Transient Division in this period in the central supervision of the work as well as the cost of maintaining 33 registration centres, seven camps and one rehabilitation centre averaged $29,334 per month, or 9.7 per cent of the total cost of caring for transients.

The cost of the administration of other special Federal programs whose policies were not controlled by the Temporary Emergency Relief Administration including surplus foods, cattle and cotton, averaged $12,195 per month during the period, paid entirely by the Federal Government. No State funds were used.

TABLE II
CENTRAL ADMINISTRATIVE EXPENSES*

	Average per Month April 1, 1934 to March 31, 1935
Salaries of TERA Central and field organization........	$106,434 63
Salaries of State Comptroller's Staff assigned to TERA.....	4,567 47
Travel	17,386 56
Telephone and Telegraph................................	3,090 18
Furniture and Equipment...............................	5,542 82
Stationery and Supplies...............................	4,294 68
Safety Supplies	36 69
Rental of Equipment...................................	494 73
Printing	10,003 49
Printing—Local Districts	4,240 70
Express and Postage...................................	2,565 98
Rent and Light..	5,294 33
Carfares	20 80
Expenses re bond sales................................	7,019 82
Miscellaneous	1,471 91
TOTAL	$172,464 79*

* In addition, special Federal programs in which the policies were not controlled by the Temporary Emergency Relief Administration averaged in administrative expense $41,529 a month, of which $29,334 was for the Transient and $12,195 for other special programs. No State funds were used.

In its central responsibility for the whole administration of relief in New York State, the Temporary Emergency Relief Administration, in accordance with the Emergency Act, consists of six members, appointed by the Governor. They serve without pay, the Chairman having declined an $11,500 salary set by Legislative enactment.

As of March 20, 1935, this Administration employed 994 persons in all its activities—in its regular administrative function as well as in its transient and other special programs: 90 at salaries of less than $1,000 a year; 361 at salaries between $1,000 and $1,499; 263 at salaries between $1,500 and $1,999; 131 at salaries between $2,000 and $2,499; 84 at salaries between $2,500 and $2,999; 18 at salaries between $3,000 and $3,499; 22 at salaries between $3,500 and $3,999; 13 at salaries between $4,000 and $4,499; 4 at salaries between $4,500 and $4,999; 4 at salaries between $5,000 and $5,550; one at a salary between $6,000 and $6,200; two at salaries between $7,000 and $7,200; and one at a salary of $10,415. All figures are for salaries actually paid at the present reduced scale.

With this staff, the total expenditure of the State Temporary Emergency Relief Administration for administrative expenses was seven-tenths of one per cent of the total relief operation.

Its task has in many ways been easier than that of the local relief organizations. Non-partisan and non-political itself, it has never been involved in political warfare, since by happy coincidence all major State decisions in relief in New York State have been taken upon agreement by the Governor and Legislative leaders of both parties. With such thorough-going support from State leaders it has been able to give increasing force to the principle enunciated at the outset in consonance with the plain mandate of the Wicks Act, that relief be given to the needy without discrimination on grounds of political adherence, religion, race, color, or non-citizenship.

The primary responsibility of the Temporary Emergency Relief Administration has been to see that relief to the needy was given in accordance with State and Federal laws. That responsibility it has discharged; relief has continued from the start of the Administration on November 1, 1931, under such orderly procedure that there has been no break or let-down in the distribution of State and later of State and Federal funds.

PROTECTION OF PUBLIC FUNDS

As custodians of State relief funds the State Temporary Emergency Relief Administration would without hesitation judge the quality of personnel to be one of the most important problems in the relief administration of the local districts, both from the point of view of humanity and of saving to the taxpayers. Since the administration of mass relief was unprecedented—to this day New York is operating under an emergency relief law—civil service requirements and advantages have not, by specific provision of the Wicks Act, applied to relief personnel. The choice was between chaos from lack of any standards, which would result in the most widespread exposure to political patronage, favoritism, inefficiency and waste and the setting up of minimum standards by the Temporary Emergency Relief Administration in cooperation with welfare commissioners and experts in various technical fields.

Complicated as the problem of personnel was throughout the State, the most serious difficulty was in New York City which, by a charter provision, had been prevented from giving outdoor public relief even on a small scale previous to the passage of the Wicks Act. New York City, therefore, unlike many upstate cities and other large cities throughout the country, had to start from scratch in the public administration of relief.

The Wicks Act, seeking to ensure proper conservation of relief funds, required investigation of relief cases. It stipulated as well that the State Temporary Emergency Relief Administration "make and enforce rules . . . which will best promote the efficiency and effectiveness of the relief which this act is intended to furnish," and laid upon it the responsibility of approving standards of personnel in the local offices.

In setting up minimum standards, the Temporary Emergency Relief Administration has taken into consideration the emergency and has required experience which is somewhat less than that for comparable positions in the civil service. The recommendation of the Temporary Emergency Relief Administration has been that the local relief authorities choose local persons wherever local trained persons were available. The actual selection of the personnel was the responsibility of the local relief authorities, with the State Temporary Emergency Relief Administration merely approving the appointment, except as to its own staff.

These standards, while far from perfect, have been evolved on the principle of merit and efficiency and not on the principle of local patronage.

The non-political basis of selection of personnel as required by the State Temporary Emergency Relief Administration has resulted in the State of New York's being outstanding in the union for infrequency of graft and political exploitation of misery.

As the number of those on relief grew, local relief officials increasingly recognized the need for qualified workers and it was easily demonstrated that the State Administration's rules relating to investigation of applications resulted in economy in relief expenditures through giving aid only to those in actual need. An immediate result of the employment of workers trained for this service was the elimination from the poor relief lists of many welfare districts of considerable numbers of long-time beneficiaries, with a consequent saving of funds for the relief of families whose needs were real and urgent.

The Administration frequently called attention to the fact that although the large numbers of applications that must be looked into without undue delay frequently necessitated the use of untrained staff, the objective should be to provide such service that applicants would be treated with consideration and understanding and their needs met intelligently and economically. They pointed out that such service required special training and experience, equally important in the first interview with an applicant for relief, in the home visit and other inquiries into needs and resources, and in later contacts with families receiving relief.

The experienced workers who have carried forward this program have done so with practically no increased cost per case for social service, despite the great improvement of the service, both in the impartial determination of the legitimacy and the accurate determination of the extent of the need. They have been the great bulwark in this State against favoritism and injustice in relief.

In carrying out the mandate of the Wicks Act by setting standards and drawing up requirements for local administrative positions in all branches, to insure that they were capably filled and exempt from personal favoritism and political pressure, the Temporary Emergency Relief Administration followed the natural lines of universal experience: for typists, it required experience in typing; for general office administrators, experience in administration; for engineers, those with experience in engineering; for social workers, those with practical experience in dealing with people and with training to make them alive to the fundamental problems involved and the most efficient procedures.

The administration of relief, in most of its phases, cannot be well carried on by work relief labor. Work relief recipients have to leave the job as soon as they become ineligible, and the turnover is large. It would be impossible to run an administrative office efficiently with such a changing staff. In the case of investigators there must also be considered the lowered efficiency of having persons on relief determine how much relief others are to get. Therefore, these staffs for the most part have been placed on a straight non-relief salary basis. The largest part of those on non-relief administrative salaries came themselves from relief rolls and would themselves be in need of relief were it not for these jobs.

There can be no question that the efficiency of the local administration of relief in New York State has increased steadily despite the increasing demands upon it. Improvement is still going on and must continue to be striven for.

In view of the immense amount of public money required for relief, orderly procedures have been necessary to protect it from misuse. The objective has been to provide the safeguards by flexible procedures, modified according to experience, so that regulations might not thwart the purpose of the Wicks Act that relief reach the needy speedily and effectively.

In reaching this objective the State Temporary Emergency Relief Administration has been forced to disappoint many private interests and public officials who have applied for relief funds for materials needed by them but not constituting legitimate relief expenditures. These requests have ranged from outright grants for which little explanation was given to demands for cutlery for city restaurants.

The regulations of the State Temporary Emergency Relief Administration and the State Comptroller have prevented the diversion of millions of dollars to non-relief costs promoted by partial interests. Flexible and temporary in its character, the State Temporary Emergency Relief Administration has simplified its regulations as far as is consonant with orderly procedure, while complying with the legal requirements inherent in an accounting to three different governments. In the simplified purchasing procedure of the State Temporary Emergency Relief Administration the overhead of its own purchase department has been 1.3 per cent of its orders.

COMPARATIVE COSTS OF HOME RELIEF AND WORK RELIEF

Public unemployment relief is the provision out of public funds of a reasonable minimum living for otherwise destitute families or individuals. Home relief is the provision of that living in cash or in kind with no immediate return to society on the part of the recipient. Work relief is its provision in the form of hourly wages in cash for work useful to the community, the number of hours depending on the need.

Thus, even apart from its support of the morale of the recipient, work relief, as a dividend on the additional outlay necessary for materials and supervision, gives an actual physical return to the taxpayer in the form of public improvements.

Work relief necessarily involves added costs for materials and supervision, and such added costs are easily measurable in dollars and cents. On the other hand, increased benefits to the morale of the work relief recipient from having a job instead of a grocery order cannot be so measured. Such added values are imponderables,

TABLE III

New York State—October, 1934

HOME RELIEF AND WORK RELIEF EXPENDITURES COMBINED

(As reported by the local welfare districts)

	Amount	Per Cent
Amount of Relief Given........................	$22,125,380	78.6
Local Supervisory and Administrative Costs......	2,946,462	10.5
Materials	3,081,866	10.9
TOTAL	$28,153,708	100.0

HOME RELIEF AND WORK RELIEF EXPENDITURES ANALYZED

	Home Relief Amount	Per Cent	Work Relief Amount	Per Cent
Total Relief Given...........	$11,226,057	91.5	$10,899,323	68.6
Local Administration:				
Social Service Salaries......	458,609*	3.7	246,944*	1.6
Office Adm. Salaries........	461,559	3.8	492,786	3.1
Other Operating Costs......	122,890	1.0	133,132	0.8
TOTAL	$1,043,058	8.5	$872,862	5.5
Technical and Supervisory Salaries	....	....	1,030,542	6.5
Materials	....	....	3,081,866	19.4
GRAND TOTAL	$12,269,115	100.0	$15,884,593	100.0

* Division of social service costs between home relief and work relief estimated on the basis of cases served by these programs.

19

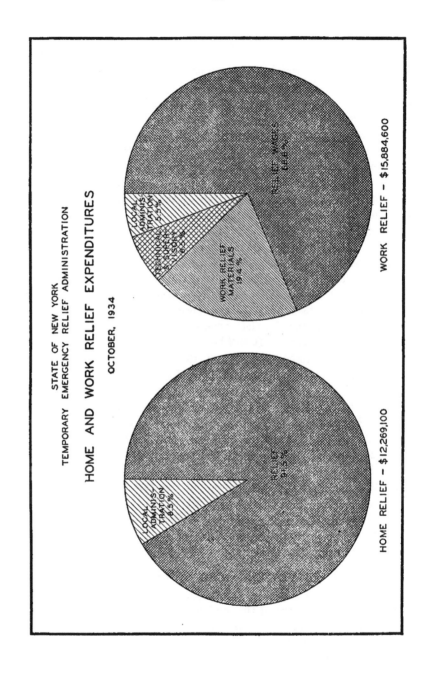

STATE OF NEW YORK
TEMPORARY EMERGENCY RELIEF ADMINISTRATION

HOME AND WORK RELIEF EXPENDITURES

OCTOBER, 1934

WORK RELIEF – $15,884,600

HOME RELIEF – $12,269,100

not amenable to statistical analysis, but they must nevertheless be taken into consideration in any proper appraisal of the costs and results of relief expenditures. The significant difference between a job well done for which wages are paid and a pension for idleness, however enforced, is so well recognized by the hundreds of relief officials throughout the State that they tend to allow somewhat greater relief if the recipients work for it than if they do not. Other factors, such as that those with the largest budget deficits are ordinarily assigned to work relief, tend to swell the average relief per month per family on work relief above the average on home relief. Home relief is sometimes confined to fuel only, medical care only, or other supplementation of inadequate income. Such averages by themselves therefore mean nothing.

For the month of October, 1934, special studies were made at the instance of the Federal Government which facilitate a detailed analysis of the relative costs of giving home relief and work relief. Such an analysis of these relative costs is impracticable month by month because of the great accounting cost involved and because of the intricate task of assigning appropriate costs between the two programs in the districts where there are consolidated home and work relief bureaus. It will be seen that the figures for October did not deviate importantly from the general average for the twelve-month period indicated in Table I.

Of $28,153,708 spent in the local* giving of home relief and work relief in October 1934, $22,125,380, or 78.6 per cent, was for relief given; $2,946,462, or 10.5 per cent, for local non-relief administrative costs, and $3,081,866, or 10.9 per cent, for work relief materials, as reported by the local welfare districts and detailed in Table III.

In that month 323,254 families and non-family persons, or 63 per cent, received home relief only, while 156,115, or 30 per cent. received work relief wages only and 38,486 families, or 7 per cent, received relief partially in the form of work and partially by a home allowance. The total number of these cases was 517,855.

Home Relief: The Basic Cost of the Relief Operation

In the month of October, for $11,226,057 given in home relief, comprising 91.5 per cent of the total cost of the operation, total local non-relief administrative salaries and costs were $1,043,058, or 8.5 per cent, divided as follows: social service salaries $458,609, or 3.7 per cent; other administrative salaries $461,559, or 3.8 per cent;

---

* State and Federal administrative costs, infinitesimal in proportion in any case, would split roughly proportionate to the home and work relief local administrative costs.

and other operating costs, rent, light, travel and supplies, and so forth, $122,890, or 1.0 per cent.

These administrative costs for home relief may be considered basic and may be expected no matter in what form relief is given; they are the costs of meeting those in need, determining their need and dispensing relief.

Work Relief: Dividends From Its Added Costs

Work relief projects, operating on an entirely different principle than public works or contract labor, pay wages to needy men and women who would otherwise receive approximately the same subsistence in the form of home relief allowances. Work relief is a way of giving relief that provides dividends in the form of public improvements. But it is primarily relief, by the very terms of the Wicks Act.

For this reason labor is used as much as possible in work relief even where labor-saving devices might do the job, as a job, more quickly and cheaply. The cost of the improvement itself, above the cost of giving needed relief to the same number of people if they were kept at home in idleness, is properly the non-relief cost of the operation.

It was to be assumed from the start that improvements made under this plan, with as much of the money as possible going to labor, could not be completed as economically as under private contract. The program is, however, cheaper than doing the job on the one hand and giving relief on the other.

A cost analysis of work relief projects drawn up by the Utica Work Division for the period from April 1, 1934 to December 27, 1934—the only complete analysis of this kind ever made for a district (summarized in the appendix, Table IV)—gives an indication of what is probably illustrative of work relief throughout the State. The total of relief wages paid was $431,362 while other costs, the non-relief costs for materials and supervision, amounted to $295,193. Substantially the amount of the relief wages would have had to be paid in any case in home relief allowances to the destitute if there had been no work program at all. By spending an additional $295,193 from local, State and Federal funds, the community obtained improvements whose value or contract price totaled $528,441.

The emphasis placed on work relief in New York State under mandate of the Legislature in the Wicks Act has been made possible by Federal contributions without which New York could not have been able to continue to carry on work relief at current levels.

In the month of October, 1934, $10,899,323, or 68.6 per cent of the whole cost of the work relief operation, went for work relief wages to support 194,601 families and non-family persons.

In the same month local administrative salaries and costs, corresponding in general to those given in the preceding section for home relief, were $872,862, or 5.5 per cent, divided: social service salaries, $246,944, or 1.6 per cent; office administrative salaries, $492,786, or 3.1 per cent; and other operating costs, $133,132, or 0.8 per cent.

In the work bureaus these non-relief costs included not only the functions already described in the local administration of home relief but the cost as well of the engineering operation of drawing up plans and specifications for work projects, and the central supervision to see that the jobs were properly done.

In addition, technical and supervisory salaries, providing time-keepers, foremen and engineers necessary to supervise the job on the spot and other services amounted to $1,030,542, or 6.5 per cent of the total, while materials—cement, steel and other needed materials, tools, and the rental of such equipment as was essential— amounted to $3,081,866, or 19.4 per cent of the total work relief cost.

In the way that has been described in regard to home relief administration, the non-relief salaries on work relief went in large part to people originally taken from relief rolls who would themselves have been in need of relief if they had not had these jobs, but who could not be used on a relief basis because their work demanded continuity. The expenditures for work relief materials, in addition to providing public improvements of value, have in themselves been a great factor in keeping thousands employed in the country's heavy industries and have thus been a factor for recovery.

The non-relief costs of work relief, the approximately 25 per cent of the total spent in October for necessary supervision and materials, were a cheap price for the communities to pay for the public improvements that work relief brought them.

Despite the overwhelming public preference for work relief over home relief from the time the State of New York first came to the assistance of its localities in furnishing relief, there has never been any generally clear understanding of this quasi-public-works status of which a successful work relief program must necessarily partake.

Throughout the State of New York in the month of October, there were nearly 2,800 work relief projects in operation. Some three-fifths of the non-administrative projects were for the direct improvement of public property, including the construction, repairing and maintenance of highways and streets, the building of grade-crossings and bridges, construction of public buildings, the laying of sewers and their maintenance, construction of recreational facilities of all types, construction of waterways, levees and reservoirs; landscaping, grading and erosion control; eradication and control of pests, disease bearers and poisonous plants; conservation of fish and game; and scores of other projects for the enhancement of property values in communities throughout the State.

The remaining projects were for the production and distribution of goods needed by the unemployed; to provide housing; to promote public education, arts and research; public welfare projects; and sundry projects to provide tools, materials and equipment needed in the prosecution of the public works projects.

Among the public welfare and public education, arts and research projects, were projects providing employment principally to persons in the white collar group, themselves in need, and through this work augmenting the relief available to and promoting the welfare of other unemployed. Such projects were nursing, nutritional and other programs for health advancement; safety campaigns to increase the safety of relief workers; and drama, arts, research, music and other special service projects providing employment to utilize the skills of white collar workers.

If these white collar persons had not been given work relief they would have been idle at approximately the same cost to the taxpayer because they were destitute and needed either home or work relief not to starve. White collar projects, on the whole, do not create the permanent improvements of the purely physical construction. Nevertheless, they have a much smaller cost for operation and materials; their cost is almost all relief.

The number of workers and the payrolls, relief and non-relief, on all work relief projects in the State in the week ending March 21, 1935, are shown in the Appendix, Tables V and VI.

Throughout the development of the work relief program, the Temporary Emergency Relief Administration has adhered to its policy of avoiding competition with private industry and business while selecting projects on the basis of their usefulness. It has insisted, as well, that the localities should not utilize work relief to cut down on their own staffs or to do work for which they could find funds elsewhere.

Despite the extra costs for foremen, time-keepers and the whole wage disbursement machinery that comes inevitably by employing men and women instead of using machines, it will be seen from Table III that supervisory costs on work relief compared favorably with the 10 per cent to 12 per cent for preliminary studies, engineering fees and supervision that is the general practice in ordinary private contract work.

Figures available for certain of the largest work relief projects indicate that at its most efficient, the program has compared closely with private contract in the actual cost of the finished job, so that the relief given has cost nothing above the ordinary cost of the improvement.

The George Perkins Memorial Drive over the top of Bear Mountain was constructed at a cost of approximately $1,350,000 of which only about 6 per cent was for salaries to engineers, supervisors, clerical staff and for other such costs. The Tompkins Cove Road, also in the Bear Mountain region, constructed under private contract, required the approximate expenditure of from 9 per cent to 12 per cent for salaries to engineers, clerks, supervisors, machinery and tool repair. In the latter work comparatively little labor was used, most of the job being done by machinery, whereas the Perkins Memorial Drive, constructed under more severe and difficult conditions, was completed with 90 per cent of hand labor. The average cost per mile of these two projects was about the same.

A concrete warehouse and machine shop in Utica was built for the Division of Canals and Waterways of the State Department of Public Works for approximately 13 per cent less than it would have cost under private contract. This saving may be attributed . in part to the lack of a contractor's overhead and profits, and the direct supervision supplied by the Division of Canals and Waterways.

On the Ontario Street Sewer project in Buffalo, a $400,000 job, the cost of work relief supervision was about 3 per cent of the total expenditure, comparing with an estimated cost of 10 per cent for supervisors and overhead had the project been done under private contract.

The supervisory and administrative expense on the Bleecker Stadium in Albany amounted to between 7 per cent and 8 per cent as compared with a private contractor's estimate of between 10 per cent and 12 per cent for the same costs.

In the beginning, material costs were kept low and many projects were of the "leaf raking" variety which brought minimum returns both in the morale of the relief workers and in public improvements. As time has gone on, every effort has been made to increase the value and permanence of the work relief projects, necessarily involving an increase in the materials and engineering and supervisory costs.

The work relief program in New York State is now a vast public improvement operation with varied accomplishments of the public works type.

Following demobilization of the CWA last April, the Temporary Emergency Relief Administration called upon a firm of eminent consulting engineers to go over the whole relief machinery with a view to changes that would result in greater efficiency and reduced costs. One of the first recommendations in the course of a five month study was for the improvement of personnel standards and compensation in the work bureaus—they were speaking particularly in this connection of the Works Division in the City of New York:

"The Works Division should be administered and operated as a business enterprise and while full recognition should be given to the fact that the great body of the employees are selected from those in need, still every effort should be made to see that full value is returned and that the work accomplished is worth its cost. This means that the projects must be intelligently selected and that their execution must be well administered. This calls for the setting up of personnel within the Works Division competent in judgment to select the projects and in administrative ability to see that they are efficiently conducted and controlled. Executives should be paid salaries more nearly commensurate with their responsibilities and proper wage classifications and rates should be established."

There can be no doubt that for the greatest efficiency and the greatest economic return to the public from work relief, the tremendous responsibilities of the direction of this great program should be in thoroughly competent hands.

THE NEW FEDERAL WORKS PLAN

The new Federal Works program whose announced objective is to provide, as a Federal responsibility, work and wages for all employables on relief, is to mark the end of the tripartite adminis-·tration of relief. With only Federal funds used on work relief, accounting will be made only to the Federal Government, and procedures will therefore admit of simplification. At the same time, the announced Federal intention is to take no further part in home relief, leaving the States and their localities to bear the burden of caring for those on relief who are unemployable. Thus in home relief, too, administration will be simplified, with accounting made to two governments instead of three.

While awaiting detailed plans of the Federal program the National and State Employment Services functioning under the Federal and State Departments of Labor, respectively, have reported occupational classification of more than one-half of the employable members of all families on relief in all up-State areas and New York City. This work is being pushed to completion.

In most parts of the State, local relief agencies have also set up central occupational indexes, as recommended by the State Temporary Emergency Relief Administration in all industrial centres. To prevent duplication of function and resulting increase in the cost to the taxpayers it has been recommended by both the State Temporary Emergency Relief Administration and the Governor's Commission on Unemployment Relief that the work of classification begun by the National and State Employment Services be completed by them.

To enable the State of New York to take full and early advantage of the new Federal program when it starts, the localities have been drawing up in advance projects for work needed by the respective communities, for which work relief funds are insufficient at this time. On the basis of such projects already set up and as yet inactive, work can begin in all parts of the State almost immediately when Federal funds become available, and within sixty days the number of persons on work relief, nearly 190,000 in March, can be doubled, with further increases as the program expands.

THE NEED TODAY

It was not as a charity to those in need that the State of New York came to the assistance of the localities in 1931 to share the burden of relief. It was the need of the State herself, not the plight of her unfortunates, that forced her to take action. It was the peril to the public health and safety from widespread destitution that was recognized by the Legislature as the compelling reason for the Emergency Act. It was the economic need of the State as well, for her strength lies in her human resources, the sum of the skills, capacities, courage and health of all her people.

Now after five years of depression, despite the upturn in private employment of the last twenty-four months, the need has been greater than ever. The peak in the relief need lags behind the peak of unemployment because of the multitude whose accumulated savings against this rainy day have tided them over until the present time but have finally given out.

In the great human ebb and flow from and to relief rolls as some get jobs and others find their resources exhausted, more men and women and children were supported by public unemployment relief in February and March than at any previous time, though the rate of increase had been lessening, giving hope that the end of the increase in need might be in sight. The hope was strengthened by the fact that for the first time in the four winters of the Temporary Emergency Relief Administration's existence the number of families and non-family persons on relief in March did not increase over the February total, where in March, 1934 it had increased by 9.3 per cent, and in March, 1933 by 12 per cent.

In the period from May 1, 1934 to March 31, 1935, more than 225,000 families and non-family persons, including approximately 900,000 individuals, who had never before needed aid in the present emergency had to be added to the rolls. But in the same period the relief rolls increased actually only by approximately 67,000 families and non-family persons. This means that there is not a stable population on relief, but that there is a real turn-over in the people who are in need. Relief has two doors, and the great majority of those forced to enter are striving constantly to step forth once more along the normal road to self-support.

With the tremendous increase in the need, public unemployment relief is today, even more than in 1931, a necessity and not a choice. The same considerations of thrift and morale that made work relief the instinctive American choice in 1931 operate today with magnified force.

There is no question of the necessity for a continuing of the intensive drive for capable, energetic and far-sighted administration of the whole gigantic task. At this time there is no other factor in that continued progress so essential as a public understanding of the nature of that task, complete enough to ensure public support of administrative expenditures proper to the economy and efficiency of a job well done.

Faced with the necessity of preventing human suffering without being able to know in advance what the need would be, the State of New York took the only possible course in creating an emergency organization with sufficient flexibility to meet changing conditions. The Temporary Emergency Relief Administration, thus created, recognizing the weaknesses inherent in temporary emergency administration of relief, however necessary in the circumstances, last June requested the Governor to undertake an impartial investigation and study of the present emergency relief machinery so that methods of improving it might be devised. It has offered to the Commission on Unemployment Relief, subsequently appointed by the Governor, all deductions from its own experience pertinent to structural improvements which might be made under new legislation.

In presenting this report of actual administrative conditions, the State Temporary Emergency Relief Administration wishes to emphasize again its belief that the time has now come for more long-time planning than is possible under the present temporary emergency structure.

APPENDIX

WORK RELIEF ANALYSES

[29]

TABLE IV
UTICA WORK DIVISION—COST ANALYSIS OF WORK RELIEF PROJECTS
APRIL 1, 1934—DECEMBER 27, 1934

LOCAL PROJECTS	Work relief wages paid	Cost above relief wages (materials and equipment and non-relief supervisory and administrative costs)	Net cost to city above relief (Deducting State and Federal reimbursement for non-relief costs)	Value or contract price
Trolley track removal.....................	$48,269 27	$79,334 93	$27,033 22	$100,000 00
Starch factory creek.....................	25,473 38	4,364 12	1,876 29	14,900 00
Engineering survey.....................	5,462 26	7,508 81	1,993 95	12,971 07
Cleaning sewers.....................	26,024 89	6,160 01	2,521 24	966
Painting in fire stations.................	2,557 46	1,342 90	512 12	200
Cinder sidewalks.....................	1,506 00	475 57	141 29	,000
General hospital improvements...........	6,761 93	2,999 05	971 42	,000
Halleck's and Nail creeks...............	9,997 83	1,670 10	561 99	29,100
Rep. comfort station and bath house.......	816 50	88 62	30 30	,012
City Hall improvements..................	3,740 59	1,729 67	907 96	3,200
Storm sewer in Niagara street............	564 00	304 46	101 73	350
Storm sewer in Arthur street.............	28,412 37	8,438 14	4,293 29	19,
Storm sewer in Albany street.............	752 00	454 85	275 25	500 90
Storm sewer in Sherman drive............	970 75	256 42	80 08	860 00
Sanitary sewer — Broad — Turner.........	4,626 35	1,509 99	622 28	3,050 00
Sanitary sewer — Broad — Gilbert........	276 00	75 37	49 93	225 00
Clerks and assistants to NRA.............	299 70	313 35	120 92	613 05
Coast and geodetic survey................	....	2,140 44	554 38	2,140 44
Municipal clothing bureau...............	9,790 77	1,670 59	516 63	11,461 36
Map for fire department.................	335 02	792 05	208 16	1,127 07
Map for city assessors..................	1,164 70	2,594 36	706 50	3,759 06
Storm sewer in Dudley avenue...........	1,056 79	540 18	288 43	1,050 00
Sanitary sewer — Brookline drive........	4,745 91	1,224 98	392 85	3,460 00
Storm sewer in Sunset avenue...........	1,414 65	547 45	207 49	1,200 73
Storm sewer in Wurs avenue.............	2,669 88	1,863 79	883 43	2,700 00
Population and unemployment census......	157 98	4,010 40	1,379 25	4,168 38
Clerks, assistants, city administration......	6,331 60	11,137 41	2,946 22	17,469 01
Rep. reconstruction Ballou creek..........	16,018 00	4,727 79	1,507 03	15,500 00
Improvement to Utica airport.............	54,986 48	40,428 72	9,687 03	46,500 00
Tool and sundry equipment..............	2,941 33	821 94	256 10	3,763 27
Sanitary sewer — Eastwood avenue.......	1,260 75	569 74	189 37	850 00
Metal ceilings — Baggs school...........	625 90	143 31	117 96	1,146 67
Law library — Supreme Court............	2,224 43	748 33	221 24	2,972 76
Municipal golf course....................	5,934 74	2,525 28	1,966 28	6,100 00
Clerks, assistants to Deans U. F. A......	767 34	291 11	82 30	1,058 45
Paint, interior of schools................	5,089 71	1,331 74	609 15	5,391 17
Sewer and water lines to zoo............	6,603 13	3,139 71	1,039 52	7,168 40
Point foundation to public schools.........	11,371 15	3,174 82	910 86	11,000 00
Adult education and recreation...........	453 73	176 35	49 76	630 08
Demolishing old police station............	2,605 07	1,452 92	477 23	3,167 67
Subsistence gardens.....................	1,858 10	1,125 12	308 13	2,983 22
Maintenance public buildings............	1,526 40	896 61	245 62	2,423 01
Alteration and addition, Miller school......	9,786 74	10,307 81	2,902 29	16,000 00
Painting interior police station...........	1,036 44	923 97	241 13	1,500 00
Janitors — public welfare................	2,076 84	1,211 84	360 35	3,288 68
Safety campaign........................	607 20	33 53	14 14	640 73
Storm sewer in Tilden avenue............	11,161 35	9,274 54	3,703 54	15,723 05
Storm sewer in Higby road...............	1,077 77	808 47	242 17	1,210 39
Repainting air-markings.................	523 62	34 00	13 47	441 44
Surplus food and milk distribution........	5,263 74	2,988 19	821 33	8,251 93
Installation new floors U. F. A. Brandegee..	1,522 95	2,661 04	679 95	3,793 69
Sanitary sewer — Blandina street.........	7,831 29	4,178 70	1,541 74	7,182 05
Sanitary sewer — Lenox avenue..........	7,766 81	3,142 90	1,136 83	6,795 00
Clerks, assistants, NRA Code Authority.....	230 10	22 71	15 36	252 81
Canning project........................	180 39	590 69	151 30	771 08
Janitor service, N. Y. S. E. S............	253 50	26 00	17 92	279 50
Widen Sunset and Shepherd place.........	927 46	976 68	315 13	1,667 95
Repaving North Genesee street...........	27,044 92	29,854 39	24,317 08	32,500 00
Storm sewer in Tilden lane..............	977 24	659 32	175 45	1,000 00
Storm sewer — Lorraine avenue..........	1,001 98	1,455 36	489 96	2,066 75
Sanitary sewer — Elizabeth street........	1,548 93	865 00	267 03	1,500 00
Visiting housekeepers...................	594 08	89 58	28 55	684 26
Federal housing campaign...............	2,731 68	150 88	63 66	2,882 56
Clerk, assistant to N. Y. S. E. S.........	334 95	33 50	22 80	368 45
Orthopedic work.......................	251 77	13 90	5 86	265 69
School safety patrol....................	4,732 16	324 84	126 73	5,057 00
Traffic survey.........................	3,084 62	193 10	89 63	3,277 72
Storm sewer in Keok place..............	1,227 58	795 11	461 63	1,200 00
Barge Canal warehouse.................	2,719 75	1,294 50	1,035 85	3,400 00

TABLE IV—Concluded

STATE PROJECTS	Work relief wages paid	Cost above relief wages (materials and equipment and non-relief supervisory and administrative costs)	Net cost to city above relief (Deducting State and Federal reimbursement for non-relief costs)	Value or contract price
Nurses — Utica State Hospital...............	....	$104 67	$2 31	$104 67
Department Taxation and Finance.........	$1,672 58	1,185 39	63 39	2,857 97
Division of Parole.......................	933 83	687 81	35 86	1,621 64
A. B. C. Board..........................	655 62	498 98	25 51	1,154 60
Visiting nurses..........................	2,249 13	1,504 36	82 88	3,753 49
Adult education and recreation.............	19,789 35	12,546 32	714 16	32,335 67
State traffic census......................	1,029 77	652 86	37 16	1,682 63
Total — State projects................	$26,330 28	$17,180 39	$961 01	$43,510 67
GRAND TOTAL — local and State projects.	$431,361 58	$295,193 04	$108,046 07	$528,440 60

ADMINISTRATIVE PROJECTS*

Works Division administration.............	$5,457 96	$31,062 51	$12,701 37	$36,520 47

** Note.— The above figures, prepared by the Utica Work Bureau, include estimates, final records being unavailable until all credit abstracts and claims have been audited.

*Administrative project shown separately because most of these costs are included in the other projects under " Cost above relief."

TABLE V
WORK RELIEF IN NEW YORK STATE—WEEK ENDING MARCH 21, 1935
NUMBER OF NON-ADMINISTRATIVE PROJECTS, PERSONS WORKING, MAN-HOURS, AND EARNINGS BY TYPE OF PROJECT

Relief Personnel

		Number of projects covered	Number of Persons Working			Man-hours worked	Earnings
			Total—all persons	Male	Female		
PLANNING PROJECTS............	A	99	3,249	2,810	439	100,002	$72,153 84
PROJECTS ON PUBLIC PROPERTY							
Roads, streets, bridges, etc.							
New construction of streets, highways, etc....	B 1 (a)	304	11,460	11,459	1	263,990	116,559 91
Repair and maintenance of streets, highways, etc....	B 2 (b)	238	11,759	11,758	1	302,261	159,529 61
New construction of bridges, grade crossings, etc....	B 5 (e)	7	134	134	....	2,919	1,330 95
Repair and maintenance of bridges, etc....	B 6 (f)	10	526	526	....	12,862	10,819 17
Total........		559	23,879	23,877	2	582,032	288,239 64
Public building							
New construction of public buildings....	B 3 (c)	74	3,016	3,016	....	53,965	38,266 37
Repair and maintenance of public buildings....	B 4 (d)	493	12,301	12,158	143	304,428	246,459 03
Total........		567	15,317	15,174	143	358,393	284,725 40
Sewers, drainage and public utilities							
New construction of sewers, and sanitation....	B 7 (g)	168	13,380	13,380	....	339,092	180,413 97
Repair and maintenance of sewers, and sanitation....	B 8 (h)	19	348	348	....	8,441	3,857 00
New construction of public utilities....	B 9 (j)	93	4,478	4,477	1	107,402	53,929 70
Repair and maintenance of public utilities....	B10 (k)	33	5,754	5,754	....	158,962	84,281 71
Total........		313	23,960	23,959	1	613,897	322,482 38
Recreational facilities, conservation, etc.							
New construction of recreational facilities....	B11 (m)	34	1,909	1,909	....	49,227	27,377 24
Repair and maintenance of recreational facilities....	B12 (n)	18	802	802	....	19,066	10,210 65
Conservation of fish and game....	B16 (s)	3	53	53	....	1,184	446 44
Total........		55	2,764	2,764	....	69,477	38,034 33

Waterway and flood control						
New construction of waterways, levees, etc........B13 (p)	14	475	475		10,853	4,986 18
Repair and maintenance of waterways, levees, etc....B14 (q)	23	1,612	1,612		34,614	15,908 21
Total.........	37	2,087	2,087		45,467	20,894 39
Landscaping, parks and airports						
Landscaping, grading, erosion control, etc........B15 (r)	135	26,106	25,877	229	746,288	465,216 22
Eradication and control of pests and disease bearers						
Eradication and control of disease bearers........B17 (t)						
Eradication and control of pests........B18 (u)	3	316	315	1	7,226	3,726 11
Eradication and control of poisonous plants......B19 (v)						
Total.........	3	316	315	1	7,226	3,726 11
All other public projects						
Other........B20 (z)	8	211	211		4,734	2,996 65
Total projects on public property........	1,677	94,640	94,264	376	2,427,514	1,426,315 12
PROJECTS TO PROVIDE HOUSING						
*Remodeling and repair of houses in lieu of rent......*C 1 (e)	1	65	63	2	2,504	2,553 30
Resettlement housing for resettled families........C 2 (b)						
Resettlement housing for subsistence homesteads....C 3 (c)	1	1	1		30	19 23
Demolition of houses........C 4 (d)	2	760	750	10	26,172	17,545 28
Other........C 5 (z)	6	245	188	57	4,736	3,493 75
Total.........	10	1,071	1,002	69	33,442	23,611 56
PRODUCTION AND DISTRIBUTION OF GOODS NEEDED BY THE UNEMPLOYED						
Clothing — sewing of garments, etc........D 1 (a)	124	3,036	518	2,518	69,165	31,121 10
Food — canning and preserving, etc........D 2 (b)	90	1,973	1,773	200	55,899	31,471 97
Fuel — cutting wood, digging peat, etc........D 3 (c)	35	4,286	4,262	24	117,193	61,020 80
Garden products........D 4 (d)	6	14	6	8	532	286 50
Household goods........D 5 (e)	10	292	101	191	7,752	3,812 19
Construction materials........D 6 (f)						
Other........D 7 (z)	1	14	14		202	83 80
Total.........	266	9,615	6,674	2,941	250,743	127,796 36

* Repair and remodeling of municipally owned tenement houses, New York City only.

WORK RELIEF IN NEW YORK STATE—WEEK ENDING MARCH 21, 1935—Concluded
Relief Personnel

	Number of projects covered	Number of Persons Working			Man-hours worked	Earnings
		Total—all persons	Male	Female		
PUBLIC WELFARE						
Nursing .... E 1 (a)	24	1,514	424	1,090	41,761	$27,884 93
Nutritional .... E 2 (b)	9	1,367	214	1,153	38,530	16,360 61
Other public health campaigns ... E 3 (c)	9	92	27	65	2,600	1,808 45
Public recreation, instruction, etc. E 4 (d)	28	1,909	1,220	689	55,716	40,343 10
Safety campaigns and traffic controls E 5 (e)	11	433	391	42	10,177	5,671 55
Other .... E 6 (z)	6	295	49	246	8,904	4,368 75
Total	87	5,610	2,325	3,285	157,688	96,437 39
PUBLIC EDUCATION, ARTS AND RESEARCH						
Education .... F 1 (a)	21	3,912	1,635	2,277	97,767	79,286 21
Research and special surveys .... F 2 (b)	218	5,169	4,037	1,132	150,328	103,233 36
Public works for art .... F 3 (c)	10	419	317	102	11,821	9,344 88
Records and clerical work .... F 4 (d)	326	8,063	5,374	2,689	244,451	139,087 79
Music .... F 5 (e)	8	1,220	909	311	32,900	27,515 80
Dramatic activities .... F 6 (f)	4	917	606	311	27,200	21,616 30
Library and museum .... F 7 (g)	45	1,321	491	830	39,520	25,170 78
Other .... F 8 (z)						
Total	632	21,021	13,369	7,652	603,987	405,255 12
TOOL AND SUNDRY EQUIPMENT PROJECTS ...... H	47	535	535	....	13,169	8,954 45
Grand total — All fields of activity	2,818	135,741	120,979	14,762	3,586,545	$2,160,523 84

TABLE VI
WORK RELIEF IN NEW YORK STATE—WEEK ENDING MARCH 21, 1935
NUMBER OF NON-ADMINISTRATIVE PROJECTS, PERSONS WORKING, MAN-HOURS, AND EARNINGS BY TYPE OF PROJECT

Non-Relief Personnel

A	Number of projects covered	Number of Persons Working			Man-hours worked	Earnings
		Total—all persons	Male	Female		
PLANNING PROJECTS......A	99	694	682	12	22,830	$22,090 55
PROJECTS ON PUBLIC PROPERTY						
Roads, streets, bridges, etc.						
New construction of streets, highways, etc. ......B 1 (a)	304	90	90	......	3,371	2,252 36
Repair and maintenance of streets, highways, etc. ......B 2 (b)	238	69	69	......	2,462	1,794 74
New construction of bridges, grade crossings, etc. ......B 5 (e)	7	4	4	......	118	110 00
Repair and maintenance of bridges, etc. ......B 6 (f)	10	1	1	......	20	12 00
Total......	559	164	164	......	5,971	4,169 10
Public buildings						
New construction of public buildings......B 3 (c)	74	52	52	......	2,016	1,849 90
Repair and maintenance of public buildings......B 4 (d)	493	132	132	......	4,550	4,032 45
Total......	567	184	184	......	6,566	5,882 35
Sewers, drainage and public utilities						
New construction of sewers, and sanitation......B 7 (g)	168	81	81	......	2,949	2,408 30
Repair and maintenance of sewers, and sanitation......B 8 (h)	19	3	3	......	105	87 60
New construction of public utilities......B 9 (j)	93	54	54	......	2,047	1,617 70
Repair and maintenance of public utilities......B10 (k)	33	25	25	......	1,022	756 95
Total......	313	163	163	......	6,123	4,870 55
Recreational facilities, conservation, etc.						
New construction of recreational facilities......B11 (m)	34	20	20	......	761	564 20
Repair and maintenance of recreational facilities......B12 (n)	18	2	2	......	78	59 00
Conservation of fish and game......B16 (s)	3	2	2	......	45	36 50
Total......	55	24	24	......	884	659 70

WORK RELIEF IN NEW YORK STATE—WEEK ENDING MARCH 21, 1935—Concluded
Non-Relief Personnel

	Number of projects covered	Number of Persons Working			Man-hours worked	Earnings
		Total—all persons	Male	Female		
PROJECTS ON PUBLIC PROPERTY—*(Continued)*						
Waterway and flood control						
New construction of waterways, levees, etc....B13 (p)	14	7	7	....	163	$94 80
Repair and maintenance of waterways, levees, etc....B14 (q)	23	9	9	....	354	285 10
Total....	37	16	16	....	517	379 90
Landscaping, parks and airports						
Landscaping, grading, erosion control, etc....B15 (r)	135	1,996	1,966	30	60,984	68,098 13
Eradication and control of pests and disease bearers						
Eradication and control of disease bearers....B17 (t)	....	....	....	....	....	....
Eradication and control of pests....B18 (u)	3	8	8	....	312	297 50
Eradication and control of poisonous plants....B19 (v)	....	....	....	....	....	....
Total....	3	8	8	....	312	297 50
All other public projects						
Other....B20 (x)	8	9	9	....	351	245 00
Total projects on public property....	1,677	2,564	2,534	30	81,708	84,602 23
PROJECTS TO PROVIDE HOUSING						
*Remodeling and repair of houses in lieu of rent....*C 1 (e)	1	17	17	....	510	569 00
Resettlement housing for resettled families....C 2 (b)	....	....	....	....	....	....
Resettlement housing for subsistence homesteads....C 3 (c)	1	....	....	....	....	....
Demolition of houses....C 4 (d)	2	38	37	1	1,185	1,190 00
Other....C 5 (x)	6	2	2	....	87	66 00
Total....	10	57	56	1	1,782	1,825 00

PRODUCTION AND DISTRIBUTION OF GOODS NEEDED BY THE UNEMPLOYED

D 1 (a) Clothing — sewing of garments, etc.	124	58	10	48	1,879	1,167 48
D 2 (b) Food — canning and preserving, etc.	90	1,001	942	59	30,092	20,964 26
D 3 (c) Fuel — cutting wood, digging peat, etc.	35	32	32		970	1,003 30
D 4 (d) Garden products	6	8	8		294	245 00
D 5 (e) Household goods	10	2	2		69	58 00
D 6 (f) Construction materials						
D 7 (z) Other	1					
Total	266	1,101	994	107	33,304	23,438 04

PUBLIC WELFARE

E 1 (a) Nursing	24	54	18	36	1,389	1,326 56
E 2 (b) Nutritional	9	279	157	122	8,269	5,747 05
E 3 (c) Other public health campaigns	9	2		2	69	55 25
E 4 (d) Public recreation, instruction, etc.	28	79	60	19	2,433	2,354 00
E 5 (e) Safety campaigns and traffic controls	11	2	2		69	66 00
E 6 (z) Other	6	5	3	2	177	151 00
Total	87	421	240	181	12,406	9,699 86

PUBLIC EDUCATION, ARTS AND RESEARCH

F 1 (a) Education	21	166	72	94	4,617	4,482 76
F 2 (b) Research and special surveys	218	289	238	51	9,676	8,594 04
F 3 (c) Public works for art	10	16	12	4	516	531 00
F 4 (d) Records and clerical work	326	1,357	760	597	50,333	31,795 28
F 5 (e) Music	8	33	23	10	1,047	942 00
F 6 (f) Dramatic activities	4	16	9	7	510	510 50
F 7 (g) Library and museum	45	15	13	2	529	431 00
F 8 (z) Other						
Total	632	1,892	1,127	765	67,228	47,286 58

TOOL AND SUNDRY EQUIPMENT PROJECTS H	47	20	20		786	604 96
Grand total — all fields of activity	2,818	6,749	5,653	1,096	220,044	$189,547 22

* Repair and remodeling municipally owned tenement houses, New York City only

J. B. LYON COMPANY, PRINTERS, ALBANY, N. Y.

PUBLIC UNEMPLOYMENT RELIEF IN NEW YORK STATE — FOURTH YEAR

SEPTEMBER 1, 1934 — AUGUST 31, 1935

TEMPORARY EMERGENCY RELIEF ADMINISTRATION
STATE OFFICE BUILDING, ALBANY, N. Y.
NEW YORK OFFICE, 79 MADISON AVENUE

October 15, 1935

MEMBERS

ALFRED H. SCHOELLKOPF OF BUFFALO, Chairman
ROBERT J. CUDDIHY OF NEW YORK
FREDERICK I. DANIELS OF NEW YORK
SOLOMON LOWENSTEIN OF NEW YORK
VICTOR F. RIDDER OF NEW YORK
JOSEPH P. RYAN OF NEW YORK

DAVID C. ADIE of Albany, ex officio
    State Commissioner of Social Welfare

FREDERICK I. DANIELS, Executive Director
HENRY EPSTEIN, Solicitor General, Counsel

PUBLIC UNEMPLOYMENT RELIEF IN NEW YORK STATE—FOURTH YEAR

TABLE OF CONTENTS

PUBLIC UNEMPLOYMENT RELIEF IN
NEW YORK STATE—FOURTH YEAR

*To His Excellency, Herbert H. Lehman, Governor, and to the
Honorable Members of the Senate and the Assembly of the
State of New York:*

With the development of the Federal Works Program that is to
utilize the capabilities of large numbers of those on relief by giving
them employment, the Federal Government has announced its intention of withdrawing its support of direct relief to those that
remain, leaving them to the care of the state and local governments.
Thus it is of the utmost urgency, in the present period of transition
to the new program, that the State of New York determine with
such precision as may be, the extent of the need the State and its
localities must expect to meet when the Federal program has reached
its maximum.

Accordingly, following instructions in Section 21 of Chapter 798
of the Laws of 1931, directing the Temporary Emergency Relief
Administration of New York State "to report to the Governor and
the Legislature from time to time in such detail as may be required,
the operations of the Administration together with the condition of
unemployment and the relief afforded unemployed persons in the
State," there is submitted herewith an analysis of the probable relief
needs in the coming year, together with a review of State aid in
public unemployment relief from September 1, 1934 to August 31,
1935.

The attached report presents as simply as possible an accounting
of the Administration's stewardship during the past twelve months
in the State's great effort to conserve the human resources upon
which her well-being and wealth are based.

From the estimate of the residual relief load to be anticipated in
the coming months, you will see that on the basis of past experience, in the absence of a decided upturn in private employment, the
burden upon the State and her localities for unemployment relief
may be expected to remain as great as in the past year—if not
greater—even after the Federal program has reached its announced
objective. State aid to the localities in meeting this burden remains
as vital as in the past.

[3]

By Chapter 505 of the Laws of 1935, the Legislature authorized submission to the people at the coming November election of a $55,000,000 relief bond issue, of which not more than $20,000,000 may be appropriated for needed public works. This bond issue was agreed upon by the Governor and the Legislative leaders of both parties as the only practicable way at this time of continuing the State's contribution to the relief costs of the localities, which now, after the years of the depression, are less able than ever to bear the burden alone.

ALFRED H. SCHOELLKOPF, *Chairman*
ROBERT J. CUDDIHY
FREDERICK .I. DANIELS
SOLOMON LOWENSTEIN
VICTOR F. RIDDER
JOSEPH P. RYAN

THE NEED OF STATE AID

Initiation of State Aid

In 1931 the State of New York came to the assistance of its localities in their relief of the unemployed, appropriating State funds and creating the Temporary Emergency Relief Administration to administer them. Public-spirited citizens who had attempted to meet the growing need by private subscription had found the burden too great. They were among the foremost in urging that the State meet its share of responsibility in the prevention of suffering. Previous reports have related the continued and unpredictable growth in the need of the unemployed as the depression went on, detailed the relief given from November 1, 1931, when the Temporary Emergency Relief Administration was organized under the Wicks Act, through August 31, 1934,* and analyzed administrative services and costs.** Subsequent sections of the present report give an accounting of the relief afforded in the year from September 1, 1934 to August 31, 1935, and of the State and Federal funds disbursed to the localities through the State Temporary Emergency Relief Administration, which have thus lightened the burden of local taxation whose chief source of revenue is real estate. Without State and Federal aid the localities could not have maintained relief of any adequacy in this fourth year of the emergency.

There will be few to question the need of State aid in the past year, or the wisdom of the Legislature which in 1931 declared the existence of an emergency in which "the public health and safety of the State and of each county, city and town therein was imperilled by the existing and threatened deprivation of a considerable number of their inhabitants of the necessaries of life," and found State assistance "vitally necessary to supplement the relief work accomplished or to be accomplished locally and to encourage and stimulate local effort in the same direction.

The extent to which such aid will be needed in the year to come, when the Federal Government has taken over and expanded the work

---

* Cf. Three Years of Public Unemployment Relief in New York State: The Need and How It Has Been Met: 1931-1934 (October 15, 1934).
** Cf. Administration of Public Unemployment Relief in New York State: Its Scope, Accomplishments and Cost: April 1, 1934—March 31, 1935.

relief program and left to the State and its localities the entire responsibility for direct relief to those not included in this Federal plan is discussed in the following sections.

The Changing Relief Population

Throughout the whole emergency period there has been a steadily changing population in need of public unemployment relief. Thousands have received relief for longer or shorter periods and then once more stepped forth to self-support, contributing directly and indirectly as taxpayers to provide for the new thousands who, their resources exhausted and unable to find work, were forced to seek public aid. So great has the turnover been that nearly 10 per cent more families and non-family persons are cared for in the course of a month than the daily average on relief during the month. Thus, though the number of families and unattached people on relief as of September 1, 1934, was approximately 468,000, the number cared for in the course of the month was approximately 508,000, while enough of these became able to support themselves before the month was over so that as of September 30, 1934 the number was approximately 483,000.

Over long periods the cumulative magnitude of this turnover has been of the greatest significance. It means that, for the most part, we do not have a great body of our population resigned to continuance on relief, but that the majority are still struggling to make their way in the economic world and are in need only of temporary or intermittent assistance.

In the eleven-month period from September 1, 1934, when these 468,000 families and non-family persons were on relief, to July 31, 1935,* there were 412,642 additions to the rolls where people had become destitute and 367,764 closings on the books where people became able to support themselves once more, at least temporarily, and no longer needed relief. In many instances the same people were forced onto relief and found their way to self-support more than once during the period, but to a large extent these figures represent a real change in that part of the population supported by public unemployment relief.

---

* Omitting August, 1935, from the calculation because transfers to the Federal Works Progress Administration began in that month. All figures given in this report, except those directly concerning the Administration itself, are as reported by the local welfare districts.

Of the 412,642 additions to the rolls in the eleven-month period, 204,968, or nearly half, had never before had public assistance during this depression, and now for the first time found themselves at the end of their resources and in need of relief.

To some serious students of the problem it has appeared puzzling that so many who were able to weather the years of worst unemployment and the lowest ebb of business should now be seeking relief for the first time. It is to be remembered that there is a human ebb and flow off and onto the payrolls of private employment, just as there is in the population on relief. Even in a time of rising private employment, healthy businesses are expanding in some fields and contracting in others, whole enterprises are still failing while others are surging forward. The man who in this constant flux of employment loses his place in the economic world today may find himself more quickly at the end of his resources—after years of irregular or reduced earnings—than if the blow had struck in 1930 or 1931, following closely upon more prosperous years.

Of the remaining 207,674 instances recorded in the eleven months where people who had previously been on relief, had left to support themselves for a time and now once again had to be placed on the rolls, no absolute data are available as to the number of different people actually involved. On the basis of figures gathered for part of the period, however, it is conservative to estimate that, with the approximately 468,000 families and non-family persons on relief at the beginning of the period, at least 800,000 different families and non-family persons received relief in the course of the year ended August 31, 1935, though the largest number at any one time was approximately 562,000 in the peak reached at the end of the month of February.

The mere figures seem tremendous. They are. But they do not mean that this number of people rely entirely upon public support to live. Heavy as the burden of aid to the needy unemployed has been, it would have been crushing if it had involved total support. For the largest number of those aided, public unemployment relief in New York State is on a partial assistance or supplementary basis.

Scores of thousands monthly who still are unable to push earnings to the point where public aid is no longer needed, struggle on with irregular and insecure employment for the breadwinner and whatever jobs come for juniors of the family group, failing by greater or lesser margins to get their hoped-for foothold once more on the road to security.

Relief Trends—1934-1935

From the beginning of the emergency through the Spring of 1935, cumulative exhaustion of resources of those who were or became unemployed forced larger and larger numbers of our citizens to seek public support. In the past year, however, the curve of the relief load had been flattening and on May 1, last, the Temporary Emergency Relief Administration was able to report that, although "more men and women and children were supported by public unemployment relief in February and March than at any previous time, the rate of increase had been lessening, giving hope that the end of the increase in need might be in sight."

This hope that a limit had been reached in totals of those needing relief—if private employment maintained current levels—appears confirmed by the experience of subsequent months. For the first time in the four winters of the emergency, the number of persons on relief during the month of March did not increase over the February total.

As time has gone on, smaller families among the unemployed, more mobile and able longer to keep off relief by eking out their own support, have at last found their resources at an end and have been forced to rely upon public aid. In the same way more and more unattached persons have found themselves unable longer to continue without relief. Of the total increase in families and non-family persons from 498,835 receiving public assistance during July, 1934, to 549,882 during July, 1935, the increase in families was only 3,554, from 435,552, to 439,106, while the number of unattached persons increased 47,493, from 63,283 to 110,776. The total number of individuals aided by public unemployment relief in July, 1935 was actually no larger than in July 1934: slightly under 2,000,000.

For the first time since the beginning of the emergency, the summer of 1935 saw no more people on relief in New York State than in the corresponding months of the previous year.

Relief During the Federal Works Program

The problem of relief remains tremendous, and will continue to be a heavy public burden through a lengthy period of readjustment even if private employment should mount once more in step with increasing production.

The Federal Government has set approximately 396,000 as the number to be taken from New York State relief rolls by its employment program.

At the peak last winter, 594,748 families and non-family persons were on relief during the month of February. Obviously, if at that time 396,000 had been given jobs, as the Federal Government now proposes, there would have remained in New York State approximately 200,000 families and non-family persons on direct relief.

Even if the trends indicated above are borne out in experience, however, and the spring peak of relief need is no higher in 1936 than it was in 1935, this figure of 200,000 is very conservative.

Since the group of the unemployed left to home relief will include those actually unemployable, the closing of cases will be proportionately fewer, while openings may continue as at the present.

This means that direct relief will be necessary this winter to aid from 700,000 to 1,000,000 individuals monthly. In addition, supplementary relief will have to be given in those cases where Federal security wages under the Works Progress Administration fail seriously to meet family budgetary needs. With the Federal Government not yet on record as to its policy in regard to this part of the cost of caring for employable persons on Works Progress Administration jobs, the extent of necessary relief expenditures by the State of New York and its localities in the months to come cannot be calculated definitely.

In recent months the State and its localities have contributed approximately $11,500,000 monthly as their share of the total cost of relief. It is difficult to see, in view of the Federal Government's contemplated withdrawal from direct relief, how the total home relief cost, to be paid entirely by State and local contributions can be any lighter than this $11,500,000 monthly contribution that State and localities have been making.

The State's share of current relief costs is being met from a bond issue of $40,000,000 approved by the electorate last November, together with an appropriation of $10,000,000 from general funds. These State funds have been budgeted to last until the Legislature will have had a chance to act at the coming session in 1936.

To provide for the continuance of State aid to the localities in the coming year, the Legislature has authorized submission to the electorate at the coming general election of a $55,000,000 bond issue, of which $35,000,000 is to be for relief until February 15, 1937, and not more than $20,000,000 for public works, such as needed construction and improvement of State hospitals and prisons. This reduction in the amount asked for relief purposes, like the $20,000,000 reduction in the 1934 relief bond issue over that of the previous year, "did not reflect any reliance upon a reduction in the anticipated need in the next year but followed the policy enunciated by the Honorable Herbert H. Lehman, Governor, in his special message, after consultation and agreement with the Legislative leaders, advising that the State should not 'continue indefinitely to pay for its relief out of the proceeds of bond issues' but that 'gradually the amount obtained from bond monies should be reduced until within a reasonable time the entire cost of unemployment relief will be borne from current revenues.' "*

---

* Three Years of Public Unemployment Relief in New York State—page 7.

RELIEF GIVEN

SEPTEMBER 1, 1934 — AUGUST 31, 1935

Total Relief Costs of $352,620,000

In the twelve months from September 1, 1934 to August 31, 1935, total home relief* and work relief wages given to aid a monthly average of some 2,000,000 individuals in New York State was $271,356,942 from local, State and Federal funds. Among the individuals aided was a monthly average of approximately 825,000 children, nearly one-quarter of all the children in the State.

Of this relief given in the period, $152,441,220* was in home relief, while $118,915,722 was in work relief wages. Home relief aided a monthly average of 397,340 families and unattached persons; work relief, 189,444 families and unattached persons; while a monthly average of 19,252 local homeless was cared for throughout the State. Eliminating duplication of families who received relief partly in the form of work relief wages and partly in the form of home relief, a monthly average of 549,307 families and unattached persons was aided altogether. The accompanying chart, page 12, shows monthly totals of home relief and work relief wages given since 1931.

Supplementary relief programs, work relief materials and supervisory expense, as shown in Table I, page 13, brought the total cost of the relief operation in the twelve months to $352,620,419.

Home relief is the provision in the domicile of necessary food, shelter, light, heat, clothing, medicine and medical attendance and household supplies, or the cash equivalent. Work relief has been in the form of cash wages.

---

* Including care of local homeless; see Table I, page 13.

12

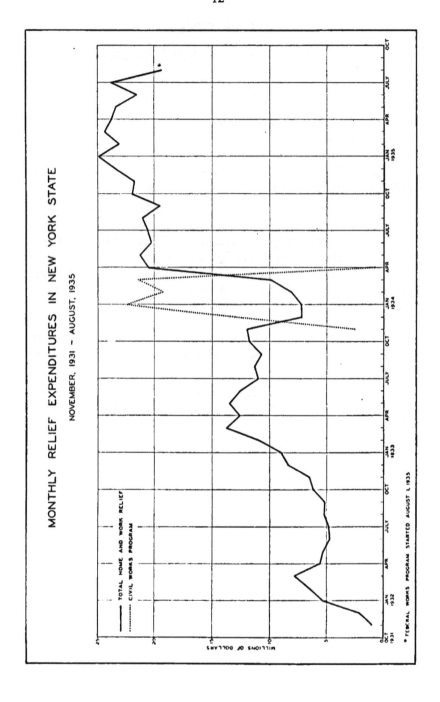

MONTHLY RELIEF EXPENDITURES IN NEW YORK STATE

NOVEMBER, 1931 – AUGUST, 1935

13

MUNICIPAL, STATE AND FEDERAL OBLIGATIONS INCURRED FOR UNEMPLOYMENT RELIEF PURPOSES
NEW YORK STATE: SEPTEMBER 1, 1934 — AUGUST 31, 1935

Policies Controllable by TERA

Home Relief (a)	$151,052,143
Care of Local Homeless	1,305,949
School Lunches	969,234
Free Milk	1,686,287
Death and Disability Benefits (b)	83,128
Rural Rehabilitation (loans)	78,654
Special Flood Relief (c)	103,899
Work Relief Wages	118,915,722*
Materials for Work Projects	28,461,711
Salaries of Workers on Continuous, Non-Relief Basis, in Supervisory and Administrative Work (d)	35,489,147
Miscellaneous Reimbursable Expense	93,050
State Departments—Materials for Work Projects	1,669,172
Central State Administration	2,319,252
Total	$342,227,348
Preparation and sale of Relief Bonds	51,974
Governor's Commission on Unemployment Relief	51,370
	$342,330,692

Federal Programs in which the TERA acted only as Federal Agent

Transient Program—Federal and State:	
Relief in Bureaus and Camps	4,429,475
Administrative Expense	425,842
National Re-employment Service	775,159
College Students' Aid	1,249,565
Cabbage Program	122,100
Cattle Program	2,468,533
Cotton Program	20,901
Potato Program	95,181
Other	702,971
Total	$ 10,289,727
Grand Total	$352,620,419

(a) In addition to this amount the welfare districts reported expenditures of $454,525 classified as non-reimbursable.

(b) Includes compensation awards for death or permanent disability of workmen on relief payrolls injured on work projects.

(c) Funds for this purpose were made available by the Rural Rehabilitation Corporation. They are being expended for families needing relief in flood disaster areas.

(d) Included in these amounts are expenditures of $11,400 for students' fellowships for social workers in training. In addition the welfare districts reported non-reimbursable expenditures of $358,600 for salaries, $4,399,973 for other administrative costs.

(e) Work Relief wages resulting from these projects are included above.

* Includes in August, 1935, $1,847,760 in wages on New York City projects administered under the Federal WPA but not yet officially accepted by it. The TERA reimbursed 100% on these projects to insure continuity of the program during the period of transition.

A study made last December of the adequacy of relief among 2,172 families on relief throughout the month, picked at random from nine up-State welfare districts, showed that 10 per cent received monthly assistance of less than $20; 10 per cent, assistance of between $20 and $30; 19 per cent, between $30 and $40; 23 per cent, between $40 and $50; 18 per cent, between $50 and $60; 8 per cent, between $60 and $70; 4 per cent, between $70 and $80; 3 per cent, between $80 and 90, and 5 per cent, more than $90.

In the month of August, 1935, the dollar given in home relief was budgeted: food, 59.7 cents; shelter 30.1 cents; fuel and light, 4.4 cents; medical service, 2.6 cents; miscellaneous necessities, 3.2 cents.

Medical care to those on relief, under the terms of the Wicks Act itself, by which the State of New York recognized such aid as among the necessities of life on a par with food, clothing and shelter, has been of such importance as to warrant special mention. Of the total home relief expenditures in the twelve-month period, $3,166,213 were for this type of aid, in addition to the care given through all previously established medical services.

Since the Administration from the inception of the program urged that such medical care under relief should supplement rather than supplant existing facilities, a large part of this money from local, State and Federal relief funds went to provide medical services to the needy in rural areas to an extent that they never had them before. This means, not that the rural communities received more than their share of relief monies, but that, lacking extensive public medical facilities, they spent a larger portion of the money to provide needed medical care, while in New York City, for instance, where the hospital and out-patient facilities were numerous, such money went for food and shelter.

Thus of the total, $1,065,423, or an average of 38 cents a month per home relief family, was spent by New York City from relief funds to provide this additional medical aid, while $2,100,481, or $1.08 monthly per home relief family was spent up-State. About $1,400,000, or nearly half of the money spent for this additional medical care of those on relief outside of New York City was spent in the non-urban areas of the counties, which had about one-sixth of the relief load. This made an average of $1.76 a month per home relief family in the counties.

Work relief families have provided their own medical care, or, if unable to do this, have been cared for on a supplementary basis under home relief.

In addition, the State-wide nursing service, operating in about 108 of the welfare districts, and furnishing work relief wages to an average of 650 formerly unemployed nurses at an expenditure of nearly $50,000 a month, has provided care never before available to the needy in rural and semi-rural districts. Thus the program provides double relief—giving employment to needy nurses as well as giving bedside and health care to the unemployed who need it. These relief nurses in a year made approximately 750,000 visits at an average cost of less than 75 cents a visit.

$260,000,000 In Aid To Local Communities

The Wicks Act made no change in the traditional policy of the State of New York that responsibility for the care of the needy rests with the local governments.* Under it local agencies have carried on the function of relief from the first interview to the investigation of the genuineness and extent of the need, and continued the job of actually giving needed aid. The local governments have appropriated and scrutinized all the money spent locally for relief though the Temporary Emergency Relief Administration in the year covered by this report has reimbursed them from State and Federal funds by 75 per cent of these approved expenditures.

Despite the large portion of State and Federal funds, the cities and counties have not shirked their responsibility. They have made a noteworthy record in continuing to carry their heavy share of the relief burden. In the year under discussion their relief expenditures have been greater than in any previous twelve months. Especially are they deserving of praise for their cooperation with the Administration in its efforts to raise relief standards, assure efficient and economical use of public funds and give relief with fairness and impartiality, without discrimination on grounds of non-citizenship, political adherence, religion, race or color.

From September 1, 1934 to August 31, 1935 the Temporary Emergency Relief Administration reimbursed the local welfare districts by $252,025,238** for their relief expenditures, with estimated

---

* Except that in New York City the Wicks Act set aside a charter provision forbidding the granting of home relief.
** For details by districts, see Table IV, page 36.

commitments of $35,655,295 outstanding at the close of the period, $7,924,799 more than were outstanding at the beginning of the period. Adding disbursements and this excess of commitments, total disbursements and commitments by the Temporary Emergency Relief Administration chargeable to the period were $259,950,037, lightening the burden of relief on local resources, dependent chiefly upon taxes on real estate.

Total expenditures and commitments of the Administration applying to the same period for all purposes including transient relief and other special Federal programs and its own administrative expense, were $275,984,562. Of this amount, its own central administrative expense was $2,319,252, which with a central administrative expense of $185,662 for transient and other special Federal programs, makes a total central administrative expense of $2,504,914, or less than one per cent of the total. "This has included the salaries of a trained social work staff to help relief bureaus organize and establish policies; of engineers to cooperate in planning valuable work projects suitable for local needs; of advisors on medical services, nutrition and garden activities for the unemployed; and of an auditing staff employed to insure sound business and accounting methods in the local relief bureaus to which the State contributes funds."*

In furtherance of the effort of the Administration to keep administrative costs as low as possible consistent with ultimate economy, its own central administrative staff contracted 26 per cent from July 1, 1935, when the Federal Works Progress Administration began organizing to take over and expand the work relief program, to August 31, the close of the period of this report. On July 1, the Administration supervised the giving of relief with a central administrative and field staff of 922 persons. By August 31, with the Works Progress Administration operating all work relief in New York City but only beginning to take over the program up-State, this staff had contracted to 681 persons.

Special Federal programs over which the TERA had no control in policy, including the Transient and Surplus commodities programs, employed through the TERA 229 persons in administrative functions as of July 1, and 256 as of September 1, the increase having been in the Transient Division, owing to the large-scale work

---

* Three Years of Public Unemployment Relief in New York State—1931-1934—page 12.

projects for transients set up in the emergency to aid the flood-stricken sections of south-central New York State.*

Work Relief

From November, 1931 to the current taking over of the program by the Federal Works Progress Administration, work relief in New York State has evolved under local administration with continuous State-wide supervision. During the period of the Federal Civil Works Administration from November 20, 1933, to April 1, 1934, the State Temporary Emergency Relief Administration acted as the Federal Civil Works Administration for New York State and for the most part the local work bureaus continued on as the local Federal agencies, becoming work relief bureaus once more at the close of the program. From the beginning every effort was made to increase the value and permanence of the work done, involving a necessary increase in the cost of materials and supervision.

This trend was accelerated during the period of the Civil Works Administration, and without the continuing availability of Federal funds, the State of New York could not have carried on its work relief program at the levels maintained thereafter. An analysis of work relief payrolls in April, 1935, gives an idea of the relative importance of different types of projects:

Type of Project		Man Hours	Per Cent of Total Man Hours
Planning		347,329	1.9
Public Property, Construction and Improvement		10,211,317	55.6
Highways	2,144,925		11.6
Other	8,166,392		44.0
Providing Housing		66,376	0.3
Production and Distribution of Goods Needed by Unemployed		1,011,852	5.5
Public Welfare, Health and Recreation...		657,045	3.5
Public Education, Arts and Research......		2,686,150	14.5
Administrative		3,406,295	18.4
Tools and Equipment		51,902	0.3
TOTAL		18,538,266	100.0

* See section on flood relief, beginning page 24.

Work relief was primarily relief, undertaken to utilize the skills of the unemployed on relief. The basic consideration in planning work was to distribute employment, as far as possible, in proportion to the labor classifications represented on the relief rolls. As a means of helping local work bureaus to plan projects with this ever in mind, the Administration arranged that the National Reemployment Service supply it with periodic reports showing the classifications of relief labor available in welfare districts.

Second only in importance to these limits automatically imposed by the very nature of the program, the Administration emphasized the constructive value of work projects and unqualifiedly encouraged local planning efforts to that end. The extent to which the localities did cooperate is demonstrated by the fact that in sixty-six of the one hundred and one participating work bureaus, about two hundred planning and closely related projects were approved, of which forty-six were for the specific purpose of developing an integrated work relief program.

To further promote foresight and adherence to a well-rounded program in each welfare district, as well as for its own guidance, the Administration at intervals requested work bureaus to submit a complete inventory of approved and contemplated projects intended to operate during the succeeding months.

The local bureaus, besides enlisting the advice of local planning commissioners, where such existed, cooperated with other public officials, prospective sponsors of projects, and civic organizations in developing sound work relief projects. Moreover, in special and technical fields of activity, the Administration procured qualified experts who cooperated closely with the regular local public agencies. Thus, the Administration's Director of Medical Care, working with the State Department of Health, formulated and guided a State-wide public health and nursing program. The educational adviser collaborated with the Department of Education in developing educational and recreational work relief activity throughout the State. Similarly, garden and airport projects were planned by experts in agriculture and aeronautics respectively, while the Social Service Division shared in developing projects related to its field. In this way, through the resultant interchange of technical knowledge and merging of organizational facilities, the planning of work relief proceeded.

In spite of the temporary nature of some individual projects, the constructive accomplishments of work relief, for which funds could not have been found otherwise at this time, have been so vast and varied as to make description in small compass difficult. Following are descriptions of work continuing into or initiated in the period, April 1, 1934 to June 30, 1935.

The City of Buffalo's recently completed project for the Germania Street Storm Water Drain is outstanding not only from the point of view of social utility but as an engineering achievement. This project, begun in July, 1934, has transformed a wide area of swamp and semi-swamp land into potentially valuable industrial property, and has relieved from seasonal floods a densely settled area of small homes covering nearly 40 city blocks. Altogether, about 1,075 acres in South Buffalo are benefited. The section is one in which considerable future development is indicated.

The Germania Street project involved the laying of twin concrete drain pipes, tapering from 78-inch widths in the main sections of the line to 60-inch widths as they reached back into higher ground. The double lines extended a distance of two and one-third miles.

Most formidable among the many physical obstacles to construction was the prevailing high ground-water level. Soil conditions were everywhere extremely bad. On one section, designated as the Germania Outlet, steel sheet piling was necessary for the first 400 feet. In the face of such conditions the project, estimated at $908,819, was completed for $559,227, of which $267,043 was for labor. Excavation totalled 50,000 cubic yards, back-fill 20,000 cubic yards, brick paving 1,800 square yards, asphalt paving 150 square yards and concrete sidewalks 20,000 square feet.

Throughout the work a reasonable but determined discipline was maintained, and the work was carried through with miscellaneous relief labor at nearly the same level of efficiency that a private contractor could have secured with trained men. The Germania Street project provided about 470,000 man-hours of work for an average of 579 men.

In the fifteen months following the end of the Civil Works Administration work relief throughout the State resulted in construction of 1,790 miles of road, and improvement and repair of 2,304 miles, with 123 bridges built and 190 improved, 304,500 cubic yards of stone quarried for road work, and 32 miles of single car track removed. In all, 500 miles of sanitary and storm sewers were constructed, 270 miles of water mains laid, 108 reservoirs constructed and 23 sewage disposal plants and as many garbage disposal plants constructed, with improvement of 29 of such plants. Thirteen miles of underground telephone wire, and nearly 5,000 feet of underground electric cable and 2,000 feet of fire alarm ducts were installed.

The work relief program was a means of aiding many smaller localities in overcoming problems resulting from emergencies such as fires and floods, with the consequent property damage and disruption of the normal tenor of community life.

In December 1933, fire destroyed the old classroom part of the Lyndonville (Orleans County) High School, leaving the newer gymnasium section standing. The urgency to provide a suitable school building was obvious. Although the school district had almost reached the limit of its bonded indebtedness, a sum was raised sufficient to cover material costs. A work relief project was approved providing for the construction of a modern two-story structure at an estimated cost of $105,000. The new fireproof building is of the wall-bearing type of construction, two stories high on a concrete foundation, and has 12 classrooms with adequate storage space in the basement.

Work started on June 1, 1934 and was 95 per cent complete as of September 26, 1935. Commitments to that date, amounting to $76,205, included a wage and salary item of $37,626 paid to an average working force of 60 men for nearly 50,000 man-hours of labor.

Aside from providing work to the skilled building trade workers on relief at a time when very little construction work was going on, the new structure gives the village and school district a much larger and more modern school than its predecessor.

Other public buildings constructed by work relief since April, 1934, include 31 schools, 7 hospitals, 4 museums, 74 garages, 12 offices, and 48 storage buildings, together with five town halls, an armory and many others, a total of 388 buildings without including recreation and airport construction. In addition 4,490 public buildings were repaired or improved.

One of the undertakings of the work bureau of the City of Rochester was the construction of a grandstand to provide a suitable arena for exhibitions, shows, athletic contests, and similar events. The old timber structure, after twenty years of hard usage and exposure to the weather, was badly in need of repair, and a source of considerable yearly expenditure for maintenance.

Full operations started May 23, 1934. Built entirely of steel and concrete, the stadium is 254 feet long by 85 feet deep. Over 280 tons of structural steel were used. The roof is of three-ply asphalt composition over a two-inch wooden base supported by steel purlins. There are two rows of box seats in front and graded passageways leading from the rear to the main circulating aisle. The seats are of a comfortable, individual, type, resting on pre-cast reinforced concrete slabs.

Utilizing material from the old grandstand, a plant was set up on the site of operations to manufacture the concrete floor slabs. A casting bed, covering some 1,700 square feet, was erected, with a capacity of 84 complete units per day.. Some 2,000 of these units, steam cured and reinforced with wire mesh, were made. Sufficient additional units to allow for breakage are stored on the site for future use. Other incidental work involved the construction of service buildings, and the laying of adequate sewer and water lines.

The total cost of this project, including the service buildings, sewer and water lines, was about $120,000, of which $64,000 was paid in wages and salaries for nearly 94,000 man-hours of labor. The grandstand structure was finished on July 21, 1934.

Other recreation facilities constructed include 60 athletic fields, 75 baseball diamonds, 112 playgrounds, 11 golf courses, 33 fair buildings, 8 community centers, 22 park cafeterias and restaurant buildings. Ground improvement in public parks included clearing and grading of approximately 12,000 acres, planting of approximately 862,000 trees and 308,000 shrubs, removal of nearly 1,500 dead trees and 60,000 tree stumps, clearing of 2,300 acres of wooded land and improvement of 722 acres more, and landscaping of 15 acres of school grounds and 140 acres of hospital grounds.

One of the most outstanding operations from the local viewpoint was undertaken by the Suffolk County work bureau. A mosquito extermination project, sponsored by a special county commission and planned in cooperation with the Bureau of Entomology of the United States Department of Agriculture and the State Entomologist, secured wholehearted support of property owners and business interests. It was, therefore, comparatively easy to obtain easements to operate on private property.

After preliminary surveys it was decided to improve several miles of the already existing drainage ditches and to center new operations along the south shore bordering the Great South Bay. The ditches measured about 12 by 20 inches and were excavated entirely by hand labor with special ditching shovels, each manned by two men. This work was conducted over a wide front, the construction force consisting of some 40 units comprised of about 12 men each. Besides the improvement and maintenance of several hundred miles of previously existing drainage ditches, over 1,200 lineal miles of new ditches were dug, many wooden sluice gates constructed and installed, and over 2,000 gallons of oil used as a larvicide.

Further analysis of this project reveals how well it has been adapted to the work relief program. Begun prior to the Civil Works Administration, it has been carried on practically without interruption except for a short period during the winter months, when the severity of the weather prohibited operations. It has provided over 660,000 man-hours of almost continuous work for about 500 persons, of whom 450 were laborers. Furthermore, the analysis of costs reveals that about 98 per cent of the expenditures, representing over $350,000, has gone for wages and salaries, and the total cost per lineal mile has averaged under $300.

The project as originally planned is now nearing completion. Without the aid of Federal and State funds this vitally necessary mosquito eradication, affecting an area of 200 square miles and 2,000,000 persons, would not have been possible. The constructive nature of the project is further evidenced by the fact that the sponsoring commission has formulated plans for the permanent maintenance of this improvement, and has received public support to extend this system of drainage ditches an additional 1,000 miles.

Important in the field of public health, though relatively small in cost, was a project developed in New York City to determine the incidence of tuberculosis in that part of the population on home relief. Sponsored by the Commissioner of Health, the survey afforded over $40,000 in wages and salaries to doctors, nurses and clerks who otherwise would have been on relief.

A clinic was opened and a pathological classification of cases made on the basis of various stages of active tuberculosis, tuberculosis suspects, healed primary tuberculosis, cardiac conditions and anomalies. The resulting data were distributed among hospitals and clinics, where the follow-up work was undertaken. Individuals who from this preliminary analysis revealed a need of more thorough physical diagnosis were requested to report for examinations, in which the nurses assisted, making such home visits as were necessary to secure the fullest cooperation.

Altogether, nearly 21,000 families, involving over 56,000 individuals above 10 years of age, were reached, and a total of 25,170 X-rays taken. Of the patients X-rayed, 13 per cent were found to require further clinical examination. The number of persons so examined totalled 2,792 or 11 per cent. These clinical diagnoses revealed 951 cases of definite tuberculosis infection and 610 cardiac cases. Of the 274 cases diagnosed as active tuberculosis, over 44 per cent were recommended for hospitalization, and about one-half of the latter were actually admitted to institutions.

It was further disclosed that over 89 per cent of the tuberculosis cases found had been previously unknown, and were discovered for the first time by this survey.

Other research, public welfare and public education projects provided employment principally to persons themselves in need, who earned by their services approximately the same amounts they would have received in idleness on home relief if these projects had not been instituted. "Such projects were bedside and public health nursing, nutritional and other programs for health advancement; safety campaigns to eliminate hazards for relief workers; and drama, arts, research, music and other special service projects providing employment to utilize the skills of white collar workers. White collar projects, on the whole, have not created the permanent visible improvements of the purely physical construction, although their permanent results in terms of conservation of the public health and morale can never be measured. Furthermore they have had a much smaller cost for operation and materials; their cost has been almost all relief."*

---

* Administration of Public Unemployment Relief in New York State: April 1, 1934—March 31, 1935. P. 23.

Other projects were developed for the employment of those on relief rolls to make and distribute goods for others on relief—the distribution of the Federal surplus foods, the making and repairing of clothes.

At its outset, the work relief program was faced with the problem of providing employment for women who had little or no occupational training outside of the home. To meet the need of these women and their capabilities, many sewing projects were initiated. One such was in New York City, set-up about a year ago for the sewing of quilts.

Beginning with fifty women, the project soon demonstrated its practicality and a former factory building with floor space of 13,000 square feet was secured, equipped with twenty power sewing machines and thirty-one large tables. Over 160 women from all parts of the City were employed receiving relief in the form of wages, producing nearly 110,000 woolen quilts in a year from materials largely supplied by the Federal surplus commodities program.

There was little competition with private industry; quilts produced were distributed to unemployed relief clients who could not otherwise have had warm bedding. Like more than 200 others throughout the State, this sewing project was the object of considerable attention and interest from those familiar with its operation.

Flood Relief

The worst flood disaster in the history of the State occurred in south-central New York on July 8 and 9, 1935, following unprecedented rains.

On the morning of July 9 all available relief workers in districts such as Corning, Hornell and Steuben, Broome, Schuyler and Tompkins Counties were mobilized for flood rehabilitation work.

The Temporary Emeregency Relief Administration made special allotments on a 100 per cent reimbursement basis, beyond the regular monthly relief allocations, providing for necessary materials, equipment and non-relief personnel as well as work relief wages for flood relief projects, the Federal Government making additional money available. In all phases of the work as hereinafter described more than $1,000,000 from State and Federal relief funds was provided for emergency flood relief.

The Administration's Project Division gave blanket approval to flood relief projects from the afflicted welfare districts, and in the emergency all rules and regulations pertaining to the number of hours a person was permitted to work, and to the budgets of such persons, were suspended. In addition, the Administration concentrated its field staff to initiate relief activities and coordinate them with those of other agencies in the field, provided Federal surplus foods to isolated stricken areas and made transient labor and equipment available wherever they could be of service.

The break-down of public water supplies and the pollution of private wells by surface water presented an imminent danger to public health throughout the region that was met by relief labor in cooperation with the State Department of Health. Private wells were chlorinated and emergency repairs to water and sewage systems effected, with such thoroughness that despite the usual association of floods with typhoid fever not a single case of typhoid or other serious enteric disorder was traceable to the flood. In cooperation with the State Department of Highways and the local and county authorities, roads were opened to traffic, and temporary by-passes constructed where bridges had been washed out. Wreckage was cleared away from and temporary repairs made to public property, and debris removed from private property insofar as it constituted a menace to public health and safety.

Following a visit to the scene by Governor Lehman, division of functions between the various agencies in the field was clearly defined. Projects under the Temporary Emergency Relief Administration were limited to temporary repairs to public property and other work involving public health and safety. Because the Federal Works Progress Administration was in process of taking over the work relief program, new projects for permanent reconstruction of damaged public property could not be entertained by the Temporary Emergency Relief Administration and were to be taken care of by the Federal agency. Rehabilitation of damaged private property for distressed families was to be undertaken by the American Red Cross except as to grants to farmers by the Rural Rehabilitation Corporation. Actual succor to those whose homes had been washed away and who lacked immediate means of support was given in each locality by whichever agency was best equipped at the moment to meet the emergency.

Under the supervision of the Corning and Hornell Emergency Work Bureaus and the Steuben County Work Bureau, approximately 2,000 relief workers employed on the emergency flood program cleared and removed tons of debris, built temporary bridges, restored water systems, etc., in Steuben County.

In the City of Hornell, relief workers repaired four miles of water lines leading from the principal reservoir to the filter plant. In addition, repairs were also made to the water lines in the city system, all of which was out of service. In the same city between 300 and 400 catch basins were cleared of debris and put in serviceable condition.

In Hammondsport, one of the most seriously affected towns in Steuben County, 90 per cent of the emergency work done consisted of clearing up debris—approximately 24,000 cubic yards of it being removed from the city streets, public and private properties, etc. In addition to doing general clean-up work in the City of Corning, relief workers repaired the sewage disposal plant there. They also dredged several thousand feet of creek and river beds.

In Steuben County 47 temporary bridges, having an average span of 30 feet, were built; 1,216 feet of culvert pipes were installed; 1,645 cellars were pumped or cleaned and disinfected. Approximately 2,600 lineal feet of cribbing work was done along the banks of creeks and rivers. The cribbing work averaged six feet in height. Thirty-seven hundred cubic yards of dry stone wall were laid up and 3,500 lineal feet of earth diking were constructed.

More than 225 miles of town roads and approximately 84 miles of county roads were repaired and made passable by relief labor. Steuben County carried on its emergency flood program through September.

Emergency floor projects in Broome County were carried on by the Broome County Emergency Work Bureau and the Binghamton Emergency Work Bureau. Repairs were made to about 2,600 feet of water lines in the City of Binghamton and in the various towns of the county. Relief workers made 500 mattresses which were distributed through the Red Cross to families in the flood zone. Work relief recipients were also employed on projects assisting the staff of the State Board of Health in the inoculation of between 3,000 and 4,000 persons in the county. Relief workers repaired and regraded 20 miles of town, city and county thoroughfares. In addition, about 25 miles of town and city streets were cleaned of debris. Forty-five temporary bridges were erected and repairs were made to five additional bridges throughout the county. More than 2,400 wells were chlorinated, and approximately 1,400 cellars of private homes and public buildings were pumped and cleaned. There were approximately 1,000 relief workers employed during the emergency period throughout the county.

In Schuyler County, where flood repairs continued through the month of September, relief workers, under the supervision of the Schuyler County Emergency Work Bureau, dredged and cleaned approximately 47,100 lineal feet of creek and river bed. In addition, relief labor was used to repair or rebuild fifty miles of town roads. Besides doing general clean-up work, relief workers pumped and cleaned 595 cellars in Schuyler County and constructed 96 temporary bridges. Relief labor assigned to the Schuyler County Supervisor of Highways cleaned and dredged 22,500 lineal feet of stream channels and repaired or rebuilt ten miles of county roads. Approximately 1,200 relief workers were used during the emergency flood period here.

Following the flood disaster, flood relief projects were carried on in a total of 24 districts of the State, at a cost of $993,544. Wages paid on relief payrolls amounted to $498,589, while non-relief payrolls totaled $65,179. There were 7,722 men on relief payrolls in July and 5,177 in August. Non-relief payrolls carried 1,819 workers in July and 486 in August. Materials and rental of equipment amounted to $429,776, including $13,861 of non-reimbursable expenditures. Details, by counties, are given in Table II.

Transients sent into the flood areas from surrounding transient centers and camps were not put on a work relief wage basis, but were given, in addition to maintenance, a weekly three-dollar cash allowance, raised early in the month of August to seven dollars. After the immediate emergency had passed they worked largely under the supervision of the Federal Soil Erosion Service, which also employed youths from Civilian Conservation Camps in the clearing and straightening of creek beds and the restoration of natural drainage to minimize the danger from further floods. Contingents of these men were sent to twelve welfare districts, ten counties and two cities. In addition to local relief workers a total of 740 transient men worked on flood rehabilitation during July and 1,137 in August, under direction and supervision of the Soil Erosion Service of the Federal Department of Agriculture. Total cash allowances paid to these men amounted to $25,770 in the two months.

Equipment was furnished from a fund of $300,000 set aside by

July, August and September, 1935

WELFARE DISTRICT	Total	EXPENDITURES			WORKERS			
		Wages on Relief Payrolls	Wages on Non-Relief Payrolls	Materials and Rental of Equipment	JULY		AUGUST	
					Relief Payrolls	Non-Relief Payrolls	Relief Payrolls	Non-Relief Payrolls
TOTAL	$993,543.58	$498,588.66	$65,178.89	$429,776.03 (a)	7,722	1,819	5,177	486
Allegany County	4,638.84	4,638.84			128		14	
Broome County	35,505.43	28,830.60	1,404.00	5,270.83	670	10	110	5
Binghamton	32,962.22	21,740.07	87.50	11,134.65	354	1	286	1
Chemung County					313		313	
Elmira	2,063.13	1,361.76	228.46	472.91	472	5	262	
Chenango County	28,359.34 (b)	16,595.30 (b)	4,123.80	7,640.24	137	62	161	53
Norwich					68		67	
Cortland County	32,147.60 (c)	17,806.20 (c)	686.10	13,655.30	227	5	218	5
Cortland					39		46	
Delaware County	22,706.41	12,906.48	829.14	8,970.79	177	4	157	5
Greene County	13,232.84	5,580.10	706.80	6,945.94	96	6	87	5
Ontario County	14,775.39	8,658.40	52.20	6,064.79	181		160	1
Otsego County	6,494.10	4,455.80	188.80	1,849.50	97	4	61	1
Oneonta	4,862.71	4,078.90		783.81	42		40	
Saratoga County	26,891.98	23,347.72		3,544.26	645		269	
Schuyler County	292,578.86 (d)	134,784.66 (d)	13,197.44	144,596.76	601	261	502	74
Seneca County	24,393.06	14,793.88	528.72	9,070.46	162	5	164	5
Steuben County	238,538.09 (e)	77,007.10 (e)	37,958.04	123,572.95	958	1,406	764	289
Corning	15,387.17	10,621.29		4,765.88	241		232	
Hornell	78,344.05	37,032.10	2,184.85	39,127.10	589	20	372	16
Tioga County	7,474.17	5,585.84	668.20	1,220.13	139	11	57	8
Tompkins County	30,269.16	15,139.21	979.89	14,150.06	261	6	235	6
Ithaca	39,400.27	23,623.89	383.33	15,393.05	276	2	265	2
Ulster County	11,958.54	6,672.00	353.15	4,933.39	188	2	127	8
Kingston	8,980.33	5,881.03	91.67	3,007.63	78	1	91	
Warren County	3,045.40	2,580.00	340.80	124.60	150	6		
Washington County	18,534.49	14,867.49	186.00	3,481.00	433	2	117	2

(a) Includes $13,860.75 non-reimbursable expenditures for materials and rental of equipment.
(b) Includes $5,275.90 of relief wages paid to Norwich residents working on Chenango County flood projects.
(c) Includes $3,943.42 of relief wages paid to Cortland City residents working on Cortland County flood projects.
(d) Includes $35,897.25 of relief wages paid to Chemung County residents, $39,236.66 of relief wages paid to Elmira residents and $2,768.17 of relief wages paid to Corning residents working on Schuyler County flood projects.
(e) Includes $4,296.93 of relief wages paid to Corning residents working on Steuben County flood projects.

the Administration for this purpose. To meet the need of emergency relief for many persons who had hitherto been self-supporting and were now in need of public support temporarily because of the flood disaster, the Temporary Emergency Relief Administration also set up a procedure for temporary certification of eligibility for relief by which flood sufferers were made eligible for thirty days. At the end of that time the cases either were closed or, upon investigation, were transferred to regular relief status. Details, by counties, are given in Table III.

Grants to farmers for rehabilitation of their farms, mentioned previously, were from an appropriation of $150,000 made available by the New York State Rural Rehabilitation Corporation, this sum being part of the unexpended balance on hand after the transfer of the Corporation's regular activities to the Federal Resettlement Administration. Grants from this fund are being made under the supervision of the Rural Activities Division of the TERA to cases authorized by local Rural Rehabilitation agents and Rural Rehabilitation County Committees. In July and August, 883 farmers stricken by the flood received a total of $103,899 in such grants. These grants were made to farmers whose land, buildings, or live stock were damaged or destroyed, and who lacked resources for meeting their own rehabilitation needs.

The foregoing summary of flood relief has, necessarily, been restricted to the part played by the Temporary Emergency Relief Administration and the chief cooperating agencies. Other State departments and volunteer organizations that played a vital part in the work of protection, relief and reconstruction included the State Police, the National Guard, the Conservation Department, the American Legion, and local chapters of the American Red Cross.

TABLE III

Relief Granted to Cases with Temporary Certification of Eligibility for Relief Because of Flood Disaster, July and August, 1935

WELFARE DISTRICT	EXPENDITURES			CASES					
				JULY			AUGUST		
	Total	Home Relief	Work Relief	Total‡	Home Relief	Work Relief	Total‡	Home Relief	Work Relief
Broome County.........	$10,714.12	......	$10,714.12	378	...	378	...	...	...
Cortland County........	7,074.53	$32.24	7,042.29	177	7	174	...	...	...
Delaware County........	300.00	......	300.00	4	...	4	3	...	3
Schuyler County........	13,153.12	......	13,153.12	228	...	228	172	...	172
Steuben County.........	16,034.64	189.76	15,844.88	290	21	286	168	2	168
Hornell................	22,676.35	443.35	22,233.00	541	77	484	185	...	185
Total..............	$69,952.76	$665.35	$69,287.41	1,618	105	1,554	528	2	528

‡ Excluding duplication of cases receiving both Home Relief and Work Relief.

SUPPLEMENTARY RELIEF ACTIVITIES

FEDERAL SURPLUS COMMODITIES

The estimated retail value of 108,105,000 pounds of Federal Surplus foods distributed from September 1, 1934 to August 31, 1935, was $13,540,000. These surplus foods were purchased by the Federal Government as part of its agricultural adjustment and drought relief program and turned over to the States for distribution. In New York State they were allocated to the welfare districts by the Federal Surplus Commodities Division of the State Temporary Emergency Relief Administration, as the Federal agent. The food was given the needy in supplementation of relief, over and above regular budgetary allowances. In addition the Federal Government sent to New York State 13,000,000 yards of cotton piece goods which were processed and issued to clients.

TRANSIENT RELIEF

The Federally financed program for transients was organized in New York State to house, feed, give medical treatment and work, when possible, to those persons—both individuals and families—who were not residents of the State but who represent, for the most part, migrants in vain search of work. From September 1, 1934 to August 31, 1935, an average of 31,830 families and unattached individuals were cared for monthly. During the year's period a total of $4,429,475 was expended for relief under this program. A net-work of transient bureaus and centers are located in geographically strategic points to deal with this problem. Included in the transient program is the transporting back to their homes of individuals and families who could be assured of aid there.

The ten transient camps now open are: Elks Park Camp at Port Jervis; Elmsford Camp at Elmsford; Camp Frontier at Langford; Camp Greenhaven at Stormville; Camp Hartwick at Hartwick Seminary (school of boys); Camp Roosevelt at Southfields; St. Johnsville Camp at St. Johnsville; Saratoga Springs Camp at Saratoga Springs; Schenectady Camp at Schenectady; and Stony Brook Camp at Dansville.

Registration of new transient cases was discontinued September 20, 1935, in line with the Federal government's decision to taper off the program. Some of the employable transients registered prior to September 20 and at present under the care of the transient program are expected to be absorbed by WPA projects, but if the Federal Government does withdraw from transient relief it will mean a heavy charge for which State funds are not available under the Wicks Act.

RURAL REHABILITATION

The New York State Rural Rehabilitation Corporation was formed as part of the Temporary Emergency Relief Administration under a charter granted by the Legislature at the last session. The purpose was to rehabilitate farm individuals and families from relief rolls and on the margin of relief and make them self-sustaining by enabling them to secure subsistence and gainful employment from the soil.

The Corporation was empowered under the charter: To accept loans, grants and assistance from the United States, or its agencies; or from New York State or any other sources for carrying out rehabilitation activities and to acquire and dispose of all classes of property. It was also empowered to make loans or give financial aid for rehabilitation purposes.

Beginning late in May the Corporation made loans of $78,654 to 161 sub-marginal farm families to enable them to become self-sustaining. Unused checks for $11,648 were returned in 27 cases and partial repayment of $1,251.58 has been made on the loans in 23 cases.

On June 30th, due to a ruling of the United States Comptroller-General that no Federal grants from the four billion dollar appropriation for the fiscal year 1935-1936 could thereafter be made to a corporation, it became necessary for the Federal Government to revise its rural rehabilitation procedure and to itself take over the administration of the plan. Hence the creation of the Federal Resettlement Administration and the transfer thereto of the objectives and operations of the New York State Rural Rehabilitation Corporation, as of July 1st, 1935. Therefore, except to administer or "service" the 161 loans theretofore made, the functions of that New York Corporation largely ceased on that date, although it may be of material assistance in meeting special rural relief problems as was exemplified in its work and contribution in the flood areas.

The Corporation, financed entirely by Federal funds, found itself with an unexpended balance of some $150,000 which, by the terms of its charter, it could not turn back to the Federal Government. By agreement this money was allocated for grants to farmers whose property was damaged in the July flood, as described in the previous section on flood relief. These grants could be made only to farmers eligible for rehabilitation under Federal regulations. All grant applications were cleared through county advisory rehabilitation committees.

Subsistence Gardens

Subsistence Gardens, encouraged by the TERA from the start as part of its effort to stretch the relief dollar to its utmost by aiding the unemployed to serve their own needs and the needs of others on relief, were continued in the past season on an even greater scale in virtually all the welfare districts. Fresh vegetables, with an estimated retail value of $2,500,000, were obtained in the summer of 1935 from 80,000 gardens planted last spring with the assistance and technical supervision of the Temporary Emergency Relief Administration. The total expenditure for this food was approximately $400,000 for the purchase of seeds and small garden tools, the plowing of land, etc., of which the State reimbursed the local welfare districts 75 per cent. Most of the crop was consumed by the 80,000 relief families that cultivated the gardens, making possible an increase in their standards of living and health. About ten per cent of the vegetables harvested were grown in community gardens operated with the workers receiving regular relief wages. It is interesting that about 6,000 of the gardens were within the limits of greater New York, Manhattan having been the only borough that had none. From the products of the gardens between 1,500,000 and 2,000,000 units of canned vegetables have been made available to about 15,000 families in the coming winter.

Federal Student Aid

In the academic year 1934-1935 Federal Student aid was given by the TERA to a monthly average of 9,222 needy students to make possible their attendance at 81 institutions of college rank in New York State. The total of $1,249,566 paid in wages to the students represented an average monthly earning per student of $13.55 for useful work that the institutions could not otherwise have had done. Clerical and office work that the colleges could not provide for in their regular budgets, work in libraries and museums, laboratory and research work, and assistance in education, recreation, health and welfare were among the accomplishments of the program. This form of aid is to be continued henceforth by the National Youth Administration.

CAMP TERA

Camp Tera on the shores of Lake Tiorati near Bear Mountain was established for unemployed young women between the ages of eighteen and forty who need physical and mental aid, relaxation and up-building, but who have not the resources to meet this necessity. It is financed by the Federal Relief Administration and is under the direct supervision of the State Temporary Emergency Relief Administration. Since it opened twenty-eight months ago, in June, 1933, it has provided rehabilitation opportunities for 1,521 young women. The cost of maintenance of the camp per girl is exceptionally low, being about fifty cents per day, or $3.52 per week. This includes expenditures for food and housing, ice, coal, electricity, laundry, medical supplies, office supplies, telephone, small equipment and transportation. During the summer 150 girls at a time are housed and cared for at the camp. The addition of a new steam-heated dormitory has increased accommodation during the winter to ninety girls and women.

MILK FOR CHILDREN

In the year ending August 31, 1935, $1,686,287 was spent in distributing over 18 million quarts of fresh milk to babies, children and nursing and expectant mothers throughout the state, under a special $1,500,000 appropriation of relief monies made by the Legislature in July, 1934, providing for 100 per cent reimbursement of the local districts for their expenditures for milk. February was the peak month when over a quarter of a million children were benefited by the program. Of the total, New York City distributed 14 million quarts at a cost of $1,167,031. After the special appropriation was exhausted, many of the local districts continued the program and now, under an amendment to the Wicks Act, are being reimbursed at the same rate as home relief by the Temporary Emergency Relief Administration.

School Lunches

Holding the prevention of undernourishment of children to be a most vital part of the relief program, the Temporary Emergency Relief Administration continued reimbursement of municipalities for school lunches, including milk, served to needy children to supplement other forms of relief. In the year ended August 31, 1935, $969,236 was expended in the State for such aid.

Civilian Conservation Corps

In the course of the year beginning September 1, 1934, approximately 50,000 New York State boys worked in camps of the Federal Civilian Conservation Corps, with an average of approximately 25,000 in the camps throughout the period. Beginning with June, 1935, all boys recruited for the camps have come from relief families and before that time practically all came either from relief families or from families on the margin of relief who were enabled to keep off relief rolls by the monthly contribution from the boys' earnings. It is estimated that in the year the boys contributed more than $7,000,000 to their families, thus lessening the burden of local relief expenditures.

36

TABLE IV.
TEMPORARY EMERGENCY RELIEF ADMINISTRATION FOR NEW YORK STATE
EXPENDITURE STATEMENT

TABLE showing disbursements of the Temporary Emergency Relief Administration to welfare districts from September 1, 1934 to August 31, 1935.

WELFARE DISTRICT	HOME RELIEF	WORK RELIEF	TOTAL PAID	ESTIMATED COMMITMENTS
Albany County	$118,942.60	$239,408.81	$358,351.41	$5,289.95
Albany	462,332.88	657,909.12	1,120,242.00	233,406.92
Cohoes	471,537.90	283,139.49	754,677.39	143,274.81
Watervliet	49,087.48	—(a) 4,303.40	44,784.08	31,162.20
Allegany County	75,653.67	84,577.54	160,231.21	29,700.96
Broome County	151,375.82	232,050.56	383,426.38	63,156.22
Binghamton	292,480.30	149,993.98	442,474.28	83,045.86
Cattaraugus County	58,392.86	176,751.60	235,144.46	50,295.67
Olean	42,295.79	148,299.74	190,595.53	12,269.35
Salamanca	114,876.10	38,238.04	153,114.14	13,184.19
Cayuga County	62,699.14	84,619.09	147,318.23	22,414.10
Auburn	189,340.52	281,813.37	471,153.89	51,126.51
Chautauqua County	160,411.64	210,424.78	370,836.42	62,380.07
Dunkirk	177,848.93	139,257.65	317,106.58	55,537.22
Jamestown	220,555.18	263,753.25	484,308.43	169,867.38
Chemung County	217,137.78	136,182.15	353,319.93	65,775.56
Elmira	436,844.51	210,381.39	647,225.90	122,914.33
Chenango County	39,105.79	56,197.76	95,303.55	6,189.10
Norwich	29,097.49	—(a) 1,390.84	27,706.65	6,566.65
Clinton County	52,702.25	105,205.76	157,908.01	20,768.68
Plattsburgh	52,172.73	48,903.95	101,076.68	11,342.93
Columbia County	44,077.70	105,663.42	149,741.12	19,512.60
Hudson	68,058.51	139,070.90	207,129.41	18,669.42
Cortland County	31,465.46	68,607.46	100,072.92	7,931.14
Cortland	56,991.01	41,851.84	98,842.85	14,395.86
Delaware County	69,702.70	115,823.37	185,526.07	25,924.12
Dutchess County	174,151.49	247,335.81	421,487.30	47,420.95
Beacon	43,629.46	118,814.24	162,443.70	9,162.50
Poughkeepsie	291,948.41	239,338.52	531,286.93	55,421.49
Erie County	1,924,280.05	2,302,619.88	4,226,899.93	858,203.92
Buffalo	6,980,856.59	6,770,832.94	13,751,689.53	1,852,610.68
Lackawanna (b)	....	....	....	....
Tonawanda	4,459.12	76.74	4,535.86	....
Essex County	135,338.74	228,435.06	363,773.80	110,459.04
Franklin County	243,203.55	202,098.60	445,302.15	66,073.77
Fulton County	46,664.41	50,947.40	97,611.81	11,459.28
Gloversville	64,525.00	79,620.11	144,145.11	13,177.44
Johnstown	15,893.21	32,036.91	47,930.12	4,155.87
Genesee County	83,482.03	81,525.36	165,007.39	24,994.87
Batavia	84,723.92	113,666.20	198,390.12	11,430.89
Greene County	35,723.74	72,213.36	107,937.10	11,776.43
Hamilton County	10,190.26	32,786.95	42,977.21	1,948.46
Herkimer County	196,957.80	239,943.60	436,901.40	64,160.10
Little Falls	31,327.43	62,220.50	93,547.93	2,222.27
Jefferson County	285,068.19	146,123.52	431,191.71	72,994.46
Watertown	198,060.90	293,083.76	491,144.66	62,941.43
Lewis County	46,292.48	116,822.07	163,114.55	9,516.72
Livingston County	136,491.94	124,796.95	261,288.89	46,291.00
Madison County	32,076.95	62,502.49	94,579.44	17,731.71
Oneida	17,450.57	34,814.70	52,265.27	4,764.39
Monroe County	943,632.59	1,422,888.80	2,366,521.39	380,555.97
Rochester	3,638,669.25	2,640,830.99	6,279,500.24	1,187,543.44
Montgomery County	82,099.22	104,001.20	186,100.42	17,066.67
Amsterdam	237,582.16	256,195.55	493,777.71	38,198.58
Nassau County	2,660,730.48	3,356,302.28	6,017,032.76	866,390.02
Glen Cove (c)	....	....	....	....
Long Beach (c)	....	....	....	....
New York City	86,116,784.95	81,456,580.48	167,573,365.43	14,594,360.67
Niagara County	52,953.09	100,487.96	153,441.05	25,645.01
Lockport	153,305.22	140,433.00	293,738.22	55,303.37
No. Tonawanda	118,039.36	260,000.52	378,039.88	22,049.06
Niagara Falls	515,411.90	888,755.25	1,404,167.15	160,064.03

(a). Refunds received by T. E. R. A. of advances made to districts for Work Relief payrolls and carried as a disbursement on August 31, 1934.

(b). Included in Erie County.

(c). Included in Nassau County.

TABLE IV—Continued
TEMPORARY EMERGENCY RELIEF ADMINISTRATION FOR NEW YORK STATE
EXPENDITURE STATEMENT

TABLE showing disbursements of the Temporary Emergency Relief Administration to welfare districts from September 1, 1934 to August 31, 1935.

WELFARE DISTRICT	HOME RELIEF	WORK RELIEF	TOTAL PAID	ESTIMATED COMMITMENTS
Oneida County.......	$200,543.60	$98,253.07	$298,796.67	$30,193.77
Rome..........	186,734.10	253,407.18	440,141.28	66,756.68
Utica..........	817,307.32	580,187.10	1,397,494.42	180,623.22
Onondaga County....	417,180.03	527,514.68	944,694.71	191,509.95
Syracuse........	1,598,632.14	2,254,595.84	3,853,227.98	593,988.88
Ontario County......	252,478.40	155,315.94	407,794.34	61,716.60
Orange County......	118,973.81	340,481.68	459,455.49	50,908.63
Middletown......	32,616.78	78,574.54	111,191.32	10,180.15
Newburgh.......	161,701.90	234,716.85	396,418.75	39,137.12
Port Jervis......	50,404.71	184,283.27	234,687.98	18,423.54
Orleans County	45,798.23	157,041.05	202,839.28	21,014.41
(Oswego County).....				
Fulton..........	96,224.73	186,286.08	282,510.81	35,384.38
Oswego..........	196,963.80	334,032.37	530,996.17	36,854.84
Otsego County......	52,180.91	88,001.40	140,182.31	30,010.79
Oneonta........	10,357.21	68,921.82	79,279.03	3,750.11
Putnam County......	52,475.67	75,963.50	128,439.17	23,730.34
Rensselaer County....	75,387.26	13,222.48	88,609.74	42,295.30
Rensselaer.......	36,199.62	73,068.81	109,268.43	15,280.93
Troy............	255,968.57	384,622.20	640,590.77	100,823.37
Rockland County.....	192,749.17	224,212.46	416,961.63	65,773.92
St. Lawrence County..	233,879.97	341,345.25	575,225.22	97,247.58
Ogdensburg......	40,331.89	189,544.12	229,876.01	2,454.64
Saratoga County......	107,209.38	280,561.30	387,770.68	49,480.60
Mechanicville....	27,234.32	43,334.44	70,568.76	5,525.23
Saratoga Springs.	48,009.83	121,454.12	169,463.95	47,415.52
Schenectady County..	215,292.00	354,664.56	569,956.56	132,560.45
Schenectady.....	517,689.82	784,729.47	1,302,419.29	322,085.01
Schoharie County....	15,413.86	57,402.06	72,815.92	11,142.22
Schuyler County....	70,125.92	186,678.35	256,804.27	9,170.24
Seneca County......	69,253.79	104,221.43	173,475.22	29,903.34
Steuben County......	102,355.97	324,955.35	427,311.32	52,831.09
Corning.........	54,696.06	121,719.35	176,415.41	14,679.37
Hornell.........	36,008.54	136,815.86	172,824.40	19,453.21
Suffolk County.......	638,240.53	1,249,743.09	1,887,983.62	292,487.47
Sullivan County......	33,078.63	88,102.05	121,180.68	14,288.98
Tioga County.......	88,937.39	61,718.75	150,656.14	24,207.51
Tompkins County....	43,633.47	132,840.57	176,474.04	25,894.00
Ithaca..........	103,170.90	208,624.62	311,795.52	36,994.39
Ulster County......	135,663.05	233,859.77	369,522.82	37,115.54
Kingston........	160,978.98	338,403.80	499,382.78	51,801.38
Warren County......	45,510.08	70,941.21	116,451.29	15,979.76
Glens Falls......	80,982.24	174,567.60	255,549.84	25,044.02
Washington County...	180,935.82	258,770.82	439,706.64	65,778.79
Wayne County......	119,697.72	170,420.49	290,118.21	52,174.92
Westchester County..	1,393,238.02	1,932,688.88	3,325,926.90	746,731.11
Mt. Vernon......	531,457.15	453,857.85	985,315.00	106,832.02
New Rochelle....	459,778.06	681,272.39	1,141,050.45	249,619.14
White Plains.....	503,409.10	336,952.73	840,361.83	118,620.59
Yonkers........	1,029,427.00	956,371.04	1,985,798.04	568,553.01
Wyoming County	102,784.58	116,861.01	219,645.59	20,110.71
Yates County......	56,882.49	....	56,882.49	14,302.53
State Improvements Allocated on a State-wide Basis.........	....	7,464,175.24	7,464,175.24	8,724,251.88
	$121,443,375.72	$130,581,862.37	$252,025,238.09	$35,655,295.47

STATE OF NEW YORK

BUDGET MANUAL

THE FAMILY BUDGET AS A BASIS
FOR HOME RELIEF

November 1st, 1935

TEMPORARY EMERGENCY RELIEF ADMINISTRATION

State Office Building, Albany

79 Madison Avenue, New York

STATE OF NEW YORK

TEMPORARY EMERGENCY RELIEF ADMINISTRATION

BUDGET MANUAL

THE FAMILY BUDGET AS A BASIS
FOR HOME RELIEF

November 1st, 1935

BUDGET MANUAL

The Family Budget as a Basis for Home Relief

SECTION ONE

SECTION TWO

SECTION THREE

SECTION FOUR

FOREWORD

As stated in the Public Welfare Law of the State of New York, it is the duty of the public officials "to provide adequately for those unable to maintain themselves". The Emergency Relief Act of the State of New York has reaffirmed this duty for those in need because of unemployment. The giving of relief is rightly considered a difficult procedure, but training and experience have developed several approaches, of which budgeting is one of the most clearly defined and widely accepted methods. The principles of the budget are quite simple and easily mastered but the amounts given in each locality must be constantly reviewed in order to adapt allowances to conditions in small towns, large cities, rural areas; as well as to differing standards of living and cultural habits. The suggestions in this manual are neither absolute nor final but should prove helpful in standardizing and rendering more effective the purposes of sound relief administration.

Section One

PLANNING FOR ASSISTANCE TO FAMILIES

Needs and Resources

Two factors in planning relief are, first, the needs of the families and second, the resources in a community to meet those needs.

Relief should always be given on the basis of need. The usual items for a family include: shelter, food, clothing, light, fuel for heating and cooking, household necessities, medicine, medical supplies and medical care.

Other items which seem less usual may be essential in certain families or under certain conditions. Examples of such items are insulin, ice, carfare, lunch money, etc.

When community resources are so limited, however, that minimum requirements cannot be met, the economies made should be such as not to reduce the family's living standards below the point of safety.

Cash Relief

The substitution of cash for commodity relief has proceeded slowly but is now beyond the experimental stage. Cash, rather than relief in kind, is the medium for both mothers' allowance and old age assistance throughout the State, and has been successfully given to over half a million home relief families. Agreement is now quite general that for the average family cash allowances should be granted. In instances where cash cannot be managed by the family, grocery or other orders may be issued. Certain conditions must be met before a bureau is granted permission to give home relief in cash.*

Budgeting Family Needs

In the past it was frequently the practice to issue a grocery order or fuel order which would "tide the family over". Nowadays an attempt is made to give "adequate" relief, which is relief sufficient

*See Manual of Procedure for Local Relief Administration, Section 200, Item 212.

8

to maintain not only subsistence but reasonable health and well-being. In determining relief allowances a budget plan is necessary.

The Budget

A budget is an estimate of need as over against income and resources. The budgetary needs vary for different families. An individual family budget is affected by many factors, such as the age and physical condition of the individuals, the locality, the season and prices. However, there are certain general principles and measures which may be used in estimating the local allowance for the various budgetary items.

Section Two

ITEMS OF THE BUDGET

Variable Costs

Just how the standard requirements of a proper budget may best be provided, is a problem to be solved by each community. The cost will vary with market, transportation and with local resources of garden, dairy and other products. Food habits also play an important part and must be considered.

Because of the differences in cost of commodities in different parts of the State, the amount of the budget cannot easily be expressed in definite amounts of money, but must be left to relief bureaus to calculate the sums to be allowed on the basis of the actual cost of items locally.

Food

Food is apt to be the largest item of expenditure in the relief budget, and it is important that wholesome articles be provided at as low a cost as possible. The only sound basis for food relief is the quantity of food needed by individuals of different ages and physical conditions. The allowance should be large enough to provide a diet sufficient for health and growth, and to allow for a reasonable variety in the selection of foods. Damage done by inadequate food may be permanent. Lack of the proper amounts of a well balanced diet will not only handicap the individual, but may create grave community health problems.

Weekly Food Needs

For the guidance of the local relief bureau a summary of weekly food needs for all ages is given in the chart on page 11. These allowances for the various types of food represent the minimum which will protect health and will promote the growth of children. Any allowance of less than the amount stated may ultimately produce impairment of health.

For convenience the food allowance is usually translated into money terms. This should not obscure the fact that the QUANTITY and KIND of food is the basic concern.

For practical use in estimating individual family budgets it is much simpler to reduce the number of age groups used to three* groups—as follows:

Ages: Sixth month to sixth year
Sixth year to thirteenth year
Thirteenth year and over

Six groups are given in the food chart on page 11, in order to make it more valuable as a guide to food selection.

The money value of the food allowance is dependent upon the local cost of the amount of food specified for the various age groups in the chart on page 11.

The Family Food Budget

· The large family can buy more economically than the small family or a single individual. Allowance should, therefore, be made for such variations in buying power.

In calculating the food budget of a family use the allowance for the individual members according to age and make the following additions or deductions.

Number in Family   *Allowances*

Single Individual..... Adult .... plus 50%
Two................Sum of individual allowances. plus 25%
Three...............Sum of individual allowances. plus 15%
Four-five-six-seven....Sum of individual allowances. no additions
Eight................Sum of individual allowances. deduct 5% from total
(No deduction if family contains three or more pre-school children.)
Nine and over........Sum of individual allowances. deduct 5% from total

Exceptions

Pregnant women......Adult .... plus 25%
Nursing mothers......Adult .... plus 50%
Infants..............Allowance for the nursing mother provides for the breast-fed baby from birth to six months, except that ten cents should be added for fruit. In case of a bottle fed infant the cost of the formula should be allowed.

*Many bureaus recognize the special needs of adolescents by indicating another group (twelfth year to sixteenth year) and considering all above 16 as adults.

FOOD CHART—SUMMARY OF WEEKLY FOOD NEEDS FOR ALL AGE GROUPS**

FOODS	Measure	6 Mo.–2 Yrs.	2–5 Yrs.	5–10 Yrs.	10–12 Yrs.	12–16 Yrs.	Over 16***
Milk..........	quarts	7	3½–5	3½	3½	3½–7	3½
Potatoes..........	pounds	1 (potatoes & vegetables together)	1½	2	3	4	4–5
Green or Root Vegetables.....	pounds		1½	3	3	3	2½–3
Fruits: Fresh..........	pounds	2 oranges or tomato juice	3 oranges or tomato juice	1	1	1	1
Dried..........	ounces	4	3	4	6	6	6–8
Bread..........	pounds	1	1½	2	2½	3½	2½–3
Cereals and Flour..........	pounds	½	¾	1	1½	2	2½–3
Eggs..........		3	3	3	3	3	3
Cheese..........	ounces	—	1	2	3	4	4
Legumes (Dried Beans, Peas, etc.).....	ounces	—	1	2	3	4	4
Meat and Fish..........	pounds	—	—	½	1	1	1½–2
Butter and Fat..........	ounces	2 (butter)	3	6	8	·12 ·	12
Sugars..........	ounces	0–2	4	6	8	8	12–16
Cod Liver Oil..........	ounces	1–3	Include for all children if possible				

** Adapted from Good Nutrition at Minimum Cost. Published by New York Association for Improving the Conditions of the Poor. Revision and enlargement 1931.
*** At light and moderate muscular work.

Special Diets

Special diets should be allowed on the recommendation of a physician. Standard diets in common use among doctors are frequently very expensive. A special bulletin to assist the physician to adjust diet recommendations to the incomes of patients is available free to all welfare bureaus and physicians handling relief clients.*

This bulletin has received the approval of the Committee on Public Health Relations of the New York Academy of Medicine and similar committees in various counties and cities. It can, therefore, be used without hesitation by a local bureau as a basis for estimating the allowance for average cases.

When one member of a family is a special diet case, the food budget for the remaining number in the family may be calculated and the cost of the special diet needed by the patient added.

Cod Liver Oil

More emphasis is now being placed on the value of cod liver oil than ever before. It might be well for both clients and welfare officials to remember that cod liver oil should be considered as a food and not as a medicine. It is needed by the normal individual as well as by the sick, in summer as well as in winter and should be used in relief families to supplement a low cost diet. (See Section Four, Page 25, for the standard allowance for various ages.)

Shelter

The allowance for shelter, like that for food, will vary according to the locality. This can best be determined after a survey of the local housing situation, including the expenses of property up-keep, the local tax rate, fire insurance rate, prevailing rent trends and assessed valuation of the property. A housing committee, representative of the many interests involved can give material assistance to a welfare bureau in their housing problem.

In arriving at a shelter allowance, which may be either rental or allowable payment on a home, consideration should be given to the following factors:

---

*"Special Diets at Low Cost," published by the Jewish Social Service Association, Inc., 67 West 47th Street, New York.

Taxes
Interest on mortgage
Water (when separate from taxes)
Necessary repairs (safety and sanitation)
Fire Insurance (when necessary)
Other items non-payment of which might lead to loss of shelter

Shelter grants are a legitimate charge. The allowances may be in the form of rent, or in the case of a home-owner, an allowance may be applied to certain fixed charges on the home, but should under no circumstances, increase the equity in the property. (See Section Three, Page 18, for information on two-family houses, combined business and home property and other property investments.)

In the average family it is desirable to maintain as far as possible their previous standards. It is obvious that it may be necessary to restrict excessive rentals but it is equally obvious that extremely low standards of housing should not be tolerated. In establishing housing standards due attention should be given to health and safety hazards. Before any rent is paid for unsuitable quarters every effort should be made either to remove the clients or obtain the reconditioning of the premises. When a bureau assumes the responsibility of relocating clients, it should definitely check on the suitability of the new quarters especially from the standpoint of sanitation and safety.

Rents should not be paid except in most unusual circumstances to legally responsible relatives.

Clothing

Clothing probably is the most difficult item in the entire relief budget. It is not possible to plan clothing budgets with the same precision as food budgets. However, clothing budgets are necessary as a guide. Factors involved include the kinds of garments needed, the number of each and the probable durability of each. Durability of the garment depends not only on the quality of the garment, but also on the care, laundering and repair and on the fact that one child may wear out his clothes almost twice as rapidly as another. Special consideration should be given to the effect of unsuitable or inadequate clothing in the case of the adolescent child and the working member of the family. Adequacy is only reached by providing essential garments for each member of the family with an allowance made for necessary replacement and upkeep.

Communities have developed various means of meeting clothing needs such as the distribution of used clothing or clothing gifts and sewing projects. These resources may be utilized but their limitations should be clearly recognized. At best these will never be more than supplemental.

Good results are being obtained by the method of having a "cumulative clothing allowance". A definite sum is allowed in the budget. This is not granted from week to week but is allowed to accumulate. The family credit thus established is checked against whenever specific purchases are authorized. (See Section Four, Page 24, for record form.)

Light and Fuel

Light is a necessity of living. It is desirable, when possible, to grant the type of lighting, heating and fuel for cooking to which the client is accustomed, and for which the house is equipped. Safety hazards should be considered when changes are made. Local minimum charges of utility companies frequently must be met to prevent shut off of the service. Back bills should not be paid. Kerosene is usually purchased at a grocery store and a common error is to expect the client to make this purchase out of his food allowance.

The period during which fuel for heating is granted naturally depends upon geographic location and weather conditions. Such fuel is frequently furnished on the basis of a definite tonnage per month. However, the amount needed is more dependent on the character of the space to be heated and the efficiency of the equipment than on the size of the family or a period of time.

Household Supplies

Household supplies should be construed as including such miscellaneous items as household cleaning agents, laundry items, toilet tissue, matches, etc. A family can usually replace small items of kitchen and cleaning equipment out of this allowance, if their cost does not exceed twenty cents. Larger items such as brooms, mops, utensils, etc., should be provided by a special grant.

Special Needs

Certain types of special needs should be included in some budgets. Insulin is a common example of such a special need.

Ice may be provided in limited amounts in families with young children or in cases of illness where there is no adequate provision for proper care of milk and other food.

Carfare allowance for clinic visits, employment and other necessary transportation, may be included in the individual budget at the discretion of welfare officers. This should be held to an absolute minimum.

Lunch money for the working member and when necessary for school children should be included in the budget. This can be a minimum figure as lunch needs may be met in part by the food grant.

In some instances there are expenditures which must be made in order to get and retain a job; the legitimacy of these items can be easily established.

Insurance

In most welfare bureaus an insurance adjustment division has been set up which advises clients as to the assets in their insurance policies; helps them use these assets for the continuation of such insurance as is reasonable; and makes available to them in cash any asset over and above the amount necessary to keep such protection in force. In planning with clients for the expenditure of money refunded through the process of insurance adjustment, it is suggested that the important needs of the family which are not met through the allowed budget be considered on a case work basis and reasonably applied.

An allowance for insurance premiums in the regular budget may be made by individual welfare bureaus at their own discretion, however, in accordance with the terms of the Emergency Relief Act*, such allowance is not a reimbursable item. Where no allowance for insurance premiums is made, provision for the payment of such premiums should be made from the refund settlement, and it is recommended that premiums be paid for a period of from six months

*Emergency Relief in New York State. Statutes, Regulations and Opinions and Interpretations of Counsel. Second Edition, 1934, Page 99.

to a year in advance. In order to eliminate the "insurance-savings" combination, clients are limited to the whole life (straight life) type of insurance in amounts not to exceed $500 on adults and $300 on minors.

Medical and Nursing Care

Medical and nursing care *in their own home* may be provided for chronically ill patients. In communities where there is a city physician or nurse on a salary basis, the care of chronic cases should be the responsibility of the local department of public welfare and should only be included in the budget where such facilities are not available. A complete statement of policies and procedures regarding medical care in the home may be found in the Manual.*

---

*Manual of Rules and Regulations governing Medical Care Provided in the Home to Recipients of Home Relief, June, 1934. (In revision.)

Section Three

SELECTION AND CONTROL OF ITEMS
IN THE BUDGET

Families should be allowed the greatest possible freedom in the choice of foods.* It is not the intention to minimize the importance of allowing for individual preference in food, but because of their great value certain foods should be assured to the average family. This is best accomplished by providing especially for them.

Milk

An adequate milk policy is a great safety factor. It is the easiest method of protecting the health and well-being of children. Money spent for milk will bring greater returns in nutritive value than money expended for any other one food. A delivered milk system is preferable because it not only guarantees milk to the child, but may reduce the price paid. Milk need not be limited to fresh, fluid milk, but may, and should, include other forms which are frequently cheaper. Unsweetened evaporated milk is just as nutritious as fresh milk and may well constitute one-half the total milk supply of the family, especially when cheaper than fresh, fluid milk. The following is considered minimum for normal individuals:

```
Ages:  1 to  2 years  ........ 7   Quarts a week
       2 "  5   "     ........ 3½—5  "    "    "
       5 " 10   "     ........ 3½    "    "    "
      10 " 12   "     ........ 3½    "    "    "
      12 " 16   "     ........ 3½—7  "    "    "
       Adults ............... 3½    "    "    "
```

Buying Controls

Experience has shown the following controls are necessary: the adoption of a list of food and household items which gives ample range of choice, but excludes foods unsuitable in a low cost diet (See Section Four, Page 20, for this list) ; the guiding of clients to such shops as offer a sufficiently wide selection and good quality.

---

* A food guide is available through the District Offices of The Temporary Emergency Relief Administration for distribution to clients.

Grocery and Food Price Controls

The most satisfactory way of assuring the lowest possible food prices in any community is through the grocery and food price control system or a local fair food price committee. Where such a system has not been set up, prices should be collected periodically from a sufficient number and variety of stores to give a reliable index of prevailing prices. Similar quality, grades and sizes should be priced in each store so that the figures will be comparable. To be of any value the pricing must be carefully done. Prevailing price, not average price, should be used in the calculation of the individual food allowance.*

Property Considerations

ONE-FAMILY DWELLINGS—Shelter allowances to home owners are granted in lieu of rent. They should not exceed the local maximum rent schedule. Payments in lieu of rent should never reduce the principal of a mortgage, increase the value of the home, or in any way enhance the client's equity therein.

The items which may be included in such shelter allowances are taxes, interest on a mortgage, water charges and fire insurance, if necessary.

Fire insurance premiums are paid only in the most unusual cases where non-payment would lead to loss of shelter. Such insurance is usually demanded as a part of the obligation of the mortgager. As it is a protection to his investment the mortgagee can, however, usually be depended on to carry the cost of such premiums, if the mortgager (relief client) is unable to do so.

If the property is in such a state that no mortgage loan can be procured, a possible situation might also arise where a very limited fire insurance premium might be included.

It is generally assumed that the owner should have a fair equity in his property if payments of any sort are to be made. Shelter allowances in cases where the owner's equity has been lost, should be made only under special circumstances.

* The Home Economics Department of the Temporary Emergency Relief Administration will assist any bureau desiring help in the calculation of food allowances or in the periodic review of the local allowance schedules.

MULTIPLE DWELLING HOMES—Where a relief client possesses a fair equity in a multiple dwelling in which he also resides, the following policy should pertain: rent allowances in accordance with the approved scale may be made where necessary. Income from the property, such as rents from other tenants, may be applied toward the minimum carrying charges. Any income from such property over and above actual minimum carrying charges should, however, be used for the family budget requirements.

OTHER PROPERTY—If a relief client owns a parcel of property other than that used as a residence, any income from such property should be used to the fullest extent to meet family budgetary needs. Such property must be regarded as an investment rather than as shelter and no allowance can be made for its maintenance.

Exceptions should be made to this rule only in rare instances. In the case of older people who own property of this type it may mean that their future security is tied up therein. If by paying carrying charges, it seems likely that a future income may be protected and future relief avoided or reduced, it might be more logical to permit minimum carrying charges to be taken out of such property income before it is figured against a budget deficit.

Since it is obviously unfair thus to give property investments preferential treatment over investments of another sort, such exceptions should be made only in rare instances.

BUSINESS AND HOME COMBINATIONS—If a relief recipient is running a business in his home, using space other than that needed for living quarters, two factors should be taken into consideration. Where non-payment of minimum carrying charges may result in the loss of the property, the income from such business may be applied toward the payment of those charges. Where a rent allowance is granted from relief funds, care should be taken that such allowance be made only for that portion of the property which would represent living quarters, as relief allowances cannot be made for the maintenance of business.

Section Four

SUGGESTED FORMS AND SCHEDULES

Insurance Schedule

The following table on an age basis is offered as a guide for the measurement of appropriate insurance protection for relief clients:

Age	Weekly Premium	Protection
1-10	$0.05	$150-$200
10-20	.10	200- 300
20-30	.20	300- 400
30-40	.30	300- 400
40-50	.40	300- 400

Food and Household Supplies

The following list was prepared to assist communities in the revision of local lists for food and household supplies. It includes the items of greatest food value and offers as wide a range of choice as is consistent with adequate nutrition at minimum cost. In the items of meat, fish, fresh fruits and fresh vegetables, it is helpful to indicate a maximum price per pound and to permit the client to buy any variety desired up to that maximum price.

In issuing a food list it may be necessary to use another arrangement. This list is intended only to give items and not to suggest set-up. However, it is hoped that the foods will be listed in groups rather than by alphabetic arrangement. In cases where alphabetic arrangement is used for foods, household items should be listed in a separate group.

Dairy Products

Price

Milk-Fluid Grade B.....Per Qt. $............
"   Evaporated ....Per tall can ....
    (unsweetened)

Cheese—American ....Per Lb. $............
"   Cottage ...... " " ....
"   Goat (Italian). " "
Eggs—Grade B........Per Doz. $............
"   "   C........ " " ....

Meat and Fish

	Price
Beef hamburg.........Per Lb. $	
" corned .... " "	
" heart .... " "	
" kidney .... " "	
" chuck .... " "	
" rump .... " "	
" flank .... " "	
" stewing .... " "	
Lamb stewing .... " "	
Pork Liver .... " "	
Beef Liver .... " "	
Fish—Cod .... " "	
Salt Cod ..... " "	
Haddock .... " "	
Flounder .... " "	
Mackerel .... " "	
Other fish in season.	
Canned Salmon (Size ...) ... " Can	
Canned Sardines (Size of fish..) " "	

Cereals and Breads

	Price
Bread—White ... Oz. Loaf $	
" Rye ..... " "	
" Whole Wheat . " "	
Graham Crackers.....Per Lb.	
Barley (Loose)........ " "	
Cornmeal " .... " "	
Farina ....1 Lb. 12 Oz.	
Oatmeal ....1 Lb. 4 Oz.	
Whole Wheat Cereal ....Lb. Oz.	
Hominy .... " "	
Flour—White ....Per Lb.	
" —Whole Wheat... " "	
" —Rye .... " "	
Macaroni (Pkg., Size ....).... " Pkg.	
Macaroni bulk......... " Lb.	
Spaghetti (Pkg., Size ....).... " Pkg.	
Spaghetti bulk......... " Lb.	
Rice, white—bulk...... " "	
" white (Pkg., Size ....).... " Pkg.	
Rice, brown—bulk...... " Lb.	
" brown (Pkg., Size ....).... " Pkg.	
Tapioca bulk.......... " Lb.	

Canned Vegetables

	Price
Corn ....Per No. 2 Can $	
Peas .... " " " "	
String Beans ... " " " "	
Beets .... " " " "	
Tomatoes ... " " " "	
" ...... " " 3 "	
Baked Beans.... " " 2 "	
Sauerkraut ..... " "	
Tomato Paste (Size ....) .. " " "	
Spinach .... " " 2½ "	
Applesauce ..... " " 2 "	

Root Vegetables

	Price
Beets ....Per Lb. $	
Carrots .... " "	
Onions .... " "	
Potatoes (White)...... " "	
" (Sweet)...... " "	
Turnips (Yellow)...... " "	

Green Vegetables

	Price
Cabbage ....Per Lb. $	
Spinach .... " "	
String Beans.......... " "	
Others in season not to exceed 7c. per lb.	

Dried Vegetables

	Price
Beans—Pea ....Per Lb. $	
" Kidney .... " "	
" Lima .... " "	
Lentils .... " "	
Peas—Green Split...... " "	

Fruits

	Price
Apples ....Per Lb. $	
Bananas	
Oranges (No........)... " Doz.	
Others in season (not in excess of 7c per lb.)	
Dried—Prunes (No......) " Lb. $	
Raisins .... " "	
Apricots .... " "	
Figs on String.. " "	

Fats

	Price
Butter ....Per Lb. $	
" Substitutes .... " "	
Lard .... " "	
Vegetable Oil .... " Pt.	
" .. " Gal.	
" Fats .... " Lb.	
Peanut butter .... " "	

Miscellaneous

	Price
Sugar—Granulated ....Per Lb. $	
" Brown ...... " "	
Molasses (Size ....)... " Can	
Pepper .... " Oz.	
Salt .... " Lb.	
Baking Powder (Size ....) " Pkg.	
Soda (Size ....)..... " "	
Spices (2 oz.)........ " "	
Flavoring	
Vinegar (bulk)........	
Yeast—Dry	
" Fresh	
Cornstarch ....Per Pkg. $	

Beverages

	Price
Tea—Green ....Per Lb. $	
" Black .... " "	
Coffee	
Cocoa (Size ....)..... " Can	

Household Supplies

	Price
Soap--Toilet	
" Laundry, White naphtha (or similar)	
Washing Soda	
Blueing	
Starch	
Scouring Powder	
Matches (Size .... Box) Box	
Toilet Paper .... Roll	
Broom	
Kerosene	
Lamp Chimney	
Wicks	
Clothes Line...(Length)	
" Pins .... Per Doz.	
Mop Handle	
Scrubbing Brush	

Clothing List

A list similar to the one given below is helpful as a check list for supplying immediate needs. (Local average price per article should be inserted.)

MAN AT WORK OR LOOKING FOR WORK

ARTICLE	COST PER ARTICLE
Hat or Cap...............................	
Coat or Jacket..........................	
Suit	
Overalls*	
Shirts	
Underwear	
Night Clothes	
Shoes	
Socks	
Rubbers	
Suspenders or Belt......................	
Tie.......................................	

* If type of work requires.

BOYS—6 TO 16 YEARS

ARTICLE	COST PER ARTICLE
Cap......................................	
Winter Coat.............................	
Jacket or sweater***J..................	
Knickers or trousers...................	
Blouses or shirts......................	
Underwear..............................	
Night Clothes..........................	
Shoes...................................	
Rubbers.................................	
Tie......................................	

*** Jacket—Sheeplined leatherette coat.

CHILDREN—1 TO 5 YEARS

ARTICLE	COST PER ARTICLE
Cap or Hat..............................	
Coat or sweater*.......................	
Dress, Suit or Rompers.................	
Underwear..............................	
Night Clothes..........................	
Shoes...................................	
Stockings or socks.....................	
Rubbers.................................	

* Might include coat, cap and leggings.

WOMAN AT HOME OR AT WORK

ARTICLE	COST PER ARTICLE
Hat...	
Coat..	
Street Dress.................................	
House Dress..................................	
Underwear....................................	
Brassieres....................................	
Corset or Girdle**...........................	
Slips or Petticoat............................	
Night Clothes................................	
Shoes...	
Stockings.....................................	
Rubbers......................................	

** If needed.

GIRLS—6 TO 16 YEARS

ARTICLE	COST PER ARTICLE
Hat or beret.................... S.............	
Coat or Sweater C............................	
Dress...	
Underwear....................................	
Slip..	
Night Clothes................................	
Shoes...	
Stockings or socks...........................	
Rubbers......................................	

INFANTS

ARTICLE	COST PER ARTICLE
Coat or Wrap*...............................	
Dress...	
Slips or Gertrudes............................	
Shirts or Vests...............................	
Night Clothes................................	
Diapers.......................................	
Stockings or socks...........................	

*Might include cap and leggings.

Shoe repair in all groups.

Articles obtainable from local sewing projects and clothing bureaus may be indicated by #.

24

Clothing Allowance Record Form

The following form is used as a file record in bureaus having a cumulative clothing allowance. A weekly sum is credited to the family according to the number in the family and the ages of the individual members.

Name......................						Address.....................						
Case No....................						Date........................						
Budget.....................						Visitor.....................						

	1	2	3	4	5	6	7	8	9	10	11	12	13
Budget													
Clothing													
Balance													
	14	15	16	17	18	19	20	21	22	23	24	25	26
Budget													
Clothing													
Balance													
	27	28	29	30	31	32	33	34	35	36	37	38	39
Budget													
Clothing													
Balance													
	40	41	42	43	44	45	46	47	48	49	50	51	52
Budget													
Clothing													
Balance													

Clothing is given on the "as needed basis". Up to date lists of clothing prices are furnished to the visitor. When requests for clothing are received, the visitor can quickly find out not only the approximate cost of the articles requested but can easily check on the amount remaining in the family clothing allowance. An allowance according to age groups has been found more satisfactory than a flat per person rate.

Cod Liver Oil

Cod Liver Oil is a valuable food because it is a very rich source of two food substances, vitamin A and vitamin D.

Liberal amounts of these two vitamins are needed both in summer and in winter to promote growth and to build up resistance. The food purchased by the average relief client is usually low in vitamin A.

In the interest of health it is desirable to have the widest possible distribution among young children, pregnant women and nursing mothers and the undernourished of all ages.

Dosage

The average daily dose recommended by the U.S.P.* Vitamin Advisory Board for the oil specified below is:

Infants: 3 teaspoonfuls daily
Adults: 6 teaspoonfuls daily

Strength

The dosage recommended above applies to cod liver oil containing at least 600 U.S.P. units of Vitamin A per gram and at least 85 U.S.P. units of Vitamin D per gram. Inasmuch as cod liver oil is ordinarily prescribed in the dosage given above, it is not necessary to purchase oil greatly in excess of the strength described above.

Purchase Plan

The purchase of standard grades is advised. The following specifications may be used in asking for bids as they conform to official standards:

"Oil of good quality containing at least 600 (U.S.P.) units of Vitamin A per gram and 85 (U.S.P.) units of Vitamin D per gram".* It is desirable to explain that oil of a higher vitamin content is not desired if it entails additional cost.

Bottled Oil

It is more economical to purchase bottled oil in packages of not less than eight ounces or more than sixteen ounces. The sixteen ounce bottle is preferred because it corresponds roughly to the bi-weekly requirement of persons over six months of age. A material saving may be made if it is purchased in at least six dozen lots.

*The Pharmacopeia of the United States, 1934 Supplement. Published by the Board of Trustees, United States Pharmacopoeial Convention.

Bulk Oil

Bulk purchases are only desirable in communities where the necessary facilities for handling and storing are available. When purchased in twenty gallon containers the oil will cost approximately one-half as much as oil purchased in sixteen ounce packages. The cost of bottles, labor and wastage will considerably reduce these savings. There is also the risk of spoilage due to improper storage and the difficulty of cleaning and sterilizing bottles for re-fills.

Storage

Both bottled and bulk oil should be stored in a cool, dark place.

Selected List of References to Official Rulings on the Family Budget

For original statements of policy in regard to budget problems see the following official Temporary Emergency Relief Administration Publications. For convenience these references have been indexed according to subject.

TITLE

TEMPORARY EMERGENCY RELIEF ADMINISTRATION—PERIODIC PUBLICATIONS

Official Bulletins
Official Letters to Commissioners of Public Welfare and Executive Directors of Emergency Relief Bureaus
Departmental Letters—Social Service Series

EMERGENCY RELIEF IN THE STATE OF NEW YORK—STATUTES, REGULATIONS AND OPINIONS AND INTERPRETATIONS OF COUNSEL. SECOND EDITION—REVISED TO NOVEMBER 1ST, 1934.

MANUAL OF PROCEDURE FOR LOCAL RELIEF ADMINISTRATION

SUBJECT REFERENCE

Home Relief—Definition and Budget Items:

Statutes—Pages 7, 10, 188
Manual, Section 000, Item 021; Section 100, Item 119; Section 200, Items 209, 210, 211, 222, 223.

Shelter

Statutes—Pages 10, 103-106.
Official Bulletin 6, Item 33.
Official Bulletin 9, Item 62.
Official Letter, May 6th, 1935.

Carfare

Departmental Letter—Social Service Series No. 18, May 3rd, 1935.

Household Supplies

Statutes—Page 30.

Cash Relief

Statutes—Pages 7, 12.
Official Bulletin 54, Item 236.
Manual, Section 200, Item 212.

Insurance

Statutes—Pages 99, 100.
Departmental Letter—Social Service Series No. 10, October 11th, 1934.

Ice

Statutes, Page 86.
Departmental Letter—Social Service Series No. 5, July 16th, 1934.

Cod Liver Oil

Official Bulletin 30, Item 153.
Official Letter, May 17th, 1934.

 60
BURLAND PRINTING CO.
45 ROSE ST., N. Y. C.

STATE OF NEW YORK

A MANUAL ON LEGAL SETTLEMENT

FOR

PUBLIC WELFARE AGENCIES

IN

NEW YORK STATE

TEMPORARY EMERGENCY RELIEF ADMINISTRATION

State Office Building, Albany

79 Madison Avenue, New York

STATE OF NEW YORK

TEMPORARY EMERGENCY RELIEF ADMINISTRATION

––––––

An Interpretation of the Provisions of the Public Welfare Law Relating to Settlement

––––––

Compiled and Arranged

by

HASKELL C. JACOBS

Consultant on Settlement

––––––

FEBRUARY 1, 1936

––––––

BURLAND PRINTING CO., INC.
45 ROSE STREET, N. Y. C.
60

ANNO DUODECIMO RICHARD II
CHAPTER SEVEN

Statute Enacted 1388

"ITEM, it is accorded and assented . . . that the beggars impotent to serve, shall abide in the cities and towns where they be dwelling at the time of the proclamation of this statute, and if the people of the cities or other towns will not or may not suffice to find them, that then the said beggars shall draw them to other towns within the hundreds, rape and wapentake, or to the towns where they were born, within xl. days after the proclamation made, and there shall continually abide during their lives . . ."

FOREWORD

A MANUAL on Legal Settlement is one of the documents which needs to come to the attention of the public and private social agencies and their workers because there is probably no other aspect of social welfare administration which is so confused. This is probably because existing sources of information are set before us in a strictly legal manner, and the confusion in our thinking and acting which results is really quite startling. These individual problems never present the same picture and the task of making a decision in terms of the legal presentation is not an easy one.

Mr. Jacobs has given a presentation of the law, backed up by case illustrations which give body and meaning to the law itself. I am very hopeful then that this pamphlet will become a desk companion to "Compilation of Settlement Laws of All States in the United States," prepared by Mr. Harry M. Hirsch, of the New York State Department of Social Welfare. Combined, they provide a guide which will be helpful to the worker, and materially serve to lighten the burdens of the growing number of people who, from one cause or another, find themselves dependent and temporarily detached from the normal public welfare service in a specific community. Without question Mr. Jacobs has given us a much needed instrument for a more intelligent social service.

DAVID C. ADIE,
Commissioner of Social Welfare.

January 1, 1936.

TABLE OF CONTENTS

PART II

VERIFICATION OF SETTLEMENT

PART III

PUBLIC WELFARE LAW

Selected Sections

—8—

INTRODUCTION

WITH the advent of thousands of new workers in the public welfare field within the past four or five years, there has developed a real need for general training programs so that these persons coming from many varied fields might better be able to cope with the intricacies of a public welfare department.

Along with this general program has been a specific need for clarification of the legal aspect of this relief picture, especially in the problem of legal settlement. To aid in answering that need is the purpose of this manual.

The material herein is confined solely to a discussion of "settlement" under the Public Welfare Law. This is to be distinguished from the "residence" requirement in the Emergency Relief Act. The two problems are distinct.

The "settlement" requirement is solely for the purpose of designating the local financial responsibility for relief in the first instance.

·"Residence" under the Emergency Relief Act ("Two years' residence in the state prior to the date of application for aid under this act . . .") is necessary only in the problem of reimbursement to local communities by the Temporary Emergency Relief Administration for relief granted by these communities under the provisions of the act.

The opinions in the cases presented in this manual are based on decisions of the State Department of Social Welfare, the Attorney General and the Appellate Courts. In a few instances where the opinions have been of an informal nature they are so identified. The same applies in those cases on which no decisions have been rendered. The manual has been compiled primarily for reference purposes, so that ultimate opinions on actual cases rest with the State Department of Social Welfare and contested statements of facts should be referred to that department for decision.

The writer wishes to acknowledge his appreciation to Mr. Henry Epstein, Solicitor General for New York State, and to Mr. Harry M. Hirsch, Assistant Commissioner of the State Department of Social Welfare, for their kindness in perusing the pages of this manual and for offering many valuable suggestions.

January 30, 1936.

PART I

AN INTERPRETATION OF THE LAW OF SETTLEMENT

PUBLIC WELFARE LAW

PUBLIC WELFARE DISTRICTS
(Reference—Sections 12, 13, 17, and 18—Part III)*

NEW YORK STATE:

The local units of responsibility for relief in the state are the public welfare districts. It is, therefore, essential to have a clear picture of the state as thus divided to better understand the respective duties and responsibilities of state, county and local welfare officials.

The state is divided into counties which are in turn divided into towns and cities. For the most part, each county is a separate county public welfare district. The cities of New York, Kingston, Oswego, Poughkeepsie and Newburgh are separate city public welfare districts. The territories of the counties outside of these cities are separate county public welfare districts. A city (other than those mentioned above) is only a part of the county public welfare district in which it is situated.

In each public welfare district is a commissioner of public welfare who has the duty of administering the public relief and care for which the district is responsible.

Each town and city in a public welfare district may have a welfare officer or city commissioner who has jurisdiction only in the locality in which he serves.

It should be carefully noted that "town" is synonymous with township rather than with village, and is a geographical sub-

---

* Legislative amendments enacted subsequent to the date of publication of this manual should be consulted for possible changes in the text.

division of a county, so that all the towns in a county will make up the county, just as all the counties make up the state. ‾

The city of New York (including the boroughs of Manhattan, Bronx, Kings, Queens and Richmond) under the law is a city public welfare district.

SETTLEMENT

(Reference—Sections 53-60 Part III)

Sec. 53—SETTLEMENT

WHY DO WE HAVE SETTLEMENT?

Case 1—Family lives in Albany for 15 years, then goes to New York City. Lives there *8* months, and makes an application for relief.

Case 2—Same facts, only family lives in New York City *18* months, and makes an application for relief.

Discussion: In both cases, if there were no law on settlement, New York City would argue that, inasmuch as this family lived in Albany for 15 years, and spent its money there, etc., that Albany should be responsible for taking care of it, now that it needs relief.

Albany, on the other hand, would argue in both cases, that it is true that a community should be responsible for its own destitute inhabitants, but that the family now lives in New York City and, therefore, that city has the responsibility.

By going to the Public Welfare Law (P.W.L.), both cities find that in Case 1 the family has an Albany settlement, and in Case 2 New York City would have to assume the financial responsibility.

In other words, THE LAW OF SETTLEMENT WAS DESIGNED TO CLARIFY AND DESIGNATE THE *FINANCIAL* RESPONSIBILITY OF THE VARIOUS TOWNS, CITIES, COUNTIES, AND OF THE STATE ITSELF, IN RESPECT OF DESTITUTE PERSONS.

In view of the above, it is evident that a knowledge of the law of settlement is a necessary prerequisite to handling intelligently and efficiently the relief problem of a community.

WHAT CONSTITUTES SETTLEMENT?

LAW: ". . . shall be a resident and inhabitant of a town or city for one year . . ."

Case 3—The Jones family has a settlement in Rochester. On January 1, 1932, the family moves to New York City, taking its furniture, Mr. Jones gets a job there, Mrs. Jones joins a bridge club, the children go to school there. After living there for over one year, Mr. Jones loses his job and makes an application for relief.

Discussion: In this case the facts all show an intention on the part of the Jones family to make a permanent home in New York City.

Case 4—The Smith family has a settlement in Rochester. On January 1, 1932, Mr. Smith procures a job in New York City. He is employed on this job until March 1933. During this period he sends money home regularly to his wife and visits his wife in Rochester whenever he can. On March 1, 1933, he loses his job and returns to Rochester. On April 1, 1933, the family makes an application for relief.

Discussion: While Mr. Smith is employed in New York City his home is in Rochester. His maintaining a home there shows his intention of considering Rochester as his permanent residence.

Case 5—The Johnson family has a settlement in Rochester. On January 31, 1932, Mr. and Mrs. Johnson disagree and Mr. Johnson moves to New York City. He lives in New York City until April 1933, when his wife makes an application for relief in Rochester for herself and the children.

Discussion: In this case when Mr. Johnson separated from his family and moved to New York City, his home was in the latter place. He could have no intention of keeping Rochester as his home while actually residing in New York City separated from his family.

Case 6—The Adams family has a settlement in New York City. On January 1, 1932, Mr. Adams enlists in the Army and is assigned to Panama. He remains there for 2 years, and is then discharged. He immediately returns to New York City to his family in January 1934. In June 1934 he makes an application for relief.

Discussion: The fact that Mr. Adams was transferred to Panama during his enlistment shows no intention of his residing there permanently, especially in view of his maintaining a home in New York City in the meantime, and his returning to his home when his enlistment period was at an end.

In other words, SETTLEMENT IS THE COMBINATION OF THREE ELEMENTS:—(1)—RESIDENCE plus—(2) *AN INTENT*, plus (3) THE PROVISIONS OF THE P.W.L.

SETTLEMENT: (Considering the family as a single unit)

LAW: "Every person of full age who shall be a resident and an inhabitant (Case 3) of a *town or city* (Case 8) for one year (Case 7) without receiving public relief (See P.W.L. Sec. 56 and cases), shall be deemed to have a settlement in such town or city, which shall continue until he shall have gained a like settlement in some other town or city of this state (Case 9) or shall have removed from this state and remained therefrom for one year (Case 11). Settlement in a county public welfare district shall be acquired by settlement in a town or city thereof."

Case 7—Mr. Roe and family live in Rochester from January 1, 1930 to February 1, 1931. They move to Syracuse and on May 1, 1931, they apply for relief.

Discussion: The Roe family had lived in Rochester for over a year and, therefore, had a settlement in Rochester on February 1, 1931. On May 1931 it had not lived in Syracuse a year, so, therefore, still had a Rochester settlement.

Case 8—On January 1, 1930, Mr. Locke and family move to Rochester and live there until February 1, 1931. They then move to Syracuse (in Onondaga County), living there for six months; then they move to Liverpool (also in Onondaga County) and live there for six months, then move back into Syracuse, live there another month and then make an application for relief.

Discussion: It should be very carefully noted that even though the Locke family lived in Onondaga County for over one year, it did not live in "a town or city" for one year and, therefore, the settlement reverts back to Rochester.

Case 9—Mr. Bridge and family lived in Albany for several years. On January 1, 1933, they move to Brooklyn and live there for six months. They then move to Manhattan, living there for six months. They then move to the Bronx and live there for seven months and make an application for relief.

—16—

Discussion: As all of the boroughs are part of the city of New York, the Bridge family lived in a city for one year and, therefore, acquired a settlement in New York City.

Case 10—Mr. Doe and family live in New York City from January 1927 to February 1931. They then move to Rochester to live. They remain there for seven months, then move to Albany where they live for seven months, up until April 1, 1932, when they make an application for relief.

Discussion: The Doe family did not lose its settlement in New York City in spite of the fact that it left New York City and was away for over a year, inasmuch as it did not acquire another settlement by residing in a town or city for a year after living in New York City.

Case 11—On January 1, 1930, Mr. Keye and family move to Rochester and live there until February 1, 1931. The family then moves to Philadelphia for six months; then to Chicago for five months; then to Cleveland for three months, and then they move to New York City. After they live there for one month they apply for relief.

Discussion: While the facts in Case 11 seem to be similar to Case 10, it should be noted that in Case 11 the family moved from Rochester *out of the state,* and although it did not live in any one place for one year it "removed from the state and remained therefrom for one year", and therefore, lost its settlement in the state.

The question arises, of course, as to where the responsibility rests for the granting of relief to those clients who have no settlement in any town or city in the state. This is discussed in the following section.

Annotation: *A*—Where a man was out of the state for over a year in a Pennsylvania penitentiary, it was *held*, he did not lose his settlement in the state as "the absence must be voluntary."

B—Where a family went to Syracuse on March 2, 1932, and made an application for relief on March 2, 1933, it was *held*, that the family had lived there for one year. The year was completed midnight March 1, 1933. (Substantial compliance is more important than meticulous adherence to the letter of the law.)

Sec. 18—RESPONSIBILITY FOR PUBLIC RELIEF, CARE AND SUPPORT

STATE POOR:

LAW: "1. *The state shall be responsible for:*

> (a) The support of any person having no settle-
> ment in any public welfare district in the state,
> who shall not have resided in any public welfare
> district in the state for sixty days during the year
> prior to an application for public relief and care.
> . . .

"2. *Each public welfare district shall be responsible for:*

> (d) The relief and care of any person found in its
> territory for whose support the state is respon-
> sible, subject to reimbursement by the state in ac-
> cordance with the provisions of this chapter. . . ."

Case 11-a—Mr. Johnson and family resided in New Jersey
for several years. They then moved to Schenectady and after living there for one month they applied for relief.

Case 11-b—Mr. Morris and family reside in Pennsylvania
for several years. On January 1, 1935, they move
to Albany, residing there for thirty days; then to
Utica where they live for forty-five days. The
family then moves to Rochester, and after it is
there for forty-five days, an application for relief
is made.

Discussion: In Cases 11-a and 11-b, neither family has
"resided in any public welfare district in the state
for sixty days during the year prior to an application for public relief and care," and in both cases,
therefore, they will be a state poor charge. The

state, through the State Department of Social Welfare, will reimburse the public welfare district 100% for the care granted, but the *administration* of this relief is the initial responsibility of the public welfare district where the client resides.

LOCAL SETTLEMENT:

LAW: *"2· Each public welfare district shall be responsible for:*

> (a) The relief, care and support of any person who resides and has a settlement in its territory."

Discussion: This section is self explanatory.

NON-RESIDENT:

LAW: *"2. Each public welfare district shall be responsible for:*

> (b) The relief, care and support of any person found in its territory not having a settlement in the state, for whose support the state is not responsible. . . ."

Case 11-c—Mr. Mack and family lived in California for several years. On January 1, 1935, they move to Syracuse and live there for one month. They then move to Albany for three months, then to Utica for one month, and an application for relief is made on June 1, 1935.

Case 11-d—Mr. Jones and family lived in California for several years. On January 1, 1935, they move to Syracuse and live there for one month. They then move to Albany and live there for one month; then to New York City for one month; then back to Syracuse for one month; then to Utica for one month, after which they make an application for relief.

Discussion: Cases 11-c and 11-d are illustrative of "non-resident" cases, that is, in neither case does the family have a settlement in any town or city in New York State, nor are they "state poor" cases inasmuch as the families in both cases did reside for sixty days in a public welfare district during the year prior to their application for relief. Therefore, the local public welfare district has both the financial responsibility and the administrative responsibility for the granting of relief. In Case 11-d, the two periods of one month each in Syracuse would constitute the sixty days, and the case would, therefore, be "non-resident," and the local public welfare district (Onondaga County —not the city of Syracuse) is responsible.

"CHARGE-BACK":

LAW: *"2. Each public welfare district shall be responsible for:*

(c) The relief and care of any person found in its territory who has a settlement elsewhere in the state, subject to reimbursement by the public welfare district of the person's settlement in accordance with the provisions of this chapter.

(e) The payment of the cost of the relief and care of a person having a settlement in its territory given by some other public welfare district."

Case 11-e—The Fay family has a settlement in Rochester, New York. They move to Syracuse, and after residing there for two months make an application for relief.

Discussion: The relief here would be administered in Syracuse, and the cost of relief would be charged back to Rochester.

Case 11-f—Mr. Gray and family have a settlement in New
York City and move to Rochester. After residing
in Rochester for six months they make an application for relief.

Discussion: New York City: New York City has had
a provision in its charter forbidding the granting
of outdoor relief. The result has been up to the
present time, that the city could neither reimburse
up-state communities for clients receiving relief
and having a settlement in New York City, nor
could they receive reimbursement from up-state
communities for relief granted to persons in New
York City and having a settlement up-state. At
the present time there is an amendment contemplated which will bring New York City under the
provisions of the Public Welfare Law. Until that
time it appears that the respective responsibilities
will be limited to the authorization of returning
the clients to their respective places of settlement,
or granting the relief as a total local responsibility.
In Case. 11-f, therefore, Rochester could at the
present time procure authorization for the return of the Gray family to New York City, or
accept the responsibility as a local charge.

General Discussion:
In the "non-resident" and "state poor" group,
while the client does not have a settlement in any
town or city in New York State, he may have
a settlement in some other state.
In "state poor" cases the State Department of Social Welfare will take the necessary steps to procure verification of client's settlement. In the
"non-resident" group, the State Department will
assist the local communities whenever called upon
to do so.

Though a person is found to have a settlement
in another state, there may be no reimbursement

from the other state for any relief granted, as in the case of charge-backs. This is due to the lack of uniformity of the laws of the different states. In examining the sections involving the responsibility of a public welfare district, it will be noted that the public welfare district, in effect, has the responsibility for the *administering* of relief to *all* destitute persons residing therein. The financial responsibility will rest either upon that public welfare district, another public welfare district in the state, or on the state itself.

Sec. 54—SETTLEMENT OF A MARRIED WOMAN

EFFECT OF MARRIAGE:

LAW: "The settlement of a married woman shall be that of her husband except as otherwise herein provided. . . ."

Case 12—Mr. Jones, having a settlement in Syracuse, marries Miss Smith, whose settlement is in Rochester. They then live in Rochester.

> *Discussion:* Even though this couple lives in Rochester, the woman's settlement, after the marriage, will be in Syracuse (that of the husband) until they have lived in Rochester "one year without receiving public relief," thus establishing a settlement there.

EFFECT OF DEATH, DIVORCE OR LEGAL SEPARATION:

LAW: "A widow (Case 13) or a woman who is divorced (Case 14) or separated by judicial decree (Cases 15, 16, and 17) from her husband shall have the same settlement which she had at the time of the death of her husband or of her divorce or separation, but may subsequently gain a new settlement."

Case 13—Mr. and Mrs. White have a New York City settlement. On January 1, 1931, Mr. White dies and Mrs. White moves to Rochester. On January 1, 1932, Mrs. White applies for relief at Rochester.

Case 14—Mr. and Mrs. Grey have a settlement in New York City. On January 1, 1931, a final decree of divorce is granted to Mr. Grey. Mrs. Grey, on that date, moves to Rochester and Mr. Grey moves to Utica. On January 1, 1932, Mrs. Grey makes an application for relief. Mr. Grey is still living in Utica.

Case 15—Mr. and Mrs. Brown have a settlement in New York City. On January 1, 1931, Judge Lewis grants a judicial decree legally separating Mr. and Mrs. Brown. Case was tried in Supreme Court in New York City. On that date Mrs. Brown moves to Rochester and on January 1, 1932, applies for relief.

Discussion: In Cases 13, 14, and 15, the same principle applies. On January 1, 1931, the wife has a settlement in New York City, and on January 1, 1932, she has acquired a settlement in Rochester, as stated in the law (Sec. 54), having lived in Rochester one year since the death, divorce or legal separation from the husband.

Case 16—Mr. and Mrs. Black have a settlement in New York City. They can't get along so their respective attorneys draw up a separation agreement, making arrangements for Mr. Black to support his wife, etc. It was signed by both parties on January 1, 1931. On that date Mr. Black moves to Utica where he still resides. The same date, Mrs. Black goes to Rochester and on January 1, 1932, she applies for relief, as her husband lost his job.

Discussion: This case illustrates a statement of facts often confused with "legal separation" as illustrated by Case 15. The separation in Case 16 is not a separation "by judicial decree," but rather a "separation agreement," and no special provision being made in the law, the wife continues to follow the husband's settlement, which would be Utica.

Case 17—Mr. and Mrs. Gray have a settlement in New York City. Mr. Gray is brought into Police Court on a charge of non-support and cruelty. He is given a sentence "suspended on condition that he stay away from his wife."

Discussion: While the sentence of the judge may appear to be a legal separation, this is a criminal action, and it is not considered, therefore, as a legal separation under the law, so that the wife would continue to take her husband's settlement.

Annotation: C—Where a man had been convicted of murder and was given a prison sentence (not for life), it was *held,* that this was not a "separation by judicial decree." The opinion states that "a matrimonial action was implied" in construing this section of the law.

D—Where a husband and wife had settlement in Albany, they went to New York City and lived there six months, after which the husband died. The wife continued to live in New York City for seven months longer. It was *held,* that the wife did not acquire a settlement in New York City inasmuch as she took the settlement of her husband at the time of his death, which was Albany, and she would have to reside in New York City for one year after his death without public relief before she could have acquired the New York City settlement.

EFFECT OF DESERTION, husband's whereabouts unknown:

LAW: ". . . A married woman whose husband has deserted her shall continue to have the settlement of her husband at the time of such desertion, except that, if her husband's whereabouts continue unknown, she shall, after a period of one year have the right to acquire a separate settlement. . . ."

Case 18—Mr. and Mrs. Ace have a settlement in Syracuse. On January 1, 1930, Mr. Ace deserts his family and is not heard from since. On that date, Mrs. Ace and family move to Rochester, living there until January 1, 1931, when she moves to Utica, lives there until January 1, 1932, and then applies for relief.

Discussion: On January 1, 1931, Mrs. Ace's settlement is still Syracuse (not Rochester), as she cannot *begin* to acquire her own settlement until one year after her husband deserts, which in this case is January 1, 1931, so that on January 1, 1932, Mrs. Ace would have acquired her own settlement in Utica.

EFFECT OF DESERTION, husband's whereabouts is known or becomes known:

LAW: ". . . Such separate settlement shall continue while her husband's whereabouts is unknown, and until he is known to have established a settlement in some town or city of this state or in some other state."

Case 19—Husband deserts, but is known to have gone to New York City, where he lives for over a year. Wife is living in Syracuse without public relief.

Discussion: Where the husband is separated from the wife and his whereabouts are known, the wife continues to follow his settlement, so the wife would have a settlement in New York City as soon as her husband had acquired his settlement there.

Case 20—Mr. and Mrs. Smythe have a settlement in Syracuse. On January 1, 1930, Mr. Smythe deserts and his whereabouts is unknown; on that date Mrs. Smythe goes to Rochester, lives there until February 1, 1932, and then procures relief in Rochester. On April 1, 1932, Mr. Smythe appears and it develops that he had lived in New York City from January 1, 1930, to March 1, 1931, when he moved to Utica, living there until April 1932, when he went to Rochester.

Discussion: Mrs. Smythe on January 1, 1932, would have acquired a settlement in Rochester, so would have a Rochester settlement on February 1, 1932, when she applied for relief. When Mr. Smythe turns up, however, his settlement is investigated, and the wife thereupon again follows the settlement of her husband. According to the facts here, Mr. Smythe had acquired a settlement in New York City on January 1, 1931. To have gained a settlement in Utica, he must have lived there for one year. He did live there from March 1, 1931 until April 1932, but his wife received relief in February 1932, before a year had elapsed. Therefore, on April 1, 1932, when Mr. Smythe reappears, both Mr. and Mrs. Smythe would have a settlement in New York City.

Annotation: E—Where a husband had left the state and had remained outside of the state for over one year, and the woman in the meantime acquired a settlement in Syracuse, it was *held*, that when the man had lost his settlement by being outside of the state for over one year, the woman and children would follow his settlement and would, therefore, lose their Syracuse settlement and would become a County charge.

Sec. 55—SETTLEMENT OF MINORS

IN GENERAL:

Note: Under the Public Welfare Law a minor is a male or female under the age of 21. In the following discussion "Minor" will represent a child under 21 years of age.

LAW: "The settlement of a minor born in wedlock shall be that of his parents (Case 21) or surviving parent (Case 23). . . ."

Case 21—Mr. and Mrs. Smith have a settlement in Syracuse. On January 1, 1932, they visit some relatives in Rochester and on February 1, 1932, a child is born in Rochester.

Discussion: Even though the child was not born in Syracuse, under the law quoted, the child takes the settlement of its parents, which is Syracuse.

Case 22—Mr. and Mrs. White and Minor have a settlement in Syracuse. Minor leaves parents and goes to Rochester where he lives with friends who help him. After he lives in Rochester for over a year he makes an application for relief there.

Discussion: Where the parents are living, the minor retains their settlement, which is Syracuse, and he cannot acquire a separate settlement except in the specific manner found in Section 55—Sub. 4, as hereinafter discussed.

Case 23—Mr. and Mrs. Jones and Minor have a settlement in Syracuse. Mr. Jones dies on January 1, 1932, and on that date Mrs. Jones and Minor move to Rochester. They live in Rochester for over one year without receiving relief.

Discussion: Mrs. Jones lived in Rochester for over a year after her husband died, and therefore, takes a Rochester settlement. Minor would follow her settlement, as she is the "surviving parent."

EFFECT OF SEPARATION OF PARENTS:

LAW: ". . . in case of divorce, legal separation or desertion," the settlement of a minor shall be that "of the parent having his custody . . ."

Case 24—On January 1, 1931, Mr. and Mrs. Locke and Minor have a settlement in Syracuse. On that date, Mr. Locke procures a divorce from his wife, and the Court Order states that he has legal custody of the child. On the same date, Mr. Locke moves to Rochester with Minor and lives there for one year. Mrs. Locke in the meantime moves to Watertown and lives in Watertown for over one year. Mr. Locke then loses his job and it is agreed that Mrs. Locke should have the custody of the child until Mr. Locke procures employment again. After Minor is with Mrs. Locke for three months, she makes an application for relief.

Discussion: In Case 24, it is to be noted that Minor follows the settlement of the father while they are together in Rochester. When Mrs. Locke procures the actual custody of Minor and Mr. Locke has legal custody, it will probably be *held*, that Minor follows Mr. Locke's settlement, though that question has not been definitely determined by the State Department as yet. Where there is no Court Order (e.g., man deserts, leaving wife and child), the child would follow the wife's settlement. Where the legal and actual custody coincide, the problem is not difficult. Where they do not coincide, the ultimate answer will rest with the State Department.

Case 25—On January 1, 1931, Mr. and Mrs. Briggs and Minor have a settlement in Syracuse. On that date Mrs. Briggs procures a divorce and gets the custody of Minor, and Mr. Briggs is ordered to pay $5.00 per week for the support of the child. Mrs. Briggs goes to Rochester, living there for a year and acquiring a settlement in Rochester. Mr. Briggs thereafter stops making payments, and Mrs. Briggs applies for relief for herself and Minor. The Welfare Department claims that inasmuch as Mr. Briggs has a settlement in Syracuse, and he is liable for the support of his son, when he stops making payments, it would logically follow that the son would have his settlement.

Discussion: While the argument may seem logical, it should be very carefully noted that *liability for support has nothing to do with the problem of settlement,* inasmuch as the latter is statutory. In Case 25, Minor takes the settlement of the mother regardless of the court order directing Mr. Briggs to pay for the support of the minor.

ILLEGITIMATE CHILDREN:

LAW: ". . . The settlement of a minor born out of wedlock shall be that of his mother . . ."

Case 26—Gladys Doe, unmarried, has a settlement in Syracuse. A child is born out of wedlock. The putative father is brought into Court and is adjudged by the Court to be the father of the child as outlined in the Domestic Relations Law. His settlement is in Rochester. Miss Doe makes an application for relief in Syracuse for herself and Minor. Syracuse claims that Minor has a Rochester settlement as paternity was established.

Discussion: Inasmuch as the law explicitly states that "the settlement of a minor born out of wedlock shall be that of his mother," the Minor will follow the mother's settlement in spite of the illegitimacy proceedings, so the child's settlement will be in Syracuse.

EFFECT OF DEATH OF PARENTS OR SEPARATION OF PARENTS FROM MINORS:

LAW: ". . . . In case of the death of the parent having custody, the settlement of a minor shall be that of his surviving parent . . ."

Case 27—Mr. and Mrs. Keye are divorced. Mr. Keye had a settlement in Syracuse. Mrs. Keye has the legal and actual custody of Minor. She remarries Mr. White who has a Rochester settlement. Three months later she dies.

> *Discussion:* The problem arising in this case depends on the construction of "surviving parent," whether or not this phrase would include "step-parents." In a recent opinion it was *held*, that where both parents died, Minor would follow the settlement of the step-parent, and this would probably be followed in a case such as Case 27, so that Minor would have a Rochester settlement.

LAW: ". . . In case of the death of both parents (Case 28), or of the mother of a minor born out of wedlock, or in case of permanent separation from his parents by Court Order (Case 29), or by surrender by an instrument in writing in accordance with the provisions of the state charities law, the settlement of a minor at the time of such death or separation shall continue until his majority, unless he shall gain a separate settlement as hereinafter provided . . ."

Case 28—Mr. and Mrs. Brown and Minor have a settlement in Syracuse. Both parents die and Minor goes to Auburn to live with an aunt and uncle for two years. The relatives then make an application for relief for themselves and Minor.

Discussion: Minor's settlement at the time of the death of both parents is, of course, Syracuse. Even though he lives in Auburn for two years thereafter, his settlement does not change, nor does he follow the settlement of his guardian, as the law clearly states that his settlement will be Syracuse until he is twenty-one years of age, unless he gains his own settlement as specifically provided in Section 55, Sub. 4 (see below).

Case 28a—Minor lives with parents in Oswego. They have an Oswego settlement. He leaves home at 18, and goes to Albany, where he remains with relatives. He is unemployed. Six months after his 21st birthday, he applies for relief.

Discussion: As he has not lived in Albany for one year without relief after his 21st birthday, his settlement is still in Oswego.

Case 29—Mr. Black procures a divorce from his wife. At that time they have a settlement in Syracuse. The order of the Court states that neither parent is to have custody of Minor, and the Court further states that Minor is to be placed in the custody of the Children's Bureau, a child-placing agency.

Mr. Black moves to Auburn and lives there for two years. He then fails to support Minor and relief is requested for Minor's care in the foster home.

Discussion: At the time of the order of the Court, the child has a settlement in Syracuse. The order separating Minor from both parents is similar in effect to the death of the parents, and the Minor will take the settlement which it had at the time of the Court Order, keeping it until Minor reaches twenty-one years of age.

Case 30—Mr. and Mrs. White and Minor have a settlement in Syracuse. Minor leaves parents and goes to Rochester, where he lives with friends who help him. After he lives in Rochester for over a year, he makes an application for relief there.

> *Discussion:* Where the parents are still living, Minor retains their settlement, which is Syracuse, and cannot acquire a separate settlement except in the specific manner found in Section 55, Sub. 4 (see next paragraph).

MINOR ACQUIRING A SEPARATE SETTLEMENT:

LAW: " . . . A minor may gain a separate settlement as follows:

BY MARRIAGE

"(a) If a male, by marrying and residing separately from the family of his father or mother for one year.

(b) If a female, by marrying and living with her husband."

Case 31—Mary, 19, and John, 19, get married on January 1, 1931. On that date Mary's parents have a Rochester settlement, and John's parents have a settlement in Syracuse. After the marriage, the young couple live with the bride's parents in Rochester, until January 2, 1932.

> *Discussion:* Even though the couple were living in Rochester, Mary, "by marrying and living with her husband," would take her husband's settlement—Syracuse. On January 2, 1932, John had married and lived away from home for a year, and therefore, established his own settlement in

Rochester, and of course, Mary's settlement would again revert to Rochester.

BY EMPLOYMENT

LAW: ". . . (c) By being lawfully employed for one year when wages are paid to such minor."

Case 32—On January 1, 1932, Minor has a settlement in New York City, where his parents are living. On that date he goes to Syracuse and gets a job. His wages are $35.00 per week. He works for six months and loses his job. During the next two months he gets along on his savings, and then gets another job on a farm which is located near the outskirts, but within the city limits, of Syracuse, where he gets his room and board and clothes, but no money. He works on the farm for five months, and then loses his job and makes an application for relief.

Discussion: Case 32 points out several problems arising under this section of the law. There are two reasons why Minor has not acquired his own settlement in Syracuse.

His working for six months and then for five months, with a two-months' period of unemployment is *not* being "employed for one year." His getting room and board and clothing on the farm job, does *not* constitute "wages" in the law.
It is to be noted that this law, abrogating the common law, is to be "strictly construed."

In some cases, however, where the actual employment has been slightly less than a year (e.g., 51 weeks, etc.), it has been held that this is a "substantial compliance" with the law, and that Minor had acquired his own settlement. It should be noted that the dividing line is not definite, and in these close cases, a decision should be requested.

LAW: ". . . (c) . . . This provision shall not apply in the case of a minor serving an apprenticeship or securing an education in a regularly organized training school (Case 34), or other educational institution (Case 33), or where such minor is dependent in whole or in part upon his or her parent or guardian for support (Case 35) . . ."

Case 33—Family has a settlement in Rochester. On January 1, 1930, Minor goes to New York City and attends High School, working nights at $10.00 per week. During the summer he works at the same job during the day at $15.00 per week, and in the fall he returns to school and resumes his night work. He is entirely self-supporting and even sends money to his parents occasionally. This continues for two years.

Discussion: Minor did not gain his own settlement as he was going to school while working. It is to be especially noted that a person *under* twenty-one cannot gain a separate settlement while he is going to school, as the law so states.

In the case of a person *over* twenty-one, the intention of the person is the governing factor in the establishing of a settlement. There is a presumption that a person attending a school or university is not intending to acquire a settlement. This presumption may be overcome by facts showing that the person has an intention of permanently residing in the place where the school is located (for example, marrying and setting up a home, etc.).

Case 34—Minor (in Case 33) has a sister, 19, who also goes to New York City and takes a nurse's training course, getting room and board and $10.00 per month wages. She keeps this up for two years.

Discussion: The sister does not acquire a separate settlement, as a nurse's training course is an apprenticeship rather than employment.

Case 35—Another brother, 18, goes to Utica and gets a job at $5.00 per week. Not being able to get along on that, his parents send him $2.00 per week extra.

Discussion: The brother does not establish his own settlement as he is "dependent in whole or in part upon his parents." A regular weekly allowance or washing and sewing would constitute dependency, though the dividing line is not clearly defined in the interpretation of the law.

BY ADOPTION

LAW: ". . . (d) By being adopted, in which case he shall have the settlement of his foster parents or parent . . ."

Discussion: This is self-explanatory. The minor would take the settlement of the foster parents at the time the adoption was effected.

Sec. 56—QUALIFICATION ON THE ACQUISITION OF SETTLEMENT

EFFECT OF BEING INSTITUTIONALIZED:

LAW: "No settlement shall be gained by reason of the place of birth (Case 36) nor by residence as a patient in a hospital or as an inmate of any public institution (Case 37) or incorporated private charitable institution (Case 38)."

Case 36—The Adams family has a settlement in Albany. It moves to Syracuse, and two months later a child is born in Syracuse.

   Discussion: Inasmuch as the place of birth is immaterial, the child will still follow the settlement of the parents, which is Albany.

Case 37—Mr. Jones has a settlement in Syracuse on January 1, 1932. He is sent to Willard State Hospital, leaving his family in Syracuse. After he is in Willard over a year, his family makes an application for relief.

Case 38—Same facts, only Mr. Jones is sent to a Home for the Aged instead of Willard.

   Discussion: In Case 37, Mr. Jones still has a Syracuse settlement, as he could not gain one while in an institution. Same in Case 38, if the Home was an "incorporated private charitable institution."

   One problem which has arisen, but is not adequately covered by the law, is illustrated in the next four cases.

Case 39—Mr. Jones and family have a settlement in Rochester on January 1, 1930. They go to Syracuse, live there for three months and Jones is then arrested and sent to the Penitentiary for two months. He returns home, lives there *nine* months and then makes application for relief.

Case 40—Same facts, except that he returns from jail, lives in Syracuse *eight* months and makes an application for relief.

Case 41—He goes to Syracuse with family, lives there three months, and then is sent to jail for ten months.

Case 42—Mr. Jones, an unattached man, is involved in the same facts as above three cases.

Discussion: In the above group of cases, the question arises as to the effect of the confinement in the institution on the family's settlement. According to the law quoted above, Jones could not acquire a settlement in a town or city in which the Penitentiary is located, but there is nothing in the law on the effect of this period on a man's settlement elsewhere, as in Cases 39 to 42, inclusive.

In Cases 39, 40 and 41, it has been held that a settlement had been established in Syracuse on the basis that the jail sentence is considered a "constructive residence" in Syracuse, as the family having resided there in the meantime, had the intention to make Syracuse the place of settlement.

In Case 42, Jones would not have established a settlement in Syracuse unless he could show sufficient facts to constitute a one year's residence, as, for example, keeping up an apartment, or paying rent in Syracuse, while in the institution; otherwise his settlement is broken by the period in the penitentiary.

Annotation F: Where a man moved to Rochester with his family on September 2, 1930, and was sent to an out-of-town hospital from January 1931 to November 1931, his family living in Rochester in

the meantime, the Attorney General *held*, that
the man had acquired a Rochester settlement.
He stated in his opinion that the facts showed
"an intent to make that city or town (Rochester)
his home, and while at such charitable institution
(the hospital) he cannot acquire a settlement there
because of the provisions of Section 56."

EFFECT OF RELIEF IN ESTABLISHING SETTLEMENT:

LAW: " . . . No person shall gain a settlement in a town or
city except by residing for one year (Case 43)
continuously (Case 44) without receiving public
relief (Cases 45 to 51), or care at the expense
of any such town or city or of any other town, city
or county or of any other state or civil division
thereof (Case 53) for himself or herself or for
his wife, or minor child for whose support either
is responsible; the burden of proof of relief and
care at public expense in any other state shall be
upon the public welfare official alleging the same."

Case 43—The Black family have a settlement in New York
City. On January 5, 1934, they move to Poughkeepsie. On January 5, 1935, they make an application for relief.

Discussion: It has been held that this did constitute one
year's residence in Poughkeepsie, and the family
thereby established a settlement there. The State
Department has held that the year elapsed on
midnight of January 4, 1935.

Case 44—Mr. Jackson and family have a settlement in
Utica. On January 1, 1932, they move to Syracuse. On June 1, 1932, Mr. Jackson goes to Buffalo on business and returns to Syracuse one
month later. The family continues living there until February 1933, when an application for relief is
made.

Discussion: In interpreting "one year continuously," it has been *held,* that this does not preclude absences from the city on visits or business, if there is an intention to return and the person does return when visit or business is completed. Therefore, Mr. Jackson has established a Syracuse settlement.

Case 45—Mr. Smith and family move from Rochester to Syracuse on January 1, 1932. At that time their settlement is in Rochester. On December 30, 1932, Mr. Smith makes an application for relief in Syracuse. He receives a grocery order on that date.

Discussion: Mr. Smith received "public relief" before he had lived in Syracuse for one year, and therefore, his settlement reverts back to Rochester as he had not completed a settlement in Syracuse.

Case 46—Same facts, except that Mr. Smith does not receive the grocery order until after an investigation is made in the home on January 2, 1933.

Discussion: Even though he made the application on December 30, Mr. Smith did not "receive public relief" until after he had been in Syracuse for one year, and therefore, acquired a Syracuse settlement. An application alone does not constitute "public relief."

Case 47—Same facts as in Case 45, and the Syracuse Welfare Department continues relief until June 1933, when they discover that the family has a Rochester settlement.

Discussion: This case is included here to illustrate the fact that even though a welfare department accepts a case by mistake, that fact does not preclude the department from later referring it back to the proper welfare district, inasmuch as the family could not have acquired a Syracuse settlement while they were receiving public relief. This was so held in an interpretation by the State Department.

Case 48—Mr. Smith has lived in Syracuse for over a year but received a pair of glasses through the Department of Public Welfare before he lived in Syracuse for one year.

Case 49—Mr. Smith's son is placed in a foster home, the cost of which is paid for by the Department of Welfare.

Case 50—Mr. Smith makes an application for entrance to Ray Brook Sanatorium, and being destitute, the Department of Welfare pays for transportation.

Case 51—Mr. Smith's wife is hospitalized, and being destitute, the Department of Welfare pays the hospital bill.

Discussion: In all of these cases, Mr. Smith "received public relief." One general test as to whether it is "public relief," is whether it is paid out of "public funds," i.e. governmental funds, whether federal, state or local. This, however, is not a true test, inasmuch as being in a state institution does not constitute public relief. It is definite, however, that relief granted by a private agency supported by a Community Chest does not constitute public relief (e.g., Associated Charities, Charity Organization Societies, etc.)

Another general test which appears to be fairly accurate is deciding whether the settlement of the person is involved in the granting of that particular relief. If so, it does constitute "public relief." Cases may come up, however, requiring an opinion.

Case 52—On January 1, 1934, the Smith family has a settlement in New York City. On that date the family moves to Albany, and receives relief in Albany
from February 1, 1934, until May 1, 1934. Relief
is terminated as a twenty year old son has entered
a C.C.C. camp and his monthly earnings cover
the budget deficiency. He remains in the C.C.C.
camp from April 1934 until April 1935, after
which he returns home to his family in Albany.
On June 1, 1935, the family makes an application
for relief.

Discussion: The question has arisen as to the effect of
the earnings in C.C.C. camps on settlement. In
this case the family has acquired a settlement in
Albany inasmuch as it has lived there for one
year and wages received in C.C.C. work do not
constitute public relief. It should also be noted
that even if a person worked in a C.C.C. camp for
over a year, he could not acquire a settlement at
the place of the camp because, of course, he could
have no intention of making that a permanent
home.

Annotation G: The above should be distinguished from
a period spent in a Transient camp, which does
constitute public relief.

Case 53—Mr. Smith lives with his wife and family in Cleveland, Ohio, for several years. On January 1, 1933,
he deserts his family, goes travelling, and comes
to New York City on October 1, 1934, where he
has been living ever since. On April 1, 1933, Mrs.
Smith had to apply for relief in Cleveland, and
has been receiving relief for herself and children
since that date. Mr. Smith applies for relief in
New York City on November 1, 1935.

Discussion: A recent amendment to the Public Welfare
Law results in Mr. Smith not acquiring a settle-

ment in New York City even though he has resided there for over a year. This amendment is
to the effect that public relief, even though received outside of the state, affects settlement in
the same way as if granted within New York State.
So that, in Case 53, Mr. Smith could not acquire
a settlement in New York City inasmuch as his
wife was receiving public relief in Cleveland.
The State Department of Social Welfare has held
that the amendment is not retroactive and, therefore, only relief granted out of the state subsequent to April 25, 1935, would affect settlement
in the above law.

LAW: " . . . provided, however, that the receipt of relief and
care of any of the following types shall not prevent the acquiring of a new settlement:

(a) Care of a wife or minor child of such person in a state
institution or in any institution on commitment for
delinquency.

(b) Relief given by reason of quarantine because of a communicable disease under the provisions of the public health law.

(c) Relief for the cost of which the recipient has repaid
the public welfare district in full.

(d) Relief given at the request of a school or other public
agency as part of its program of health betterment. . . ."

Discussion: (a)—It is to be noted that if the husband
were in a state institution, the wife could not be
acquiring her own settlement, but the wife or the
minor child in an institution does not prevent the
man from acquiring a separate settlement.

(b)—(c) and (d)—These are self-explanatory.

—44—

EFFECT OF RELIEF TO MINORS WHEN MOTHER REMARRIES:

LAW: " . . . When a widow, divorced woman or unmarried mother gains a new settlement by marriage, if, at the time of such marriage her child is receiving care at public expense, the settlement of such child shall not follow that of its mother until such time as the child has been returned to the custody of its mother and has remained in her care without receipt of public relief for the period of one year."

Case 54—Mr. and Mrs. Smith are married and have a child, a minor. On January 1, 1932, they are residing and have a settlement in Syracuse. On February 1, 1932, Mr. Smith dies. On March 1, 1932, Mrs. Smith makes an application to have minor placed in a foster home. This plan is carried out and the foster home care is paid for by the Department of Welfare in Syracuse. On June 1, 1932, Mrs. Smith remarries a Mr. Jones who has a settlement in Rochester. After her remarriage the Syracuse Department claims that inasmuch as the child follows her settlement, the care in the foster home should now be assumed by Rochester.

Discussion: This case illustrates one example in which the mother and child may have separate settlements. When Mrs. Smith remarried, her child was receiving "care at public expense," and therefore, even though Mrs. Smith did have a Rochester settlement, minor would retain its Syracuse settlement until it "had been returned to the custody of its mother and had remained in her care without receipt of public relief for one year. . . ."

Case 55—Same facts, only Mrs. Smith, instead of placing minor in a foster home, keeps the child with her and receives relief for herself and minor until

June 15, 1932. Relief was then terminated inasmuch as it was discovered that she had remarried on June 1, 1932.

Discussion: In this case it has been *held,* that even though the child is "receiving care at public expense," the child would follow the settlement of the mother after her remarriage, as this section only applies to relief to child *away from the custody* of the mother; otherwise, the statute is meaningless.

Annotation H: Where a minor was an inmate in a state institution when the mother remarried, it was *held,* that the minor takes the mother's new settlement (i.e., this section does not apply).

Sec: 57—RESTRICTION OF SETTLEMENT IN CERTAIN COUNTIES

LAW: "No person, nor any member of his family, who shall have become a resident of any town in' the county of Franklin, Greene, Essex, Ulster, Orange, Rockland, or Sullivan, while afflicted with tuberculosis, and no person who shall become a member of the National Soldiers' Home of Bath, New York, from any cause whatever, and no member of his family, who shall become a resident of any town in the county of Steuben, shall gain a settlement in such town until he has resided therein for five years. No person, nor any member of his family, who shall have become a member of the veterans' administration facility in the county of Ontario, shall gain a settlement in such county or in any town or city therein until he has resided in such county for five consecutive years. . . ."

Case 56—Mr. Payne and family have a settlement in New York City. Mr. Payne develops tuberculosis, and on January 1, 1930, is sent to Middletown, Orange County, where he lives in a private nursing home until January 15, 1932. On that date his family moves up from New York City, and Mr. Payne continues to live with his family in Middletown until March 1934, when they are compelled to apply for relief.

Discussion: Mr. Payne and family have resided in Middletown for over a year before applying for relief. Inasmuch, however, as Mr. Payne was suffering from tuberculosis when he moved to Middletown, Orange County, neither he, nor any member of his family, could acquire a settlement in Middletown until he had lived there for five years; and their settlement, therefore, is in New York City.

Case 57—The McKnight family has a settlement in Binghamton. On January 1, 1931, Mr. McKnight, a
veteran, is sent to the National Soldiers' Home in
Bath, Steuben County, to be treated for illness
caused by having been gassed in the war. He does
not recuperate as soon as expected, and on September 15, 1931, his wife moves to Hornell, which
is also in Steuben County, to be near her husband.
A year later, in October 1932, Mrs. McKnight
applies for relief in Hornell.

Discussion: In the same manner Case 57 illustrates the
five year restriction in acquiring settlement in Steuben County because of Mr. McKnight's residence
in the Soldiers' Home at Bath. The family's settlement remains in Binghamton until Mr. Mc-
Knight has resided in Bath for five years.

The purpose of these restrictions is obvious—a
desire to protect these counties from acquiring a
heavy relief load because of special community
facilities.

PART II

VERIFICATION OF SETTLEMENT

IN GENERAL:

In the practical routine of a department of public welfare, the foregoing information on the law of settlement will be of value, of course, only if the statement of facts on which the law is based is accurate.

When a client makes an application for relief, the information which he gives regarding his past residences may or may not be correct, and like all information regarding assets, employment, etc., should be verified. Failure to do this may mean as much financial loss to a public welfare district as the failure to discover a large bank account.

It is important to keep in mind that an applicant for relief is usually not acquainted with the legal requirements of settlement and residence. Very frequently inaccurate information may be the result of the client's not remembering his previous places of residence, or he may give this information without carefully considering it, merely to complete the application as quickly as possible.

Both the intake worker and the field investigator should consider this in their contact with the client. The suggested procedure which follows is presented so that the worker may assist the client in completing this phase of the work as efficiently as possible.

The procedure set forth below will undoubtedly require certain changes to conform with peculiar local problems, and is presented only as a suggested plan for handling this problem. The verification may be made by following *any or all steps, as may be necessary*. In the outline below if the settlement given at the time of application is found incorrect, the field investigator should work toward finding and verifying the correct settlement.

SUGGESTED METHODS IN THE VERIFICATION OF SETTLEMENT

CASE HISTORY:

There should appear in the case history a separate paragraph titled "Settlement Verification." This paragraph should contain:

(1) A summary of the relief history,

(2) The period to be proved, and

(3) The procedure used in the verification.

This will be illustrated below.

RELIEF HISTORY:

Inasmuch as the "receipt of public relief" affects settlement, a careful check should be made regarding the exact periods during which a client has received public relief.

This will mean a careful examination of records as follows:

1. Previous case history of client within the agency.

2. Relief history of other agencies known to have had contact with client.

3. Contact agencies registered by S. S. E. ("Social Service Exchange," or "Central Index") as having had contact with client. This step is very valuable also in procuring other essential data regarding the client.

All members of the family should be included in the application form. Any members missing during the past two years should be accounted for. This may be important if some one of the family was receiving public relief from some other agency or institution.

"SETTLEMENT PERIOD":

From the above information the worker may compute the period which will require verification.

Illustration: Client receives relief from Home Relief Division from January 15, 1933, to August 1934, and from June 1935 to August 1935. Client now re-applies for relief. He could not have acquired another settlement since January 15, 1933, so the period to be verified would be the year or more preceding January 15, 1933.

VERIFICATION:

Documentary Proof: Client may have available documents of many types such as are listed below which may constitute a perfectly adequate verification. The details should be included in the case history to show exactly what the worker is depending upon as verification.

Illustration: "Worker saw receipts from Edison Electric Company for John Smith, 105 East 42nd Street for all months from January 1933 to February 1935, and from July 1935 to August 1935, inclusive."

Proof by Reference: The worker may often be able to verify settlement by communicating with references given by the client. Wherever possible it is desirable that the worker communicate directly with the prospective source of information rather than instruct the client to do so. (For example, having client get a note from the landlord as to the period of residence.) This will lead to more accurate and incidentally more trustworthy information. This procedure should also be entered in the case history.

Illustration: "Worker phoned John Smith & Company regarding Jack Jones and according to their records Jack Jones was employed there from January 1927 until August 1935. They had his last address as 120 Simpson Street. Worker also checked the school records of Mr. Jones' child, Robert, and found that he attended School No. 63 from September 1929 until June 1931, home address given as 123 Monroe Street, and School No. 103 from September 1931 until date, home address given as 120 Simpson Street."

SUGGESTED SOURCES OF INFORMATION:

The following lists are offered as suggesting many of the possible sources by which the client may be assisted in verifying his settlement:

Documentary Proof	*References*
Receipts—	Social Service Exchange, or,
rent	Central Index
gas .	Employers
electric	Social Agencies
water	Churches
telephone	Sunday schools
insurance	Insurance agents
Voting certificates	Schools
Literacy certificates	Employment agencies
Hospital cards	Furniture moving companies
Clinic cards	Landlords
Union cards	Tradesmen
Library cards	Civil Service records
Military service certificates	Loan Associations
Letters of reference	Voting records
Children's report cards	Hall of Records
Children's birth certificates	real property information
Postmarked envelopes	vital statistics
Auto registration certificates	Court proceedings, etc.
Newspaper items	Telephone directories
Passports	City Directory.
Bank books and statements	
State and city licenses	
fishing, peddling, etc.	
Leases	
Evictions and dispossess notices	
Mortgages and deeds	
Cancelled checks	
Etc., etc.	

Aside from the above information procured, the comparison of the information given by different members of the family, as also the integration of the individual client's story, should assist in many cases in working out an adequate solution of this problem.

PART III

PUBLIC WELFARE LAW*

SELECTED SECTIONS

PUBLIC WELFARE DISTRICTS AND THEIR RESPONSIBILITY FOR PUBLIC RELIEF AND CARE

ARTICLE VII—SETTLEMENT

STATE POOR

*Legislative amendments enacted subsequent to the date of publication of this manual should be consulted for possible changes in the text.

PUBLIC WELFARE DISTRICTS AND THEIR RESPONSI-BILITY FOR PUBLIC RELIEF AND CARE

Sec. 12—CITY PUBLIC WELFARE DISTRICTS

The city of New York, the city of Kingston, the city of Oswego, the city of Poughkeepsie and the city and town of Newburgh shall on January first, nineteen hundred thirty, be constituted city public welfare districts. Such cities and the corporation known as the commissioners of the home of the city and town of Newburgh shall have all the powers and duties of a public welfare district insofar as consistent with the provisions of the special and local laws relating to such cities and to said corporation. The officers charged with the administration of public relief and care in such cities and the officers of said corporations shall have additional powers and duties of a commissioner of public welfare not inconsistent with the laws relating to said cities and said corporation.

Sec. 13—CITIES FORMING PART OF A COUNTY PUBLIC WELFARE DISTRICT

Each city, other than those constituted city public welfare districts, as provided in subdivision one of section seventeen of this chapter, shall, when this act takes effect, form part of the county public welfare district of the county in which it is situated and, in addition to the powers conferred on it by subdivision two of section twenty-five of this chapter, may continue to exercise any other power which it heretofore has exercised in regard to the poor having a settlement in its territory. Nothing contained in this chapter shall deprive any city of the independent exercise of all powers of such city theretofore conferred by law.

Sec. 17—PUBLIC WELFARE DISTRICTS

For the purpose of administration of public relief and care the state shall be divided into county and city public welfare districts as follows:

1. The city of New York, the city of Kingston, the city of Oswego, the city of Poughkeepsie and the city and town of

Newburgh are each hereby constituted a city public welfare district.

2. The territory of the county of Dutchess, exclusive of the city of Poughkeepsie, is hereby constituted a county public welfare district. The territory of the county of Orange, exclusive of the city and town of Newburgh, is hereby constituted a county welfare district. The territory of the county of Oswego, exclusive of the city of Oswego, is hereby constituted a county public welfare district. The territory of the county of Ulster, exclusive of the city of Kingston, is hereby constituted a county public welfare district.

3. Each of the counties of the state not included in subdivisions one and two of this section is hereby constituted a county public welfare district.

Sec. 18—RESPONSIBILITY FOR PUBLIC RELIEF, CARE AND SUPPORT

A person in need of relief and care which he is unable to provide for himself shall be relieved and cared for by and at the expense of a public welfare district or the state as follows:

1. *The state shall be responsible for:*

(a) The support of any person having no settlement in any public welfare district in the state, who shall not have resided in any public welfare district in the state for sixty days during the year prior to an application for public relief and care.

(b) The support of any Indian who is eligible for relief from the state under the provisions of section sixty-five of this chapter.

(c) The expense of transportation of any alien poor person who is returned to his own country and of any non-resident poor person who is returned to the state in which he has a settlement or in which he has friends or relatives willing to support him.

2. Each public welfare district shall be responsible for:

(a) The relief, care and support of any person who resides and has a settlement in its territory.

(b) The relief, care and support of any person found in its territory not having a settlement in the state, for whose support the state is not responsible.

(c) The relief and care of any person found in its territory who has a settlement elsewhere in the state, subject to reimbursement by the public welfare district of the person's settlement in accordance with the provisions of this chapter.

(d) The relief and care of any person found in its territory for whose support the state is responsible, subject to reimbursement by the state in accordance with the provisions of this chapter.

(e) The payment of the cost of the relief and care of a person having a settlement in its territory given by some other public welfare district.

ARTICLE VII—SETTLEMENT

Sec. 53—SETTLEMENT

Every person of full age who shall be a resident and an inhabitant of a town or city for one year, and the members of his family who shall not have gained a separate settlement, shall be deemed to have a settlement in such town or city, which shall continue until he shall have gained a like settlement in some other town or city of this state or shall have removed from this state and remained therefrom for one year. Settlement in a county public welfare district shall be acquired by settlement in a town or city thereof.

Sec. 54—SETTLEMENT OF A MARRIED WOMAN

The settlement of a married woman shall be that of her husband except as otherwise herein provided.

A widow or a woman who is divorced or separated by judicial decree from her husband shall have the same settlement which she had at the time of the death of her husband or of her divorce or separation, but may subsequently gain a new settlement.

A married woman whose husband has deserted her shall continue to have the settlement of her husband at the time of such desertion except that, if her husband's whereabouts continue unknown, she shall, after a period of one year, have the right to acquire a separate settlement. Such separate settlement shall continue while her husband's whereabouts is unkown, and until he is known to have established a settlement in some town or city of this state or in some other state.

Sec. 55—SETTLEMENT OF MINORS

1. The settlement of a minor born in wedlock shall be that of his parents or surviving parent, or, in case of divorce, legal separation or desertion, of the parent having his custody.

2. The settlement of a minor born out of wedlock shall be that of his mother.

3. In case of the death of the parent having custody, the settlement of a minor shall be that of the surviving parent. In case of the death of both parents or of the mother of a minor born out of wedlock, or in case of permanent separation from his parents by court order or by surrender by an instrument in writing in accordance with the provisions of the state charities law, the settlement of a minor at the time of such death or separation shall continue until his majority unless he shall gain a separate settlement as hereinafter provided.

4. A minor may gain a separate settlement as follows:

(a) If a male, by marrying and residing separately from the family of his father or mother for one year.

(b) If a female, by marrying and living with her husband.

(c) By being lawfully employed for one year when wages are paid to such minor. This provision shall not apply in the case of a minor serving an apprenticeship or securing an education in a regularly organized training school or other educational institution, or where such minor is dependent in whole or in part upon his or her parent or guardian for support.

(d) By being adopted, in which case he shall have the settlement of his foster parents or parent.

Sec. 56—QUALIFICATION ON THE ACQUISITION OF SETTLE-MENT

No settlement shall be gained by reason of the place of birth nor by residence as a patient in a hospital or as an inmate of any public institution or incorporated private charitable institution. No person shall gain a settlement in a town or city except by residing for one year continuously without receiving public relief or care at the expense of any such town or city or of any other town, city, or county or of any other state or civil division thereof for himself or herself, or for his wife, or a minor child for whose support either is responsible; the burden of proof of relief and care at public expense in any other state shall be upon the public welfare official alleging the same; provided, however, that the receipt of relief and care of any of the following types shall not prevent the acquiring of a new settlement:

(a) Care of a wife or minor child of such person in a state institution or in any institution on commitment for delinquency.

(b) Relief given by reason of quarantine because of a communicable disease under the provisions of the public health law.

(c) Relief for the cost of which the recipient has repaid the public welfare district in full.

(d) Relief given at the request of a school or other public agency as part of its program of health betterment.

When a widow, divorced woman or unmarried mother gains a new settlement by marriage, if, at the time of such marriage her child is receiving care at public expense, the settlement of such child shall not follow that of its mother until such time as the child has been returned to the custody of its mother and has remained in her care without receipt of public relief for the period of one year.

Sec. 57—RESTRICTION ON SETTLEMENT IN CERTAIN COUNTIES

No person, nor any member of his family, who shall have become a resident of any town in the county of Franklin, Greene, Essex, Ulster, Orange, Rockland, or Sullivan, while afflicted with tuberculosis, and no person who shall become a member of the National Soldiers' Home of Bath, New York, from any cause whatever, and no member of his family, who shall become a resident of any town in the county of Steuben, shall gain a settlement in such town until he has resided therein for five years. No person, nor any member of his family, who shall have become a member of the veterans' administration facility in the county of Ontario, shall gain a settlement in such county or in any town or city therein until he has resided in such county for five consecutive years. Such person shall retain any former settlement which he may have gained in another town or city and be subject to support by such town or city, or by the county public welfare district in which such town or city is located, until he shall have gained a settlement as above provided. If he has no settlement within the state he shall be a state poor person and be cared for as provided in article eight of this chapter unless he has resided in the several towns of such county for an aggregate of five years, in which case the county public welfare district shall be liable for his support.

Sec. 58—PROCEEDINGS TO ESTABLISH SETTLEMENT

1. *Between public welfare districts:*

When a person alleged to have a settlement elsewhere in the state is in need of relief and care, the commissioner of the public welfare district where such person is found shall provide the relief and care necessary, but shall, as soon as possible, and not later than thirty days after the application for relief and care for such person, send a written notification of the facts of the case to the commissioner of the public welfare district in which such person is alleged to have a settlement.

The commissioner receiving such notification shall cause an investigation to be made as to the settlement of such person. He may accept the responsibility for the support of the person in need and for repayment of any reasonable cost of such relief and care given by the public welfare district where such person is found, or he may within thirty days from the date of the receipt of such notification contest the allegation that the person has a settlement within his public welfare district.

If the type of relief and care needed is such that the cost would be charged to the town or city of the person's settlement, the commissioner on receipt of the notification shall immediately notify the town or city public welfare officer of the allegation that the person needing relief has a settlement in such town or city. Such town or city public welfare officer may, within ten days of the receipt of such notice, file a protest with the county commissioner, which protest shall be communicated to the commissioner from whom the first notification was received.

If such protest is made and the commissioner of the public welfare district where the person is found does not accept the facts therein presented, the question of responsibility may, within thirty days of the receipt of the protest, be referred to the state department of charities. The state department of charities within ten days of the receipt of a request for decision shall render a decision or shall set a date for a hearing, notifying the public welfare officials involved. The state department of charities upon rendering the decision shall file copies thereof in the offices of the commissioners of the public welfare districts involved. The decision of the state department of charities shall be final unless the commissioner, against whose public welfare district the decision is rendered, shall, within thirty days of the rendering of such decision, enter a proceeding in the supreme court.

2. Between towns and cities in a county public welfare district:

When a person alleged to have a settlement elsewhere within the same county public welfare district makes application for relief or care in a town or city, the public welfare officer shall furnish such temporary relief and care as may be necessary, and shall immediately notify the county commissioner of the facts of the case. The commissioner shall notify the public welfare officer of the town or city in which such person is alleged to have a settlement, and shall cause an investigation to be made to determine the question of settlement of such person. If no agreement can be reached, the commissioner shall fix a date for a hearing, giving the public welfare officer of each town or city involved not less than ten days nor more than thirty days' notice in writing. The commissioner, after making any further investigation necessary and in his discretion securing a ruling from the state department of charities, shall render a decision in the case and shall file a copy thereof with each such public welfare officer involved. The decision of the county commissioner in such case shall be final unless the town or city public welfare officer against whose town or city the decision was rendered shall, within thirty days of the receipt of a copy of the commissioner's decision, take an appeal to the county court and serve upon the other parties interested therein a notice of appeal, specifying the ground of appeal. The hearing of such an appeal may be brought on by either party in or out of term, upon notice of fourteen days. Upon such appeal a new trial of the matters in dispute shall be had in the county court without a jury. A decision of the county court therein shall be final and conclusive, and the same costs shall be awarded as are allowed on appeals to said court.

3. The notification and protest required by subdivision one and two shall be made in the form prescribed or approved by the state department of charities and shall be sent by registered mail. Failure to so notify, contest or appeal within the time specified shall be considered an acceptance of responsibility for the support of such person and shall bar any subsequent action to contest the responsibility.

Sec. 59—REMOVAL OF A PERSON TO THE PUBLIC WELFARE DISTRICT OF HIS SETTLEMENT

When a person cared for in the public welfare district where he is found shall have a settlement in some other public welfare district within the state, the public welfare official responsible for his support may send for and remove such person and care for him in his own public welfare district, or elsewhere, when it shall seem for the best interests of such person that he be so removed. If such person shall refuse to be so removed, the commissioner of the public welfare district responsible for his support may apply to the county judge of his county for the issuance of an order to the sheriff of the county, or to some other person or persons, for the removal of the person to the public welfare district legally responsible for his support. If the person is not so removed, the commissioner shall continue to be responsible for his support in the public welfare district where he is found.

Sec. 59-a—REMOVAL OF A PERSON WITHIN A COUNTY PUBLIC WELFARE DISTRICT TO THE TOWN OR CITY OF HIS SETTLEMENT THEREIN

Except in a county public welfare district where the cost of all relief and care is a charge on such district as a whole, when a person cared for where he is found by a town or city within a county public welfare district shall have a settlement in some other town or city within the same county public welfare district, the public welfare official of the town or city responsible in whole or in part for his support may send for and remove such person and care for him in the town or city wherein he has a settlement, when it shall seem for the best interests of such person and of the town or city wherein he has a settlement that he be so removed. If such person shall refuse to be so removed the commissioner of public welfare of the county may apply to the county judge of his county for an issuance of an order to the sheriff of the county, or to some other person or persons for the removal of the person to the town or city legally responsible in whole or in part for his support. Such application shall be made upon notice to the person sought to be removed of at least five days or such less time as the court may direct, and service thereof shall be made personally or in such other manner as the court may direct. If the person is not so removed, the commissioner of public welfare of the county wherein such person has a settlement shall continue to be responsible for his relief in the town or city where he is found, in the same manner as if such application had not been made.

Sec. 60—COLLECTION OF SUPPORT FROM A PUBLIC WELFARE DISTRICT

If a public welfare district shall fail to pay for the care given by another public welfare district to a person for whose support it is responsible, the commissioner of the public welfare district where such person is cared for may enter a proceeding in the supreme court.

STATE POOR

Sec. 65—STATE POOR

The state shall be responsible for the necessary public care and support of:

1. Any person who has no settlement in any public welfare district in this state and who shall not have resided in any public

welfare district in this state for sixty days during the year prior to an application for public relief and care, and

2. Any Indian, who has resided upon any of the Indian reservations in this state at least six months during the year prior to an application for public relief and care or who has within one year prior to the application for public relief and care received relief from the state for himself or any member of his family.

State poor persons shall be cared for and supported at the expense of the state, if written notice of the application for relief and care, with a statement of the facts in the case, is sent to the state department of charities as required by section sixty-eight of this chapter.

Sec. 68—CARE TO BE GIVEN STATE POOR

When a commissioner shall receive an application for relief and shall find upon investigation that such person is a state poor person, he shall, within five days of the time the case is brought to his attention, report the fact to the state department of charities, in such form as the department may prescribe. The commissioner shall cause such state poor person to be given relief and care as in the case of any other person in need, subject to the approval of the superintendent of state and alien poor.

Sec. 73—REMOVAL OF NON-RESIDENT AND ALIEN POOR TO OTHER STATES AND COUNTRIES

When any person who is an inmate of any public home or is otherwise cared for at the expense of the state or of any public welfare district belongs to or has friends willing to support him or to aid in supporting him in any other state or country, the state department of social welfare may cause his removal to such state or country, provided in the judgment of the state department of social welfare, the interest of the state and the welfare of such person will be thereby promoted. After notification of the proposed removal, if such person shall refuse to be so removed, the commissioner of the public welfare district wherein such person is being cared for may apply to the county judge of his county for the issuance of an order to the sheriff of the county, or to some other person or persons, for the removal of the person to the state or country or district therein legally responsible for or willing to support him, and cause his removal thereto. The expense of such removal shall be paid from the state treasury on the warrant of the comptroller pursuant to a verified account submitted by the proper officer of the state department of social welfare.

INDEX

·OF·

MEDICAL CARE

RULES AND REGULATIONS

GOVERNING

Medical Care Provided in the Home To Recipients of Home Relief

(First defined and issued on December 8, 1931)
Adopted March 3, 1933; amended from time to time; now completely
rewritten and revised to conform with F.E.R.A. Rules and
Regulations No. 7, issued September 8, 1933; adopted
in revised form, June 8, 1934, to take
effect on July 1, 1934

(Reprinted with minor revisions, March 1, 1936;
to take effect on April 1, 1936)

March, 1936

STATE OF NEW YORK

TEMPORARY EMERGENCY RELIEF ADMINISTRATION
79 MADISON AVENUE, NEW YORK, N. Y.

TO: COMMISSIONERS OF PUBLIC WELFARE
CHAIRMAN OF ERB

FROM: FREDERICK I. DANIELS

A copy of the revised Manual of Medical Care, effective April 1st, 1936, has been forwarded to you. Your attention is directed, by page reference, to certain features of the new manual.

1. **Title; Index.** The manual may hereafter be referred to by the short title "Manual of Medical Care." A complete index has been added for easy page reference (see pages 51-56).

Distribution of synopsis, covering only services reimbursable in your district, is recommended. Because the medical relief program is restricted to supplementation of already existing facilities, the scope of the program varies from district to district. For a given district, only a portion of the services covered by the manual may apply. For this reason, many welfare districts have made excerpts covering only the services which are reimbursable for their respective districts, and have released such excerpts to participating professional personnel and authorizing officials, in preference to issuing the complete manual.

2. **Medical Compensation Board may act as professional advisory committee.** The local Medical Compensation Board may be empowered locally to act as the professional advisory committee to the local relief organization (see page 10).

3. **Equitable distribution of work to physicians.** It is one of the objectives of the medical relief program to provide an equitable distribution of work where medical care is given on a fee basis (see page 9). It is recommended for such districts that the local welfare official maintain an approved list of physicians or other professional attendants, who have filed with him the statement appearing at the head of page 13 of the manual. A patient requesting medical care may be assigned the physician of his choice, but when a patient does not designate a physician or professional attendant by name, assignments should be made from the approved list alphabetically and in rotation (see page 12).

A limit may be imposed on income from relief work. To spread the work equitably, a welfare officer may establish a monthly maximum (see page 12). (For example, in a populous upstate county, the limit established for physicians is $150.00 per month, excluding obstetrics; if, prior to the end of the month a physician has earned $150.00 by attending relief cases, he may desire to treat certain of his patients free of cost for the remainder of the month; otherwise, no further authorizations are issued to him, and subsequent requests are assigned in rotation to other physicians on the approved list.)

[1]

4. **Optional procedure for control of number of visits.**

Original authorization for one visit. The local welfare officer may limit the original order for medical care to one diagnostic visit; authorization for additional visits may be based on the diagnosis and the number requested by the attending physician (see page 14). It has been the experience of several welfare districts that available funds for medical care can be used to provide more adequate care for a greater number of clients when the above procedure is established.

Number of subsequent visits based on diagnosis. Set up in conjunction with local professional advisory committees, such a plan provides that the original authorization, limited to a single diagnostic visit, is issued as usual on form 277. Participating physicians are furnished with a supply of stamped, addressed, postcards (of a type which may be sealed to keep the information confidential). On completing the diagnostic visit, the physician records on the postcard the name of the patient, the case number and order number, the tentative diagnosis, and his estimate of the number of visits subsequently needed, and mails the card to the authorizing official. On receipt of the card, the local welfare officer or his medical supervisor may discuss the case with the physician if the number of visits does not appear to be justified by the diagnosis, and the estimated number of visits may be revised. The physician's estimate (revised if necessary) is then posted on the copy of form 277 retained by the authorizing official—or, the postcard may be attached to the form.

The physician's bill is presented in the usual manner, compared with the copy of the authorization and postcard on file, and, if necessary, revised to come within the estimate on the postcard or file copy.

5. **Prior authorization not required for appliances costing $7.00 or less.** Prior authorization is no longer required for the majority of prosthetic appliances, i.e., those costing $7.00 or less. For those appliances, including eyeglasses, which cost more than $7.00, prior authorization, obtained from the Division of Medical Care on form 3486, is required as heretofore (see page 28).

Prior authorization required for certain services. The established procedure is for the usual and ordinary services which comprise the greater part of medical care to be authorized locally without prior authorization. In general, only those infrequent cases requiring expensive or prolonged care, and where an expenditure of more than $20.00 is involved, require prior authorization, if reimbursement is contemplated. Where either dental care (see page 25), or x-ray examinations (see page 20), or practical nurse-housekeeping care (see page 26), or chronic medical care (see page 15), amounts to more than $20.00 for one person, prior authorization of expenditure in excess of $20.00 is required.

Certain infrequent special services entailing considerable expenditure require prior authorization irrespective of the usual $20.00 limit: x-ray therapy (see page 20), laboratory examinations—categorical approval may be secured for certain types—

(see page 22), physiotherapy treatments in excess of 5- (see page 22), expensive and prolonged medication (see page 36), and special professional services not described in the manual (see page 34).

6. **Advice on appliances and eyeglasses.** Although prior authorization is no longer required for prosthetic appliances and eyeglasses costing $7.00 or less, the Division of Medical Care will, on request, aid welfare districts in technical matters such as the reimbursable basis for various eyeglass lens classifications. If this type of service is desired, it will be necessary only to state the specifications for the appliance or lenses—form 3486 need not be used.

7. **Application of State Education Law to needy school children.** Under Article 20-A, Section 577-b, subdivision (3-a), of the State Education Law, a school hygiene district may, where a school medical inspection has revealed physical disability, provide necessary treatment for school children whose parents are unable to do so (see page 50).

8. **Boarding care.** Board, lodging, and care given to a home relief case may be reimbursable as food and shelter, but such care is not eligible for reimbursement as bedside nursing care (see page 36).

Hospital and institutional care not reimbursable. Hospital and institutional care is specifically excluded from home relief by the Emergency Relief Act. (See page 42.) The burden of proof that a boarding case does not properly belong in a hospital or institution is that of the local welfare district. Patients for whom hospital or institutional care may be imperative should not be maintained in boarding or nursing homes.

Any establishment licensed, or required to be licensed under the State Charities Law is considered to be an institution and care therein is not reimbursable by the Administration. Your attention is directed especially to the following, which are not reimbursable when provided elsewhere than in the patient's home: maternity care, care of the tuberculous, care of children under the age of sixteen years, other types of care customarily provided in hospitals or institutions.

Eligibilty for reimbursement; reimbursable charges. It is suggested that the written opinion of the Social Service Division of the Administration, as to the reimbursability and the basis therefor, be obtained prior to, or as soon after as possible, authorizing such care. Where a case presenting medical conditions is cared for in a boarding home the attending physician's written recommendation as to the desirability of such care should be submitted also.

9. **Corrections; Eyeglass schedule, page 39.** The column under "single vision" which is now headed $+\subset-$ is corrected to read $+\subset+$. The footnote (*) to the schedule is corrected to read "*Bausch and Lomb or American Optical Company standards, or their equivalent, and of U.S.A. manufacture."

10. **Venereal disease treatment—co-operative policy.** In co-operation with the New York State Department of Health in its campaign against venereal disease, the following policy (see page 27) has been established in regard to venereal disease treatment, which is now a dual responsibility under the Public Health and Public Welfare Laws.

Not reimbursable in cities and county health districts. In all cities (including those cities which are not public welfare districts), and in those counties having a county health department (Cattaraugus, Columbia, Cortland, Suffolk, Westchester) venereal disease treatment of those unable to pay for such treatment by a private physician is the responsibility of the local board of health under section 343-p of the Public Health Law. Such treatment does not constitute a basis for reimbursement by the Administration.

Reimbursable except in cities and county health districts. Except in cities and county health districts, treatments for relief recipients may be authorized under section 83 of the Public Welfare Law and shall be eligible for reimbursement by the Administration on the basis of regular office visits. Specific drugs for the treatment of syphilis may be obtained, free of cost, from the State Department of Health.

Co-operation of health and relief officials; existing facilities to be utilized. In authorizing treatment, the relief official should co-operate fully with the local health officer in the conduct of his syphilis control program. Already existing local facilities, such as clinics which are supported in whole or in part by local and/or State funds, shall continue in undiminished volume their services to relief and non-relief cases who are unable to pay for such treatment. However, treatments given in clinics do not constitute a basis for reimbursement by the Administration.

11. **Laboratory examination of sputum for pneumonia.** One of the most important factors in the state-wide campaign being waged to reduce deaths from pneumonia is quick, accurate, examination of sputum. In many cities and counties this service may be obtained, without additional cost to the relief or welfare department, from state-approved laboratories maintained by, or paid on a contract basis from, public funds.

Sputum typing reimbursable in certain districts. In public welfare districts not having established laboratory service provided from public funds, necessary diagnostic laboratory examinations may be reimbursable upon prior authorization by the Administration (see page 22). Rather than obtaining prior authorization for individual examinations, categorical authorization may be obtained for certain types of examinations, such as sputum typing for pneumonia. The Division of Medical Care will be glad to advise you promptly as to whether or not sputum typing is a reimbursable service in your district, and as to the name and address of the nearest approved laboratory. Where such examinations are reimbursable, the basis for reimbursement is . 2.00.

MANUAL

OF

MEDICAL CARE

RULES AND REGULATIONS

GOVERNING

Medical Care Provided in the Home
To Recipients of Home Relief

(First defined and issued on December 8, 1931)
Adopted March 3, 1933; amended from time to time; now completely
rewritten and revised to conform with F.E.R.A. Rules and
Regulations No. 7, issued September 8, 1933; adopted
in revised form, June 8, 1934, to take
effect on July 1, 1934

(Reprinted with minor revisions, March 1, 1936;
to take effect on April 1, 1936)

March, 1936

STATE OF NEW YORK

TEMPORARY EMERGENCY RELIEF ADMINISTRATION
79 MADISON AVENUE, NEW YORK, N. Y.

STATE OF NEW YORK

Temporary Emergency Relief Administration

353 BROADWAY, ALBANY, N. Y.

NEW YORK OFFICE
79 MADISON AVENUE
Telephone LExington 2-8901

MEMBERS

FREDERICK I. DANIELS OF NEW YORK, Chairman

THOMAS CRIMMINS OF NEW YORK

PAUL S. LIVERMORE OF ITHACA

SOLOMON LOWENSTEIN OF NEW YORK

JOSEPH P. RYAN OF NEW YORK

ALFRED H. SCHOELLKOPF OF BUFFALO

DAVID C. ADIE OF ALBANY—Ex Officio
State Commissioner of Social Welfare

FREDERICK I. DANIELS, Executive Director

GLENN E. JACKSON, Assistant Executive Director

PAUL MAYER, Assistant Executive Director

NOTE

THIS MANUAL WAS PREPARED BY THE T.E.R.A.
DIVISION OF MEDICAL CARE:

H. JACKSON DAVIS, M.D., Dr.P.H., Director of Medical Care

T. E. R. A.

MANUAL of MEDICAL CARE

RULES AND REGULATIONS
Governing

Medical Care Provided in the Home to
Recipients of Home Relief

(Adopted in revised form, June 8, 1934, to take effect on July 1, 1934)

(Reprinted with minor revisions, March 1, 1936;
to take effect on April 1, 1936)

TABLE OF CONTENTS

T.E.R.A. Authorization, Invoice and Voucher for Medical, Dental, Nursing and Other Professional Services

Note: See Regulation 1, *Items 1* and *6* on page 14 and Regulation 10, *Item 3* on page 40.

TERA Form 217. 12-4-34-100,000 Sets (26-3036)

AUTHORIZATION, INVOICE AND VOUCHER FOR PROFESSIONAL SERVICES

Work Relief Disability ☐   Home Relief ☐

EMERGENCY RELIEF BUREAU OF_____
City _____   County _____

Voucher No. _____

AUTHORIZATION: DATE_____ 193___

Relief Order No. _____

TO_____
(Name of Physician, Dentist, Nurse or Institution—Indicate which)

Home Relief Case No. _____

ADDRESS_____
(Street and Number)   (City or Town)

Disability No. _____

USE FOR HOME RELIEF — You are hereby authorized to supply medical, dental and/or nursing service within the restrictions and according to the Regulations given in the TERA "Manual of Rules and Regulations Governing Medical Care Provided in the Home to Recipients of Home Relief" to:

USE FOR WORK RELIEF DISABILITY — The bearer, or the patient whose name and address appears immediately below, is an employee of the Work Bureau on Project _____ and alleges that he met with an injury or disability in the course of his employment, on Date_____, 193___ You are hereby authorized to give NECESSARY TREATMENT for a period of_____days from date hereof to:

FAMILY NAME_____   HEAD OF FAMILY_____

ADDRESS_____   AUTHORIZED BY_____
(Street Address or RFD. No. and Name of City or Town)

FOR: (Indicate purpose)_____   TITLE_____

Following statement to be prepared, invoice dated and signed, and affidavit executed, by Professional Attendant:

DATE 193 (1)	INDICATE HOME OR OFFICE CALL (*) (2)	PATIENT'S NAME (3)	AGE (4)	SEX (5)	DIAGNOSIS (6)	SERVICES RENDERED (7)	(**) STATUS (8)	CHARGES (9)

(*) Use symbol "H" for home visit and "O" for office visit

(**) C—CURED   T—NEEDS FURTHER TREATMENT   H—HOSPITALIZED (name and date as shown)   D—DEAD

NAME OF HOSPITAL_____ 193___   Date_____ 193___   TOTAL

DATE INVOICE PREPARED:_____ 193___

NOTE (to physician, dentist, nurse or hospital): Enter on the original and duplicate yellow copy of this form the information called for above in columns 1 to 9, specify date invoice is prepared, sign under "received payment," execute affidavit on both copies, and send to local relief headquarters. Keep the triplicate copy for your records.

RECEIVED PAYMENT:_____

STATE OF NEW YORK
_____ County } ss.:   (DO NOT NOTARIZE INVOICES LESS THAN $5)

_____being duly sworn says that he actually resides at _____; that the services rendered or charged in the above bill or account were actually rendered to the relief case named herein residing in_____
(City or County)

on the order of_____
(Name and Title of Authorizing Officer)

at the dates and for the prices herein named, which are just and reasonable for the services rendered; that said bill or account is just and true; that there are no Federal or New York State Taxes included and that there is due hereon $_____and no part of same has been paid

Subscribed and sworn to before me

this_____day of_____ 193___   _____
Signature

_____
Notary Public or Commissioner of Deeds   (PROFESSIONAL ATTENDANT—DO NOT WRITE BELOW THIS LINE)

(LEAVE BLANK)	ACCOUNTING CLASSIFICATION		(THIS SPACE FOR LOCAL ACCOUNTING OFFICE)
	Charge	Amount	Account Verified; Correct for—

(Signature)_____

I certify that the records of this office show that the services covered by this voucher were rendered, and that the prices charged are in conformity with the authorized scale.

Certified for $_____   _____
Accounting Officer

TERA

Paid by the_____
(Title of Fiscal Officer)   (Local Governmental Unit)   with Check No._____

Dated_____ For_____   Drawn on the_____ of_____
(Amount)   (Name of Bank)   (City)

[6]

STATE OF NEW YORK
Temporary Emergency Relief Administration
MANUAL of MEDICAL CARE

RULES AND REGULATIONS
Governing Medical Care Provided in the Home to
Recipients of Home Relief

(First defined and issued on December 8, 1931.)

Adopted March 3, 1933; modified by official interpretations as issued in T. E. R. A. Official Bulletin Number 1, and in official letters from the Administration to Commissioners of Public Welfare; now completely rewritten and revised to conform with Federal Emergency Relief Administration Rules and Regulations Number 7, issued September 8, 1933; and adopted in the revised form, June 8, 1934, to take effect on July 1, 1934. (Reprinted with minor revisions, March 1, 1936, to take effect on April 1, 1936.)

Note—*Page* references in text and footnotes below refer to *This Manual.*

INTRODUCTION

The conservation and maintenance of the public health is a primary function of Government. In the present economic depression, the ingenuity of Federal, State, and local relief officials is being taxed to conserve available public funds and, at the same time, to give adequate relief to those in need.

For the purpose of facilitating the discharge of these obligations with regard to medical care, the following rules and regulations governing medical care provided in the home to recipients of home relief are hereby established.[1]

CHAPTER I

Statement of Policy

Section A.—**Definitions.** As used in these rules and regulations:

Item 1. "Medical care provided in the home" means medicine, medical supplies, and medical attendance furnished by a municipal corporation or a town, where home relief is a town charge, to persons or their dependents in their abode or habitation whenever possible and *does not include hospital or institutional care.*

a. It does not include medical, nursing and dental services, given either "in the home," in the office, or in a clinic, where such services are already established in the community and paid for, in whole or in part, from local and/or State funds in accordance with local

---

[1] Basic legislation, a summary of prior regulations, and quotations from the Public Welfare Law, may be consulted in Chapter III, pages 42–50.

8

statutes or charter provisions. Federal and State Emergency Relief Funds shall not be used in lieu of such local and/or State funds to pay for these established services.

b. The scope of "medical care" as above defined shall be construed to include: *Bedside nursing care,* as an adjunct to medical attendance; and *emergency dental care*—subject to the restrictions stated in the preceding paragraph.

c. "Medical care" as above defined shall be construed ordinarily to include only necessary care for conditions that cause acute suffering, interfere with earning capacity, endanger life, or threaten some permanent new handicap that is preventable when medical care is sought.

d. "Emergency dental care" shall in general be restricted to those extractions, fillings, treatments and repairs which are necessary for the relief of pain and other conditions referred to in the preceding paragraph.

e. "Medicine" and necessary drugs shall be restricted to a formulary which excludes expensive drugs where less expensive drugs can be used with the same therapeutic effect. Proprietary or patent medicines shall not be authorized.

f. "Medical supplies" shall be restricted to the simplest *emergency* needs of the patient consistent with good medical care.

g. The phrase "in the home" shall be interpreted to include medical and dental office service for ambulatory patients: Provided, that such medical and dental office service shall not supplant the services of clinics and/or salaried physicians and dentists already provided in the community.

Item 2. *"Recipients of home relief"* means all cases of home relief who have been duly investigated, as required by section 13 of chapter seven hundred and ninety-eight of the laws of nineteen hundred and thirty-one, and found to be eligible for home relief.

Section B.—Objectives. The common aim of the state-wide medical relief program is the provision of good medical care at a low cost—to the mutual benefit of the indigent patient, professional attendant and taxpayer. This program has the following objectives:

Item 1. *Uniform policy.* Medical care is to be provided to recipients of home relief, under these regulations, in accordance with a uniform policy formulated by the Temporary Emergency Relief Administration in consultation with representatives of the organized State medical, dental and other participating professions.

Item 2. *Maintenance of professional standards.* This policy recognizes, within legal and economic limitations,[2] the traditional relationships existing between the patient and physician or other professional attendant, and provides that authorized professional attendants shall furnish to recipients of home relief the same quality of service as would be rendered to a private patient, with the under-

[2] See Section D, *Item 1,* on page 11.

standing that such authorized service shall be a minimum, consistent with good professional judgment, and shall be charged for at an agreed rate which makes due allowance for the conservation of relief funds.

Item 3. More adequate medical care. *a.* The policy adopted shall be to augment and render more adequate, facilities already existing in the community for the provision of medical care by medical, dental and nursing professions to indigent persons.

b. This policy and the scope of the program of medical care adopted locally, under the provisions of these regulations, shall be restricted to supplementation of local facilities and services, and shall imply continuance in the use of hospitals, clinics and medical, dental and nursing services already established in the community. and paid for, in whole or in part, from local and/or State funds in accordance with local statutes or charter provisions or in accordance with provisions of the Public Welfare Law[3] which require or permit services not within the scope of the Emergency Relief Act of the State of New York.

Item 4. Uniform procedure. *a.* In the interest of simplified administration and accounting, as well as the provision of adequate medical care at a low cost, a uniform procedure for authorization of medical, dental, and nursing care in the home shall be established by each local department of public welfare. This procedure shall not be in conflict with the detailed requirements stated in Chapter II, on pages 13 to 42, of these regulations.

b. The purpose of the uniform procedure adopted is to provide more adequate medical care to recipients of home relief and to provide an *equitable distribution* of authorization to professional attendants participating in the program. Hence, the Administration and the professional advisory committees are opposed to any undue stimulation of demands for medical care on the part of individual physicians, dentists and nurses. If such stimulation is discovered in any local welfare district, the local commissioner of public welfare shall report the facts in writing to the welfare advisory committee[3a] of the local county medical society or comparable professional advisory committee, and send a copy of the written complaint to the Director of Medical Care, T. E. R. A., 79 Madison Avenue, New York, N. Y. All authorizations for medical care are a responsibility of the local commissioner of public welfare and should not be unduly stimulated by the physician, dentist or nurse.

c. Recipients of home relief shall be notified by the local commissioner of public welfare that application for necessary medical care should be made to the welfare office from which orders for other forms of relief are issued. The welfare office is responsible for calling the physician, dentist or nurse instead of the medical attendant being responsible for initiating the call upon the welfare office. Hence, if authorization is desired, physicians and dentists should

[3] Chapter 565, Laws of 1929, with subsequent amendments; see Chapter III. Section C, on page 46. [3a] Or Medical Compensation Board established under subd. 1, § 13-b, of the Workmen's Compensation Law, as amended.

not encourage ambulatory patients to come to their offices in the first instance, but shall, during the hours when the local welfare office is open, refer patients requesting medical care to such welfare office. Exceptions to this rule are covered in Regulation 1, page 14.

Section C. **Professional supervision and advice.** The Administration has recognized the need for professional supervision and advice in the administration of medical care provided in the home to recipients of home relief. To meet this need the following steps have been taken.

Item 1. Division of medical care. a. The Administration, under the provisions of section 5 of the Emergency Relief Act,[4] has received advice and expert assistance from the State Department of Health, and has appointed a member of the staff of said department as director of medical care.

b. The Administration has further established a division of medical care to provide additional expert supervision over medical and related problems confronted in the administration of both home and work relief.

c. The duties of the staff of the division of medical care are to make surveys, formulate procedures, promote professional standards, and suggest policies for the more effective provision of adequate medical care to recipients of home relief.

d. The director of medical care also acts as liaison officer with respect to medical problems between the Administration, other State and Federal agencies, State and local professional organizations, and local Departments of Public Welfare and Health.

Item 2. Professional advisory committees. a. The Administration has requested the State medical, dental and nursing organizations, respectively, to designate an existing committee or appoint a special advisory committee, to assist in the formulation and adoption of an adequate program for medical, dental, and nursing care in the home, for recipients of home relief. These advisory committees assist the Administration both in maintaining proper professional standards and in enlisting the co-operation of the constituent professional membership, in the State and local programs for medical care.

b. The State medical and dental organizations have recommended that similar professional advisory committees[5] be appointed locally to serve in each public welfare district. If such committees have not already been appointed, the local commissioner of public welfare should request such a committee[6] from the appropriate local professional organization to advise with him both in the promotion of the State and local program of medical care and with regard to disputed problems of medical, dental and nursing policy and practice.

---

[4] Chapter 798, Laws of 1931. [5] Or Medical Compensation Board established under subd. 1, § 13-b, of the Workmen's Compensation Law, as added by Chapter 258, Laws of 1935.

c. The local professional advisory committees[6] may be asked by the local Commissioner of Public Welfare to assist in the formulation of a mutually satisfactory schedule of flat-rate charges which, in general, shall not exceed: two-thirds of the usual minimum local fees; nor the fees ordinarily charged indigent persons; nor, for the purpose of reimbursement by the Administration, shall the schedule exceed the charges listed in Regulation 9, pages 29 to 39.

d. The local professional advisory committee[6] may submit to the local commissioner of public welfare, a list of physicians or dentists who have agreed to co-operate under this program. To this list, may be added the names of other reputable local physicians or dentists, licensed to practice in the State of New York, who are not members of the local professional organizations. These additional practitioners may be cleared with the local professional advisory committees however, to insure that their licenses and professional standing are checked up, and that they are otherwise qualified.

e. Local professional advisory committees[6] are recommended by the Administration, even in public welfare districts where professional participation is restricted.[7]

Section D. **Scope of participation.** The scope of participation in the state-wide program of medical care, provided in the home to recipients of home relief under the Emergency Relief Act[8] of the State of New York, is subject to statutory and/or charter limitations applying either, or both, to municipal corporations or/and to professional personnel.

Item 1. Municipal corporations (cities and counties) and towns, where home relief is a town charge, are eligible for participation in this state-wide program of medical care, subject to the following restrictions:

a. A municipal corporation or a town, where home relief is a town charge, with clinics and/or medical, dental and bedside nursing services already established in the community and paid for in whole or in part from local and/or State funds in accordance with local statutes or charter provisions requiring employment of city, county or town physicians and/or other professional personnel on a salary basis, is eligible for reimbursement, by the Administration, only for such items of medical care as can be accounted for on a unit basis (i. e., drugs, medical supplies, and prosthetic devices) and, in addition, only for such professional services as have been specifically authorized by the Administration to render more adequate, but not to supplant, existing local services.

b. A municipal corporation or a town, where home relief is a town charge, where there are no such established salaried services for providing medical care to recipients of home relief (i. e., communities where medical care is provided primarily on an individual fee basis), is eligible for reimbursement by the Administration, for all types of medical care covered by these rules.

---

[6] Or Medical Compensation Board, see footnote 6, page 10.
[7] See Section D, *Item 1, a,* below on this page.
[8] Chapter 798, Laws of 1931, with subsequent amendments.

Item 2. Professional personnel. a. Only physicians, dentists, nurses and other professional personnel who are licensed and/or registered to practice their respective professions in the State of New York, shall be authorized to participate, with a view to reimbursement from the Administration, in the provision of medical care in the home to recipients of home relief: Provided, that authorization of such professional personnel and services is restricted to welfare districts eligible [9] to provide professional services, on a fee basis.

b. The traditional relationships existing between patient and professional attendant shall be recognized in the authorization of medical care under this program, subject to the restrictions imposed by charter provisions, local statutory limitations, and the provisions of these Rules and Regulations.

c. In recognition of the principle of maintaining traditional relationships between patient and professional attendant, where a preference is expressed by the patient, midwives, licensed to practice in the State of New York, may be authorized to provide obstetrical care in the home to recipients of home relief, subject to restrictions imposed by law and the provisions of these Rules and Regulations.

d. In order to provide adequate medical care it is recommended that commissioners of public welfare maintain on a district basis, approved lists or files of physicians and other licensed professional attendants who have agreed in writing to comply with these Rules and Regulations. In general, authorizations for medical care, in districts eligible to issue such authorizations with a view to reimbursement by the Administration, shall be restricted to those professional attendants who are already on such approved lists. When a patient does not choose a physician or other professional attendant at the time that medical care is requested, *assignments should be made from the approved list by the local welfare office, alphabetically and in rotation.* When a patient requests the services of a physician or other professional attendant who has not applied for inclusion on the approved list, as indicated above, such attendance may be authorized, provided that the written authorization is accompanied by a copy of these Rules and Regulations and a statement that acceptance of the order automatically implies compliance with these rules in giving professional care. No limited number of physicians or other professional attendants should secure an excessive amount of the work. To spread the work equitably, a welfare officer may establish a monthly maximum.[9a]

e. If a recipient of home relief, who needs continued care, happens to be under the care of a physician or other professional attendant, who is not on the authorized list, or who is not willing or legally eligible to be on such a list, the welfare officer should ask the physician or other attendant if he wishes to continue to care for the patient without compensation. If the physician or other attendant does not wish to continue such care, the patient may be requested to select another from the authorized list.

---

[9] See Section D, *Item 1, a* and *b*, page 11. [9a] $150 per month, excluding obstetrics. is the limit established for physicians in a populous upstate county.

f. The Administration recommends that the local commissioners of public welfare require signature on the following statement as a prerequisite to being placed on the authorized list of physicians or other professional attendants:

"I, the undersigned, a regularly licensed and/or registered ———————— (physician, dentist, nurse, other) hereby certify that I am desirous of participating in the officially adopted program for providing medical care in the home to recipients of home relief; that I have carefully read the Rules and Regulations, adopted by the Temporary Emergency Relief Administration to govern such medical care; and that I hereby agree to conform to the provisions of said Rules and Regulations and to co-operate fully with the ——————————(City or County) department of public welfare and the Temporary Emergency Relief Administration. My license is No. ——————, issued by the State of New York, and my current registration is No. ——————, date ————, 19—, County of ————. My specialty, for which I am qualified, is ———— My Official Compensation No. and Symbol is ———— (under § 13-b, Workmen's Compensation Law).
Dated this ————, day of ———— 193–.
Address ———————————— (Signed) ————————"
(Street) (City, Village, etc.)

Section E. Qualifications of recipients of medical care.

Item 1. Person eligible. Medical care, under the provisions of these Rules and Regulations, shall be restricted to persons who are recipients of home relief or who, upon investigation by the welfare officer, are found to be eligible for home relief.

Item 2. Other restrictions. Types of cases usually referred to physicians or other professional attendants who are paid on a salary basis from local and/or State funds, shall continue to be so referred: Provided, that adequacy of medical care can be maintained for these patients.

Item 3. Persons not eligible: procedure. Patients who request medical care from the welfare office, but who do not qualify under the above requirements, should be referred to their family physicians or other professional attendants for free treatment, or for credit given by such family physicians or attendants, provided the physicians or attendants agree to give the necessary care.

CHAPTER II

Regulations Governing Procedure

In welfare districts eligible to participate[10] in the state-wide program of medical care provided in the home to recipients of home relief, a uniform procedure for the authorization and provision of medical, dental and bedside nursing care shall be established, which shall not be in conflict with the following regulations.

[10] See Chapter I, Section D, *Item 1, a* and *b*, page 11.

Regulation 1. **Written order required.** *Item 1. General.* All authorizations for medical, dental and bedside nursing care shall be issued in writing, by the proper local welfare officer, on T.E.R.A. Form No. 277, prior to giving such care; except that telephone authorization shall immediately be followed by such a written order; and provided, that in the case of an emergency call the physician or other professional attendant shall request authorization from the local department of public welfare within 48 hours after making such call. The local welfare officer may limit the original order to one diagnostic visit; authorization for additional visits to be based on the diagnosis and the number requested by the attending physician.

Item 2. Retroactive. Any authorization for medical, dental or bedside nursing care issued more than 48 hours after the first call authorized shall be considered to be retroactive and payment for care rendered under such a retroactive authorization shall not be eligible for reimbursement by the Administration.

Item 3. Dental care. Authorizations for dental care may, in cases where extensive treatment seems indicated, be restricted to authorization for one visit only, for the purpose of examination and estimate of necessary treatment. In such cases, additional written authorization, based upon the dentist's estimate, shall be required, prior to starting extensive treatment. Authorized dental care shall be limited to such work as is specifically indicated in the written order, and such order shall not be valid for more than thirty days from the date of issue.

Item 4. Bedside nursing care. Authorization for bedside nursing care, in welfare districts eligible to provide such care on a fee basis, shall as a rule be based on a recommendation by the attending physician, who shall certify to the need for bedside nursing service as an adjunct to the medical care.

Item 5. Medicine, medical supplies, etc. Authorizations for medicine, medical supplies and prosthetic devices shall also be issued in writing, prior to the provision of such materials and supplies, and, such authorizations shall not be issued except upon the written request of the physician authorized to attend the person for whose use they are desired.

Item 6. Submission of bill. Bills shall be submitted on T.E.R.A. Form No. 277, which is a combination authorization and invoice for professional services, upon completion of the services specifically authorized.

Regulation 2. **Acute illness.** *Item 1. Medical care.* Authorizations for medical care for acute illness shall be limited to: not more than two weeks; not more than ten home and/or office visits; and an expenditure, as a basis for reimbursement by the Administration, of not more than twenty dollars ($20).

Item 2. Bedside nursing care. Authorizations for bedside nursing care for acute illness, in districts eligible to provide such care on a fee basis, shall be limited to: not more than two weeks; not more than ten home visits; and an expenditure, as a basis for reimbursement by the Administration, of not more than ten dollars ($10).

Item 3. Renewal of order. Medical and bedside nursing care in excess of this period or expenditure shall not be authorized until after a reinvestigation of the case in the home by an accredited representative of the local department of public welfare.

Item 4. Consultant or specialist. When in the course of an acute illness, the physician in attendance, the patient, or his family, desires the services of a consultant or a specialist, such services may be authorized in writing, subject to the restrictions imposed by *Items 1* and *2* of Regulation 5, page 19.

Item 5. Emergency; first aid. When a physician makes an emergency call or gives first aid treatment to a recipient of home relief under circumstances which prevent him from obtaining prior authorization, a written authorization may be issued to him to cover such emergency call or first aid treatment provided it is requested within 48 hours. Subsequent care for the same patient shall be provided only after further written authorization, if reimbursement from the Administration is contemplated.

Item 6. Additional patients in household. When advice and/or care is given to other members of the same household by a physician or nurse in the course of an authorized home visit, an allowance for extra compensation for such additional care shall not be eligible for reimbursement; nor shall an allowance for more than one member of the same household, seen in the course of an authorized office visit, be eligible for reimbursement.

Regulation 3. **Chronic illness.** *Item 1. Medical care.* Medical care for prolonged illnesses, such as chronic asthma, chronic heart disease, chronic rheumatism, diabetes, etc., shall be subject to the restrictions imposed upon authorization for medical care for acute illness in Regulation 2, page 14; except that care for chronic illness shall be authorized only on an individual basis, and such written authorization shall be limited to: not more than one visit per week for not more than ten weeks or, not more than ten home and/or office visits made at longer intervals; and an expenditure, as a basis for reimbursement by the Administration, of not more than twenty dollars ($20) unless a history of the case is submitted to, and prior authorization secured from, its Division of Medical Care.

Item 2. Bedside nursing care. a. Bedside nursing care for chronic illnesses shall be provided: through existing community services, such as visiting nurses associations, public health nurses, etc., paid for in whole or in part from local and/or State funds; through nurses employed, on work relief under the state-wide bedside nursing service; and by written authorization of registered nurses, only in communities where, and to the extent which, existing services are not adequate to carry the load, and then only in accordance with the need for such bedside nursing care as indicated by the attending physician.

b. Authorizations for bedside nursing care for chronic illnesses, in communities eligible to issue such authorizations as a basis for reimbursement shall be limited to not more than ten visits, at the intervals and for the period indicated by the attending physician. The purpose of authorized nursing visits shall be demonstration and instruction to some member of the household in the necessary care, in addition to giving such care.

Item 3. Acute attack. If necessary, more frequent visits, by the physician and/or nurse, for an acute attack occurring in the course or during the critical terminal phase, of a chronic illness, may be authorized: Provided, that a request is made, by the physician and/or nurse in attendance, for additional written authorization for more frequent visits, stating the need for such visits. Such additional written authorization shall be subject to the limitations placed upon medical and/or bedside nursing care for an acute illness under the provisions of Regulation 1, page 14.

Item 4. Care restricted. Care for chronic illness authorized under this regulation shall supplement and not supersede existing community services, such as visiting nursing service, salaried physicians, public clinics, or institutional care.

Regulation 4. **Obstetrical Care.** *Item 1. Scope.* Authorization for obstetrical service in the home[11] shall include: prenatal care, delivery in the home, and postnatal care; and a requirement that, as far as possible, such obstetrical service shall conform, both in frequency of visits and in quality of care, at least to the standards of maternity care adopted by the regional consultants in obstetrics of the New York State Department of Health.

Item 2. Not emergency service. Maternity care should not be considered an emergency service to be authorized late in pregnancy. Local welfare and health officials, public health nurses, social workers, family physicians, and families on home relief should cooperate to the end that continuous medical supervision should begin for every expectant mother as soon as pregnancy is suspected.

Item 3. Minimum standards. The following standards of maternity care shall be maintained.

a. *Prenatal care* shall, wherever possible, conform to the following minimum requirements: 1. First visit at or prior to the fifth month of pregnancy. This first visit should include: histories of previous pregnancies and labors; determination of expected date of confinement; and instruction in the hygiene of pregnancy. 2. A general physical examination as early in pregnancy as possible, with special attention directed to determination of blood pressure, urinalysis, heart, lungs and kidneys, general nutrition, and a blood

---

[11] Written authorization for obstetrical care shall be requested and issued within 48 hours of the date of the first prenatal visit.

Wassermann, or comparable test. 3. Pelvic measurements and examination at or before the seventh month. 4. Visits at least monthly until the ninth month and weekly thereafter, with urinalysis, blood pressure determination, and abdominal examination made at each visit. 5. Treatment as needed for ordinary disturbances incident to pregnancy. 6. Social service or visiting nursing service adequate to insure the patient's cooperation with the attending physician and prenatal clinic.

b. *Delivery in the home* shall include, in addition to obstetrical attendance for the mother, treatment for the infant as needed, including the administration of prophylaxis, as required by law,[12] to prevent blindness.

c. *Postnatal or postpartum care* shall include care for both mother and infant as often as may be needed, and bedside visits should be made at least on the first, third and fifth days after delivery. Authorization for obstetrical care shall include provision for a final gynecologic examination of the mother about six weeks after delivery or before she resumes usual activities.

Item 4. Restrictions and precautions. Due caution shall be exercised that authorization for delivery in the home does not involve undue risk to a patient for whom hospital care may be imperative. The judgment of the attending physician shall be a decisive factor in issuing such an authorization. The physician authorized to attend the confinement in the home shall be responsible for certifying to the local commissioner of public welfare, that, in his professional judgment, delivery in the home will be safe. In those cases where it is the professional opinion of the attending physician, that confinement in the home will be hazardous he should notify the local commissioner of public welfare immediately, in order that hospitalization may be authorized in accordance with the provisions of Article X, sections 83 and 85 of the Public Welfare Law.[13] However, expenditures for such authorized hospitalization and hospital care shall not be eligible for reimbursement by the Administration.

Item 5. Complications of pregnancy. Authorization for obstetrical care in the home shall include the items of maternity care specified in the preceding paragraphs. Where complications and/or intercurrent illnesses arise in the course of pregnancy and/or the puerperium and require medical care in addition to that outlined above, the attending physician may request, giving full reasons, additional written authorization for giving supplementary care. Reimbursement may be granted by the Administration on the basis of regular home and/or office visits for medical care given under such additional authorization. Some of the complications of pregnancy which may justify additional authorization and reimburse-

---

[12] See Penal Law, § 482, subd. 3, and the State Sanitary Code, Chapter II, Regulation 12. "Precautions to be observed for the prevention of ophthalmia neonatorum."

[13] See Chapter III, Section C, Appendix, pages 46 and 47.

ment are: any acute intercurrent infection; pernicious vomiting of pregnancy; uterine hemorrhage; eclampsia, pre-eclampsia and/or any toxemia of pregnancy; and threatened miscarriage.

Item 6. Miscarriage, etc. When pregnancy is terminated prior to the full term, a pro rata allowance may be reimbursable on the basis of the authorized home and/or office visits actually made: Provided, that in case of any early miscarriage (prior to the sixth month of gestation), where a dilatation and curettage is performed, or care is given for any miscarriage at or after the sixth month, an extra allowance may be granted for such service. The total allowance, as a basis for reimbursement, for all such authorized care where the pregnancy is terminated prior to the full term, shall not exceed the allowance made for authorized complete obstetrical care of a normal confinement in the home.

Item 7. Prenatal clinic. Prenatal care given in a local clinic by arrangements approved by the authorized attending physician shall count for regular prenatal home and office visits, and, if the dates of visits to the clinic are entered in the physician's bill, the regular flat obstetrical fee may be allowed, as the basis for reimbursement.

Item 8. Emergency hospitalization. a. When, in the course of a delivery in the home, complications arise, during the *second* stage of labor, which make transfer to a hospital imperative, and such delivery is subsequently performed by the authorized attending physician or by another physician, reimbursement may be allowed for payments to the physician originally authorized to attend the confinement in the home, on the basis of a sliding scale, up to 80 per cent of the flat obstetrical fee, depending upon the adequacy of prenatal care given.

b. In certain cases, for whom delivery in the home was originally authorized, but for whom hospitalization was ordered prior to the onset of labor, allowance may be made for the prenatal and postpartum care actually given, on the basis of the regular home or office charges for each visit.

Item 9. Major obstetrical operations. To safeguard the lives of both mother and child major obstetrical operations shall not be undertaken in the home, except where there are no hospital facilities within a reasonable distance. Wherever possible, hospitalization should be authorized locally,[14] for such obstetrical operations as mid or high forceps application, internal podalic version with or without subsequent extraction, Cesarean operation, and the introduction of a Voorhees bag.

Item 10. Obstetrical nursing. Bedside nursing care, as an adjunct to the obstetrical service, is provided in many communities through local public health nurses employed on work relief. As a supplement to the existing community services, bedside nursing

---

14 Under § 85 of the Public Welfare Law, see Chapter III, Section C, page 47.

care for expectant mothers and young infants, may be authorized on an individual basis, at the request of the attending physician.

Item 11. Care by midwife. Whenever an expectant mother eligible for home relief requests the attendance of a licensed midwife at her confinement, such service may be authorized, and arrangements should be made for adequate prenatal and postnatal care through existing community services. If there is doubt about the normal progress of pregnancy or delivery, the patient should be transferred immediately to a physician or to a hospital. Authorized obstetrical service provided by a licensed midwife may be eligible for reimbursement by the Administration on the basis of not to exceed one-half of the fee paid to a physician for the same type of service.

Regulation 5. **Special services.** Medical care not covered above shall be authorized only on an individual basis under the restrictions stated below and elsewhere[15] in these regulations. Such special medical care shall not ordinarily be authorized by welfare officials for conditions that do not cause acute suffering, interfere with earning capacity, endanger life, or threaten some permanent new handicap that is preventable when such medical care is sought.

The types of special medical services which may be authorized under the provisions of this regulation are as follows:

Item 1. The usual services of a specialist. a. A specialist may be authorized to provide necessary care for those types of illness which are not amenable to treatment by the general practitioner: Provided, that such authorization shall not be issued in communities where specialized services are already provided in clinics or by salaried physicians supported or paid in whole or in part from public funds. As a rule, such special service shall only be authorized upon the written recommendation of the physician in attendance upon the case. Authorizations for the usual services of a specialist shall be subject to the limitations stated on page 14, in *Item 1* of Regulation 2 in this chapter.

b. A specialist is defined,[16] under these rules, as a licensed practitioner of medicine who has had special training and experience in the treatment of a special disease or class of diseases, and who is restricting his practice in whole or in part to such specialty. The services of a specialist shall not be authorized, with a view to reimbursement by the Administration, except for cases and types of illness ordinarily referred to a specialist in that welfare district.

c. Reimbursement for expenditures made for the usual services of an authorized specialist shall be on the basis of an ordinary home or office visit: Provided, that in no instance shall that basis exceed the charge for a home visit.

---

[15] See Chapter I: Section A, *Item 1*, page 7; Section B, *Items 2* and *3*, pages 8 and 9; and Section D, *Items 1* and *2*, pages 11 and 12.

[16] The Administration recognizes certification as a specialist under the provisions of the Workmen's Compensation Law, subdiv. 2, § 13-b, added by Chapter 258, Laws of 1935. See footnote [54], page 40.

Item 2. Consultations. The services of a consultant may be authorized when they are requested by the patient, his family, or the physician in attendance. Reimbursement may be granted for such authorized services, provided the charge does not exceed the charge for a home visit.

Item 3. First aid and/or emergency treatment. Authorized first aid and/or emergency treatment shall be eligible for reimbursement by the Administration: Provided, that such treatment is given in the patient's home, at the physician's office or at the place of accident, and provided further that the claim for such first aid treatment shall not exceed the charge for a home visit under these rules.

Item 4. X-ray diagnosis and treatment. a. X-ray examinations may be authorized, with a view to reimbursement from the Administration, only when essential to the proper diagnosis and treatment of the case and then only in those communities where x-ray examination and treatment service is not available[17] in clinics and hospitals supported in whole or in part from public funds. Under these rules, reimbursement may be obtained only on the basis of authorizations,[18] issued for x-ray examinations and treatment provided in the office of a recognized roentgenologist. The advisory committee of the New York State Medical Society on February 14, 1934, recommended that the basis of reimbursement for all x-ray examinations authorized in physician's offices should be at a rate not to exceed fifty per cent more than the schedule adopted, by the United States Employees Compensation Commission for use in hospitals, for injured Civil Works Administration Employees. This schedule, with the fifty per cent increase added is given in Regulation 9, *Item 7,* page 30.

b. X-ray treatment, either deep or superficial, may be authorized with a view to reimbursement only after prior authorization by the Division of Medical Care, and then only when no satisfactory alternative treatment is available. Requests for prior authorization shall include a detailed account of the condition, and the physician's statement of the need for x-ray therapy.

c. Dental x-rays may be authorized according to the provisions of Regulation 6, *Item 5,* page 24, for diagnostic purposes only.

Item 5. Minor surgery. a. Minor surgery, involving the less formidable manual and operative procedures for relieving traumatic and pathological conditions may be authorized, either on the basis of ordinary office calls or on an individual basis, in communities eligible to participate,[19] if it is to be performed in the patient's home, at the place of accident, or in the physician's office. The charge for such medical care shall be, for the purposes of reimbursement, either on the basis of a regular home or office visit, or

---

[17] Under provisions of §§ 83 and 85 of the Public Welfare Law; see Chapter III, Section C, *Item 1,* on page 46.
[18] Not to exceed $20, unless physician's tentative diagnosis and history of the case is submitted to, and prior authorization is secured from, the T.E.R.A. Division of Medical Care.
[19] See Chapter I, Section D, *Item 1,* page 11.

on a basis agreed upon by the attending physician and the local welfare official for the individual case, within the limits set by Regulation 9, Section A, *Items 4* and *6*, page 30, and *Item 8*, page 32.

b. The charge for the minor operation shall include the administration of the necessary anesthetic, if local in type, and necessary dressings and secondary services at the time of the operation. If a general anesthetic is given, a separate claim for reimbursement shall be submitted by the physician authorized to administer such general anesthetic.

c. Follow-up visits, when authorized, shall be eligible for reimbursement on the basis of regular office visits, and the written authorization shall be subject to all the limitations imposed for attendance upon acute illness by Regulation 2, pages 14 and 15. The name of the operation and description of the work done shall be entered in the physician's bill, if reimbursement is expected.

Item 6. Reduction of fractures. a. Authorizations may be issued for reduction, splinting, and after care of simple fractures, when such procedures are to be undertaken in the patient's home, at the place of accident, or in the physician's office. Such authorizations shall be issued only as a supplement to existing community services, where services supported locally in whole or in part from public funds, are available to provide this type of treatment.

b. Reimbursement for the reduction of fractures, may be allowed for charges not to exceed the schedule listed under Regulation 9, below. The charge should be dependent on the relative amount of work done, in relation to the maximum charge eligible for reimbursement.

c. When the fracture is compound, involving prolonged treatment in bed with the use of plaster casts and/or traction, such treatments shall be given in a hospital[20] whenever possible, and reimbursement shall not be allowed for treatment provided to such cases in the home, except on an individual basis, and following a review, by the authorizing official and the Administration, of the reasons for giving such treatment in the home.

d. After care and follow-up treatment of fractures shall be on the basis of regular home and/or office visits: Provided, that such treatment for fractures which do not impair the patient's ability to walk, shall be reimbursable only on the basis of regular office visits.

Item 7. Major surgery. a. Authorizations for major surgery for recipients of home relief shall not ordinarily be eligible for reimbursement. However, such authorizations may be issued on an emergency basis and in instances where it is not practicable to move the patient to a hospital for necessary care, and full reasons must be given in writing for performing the more important and dangerous operations in the home, at the site of the accident, or in the physician's office.

---

[20] In accordance with § 85 of the Public Welfare Law, See Chapter III, Section C, on page 47.

b. Reimbursement for authorized major surgery may be allowed on the basis of charges not to exceed two-thirds of the minimum county fee schedule: Provided, that in no instance shall the reimbursable basis exceed the limit set by Regulation 9, *Item 10*, page 33.

Item 8. General anesthesia, surgical assistance and physiotherapy. a. When authorized, the physician giving the general anesthetic or acting as assistant at a major operation performed in the home, at the site of the accident, or in the physician's office under the restriction of *Items 5 to 7* of this regulation, shall submit a separate claim for reimbursement, which may be allowed on the basis stipulated in Regulation 9, Section A, *Item 11*, page 33.

b. Physiotherapy shall not ordinarily be authorized for recipients of home relief. Physiotherapy may be reimbursable on a limited scale, only when a special written authorization is issued by the welfare official, following the submission in writing of full details of the case by the authorized attending physician. Such special authorization shall be limited to five consecutive treatments. Reimbursement for further treatment shall be allowed only on authorization issued following submission of the request, and full details of the case, to the Division of Medical Care of the Administration[21] and after prior approval has been given by that division.

Item 9. Laboratory diagnostic service. a. The facilities of state, county and city laboratories and other laboratories approved by the State Department of Health for performing specified examinations and procedures shall continue to be used, by physicians authorized to provide medical care to recipients of home relief, for performing such diagnostic examinations under the existing procedures.

b. Laboratory diagnostic examinations authorized under the provisions of these Rules and Regulations shall be only as a necessary supplement[22] to the full use of existing facilities maintained under local statutes and/or charter provisions and paid for, in whole or in part, from local and/or state funds. Such authorized diagnostic examinations should be confined to making more adequate a program of medical care which is restricted to conditions that cause acute suffering, interfere with earning capacity, endanger life, or threaten some permanent new handicap that is preventable when medical care is sought.

c. Routine diagnostic examinations, such as urinalysis, made as part of an authorized office visit to a physician, shall be considered as part of such authorized office visit, and shall not be considered as a basis for additional reimbursement.

d. Reimbursement for authorized laboratory diagnostic examinations, provided under this regulation shall be on the basis of charges not to exceed two-thirds of the minimum rate charged persons in the lowest income class by local state approved laboratories.

---

[21] T.E.R.A., 79 Madison Avenue, New York, N. Y.
[22] For which prior approval shall be obtained by the public welfare district, from the Administration, before it shall take effect.

e. Authorization for a specified laboratory examination shall be restricted to laboratories approved, for making that examination, by the New York State Department of Health.

Item 10. Other special services. Other special services not covered above or in Regulations 6, 7, 8 and 9 of this chapter, shall be authorized only on an individual basis subject: to the restrictions, imposed by Chapter I; and to an expenditure, as a basis for reimbursement, which shall not exceed the maximum specified for each type of service in these Rules and Regulations.

Regulation 6. **Dental care.** *Introduction.* *a.* Emergency dental care in welfare districts eligible[23] to provide such care under these Rules and Regulations, shall be restricted to those extractions, fillings, treatments and repairs which are necessary for the relief or prevention of pain and for the correction of conditions that interfere with earning capacity or endanger life.

b. Such dental care shall be authorized only as a supplement to existing community services or to services provided on a work relief basis, except in welfare districts with no available dental services supported in whole or in part from local and/or State funds.

c. No dental program for school children shall be set up, under these regulations, which supplants a school dental service already supported by local and/or State funds.

Note: Under the Education Law, *the correction of physical defects for any pupil,* whose parents are unable to provide necessary treatment, is the duty of the district director of school hygiene, under the provisions of subdivision (3-a), Section 577-b, added by Chapter 754, Laws of 1935.

Authorization and provision of dental care to recipients of home relief shall be subject to the following requirements:[24]

Item 1. Extractions. Dental extractions may be authorized when indicated: Provided, that extractions of one or more permanent teeth, the loss of which would necessitate a denture which could not be provided from local funds, or which serve as key teeth for the retention of a denture, and extractions of one or more temporary teeth, the loss of which may result in the malocclusion of the permanent teeth in a child, shall not be authorized or undertaken, except in cases of infection.

Item 2. Fillings. *a.* Authorization of necessary dental fillings shall require that an approved method of pulp protection be a necessary preliminary procedure. All fillings shall be thoroughly polished after being properly contoured, constructed with correct contact points and with grooves and cusps carved to occlusion. Both work and material shall conform to the highest standards, except that gold shall be used only when prosthetic repairs are authorized. Designation of teeth filled and surfaces involved in the fillings shall be given on the dentist's voucher.

23 See Chapter I, Section D, page 11.
24 See also Chapter I, Section B, *Item 2,* page 8.

b. Pit and fissure cavities shall not be considered as in need of "emergency dental care," and expenditures for filling such cavities shall not be reimbursable by the Administration.

Item 3. Treatment.[25] *a.* Emergency treatment may be authorized for the relief of pain and/or any acute oral pathological condition which endangers the health of the patient. Authorizations for emergency treatment shall be subject to the restrictions of *Item 3* of Regulation 1, page 14, and of *Item 8* of Regulation 6, page 25.

b. Emergency treatment shall include treatment for inflammation of the pulp and/or draining an alveolar abscess, also recementing of crowns, bridges and inlays.

c. Bills submitted for authorized treatment of Vincent's stomatitis shall be accompanied by a report from a laboratory approved by the State Department of Health, to make such an examination.

Item 4. Dental prophylaxis. a. The policy followed under these rules in the authorization of dental prophylaxis shall be restricted in scope.[26] Prophylaxis shall be authorized, with a view to reimbursement, only in cases where the patient suffers from diseases of the supporting tissues of the teeth, such as pyorrhea, Vincent's stomatitis, marked gingivitis, etc., or when heavy deposits of calculus endanger the healthy condition of the soft tissues of the oral cavity.

b. Dental prophylaxis, when authorized, shall consist of both thorough scaling and polishing of the teeth. When expenditures are made for cleaning and polishing of the teeth for purely aesthetic reasons, such expenditures shall not be eligible for reimbursement by the Administration.

c. Authorized prophylactic and other dental treatment should include detailed instructions in mouth hygiene and the proper use of the tooth brush.

Item 5. Dental x-ray examinations. a. Authorization of dental x-ray examinations shall be restricted to a minimum consistent with good dental care, and shall be for the purpose of diagnosis only.

b. X-ray films, taken under an authorization for dental care shall be the property of the Department of Public Welfare, from which the authorization was obtained, and shall be given to it upon request without further charge.

Item 6. Special dental services. Special dental services not covered in the preceding items of this regulation, shall be authorized only on an individual basis, and then only when they cannot be provided through existing local agencies. The types of special dental service which are included in the scope of this program are as follows:

---

[25] See also Chapter I, Section A, *Item 1, c* and *d,* page 8.
[26] See Regulation 6, Dental care, *Introduction,* page 23.

a. Root canal therapy, which is to be authorized only when a key tooth, by such therapy, can be made to remain useful in the retention of a denture already present or, where the removal of an anterior tooth or teeth would necessitate a denture which could not be provided from local funds; and

b. Dental surgery, other than simple extractions, which may include such necessary operative procedures as removal of cysts, impacted teeth, or infected areas.

Item 7. Repair of dental prosthetic devices. a. The provision of dentures is not interpreted as within the scope of the Emergency Relief Act of New York State or of these Rules and Regulations. Paragraph six, of *Item 1, f,* Section A, Chapter I, of these regulations states that "Medical" (dental and nursing) "supplies shall be restricted to the simplest *emergency* needs of the patient consistent with good medical" (dental and nursing) "care."

b. These *emergency* needs are interpreted to include the repair of vulcanite dentures and/or the replacement of teeth and clasps on such dentures. Work and material used in making such repairs shall conform to the highest standards and only 18.3 carat gold shall be used in making clasps.

c. Dentures may be authorized for recipients of home relief under the provisions of the Public Welfare Law[27] but such authorized expenditures shall not be eligible for reimbursement by the Administration.

(NOTE.—*Re dentures.*—For the guidance of local commissioners of public welfare authorizing dentures under § 83 of the Public Welfare Law, a schedule of charges for such dentures recommended by the Dental Society of the State of New York, is on file in the Division of Medical Care, T.E.R.A., 79 Madison Avenue, New York City. It will be sent to any commissioner of public welfare upon request.)

Item 8. Maximum expenditure.[28] To conserve Federal and/or State relief funds in the provision of adequate dental care to all recipients of home relief needing such care, the maximum charge for all dental care provided, under these Rules and Regulations, to one patient, shall not exceed twenty dollars ($20) as a basis for reimbursement.

Regulation 7. **Bedside nursing care.**[29] *Introduction. a.* Bedside nursing care to recipients of home relief shall be provided, whenever possible, by registered nurses employed on a work relief basis, under the statewide bedside nursing service supervised by the New York State Department of Health in more than ninety public welfare districts in the State.

b. Bedside nursing care shall continue to be provided through existing community services, such as visiting nurses associations, public health nurses, etc., paid for in whole or in part from local and/or State funds, in accordance with local statutes and/or charter provisions.

---

[27] § 83, see Chapter III, Section C, *Item 1,* page 46.
[28] Unless prior authorization is obtained from the Division of Medical Care.
[29] See Regulation 9, Section C, page 36.

Item 1. Bedside nursing, per visit. *a.* Bedside nursing care shall be authorized, on a per visit basis, only in communities where and to the extent to which work relief nurses are not available or where existing community services, mentioned above, are not adequate to carry the load, and then, only in accordance with the need for such bedside nursing care as indicated by the attending physician. Authorizations for bedside nursing care shall be issued, subject to the restrictions imposed by Regulations 1, 2, 3, 4, 7, 9 and 10 of this chapter, on pages 14, 15, 16, 25, 36 and 39.

b. Standards of accredited local nursing organizations shall be followed by registered graduate nurses authorized to give bedside nursing care to recipients of home relief in their homes.

Item 2. Bedside nursing, per day. Bedside nursing care for acute and serious illnesses, when recommended in writing by the physician in attendance on the case, may be authorized, for not more than 10 days' care, on a per diem basis where hospitalization is not possible or practicable and where such bedside nursing care is not available through work relief nurses or other existing local agencies. The physician's written recommendation shall accompany the bill, which may be reimbursable for not more than 10 days' care.

Item 3. "Home helps," practical nursing. In isolated communities where the services of a registered graduate nurse are not available and for the care of chronic illnesses not requiring expert attention or institutional care, "home helps" or practical nurse housekeepers may be authorized to provide necessary service in the home of the patient, on a per diem basis, provided that the employment of such "home helps" is recommended in writing by the attending physician, such written recommendation to accompany the bill.

Regulation 8. **Medicine, drugs, sickroom supplies and prosthetic devices.** Such materials and supplies as are necessary to provide adequate medical care to recipients of home relief shall be authorized, subject to the following restrictions imposed on each type, if reimbursement from the Administration is contemplated for such authorized expenditures.

Item 1. Medicine and drugs. *a.* Physicians providing authorized medical care to recipients of home relief shall use a formulary which excludes expensive drugs where less expensive drugs can be used with the same therapeutic effect.

- *b.* When expensive and prolonged medication is considered essential by the attending physician, prior authorization shall be obtained from the Division of Medical Care, if reimbursement from the Administration is contemplated.

c. Certain special remedies[30] which are in general use for the treatment of specific maladies and which have been accepted and officially approved in "New and Non-official Remedies" by the

[30] These are insulin for diabetes, liver and/or stomach extract for pernicious anemia, digifolin and similar compounds of digitalis for heart disease, and ephedrin and its compounds.

Council of the American Medical Association may be authorized with a view to reimbursement, upon the prescription of the attending physician, without further consultation, except as noted in paragraph *b*.

d. With the exceptions noted above, prescriptions for necessary drugs and medicine shall be restricted to those listed in the *latest* edition of the National Formulary and/or the United States Pharmacopeia; and proprietary or patent medicines, patent infant foods, and prescriptions containing proprietary remedies, shall not be eligible for reimbursement by the Administration. Substitutions should be made by the attending physician, from the National Formulary or the United States Pharmacopeia, for certain proprietary remedies, for example: phenobarbital should be substituted for luminal; hexamethylenamin for urotropin; etc.

e. Arsphenamine or neo-arsphenamine may be eligible for reimbursement only for the treatment of other than venereal infections. These and other specific remedies for the treatment of venereal disease may be obtained by the attending physician, free of charge, from the State Department of Health, for the treatment of indigent patients. Expenditures for the *treatment of venereal disease* in recipients of home relief shall not be eligible for reimbursement by the Administration, except on the basis of regular office visits in county public welfare districts not covered by a county health department.[31] In all city and county health districts such treatment is by law[32] a responsibility of the local board of health.

f. Certain approved sera, vaccines and biologicals, may be obtained free of charge from the Division of Laboratories and Research of the State Department of Health; expenditures for such therapeutic or diagnostic materials shall not be reimbursable.

g. Medicine dispensed directly by a physician in the course of an authorized home or office visit is ordinarily included in the flat charge for such a visit. In certain instances where an expensive drug is used or a large quantity of an ordinary medicine is required, the physician may submit an additional claim for the medicine he dispenses: Provided, that such a claim shall be eligible for reimbursement only if it is itemized to include the name and amount of each ingredient. See Section D, *Item 1, f,* page 37.

Item 2. Sickroom supplies. Authorization for medical and sickroom supplies shall be restricted to the simplest *emergency* needs of the patient consistent with good medical care. Such authorizations shall be issued only on the basis of a physician's prescription for an individual patient and shall be confined to such necessary items as gauze, adhesive tape, cotton, ear syringe, eye cup, ice bag, clinical thermometer, hot water bottle (not electric pad), and hypodermic syringe and needles (for diabetics).

Item 3. Prosthetic devices and surgical appliances. a. Authorizations for necessary prosthetic devices shall be issued to meet emergency needs only, and shall *not* include, with a view to reimburse-

---

[31] Only Cattaraugus, Columbia, Cortland, Suffolk and Westchester counties have county health departments.

[32] Article XVII-B, §§ 343-m to 343-t (added by Chapter 264, Laws of 1918)

ment, such expensive devices as artificial limbs for unemployables, vulcanite dentures, etc. Such devices may be authorized by the local commissioner of public welfare,[33] but expenditures on the basis of such order shall not be reimbursable by the Administration.

b. Expenditures for authorized repairs of dentures shall be eligible for reimbursement subject to the restriction imposed by these Rules and Regulations.[34]

c. Necessary surgical and orthopedic appliances, including simple braces and other devices, may be authorized under these Rules and Regulations, upon the written order of a competent physician, for the rehabilitation of recipients of home relief who are twenty-one or more years of age: Provided, that prior authorization[35] shall be required, if reimbursement is contemplated, where the proposed expenditure is more than $7.

NOTE.—In granting authorizations for expensive prosthetic devices, consideration will be given to the age of the patient, his probable re-employability with the proposed appliance, and the underlying physical condition.

d. Claims for reimbursement for authorized orthopedic appliances may be subject to review by the Division of Orthopédics, or an orthopedic consultant of the State Department of Health.

e. Expenditures for such prosthetic devices for persons under twenty-one years of age shall not be eligible for reimbursement by the Administration. Care and necessary prosthetic devices for a "physically handicapped child" comes under the jurisdiction of the State Education Law.[36] Under subdivision seven-a of section two of the Children's Court Act:[37] "A 'physically handicapped child' is a person under twenty-one years of age who, by reason of a physical defect or infirmity, whether congenital or acquired by accident, injury or disease, is or may be expected to be totally or partially incapacitated for education or for remunerative occupation, but shall not include the deaf and the blind."

Exceptions to this exclusion may be made in the case of an expenditure of less than $10 in view of the fact that a children's court does not usually entertain applications for appliances costing less than that amount.

f. Optical supplies, including eye glasses, shall be authorized, with a view to reimbursement, only upon the written prescription of a licensed physician who, in his specialty as an oculist or opthalmologist, is permitted to use drugs in examining eyes. The reimbursable claim for such an examination and prescription shall be restricted by the provisions of *Item 4* of Regulation 9, page 30.

Expenditures for eye glasses shall be eligible for reimbursement only when they are provided under the following conditions: 1. When glasses are necessary in order to enable a recipient of home relief to secure employment; 2. When, in the opinion of the examining physician-oculist eyesight is endangered because of lack of

[33] In accordance with § 83 of the Public Welfare Law, see page 46.
[34] See Regulation 6, *Item 7*, page 25, and Regulation 9, Section D, *Item 3, b.*
[35] Division of Medical Care, T.E.R.A., 79 Madison Avenue, New York, N. Y.
[36] For details write the Physically Handicapped Children's Bureau, State Education Department, Albany, N. Y. See also subd. (3-a), § 577-b, Education Law.
[37] Chapter 547, Laws of 1922, with subsequent amendments.

glasses; 3. When the patient cannot attend to usual household tasks, or a child cannot make proper progress in school, without glasses; and 4. When, according to the attending physician-oculist or opthalmologist, the patient has a disease or defect of the eye which requires glasses for its cure or correction.

Regulation 9. **Schedule of reimbursable charges.** *Introduction.* *a.* It is realized by the Administration that with the funds available, it is impossible to compensate fully the physician, dentist or nurse for his or her professional services. The following schedule of charges, therefore, should not be considered as complete compensation for services rendered, but rather as a maximum basis for reimbursement, with due consideration for the conservation of relief funds to the mutual benefit of the patient, the professional attendant and the taxpayer.

The following schedule of reimbursable charges was prepared following a conference, in Albany, N. Y., on April 16, 1934, between authorized representatives of the Medical and Dental Societies of the State of New York, the Administration, and the State Commissioner of Health.

b. The charges listed are hereby established by the Administration as the maximum eligible for reimbursement, under these Rules and Regulations. However, no statement in these regulations shall be construed to prevent a local commissioner of public welfare from making additional payments, for specified services, from local funds;[38] or from making payment at less that the maximum charges stated in these regulations, where the local professional organization has agreed to the authorization of specified services at a lower rate.

Section A. *Medical Care.* (**Personal Services.**) The services of a physician, authorized with a view to reimbursement by the Administration, shall be subject to the restrictions imposed by these Rules and Regulations, and expenditures for such services shall be eligible for reimbursement at not to exceed the following schedule of charges.

Item 1. Home visit. Authorized home visits, subject to the restrictions imposed by Section D, page 11, and Regulations 1, 2,[39] and 3, above, shall be reimbursable at a rate per visit not to exceed...................... $2.00

Item 2. Office visit. Authorized office visits, subject to the restrictions stated for *Item 1*, above, shall be reimbursable at a rate per visit not to exceed.......... 1.00

Item 3. Obstetrical care. Authorized obstetrical care in the home including necessary prenatal care, delivery in the home and postnatal care, subject to the general restrictions and requirements imposed by these Rules and Regulations and the specific requirements of Regulation 4, above, shall be eligible for reimbursement:

---

[38] Under § 83, of the Public Welfare Law, See Chapter III, page 46.
[39] Note especially *Item 6*, page 15. Also, mileage is not reimbursable.

a. For the services of a physician, on the basis of an all inclusive flat rate which shall not exceed.......... $25.00
or,

b. For the services of a physician, on the basis of a flat rate for delivery in the home and necessary post-natal and postpartum care at not to exceed.......... 15.00
and, prenatal care at a rate not to exceed $1.00 per visit, with a maximum for such prenatal care at a rate not to exceed 10.00
The total charge, under this plan, for prenatal, delivery and postpartum care, not to exceed, as above........ 25.00

c. For the services of a midwife, subject to the requirements of *Item 2, c,*[40] Section D and *Item 11,*[41] of Regulation 4, above, on the basis of a rate not to exceed 12.50

d. For authorized obstetrical services not covered above, see Regulation 4, *Items 5, 6* and *8,* pages 17–18.

Special Services

Item 4. The usual services of a specialist. Authorized services of a specialist, shall be subject, for the purposes of reimbursement, to the general restrictions of these Rules and Regulations and the specific requirements of *Item 1* of Regulation 5,[41] and shall be eligible for reimbursement at a rate not to exceed............ 2.00

Such services include: complete refraction; eye, ear, nose, throat and skin treatment; etc.

Item 5. Consultation. The services of a consultant, authorized under these Rules and Regulations,[42] shall be eligible for reimbursement at a rate not to exceed...... 2.00

Item. 6. Emergency or first aid treatment. Authorized emergency or first aid treatment, including necessary dressings, to be provided in the home, at the place of accident or in the physician's office, shall be eligible for reimbursement at a rate not to exceed.......... 2.00

Item 7. X-ray examinations and treatment. a. Diagnostic x-ray examinations authorized[43] subject to the requirements of *Item 4,* Regulation 5, above, shall be eligible for reimbursement on the basis of a rate not to exceed 50 per cent more than the schedule of charges adopted by the United States Employees Compensation Commission for use in the examination of injured Civil Works Administration employees. The 50 per cent additional charge was recommended for x-ray examinations restricted to physicians' offices, by the Advisory Committee of the Medical Society of the State of New York, at a conference on January 16, 1934.

[40] See page 12. [41] See page 19. [42] See Regulation 5, *Item 2,* on page 20.
[43] Not to exceed $20, unless physician's tentative diagnosis and history of the case is submitted to, and prior authorization secured from, the T.E.R.A. Division of Medical Care.

The following schedule of charges for specified x-ray examinations made in physicians' offices shall be the maximum basis for reimbursement by the Administration:

	No. of films	Maximum Reimbursable Charge[44]
Ankle joint, antero-posterior and lateral views...	2	$3.75
Arm, humerus, antero-posterior and lateral views.	2	3.75
Bladder, with injection, antero-posterior view...	1	7.50
Chest, for pulmonary or cardiac diagnosis, plain.	1	5.75
Chest, for pulmonary or cardiac diagnosis, stereoscopic	2	7.50
Clavicle, postero-anterior view	1	3.75
Elbow, antero-posterior and lateral views	2	3.75
Fluoroscopy, when required, without film	1	1.50
Foot, antero-posterior and lateral views	2	3.75
Forearm, radius and ulna, antero-posterior and lateral views	2	3.75
Foreign body in eye, location of (the fragment charted in three planes and its dimensions ascertained by the method of Sweet or equivalent as needed)	..	18.75
Gall bladder, Graham technic, including cost of dye	1	15.00
Gastrointestinal tract, complete x-ray study, including fluoroscopy, 6 hour examination and 24 hour re-examination with barium clysma, as needed	..	18.75
Hand, antero-posterior and lateral views	2	3.75
Hip joint, plain, antero-posterior view	1	5.75
Hip joint, stereoscopic, antero-posterior view	2	7.50
Intestine, barium clysma, 14 x 17 films for position and outline, as needed	..	11.25
Jaw, upper or lower	1	3.75
Kidneys, right and left, for comparison, 11 x 14 films as needed	..	7.50
Knee joint, antero-posterior and lateral views	2	3.75
Leg, tibia and fibula, antero-posterior and lateral views	2	3.75
Lipoidol injection for bronchiectasis, etc. including Roentgenograms and interpretation, as needed	..	18.75
Pelvis, 14 x 17, single film, antero-posterior view	1	7.50
Pyelography, using uroselectan or similar preparation (including cost of drug)	4	15.00
Ribs, plain view over suspected area, 10 x 12 film	1	5.75
Scapula	1	3.75
Shoulder joint, plain, antero-posterior view...	1	3.75

[44] Only when taken in the office of a recognized roentgenologist.

	No. of films	Maximum Reimbursable Charge[45]
Shoulder joint, stereoscopic, antero-posterior views	2	$7.50
Sinuses, frontal and ethmoid, antero-posterior and lateral views	2	7.50
Sinuses, mastoid, right and left sides for comparison	2	7.50
Sinuses, maxillary, antero-posterior and lateral views	2	7.50
Skull, ventriculogram, air injection, as needed	..	11.25
Skull, antero-posterior and lateral views	2	7.50
Skull, stereoscopic	2	11.25
Spine, cervical, antero-posterior and lateral views	2	7.50
Spine, dorsal, antero-posterior and lateral views	2	7.50
Spine, lumbo-sacral, with coccyx antero-posterior and lateral views	2	7.50
Stomach, barium or bismuth meal, 14 x 17 film, after ingestion, four 8 x 10 films for detection of duodenal cap; total of four 8 x 10 films, including fluoroscopy	4	18.75
Teeth, see *Item 5*, Section B, Regulation 9, page 35.		
Thigh, femur, antero-posterior and lateral views	2	5.75
Ureters, right and left, for comparison	(1 or 2)	11.25
Wrist, antero-posterior and lateral views	2	3.75

b. X-ray treatments authorized subject to the requirements of *Item 4*, Regulation 5, page 20, shall be eligible for reimbursement at a rate not to exceed:

for low voltage or superficial treatments	2.00
for high voltage or deep x-ray therapy	3.00
to	5.00

Item 8. Minor operations. a. Minor surgery, authorized to be performed *in the home* or *in the physician's office*, shall be subject to the general restrictions imposed by these Rules and Regulations and the specific requirements of *Item 5*, of Regulation 5, page 20, and shall be eligible for reimbursement on a sliding scale, dependent upon the services rendered,[46] at a rate not to exceed 3.00

to 10.00

Such reimbursable charges for minor surgery shall include necessary dressings at the time of the operation.

---

[45] Only when taken in the office of a recognized roentgenologist.

[46] Examples of claims submitted for reimbursement which have been approved by the Administration are: circumcision of an infant—$5.00, for an older boy or adult—$10.00; blood transfusion, artificial pneumothorax, paracentesis abdominalis—$5.00; myringotomy—$3.00; tonsillectomy and adenoidectomy—$6.00 to $10.00; minor incisions and excisions—$2.00 to $5.00; etc.—all performed in the home or in the physician's office.

b. Authorized follow-up visits shall be eligible for reimbursement on the basis of a charge not to exceed that for an authorized office visit, namely............ $1.00

Item 9. Reduction of simple fractures. Reduction and splinting of simple fractures shall be authorized subject to the general restrictions imposed by these Rules and Regulations and the specific restrictions imposed by *Item 6* of Regulation 5,[47] above, and shall be eligible for reimbursement on a sliding scale, dependent on the relative amount of work involved, on the basis of (except for a fracture of the pelvis or the surgical neck of the femur) a charge not to exceed.... 10.00
Expenditures for authorized reduction (including cast) of a fracture of the pelvis or the surgical neck of the femur shall be on the basis of a charge not to exceed.. 25.00
Authorized after care and follow-up treatment of fractures shall be eligible for reimbursement subject to the restrictions imposed by *Item 6, d*, Regulation 5,[47] above.

Item 10. Major operations. Authorizations for major surgery on recipients of home relief shall not generally be eligible for reimbursement by the Administration. However, subject to the general restrictions imposed by these Rules and Regulations and the specific restrictions imposed by *Item 7*, Regulation 5,[47] above, emergency major surgery authorized in the home, at the site of the accident, or in the physician's office, shall be eligible for reimbursement on the basis of a charge not to exceed two-thirds of the minimum county fee schedule: provided that, in no instance shall such basis of reimbursement exceed..................... 25.00

Item 11. General anesthesia, surgical assistance, and physiotherapy. Subject to the general restrictions imposed by these Rules and Regulations and the specific restrictions imposed by *Items 5 to 8*, inclusive, Regulation 5,[47] above, *separate claims* for the above services, when authorized, shall be eligible for reimbursement on the basis of a charge not to exceed the following schedule of charges:
a. General anesthesia given by a physician in the home or at the physician's office, not to exceed........ 5.00
b. Surgical or obstetrical assistance given by a physician, not to exceed........................... 5.00
c. Physiotherapy, restricted to a maximum of 5 visits, at a rate per treatment not to exceed......... 1.00

Item 12. Laboratory diagnostic services. Authorized laboratory diagnostic examinations, subject to the requirements and restrictions imposed by *Item 9* of Regulation 5,[47] shall be eligible for reimbursement on the basis of a rate not to exceed two-thirds of the minimum rate charged by local State approved laboratories.

---

[47] See pages 21, 22 and 23.

Item 13. Other special services.[48] Special services, not covered above shall be eligible for reimbursement, when authorized, only on the basis of a rate not to exceed two-thirds of the local minimum fee schedule: Provided, that in no instance shall the basis of reimbursement exceed $25.00
and provided, further, that a request for prior authorization is submitted to, and approved by, the Division of Medical Care.

Section B. *Dental Care.* (**Personal services.**) The following schedule of charges for authorized dental care is hereby established, as the basis for reimbursement, by the Administration, after consultation[49] with authorized representatives of the Dental Society of the State of New York.

Item 1. Extractions. Authorized dental extractions subject to the restrictions imposed by *Item 1* of Regulation 6, page 33, shall be reimbursable at not to exceed the following charges:

a. First tooth, including necessary anesthetic and postoperative treatment 1.50

b. Each additional tooth extracted from the same patient, not necessarily extracted at the same visit.... 1.00

c. Maximum charge for authorized extraction of teeth from any one patient shall not exceed.............. 10.00

d. All gold crowns and bridge work removed by a dentist authorized to extract teeth, shall be given to the patient in return for a signed receipt, which shall be attached by the dentist to the voucher, when he submits his claim for performing such authorized extractions.

Item 2. Fillings, including an approved method of pulp protection, and subject to the requirements and restriction imposed by *Item 2,* Regulation 6, page 23, shall be reimbursable at charges not to exceed the following:

a. Silver amalgam meeting specifications approved by the American Dental Association: one surface........ 2.00
two or more surfaces............................. 3.00

b. Silicious cement meeting specifications approved by the American Dental Association (restricted to fillings in anterior teeth only)............................. 3.00

c. Other cements, meeting specifications approved by the American Dental Association, restricted to conditions for which a temporary filling is indicated: for a permanent tooth 1.00
temporary tooth 0.50

---

[48] Dental services are covered in Regulation 6, pages 23 to 25, and *Items 1* to 7, inclusive in Section B, of Regulation 9, pages 34 and 35.
[49] In Albany, N. Y., April 16, 1934.

Item 3. Treatment. Emergency treatment for conditions listed under *Item 3,* Regulation 6, page 24, shall be reimbursable at a rate per visit not to exceed....... $1.00
<small>(Same rate applies to recementing inlays, crowns and bridges.)</small>

Item 4. Dental prophylaxis, subject to the general restrictions imposed by these Rules and Regulations and the specific restrictions and requirements of *Item 4,* Regulation 6, page 24, shall be reimbursable at a rate not to exceed 2.00
<small>(Note.—Prophylaxis for purely esthetic reasons shall not be eligible for reimbursement.)</small>

Item 5. Dental x-ray examinations, for diagnosis only and subject to other restrictions of *Item 5,* Regulation 6, page 24, shall be eligible for reimbursement at a rate not to exceed:
Single film 0.50
Each additional film for the same patient, not necessarily taken at the same visit, up to and including the tenth.. 0.25
Full mouth x-ray series, not less than eleven films.... 3.00
<small>(For x-ray of jaw, upper or lower, see page 31.)</small>

Item 6. Special dental services, authorized only on an individual basis, and subject to the restrictions imposed by *Item 6, a* and *b,* Regulation 6, page 25, shall be reimbursable at charges not to exceed the following:
a. Root canal therapy, including silicate filling and at least one extra x-ray when the therapeutic procedure and filling is completed, for the first root canal....... 5.00
for the second root canal treated in the same tooth.... 3.00
for the third root canal treated in the same tooth.... 2.00
b. Dental surgery, other than simple extractions, to include such necessary operative procedures as removal of cysts, impacted teeth and/or infected areas, from.... 5.00
to 10.00
depending upon the time spent and the skill required: Provided, that the total reimbursable charge for dental surgery, for any one patient shall not exceed........ 10.00
With the exception of reduction and fixation of a fracture of the jaw, at a rate not to exceed........... 20.00

Item 7. Maximum expenditure, for all reimbursable dental care provided for any one person under these Rules and Regulations, shall be, for the reasons stated in *Item 8,* Regulation 6, page 25, on the basis of total charges not to exceed............................. 20.00
a. Should a patient fail to return for the completion of authorized treatment, the dentist may receive a pro rata share of remuneration for the authorized work actually completed.

Section C. *Bedside nursing care.* (**Personal services.**) The following schedule of charges for authorized bedside nursing care and authorized service of "home helps" is hereby established by the Administration as its basis for reimbursement.

Item 1. Registered nurses on a per visit basis. Subject to the general restrictions imposed by these Rules and Regulations,[50] and the specific restrictions imposed by *Item 1*, Regulation 7, page 26, bedside nursing care provided by registered nurses authorized on a per visit basis, shall be reimbursable at a rate per visit not to exceed $1.00

Provided, that no additional allowance shall be reimbursable for advice and/or care given to other members of the same household by the nurse in the course of an authorized home visit.[51]

Item 2. Registered nurses on a per diem basis. Subject to the general restrictions imposed by these Rules and Regulations, and the specific restrictions imposed by *Item 2*, Regulation 7, page 26, necessary bedside nursing care provided by registered nurses authorized on a per diem basis, shall be reimbursable, for not more than 10 days' care, at charges, per 12 hour day, not to exceed the following:

a. For acute non-communicable diseases............ 4.00

b. For acute communicable diseases.............. 5.00

Item 3. "Home helps" on a per diem basis. a. Subject to the general restrictions imposed by these Rules and Regulations, and the specific restrictions imposed by *Item 3*, Regulation 7, page 26, the necessary services provided in the home of the patient by "home helps" or practical nurse housekeepers authorized on a per diem basis, shall be reimbursable at charges per day not to exceed 1.50
to 2.00

Provided, that unless a history and prognosis of the case by the attending physician is submitted to, and prior authorization secured from, the Division of Medical Care, the maximum reimbursable expenditure shall not exceed................................... 20 00

b. In a *nursing home* or a *boarding home*, the authorized board, lodging and care given to a home relief case may be reimbursable as food and shelter, but no part of such care shall be eligible for reimbursement as bedside nursing care.

---

50 See Chapter II; Regulations 1, 2, 3, 4, 7, 9 and 10.
51 See Chapter II, Regulation 2, *Item 6*, page 15.

Section D. *Materials and Supplies. Introduction.*
a. The scope of materials and supplies which may be
provided to recipients of home relief shall include necessary medicine, drugs, sickroom supplies and prosthetic
devices, subject to the restrictions imposed by these
Rules and Regulations.

b. Commissioners of public welfare are urged to make
trade agreements or request bids for the provision of
these materials and supplies, in order that available
relief funds may be conserved.

Item 1. Medicines and .drugs. a. Physicians providing authorized medical care to recipients of home relief
shall use a formulary which excludes expensive drugs
where less expensive drugs can be used with the same
therapeutic effect. Medicine and drugs, ordered in writing by a physician, shall be authorized subject to the
general restrictions of these Rules and Regulations and
the specific requirements of *Item 1* of Regulation 8,
above,[52] and shall be eligible for reimbursement at
charges not to exceed the following:

b. Compounded prescriptions containing no rare or
costly drugs $0.75

c. Uncompounded prescriptions for ordinary drugs.. 0.50

d. Uncompounded prescriptions for the more expensive drugs 0.75

e. Compounded or uncompounded prescriptions for
special and more costly medicines and preparations,
such as insulin, at prices not to exceed: 20 per cent more
than the wholesale price listed in the current "Druggists' Circular"
plus a service charge not in excess of................ 0.25
in cases where these drugs are compounded.

f. Simple drugs furnished by a physician in the course
of a home or office visit shall not ordinarily be eligible
for reimbursement except as part of the service provided
under an authorized visit. In certain instances where a
physician, in the more isolated communities, dispenses
large quantities or more expensive drugs, a claim may
be submitted for reimbursement at a rate not to exceed. 0.50
Provided, that the claim lists the name and quantity of
each drug, and complies with the restrictions imposed by
Item 1 of Regulation 8, page 26.

g. Not more than one prescription for the same drug
or drugs may be authorized for the same patient, with
a view to reimbursement, in a given week.

---
[52] See page 26.

Item 2. Sickroom supplies. Necessary sickroom supplies shall be authorized as a rule only on the order of a physician, and expenditures for such materials, subject to the restrictions imposed by *Item 2* of Regulation 8, page 27, shall be eligible for reimbursement either:

a. On the basis of the price secured by competitive bids, or

b. In any case at a price not to exceed.............. 20% more than the standard current wholesale price for such materials.

c. Provided, that the name of the physician issuing the order for necessary sickroom supplies shall be made a part of the claim for reimbursement.

Item 3. Prosthetic devices and surgical appliances. Introduction. Subject to the general restrictions imposed by these Rules and Regulations and the specific requirements of *Item 3* of Regulation 8, page 27, necessary prosthetic devices and appliances (including glasses, glass eyes, simple braces, repair of dentures, etc.) may be authorized for recipients of home relief, with a view to reimbursement by the Administration. Prosthetic devices shall be purchased, whenever possible, on the basis of the lowest bid submitted to the commissioner of public welfare for such devices.

a. Orthopedic and surgical appliances. Subject to the restrictions imposed by *Item 3* of Regulation 8, page 27, authorized expenditures for orthopedic and surgical appliances shall be eligible for reimbursement at a charge obtained upon competitive bid and/or at an appreciable reduction from the current retail price.

b. Repair of dentures. The repair of dental prosthetic devices, including repairs of vulcanite dentures and/or the replacement of clasps on such dentures shall be subject to the requirements of *Item 7*, Regulation 6, page 25, and shall be reimbursable at a rate not to exceed:

1. Vulcanizing charge including repair of all cracks, fissures and/or fractures; replacement of one or more teeth; and attaching by vulcanization one or more clasps —in any one vulcanite denture...................... $3.00

2. Additional charge for first tooth replaced in such a vulcanite denture 1.00

3. Additional charge for each additional tooth, after the first, replaced in any such vulcanite denture...... 0.50

4. Additional charge for making and fitting a clasp, only in cases where a new clasp is required, to replace a broken clasp or to change the point of retention due to loss of a key tooth, to insure an accurate fit of any such vulcanite denture 4.00

Provided, that only 18.3 carat gold shall be used in making clasps, laboratory technician shall be given to the patient in return for a signed receipt, which shall be submitted with the voucher for making and fitting a clasp.

c. Optical supplies. Subject to the general restrictions imposed by these Rules and Regulations and the specific requirements of *Item 3, f* of Regulation 8, above,[53] authorized expenditures for *eyeglasses* shall be eligible for reimbursement preferably on the basis of prices obtained by competitive bids, at charges not to exceed the following:

REIMBURSABLE CHARGES PER PAIR FOR EYEGLASSES, COMPLETE WITH FIRST QUALITY LENSES * AND FRAMES †

LENS STRENGTH IN DIOPTERS	SINGLE VISION Toric, flat or meniscus lenses		BIFOCALS Lenses with fused bifocal segments up to 4.50D	LENS STRENGTH IN DIOPTERS	SINGLE VISION Toric, flat or meniscus lenses		BIFOCALS Lenses with fused bifocal segments up to 4.50D
Spheres	Convex	Concave	+ or −	Sphero Cylinders	+○+	−○+	+○− or −○−
Plano to 2.00.....	$3.00	$3.00	$6.00	0.12 ⎧ 0.12 to 2.00 Cyl.	$3.50	$3.75	$6.25
2.25 to 4.00.....	3.25	3.25	6.00	to ⎨ 2.25 to 3.00 Cyl.	3.75	4.00	6.25
4.25 to 6.00.....	3.50	3.50	6.25	2 00 ⎨ 3.25 to 4.00 Cyl.	4.00	4.25	7.00
6.25 to 9.00.....	4.25	4.25	7.75	Sph. ⎩ 4.25 to 6.00 Cyl.	4.75	5.00	7.75
9.25 to 12.00.....	5.25	5.25	8.75				
12.25 to 16.00.....	6.25	6.25	9.75	2.25 ⎧ 0.12 to 2.00 Cyl.	4.00	4.25	6.75
16.25 to 20.00.....	7.25	7.25	10.75	to ⎨ 2.25 to 3.00 Cyl.	4.25	4.50	7.00
				4 00 ⎨ 3.25 to 4.00 Cyl.	4.50	4.75	7.75
Plano Cylinders.....	+	−	− only	Sph. ⎩ 4.25 to 6.00 Cyl.	5.25	5.50	8.25
0.12 to 2.00 Cyl.	3.50	3.75	6.25	4.25 ⎧ 0.12 to 2.00 Cyl.	4.75	5.00	6.75
2.25 to 3.00 Cyl.	3.75	4.00	6.25	to ⎨ 2.25 to 3.00 Cyl.	5.25	5.50	7.00
3.25 to 4.00 Cyl.	4.00	4.25	6.75	6.00 ⎨ 3.25 to 4.00 Cyl.	5.75	6.00	7.75
4.25 to 6.00 Cyl.	4.75	5.00	7.00	Sph. ⎩ 4.25 to 6.00 Cyl.	6.50	6.75	8.25

* Bausch and Lomb or American Optical Company standards, or their equivalent.
† Frames shall be of white metal, military style, or its equivalent, and of U. S. A. manufacture.
For prism values combined with lenses, add to price of complete eyeglasses $1.50.
For the maximum reimbursable basis for eyeglasses with lens combinations or strengths other than those listed, refer to the T.E.R.A. Division of Medical Care, for prior authorization before purchase.

The above reimbursable charges do not include the charge for complete refraction, including the prescription for the glasses, which is subject to the restrictions imposed by *Item 4*, Section A, page 30. A supplier's invoice for eyeglasses shall include a description of the type, and optical strength in diopters of lenses supplied, as well as a copy of the physician's prescription.

Regulation 10. **Bills.** The following procedure is hereby established for the submission of bills for services and materials authorized for the purpose of providing more adequate medical care to recipients of home relief.

Item 1. General requirements. a. Physicians, dentists, nurses, druggists and others who are providing authorized medical care, to recipients of home relief, under the requirements of these Rules and Regulations, shall submit to the local welfare official, monthly (within 10 days after the last day of the calendar month in which such medical care was provided), an itemized bill for each patient.

b. Each bill shall be chronologically arranged and shall contain full details as required in *Items 2 to 4*, below, to permit proper audit.

53 See pages 28 and 29.

c. All vouchers for medical care (provided by physicians, dentists, nurses, druggists, others) shall be submitted to the Administration under a separate claim, not later than the last day of the calendar month next succeeding the month during which the provision of such care and/or medical supplies was authorized. Claims submitted later than such date may not be audited until after audit of current claims is completed with corresponding delay in reimbursement to local welfare districts. In order that proper evaluation may be made of medical care for individual patients, so far as possible, the claims for reimbursement for medicines, drugs and medical supplies shall be submitted with the claim for medical, dental and nursing care for the same patients.

Item 2. Specific requirements. a. Physicians, dentists, nurses and other professional personnel providing authorized personal services to recipients of home relief shall submit, in their bills, the following details: date and number of written order; name, age, case number, and address of patient (also name of the head of the household receiving home relief, unless he or she is the patient); diagnosis, or specific indication of the nature of the illness (acute or chronic); whether treatment was given in the patient's home or in the office of the physician or dentist, with full details, if unusual services were given;[54] a chronological list of the dates on which services were rendered; and the status of the case at the end of the month, namely, "cured, needs further treatment, hospitalized (give date and name of hospital), dead (give date of death), etc."

b. Druggists or pharmacists authorized to provide drugs and/or medical supplies under the general and specific restrictions of these Rules and Regulations, to recipients of home relief shall submit, in their bill, the following details: date and number of written order; name, age, case number and address of patient (and head of household if other than the patient), a copy of the prescription or, the name and amount of each drug and the name of the physician prescribing it. Bills for large amounts of medication or medical supplies, which involve unusual expenditures should give sufficient details on the case, or a reference to the bill of the attending physician, as a justification for such expenditure. For example, when insulin is given, the bill should include, the size of the vial, the number of units per cubic centimeter, and the physician's estimate of the monthly needs of the patients.

c. Medical supply houses or other firms authorized to provide prosthetic devices shall submit bills with the data required above, including a specific description of the device or material provided under the authorization, and the written order and name and address of the physician prescribing it.

Item 3. Bill form. Bills shall be submitted on T.E.R.A. Form 277, adapted to present the details required in this regulation. Bills for medical care (including personal services of physician, dentist, nurse, etc., and materials and supplies) shall be on or accompanied by the original written order, except for cases in which medical service under an authorization has not terminated during the calendar month covered by the bill, in which cases the bill shall show, in addition to the details required above, the date and serial number of the outstanding order.

Item 4. Retroactive bills. Bills submitted for services or materials and supplies provided on the basis of retroactive authorizations as defined in *Item 2* of Regulation 1, above,[55] shall not be eligible for reimbursement by the Administration.

Regulation 11. **Professional audit and arbitration.** The Administration is desirous of maintaining professional standards in the provision of medical care to recipients of home relief, and solicits the cooperation of the organized profession in establishing arrangements for providing medical and other professional advice to commissioners of public welfare. Under the provisions of Section C[56] of Chapter I of these Rules and Regulations, audit and arbitration of bills for professional service may be conducted under professional supervision[57] with regard to: reasonableness of any individual bill for authorized service; failure to maintain professional standards; proposed changes in policy and procedure; and principles to be followed in the allocation of cases to physicians.

Regulation 12. **Monthly report.** The local department of public welfare shall submit, at the end of each calendar month, a monthly report of total medical, dental, nursing services and drugs and medical supplies authorized and submitted for reimbursement for the preceding month. This report should contain a summary of relevant data for each physician, dentist, nurse and druggist, including: the number of different patients for whom care was authorized; number of home visits; number of office visits; number drugs and medical supplies shall be submitted with the claim of confinements; number of special services;[58] number of drugs and medical supplies; and total charge on all claims included in bills.

Regulation 13. **Authorization of change in scope of local program.** The local program of medical care adopted under these Rules and Regulations shall be subject to the restrictions imposed by *Items 1* and *2* of Section D, pages 11 and 12. *No change in the scope of local services,* provided under existing statutes from nonrelief funds, *shall be made with a view to securing reimbursement* from the Administration for such services, *without prior written approval by the Administration.* A request for approval in change of scope of the local program of medical care shall be accompanied by detailed monthly records of the services in question for a period of not less than the two preceding years, as well as evidence that these services are not adequate to give needed medical, dental or nursing care to recipients of home relief.

---

[55] See page 14. [56] See pages 10 and 11. [57] Preferably by the County Medical Compensation Board established under subd. 1, § 13-b, of the Workmen's Compensation Law, added by Chapter 258, Laws of 1935. [58] See *Items 4* to *13,* pages 30 to 34.

CHAPTER III

A Summary of Basic Legislation and
A Chronological Review of
Prior Regulations

With an Appendix of Quotations from the Public Welfare Law and the Education Law

Sections and regulations, governing the policy and procedures of the Administration, as adopted in Chapters I and II, above, which conflict with analogous statements in the following regulations and/or official statements, shall supersede such conflicting statements.

Section A. **Basic legislation.**

Item. 1. The Emergency Relief Act of the State of New York (Chapter 798 of the Laws of 1931) defines medical care as one of the necessaries of life to be provided to such of its inhabitants as are found to be imperilled by the existing and threatened deprivation of such necessaries of life, owing to the present economic depression. Paragraph 8 of Section 2 of this Act reads as follows:

" 'Home Relief' means shelter, fuel, food, clothing, light, *medicine or medical attendance furnished* by a municipal corporation to persons or their dependents *in their abode or habitation* and does not include relief to veterans under existing laws, old age relief or allowance made to mothers for the care of dependent children." [59]

Item 2. The Emergency Relief Act was subsequently amended on May 1, 1933 by Chapter 646 of the Laws of 1933 to read as follows:

" 'Home Relief' means shelter, fuel, food, clothing, light, necessary household supplies, *medicine, medical supplies,* relief to veterans under existing laws *and medical attendance furnished* by a municipal corporation or a town, where home relief is a town charge, to persons or their dependents *in their abode or habitation* whenever possible and does not include old age relief or allowances made to mothers for the care of dependent children or *hospital or institutional care.*" [59]

Item 3. The Act was further amended on April 27, 1934 [60] by Chapter 303 of the Laws of 1934 to read as follows:

"§ 16-a. *Work relief disability allowance.* 1. Persons employed on work relief projects under the provisions of this act as heretofore or hereafter amended and receiving "work relief" as defined

[59] Italics mine (Ed.); See Section C, *Item 1,* on page 46, below, for legal provisions for authorizing services, such as hospital or institutional care, excluded from the scope of the Emergency Relief Act.

[60] To take effect immediately and provisions thereof effective as of April 1, 1934.

herein shall not be deemed to come within the scope of the provisions or benefits provided by chapter six hundred fifteen of the laws of nineteen hundred twenty-two as amended and known as the workmen's compensation law; but all persons receiving "work relief" who shall become temporarily disabled or injured by reason of any cause arising out of and in the course of their employment shall, during the period of said disability, so caused within the duration of the emergency period as defined herein, continue to receive" *(home)* "*relief* on the basis of the budgetary needs of the said person's family as determined under the standards and pursuant to the rules and regulations of the administration and in addition thereto shall be provided with such medical services as the administration may deem necessary."[61]

Section B. **Chronological review of prior regulations.**

Item 1. The first detailed instructions on medical care under the Emergency Relief Act of 1931 were sent "To Public Welfare Officials" on December 8, 1931. They are quoted below in full:

"Interpretation of 'Medicines or Medical Attendance
to Persons or Their Dependents in
Their Abode or Habitation.'"

"This shall include medical service in the home[62] as well as medicines, and such sickroom supplies as are necessary. Other expenditures for the care of the sick may be approved depending upon the circumstances."

"Condition of Approval

"The Administration reserves the right to refuse approval in whole or part of claims by Municipal Corporations in cases:

"1. Where necessary hospital or institutional care has not been provided or has been unduly delayed: and

"2. Where full use has not been made of all existing public and private facilities providing free medical services.

"Procedure: Orders for Medical Service.

"When public welfare officers authorize expenditures for medical relief, they shall fill out the usual home relief order forms, in duplicate, and note that medical care is authorized. The original should be sent to the physician or the authorized medical agent immediately and must be returned by him with his bill. This bill should contain the following items:

"1. Diagnosis or condition of patient.

"2. Duration of treatment.

"3. Nature of services rendered.

"*Note.*—The inclusion of the above data on the physician's bill will waive the usual requirement for the countersignature (on the Home Relief Order Form) of the person receiving relief.

[61] Italics mine. (Ed.)

[62] The attorney-general has interpreted this in the interest of economy to include medical attendance at a physician's office in cases in which the patient is able to go there.

"The duplicate home relief order should be retained by the welfare officer as a memorandum for check against the bill, on receipt of which the total expenditure under this order should be noted.

"Procedure: Orders for Medicines and Sickroom Supplies

"1. A physician's prescription is required for all medicines and sickroom supplies. According to the local custom, it may be sent directly to the pharmacist or filed with the welfare officer who uses it as a basis for issuing an order to the pharmacist.

"2· The physician's prescription must show the date, patient's name and address, and specifically state the nature and quantity of medicines or supplies ordered.

"3· Countersignature of patient or a member of his family must be affixed on either the order or the prescription.

"4· Bills must indicate the nature and quality of medicines or supplies furnished. Separate bills need not be made for each relief order or physician's prescription filled; instead bill may cover a number of orders, or prescriptions filled.

"5· Either the welfare officer's order or the physician's prescription, as the case may be, should be attached to the pharmacist's bill.

"TEMPORARY EMERGENCY RELIEF ADMINISTRATION,

JESSE ISIDOR STRAUS,

Chairman."

Item 2. A detailed supplement of the above interpretation of the definition under Home Relief of "Medicine or medical attendance furnished by a municipal corporation to persons or their dependents in their abode or habitation . . ." was issued on January 7, 1932 as a "Memo for Field Workers."

Item 3. On March 3, 1933, the Administration adopted "Rules and Regulations Governing Medical Care to Home Relief Clients," in the form approved by the Special T.E.R.A. Advisory Committee, of the Medical Society of the State of New York, and the State Commissioner of Health. These rules included in their scope preceding statements of policy and procedure.

Item 4. On April 11, 1933, Harry L. Hopkins, then chairman of the Administration wrote to "Public Welfare Commissioners" as follows:

"The Administration would like you to know that the Rules and Regulations Governing Medical Care were established for the fundamental purpose of providing more adequate medical care, as well as establishing an official liaison between the public welfare officials and the local county medical societies. The Executive Committee of the State Medical Society has felt that the arrangement now established will result in the use of a great many more physicians in providing necessary medical care to home relief clients.

"For the reasons above stated, the Administration is considering the $2 fee for a home visit and the $1 fee for an office visit as its uniform basis for reimbursement. This does not preclude payment of an additional amount by welfare commissioners where unusual circumstances, such as large mileage, etc., seem to warrant such payment, but the Administration will not be able to assume this additional charge.

"Our present records indicate that in the course of a year, the number of calls for which more than the usual payment is authorized constitutes a relatively small percentage of the total expenditure, hence, payment of this additional expense in unusual instances would not seem to work any undue hardship on any welfare district."

Item 5. A request that all vouchers for medical care be submitted to the T.E.R.A. under a separate claim and detailed instructions with regard to filing of claims by physicians and other authorized professional personnel, were issued on May 26, 1933. (Effective June 1, 1933.)

Item 6. On July 11, 1933, T.E.R.A. Official Bulletin Number 1 was issued. Section B of this bulletin was an "Amendment to Rules and Regulations Governing Medical Care to Home Relief Clients." which stated " . . . the policy of the Administration with respect to reimbursement for the services of a consultant physician in the home, the usual authorized services of a specialist in his office and professional services given to additional patients in the course of an authorized home visit by a physician."

Item 7. Finally, on September 8, 1933, the Federal Emergency Relief Administration issued "Rules and Regulations No. 7 Governing Medical Care Provided in the Home to Recipients of Unemployment Relief."

These rules were based on experience under the Emergency Relief Act of 1931 in New York State and recognized, on a nation-wide scale, that "The conservation and maintenance of the public health is a primary function of our Government." It was further noted that "To assist State and local relief administrations in the achievement of these aims, with regard to medical care, two steps have been taken: First, to define the general scope of authorized medical care, where the expenditure of Federal Emergency Relief Funds is involved; and second, to establish general regulations governing the provision of such medical care to recipients of unemployment relief."

In a letter to the governors and state relief administrations transmitting the Federal Emergency Relief Administration Rules and Regulations No. 7, Harry L. Hopkins, Administrator, said:

"I particularly call to your attention the common aim of these regulations—the provision of good medical service at low cost—to the mutual benefit of indigent patient, physician and taxpayer."

Section C. **An appendix of quotations from the Pubic Welfare Law of the State of New York.**[63]

The public welfare law, to which the Emergency Relief Act of 1931 was a supplement to meet some of the additional needs occasioned by the "present economic depression," governs the basic procedures by which the State of New York and its component political subdivisions discharge their responsibility "to provide adequately for those unable to maintain themselves."

The quotations were selected to present general and special sections of the public welfare law which have both a direct and an indirect bearing on the provision of medical care "for those unable to maintain themselves."

These, and other sections of the public welfare law allow methods of providing medical care in the home to recipients of home relief, which do not fall within the scope of the emergency relief act, and in addition make provision for such vitally essential services as hospitalization, dispensary and institutional care to recipients of home relief, and to "such persons otherwise able to maintain themselves, who are unable to secure necessary medical care . . ."

Item 1. Sections of the public welfare law *directly* relating to medical care:

"ARTICLE X

" MEDICAL CARE[64]

"§ 83. *Responsibility for providing medical care.* The public welfare district shall be responsible for providing necessary medical care for all persons under its care, and for such persons otherwise able to maintain themselves, who are unable to secure necessary medical care. Such care may be given in dispensaries, hospitals, the person's home or other suitable place.

"(As amended by chapter 494, Laws of 1935.)

"§ 84. *Physicians in public welfare districts.* When a legislative body shall make an appropriation for the purpose, one or more physicians shall be appointed to care for sick persons in their homes. In a county public welfare district, such physician or physicians shall be appointed by the county commissioner. In a city, such physician or physicians shall be appointed in accordance with the provisions of the general or local law, relating to such city. In a town, such physician shall be appointed by the town board. Where no physician is so appointed, the public welfare official shall employ a physician or physicians to visit sick persons in their homes whenever necessary.

---

[63] Chapter 565, Laws of 1929, with subsequent amendments, constituting chapter forty-two of the Consolidated Laws.
[64] As amended by chapter 620, Laws of 1930.

"§ 85. *Care in hospitals.* A public welfare district shall provide needed care for sick and disabled persons in a hospital maintained by the municipality or in any other hospital visited, inspected and supervised by the state board of charities. It may contract with such other hospital to pay such sum for the care of sick persons as may be agreed upon.

"As far as practicable, no patient whose care is to be a charge on a public welfare district, or a subdivision thereof, shall be admitted to a hospital without the prior approval of the public welfare official responsible for his support. Acceptance of any patient as a public charge shall be in the discretion of the public welfare official. In any case where the patient is a public charge, the public welfare official may, when the condition of the patient permits, transfer such patient to another hospital or provide care in any other suitable place.

"If, in case of emergency, a patient is admitted without prior authorization of the public welfare official empowered to approve payment for such care, and the hospital wishes to receive payment from public funds for such patient, the hospital shall, within forty-eight hours of the admission, send to such official a report of the facts of the case, including a statement of the physician in attendance as to the necessity of the immediate admission of such patient to the hospital. If the settlement of the patient is not known by the hospital, such notice shall be sent to the commissioner of the public welfare district in which the hospital is located, and such commissioner shall be responsible for making an investigation to discover whether any public welfare district or the state is liable for payment for the care of such patient. The cost of the care of such a patient shall be a charge against the public welfare district only when authorized by the commissioner.

"§ 86. *Care of patients suffering from tuberculosis.* The public welfare district shall likewise provide suitable care for patients suffering from tuberculosis in a county or city tuberculosis hospital or in any other hospital or sanitarium approved by the state board of charities or in a boarding house approved in writing for this purpose by the health officer in charge of the locality where it is situated. . . .

"(As amended by chapter 481, Laws of 1931.)"

Item 2. Sections of the public welfare law, *indirectly* relating to medical care, which outline responsibilities and standards for public relief and care:

"Public Welfare Districts and Their Responsibility for Public Relief and Care

"§ 17. *Public welfare districts.* For the purpose of administration of public relief and care the state shall be divided into county and city public welfare districts. . . .

48

"§ 18. *Responsibility for public relief, care and support.* A person in need of relief and care which he is unable to provide for himself shall be relieved and cared for by and at the expense of a public welfare district or the state as follows:

"1· The state shall be responsible for:

"(a) The support of any person having no settlement in any public welfare district in the state, who shall not have resided in any public welfare district in the state for sixty days during the year prior to an application for public relief and care.

"(b) The support of any Indian who is eligible for relief from the state under the provisions of section sixty-five of this chapter.

"(c) The expense of transportation of any alien poor person who is returned to his own country and of any non-resident poor person who is returned to the state in which he has a settlement or in which he has friends or relatives willing to support him.

"2· Each public welfare district shall be responsible for:

"(a) The relief, care and support of any person who resides and has a settlement in its territory.

"(b) The relief, care and support of any person found in its territory not having a settlement in the state, for whose support the state is not responsible.

"(c) The relief and care of any person found in its territory who has a settlement elsewhere in the state, subject to reimbursement by the public welfare district of the person's settlement in accordance with the provisions of this chapter.

"(d) The relief and care of any person found in its territory for whose support the state is responsible, subject to reimbursement by the state in accordance with the provisions of this chapter.

"(e) The payment of the cost of the relief and care of a person having a settlement in its territory given by some other public welfare district."

"§ 25. *Responsibility for public relief and care in a county public welfare district.* The responsibility for the administration of public relief and care in a county public welfare district and the expense thereof may either be borne by the county public welfare district or be divided between such district and the towns and cities therein as hereinafter provided.

"1· Unless otherwise determined by the board of supervisors as hereinafter provided, each town shall be responsible for the expense of providing home relief and medical care given at home for persons having a settlement and residing in such town, except defective or physically handicapped children and children born out of wedlock. . . .

"2. Unless otherwise determined by the board of supervisors as hereinafter provided, a city forming a part of a county public welfare district shall be responsible for the expense of providing home relief and medical care given at home or in a hospital for any person having a settlement and residing in its territory except defective or physically handicapped children and children born out of wedlock. . . .

"3. A county public welfare district shall be responsible for the expense of providing all relief and care for persons having a settlement in a town or city in its territory for which such towns and cities may not be responsible under the provisions of subdivisions one and two of this section, and for the relief and care of any person found in its territory who has no settlement in any such town or city. . . .

"The cost of relief and care of any or all of the following types administered by the county commissioner to a person having a settlement in a town or city in the county public welfare district may be charged back to such town or city if the regulations established by the board of supervisors so direct:

"(a) Institutional care of an adult.

"(b) Relief and care for any child who is cared for away from his parents, for defective or physically handicapped children, and for children born out of wedlock.

"(c) Hospital care.

"(d) Home relief and medical care of persons residing in the district but in a town or city other than that of their settlement.

"(e) Home relief and medical care of persons residing in another public welfare district.

"The county commissioner shall immediately notify the town or city public welfare officer of any person alleged to have a settlement in his town or city, the cost of whose relief and care is to be charged back to such town or city. Commitments to a county home may be made by town and city public welfare officers subject to the approval in writing of the county commissioner. All other commitments to hospitals or other institutions at the expense of the county public welfare district shall be made by the county commissioner."

"§ 31. *Powers and duties of city public welfare districts.* A city public welfare district shall be responsible in its territory for the administration of public relief and care and the expense incident thereto. . . ."

"ARTICLE IX

"Relief and Service

"§ 77. *Care to be given.* It shall be the duty of public welfare officials, insofar as funds are available for that purpose, to provide adequately for those unable to maintain themselves. They shall, whenever possible, administer such care and treatment as may restore such persons to a condition of self-support, and shall further give such service to those liable to become destitute as may prevent the necessity of their becoming public charges.

"As far as possible families shall be kept together, and they shall not be separated for reasons of poverty alone. Whenever practicable, relief and service shall be given a poor person in his own home; the commissioner of public welfare, may, however, in his discretion, provide relief and care in a boarding home, the home of a relative, a public or private home or institution, or in a hospital.

"§ 78. *Investigation.* Whenever a public welfare official receives an application for relief, or is informed that a person is in need of care, an investigation and record shall be made of the circumstances of such person. . . . If it shall appear that such person is in immediate need, temporary relief shall be granted pending completion of the investigation.

"§ 79. *Supervision.* When relief is granted to a person in his own home, or in any place outside of an institution, such person shall be visited once a month, or as often as necessary, in order that any care or service tending to restore such person to a condition of self-support and to relieve his distress may be rendered and in order that relief may be given only as long as necessary for this purpose. . . .

"§ 80. *Cooperation of public welfare officials.* It shall be the duty of every public welfare official to render assistance and cooperation within his jurisdictional powers to children's courts, boards of child welfare and all other governmental agencies concerned with the welfare of persons under his jurisdiction. Every public welfare official shall also cooperate whenever possible with any private agency whose object is the relief and care of persons in need or the improvement of social conditions in order that there may be no duplication of relief and that the work of agencies both public and private may be united in an effort to relieve distress and prevent dependency."

A Quotation from the Education Law[65]
"ARTICLE 20-A   Medical Inspection

"§ 577-b. *School hygiene districts.* . . .

"(3-a) If it be ascertained upon any test or examination held by a medical inspector under the provisions of section five hundred seventy-three of this article in any of the school districts within a school hygiene district that any of the pupils are afflicted with defective sight or hearing or other physical disability and the parents have been duly notified as to the existence of such defects and physical disability and are unable to provide the necessary relief and treatment for such pupils and such fact is reported by said medical inspector to the district director of school hygiene, such district director shall have the power and it shall be his duty to provide relief for such pupils within the amount appropriated for such purpose by the board of supervisors.

"Subdivision 3-a added by chapter 754, Laws of 1935, in effect May 6, 1935."

---

[*] Chapter 21, Laws of 1909, as amended, constituting chapter sixteen of the Consolidated Laws.

INDEX

55

5000-April 1, 1936

J. B. LYON COMPANY, PRINTERS, ALBANY, N. Y.

UNEMPLOYMENT RELIEF IN NEW YORK STATE

SEPTEMBER 1, 1935 — AUGUST 31, 1936

TEMPORARY EMERGENCY RELIEF ADMINISTRATION

STATE OFFICE BUILDING, ALBANY, N. Y.
NEW YORK OFFICE, 79 MADISON AVENUE

October 15, 1936

UNEMPLOYMENT RELIEF
IN NEW YORK STATE

TABLE OF CONTENTS

UNEMPLOYMENT RELIEF
IN NEW YORK STATE

*To His Excellency, Herbert H. Lehman, Governor, and to the
Honorable Members of the Senate and the Assembly of the
State of New York:*

In June, 1934, this Administration, recognizing its temporary
character, urged the Governor to undertake an impartial study so
that a vehicle for a "more permanent machinery for relief might be
devised."[1] The Governor's Commission on Unemployment Relief,
subsequently appointed, served for two years and published seven
formal reports. In the 1936 Legislative session measures sponsored
by the leaders of the two major parties in the Legislature were enacted providing for termination of the Temporary Emergency Relief
Administration and transfer of its functions to a reorganized State
Department of Social Welfare.

By July 1 next the Temporary Emergency Relief Administration
will cease to exist. The need of nearly a million citizens of this
State for assistance and the need of the communities for State aid
will go on.

Under bi-partisan sponsorship the Legislature directed that there
be submitted to the people this November a relief bond issue of
$30,000,000, approximately half to be made immediately available
in the event of approval. This is the only provision that has been
made to continue State aid to the communities in unemployment relief through the coming winter.

Following the instruction in Section 21 of Chapter 798 of the Laws
of 1931 directing the Temporary Emergency Relief Administration
"to report to the Governor and the Legislature from time to time
in such detail as may be required, the operations of the Administration together with the condition of unemployment and the relief

---

[1] *Three Years of Public Unemployment Relief in New York State,* October
15, 1934, p. 3.

afforded unemployed persons in the State," there is presented herewith an analysis of the relief needs to be anticipated in the year to come together with an accounting of our stewardship, soon to end.

FREDERICK I. DANIELS, *Chairman*

THOMAS CRIMMINS

PAUL S. LIVERMORE

SOLOMON LOWENSTEIN

JOSEPH P. RYAN

ALFRED H. SCHOELLKOPF

RELIEF TRENDS — 1936

Decrease in Relief Need

A year ago the Temporary Emergency Relief Administration reported that "for the first time since the beginning of the emergency the summer of 1935 saw no more people on relief in New York State than in the corresponding months of the previous year," [1] and pointed out that experience had apparently confirmed the "hope that a limit had been reached in totals of those needing relief if private employment maintains current levels." [1]

Despite difficulties of analysis discussed below, the more-than-seasonal decrease during the spring and summer of 1936 indicates that the peaks and valleys in the year to come may prudently be expected to be lower than in the twelve months past if private employment and payrolls maintain their current levels. This record presents furthermore a testimony to the competence and loyalty of local relief administrations throughout the State which saw to it that reduction of relief rolls kept pace with the improved employment situations, confirming the wisdom of the Legislature in providing that relief during the emergency should continue in local hands, with the State acting in a supervisory capacity only, reimbursing on such local expenditures as conformed with State law.

More eloquent still as to the future has been the decrease in the numbers of those asking aid and especially in the numbers of those now for the first time in the emergency needing public assistance.

Applications for Relief Drop 55 Per Cent

Because the applications for relief, month by month, arise directly from the needs of those who become destitute and are less affected by possible fluctuations of local policy or by the amount of funds available than are the figures for relief given, they have come to be accepted as the most accurate barometer we have of relief trends.

[1] *Public Unemployment Relief in New York State—Fourth Year*, October 15, 1935, p. 8.

[5]

In the early years of the emergency when the cumulative exhaustion of resources among those long unemployed brought more and more families to seek public aid, applications rose sharply.

In 1936 this trend was strikingly reversed. During the month of January, 75,554 applications for relief were received in the local welfare districts throughout the State, whereas only 34,125 were received in August, a decrease of 55 per cent as compared with a decrease of 16 per cent between February and August of 1935 (figures for January of that year are not available).

At the same time private employment had so improved as to make possible this year a steady increase in the proportion of applicants for relief for whom work could be found or other resources developed to keep them from relief. Thus the applications rejected rose from 28 per cent of those acted upon in January to 46 per cent in August.

With both factors operating together, the number of families and unattached persons actually added to relief rolls dropped from 56,042 in January to 17,516 in August, a decrease of 69 per cent.

Within these totals "new cases"—families and unattached persons who had not previously in this emergency needed public aid—declined even more rapidly. In August, 1936, 6,077 of these new cases were added to the rolls, as compared with 18,851 in the previous January.

It is evident that the great reservoir of families being driven on to relief for the first time—the most discouraging fact of the relief situation in earlier years—is drying up in the heat of rekindled factory fires.

What Is A Relief Case?

Home relief is the provision in the domicile of necessary food, shelter, light, heat, clothing, medicine and medical attendance and household supplies. It may be provided in cash or in kind. Work relief in New York State under the Emergency Act has always been given in the form of cash wages.

In the presentation of relief statistics throughout the country it has been customary to list the number of families and unattached persons who received relief "during" the month.

Such a figure, adopted in the first instance because more easily obtained and because it tells how many received the relief granted, includes many who come on relief or go off during the month, receiving aid for only a part of the period. The relief turnover has been sufficiently great so that those receiving relief "during" a month are approximately ten per cent more than the daily average on relief.

Since the public has commonly interpreted this monthly figure to mean the number of people "on" relief at a given time, the presentation of such monthly totals has resulted in the public mind in an exaggeration of the relief load by approximately the percentage named.

Emphasizing the turnover on relief in its annual report of 1935, the State Temporary Emergency Relief Administration called attention to this difference between the daily and the monthly figures. It showed the cumulative magnitude of the turnover to mean "that, for the most part, we do not have a great body of our population resigned to indefinite continuance on relief, but that the majority are still struggling to make their way in the economic world and are in need only of temporary or intermittent assistance."

The same report also discussed the drop in the size of the average family on relief and the increasing proportion of unattached persons, which together make it difficult to compare the relief load with other years in terms of "cases": "As time has gone on, smaller families among the unemployed, more mobile and able longer to keep off relief by eking out their own support, have at last found their resources at an end and have been forced to rely upon public aid. In the same way more and more unattached persons have found themselves unable longer to continue without relief."

In the year ended August 31, 1936, these tendencies continued to be accentuated. The 498,835 families and unattached persons cared for during July, 1934, included approximately 2,000,000 individuals, or an average of four individuals per "case." The 549,882 families and unattached persons cared for during July, 1935, included slightly fewer than 2,000,000 individuals, or an average of 3.5 per "case." The 286,270 families and unattached persons cared for during the month of August, 1936, included fewer than 900,000 individuals, or an average of three per "case."

In view of the changing constitution of the average "case," comparison of the number of "cases" today with "cases" a year or two years ago again tends to overstate the actual situation.

Thus it should be borne in mind in the following discussion of the reduction last spring and summer in the number of families and unattached persons on relief that these figures do not show the full extent to which the burden has lightened in terms of population on relief.

526,361 On Relief as of July 31, 1935

As of July 31, 1935, just before the active inauguration of the Federal WPA program in New York State, 526,361 families and unattached persons were receiving public unemployment relief. As of January 31, 1936, when the wholesale transfers to the Federal program had ended, the number being thus aided—now by State and local monies only—had been reduced to 307,311 families and unattached persons.

This reduction, result of a shift from one program to another, throws little light on the total need for relief. But the reductions that followed in the spring and summer of 1936 lend strong support to the view that the long-awaited demobilization of relief is at last under way.

As of August 31, 1936, the number had dropped to 267,654, a reduction of 18 per cent from the March peak, as compared with a drop of seven per cent from the peak to July 31, 1935 (the WPA was under way in August), and a drop of eleven per cent from the peak to August in 1933. Operation of the Federal CWA in the early months of 1934 and its cessation April 1 vitiate comparisons for that year.

In the reductions of the current year, the experience of New York City has been so different from that of the rest of the State that separate analysis is called for.

Relief and Employment in the State Outside New York City

In its recent downward trend relief has shown a significant correlation with the upward movement of indices of private employment.

During the early years of recovery from the low point reached by factory employment and payrolls in March, 1933, many were puzzled that the relief need continued to rise despite improvement of business conditions. In previous reports the Temporary Emergency Relief Administration pointed out that the cumulative exhaustion of resources of those long unemployed was a chief factor in the determination of need and attention was called to the fact that even in times of expanding prosperity "there is a human ebb and flow off and on to the payrolls of private employment, just as there is in the population on relief." [1]

Obviously there must be a level where employment and payrolls are so low that through this exhaustion of resources destitution will continue to rise even though the private business situation has shown some improvement from its lowest point.

In New York State outside New York City employment in agriculture is of such importance that factory payrolls may give but a poor indication of the total private employment situation. For factory payrolls, however, we have the monthly index numbers of the State Department of Labor, the average for 1925-27 equalling 100. On this base, factory payrolls in the State outside the city reached a low of 35 for March, 1933, a point so low that it would have been unreasonable not to have expected a continuing increase in the need of relief until substantial improvement obtained.

Such an increase occurred.

The up-State experience was that not until the index number for payrolls had passed 65 and sustained itself above that level for some months did real decrease in the relief need beyond seasonal expectations take place. As may be seen from the accompanying chart, the number of families and unattached persons on relief rolls was about the same in the summer months of 1935 as in the summer of 1934, although the index of payrolls had by 1935 risen from the mid-fifties to the low sixties.

In human terms this relief experience means that not until the part-time worker rises above half-time can he relinquish the supplementary aid of relief to his family, not until the weekly wage has risen to well above half its old norm can the family capital of clothes and household goods, depleted through long years, be replenished and debts paid off so that the wage-earner can once more assume the human obligation of assisting relatives and friends, for whom he has no legal responsibility, to quit relief.

The index of payrolls is chosen for discussion here because it yields better clue to this factor of available resources than the index of employment. The accompanying chart, plotting relief "cases" and payrolls month by month since March, 1933, shows clearly how, after the arbitrary drop in relief from November, 1935, to February,

---

[1] Ibid. p. 7.

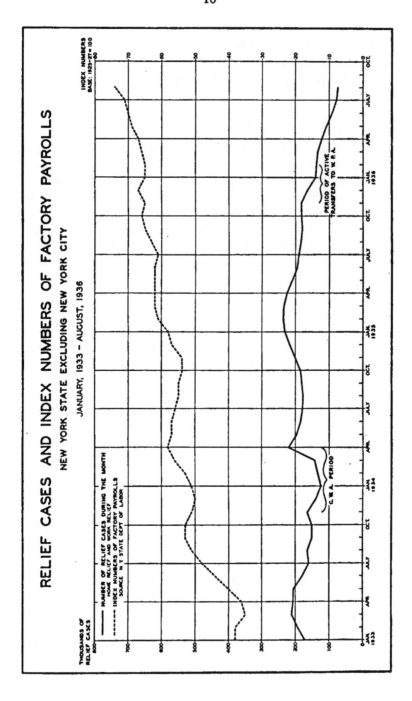

RELIEF CASES AND INDEX NUMBERS OF FACTORY PAYROLLS

NEW YORK STATE EXCLUDING NEW YORK CITY

JANUARY, 1933 - AUGUST, 1936

1936, resulting from transfer to Federal WPA jobs, the relief curve funneled downward as the index of factory payrolls rose to 73.

It is significant also that receipts from the sale of principal farm products in New York State, as reported by the United States Department of Agriculture, totaled $181,335,000 in the first eight months of 1936 as compared with $156,685,000 in the same period of 1935. For the like period of 1934 they were $143,586,000 and for 1933, $115,669,000.

The reduction in relief rolls takes on added meaning in view of a reduction of some 34,000 in the number employed on the Federal WPA in these districts, from February 1 to August 29. Thus the drop in direct relief reflected a real decrease in need and not merely a shift from one type of program to another.

As of February 29 there were approximately 126,000 families and unattached persons on relief rolls in the welfare districts outside New York City, while as of August 31 there were only approximately 70,000, a drop of 44 per cent. This should be compared with a drop of 21 per cent in 1935, 17 per cent in 1934 after the CWA and 3 per cent in 1933.

Staffs of the local relief administrations, taking advantage of this increase in private employment in 1936 greater than the seasonal experience of other years, effected the reductions without arbitrary measures and by restricting relief to those actually in need made it possible to maintain a decent standard of relief and to achieve economies at the same time.

Relief and Employment in New York City

It will be seen from the accompanying chart of relief "cases" and factory payrolls in New York City that, while the City did not slump nearly as low as the rest of the State as to payrolls, the index number having dropped to 44 as against the 35 reported for the other districts in March, 1933, neither has its recovery been so rapid. Despite an increase of six points recorded in the month, the City's index of factory payrolls stood at 68 for August, 1936, as against 73 in the other districts, relative to the 1925-27 base.

It may be noted also that, though the City's payroll index reached a peak of 68 in August, 1936, the average for the first eight months of the year was 64.

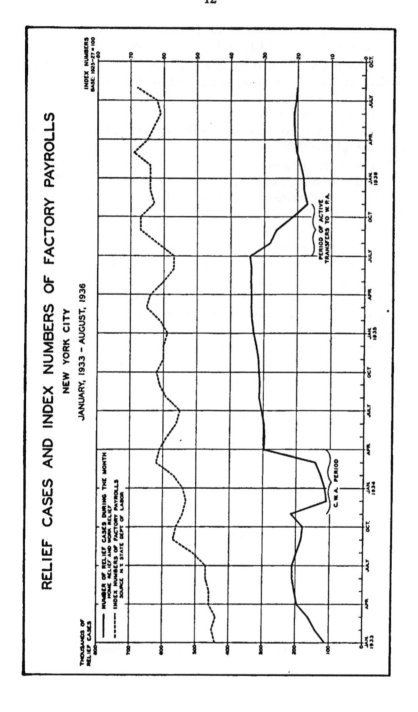

Factory payrolls give a more complete indication of the fluctuations of total payrolls in New York City than in the rest of the State, the factors of seasonal employment and recovery in agriculture being lacking.

The New York City relief load in 1936 followed its usual seasonal trend. From a peak of 207,581 families and unattached persons receiving direct relief—a State and local charge—as of April 30, 1936, the number dropped 4.8 per cent to 197,329 as of August 31.

It should be noted that from February 29 to August 29 the number employed in the City by the Federal WPA was progressively reduced by approximately 37,000.

Relief in the Future

Largely through the recovery of private payrolls the relief problem has begun to liquidate itself. It may be expected to continue in the future, slowly, especially in New York City, if payrolls continue at present levels, more rapidly as they advance. At best it will be a long-time task.

Every "case" closed from the relief rolls means an individual solution of the problem. Only by the multiplication of such individual solutions can we arrive at the eventual minimum, the human residue of lives wrecked by the economic cataclysm that struck us all. We are as yet far from that point.

During August, 1936, there were 286,270 families and unattached persons receiving public unemployment relief in New York State, 286,270 "cases" including approximately 868,000 individuals of whom more than 340,000 were children under eighteen.

Now and for a long time to come the State must stand by the local communities to assist them in giving adequate care to those who cannot yet fend for themselves if we are to prevent human suffering and hold forth the hope and possibility of rehabilitation to those still struggling to find a foothold on the road to economic independence.

In 1936 as in 1931 State aid is a necessity not a choice.

RELIEF GIVEN

SEPTEMBER 1, 1935 — AUGUST 31, 1936

Total Relief Costs of $173,574,719

In the twelve months from September 1, 1935, to August 31, 1936, total home relief and work relief wages amounted to $137,518,072 from local, State and Federal funds. The Federal participation in direct relief ended late in 1935 after the Federal Works Program was under way throughout the State.

Of this relief, $125,991,568 was in home relief and $11,526,504 was in work relief wages. The work relief was confined almost entirely to the early months of this period and to up-State welfare districts, the Federal WPA program not getting under way in these districts until late in 1935. During the period under review home relief aided a monthly average of 325,678 families and unattached persons throughout the State. The accompanying chart, page 15, shows monthly totals of home relief and work relief wages given since 1931.

Supplementary relief programs, work relief materials and administrative and supervisory expense, as shown in Table I, page 16, brought the total cost in the twelve months to $173,574,719.

In September, 1935, the first month of the period, relief given in the State totaled $17,001,468. By August, 1936, the last month, through transfers to the W.P.A. and further reduction of the relief load, relief given totaled $9,410,697, a reduction of 45 per cent.

Particularly striking was the reduction in relief given in the districts outside New York City paralleling the drop in the rolls after the wholesale transfers to W.P.A. were over. In these districts, relief given in March totaled $3,996,899, while in August it totaled $1,909,037, a drop of 52 per cent. This was greater than the decrease in the relief case load (see p. 11) because of seasonally lower needs.

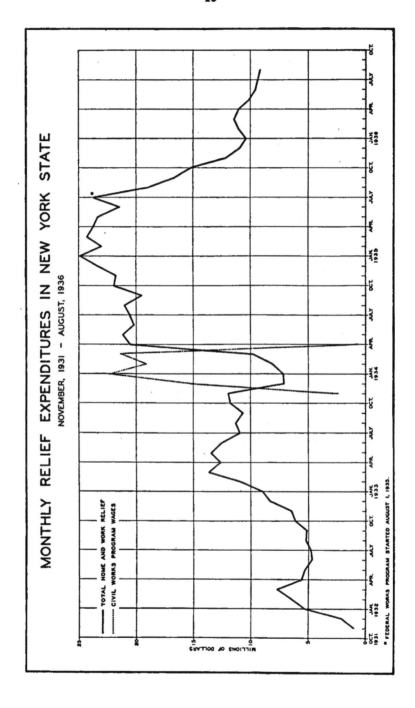

MONTHLY RELIEF EXPENDITURES IN NEW YORK STATE

NOVEMBER, 1931 – AUGUST, 1936

—— TOTAL HOME AND WORK RELIEF
········ CIVIL WORKS PROGRAM WAGES

* FEDERAL WORKS PROGRAM STARTED AUGUST 1, 1935.

MILLIONS OF DOLLARS

TABLE I

OBLIGATIONS INCURRED FOR EMERGENCY
UNEMPLOYMENT RELIEF
NEW YORK STATE: SEPTEMBER 1, 1935—AUGUST 31, 1936

Policies Controllable by T.E.R.A.

Relief:

Home Relief (a)	$125,991,568
Care of Local Homeless	1,681,230
School Lunches	1,046,966
Additional Milk	1,379,679
Death and Disability Benefits (b)	221,825
Garden Supplies	41,276
Work Relief Wages	11,526,504

Rural Rehabilitation:

Loans	9,308
Grants in Flood Disaster Areas	18,641
Materials for local Work Projects	2,354,774
Materials for work projects of state departments	307,412
Local Administrative and Supervisory Salaries (c)	24,730,224
Miscellaneous Reimbursable Expense	33,764
Central State Administration	1,577,217
Total	$170,920,388
Miscellaneous General Expenses	47,694

*Federal Programs in Which the T.E.R.A. Acted
Only as Federal Agent*

Federal Programs:

Transient Program	1,949,255
Other	657,382
Total	$ 2,606,637
Grand Total	$173,574,719—100%
State Funds	66,180,164— 38%
Local Funds	75,728,252— 44%
Federal Funds	31,666,303— 18%

(a) In addition to this amount, the welfare districts reported expenditures of $645,271 classified as non-reimbursable home relief.

(b) Compensation awards for death or permanent disability of relief workers injured on work projects.

(c) In addition the welfare districts reported non-reimbursable expenditures of $352,810 for salaries and $2,600,316 for other administrative costs.

Adequate local staffs made these cuts possible without denying essential relief to those in need. Adequate staffs were still needed at the end of the period to cull the new applications to make sure that only those genuinely in need received relief.

At the same time, the drastic reductions in relief rolls in many districts created a situation where administrative staffs needed to bring about these reductions were out of line with actual case loads and relief. This was to have been expected in a period when the total cost of relief activities administered by these staffs was dropping from approximately $30,000,000 a month in the spring of 1935 to approximately $11,000,000 in August, 1936, and in some districts was being cut by as much as 90 per cent. In view of the progressively decreasing case loads outside New York City, the reduction of local administrative staffs required constant review. Appreciating the difficulties inherent in reducing local administrative costs while maintaining full efficiency so that the relief rolls could be kept down through proper scrutiny of new applications, the State TERA provided local districts concrete assistance in reorganizing local staffs on the basis of reduced case loads. It urged that no speculation as to possible increase in relief need in the winter months be ground for delay that would prevent a present saving of relief funds.

Naturally inherent in the policy of local responsibility for relief locally administered—the policy adopted by the State of New York in the Emergency Relief Act—is a degree of local autonomy that would not exist if relief were administered directly by the State. The advantages of this policy, however, are so compelling, especially in regard to the maintenance of a quickened local interest in the problem and a searching local scrutiny of expenditures, that the wisdom of this course has been amply justified.

In line with its efforts to keep administrative costs as low as possible consistent with ultimate economy, the TERA itself has continued to reduce its own staff as its responsibilities have lessened. As previously reported, its own central administrative staff "contracted 26 per cent from July 1, 1935, when the Federal Works Progress Administration began organizing to take over and expand the work relief program, to August 31, the close of the period of this report. On July 1, the Administration supervised the giving of relief with a central administrative and field staff of 922 persons. By August 31, with the Works Progress Administration operating all work relief in New York City but only beginning to take over the program up-State, this staff had contracted to 681 persons." [1]

In the period that followed, a further contraction of 54 per cent took place, so that the central administrative staff of the TERA consisted of 310 persons as of October 15, 1936. In the year the total cost of central State administration was $1,577,217, as compared with $2,319,252 in the previous twelve months.

Federal special programs over whose policies the TERA had no control, including Transients and Surplus Commodities, employed through the TERA 256 persons in administrative functions as of September 1, 1935, and 82 as of October 15, 1936, a drop of 68 per cent. No State funds were involved in these programs.

The central administrative staff of the TERA includes "a trained social work staff to help relief bureaus organize and establish policies; advisors on medical services, nutrition and garden activities for the unemployed; and an auditing staff employed to insure sound business and accounting methods in the local relief bureaus to which the State contributes funds." [2]

It is the function of this staff to supervise the relief operations carried out locally, to ensure that monies on which reimbursement is to be claimed are spent according to the terms of the Emergency Act.

From September 1, 1935, to August 31, 1936, the TERA reimbursed the local communities by $132,531,620 for their relief expenditures, including claims for earlier months. Special programs and central administrative costs brought total expenditures to $141,215,431. Reimbursement was chiefly from State funds, Federal contributions having been withdrawn, as stated, late in 1935. No additional Federal funds are being made available to meet outstanding commitments.

During the period since Federal assistance in direct relief ended, the drain on State relief funds has been greater than ever. Nor have the local districts shirked their responsibilities. Where the need has dropped sharply, their commitments have been less. But in communities where the relief need remains at or near old levels the local burden, too, is as great as ever.

[1] Ibid. p. 16.
[2] *Three Years of Public Unemployment Relief in New York State*—1931-1934, p. 12.

The cities and counties of the State are deserving of praise for the way they have continued to meet the challenge of unemployment and for their cooperation with the TERA in its efforts to assure efficient and economical use of public funds and to see to it that relief was given impartially and fairly, without discrimination on grounds of non-citizenship, political adherence, religion, race or color.

SUPPLEMENTARY RELIEF ACTIVITIES

Supplementary relief activities, in most of which the TERA acted as Federal agent, were sharply curtailed during the period, leaving the Federal Surplus Commodities Division the most important of the agencies still carrying on these functions.

Federal Surplus Commodities Division

In the year ended August 31, 1936, the Federal Surplus Commodities Division distributed to the local welfare districts approximately 85,200,000 pounds of surplus foods whose retail value is estimated at $9,000,000. These surplus foods, removed from the market through purchase by the Agricultural Adjustment Administration, were given to the needy by local relief officials over and above regular budgetary allowances. The TERA acted merely as Federal agent, chiefly in the allocation of commodities to the local districts.

During the year the AAA, in cooperation with the New York State Department of Agriculture and Markets, bought directly from New York State farmers $340,000 worth of surplus products which included approximately 255,000 bushels of apples. In addition to these surplus commodities the Federal agencies bought from New York State farmers and dairymen milk for the manufacturing in the State of 3,883,511 pounds of dry skim milk, and 2,505,870 pounds of evaporated milk and sent to New York State during the 1935-36 period 26,000,000 yards of cotton piece goods which were processed and distributed to needy persons on relief with the cooperation of the Federal W.P.A.

Transients

In December, 1935, the federally financed program for transients in this State was terminated. During the four month period in 1935 the transient program, which was organized to house, feed, give medical treatment and work, when possible, to those persons—both individuals and families—who were not residents of this State, cared for approximately 97,000 different individuals at a total cost of $1,949,254.

Camp TERA (Now Camp Jane Addams)

Supervision of Camp TERA for unemployed women at Lake Tiorati near Bear Mountain was transferred from the TERA to the National Youth Administration on January 1, 1936. From June, 1933, when it was opened, through December 31, 1935, the camp had provided rehabilitation opportunities for 1,616 unemployed young women at a cost of about forty cents per day per person for food and housing, ice, coal, laundry, electricity, medical supplies, equipment and transportation.

CCC Camps

Approximately 35,000 New York State boys and men worked in camps of the Civilian Conservation Corps in the year ended August 31, 1936, with an average of about 20,000 enrollees in the camps throughout the period. All of the boys and men recruited have come from families on public relief, picked by local relief authorities, to whom the TERA delegated its functions as selecting agent for the State.

It is estimated that in the twelve month period the New York State enrollees contributed approximately $5,500,000 to their families, thus reducing the burden of local relief expenditures. The basic cash allowance for enrolled boys and men is $30 a month, of which they allot from $22 to $25 a month to their families.

State Activities

The New York State Rural Rehabilitation Corporation, formed in May, 1935, as part of the TERA under a Legislative charter, in the fall of 1935 had made farm flood relief [1] grants to 1,164 farmers, totaling $131,827. These grants were given to farmers eligible for rehabilitation loans and the maximum grant to any farm family was $300. In the spring of 1936 the Corporation made supplementary loans of $7,900 to clients who had received original loans in the previous year. As of September 1, the Corporation has had

---

[1] See *Unemployment Relief in New York State—Fourth Year*, p. 24, et seq.

more than $10,000 or 16 per cent of its loans repaid and only once has it been necessary to close an account at a financial loss. Besides its financial aid, the Corporation has furnished technical services, assisted in moving farm families to better locations and has given needed legal advice and assistance.

During the year ending September 30, 1936, a total of $1,379,679 was expended in providing milk for undernourished children in schools, camps and other institutions, or to children and nursing or pregnant mothers in families not on relief but with subsistence incomes. Of this, $230,000 was left over from the previous year's grant by the Legislature, of one million and a half dollars for a free milk program, some districts having failed to use their whole allotment in the previous period. The remainder was spent by local districts on the basis of reimbursement at the same rate as home relief.

In New York City, in addition, reimbursement was granted on the same basis as home relief for giving school lunches to undernourished children. For this purpose a total of $1,046,966 was expended during the year.

Continuing the policy of encouraging the unemployed to serve their own needs through a garden program, approximately 40,000 individual and community subsistence gardens were planted this past season in welfare districts of the State, New York City excepted. In New York City, this year's gardens were planted under the supervision of the Works Progress Administration. Fresh vegetables with an estimated retail value of $1,500,000 were obtained in the summer of 1936 from the gardens planted with the assistance and technical supervision of the TERA. The total expenditure for this harvest, all of which was or will be consumed by persons on relief, was approximately $265,000.

TABLE II

TEMPORARY EMERGENCY RELIEF ADMINISTRATION FOR NEW YORK STATE

EXPENDITURE STATEMENT

Table showing expenditures by the Temporary Emergency Relief Administration in reimbursement of local welfare districts charged during the period September 1, 1935 to August 31, 1936 and during the period November 1, 1931 to August 31, 1936.

WELFARE DISTRICT	Expenditures Charged September 1, 1935 to August 31, 1936			Estimated Commitments as of Aug. 31, 1936	Total Expenditures Charged November 1, 1931 to August 31, 1936		
	Home Relief	Work Relief	Total Paid		Home Relief	Work Relief	Total Paid
Albany County	$81,634.48	$94,945.62	$176,580.10	$5,037.93	$283,686.70	$528,374.55	$812,061.25
Albany	459,891.96	254,747.63	714,639.59	38,250.83	1,258,866.12	1,614,238.75	2,873,104.87
Cohoes	347,652.19	102,630.31	450,282.50	90,262.14	1,019,803.17	666,472.81	1,686,275.98
Watervliet	45,820.55	....	45,820.55	3,437.81	140,777.63	39,864.23	180,641.86
Allegany County	81,173.60	22,268.72	103,442.32	6,969.49	211,922.04	156,674.82	368,596.86
Broome County	164,763.42	88,474.32	253,237.74	29,307.51	503,873.23	453,471.21	957,344.44
Binghamton	207,090.84	84,316.18	291,407.02	17,682.40	778,939.82	554,833.41	1,333,773.23
Union (a)	2,567.65	....	2,567.65	489.63	2,567.65	....	2,567.65
Cattaraugus County	110,974.64	36,562.49	147,537.13	24,716.86	244,914.05	314,769.94	559,683.99
Olean	47,447.01	42,614.15	90,061.16	4,145.49	159,354.78	345,387.39	504,742.17
Salamanca	35,707.41	42,273.39	77,980.80	3,786.99	200,611.51	123,054.57	323,666.08
Cayuga County	51,572.12	24,505.91	76,078.03	3,512.08	149,555.64	177,860.15	327,415.79
Auburn	184,341.84	121,926.85	306,268.69	29,639.00	600,561.54	712,025.27	1,312,586.81
Chautauqua County	130,804.81	97,890.97	237,695.78	25,403.25	403,226.34	387,822.86	791,049.20
Dunkirk	175,892.85	52,949.57	228,842.42	50,708.69	497,715.61	425,165.78	922,881.39
Jamestown	423,794.53	78,294.50	502,089.03	64,769.95	865,129.62	532,509.33	1,397,638.95
Chemung County	161,621.33	32,510.87	194,132.20	23,169.87	548,141.14	311,566.13	859,707.27
Elmira	338,160.30	122,536.04	460,696.34	68,746.28	1,225,470.88	410,468.19	1,635,939.07
Chenango County	31,294.91	13,792.49	45,087.40	2,854.90	91,331.14	171,578.83	262,909.97
Norwich	23,072.83	50.40	23,123.23	1,574.29	66,375.86	43,080.48	109,456.34
Clinton County	46,455.16	47,378.01	93,833.17	5,090.07	131,558.03	195,415.18	326,973.21
Plattsburg	38,241.66	26,328.34	64,570.00	1,981.84	109,420.83	95,386.49	204,807.32
Columbia County	42,623.11	37,540.65	80,163.76	1,552.02	110,581.72	239,711.87	350,293.59
Hudson	69,440.24	45,129.01	114,569.25	2,560.65	212,733.22	308,239.48	520,972.70
Cortland County	24,699.88	17,902.88	42,602.76	1,457.87	78,570.26	125,758.52	204,328.78
Cortland	44,038.51	12,968.03	57,006.54	4,594.01	165,412.27	112,263.17	277,675.44
Delaware County	77,807.28	31,111.86	108,919.14	7,982.07	183,845.53	171,356.51	355,202.04
Dutchess County	171,592.73	84,184.47	255,777.20	25,187.83	545,500.32	444,550.17	990,050.49
Beacon	28,481.37	41,094.01	69,575.38	2,339.96	107,174.34	237,410.04	344,584.38
Poughkeepsie	250,143.28	88,228.04	338,371.32	3,150.58	856,543.46	464,876.45	1,321,419.91

TABLE II—Continued

WELFARE DISTRICT	Expenditures Charged September 1, 1935 to August 31, 1936			Estimated Commitments as of Aug. 31, 1936	Total Expenditures Charged November 1, 1931 to August 31, 1936		
	Home Relief	Work Relief	Total Paid		Home Relief	Work Relief	Total Paid
Erie County	$1,720,114.05	$1,077,980.88	$2,798,094.93	$400,846.04	$4,905,127.43	$4,689,836.23	$9,594,963.66
Buffalo	5,561,320.77	2,807,888.77	8,369,209.54	615,780.68	20,398,391.36	13,544,550.46	33,942,941.82
Lackawanna (b)	....	....	....	....	261,419.69	256,708.65	518,128.34
Tonawanda (b)	....	....	....	....	89,306.92	92,181.72	181,488.64
Essex County	204,358.52	81,833.83	286,192.35	23,890.13	467,100.38	544,712.42	1,011,812.80
Franklin County	237,301.27	89,919.20	327,220.47	16,998.42	655,082.46	469,433.21	1,124,515.67
Fulton County	40,804.38	27,073.72	67,878.10	7,951.35	114,608.72	99,872.11	214,480.83
Gloversville	59,228.29	34,265.85	93,494.14	607.31	163,950.45	181,147.38	345,097.83
Johnstown	14,515.46	10,429.18	24,944.64	848.28	43,603.99	58,369.32	101,973.31
Genesee County	68,896.64	15,973.78	84,870.42	6,088.51	222,045.21	136,263.15	358,308.36
Batavia	78,227.40	31,864.31	110,091.71	6,016.52	259,516.82	214,911.39	474,428.21
Greene County	37,576.30	17,241.59	54,817.89	1,452.06	113,020.39	93,258.03	206,278.42
Hamilton County	12,635.57	965.59	13,601.16	489.61	28,057.18	64,399.20	92,456.38
Herkimer County	165,923.02	86,613.88	252,536.90	34,711.80	694,319.83	579,953.97	1,274,273.80
Little Falls	27,972.03	21,939.91	49,911.94	1,605.47	87,950.10	111,609.04	199,559.14
Jefferson County	222,564.77	74,134.11	296,698.88	15,202.32	688,836.57	324,309.83	1,013,146.40
Watertown	272,120.19	124,431.39	396,551.58	18,456.93	809,124.31	693,965.88	1,503,090.19
Lewis County	43,659.07	44,144.97	87,804.04	740.80	118,723.52	187,628.65	306,352.17
Livingston County	97,616.37	109,406.57	207,022.94	7,920.65	346,840.44	305,731.08	652,571.52
Madison County	52,796.87	22,053.46	74,850.33	2,599.25	125,868.66	126,785.32	252,653.98
Oneida	17,568.73	18,084.23	35,652.96	2,672.58	57,808.74	71,853.78	129,662.52
Monroe County	822,613.68	515,391.24	1,338,004.92	71,412.13	2,238,666.49	3,946,796.16	6,185,462.65
Rochester	2,864,745.62	1,598,333.55	4,463,079.17	298,530.43	9,919,588.40	5,915,977.13	15,835,565.53
Montgomery County	60,252.76	50,101.02	110,353.78	8,353.98	196,940.57	215,260.33	412,200.90
Amsterdam	122,363.30	116,158.14	238,521.44	11,566.34	608,838.50	634,260.61	1,243,099.11
Nassau County	2,195,675.63	1,311,916.17	3,507,591.80	123,723.35	6,182,551.45	9,350,432.15	15,532,983.60
Glen Cove (c)	....	....	....	....	29,567.57	13,644.17	43,211.74
Long Beach (c)	....	....	....	....	6,663.98	36,478.23	43,142.21
New York City	64,892,514.54	14,842,752.64	79,735,267.18	11,775,662.26	212,498,938.60	136,072,294.80	348,571,233.40
Niagara County	33,123.97	12,608.66	45,732.63	4,300.78	128,907.86	196,871.28	325,779.14
Lockport	138,183.76	43,199.09	181,382.85	18,293.30	406,813.41	328,434.66	735,248.07
No. Tonawanda	71,397.42	90,019.86	161,417.28	5,630.89	409,328.16	573,582.02	982,910.18
Niagara Falls	509,039.70	329,121.41	838,161.11	65,708.38	1,620,832.87	1,916,269.77	3,537,102.64
Oneida County	150,392.74	83,410.61	233,803.35	10,378.72	490,352.29	298,051.08	788,403.37
Rome	149,560.80	125,516.11	275,076.91	26,861.52	436,571.78	579,751.75	1,016,323.53
Utica	555,709.80	288,406.90	844,116.70	65,853.21	1,888,843.60	1,536,266.02	3,425,109.62
Onondaga County	401,713.04	244,657.19	646,370.23	71,100.07	1,169,130.27	1,966,203.35	3,135,333.62
Syracuse	1,596,624.72	1,031,692.77	2,628,317.49	116,240.10	4,946,042.46	5,369,460.00	10,315,502.46

25

TABLE II (Cont'd)

WELFARE DISTRICT	Expenditures Charged September 1, 1935 to August 31, 1936			Unpaid Commitments as of Aug. 31, 1936	Total Expenditures Charged November 1, 1931 to August 31, 1936		
	Home Relief	Work Relief	Total Paid		Home Relief	Work Relief	Total Paid
Ontario County	$201,594.94	$57,683.88	$259,278.82	$12,410.14	$657,235.11	$344,333.73	$1,001,568.84
Orange County	114,953.04	147,819.34	262,772.38	4,314.90	307,735.46	773,606.42	1,081,341.88
Middletown	39,031.91	39,881.47	78,913.38	84.00	91,347.90	164,805.55	256,153.45
Newburgh	175,063.58	89,349.76	264,413.34	2,094.07	514,247.72	550,858.14	1,065,105.86
Port Jervis	67,899.35	61,541.95	129,441.30	2,759.08	148,871.33	420,615.37	569,486.70
Orleans County	25,938.08	51,419.88	77,357.96	25,773.59	116,125.71	271,873.62	387,999.33
(Oswego County)							
Fulton	123,191.18	54,013.00	177,204.18	34,022.74	378,285.30	603,381.56	981,666.86
Oswego	173,094.35	122,382.29	295,476.64	14,011.70	512,346.69	1,023,129.77	1,535,340.46
Otsego County	4,689.20	33,688.52	75,377.72	10,455.36	131,283.57	166,387.82	297,671.39
Oneonta	8,917.44	28,985.95	37,903.39	3,904.04	29,649.78	155,053.34	184,703.12
Putnam County	4,815.95	29,797.45	71,160.00	15,304.47	113,427.03	134,416.55	247,843.58
Rensselaer County	84,500.60	19,228.49	103,729.09	65,420.56	221,290.31	88,988.62	310,278.93
Rensselaer	46,424.59	30,539.59	76,964.48	14,706.08	118,958.29	138,810.78	257,769.07
Troy	97,497.52	121,211.14	418,556.66	2,972.02	997,041.21	763,187.18	1,760,228.39
Rockland County	168,339.06	130,091.74	298,430.80	11,980.09	478,636.42	438,815.63	917,452.05
St. Lawrence County	238,986.97	155,621.57	394,608.54	31,983.50	688,166.29	753,048.61	1,441,214.90
Ogdensburg	57,888.93	103,234.25	161,123.18	6,314.46	140,256.13	448,895.13	589,151.26
Saratoga County	94,428.17	122,255.74	216,683.91	28,967.14	296,379.54	509,483.07	805,862.61
Mechanicville	25,375.83	19,759.46	45,135.29	4,851.09	108,998.92	119,483.72	228,482.64
Saratoga Springs	74,996.54	45,216.89	120,213.43	13,464.31	155,189.08	213,320.18	368,509.26
Schenectady County	337,626.70	104,306.57	441,933.27	54,059.88	791,689.96	894,352.12	1,686,042.08
Schenectady	520,802.87	523,746.58	1,044,549.45	68,489.82	1,565,801.83	2,275,638.84	3,841,440.67
Schoharie	15,082.97	16,016.05	31,099.02	1,431.36	38,115.98	119,069.53	157,185.51
Schuyler County	45,886.59	28,360.75	74,247.34	8,914.46	179,805.12	91,585.61	271,390.73
Seneca County	66,315.15	39,390.03	105,705.18	8,747.03	209,933.24	176,830.36	386,763.60
Steuben County	107,220.88	80,584.91	187,805.79	12,068.38	296,776.78	471,404.20	768,180.98
Corning	47,054.20	31,857.20	78,911.40	2,174.11	183,078.33	262,811.48	445,889.81
Hornell	38,389.24	23,681.50	62,070.74	3,036.79	104,650.01	243,699.76	348,349.77
Suffolk County	755,999.38	429,978.59	1,185,977.97	127,802.00	2,022,112.20	2,863,135.34	4,885,247.54
Sullivan County	37,039.02	23,274.06	60,313.10	3,922.85	93,632.50	143,970.47	237,602.97
Tioga County	72,921.39	19,470.57	92,391.96	7,311.08	221,840.33	119,306.98	341,147.31
Tompkins County	40,283.87	42,198.09	82,481.96	4,869.65	116,119.03	231,975.61	348,094.64
Ithaca	92,633.89	45,993.39	138,627.28	7,941.32	255,437.66	421,893.95	677,331.61
Ulster County	110,231.84	107,461.34	217,693.18	5,183.86	327,223.87	436,944.20	764,168.07
Kingston	163,272.64	140,791.54	304,064.18	11,188.11	440,467.38	735,688.47	1,176,155.85
Warren County	44,661.13	25,897.88	70,559.01	1,917.06	17,696.89	122,852.34	250,549.23
Glens Falls	85,992.54	71,431.18	157,423.72	13,492.55	282,837.60	334,833.13	617,690.73
Washington County	149,858.38	120,088.91	269,947.29	14,075.51	586,808.26	532,211.51	1,119,019.77

TABLE II (Continued)

WELFARE DISTRICT	Expenditures Charged September 1, 1935 to August 31, 1936			Estimated Commitments as of Aug. 31, 1936	Total Expenditures Charged November 1, 1931 to August 31, 1936		
	Home Relief	Work Relief	Total Paid		Home Relief	Work Relief	Total Paid
Wayne County............	$129,128.39	$70,392.35	$199,520.74	$7,848.92	$335,053.08	$278,247.96	$613,301.04
Westchester County........	1,499,129.03	923,008.83	2,422,137.86	272,941.33	3,712,171.55	5,284,944.92	8,997,116.47
Mt. Vernon.............	384,676.98	187,187.75	571,864.73	81,276.93	1,085,621.29	1,219,132.67	2,304,753.96
New Rochelle............	578,775.38	236,659.92	815,435.30	139,420.45	1,531,498.69	1,303,452.84	2,834,951.53
White Plains.............	351,553.99	158,526.21	510,080.20	36,806.83	1,287,343.56	666,177.84	1,953,521.40
Yonkers................	1,162,591.29	533,945.40	1,696,536.69	153,017.20	3,235,173.10	2,765,016.69	6,000,189.79
Wyoming County.........	55,798.94	28,931.04	84,729.98	1,387.42	208,367.30	219,405.18	427,772.48
Yates County............	37,707.73	....	37,707.73	2,860.54	119,970.61	414.00	120,384.61
State Improvements Allocated on a Statewide Basis	....	3,269,241.81	3,269,241.81	1,624,048.43	....	25,716,554.23	25,716,554.23
Disability and Death Awards	....	221,703.24	221,703.24	703,185.62	....	304,830.80	304,830.80
TOTAL GENERAL RELIEF..	$96,439,175.31	$36,092,444.66	$132,531,619.97	$18,094,195.41	$311,148,207.82	$258,480,596.73	$569,628,804.55
Free Milk Program........	....	....	952,032.11	142,552.04	....	....	1,357,447.96
Veteran's Aid (d)........	....	....	46,891.02	100,000.00	....	....	178,370.43
Special Federal Programs..	....	....	6,077,269.87	781,211.42	....	....	20,020,046.43
Civil Works Administration.	....	....	....	....	....	....	79,481,455.74
T. E. R. A. Central Administration..............	....	....	1,607,617.60	131,509.11	....	....	5,619,734.05
GRAND TOTAL.........	$96,439,175.31	$36,092,444.66	$141,215,430.57*	$19,249,467.98	$311,148,207.82	$258,480,596.73	$676,285,859.16

* Includes $30,048,446.93 of expenditures charged during this period to districts for obligations incurred prior to August 31, 1935 and outstanding as of that date.

(a) Included in Broome County since July 1, 1936.
(b) Included in Erie County.
(c) Included in Nassau County.
(d) This item represents only payments made by the T. E. R. A. from specific appropriations for Relief of sick and disabled veterans.

NOTE: "Work Relief" excludes projects classified as Special Federal Programs although payments may have been made direct to the welfare districts. It includes payments of $7,382,766.20 made to the welfare districts for the Civil Works Service program in 1933-1934.

FIVE MILLION PEOPLE
ONE BILLION DOLLARS

Final Report of the

TEMPORARY EMERGENCY RELIEF ADMINISTRATION

November 1, 1931—June 30, 1937

STATE OFFICE BUILDING, ALBANY, N. Y.
NEW YORK OFFICE: 79 MADISON AVENUE

June 30, 1937

MEMBERS

FREDERICK I. DANIELS OF NEW YORK, Chairman
THOMAS CRIMMINS OF NEW YORK
PAUL S. LIVERMORE OF ITHACA
SOLOMON LOWENSTEIN OF NEW YORK
JOSEPH P. RYAN OF NEW YORK
ALFRED H. SCHOELLKOPF OF BUFFALO

DAVID C. ADIE OF ALBANY, ex officio
                State Commissioner of Social Welfare

FREDERICK I. DANIELS, Executive Director
HENRY EPSTEIN, Solicitor General, Counsel

Membership of the New York State Temporary Emergency Relief Administration 1931—1937

Chairmen

JESSE ISIDOR STRAUS.........................October 1, 1931—March 22, 1932

PHILLIP J. WICKSER..........................March 22, 1932—April 23, 1932

HARRY L. HOPKINS............................April 25, 1932—June 1, 1933

ALFRED H. SCHOELLKOPF.......................June 8, 1933—October 15, 1935

FREDERICK I. DANIELS........................October 18, 1935—June 30, 1937

Members

THOMAS CRIMMINS.........................January 28, 1936—June 30, 1937

ROBERT J. CUDDIHY..................November 23, 1934—November 16, 1935

FREDERICK I. DANIELS.......................October 18, 1935—June 30, 1937

WILLIAM HODSON..........................June 15, 1933—December 28, 1933

HARRY L. HOPKINS............................March 22, 1932—June 1, 1933

PAUL S. LIVERMORE.........................October 24, 1935—June 30, 1937

SOLOMON LOWENSTEIN......................January 13, 1934—June 30, 1937

CHAS. D. OSBORNE......................April 25, 1932—September 11, 1935

VICTOR F. RIDDER.........................March 7, 1935—October 15, 1935

JOSEPH P. RYAN..............................May 11, 1933—June 30, 1937

ALFRED H. SCHOELLKOPF.......................March 9, 1933—June 30, 1937

HENRY ROOT STERN......................March 9, 1933—November 23, 1934

JESSE ISIDOR STRAUS.....................October 1, 1931—March 22, 1932

JOHN SULLIVAN..............................October 1, 1931—May 11, 1933

PHILLIP J. WICKSER.........................October 1, 1931—April 23, 1932

DAVID C. ADIE—Commissioner of Social Welfare, ex officio

HENRY EPSTEIN—Solicitor General, Counsel

FIVE MILLION PEOPLE
ONE BILLION DOLLARS

Final Report of the

TEMPORARY EMERGENCY RELIEF ADMINISTRATION

November 1, 1931—June 30, 1937

STATE OFFICE BUILDING, ALBANY, N. Y.
NEW YORK OFFICE: 79 MADISON AVENUE

June 30, 1937

MEMBERS

FREDERICK I. DANIELS OF NEW YORK, Chairman
THOMAS CRIMMINS OF NEW YORK
PAUL S. LIVERMORE OF ITHACA
SOLOMON LOWENSTEIN OF NEW YORK
JOSEPH P. RYAN OF NEW YORK
ALFRED H. SCHOELLKOPF OF BUFFALO

DAVID C. ADIE OF ALBANY, ex officio
State Commissioner of Social Welfare

FREDERICK I. DANIELS, Executive Director
HENRY EPSTEIN, Solicitor General, Counsel

LETTER OF TRANSMITTAL

To His Excellency, Herbert H. Lehman, Governor, and to the Honorable Members of the Senate and the Assembly of the State of New York:

Nearly six years have passed since the State of New York, the first to come to the substantial assistance of its communities in the crisis of unemployment, declared the existence of a temporary emergeney, appropriated funds for State aid and established this Temporary Emergency Relief Administration to administer them.

Through the months in which the emergency grew ever more acute, through the months of improvement that have followed, this program has provided an economic lifeline by which thousands of stricken families have climbed back to self-support. Now, with relief need greatly reduced and the prospect of continued reduction, the State of New York has pioneered once more in a permanent program of State aid to its municipalities and counties which include provision for meeting the residual distress to be expected after the economic convulsion through which we have passed.

Today, according to Legislative instruction, completes the transfer of the functions of the Temporary Emergency Relief Administration to the permanent State Department of Social Welfare.

Following Section 21 of Chapter 798 of the Laws of 1931 directing "report to the Governor and the Legislature in such detail as may be required, the operations of the Administration together with the condition of unemployment and the relief afforded unemployed persons in the State," there is presented herewith a final accounting of the Administration's stewardship during the five years and eight months it has been charged with the administration of State monies and policy. The record here set forth has been made possible only by the loyal, generous and continuing support of the people of the State of New York and their elected representatives, executive and legislative, of both parties.

Nor can we pass this opportunity for public acknowledgment of our debt and the debt of the people of the State of New York to Mr. Henry Epstein, Solicitor General and Counsel to the Administration from the beginning of the program, who by his liberal legal wisdom and generous availability to the Administration and staff at all times, without thought or question of recompense, gave practical effectiveness to his own early ruling "that people should not be permitted to suffer from want when the organs of the government had supplied the machinery aimed, to prevent such suffering."

FREDERICK I. DANIELS, *Chairman*
THOMAS CRIMMINS
PAUL S. LIVERMORE
SOLOMON LOWENSTEIN
JOSEPH P. RYAN
ALFRED H. SCHOELLKOPF

June 30, 1937

CONTENTS

[5]

FOREWORD

This report is as of June 30, 1937. As it reaches the hands of the reader at a later date it should be borne in mind that relief is a most unpredictable governmental program. To avoid unwarranted conclusions as to the relief situation at the time of reading, this report should be read in the light of the latest information.

[7]

THE PEOPLE AND RELIEF

70 Per Cent of Those Who Have Been on Relief Have Left It

In November 1931 the people of the State of New York recognized the existence of an emergency resulting from widespread unemployment and initiated State aid to the communities in caring for their needy unemployed. At midnight tonight by Legislative definition that emergency ends.

Necessary State aid will go on through the permanent State Department of Social Welfare. Relief will continue decentralized with the actual giving—or decision not to give—still in the hands of the municipalities and counties. New York State follows its traditional policy of local responsibility and autonomy.

The needy are to be cared for. The hungry are to be fed.

There is actually no solution to the relief problem—no one solution in the nature of the case—for there is no relief "problem" as such. Experts, officials, social workers, writers, may comfortably lump together "the relief problem," but to each destitute man-in-the-street the need of his children for food and shelter and clothes is desperately individual. There have been as many relief "problems" in New York State as there have been destitute families—and as many solutions as breadwinners leaving the rolls. Withdrawals from relief have for the most part been made possible by individual answers to individual situations—the reopening of a particular factory, the personal adaptation to a new skill that can find employment.

People "on relief" have not been an economically homogeneous group. They have been a fair cross-section of the population. "Unemployment is not confined to unskilled workmen. It includes large numbers of skilled mechanics, mercantile and office employees, as well as professional and semi-professional groups."[1] Among their number have been many formerly in independent business. "Applications for relief are being made by persons who have never heretofore received either public or private relief."[1] Their circumstances as they have come to relief have ranged from utter destitution to family earnings that approached a subsistence level. "Heavy as the burden of aid to the needy unemployed has been, it would have been crushing if it had involved total support. For the largest number of those aided, public

---

[1] Report of Governor's Commission on Unemployment Problems, January 1931, p. 1.

[9]

unemployment relief in New York State is on a partial assistance or supplementary basis."[2] Furthermore, it has for the most part involved but temporary or intermittent aid.

In the five years and eight months that this Temporary Emergency Relief Administration has supervised the giving of public unemployment relief by the local governments, the greatest number of men, women and children recorded on public support in any one month was something over 2,000,000,[3] or one in six of the population, a total that remained fairly constant, though different individuals made it up, from the winter of 1934 through the summer of 1935 and even thereafter when transfer of many of the wage earners to the Federal Works Program reduced the apparent total.

Yet over the whole emergency period reports from the local districts indicate that aproximately 5,000,000 different men, women and children, approximately 40 per cent of the population of the State, have at some time or other, for greater or lesser periods, been forced to rely upon public assistance. In this number were included more than 2,000,000 children, nearly 60 per cent of the future citizens of the State.

Total costs to the public in the nearly six years of tiding these neighbors over what were, to most of them, temporary bad times, were approximately $1,155,000,000.[4] Thus the average total cost per person aided over the whole period of five years and eight months has been about $230. At an expenditure of about $90 per capita, from local, State and Federal funds, the people of the State of New York have saved 40 per cent of their number, nearly 60 per cent of their future citizens, from the impairment of destitution.

In return for a part of this expenditure the people of the State have had the benefit of work relief improvements as well, expanded park facilities, better streets and sanitary systems, courthouses, armories and stadiums, and other additions to the value of the public physical plant, as well as improved educational, medical, nursing, library, museum and research services. Rare is the city or county where the consciousness of such improvements is not in the individual taxpayer's mind. But of greatest importance in this investment has been the sustenance of morale and public health.

---

[2] Public Unemployment Relief in New York State—Fourth Year, October 15, 1935, p. 7.

[3] All figures in this report, except those proper to the State Administration itself, are from reports by the local welfare districts.

[4] Monthly figures for relief cases and expenditures are given in Appendix Tables I and II.

Through the gravest economic dislocation of our history there have been no public disorders. All available indices show that the public health has never been better than it is today.

The great numbers forced to rely upon relief at least temporarily through the emergency gave substance to the finding of the Legislature that the public health and safety of the State was involved. Here was no Legislative hyperbole. The public health and safety of the State were indeed imperilled, with 40 per cent—two out of five of the people—needing public aid to tide them over a short time at least.

Even at the start, as the months of increasing need dragged into years, many who had been helped were once again seizing a foothold on the road to economic self-sufficiency, leaving the rolls, while still more were finding themselves at the end of their resources.

A survey conducted for another purpose by the State Department of Health showed the extent to which this was taking place. Of 1,500 relief families chosen at random in eleven representative welfare districts in December 1932, the family breadwinner had been unemployed for an average of 22 months, the family had been on relief for an average of but nine months.[5] Recheck of the same families a year later showed that more than 30 per cent had become self-supporting again. Thirty per cent of those on the rolls a year before had left relief, despite the fact that the relief rolls had increased by 10 per cent in the twelvemonth.

In this continuous turnover, reaching to 10 per cent monthly, the tide turned in the spring of 1935, ebbing slowly at first, so that the Administration was able to report that "for the first time since the beginning of the emergency the summer of 1935 saw no more people on relief in New York State than in the corresponding months of the previous year."[6]

From the spring of 1936 the ebb of relief need has been of dramatic proportion. This reduction in numbers on relief—taking place like the increase of previous years through continuous turnover, a daily withdrawal from the rolls of those no longer in need, a daily addition of those with resources gone—left approximately 660,000 men, women and children supported wholly or in part by home relief, as of June 30, 1937.

---

[5] Annual Report of the State Department of Health, 1932, p. 17.
[6] Public Unemployment Relief in New York State—Fourth Year, October 15, 1935, p. 8.

Thus, of the 5,000,000 men, women and children who had subsisted through public unemployment relief at some time or other since November 1, 1931, over 85 per cent were no longer on the rolls at the close of the emergency.

Many of those who left the unemployment relief rolls in the last two years are still supported by Federal Works Progress Administration earnings. At the start of the Federal Works Program the Federal Government emphasized through Presidential Proclamation and Executive Order that the Works Progress Administration was to give jobs at security wages, that the Federal Government had quit "this business of relief" and that those so employed were not to be subject to further investigation to determine whether their relief status continued. But with changing times this premise has been minimized. In the public mind those supported by WPA earnings are lumped with those supported by unemployment relief. As of June 30, 1937, the total of men, women and children in New York State supported by home relief and WPA earnings—taken together—was approximately 1,500,000.

Thus of the 5,000,000 men, women and children who have subsisted through unemployment relief at some time during the emergency, approximately 70 per cent were by June 30, 1937, no longer either on home relief or WPA employment rolls.[7]

The reduction in relief in New York State has been achieved without arbitrary changes of State policy, without arbitrary denial of relief through lack of appropriated money to destitute persons in any category. The very figures are testimony to the continued morale of most of those who have been on relief, to their willingness and ability to take advantage of the improved employment situation.

As the emergency continued dark beyond early expectations, the unemployed, whose succor was undertaken in the first place in the spirit of a crusade, have borne a good deal of public calumny. Not the least has been the assertion that they preferred a relief pittance forever. Particularly hard has this charge borne upon those who hung on to one job and another until 1935 or 1936 and, with sound savings behind them and every effort, managed to keep off relief until the early spirit of public crusade was over. The final figures

[7] Of the increase in Old Age Assistance, Aid to Dependent Children and to the Blind under the Social Security program, no figures are available to show how many recipients were transferred from unemployment relief. If the entire increase had come from relief, this percentage would be reduced by less than 1.5.

13

70 PERCENT OF THOSE WHO HAVE BEEN ON RELIEF HAVE LEFT IT

NOVEMBER 1, 1931 TO JUNE 30, 1937

LEFT RELIEF BEFORE JUNE 30, 1937

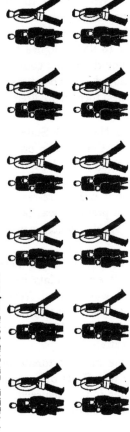

ON HOME RELIEF JUNE 30, 1937[a]

SUPPORTED BY W.P.A. EARNINGS ON JUNE 30, 1937

EACH GROUP REPRESENTS 250,000 INDIVIDUALS

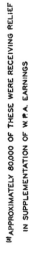

[a] APPROXIMATELY 80,000 OF THESE WERE RECEIVING RELIEF IN SUPPLEMENTATION OF W.P.A. EARNINGS

are the unemployed's own answer to the charge. The final figures are testimony as well to the loyalty and efficiency of the local administrative staffs of the emergency relief bureaus and local departments of public welfare who have worked at reducing the rolls to the jeopardy of their own jobs.

Of those at some time or other in this emergency dependent upon relief, over 85 per cent are no longer on relief—70 per cent are no longer either on home relief or supported by WPA "employment".

Relief Follows Payrolls

The 1929 market crash, dramatic symptom of the break in prosperity, impressed upon most of the market-minded a symbolic date of catastrophe. Yet the index of factory payrolls in New York State in January 1930, had dropped only to 95,[8] a figure to which it has never yet remounted, and at that time the public conscience cried out the need of caring for the unemployed. Panhandlers of new mien appeared upon the streets, breadlines formed in great cities, people formerly substantial were going under.

In 1930 when the payroll index for New York State was still higher than it has been since, the Governor's Commission on Unemployment Problems was appointed. In the spring of 1931, although the index of factory payrolls had not as yet dipped very low—when indeed it had only dropped to the point that it was to re-reach for the first time in October 1936, mighty public pressure was behind campaigns of "Give a Job" and "Share the Work," whole communities were mobilized.

In September 1935, six months after the tide of increasing relief need had turned, the index was still seven points below the figure for April 1931, when the resolution was adopted creating the Joint Legislative Committee to investigate the unemployment problem. It still stood practically at the level of August 1931, when Emergency Relief was initiated by the Legislature.

Perhaps because the strongest, the most fortunate and the most fortunately placed felt most quickly the effects of a general economic convulsion and most quickly thereafter found themselves again secure, there has come increasingly in recent months—let it be frankly faced

---

[8] Payroll index numbers are from the New York State Department of Labor (Base: 1925–27 Average—100). Payroll indices are chosen as more significant than those for employment because of natural and stimulated "spread work" efforts during the emergency, which obscured the relation of employment to need for relief.

—an innuendo quite absent in 1931 that there is something inherently and wilfully wrong-spirited about those now on relief.

"Still on relief" would be as incorrect a phrase now as in 1931, for many in the turnover of even advancing private employment reached the end of their savings but yesterday. As late as September 1935 nearly 13,000, or more than half the cases opened for relief, were new cases that never before in this emergency had had to have public aid. By January 1936 the number of such new cases had risen to nearly 19,000, though in the great increase in need of that month they represented only one-third of all cases added. From then on the decline has been fairly steady. By June 1937 fewer than 4,000 new cases were opened, an all-time low, a drop of nearly 80 per cent since January 1936.

How is it that so many—even though their numbers have been rapidly diminishing—have become so lately destitute? What is the anatomy of relief need?

Of course, few indeed of those who have needed relief for the first time in recent months were stricken in 1933 when industrial payrolls were lowest and have been subsisting on their savings since. That is not in question. But many people, despite recovery, have come finally to unemployment but recently.

In his special message urging passage of the Emergency Relief Act, Governor Franklin D. Roosevelt in 1931 called attention to the "many employers who, up to recently, with fine public spirit, have continued to use their resources to prevent the laying-off of workers, are finding they can no longer do so."

Obviously the employer who then and later drained his resources to keep people at work on the downturn has not had the resilience he might have had toward re-employment on the up. This has been but one factor. What happened as well, naturally, was that, as jobs grew more scarce, employers could pick from a higher scale, and employees with more-than-normal qualifications forced others out of jobs. Retail stores found salesgirls from among their customers; regular elevator operators lost jobs by pressure from above. The tendency reached so far that at least one large New York gasoline distributor refused applicants to change casual tires unless they had a college degree.

It is striking testimony to the thriftiness of the people of New York State that the peak of relief need lagged so far as two years behind the low point in payrolls. It is the corollary of that thrift and adaptability that the rebuilding process has taken time also. The college salesgirl who became buyer—the engineer gas salesman who eventually found an opportunity to return to his profession—has not immediately removed anyone from relief. They have made place for others to push up from below instead.

Students of the problem, in discussing the subjectivity of unemployment figures, have pointed out how the loss of one job may cause several to consider themselves unemployed—the wife who now tries to re-enter business, the son and daughter who are forced to give up their education and seek their way in the world. But quite objectively the loss of one job may cause several families to need relief, for a time at least.

An engineer-executive of wide experience loses his job. Perhaps he never reaches the relief level. Eventually he gets other work below his previous scale, displacing a junior engineer. The young engineer, in the great drop of construction, is forced on relief before postponing hopes of a professional career to live by odd jobs—say, repairing radios from door-to-door. His odd jobs displace a regular repairman whom he never met, whose family then needs relief. The radio repairman displaces someone else he never saw, getting steady employment as elevator operator and general handyman in a small hotel. The junior engineer meanwhile finds regular employment as a gasoline station attendant, displacing someone else who goes on relief for a time until he gets a job as a laborer, displacing someone. Without following the further ramifications of the family-tree of unemployment, the loss of a good job by an engineer-executive of wide experience, who never needed relief, has so far accounted for five groups of people needing relief for a greater or a lesser period.

In the same way, in improving times, the creation of one new job may take many off relief. But in the nature of the case the progress toward normal has been equally complex—and slow.

An analysis of relief families availing themselves of free clinic services in five welfare districts in 1934 showed that the average family on relief was made up of father, mother and from three to four children. The father was between 30 and 40 years of age, had been unemployed for more than a year before he applied for relief.

When the crisis struck it came after several lush years during which people might have been expected to accumulate such reserves as they could. When, after many lean months the payrolls again reached toward old norms, it would have been utter misunderstanding to expect reduction of relief need immediately to the corresponding index number,

17

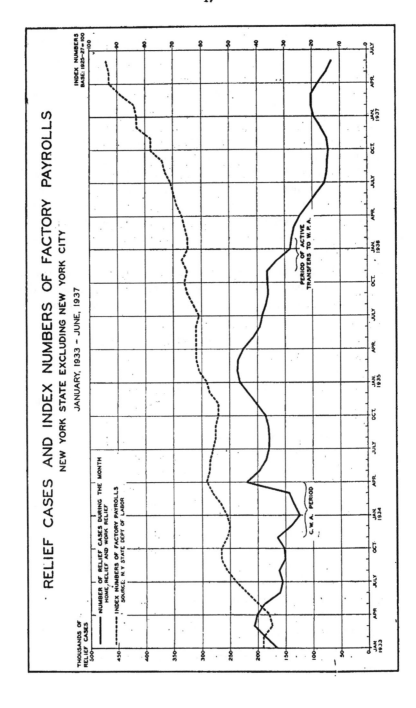

RELIEF CASES AND INDEX NUMBERS OF FACTORY PAYROLLS
NEW YORK STATE EXCLUDING NEW YORK CITY
JANUARY, 1933 – JUNE, 1937

In a previous report the Administration pointed out that:

"Not until the index for payrolls had passed 65 and sustained itself above that level for some months did real decrease in the relief need take place. As may be seen from the accompanying (up-State) chart, the number of families and unattached persons on relief rolls was about the same in the summer of 1934, although the index of payrolls had by 1935 risen from the mid-fifties to the low sixties.

"In human terms this experience means that not until the part-time worker rises above half-time can he relinquish the supplementary aid of relief to his family, not until the weekly wage has risen to well above half its old norm can the family capital of clothes and household goods, depleted through long years, be replenished and debts paid off so that the wage-earner can once more assume the human obligation of assisting relatives and friends, for whom he has no legal responsibility, to quit relief."[9]

"Largely through the recovery of private payrolls the relief problem has begun to liquidate itself. It may be expected to continue in the future, slowly, especially in New York City, if payrolls continue at present levels, more rapidly as they advance."[10]

That prophecy has been more than fulfilled. After the great transfer from relief to WPA there were, as of March 31, 1936, approximately 313,000 families and unattached persons receiving public unemployment relief. Fifteen months later at the end of the emergency period the number had been reduced to 207,750, a drop of more than one-third.

This was a real reduction, not a transfer to the Federal works program. In the same period the WPA itself cut the number of its workers in this State by one-third from approximately 364,000 to approximately 244,000. It must be remembered as well that the Federal government originally agreed to take care of all those employable, so that subsequent reductions of home relief rolls, after WPA had combed the lists, must have required extraordinary effort on the part of the handicapped home relief recipient. Especially must this have been true up-State where home relief has dropped so drastically since the WPA reached its maximum.

Nor is this the whole story of the year. June 30 is scarce midway in the seasonally experienced decline of relief need. If the Federal government does not cut down on WPA faster than private employ-

---

[9] Unemployment Relief in New York State, October 15, 1936, p. 9.
[10] Ibid., p. 13.

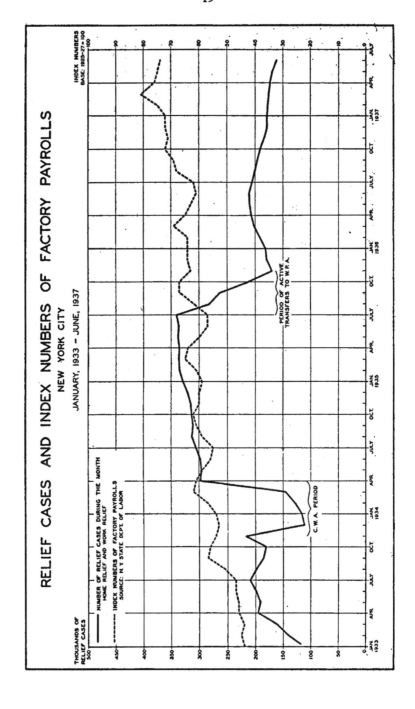

RELIEF CASES AND INDEX NUMBERS OF FACTORY PAYROLLS

NEW YORK CITY

JANUARY, 1933 – JUNE, 1937

THOUSANDS OF
RELIEF CASES

INDEX NUMBERS
BASIC 1925-27 = 100

NUMBER OF RELIEF CASES DURING THE MONTH
HOME RELIEF AND WORK RELIEF

INDEX NUMBERS OF FACTORY PAYROLLS
SOURCE: N Y STATE DEPT. OF LABOR

PERIOD OF ACTIVE
TRANSFERS TO W.P.A.

C.W.A. PERIOD

ment is picking up, there is every indication that home relief rolls will continue to decrease through the remaining summer months. On the basis of last year's experience when the rolls continued to decrease until December there would be a further drop this season to bring the total decrease for the State in the twenty months to more than 40 per cent.

In an analysis of the relation between relief figures and payroll indices it is necessary to consider New York City separately.

In the beginning of the emergency that part of the State outside New York City was hardest hit. It touched, in March 1933, the shockingly low index number of 35 for factory payrolls. The up-State relief need in the early days was greater. The relief expenditures up-State were greater and the State gave in proportion.

But in these districts the recent gain in payrolls has confounded the most sanguine prophets, the index number reaching 94 in June 1937, a point it had not previously touched since February 1930. And as of June 30 the number of families and unattached persons on relief in up-State New York was 56,727, lower than it had been at any time since January 1932. The number had dropped more than one-quarter since June 30, 1936, three-quarters since February 1935.

The gain in factory employment has caught the most sanguine prophets, but the drop in relief need has been even more astounding. For in up-State New York the need for relief has now been dropping faster than payrolls have increased.

In the City of New York payrolls have not risen in any such fashion. There is on the part of many, in other States and in this, a disposition to regard large cities as a trouble spot in "this business of relief." Yet in this State, as may be seen from the accompanying diagrams, we have been through an emergency in which the State as a whole has been involved.

The diversified industries of the City of New York did not dip so low—nor so fast—but their recovery has been even slower than their dip—much more slow.

In June 1937 the index of factory payrolls for New York State excluding New York City stood at 94. But for the City of New York it stood at only 74, the point first passed downward by New York City in the debacle of January 1931, the point passed in the recovery of up-State New York as long ago as September 1936. Recovery in New York City is still in the marginal period where effective reduction of relief is necessarily slow.

The total rise of payroll indices in New York City from August 1936 to June 1937 was only from 68 to 74. The number of families and unattached people on relief dropped in these same months by 22 per cent.

The number of applications for relief has been generally accepted as even more significant for the future than trends in relief itself. Just as the reduction in those supported by relief has proceeded in recent months more rapidly than the increase in payrolls, so also applications for relief have decreased faster than the number of those receiving relief. In January 1936 over 75,000 applications for relief were received throughout the State. By June 1937 the number had dropped nearly two-thirds to just over 26,000. In this same period the number of cases accepted declined by three-quarters, from 56,658 in January 1936 to 14,199 in June 1937.

From March 31, 1936, to June 30, 1937, the number of families and unattached people receiving unemployment relief in New York State dropped one-third, despite somewhat greater reduction of Federal WPA rolls. Even more significant for the future, from January 1936 to June 1937 the number of families and unattached people added to relief rolls during the month declined by three-quarters.

The State of New York, for its own safety and future prosperity, set out in 1931 to give relief to its needy. And without change of policy "this problem of relief" has gone far—farther than most could have expected—toward demobilizing itself.

THE STATE AND RELIEF

Spirit of an Emergency

Public unemployment relief—even on a large scale—was in the State of New York no break with tradition begotten of the late economic crisis.

A first emergency message of a Governor on this subject had come in Colonial times, addressed to the City of New York in 1685, only ten years after the permanent English occupation. In 1713 the pay-as-you-go policy had been abandoned and under Mayor Caleb Heathcote the borrowing of money for relief begun. The Brooklyn ferryboat was mortgaged for $500. In the year 1794 practically half the budget of the City of New York was for relief. During the difficult times that followed the interruption of commerce in the War of 1812, work relief was entered upon as a major solution for the same controlling reasons and later subject to many of the same criticisms voiced today.[1] From then until the present, whenever destitution has threatened the health and the very existence of large sections of its population, Government in New York State has taken whatever measures seemed necessary to preserve that resource without which its physical resources would be valueless: the courage, work capacities and integrity of its people.

It was not as a charity that the State in 1931 stepped in to aid the communities in caring for their own. It was not the plight of those in distress, but the need of the State itself, that motivated the Emergency Act. It was the peril to the public health and safety of the State and of its subdivisions that was recognized by the Legislature as the compelling reason for State aid.

When in this emergency the State of New York pioneered in substantial help to its cities and counties, local resources, private and public, had proved no longer able to bear the brunt alone. For two years before 1931 the need had been growing. Public relief in New York State had increased 32 per cent in 1930 over the year before, had increased 80 per cent again in 1931. Private charities had more than doubled their expenditures in the same two years and still the need was not met.

---

[1] All from Minutes of the Common Council, City of New York.

Typical headlines[2] recall the spirit of the day:

Aug. 22— $20,000,000 GRANT FOR JOBLESS LOOMS

Board of Estimate Studies Problem
of Record Drain on Funds with
Shrinking Revenues

Aug. 22— STATE LABOR URGES TWO RELIEF PLANS

Aug. 24— FINDS WIDE NEGLECT OF JOBLESS RELIEF

Joint Unemployment Committee Reports
Lack of Preparations in State
for Coming Winter

WORSE CONDITIONS LIKELY
Statement Says Thousands Who
Have Never Known Charity
Will Be in Need

Aug. 24— BANKERS ORGANIZE TO RAISE HUGE
FUND FOR RELIEF IN CITY

Aug. 26— **AID TO EXCEED $8,000,000**

Unemployment Problem Will Be Greater
Than Last Winter Financiers
Are Told

Two days later the Special Session convened to consider State aid in the emergency.

On September 12 the New York *Times* recorded:
Factories in State Cut Work in August
Employment Index Declined to 71.5
A New Low

On September 23 the Emergency Relief Act became law, providing $20,000,000 for State aid and establishing a Temporary Emergeney Relief Administration in charge of State policy and funds.

A simple fact had forced the State of New York into the picture. The need was too great for private resources or smaller units of

---

[2] All from the New York *Times*.

Government to bear. The Governor had said that the number of destitute might be twice as many as twelve months before. The event proved him more than right.

It is difficult now to recall those days of 1931. To many it seemed that the very foundations of the earth had faltered with the market quotations. In the two years that had passed since the first market crisis this feeling had been but intensified.

On October 1, 1931, when the first members of the Administration were sworn in the presence of Acting Governor Herbert H. Lehman, the spirit of an emergency, the fervor of a war on destitution, provided the watchword, not only for the Administration itself, but among other public officials and the people at large.

The Administration was to exist for only a brief few months. It had $20,000,000 to spend and the human need that this money was to relieve was immediate and everywhere apparent. All the Administration's efforts were bent toward seeing that the utmost possible of every relief dollar went as quickly as possible to those who needed it. Thinking and action were based on the Administration's being set up for the quick relief of an unusual situation, destined to disband after a brief period. Since the emergency though serious would be short and the need was immediate and pressing, the method was constantly to improvise rather than to set up a deliberate organization.

For the first weeks of its existence, the Administration was in almost continuous session and consultation with experts in every related field. Governor Roosevelt, Lieutenant-Governor Lehman, and the Majority and Minority Legislative leaders kept in the closest touch with the deliberations and decisions of the Administration. For the two weeks before November 1, 1931, when it began active operations, the abbreviated journal of its proceedings runs to more than 100,000 words, as voluminous as a large-sized novel. In the effort to assure that the greatest possible part of relief money went to those in need, every emphasis was placed on volunteer workers, both for the Administration itself and for the units of local government actually giving relief. Members of the Administration themselves served without pay, the first Executive Director was loaned by a private health organization on a part-time basis, and his original staff for the State organization consisted of fifteen persons of whom four were volunteers.

By November 10, 1931, the staff of the State Administration consisted of 28 paid and 32 volunteer workers.

Events beyond the control of the Administration, beyond the control of the members of the Legislature, beyond control even of the people of the State of New York, who voted the bond issues expanding relief appropriations, forced continuance of the temporary emergency program long past the time when it could properly any longer be called temporary.

As the emergency was prolonged the program in the very nature of the case gradually changed character, even though legally it retained its temporary basis. Organizations that had loaned workers, staff members who had volunteered their time for a short crisis, could not continue to afford to do so as the years dragged on. This was true with the staff of the State Administration, with the local staffs of the local administrations; a change in attitude came with the unemployed themselves.

The very proposal to give relief to large numbers hitherto self-supporting of its very nature involved certain problems and a surprising number of these inherent problems were foreshadowed in the formative discussions of the Administration and its advisors in the days when it was organizing for the start of the program on November 1, 1931.

The problem of preserving local autonomy in the administration of relief and yet assuring a fair standard as to adequacy, impartiality and efficiency and the problem as to what constitutes "adequate" relief came up at these early meetings. The conflicts in work relief between the desire to get the work done efficiently and the desire to give a maximum of relief, the conflict between the desire to have worthwhile projects and the desire not to interfere with regular employment, the determination that work relief should not operate to depress wage scales in regular employment, all had full consideration. The necessity for an accurate knowledge of the extent of the problem versus the unreliability of figures to be obtained through a census also was thrashed out. Closest to the present perhaps, was the disappointment expressed at an early session upon reports from places where industry had improved without need for additional labor.

Everyone was feeling his way in what was to be a totally different sort of effort than had ever been made before. At one time it was proposed that each case record be sent in to the State Administration by the local districts. But this was quickly vetoed in favor of monthly reports with periodic check in the field. At one time it was questioned whether the City of New York, because of its charter restrictions, could give home relief at all under the Act.

Emphasis was placed on confining the program actually to such relief as had been made necessary by the unemployment crisis. The feasibility and fairness of holding reimbursement to local expenditures above the normal was debated. As time went on these considerations in their very nature were blurred; it became difficult to define what relief had not been specifically made necessary by the unemployment crisis; total relief expenditures rose so far above normal, local resources were so strained, that the earlier distinction became academic.

Repugnance to any form of a "dole" had led to insistence in the Emergency Act upon home relief being given in kind, while wages on work relief expressly were to be paid in cash. There was a strong public opinion, reflected in the press and shared by the Administration and its advisors, that work relief was the very core of the program, that it would provide jobs for those in need through no fault of their own and that this was to be a new and different matter than the old poor relief that stemmed from the Poor Laws of Queen Elizabeth.

Work relief under the Emergency Act was to be in the hands of local work bureaus: lay, unpaid boards of public spirited citizens paralleling the organization of the State Administration itself. Such committees were in many places already functioning with private funds. So strong was the feeling that this was a new start, entirely different from the poor relief, that emphasis was placed on having a different building for intake with a separate division for women applicants, a separate investigating staff from the regular organization under the Public Welfare Law. The feeling was pushed further by Chapter 259 of the Laws of 1933, which provided for consolidated local Emergency Relief Bureaus—in effect placing the administration of emergency home relief also in the hands of non-partisan, unpaid boards.

The very first meeting of the Administration reached a determination upon certain first principles, among other things that relief must be adequate and food of proper character, and that investigation was not to be a desk job.

It was the stated intention through the State field service to enforce consideration of the needs of each individual family instead of following what was in many places the general practice of sitting at a desk, talking to an applicant and giving him some flat sum that was customary.

The question was raised as to whether adequate relief would pauperize. One answer given in the early discussions was that it was

the flat $2 a week that pauperized. "Of course," it was added, "if
the depression were.to last ten years with adequate relief given, there
would be a pauperizing effect without question. But whatever pau-
perization resulted would result from the long continuance of unemployment."

Who Needs Relief?

It was the paramount purpose of the people of the State of New
York in the Emergency Relief Act to preserve the morale of those
who had become in need through the inter-play of impersonal economic
forces far out of their control. It was obvious enough that if relief
were made harsh and degrading to obtain it would rapidly impair self-
respect. It is equally obvious that if people over long periods find
life on relief entirely satisfactory their initiative will be destroyed.
Any relief policy is in the larger sense, therefore, a compromise.

The 70 per cent of people who have left public support, the great
numbers who are still leaving, day by day, today even though the
numbers on relief are already below earlier estimates of "unemployables", indicate that the morale of the vast number of those who have
been and are on relief has not been seriously impaired in either direction. The desire to make money is deeply ingrained in the American
people. Those on relief have been on a bare subsistence basis. By
and large, as the relation of relief to employment figures shows, they
have not been slow to take any opportunity to improve their lot.

Perhaps the two greatest residual problems of the relief emergency
are the seasonal workers of low income who previously managed to
tide themselves over slack periods and the undoubted change that has
come in public sentiment whereby people no longer feel the responsibility they once felt for the support of others whom the law does not
oblige them to support. The rate at which people have left relief
and are still leaving it—more than 28,000 families and unattached
people, including more than 90,000 men, women and children went
off the rolls in June 1937, although the rolls were not reduced by
that much, because others became in need—indicates that neither of
these problems is as grave as might once have been feared.

Such problems aside, in the nature of the case, the number of people
in need of relief will depend on the definition of need. If $20 is
determined to be the subsistence level for a given family, then fewer
people will be found in need of relief than if the subsistence level had
been determined at $30. Such changes of policy, forced by the logic
of events, broadened the relief definition through the early period of

the emergency. The great significance of the contraction in relief in recent months is that it has come about without any corresponding narrowing of policy.

In consonance with the principle of local autonomy and local responsibility inherent in the Emergency Act, the State Administration consistently allowed the widest latitude possible within reasonable limits to local variations in the definition of adequacy, insisting only that each locality apply its own formula consistently and without discrimination in the consideration of the needs of each family applying for relief.

Changing policies should be considered in assessing the need for relief as reflected in the figures reported to the State Administration month by month by the local districts. Changes in the reporting system itself must also be taken into account.

Because of the sense of brief emergency there was at the beginning no plan for the development of complete statistical information with respect to the relief operations. Even after the emergency period was extended, when comprehensive statistical material became available in May 1932, the Administration concerned itself chiefly with those local expenditures which were reimbursable. In consequence, as reimbursement was broadened to include relief to veterans, work relief materials and an increasing share of local administrative costs, more and more items came to be statistically reported.

Table II in the Appendix, showing monthly expenditures from the beginning, is therefore not as all-inclusive in the earlier months, but has been compiled in part for these months from estimates based on data obtained later from the local districts.

It has been said that the logic of events forced a liberalization of relief standards. This will be seen, for instance, in the case of rents. In a brief emergency it might be reasonable to call upon landlords to forego or to postpone rent from some properties as their contribution to the alleviation of the general distress. As the emergency continued such a policy could no longer be publicly defended. Similarly with other items, the length of the emergency forced inclusion. Clothes and household goods actually wore out and actually had to be replaced.

There can be no question also but that the work relief program itself by helping remove the stigma from relief led many people to rely upon relief who would not formerly have done so. This, in fact, was part of the very purpose of work relief. When the people of the State of New York entered upon the work relief program they were convinced that this was a socially desirable aim. They wanted those in need to get work rather than to suffer through a period of privation to the consequent detriment of their and the public health. They wanted relief to go to the self-respecting to whom the idea of relief was repugnant, as well as to those with less moral resistance to public support.

Thus work relief began with the emphasis upon the work, upon the provision of jobs for the worthy. Similarly, and with even greater effect, the program of the Federal CWA in the winter of 1933–34, recruiting labor not only from relief, but from among all the unemployed, resulted in breaking down the repugnance to relief. Through these two doors marked "JOB" many entered only to find after some months that in a changed public opinion they had been in the house of relief all along.

RELIEF GIVEN

$1,039,281,359 for Relief

In the five years and six months during which the TERA operated under the provisions of the Emergency Relief Act, a total of $1,039,-281,359 was expended from local, State and Federal funds for the emergency relief program in the State. An additional $16,423,033 of Federal funds was spent by the Administration as agent of the Federal Relief Administration in carrying out Federally controlled programs such as care of transients and distribution of surplus food. The Federal Civil Works Administration,[1] during the four months of its existence in the winter of 1933–34, resulted in expenditures of an additional $99,609,709, making a grand total of $1,155,314,101.

Of the $1,039,281,359 spent for emergency relief, $860,036,139, or 82.8 per cent, was expended directly for relief of those in need. Home relief, a charge on State and local funds throughout the emergency period and shared by the Federal government from January to October 1933 and from April 1934 to July 1935, totalled $549,-643,241, or 52.9 per cent of the total. Work relief initiated before Federal participation, was solely a Federal responsibility for the four months, December 1933 to March 1934, and after December 1935 when the Works Progress Administration completed absorption of the work relief program. During the remainder of the emergency period, when the State shared in the costs of work relief, the total paid in work relief wages was $295,454,647, or 28.4 per cent of the total.

Special State relief programs amounted to $14,937,251 in expenditures, 1.4 per cent of the total. These programs, discussed in detail later,[2] were chiefly the care of local homeless and the providing of school lunches and fresh milk to needy children in marginal families.

In the prosecution of work relief, $65,078,893 was expended for materials, representing 6.3 per cent of the total. This sum, although charged to relief, represents in large measure permanent improvement in public parks, sewers, schools, highways, and buildings, as indicated elsewhere.

Costs of local relief administration, including technical supervision of work projects as well as investigation of applicants and reinvestiga-

---

[1] See p. 48 et seq.
[2] See p. 49 et seq.

tion of recipients, totalled $107,048,924, or 10.3 per cent of the total. Expenses of the State Administration, including the cost of printing and selling the relief bonds, totalled $7,117,403, or less than one per cent of the total cost of the program.

During the 68-month emergency the State Relief Administration reimbursed the local welfare districts by $586,403,331, from State and Federal Funds, with commitments of approximately $9,200,000 still outstanding. It disbursed more than $24,000,000 additional for State-wide projects under the supervision of State Departments.

Total State contributions to the program were $234,155,962 or 20.3 per cent. Total Federal contributions through the Administration, beginning in May 1933 and ending in November 1935, including direct disbursements for CWA and other special Federal programs, were $506,023,610 or 43.8 per cent. Total local contributions were $415,131,229 or 35.9 per cent. Thus State and Federal contributions lightened the burden on local real estate by more than sixty per cent of the total cost of relief.

As the emergency became prolonged and the responsibilities of the Administration increased in many directions its staff came to include "trained social workers to help relief bureaus organize and establish policies; engineers to cooperate in planning valuable work projects suitable for local needs; advisers on medical services, nutrition and garden activities for the unemployed; and an auditing staff employed to insure sound business and accounting methods in the local relief bureaus to which the State contributes funds".[3]

At the peak of its responsibilities on July 1, 1935, before the Federal WPA took over the state-wide work relief program, the central administrative and field staff of the TERA in the supervision of relief numbered 922 persons. Steadily this was contracted parallel to contracted responsibilities, until as of June 1, 1937 the staff numbered 265, a drop of 60 per cent. By June 30 there had been a further contraction to 107.

The Emergency Act provided for reimbursement of 40 per cent on home relief expenditures and discretionary reimbursement for work relief. This continued until the Autumn of 1933 when, to insure that every effort would be made to prevent suffering, Governor Lehman in consultation with the Legislative leaders announced a policy whereby local districts would be reimbursed by two-thirds of their mounting home relief expenditures, the Federal CWA having taken over work relief. After the demobilization of the CWA on April 1, 1934, the TERA reimbursed local districts from State and

[3] Three Years of Public Unemployment Relief in New York State, October 15, 1934, p. 12.

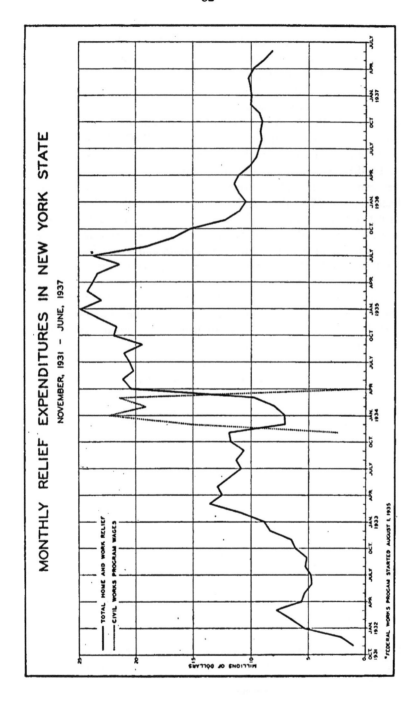

MONTHLY RELIEF EXPENDITURES IN NEW YORK STATE

NOVEMBER, 1931 — JUNE, 1937

Federal funds by 75 per cent of approved expenditures until, with
the completion of the transfer of work relief to the Federal WPA in
December 1935, reimbursement returned to the basic 40 per cent
of the Emergency Act, Federal aid in direct relief having been once
more withdrawn.

TOTAL OBLIGATIONS FOR EMERGENCY RELIEF
November 1, 1931—June 30, 1937

Relief:	Amount	Per Cent of Total
Home relief	$549,644,241	52.9
Work relief wages	295,454,647	28.4
Other relief	14,937,251	1.4
Care of local homeless	5,036,336	
School lunches	4,951,077	
Fresh milk	4,004,278	
Death and disability benefits	416,369	
Garden supplies	54,319	
Rural rehabilitation loans and grants	224,872	
Relief to sick and disabled veterans	250,000	
Total	$860,036,139	82.8
Materials for Work Projects	65,078,893	6.3
Local Administrative Costs	107,048,924	10.3
Administrative and supervisory salaries	94,587,884	
Costs other than salaries	12,461,040	
Central State Administration	7,117,403[4]	0.7
Grand Total without Federal Programs	$1,039,281,359	100.0
Special Federal Programs	16,423,033	
GRAND TOTAL, WITHOUT CWA	$1,055,704,392	
Civil Works Administration:		
Wages	$82,216,107	
Materials and other costs	17,393,602	
Federal funds	6,082,935	
Local funds	11,310,667	
Total	$99,609,709	
GRAND TOTAL	$1,155,314,101	100.0
Local funds	$415,131,229	35.9
State funds	234,155,962	20.3
Federal funds	506,023,610	43.8
Contributed	3,300	....

[4] Includes $416,548 for the cost of printing and distributing relief bonds,
$500,990 for printing forms for local districts and $179,596 for administration of
Federal programs in the period before costs for Federal programs were strictly
segregated.

It should be interesting to students of Government to note how, with the changing percentage of reimbursement, the actual responsibilities of the State Administration expanded and contracted though the legal position as a merely supervisory agency had never altered since 1931. It became necessary to supervise so closely when State and Federal funds represented 75 per cent of expenditures as to approach an operating function. With the reduction to a 40 per cent reimbursement, with a 60 per cent local interest, once more the Administration was able to withdraw to its original function—purely supervisory.

Of the more than 100 welfare districts of the State, all cooperated in the emergency program except one rural county with a population of less than 0.3 per cent of the total population of the State.

Home Relief

Home relief was the form of relief generally in existence throughout up-State districts before the Emergency Act was passed, having been legislated the basic form of relief in New York State by passage of the Public Welfare Law in 1929. This not only limited almshouse care to those cases that could not be cared for in their own homes, but set up what are now commonly accepted standards of investigation, supervision and adequate relief—standards which had not yet been put into very general practice in the State by the time the emergency situation arose. The Emergency Act, therefore, the Administration's rules based upon it, and State aid in reimbursement represented a unique opportunity to put into practice the standards laid down in the Public Welfare Law. The granting of home relief had a long history and an extensive body of tradition. The TERA in this field was faced with the problem of modernizing that tradition and helping with State money to effect the standards laid down in the Public Welfare Law.

As the basic form of relief least affected by changes in Federal policy, home relief was continuous throughout the operation of the Emergency Relief Act. During the 68 months of its administration, a total of $549,644,241 was expended in relief grants to needy citizens in their own homes. Of this amount more than 90 per cent was reimbursable in part from State or State and Federal funds whereas the remainder was wholly a charge upon local funds. The two year residence requirement in the Emergency Relief Act was the chief reason for local expenditures not subject to reimbursement.

Home relief was granted to a monthly average of approximately 265,000 families and unattached persons throughout the 68 months of the emergency, beginning with 38,074, in up-State districts in November 1931, when New York City had not yet organized home relief, and reaching a peak of 433,731 in February 1935.

When it was assumed those unemployed workers would need only to be tided over the winter months of 1931 and 1932, it was natural that the chief emphasis should be upon prevention of starvation. Accordingly, in the early months of the emergency three-fourths or more of home relief expenditures represented food vouchers. In June 1932, when information on this point was first gathered, 81 per cent of all home relief in New York City and 73 per cent up-State provided food supplies. Practically all of the remainder was spent for shelter, leaving very little for fuel and light, clothing, medical care and household necessities. As relief needs were more adequately met, food came to represent a less important fraction of the total expenditures, dropping to about 55 per cent of home relief in the final months.

The traditional home relief policy of giving relief only in kind was carried over in the Emergency Relief Act. Home Relief as defined in the Act consisted of "shelter, food, fuel, clothing, light, medicine or medical attendance furnished by a municipal corporation to persons or their dependents in their abode or habitation." This provision making voucher relief mandatory followed the special message of Governor Roosevelt on August 28, 1931, embodying this restriction, "that under no circumstances shall any actual money be paid in the form of a dole or in any other form by the local welfare officer to any unemployed or his family."

With the extension of the emergency period however, the question arose as to whether cash relief might not be both more economical as well as more salutary to the recipient in a) reducing the cost of distribution; b) making the relief recipient responsible, as he would be under normal circumstances, for planning the use of his own resources; c) reducing the stigma attached to relief vouchers presented in neighborhood retail stores; d) eliminating the possibility of abuses in the cashing of relief vouchers by retailers, and e) at the same time eliminating the inspection necessary to prevent these abuses. In 1934 this point of view gathered momentum, especially through pressure by New York City relief officials, and finally an amendment to the Wicks Act provided that "for purposes of and in order to provide wholly or in part home relief as herein defined, money may be given in cash if and when approved by and under the rules and regulations made and conditions specified by the Administration."

In May 1934 New York City began issuing cash relief and has since that time, except for medical care, used cash relief almost exclusively. Nassau County began issuing cash relief in July 1935.

After the first winter of the emergency, also, the larger questions of adequate relief standards and maximum conservation of relief funds came to the fore. From the beginning the rules of the Administration required proper investigation of relief applicants not only to determine need for relief but to determine the extent of need and to mobilize the family resources of health, employability and self-help. The rules of the Administration also required follow-up visits to relief cases at least once a month and required that the amount of relief be based upon family budgets. It had been a common practice among public relief officials to give a standard grocery order for $2.50, $3.50, $5.00, or some other fixed sum, regardless of the size of family or special diet needs.

Whereas the Act and the rules of the Administration made it possible to deny reimbursement to local districts that persistently refused to meet adequate standards of relief, this resort was, in practice, seldom used. It was recognized that practically never was there a definite policy of granting inadequate relief but rather that, insofar as inadequate standards were in effect, they stemmed back to the old Poor Law tradition which pretty generally throughout the country held that relief should be as unpleasant as possible so that the fewest number of people should apply for it. Consequently the Administration undertook a program of persuasion and education rather than of coercion with respect to adequate standards of relief. The wisdom of that course has been justified by the fact that at the present time in the State there is little disposition to grant starvation relief by relief officials nor is there indeed any extensive pressure by the public in general to keep relief on such a level.

Among the early functions of the TERA representatives in the field was the interpretation to local welfare officials of the Administration's principle of adequate relief. Furthermore, periodical studies were made of the standards of home relief in the various welfare districts to ascertain the progress in conforming to the fundamental standards set up by the Administration in its rules.

In helping to "maintain minimum relief standards" as well as "maximum efficiency and economy in furnishing relief," the Administration early prepared for the use of local relief officials food allowance schedules. The first of these, prepared by a group of nutrition experts from various social agencies, were issued in August 1932. Further suggestions crystalized in a pamphlet entitled "Reduction of Food Costs," published in May 1933 and outlining plans for price agreements with retailers, for careful periodic check of the cost of food items, for large-scale buying of staples such as milk, bread, etc.

Similarly, the Administration in February 1934 worked out with the aid of the New York State Coal Merchants' Association and the Anthracite Institute a plan for local buying of coal from local retailers under a State contract that has resulted in substantial savings. Similarly, the Administration contracted for cod liver oil on a state-wide basis.

At the beginning of the emergency period there was little disposition to include rent as a regular item of home relief grants. A study of the rent-paying practices in up-State cities in November 1931 revealed that no rents were paid in fourteen cities, paid only to avoid eviction in five, paid "seldom" or occasionally in twenty-five and paid as a matter of policy in only eleven cities. Even in these cities, inclusion of rent as a budget item was not an invariable policy. Although paying rents intermittently to avoid eviction or other hardship earlier, New York City did not have a definite policy to include rent as a regular budget item until after October 1933.

As late as December 1933 "a study of the policies and practices in paying for shelter from public funds revealed the fact that only two cities had a definite policy of paying rent in all home relief cases in which there was need for such aid . . . and five districts never paid rent or other shelter costs."[5] Many districts paid no rents except under imperative pressure by landlords or upon receipt of dispossess notice. By May 1934, when a special study was made in cities, rent payments had become part of the regular relief budget in all but one city.

A statewide program of medical service was organized by the TERA with the cooperation of Medical Societies in 1931 after a survey in seventeen cities and four counties had shown that there were twenty different programs for medical care of those on relief, ranging from those limited to strictly emergency calls and serious illness and injuries, to comprehensive plans including prevention. To

---

[5] Relief Activities of City and County Welfare Districts in Cooperation with the State Temporary Emergency Relief Administration, November 1, 1931–December 31, 1933, p. 13.

carry out the stipulation of the Wicks Act that relief be adequate, a uniform reimbursement of the localities for medical care was worked out.

From July 1, 1932, when this program went into operation, to June 30, 1937, $10,457,541 of the money expended for home relief was for medical care. In the first six months; an average of $.25 per family per month went for this type of relief. Year by year this amount increased until in 'the final six months of the period $.80 per family per month was expended.

Since the TERA insisted that the money should supplement rather than supplant existing facilities, a large part has provided medical services to the needy in rural areas. This means, not that the rural communities received more than their share of relief monies, but that, lacking extensive public medical facilities, they spent a larger portion of the money to provide needed medical care, while in New York City, for instance, where the hospital and out-patient facilities were numerous, such money went for food and shelter.

Thus, in the five years $3,886,443, or an average of $.35 per home relief family per month was spent in New York City, while $6,571,098, or $.90 per home relief family per month was spent in the State outside New York City to provide this additional medical aid. More than $4,330,000, or two-thirds of the total amount spent up-State, was spent in counties outside of the cities which had about 40 per cent of the up-State relief load. This made an average of $1.49 per home relief family per month in these areas where previously existing public medical services were not extensive.

Work Relief

The same sense of brief emergency which colored the entire relief program shaped its work aspect.

Spontaneously in many parts of the State civic-minded citizens had conducted campaigns for private funds to take care of those who could no longer take care of themselves and to forestall the necessity of governmental intervention. There was a widespread feeling that a stigma would attach to relief given by the government and that it was up to the communities to supply, through private means, work for those whose only economic difficulty was that there were no jobs to be had. Thus, when the TERA came into being, there was in many parts of the State a private work relief program already in operation.

Methods of handling the programs and the types of work prosecuted were as various as local conditions and ingenuity might be expected to make them.[4] Sporadic attempts everywhere were made to help the victims of the economic disaster that had overtaken the whole State.

In many places "man-a-block" campaigns were organized supplying odd jobs directly to the unemployed through personal canvass by committees which persuaded householders to undertake repairs, clean-up-work, the committee putting those on their lists directly in touch with the job. In New York City extensive programs were initiated recognizing the needs of the white collar worker through non-commercial enterprises which included gathering material for a new city directory. Neighborliness and the sense that everyone was close to the distress was dramatized even in large centers through such work as New York City's block aid campaign in which a committeeman sought out the needy in his block and gathered contributions within the block for assistance, the beneficiaries remaining anonymous. Throughout the State the clean-up of public parks, minor repairs to public buildings and other non-competitive work was carried on. Jamestown was one of the first to step in governmentally, enlarging its regular program of street surfacing to provide jobs for relief applicants. In June 1931 a Joint Committee on Unemployment Relief of the State Board of Social Welfare and the State Charities Aid Association reported that "Nine cities have used private relief funds to pay wages for work relief: New York, Yonkers, Utica, Schenectady, Binghamton, Troy, Poughkeepsie, Olean and Cortland. All of these cities had emergency relief funds raised by an Emergency Committee on Unemployment. In Binghamton and Cortland grants of public funds were also made to these Emergency Committees."[8]

In New York City the Emergency Unemployment Relief Committee, organized in the fall of 1930, set out to raise funds for carrying on and extending the work of private agencies. Much of its money went to the eleven established family service agencies in the five boroughs. In addition, however, it also set up a program of providing work for the unemployed. Need of relief was in the beginning not a condition of obtaining employment. This committee reported in June 1933 that $7,100,000 had been set aside for work relief, with $6,002,000

---

[8] Work relief: A Memorandum on Work as a Means of Providing Unemployment Relief, issued by the Joint Committee on Unemployment Relief of the State Board of Social Welfare and the State Charities Aid Association, June 1931, p. 8.

disbursed up to May 31, 1933. Up to the same date it reported having given 1,410,219 days of work in the ratio of 60 to 40 for men and women. At the peak, in February 1933, 23,715 persons were employed, 16,729 men and 6,986 women.

Likewise, a number of municipalities had made provision for carrying on work relief with public funds before the Wicks Act went into effect. In Rochester, in the winter of 1930–31, a Civic Committee on Unemployment developed a work relief program for which the city appropriated a total of $800,000.

A report[7] of this activity recounted how, of 12,000 applicants, 7,917 different men were given work in varying amounts on 77 projects undertaken. The report further stated that, "At the outset the policy was established of giving approximately two-thirds of the jobs to men who were not at the time of application receiving relief from any family caring agency, in the hope that the small but steady income from this source might supplement their resources and enable men to 'weather the storm' without coming into formal contact with a family caring agency. It was also established that about one-third of the jobs would be allotted to the public and private family caring agencies, to be assigned by them either as a part of case work treatment or, in some instances, as a work test."

Such was the varied picture when in the autumn of 1931 the TERA stepped in with authorization to extend State aid to work relief. The rate of reimbursement for home relief was fixed in the Emergency Relief Act at 40 per cent but the rate of reimbursement on work relief was left to the discretion of the Administration, the most significant stipulation being that work relief wages must be paid in cash "in the form of day's wages for day's work or hour's wages for hour's work." To assure that work relief would not aggravate the situation that relief was designed to help by competing with private industry or regular governmental work, the Administration early ruled that the localities should not undertake through relief any operations that they would have done otherwise with regular labor in the near future. In compliance with the State Labor Law and to prevent the general depression of wages through work relief the Administration ruled that the local prevailing rate should be paid on work relief projects, the worker receiving sufficient hours of work during the month to make up the deficit in the family budget.

---

[7] Municipal Work Relief for the Unemployed by C. Arthur Poole, Consulting Engineer, Rochester, New York, in Addresses Delivered at the Open Forum Session on Unemployment Relief of the 37th Annual Convention of the American Society of Municipal Engineers held in Pittsburgh, Pa., October 19–23, 1931, p. 35.

To stimulate the development of work projects the Administration at the start matched dollar for dollar with local money that went for relief wages on work projects. State funds did not participate in meeting the cost of materials, equipment, supervision and accident insurance and it is significant of the thinking in the early days that, although these items were met wholly from local funds, projects were not approved if such non-relief costs represented more than ten per cent of the total. At this time project approvals were sketchy and the applications gave little more than the name of the project and the estimated total cost, divided between relief wages and other items, since it was assumed that with such a high percentage of local money involved the communities would undertake work that was locally desirable. For this reason exact figures as to types of projects and the total cost of the program at this period have never been available through the State Administration, the districts at that time reporting only on their reimbursable expenditures, consisting of relief wages paid.

Such strict emphasis on having practically all the cost of work relief go into wages to relief workers, born of a determination to see that as much as possible of relief funds went for relief, naturally limited the type of project that could be undertaken. These at first were of the municipal housecleaning sort and useful projects within these limits in time became thoroughly exhausted.

After June of 1932 the standard reimbursement on work relief wages was cut to 40 per cent in line with reimbursement on home relief, project applications forms were changed to make possible a more detailed control and the limit on expenses for materials and equipment was revised upward at the request of local officials from many parts of the State. Such items continued to be non-reimbursable, however, and even in the enlarged work program that came later following the CWA only Federal funds were ever used in their reimbursement, there being no provision in the State law for such use of State funds.

A conference in the spring of 1932 with officials from the city of Jamestown, one of the factors that led to the raising of the limit on non-relief costs, brought out in essence the case for and against extended work relief which has come to be argued with greater intensity since. The local officials said that they had some street resurfacing work to be done, that if they let it out under ordinary contract it would be done by machinery, helping the labor situation very little. They said that if they could do it under work relief using all

labor and little machinery the cost of doing the job would be somewhat higher, but considerably lower than the combined costs of doing
the job under contract on the one hand and on the other hand supporting on home relief the labor that could otherwise have been employed
on that job.

The Administration decided to allow the municipality to make the
experiment it desired to make and in other communities throughout
the State the program began gradually to change in character to em-
brace more substantial work.

One of the factors inhibiting such a change was that State aid was
provided for on such a temporary basis. Local governments very
naturally did not want to start on work that might have to be abandoned before completion. When the TERA was organized it was
established first for a period of eight months, then for five-and-a-
half months, then for three months and was continued thereafter generally from year to year.

The work relief program divides itself naturally into three periods,
that prior to November 1933, when the Federal CWA took over complete financial responsibility for work relief; the CWA period through
March 1934, when although work relief was wholly a Federal responsibility, financially the TERA was the State agent for the Federal
Administration; and the period from April 1934 following the CWA
to December 1935, when the Federal Works Program completed the
absorption of all work relief. In the earlier period, as has been
said, projects were chiefly limited to the municipal housecleaning sort.
So thoroughly was the program permeated with crusading idealism
that the accomplishments were far greater than might have been expected of jobs with so little technical supervision.

With the Federal Civil Works program,[9] came a great change in
the character of work relief. The Federal Government, paying all
wages including supervisory, required local contributions for materials as well as paying largely for some materials itself. Work of
more substantial character was therefore possible and was required.
The reorganized work program of the State and local districts, following the CWA, showed this changed emphasis. Although still
enjoined by the terms of the Emergency Act from spending State
money in reimbursement of other than wages, the TERA from April
1934 reimbursed local districts from Federal funds for materials expenditures. It also insisted upon proper and competent supervision of
work by granting reimbursement for supervisory expense, allowing

---

Vide following section, p. 48 et seq.

a "budget deficiency waived" category of relief personnel by which persons in need of relief, employed in an administrative or supervisory capacity could be paid on a continuous basis regardless :of budget deficits. Under these influences the accomplishments of work relief during this period were an impressive contribution to the public physical plant.

At the beginning of the work relief program compensation of injured workers was the responsibility of the municipalities and counties, the Administration requiring coverage by compensation insurance.

Chapter 769 of the Laws of 1934 excluded persons receiving work relief from the operation of the Workmen's Compensation Law and concurrently an Amendment to the Emergency Relief Act, placed the responsibility upon the State. A compensation plan was devised so that a worker temporarily disabled continued to receive relief and was provided with medical services, with a regular scale of compensation for death or permanent disability based upon the State Workmen's Compensation Act.

The advantages of this plan to the temporarily disabled relief worker over coverage by the Workmen's Compensation Act are obvious. Since relief wages were on a subsistence basis to begin with, the regular allowance of two-thirds of such wages during a period of disability would have been below the starvation level. In large part because of the safety program developed in connection with work relief, only 113,560 accidents to relief workers took place from April 1, 1934, to December 1, 1935. Of these, 4,950, or 4 per cent, resulted in lost time and therefore presumably required medical care and home relief allowances during the period of disability. Since these services were furnished through regular home relief channels the cost of them has not been segregated. Death or permanent disability cases totalled 835, or less than one per cent of total accidents, and total allowances for these cases were $548,750. Five per cent, or 42 of the allowance cases involved either death or permanent total disability. For these cases the total compensation awards were $120,150, or an average of $2,860 per case. The remaining 793 cases involved only partial disabilities and received $428,600, or an average of $540 in allowances. While no exact comparison is possible, it is evident that expenditures were far less than they would have been if the State Workmen's Compensation Law had been applied. During the period approximately $190,000,000 was paid in relief wages and it is estimated that the normal premium for this payroll under the Workmen's Compensation Law would have been approximately $9,000,000. In contrast to this amount, the most generous estimates of costs that cannot be segregated would hardly bring the total expended for compensation to more than two or three million dollars.

Work relief wages, including neither wages to necessary supervisory personnel nor Federal CWA and WPA wages, totalled $295,454,647 during the emergency period. The work relief program was in operation by December 1931. For the 40 months thereafter during which work relief was jointly a State and local responsibility, with or without Federal participation, an average of approximately 149,000 persons a month received work relief. Beginning with about 25,000 in December 1931, the number grew to over 180,000 in November 1933, when the Federal CWA program began. The highest point in work relief was in April 1934, the first month after it had been turned back by the CWA to State and local responsibility. From that time, when there were about 260,000 persons employed, it dropped to about 185,000 in July 1935, when the Federal WPA began to take over the program.

Work projects carried on divide themselves rather naturally into three types, the largest of which was, of course, the development and improvement of public property such as parks, playgrounds, sewers, highways, museums, libraries and other public buildings. In the period following the CWA 1,790 miles of new roads were constructed and 2,300 miles of roads improved and repaired, 123 bridges were constructed and 190 improved, nearly 400 public buildings constructed and 4,500 improved, 1,942 miles of mosquito-control drainage ditches were constructed, over a million trees, vines and shrubs were planted.

A recent report of the State Commissioner of Health points out that work relief "has resulted in advancing construction of water purification and sewage treatment works by at least twenty-five years. Considering sewerage alone there will be more persons served by sewage treatment works constructed and under construction since January 1, 1933, than all such works constructed during the thirty-year period prior to that date."

A second type of project is represented by the group that furnished goods and services for the unemployed themselves—through a natural desire to have the unemployed work to increase relief without extra cost to the taxpayer. Clothing needs were met in a large part of the State by sewing projects; there were work relief projects for the distribution of surplus commodities. Some districts carried on cobbling and tailoring projects for the renovation and repair of shoes and clothing for relief clients. Garden and canning projects likewise produced food for the use of relief clients and public institutions.

During the period April 1934 to July 1935, 349 sewing rooms, employing more than 2,500 women, were operated and made over 60,000 garments. Through 21 canning projects in the State, more than 235,000 units of fruits and vegetables were canned or preserved in the summer of 1934 and made available for distribution to relief families.

Artistic, educational, recreational and research projects represented the third approach to the problem of made work—adult education and Americanization classes, playground supervision, sketching and drawing, music classes. The music and theater projects as begun under State work relief, contributed not only to the relief of unemployed actors and musicians and furnished free or inexpensive recreation for the unemployed themselves, but developed a new and broad clientele for such services that may well carry into normal times and extend permanently the demand for such services. It is estimated that the audiences for the music and drama projects totalled more than five million persons.

In addition to locally sponsored projects the various departments of the State government developed plans for employing persons of varied skills on State work. The Emergency Act in 1931, providing up to $1,000,000 for State Department projects, furnished the one exception to the rule that State funds could be used in work relief only for relief wages. The Act stipulated that not more than 10 per cent was to go for materials, the limit being raised to 15 per cent in 1933 and 20 per cent in 1934. Supervision was furnished largely by State engineers and other regular employees. Workers were selected from certified relief lists of the localities in which the projects were located. In this way vast extensions were made to the State park systems, State highways and waterways were developed and improved.

Public health projects throughout the State employed nearly 900 nurses who made over a million home visits for the supervision of infant and child health, for care and teaching with respect to tuberculosis and other communicable diseases, and for prenatal and postpartum care. Nearly three-quarters of a million children were examined in clinics and over 100,000 diphtheria immunizations were made.[9]

---

[9] For fuller discussion of the accomplishments of work projects *vide* Public Unemployment Relief in New York State—Fourth Year, October 15, 1935, pp. 17–24.

Types of work relief and their relative importance in the program are shown in the following table for April 1935—a typical period:

Type of Project	Man Hours		Per Cent of Total Man Hours
Planning	347,329		1.9
Public Property, Construction and Improvement	10,311,317		55.6
Highways	2,144,925	11.6	
Other	8,166,392	44.0	
Providing Housing	66,376		0.3
Production and Distribution of Goods Needed by Unemployed	1,011,852		5.5
Public Welfare, Health and Recreation	657,045		3.5
Public Education, Arts and Research	2,686,150		14.5
Administrative	3,406,295		18.4
Tools and Equipment	51,902		0.3
Total	18,538,266		100.0

Despite the disadvantages inherent in an emergency program, making long-time planning impossible, its flexibility is an indisputable asset in unusual or emergent situations. Such was the case in the summer of 1935 when, on July 8 and 9, the worst flood disaster in the history of the State occurred in south central New York. Fortuitously an emergency organization was in the field and the situation could be met.

The original emergency which had brought emergency relief into being had dragged on so long that in the minds of most people it was no longer emergent. But here was a new and utterly unforeseen condition for which the emergency machinery, by its very nature, was admirably adapted. By the morning of July 9 food and blankets[10] had been rushed into the devastated areas, relief workers had been transferred to flood rehabilitation work. Immediately also men from nearby Transient centers were brought to work, being housed in temporary shelters thrown up in the devastated regions.

Since the regular relief budgets of the local municipalities were unable to meet this unexpected emergency and since in any case the magnitude of the disaster called for other than local aid, the Administration "made special allotments on a 100 per cent reimbursement basis, beyond the regular monthly relief allocations, providing for necessary materials, equipment and non-relief personnel as well as work relief wages for flood relief projects, the Federal Government making additional money available."[11] Such work was limited to clearing of debris and temporary repairs to public property.

[10] Federal Surplus Commodities.
[11] Public Unemployment Relief in New York State—Fourth Year, October 15, 1935, p. 24.

The vital promptness and adequacy of flood relief depended upon cooperation with many agencies such as the State Department of Health, other State Departments and the American Red Cross, coordinated by Governor Lehman after a personal tour of the stricken areas. The activities in which the Administration shared included relief through regular home and work relief channels, relief to farmers through the Rural Rehabilitation Corporation and flood rehabilitation and soil erosion repair by Transient camp workers. The TERA staff already in the field aided mobilization of local forces and coordination of the various other agencies of Government.

A total of over $1,000,000 was expended on work projects, including, besides the clearing away of debris, temporary repairs to roads and bridges, repair of broken water mains and sewer lines and the carrying on of all emergency activities that did not involve new and permanent construction. The latter type of project, as well as long-time flood control projects, could not be embarked upon because the Federal Works Progress Administration was about to take over work relief.

In view of the great and immediate distress, provision was made for temporary certification of, *prima facie* flood sufferers without awaiting formal casework investigation. About $70,000 was expended in relief to over 1,600 cases who received such temporary certification for relief.

The Rural Rehabilitation Corporation made available $150,000 in outright grants to farmers stricken by the flood, for such purposes as replacement of farm animals and farm equipment and the restoration of soil. The Corporation gave relief to nearly 1,200 farmers at a total cost of nearly $132,000.

The flood disaster presented a signal opportunity to the men under care of the Transient Division to prove their usefulness. From nearby Transient centers men volunteered to go into the stricken areas to do whatever could be done and without waiting for details to be worked out as to adequate living quarters or wages to be paid. Temporary shelter and commissary facilities were thrown up for as many as 1,500 men. After the first harrowing days when food and water had to be brought in, roads had to be cleared, sewers and water mains repaired and debris cleared away, these contingents of transients worked under the technical supervision of the Soil Erosion Service of the Federal Department of Agriculture, and for four months thereafter worked with this bureau in its program of restoring and preserving the soil. Nearly half a million dollars was expended for flood relief by the

Transient Division, less than half of which was used for maintenance and wages of the men working. The Federal agency reported that the Transient workers were more efficient than other groups under its supervision.[12]

Federal Civil Works Administration

The winter of 1933–1934, a very cold winter which in many parts of the country recorded new lows in temperature as well as employment, brought such distress as to lead the Federal Government to attempt more drastic succor than relief.

In the bank holiday of the previous spring New York State factory payrolls had dropped to an index number of 38. The heavy construction projected under the National Industrial Recovery Act had failed to get under way with sufficient promptness in sufficient volume to be a large factor. Winter was at hand.

On November 7th President Roosevelt announced the creation of the Federal Civil Works Administration to provide work for 4,000,-000 jobless throughout the country during the winter and and to stimulate trade revival through payment of a standard living wage to those employed. Simultaneously Federal aid for direct relief was withdrawn.

To assure that the unemployed of New York State would benefit as promptly as possible, the State Temporary Emergency Relief Administration acted as agent of the Federal Civil Works Administration for the State, in turn naming the local work bureaus as its agents, so that the decentralization that had characterized New York State relief from the start was maintained as far as might be in a completely Federal program.

Actual functioning of the State CWA was begun late in November and by December 15th approximately 225,000 persons were employed, including those transferred from work relief projects which had been practically absorbed. At the height of the program early in 1934 nearly 350,000 persons were employed, of whom about 155,000 were in New York City and 185,000 were in other districts of the State.

From the middle of December on, persons employed on CWA in the State were selected through the sixty-two branch offices of the

---

[12] For a full discussion of flood relief activities *vide* Public Unemployment Relief in New York State—Fourth Year, October 15, 1935, pp. 24–30, and New York State Temporary Emergency Relief Administration Monthly Bulletin on Public Relief Statistics, July 1935, pp. 4–6; October 1935, pp. 22–23; December 1935, pp. 8 and 11.

National Re-employment Service and the New York State Employment Service, on the sole basis of qualification for the job, no preference being given to those in need of relief. This provision, mandatory under the Federal Act which made the funds available, necessarily minimized the effect of the CWA in reducing relief needs, and State and local expenditures for home relief alone were greater than their contributions for all relief had been a few months previously.

During the four months of the CWA program a total of $82,216,107 was paid in wages from Federal funds. For materials and other costs, including the administrative project, Federal expenditures totalled $6,082,935. Local districts contributed a total of $11,310,667 in materials and other non-wage costs. The total expenditures of the CWA program in New York State were therefore $99,609,709. No State funds were used.

Supplementary Relief Programs

FEDERAL SURPLUS COMMODITIES

The Surplus Commodities Division of the TERA, acting as agent for the Federal Surplus Commodities Corporation, distributed to the local welfare districts approximately 331,000,000 pounds of surplus foods to needy persons in the State in the past four years. These foods, removed from the market through the Federal Farm program and given to the needy over and above their regular budgetary allowances, had an estimated retail value of $38,200,000. The TERA acted merely as Federal agent, chiefly in allocation of amounts.

Included among the foods distributed were:

Apples	16,463,000 lbs.
Butter	11,810,800 lbs.
Flour	33,416,800 lbs.
Grapefruit	30,604,600 lbs.
Potatoes	56,804,600 lbs.
Roast Beef	39,666,200 lbs.
Smoked Pork	28,043,200 lbs.
Veal—Fresh	28,959,900 lbs.

In addition to these commodities, whose distribution was begun in October 1933, the State distributing agency provided 3,000,000 articles of clothing valued at $4,000,000 to persons in need. More than 39,000,000 yards of cotton cloth, allocated to the State by the Federal government, were used in the manufacture of the articles. Sewing shops established as work projects and the Federal WPA sewing projects made the finished products, which included 1,861,600 household articles such as sheets, pillow cases, towels, etc., and 1,728,700 finished garments. Persons on home relief and others whose earnings were on a minimum subsistence basis and who were certified as in need by the local Welfare Commissioner received these commodities.

Actual distribution of the food and clothing was through local relief authorities who orgainized 2,000 distributing stations manned by persons employed on work relief and later WPA projects.

After October 1933, the Federal government, through the Commodities Purchasing Division of the AAA and in cooperation with the New York State Department of Agriculture and Markets, purchased directly from New York State farmers more than $500,000 worth of surplus products.

Among these purchases were included 36,600,000 pounds of cabbage, 11,000,000 pounds of potatoes and 255,000 bushels of apples. Also purchased directly from New York State farmers were many of the more than 3,500,000 dozens of eggs bought in the early months of 1937 by the Federal government.

During 1936, milk was purchased directly from New York State dairymen for the manufacture within the State of 3,882,500 pounds of dry skim milk and 2,503,800 pounds of evaporated milk.

TRANSIENTS

In its twenty-nine months of operation the Federally financed program for Transients, which was terminated on March 4, 1936, provided food, shelter, medical care and, when feasible, work to more than 200,000 needy transients, namely, needy persons of less than two years' residence in the State, at a cost of approximately $8,400,000. The program was administered by the Transient Division of the Temporary Emergency Relief Administration.

To assist these individuals, who for the most part formed a migratory population in vain search of work, a State-wide network of Transient centers and camps was located at strategic points. These camps were set up in accordance with the announced Federal policy of stabilizing the transient population and eliminating the old system whereby transients were shunted back and forth from officials of one public welfare district to another. The camps were an attempt to help enable such men at least partially to regain status in society.

Ten camps were erected. The men thus provided for performed useful work in return for which they received maintenance and up to three dollars a week, depending upon willingness and ability to perform satisfactory work. The permanent camps accommodated two hundred men each at a time. In most instances the camps were erected on State property and the buildings at the termination of the Transient program were turned over to the State. Following the devastating 1935 flood of the Southern Tier of the State additional temporary camps were established and the men worked clearing up the debris, reopening roads, clearing farmlands, etc., for $7.50 a week and their food and shelter. In the liquidation of the Transient program in the fall of 1935 seven camps were taken over by the Works Progress Administration.

Three additional types of transient units were operated, treatment centers, reference bureaus and special rehabilitation units. The treatment centers afforded a complete program of care to unattached persons, including housing, meals, clothing, medical care, work programs, recreation and consultation on special types of problems, the aim being to select for treatment centers those most capable of industrial rehabilitation.

Hartford House, located in New York City, and Hartwick Academy at Cooperstown, New York, were the special rehabilitation units of the Transient Division. The former was a special service center which combined relief and vocational counseling service. This combination was designed to assist the white collar men and those with special skills and prepare them for return to private employment. Hartwick Academy was established for transient young men interested in educational and vocational opportunities.

The reference bureaus, which were operated locally under the supervision of County Welfare Commissioner provided little more than food and housing for the Transients, transferring to camps or centers those requiring such service.

Transient families were provided for in the same manner as home relief cases, that is, given vouchers or cash for maintenance, the while attempts were made either to return them to place of settlement·or to help them to self-support.

CAMP TERA

Camp TERA, in Palisades Interstate Park, was established in June 1933 as a rest camp for jobless young women in need of mental and physical rehabilitation. Founded as a work relief project sponsored by the Federal Emergency Relief Administration in cooperation with the Temporary Emergency Relief Administration, the New York State

Conservation Department and the New York City Welfare Council, it was open to unemployed women from New York City between the ages of eighteen and forty and, until its transfer to the National Youth Administration on December 31, 1935, had cared for 1,616 young women at an over-all cost of about forty cents per day per person.

The TERA acted in a supervisory capacity for the camp and disbursed Federal funds allocated for its maintenance.

CCC CAMPS

New York State's 115,000 boys and young men recruited from needy families who were enrolled in the Civilian Conservation Corps from April 1933 through June 1937, contributed to their dependents approximately $18,200,000 by alloting to them a minimum of $22 of their monthly earnings of $30.

Total obligations of approximately $70,000,000 were incurred in the State by the CCC, including wages, administrative and personnel expenses, the construction of camps throughout the State and the purchase of food, clothing, medical supplies and camp equipment.

The majority of boys and men enrolled in New York State were sent to camps in the State of which there were 33 established during the first months of the program. The number of camps was gradually increased until it reached a total of 137 in the summer of 1935. On June 30, 1937, there were 105, including 11 camps for war veterans.

Selection of veterans to be sent to camps was made by the State Veterans' Administration. The selection of young men for the remaining camps was made by local relief authorities to whom the TERA delegated its functions as selecting agent for the State. For the most part these were taken from families on public relief, thus lightening through their contributions to their families the local and State relief burden.

Originally the minimum age limits for admission to CCC camps were set at 18 and 25 years. This later was changed to allow boys of 17 and young men who had not reached their 29th birthdays to enroll. Additional requirements for admission to the CCC, veterans excepted, were that applicants be American citizens, single, unemployed, physically fit and able and willing to allot a minimum of $22 of their $30 monthly wage to their dependents.

Among the work done by the CCC in New York were reforestation, insect pest control, forest fire prevention, road and trail construction, flood control and the construction of buildings in various State parks.

One of the outstanding projects was the Walkill River flood control project designed to eliminate floods from the farming section bordering this river in Orange County. An average of 2,400 men were employed on this project beginning in April 1935.

SUPPLEMENTARY STATE ACTIVITIES

The subsistence garden program, with its objective of helping the unemployed on relief to provide through their own efforts a considerable portion of their food requirements, was launched in the spring of 1932 with the planting of approximately 13,000 gardens.

Fresh vegetables obtained from subsistence gardens so planted have had an estimated retail value of $5,170,000. This approximate $5,000,000 harvest from the gardens, sponsored by welfare districts throughout the State and planted with the assistance and technical supervision of the TERA, involved expenditures of only $1,021,000 for the planting of a yearly average of 32,000 gardens during the five year period.

Since the beginning three types of gardens have been planted: a) home or backyard gardens; b) community gardens, usually of considerable area and located near urban centers, subdivided into small plots which could be worked by individuals; c) quantity production tracts planted and operated as work relief projects, the workers receiving regular relief wages. The products from this type of garden were stored or canned for eventual distribution to families on relief. In addition the TERA provided, when requested, technical assistance in the planting of the privately-sponsored industrial gardens. Such gardens were financed by private employers to aid their part-time and unemployed workers.

Preservation of fresh vegetables for the use of the needy was begun in 1933. The State College of Home Economics through its Extension Service cooperated with the TERA and organized food canning classes and established county canning kitchens. Under this program 400,000 units of garden products were canned in 1933. The number of units canned in subsequent years was 473,000 in 1934, 1,000,000 in 1935 and 822,000 in 1936.

The first large scale subsistence garden program launched in New York City was in 1935. In that year 6,000 gardens were planted in all of New York City's five boroughs except Manhattan. The TERA reimbursed welfare districts at the regular rate for home relief on their expenditures.

The extent to which the training in gardening and in the home preservation of foods, may have aided otherwise marginal families to keep off relief cannot be measured in the statistics of the TERA.

In the period between July 1934 and June 1937 over four million dollars was expended in providing over 48 million quarts of New York State fresh milk to babies, children and nursing and expectant mothers in families on a subsistence level of income though not necessarily on relief. This program was begun under a special appropriation of $1,500,000 of relief monies by the Legislature in 1934, providing for 100 per cent reimbursement to local districts for their expenditures for milk in this category, on condition that these purchases did not cut down normal milk provision for home relief families. After the exhaustion of the special appropriation many local districts continued the program and were, by amendment to the Emergency Relief Act, reimbursed at the same rate as home relief.

Believing that prevention of undernourishment of children was a vital concern of the State, the Temporary Emergency Relief Administration, in February 1933, began reimbursement to municipalities, on the same basis as home relief, of expenditures for school lunches, including milk, served to under-nourished and needy children in public schools. This program was carried on in New York City at a total cost of $4,951,077, which sum included also an appropriation for clothing for needy school children in the winter of 1936.

The activities of the New York State Rural Rehabilitation Corporation have been previously reported at length.[18]

---

[18] Unemployment Relief in New York State, October 15, 1936, pp. 21-22.

TABLE I
NUMBER OF RESIDENT FAMILIES AND UNATTACHED PERSONS RECEIVING RELIEF
JUNE, 1932—JUNE, 1937

Month	Entire State	Up-State	New York City
	NUMBER OF RELIEF CASES		
June, 1932	171,302	94,090	77,212
July	169,256	94,027	75,229
August	183,823	104,097	79,726
September	186,602	108,209	78,393
October	199,664	116,439	83,225
November	212,600	123,273	89,327
December	247,037	148,316	98,721
January, 1933	295,208	171,450	123,758
February	342,831	192,730	150,101
March	384,058	212,294	171,764
April	412,882	207,550	205,332
May	418,334	205,474	212,860
June	398,257	179,876	218,381
July	378,410	160,041	218,369
August	372,575	165,592	206,983
September	345,168	150,216	194,952
October	342,530	151,995	190,535
November[1]	393,529	165,544	227,985
December[1]	265,279	139,969	125,310
January, 1934[1]	253,771	124,017	129,754
February[1]	279,289	134,150	145,139
March[1]	305,384	143,267	162,117
April	536,384	222,433	313,951
May	513,483	199,943	313,540
June	498,214	187,824	310,390
July	498,835	182,068	316,767
August	507,858	181,787	326,071
September	508,256	183,793	324,463
October	517,866	189,656	328,210
November	532,929	203,525	329,404
December	559,235	220,895	338,340
January, 1935	584,953	236,613	348,340
February	594,748	241,124	353,624
March	593,919	239,936	353,983
April	582,488	229,632	352,856
May	566,560	212,882	353,678
June	551,544	199,011	352,533
July	549,882	194,788	355,094
August[2]	484,924	188,555	296,369
September	459,454	183,036	276,418
October	413,033	185,167	227,866
November	369,866	186,110	183,756
December	361,643	169,395	192,248
January, 1936	339,041	142,439	196,602
February	346,535	139,954	206,581
March	354,219	136,687	217,532
April	347,717	125,217	222,500
May	331,834	109,373	222,461
June	316,663	95,432	221,231
July	295,710	81,123	214,587
August	286,272	76,974	209,298
September	282,409	76,121	206,288
October	276,349	74,856	201,493
November	271,790	77,306	194,484
December	278,439	88,434	190,005
January, 1937	290,127	99,988	190,139
February	294,139	105,051	189,088
March	292,789	105,097	187,692
April	277,911	93,924	183,987
May	255,559	77,731	177,828
June	236,242	67,584	168,658

[1] Civil Works Program in operation from November 20, 1933 through March 31, 1934.
[2] The Works Progress Administration began active operation in August, 1935.

NOVEMBER, 1931—JUNE, 1937

Type of Expenditures	November 1931	December 1931	January 1932	February 1932	March 1932	April 1932	May 1932	June 1932	July 1932	August 1932	September 1932	October 1932	November 1932	December 1932
Local Reimbursable Expenditures:														
Home relief	$894,195	$1,380,932	$1,864,841	$2,571,566	$3,431,558	$2,608,246	$2,497,724	$2,459,099	$2,552,748	$2,776,833	$2,890,580	$3,242,637	$3,683,294	$4,684,938
Care of local homeless													29,518	15,478
School lunches														
Fresh milk														
Death and disability benefits														
Garden supplies														
Work relief wages	100,453	753,406	3,495,551	3,832,412	4,308,486	2,998,254	2,820,651	2,256,391	2,244,420	2,444,587	2,464,905	2,910,722	2,815,670	3,684,301
Materials for work projects														
Administrative and supervisory salaries	24,196	45,874	54,846	59,569	66,998	69,570	70,476	65,573	67,312	69,648	93,016	97,144	98,401	100,066
Miscellaneous reimbursable expense														
Total	1,018,844	2,180,212	5,415,238	6,563,547	7,807,042	5,676,070	5,388,851	4,781,063	4,864,480	5,291,068	5,248,501	6,250,503	6,626,883	8,484,783
Local Non-Reimbursable Expenditures:														
Home relief	47,065	72,065	82,200	88,930	102,240	96,090	81,505	81,535	86,070	92,740	93,480	93,980	106,887	107,102
Materials for work projects	17,419	130,712	606,462	664,906	747,503	520,183	489,370	391,473	389,397	424,125	427,650	504,997	488,506	639,209
Administrative salaries														
Administrative costs other than salaries	12,342	25,628	55,418	66,667	78,284	59,534	54,597	47,599	48,569	53,187	53,205	62,811	66,266	86,054
Total	76,826	228,405	744,080	820,503	928,027	676,407	625,472	520,607	524,036	570,052	574,335	661,788	663,659	832,365
Relief to Sick and Disabled Veterans							2,000	2,000	4,100	4,100	4,100	4,100	4,100	4,100
Rural Rehabilitation Loans and Grants														
Materials for State Projects		8,874	41,174	45,142	50,750	35,316	33,224	24,544	24,414	26,591	26,812	31,661	30,627	40,076
Central State Administration	18,988	14,822	19,148	21,222	22,258	23,531	29,725	24,998	25,406	24,984	27,904	27,741	31,994	29,522
Total Without Federal Programs	1,114,658	2,432,313	6,219,640	7,450,414	8,808,077	6,411,324	6,079,272	5,353,212	5,442,436	5,916,795	5,881,652	6,975,793	7,357,263	9,390,846
Federal Special Programs														
GRAND TOTAL	1,114,658	2,432,313	6,219,640	7,450,414	8,808,077	6,411,324	6,079,272	5,353,212	5,442,436	5,916,795	5,881,652	6,975,793	7,357,263	9,390,846

TABLE II (Continued)

Type of Expenditures	January 1933	February 1933	March 1933	April 1933	May 1933	June 1933	July 1933	August 1933	September 1933	October 1933	November 1933	December 1933
Local Reimbursable Expenditures.												
Home relief	$4,754,454	$6,188,592	$6,825,827	$5,317,666	$5,594,825	$5,562,578	$4,581,564	$4,552,366	$4,419,364	$5,335,202	$6,216,760	$6,785,941
Care of local homeless	20,543	14,430	14,073	14,226	11,814	11,339	14,494	14,534	14,230	14,039	18,521	32,992
School lunches		70,152	109,461	87,183	115,000	109,156	44,856	55,714	73,478	75,000	100,000	129,230
Fresh milk												
Death and disability benefits												
Garden supplies												
Work relief wages	4,124,182	4,580,592	6,776,345	7,199,994	7,763,913	6,903,462	6,298,609	6,707,602	6,222,384	6,405,490	5,685,742	320,370
Materials for work projects												
Administrative and supervisory salaries	157,724	161,055	166,355	169,563	176,467	184,558	197,380	210,190	223,000	235,810	240,470	209,701
Miscellaneous reimbursable expense												
Total	9,056,903	11,014,821	13,892,061	12,788,632	13,662,019	12,771,093	11,136,903	11,540,406	10,952,456	12,065,541	12,261,493	7,478,234
Local Non-Reimbursable Expenditures:												
Home relief	131,072	129,340	154,332	148,622	136,494	101,430	85,731	76,056	74,624	74,143	79,284	69,115
Materials for work projects	715,527	794,712	1,175,665	1,249,166	1,347,003	1,197,719	1,082,780	1,163,738	1,079,555	1,111,323	986,458	
Administrative salaries												
Administrative costs other than salaries	92,647	109,253	138,963	126,323	133,722	122,220	106,892	111,953	105,815	115,804	117,713	72,147
Total	939,246	1,033,305	1,468,960	1,524,111	1,617,219	1,421,369	1,285,403	1,351,747	1,259,994	1,301,270	1,183,455	141,262
Relief to Sick and Disabled Veterans	4,100	4,100	4,100	4,100	4,100	4,100	4,100	4,100	4,100	4,100	4,100	4,100
Rural Rehabilitation Loans and Grants												
Materials for State Projects	44,861	49,825	73,710	78,318	84,452	75,092	68,513	72,962	67,684	69,676	61,847	39,573
Central State Administration	35,083	29,720	36,779	38,522	39,572	36,677	34,660	34,159	36,513	43,614	42,617	
Total Without Federal Programs	10,060,193	12,131,771	15,475,610	14,433,683	15,407,362	14,308,331	12,529,579	13,003,374	12,320,747	13,484,201	13,553,512	7,663,169
Federal Special Programs											29,760	180,951
GRAND TOTAL WITHOUT C. W. A.	10,060,193	12,131,771	15,475,610	14,433,683	15,407,362	14,308,331	12,529,579	13,003,374	12,320,747	13,484,201	13,583,272	7,844,120

TABLE II (Continued)

Item or Expenditures	January 1934	February 1934	March 1934	April 1934	May 1934	June 1934	July 1934	August 1934	September 1934	October 1934	November 1934	December 1934
Local Reimbursable Expenditures:												
Home relief	$7,192,236	$8,028,388	$9,736,739	$8,694,583	$8,741,413	$8,674,815	$8,912,005	$9,930,568	$9,423,250	$10,986,486	$11,499,972	$13,118,232
Care of local homeless	34,165	52,090	68,654	76,633	73,327	61,737	60,750	60,367	62,726	68,769	74,831	87,000
School lunches	103,234	95,235	134,941	119,597	124,099	119,193	27,815	46,535	62,324	90,513	81,210	76,957
Fresh milk							21,127	24,461	34,957	81,727	102,373	138,735
Death and disability benefits									473	2,586	1,804	1,338
Garden supplies												
Work relief wages	23,494	77,022	85,083	11,758,662	12,454,427	11,567,513	11,660,939	11,035,665	10,038,308	10,899,323	10,200,388	10,200,301
Materials for work projects				1,014,312	1,922,924	2,771,643	2,593,163	3,089,524	2,856,236	2,955,642	3,421,280	2,697,656
Administrative and supervisory salaries	265,956	279,565	312,291	1,973,209	2,784,569	2,894,244	2,587,751	2,551,966	2,410,346	2,662,064	2,631,512	2,708,110
Miscellaneous reimbursable expense												
Total	7,619,085	8,532,300	10,387,708	23,636,996	26,100,759	26,089,145	25,873,550	26,748,086	24,888,620	27,747,110	28,013,370	29,028,329
Local Non-Reimbursable Expenditures:												
Home relief	71,362	61,230	68,042	50,256	46,134	36,439	41,741	35,692	35,930	34,037	34,870	39,006
Materials for work projects				43,737	40,806	42,673	39,382	42,936	32,386	30,906	28,377	27,594
Administrative salaries												
Administrative costs other than salaries	71,805	79,885	96,447	175,000	175,419	229,863	247,806	272,691	251,095	256,021	287,267	322,344
Total	143,167	141,115	164,489	288,993	262,359	308,975	328,929	351,319	319,411	321,864	350,514	388,944
Relief to Sick and Disabled Veterans	4,100	4,100	4,100	4,100	4,100	4,100	4,100	4,100	4,100	4,100	4,100	4,100
Rural Rehabilitation Loans and Grants												
Materials for State Projects				128,073	335,291	290,163	342,552	300,597	138,017	126,224	175,145	99,282
Central State Administration	61,008	45,055	33,567	161,979	159,406	155,113	145,739	213,537	212,403	192,717	201,243	184,355
Total Without Federal Programs	7,827,360	8,722,370	10,589,884	24,200,141	26,861,915	26,847,496	26,694,870	27,617,639	25,562,551	28,392,015	28,744,372	29,705,010
Federal Special Programs	180,951	180,951	180,951	245,213	361,965	327,998	348,189	1,079,813	801,975	925,167	1,142,600	1,517,685
GRAND TOTAL WITHOUT C.W.A.	8,008,311	8,903,521	10,770,815	24,445,354	27,223,880	27,175,494	27,043,059	28,697,452	26,364,526	29,317,182	29,886,972	31,222,695

TABLE II (Continued)

Type of Expenditures	January 1935	February 1935	March 1935	April 1935	May 1935	June 1935	July 1935	August 1935	September 1935	October 1935	November 1935	December 1935
Local Reimbursable Expenditures:												
Home relief	$14,303,893	$13,473,062	$13,973,839	$13,489,702	$13,159,642	$11,666,692	$13,096,144	$12,861,229	$12,510,532	$11,279,451	$9,911,970	$10,740,810
Care of local homeless	132,229	135,679	136,054	130,830	127,293	119,865	115,321	115,452	112,749	131,265	129,273	143,994
School lunches	97,108	90,379	95,211	88,027	97,069	90,486	49,936	50,014	77,898	97,901	85,227	92,815
Fresh milk	276,345	217,750	209,255	213,678	146,016	115,717	74,842	74,892	101,348	128,726	111,537	116,183
Death and disability benefits	4,090	6,304	8,595	7,692	9,241	10,437	10,178	19,990	13,228	17,404	17,751	17,735
Garden supplies												
Work relief wages	10,573,195	9,541,591	10,303,075	10,273,301	10,228,152	9,821,307	10,631,918	6,199,863	4,185,712	3,938,263	2,351,469	237,088
Materials for work projects	2,456,187	2,033,713	2,239,245	1,919,849	2,133,926	2,281,694	2,194,607	1,240,729	1,044,811	847,641	392,737	15,602
Administrative and supervisory salaries	2,907,526	2,814,559	3,121,269	3,179,897	3,374,320	3,266,983	3,613,535	2,804,601	2,440,756	2,609,049	2,338,396	2,238,487
Miscellaneous reimbursable expense	6,160	8,884	11,266	12,810	12,810	12,810	12,810	15,500	16,995	16,770		
Total	30,756,733	28,322,321	30,102,809	29,315,636	29,288,469	27,385,991	29,799,291	23,382,270	20,504,029	19,066,470	15,338,360	13,603,714
Local Non-Reimbursable Expenditures:												
Home relief	40,336	40,066	40,212	40,753	39,193	37,293	35,628	33,701	38,323	39,495	44,222	55,704
Materials for work projects												
Administrative salaries	30,399	30,906	30,952	30,734	29,544	29,656	30,245	30,392	29,638	29,538	29,698	30,862
Administrative costs other than salaries	361,896	283,379	605,460	443,931	425,587	431,918	416,888	315,237	269,406	225,912	252,528	252,819
Total	432,631	354,951	678,624	514,418	494,324	498,867	482,710	379,330	337,367	294,945	326,448	339,445
Relief to Sick and Disabled Veterans	4,100	4,100	4,100	4,100	4,100	4,100	4,100	4,100	4,100	4,100	4,100	4,100
Rural Rehabilitation Loans and Grants					26,584	41,325	21,211	102,720	17,055	933	715	612
Materials for State Projects	155,383	104,326	170,494	247,057	120,283	63,028	132,733	137,210	103,490	157,685	45,706	531
Central State Administration	130,341	198,353	243,346	198,002	207,388	230,533	191,446	192,469	158,150	187,370	161,117	134,332
Total Without Federal Programs	31,529,189	28,984,051	31,199,363	30,279,263	30,141,148	28,213,844	30,631,491	24,198,099	21,124,191	19,711,503	15,866,446	14,081,734
Federal Special Programs	799,445	606,211	911,759	888,211	765,306	640,363	610,277	696,914	760,349	691,639	397,047	393,296
GRAND TOTAL	32,328,633	29,650,262	32,111,122	31,167,474	30,906,454	28,854,207	31,241,768	24,895,013	21,884,540	20,403,142	16,264,093	14,475,029

TABLE II (Continued)

TYPE OF EXPENDITURES	January 1936	February 1936	March 1936	April 1936	May 1936	June 1936	July 1936	August 1936	September 1936	October 1936	November 1936	December 1936
Local Reimbursable Expenditures:												
Home relief	$10,266,086	$10,946,031	$11,332,456	$11,000,309	$10,076,203	$9,528,742	$9,292,643	$9,100,335	$9,173,220	$9,004,658	$9,257,792	$9,975,237
Care of local homeless	162,410	170,030	188,435	157,364	151,351	125,236	114,239	114,239	117,232	126,496	124,945	151,735
School lunches	101,638	97,894	107,369	95,493	99,963	84,490	54,592	51,996	70,016	100,679	89,318	200,597
Fresh milk	132,915	112,837	127,394	116,155	160,362	139,283	90,422	52,516	88,272	112,743	98,096	100,558
Death and disability benefits	18,089	28,714	20,100	17,538	16,284	18,980	14,673	21,328	15,437	12,346	13,756	10,584
Garden supplies			808	9,444	14,105	7,861	5,305	3,753	3,249	2,900	2,550	273
Work relief wages	161,662	123,226	112,130	101,700	94,579	86,364	69,476	66,165	60,696	54,239	42,422	38,629
Materials for work projects	5,909	9,738	1,996	16,781	7,558	7,122	4,438	441	2,133	49	374	606
Administrative and supervisory salaries	2,162,894	1,973,720	1,957,571	1,895,992	1,831,570	1,790,568	1,766,233	1,724,986	1,695,452	1,666,586	1,649,510	1,629,716
Miscellaneous reimbursable expense										214,017	2,911	
Total	13,011,603	13,461,990	13,828,149	13,416,776	12,451,975	11,788,646	11,402,021	11,136,404	11,225,717	11,294,713	11,281,674	12,107,965
Local Non-Reimbursable Expenditures:												
Home relief	67,597	65,847	85,933	82,980	64,053	63,248	56,415	53,867	56,643	58,748	59,400	66,684
Materials for work projects												
Administrative salaries	29,821	29,201	29,518	29,427	29,069	29,279	28,291	28,469	27,903	26,869	27,193	27,166
Administrative costs other than salaries	234,475	214,702	160,712	177,047	173,529	181,197	163,720	164,507	163,239	199,232	198,481	183,047
Total	331,893	309,750	276,163	290,054	266,651	273,724	253,426	246,843	247,790	282,849	285,074	276,897
Relief to Sick and Disabled Veterans	4,100	4,100	4,100	4,100	4,100	4,100	4,100	4,100	4,100	4,100	4,100	4,100
Rural Rehabilitation Loans and Grants	156	26		2,128	4,308	1,212	244	560				
Materials for State Projects												
Central State Administration	155,733	120,356	130,968	125,222	100,653	97,712	110,561	152,907	121,619	94,994	113,963	84,533
Total Without Federal Programs	13,503,485	13,896,222	14,239,380	13,838,280	12,827,687	12,165,394	11,770,342	11,540,814	11,599,126	11,676,656	11,684,811	12,473,405
Federal Special Programs	107,765	63,176	40,009	22,666	34,117	31,904	39,846	24,067	21,516	26,961	22,031	33,160
GRAND TOTAL	13,611,250	13,959,398	14,279,389	13,860,946	12,861,804	12,197,298	11,810,188	11,564,881	11,620,642	11,703,617	11,706,842	12,506,655

TABLE II (Concluded)

Types of Expenditures	January 1937	February 1937	March 1937	April 1937	May 1937	June 1937	Grand Total
Local Reimbursable Expenditures:							
Home relief	$9,040,999	$10,091,807	$10,220,487	$9,790,112	$8,793,567	$8,128,724	$544,954,401
Care of local homeless	150,386	142,645	154,058	139,175	119,488	95,043	5,036,336
School lunches	96,726	96,260	197,399	116,875	108,604	108,525	4,951,077
Fresh milk	106,484	75,776	82,162	79,865	76,454	72,285	4,004,278
Death and disability benefits	15,213	8,960	9,624	8,369	8,398	8,730	416,369
Garden supplies	37			1,025	2,032	977	54,319
Work relief wages	33,405						295,454,647
Materials for work projects	129	704	1,609	1,222			42,183,930
Administrative and supervisory salaries	1,612,960	1,804,000	1,579,217	1,571,028	1,581,155	1,573,919	9,335,001
Miscellaneous reimbursable expense							343,743
Total	11,956,339	12,020,152	12,244,556	11,707,671	10,679,698	9,988,203	990,762,101
Local Non-Reimbursable Expenditures:							
Home relief	64,675	68,033	70,132	65,312	57,264	47,052	4,689,840
Materials for work projects							18,355,558
Administrative salaries	29,159	33,948	34,597	35,109	34,532	33,966	1,224,883
Administrative costs other than salaries	209,393	209,447	179,798	84,839	185,061	156,104	12,117,297
Total	303,227	311,428	284,527	185,260	276,858	237,122	36,397,678
Relief to Sick and Disabled Veterans	4,100	4,100	4,100	4,100	4,100	4,100	250,000
Rural Rehabilitation Loans and Grants	68	238	1,053	644	1,789	1,291	224,872
Materials for State Projects							4,539,405
Central State Administration	101,809	103,009	93,858	90,274	93,489	86,664	7,117,403[1]
Total Without Federal Programs	12,365,543	12,438,927	12,628,094	11,987,949	11,065,935	10,317,380	1,039,281,359[1]
Federal Special Programs	16,082	16,450	40,742	87,121	26,303	43,533	16,423,033
GRAND TOTAL WITHOUT C.W.A.	12,381,625	12,455,377	12,668,836	12,075,070	11,082,238	10,360,913	1,055,704,392[1]

[1] Includes $418,548 for the cost of printing and distributing relief bonds, $500,990 for printing forms for local districts, and $179,596 for administration of Federal programs in the period before costs for Federal programs were strictly segregated. Also includes $320,489 for T.E.R.A. liquidation subsequent to June 30, 1937.

Condensed Statement of Funds, Expenditures, Resources, November 1, 1931–June 30, 1937

	FUNDS MADE AVAILABLE					
1	State					$239,284,244.24
2	Federal					506,023,610.31
3	Contributed					3,300.00
4	Total Funds Made Available					$745,311,1!
	EXPENDITURES AND LIABILITIES					
	Special Federal Programs (Administered by TERA Administration)					
5	Expenditures				$8,274,009.50	
6	Liabilities				305,862.19	
7	Total Special Federal Programs					$8,579,871.69
	Arts and Crafts					
8	Expenditures				2,929.67	
9	Liabilities				370.33	
10	Total Arts and Crafts					3,300.00
	General Relief					
	Expenditures					
	Cities and Counties					
11	Home Relief		$320,331,196.67			
12	Milk for Needy Children		1,388,748.17			
	Work Relief					
13	Wages and Materials	$207,197,724.78				
14	Disability and Death Awards	419,383.14	207,617,107.92			
	Local Bureau Administration					
15	Home Relief	41,893,578.50				
16	Work Relief	18,677,071.74				
17	Printing (Furnished by T.E.R.A.)	500,990.28	61,071,640.52			
18	Total Cities and Counties			$590,408,693.28		
19	State Departments			24,385,386.91		
20	Relief of Sick and Disabled Veterans			184,283.68		
21	Losses through Burglary Reimbursed			546.93		
22	Total Expenditures — General Relief				614,978,910.80]	
23	Liabilities				10,372,782.62	
24	Total General Relief					625,351,693.42

	T.E.R.A. ADMINISTRATION				
	Central Administration (Applicable to Above)				
25	Expenditures	5,847,326.49			
26	Liabilities	172,944.06			
27	Total Central Administration		6,020,270.55		
	Administrative Costs Other Than for Direct Administration of Relief				
28	Expenditures	269,003.05			
29	Liabilities	147,545.00			
30	Total		416,548.05		
31	Total Administration			6,436,818.60	
	Special Federal Programs (Administrative Costs Charged to Programs)				
	Civil Works Administration				
32	Payrolls and Materials — Expenditures	79,081,707.21			
33	Administration — Expenditures	399,748.53	79,481,455.74		
	Civil Works Service Payrolls and Disability Compensation				
34	— Expenditures	8,779,248.16			
35	Administration — Expenditures	38,338.49	8,817,586.65		
	Miscellaneous Federal Programs				
36	Payrolls and Materials — Expenditures	10,449,583.91			
37	Administration — Expenditures	1,052,562.04			
38	Administration — Liabilities	10,000.00	11,512,145.95		
39	Total Special Federal Programs				
40	Payrolls and Materials		98,310,539.28	99,811,188.34	
41	Administration		1,500,649.06		
	Grand Total Expenditures and Liabilities				740,182,872.05
	Resources — Cash Available for Transfer to Department of Social Welfare				5,128,282.50
42	Total Expenditures, Liabilities, Resources				$745,311,154.55

TABLE IV

Statement of Expenditures for and Liabilities to Districts, November 1, 1931–June 30, 1937

GENERAL RELIEF

CITIES	Home Relief	Free Milk for Needy Children	Work Relief Wages	Work Relief Materials	Local Bureau Administration Home Relief	Local Bureau Administration Work Relief	Total Expenditures	Commitments
Albany	$1,219,423.53	$15,561.35	$1,098,890.01	$210,377.79	$193,642.27	$62,204.42	$2,800,099.37	$39,557.08
Amsterdam	600,919.07	4,506.35	512,854.16	102,238.47	54,514.15	12,666.55	1,287,698.75	7,675.17
Auburn	599,263.48	3,543.22	512,728.55	89,070.75	78,173.32	81,613.28	1,364,392.60	25,980.14
Batavia	259,472.93	1,025.75	182,032.22	16,708.29	27,228.72	12,793.68	499,261.59	3,746.53
Beacon	104,847.45	1,404.50	180,248.76	42,065.06	15,588.01	14,906.20	359,059.98	5,542.11
Binghamton	800,818.27	8,176.78	473,497.80	38,807.58	73,284.83	30,243.70	1,424,828.96	28,557.12
Buffalo	21,029,030.71	89,607.92	11,434,744.20	1,591,364.86	1,561,435.32	184,224.06	35,890,407.07	561,996.95
Cohoes	1,002,475.52	2,108.10	597,482.58	36,444.17	90,938.38	31,091.03	1,760,539.78	24,952.39
Corning	178,245.10	1,031.22	207,701.82	35,154.52	19,976.82	14,821.09	456,930.57	3,097.07
Cortland	172,386.79	1,607.16	75,966.89	8,723.48	19,327.56	22,654.99	300,662.37	5,580.75
Dunkirk	500,883.24	3,082.29	377,526.50	33,585.11	41,850.06	11,491.49	968,418.69	57,942.97
Elmira	1,236,067.92	7,599.56	305,774.03	69,487.68	121,756.56	35,696.90	1,777,382.65	......
Fulton	386,053.82	3,344.10	520,156.14	50,302.26	52,096.80	17,711.70	1,029,664.82	8,617.29
Glen Cove	26,163.27		12,886.24		3,404.30	757.93	43,211.74	
Glens Falls	284,356.64	1,711.66	252,862.07	45,831.25	29,448.15	32,878.83	647,088.60	11,484.53
Gloversville	166,640.53	889.08	133,077.75	20,649.37	21,877.76	19,735.36	362,869.85	3,650.04
Hornell	103,318.19	986.85	177,527.51	28,901.40	15,314.29	29,067.03	355,115.27	2,632.41
Hudson	194,145.93	496.84	251,880.82	13,839.75	22,371.99	38,100.50	520,835.83	
Ithaca	239,204.76	2,983.12	311,312.08	60,060.86	41,281.14	39,390.93	694,232.89	4,833.62
Jamestown	874,568.03	11,574.85	419,301.67	54,864.00	102,756.47	56,842.06	1,519,907.08	32,660.37
Johnstown	41,120.87	662.76	41,928.24	9,633.38	9,875.10	6,807.70	110,028.05	1,208.83
Kingston	448,315.94	4,122.66	536,146.99	151,395.25	42,640.04	42,874.50	1,225,495.38	16,405.85
Lackawanna	245,906.10		249,433.65		15,513.59	7,275.00	518,128.34	
Little Falls	75,791.06	1,239.44	85,611.29	17,837.11	20,183.12	8,176.40	208,838.42	1,207.29
Lockport	407,629.88	3,486.87	254,837.40	39,424.72	53,409.93	25,904.13	784,692.93	8,536.15

Long Beach	5,413.98	......	35,684.90	......	1,250.00	793.33	43,142.21	......
Mechanicville	107,354.15	463.95	94,753.38	4,460.83	12,745.94	12,919.46	232,697.71	82.57
Middletown	93,971.57	430.02	129,820.96	2,964.23	9,028.35	8,652.97	264,868.10	1,579.06
Mount Vernon	1,143,083.32	6,832.09	1,016,835.67	172,087.04	114,987.69	66,935.67	2,520,761.48	28,471.13
Newburgh	528,429.86	2,157.21	402,083.64	97,750.32	58,523.19	40,192.97	1,129,137.19	14,677.70
New	1,655,115.74	5,875.51	1,011,470.29	221,211.94	151,353.11	61,781.70	3,106,808.29	73,398.28
New York City	219,999,440.97	757,421.26	100,171,109.19	14,825,290.17	31,930,459.39	13,897,236.54	381,580,957.52	5,662,681.57
Niagara Falls	1,588,264.14	15,848.22	1,581,773.48	195,234.11	201,153.66	95,178.00	3,677,451.61	41,366.16
Nth Tonawanda	390,091.38	2,382.14	498,080.46	49,740.21	37,508.11	15,528.67	993,330.97	2,831.27
Norwich	61,516.31	690.34	37,782.63	274.67	8,961.68	1,793.96	111,019.59	2,165.38
Ogdensburg	142,492.17	1,383.32	359,705.62	63,348.13	23,680.94	11,065.38	601,675.56	4,595.78
Olean	157,786.82	661.57	275,503.43	29,598.54	21,901.08	36,820.44	522,271.88	3,578.98
Oneida	57,840.56	591.02	43,915.35	13,863.21	5,831.55	11,114.12	133,155.81	1,876.92
Oneonta	30,787.58	......	117,367.35	24,163.73	5,296.64	11,667.41	189,282.71	1,061.12
Oswego	531,609.63	3,888.93	795,858.68	120,789.44	45,139.45	76,611.18	1,573,897.31	20,043.89
Plattsburgh	111,587.95	675.00	80,021.64	4,262.35	9,724.84	7,008.28	213,280.06	3,920.58
Port Jervis	138,793.97	2,029.06	309,210.00	54,002.95	20,488.05	43,427.59	567,951.62	10,447.96
Poughkeepsie	863,551.48	5,274.09	342,416.50	65,627.74	79,660.78	58,513.82	1,415,044.41	15,649.55
Rensselaer	120,092.29	1,559.22	102,522.75	12,557.40	22,041.16	21,038.26	279,811.10	5,987.58
Rochester	10,121,054.11	72,535.21	4,708,876.34	909,528.45	807,324.00	332,471.92	16,951,790.03	303,512.83
Rome	432,714.24	5,599.74	429,359.89	109,769.98	51,473.37	17,884.41	1,046,801.63	14,310.59
Salamanca	208,011.68	1,766.43	94,970.97	18,459.71	15,226.21	8,501.09	346,936.09	3,462.32
Saratoga Springs	153,110.79	830.55	144,290.22	30,605.98	27,721.97	33,087.57	389,647.08	4,247.04
Schenectady	1,529,092.53	7,432.71	1,808,243.72	325,686.84	203,507.37	67,994.23	3,941,957.40	27,621.85
Syracuse	4,861,082.41	42,800.24	4,310,297.75	830,523.25	677,583.62	183,495.01	10,905,782.28	196,345.50
Tonawanda	85,235.36	......	81,534.95	3,247.35	4,071.56	3,753.74	177,842.96	34,732.43
Troy	949,384.87	9,857.37	573,781.63	84,853.24	150,825.55	91,720.91	1,860,423.57	72,581.98
Utica	1,824,864.37	14,273.47	1,341,314.44	95,594.52	307,244.04	99,423.34	3,682,714.18	23,741.05
Watertown	827,761.43	4,550.26	571,892.24	61,805.99	80,543.36	37,336.54	1,583,889.82	3,721.97
Watervliet	136,632.96	2,042.35	37,361.51	1,802.97	14,291.72	699.75	192,831.26	......
White Plains	1,254,116.17	5,937.14	519,875.53	96,470.69	138,064.71	34,856.39	2,049,320.63	35,074.87
Yonkers	3,231,661.42	17,242.32	2,409,766.45	225,145.93	241,959.08	101,926.80	6,227,702.00	118,585.15
Town of Union	13,941.24	......	......	......	3,068.58	......	17,009.82	3,161.05
TOTAL CITIES	$284,552,936.48	$1,163,783.19	$143,643,886.43	$21,537,489.02	$38,210,529.43	$16,332,360.91	$505,440,985.46	$7,593,578.77

TABLE IV (Continued)

GENERAL RELIEF

Counties	Home Relief	Free Milk for Needy Children	Work Relief		Local Bureau Administration		Total Expenditures	Receipts
			Wages	Materials	Home Relief	Work Relief		
Albany	$265,678.59	$311.25	$406,919.59	$47,497.43	$46,123.30	$29,956.69	$796,486.85	$10,591.76
Allegany	221,481.65	2,241.04	127,556.51	8,745.04	25,181.95	15,044.88	400,251.07	14,121.96
Broome	504,010.74	98.55	360,759.41	50,075.21	49,190.13	34,314.55	998,448.59	38,955.58
Cattaraugus	260,739.99	2,009.05	241,326.77	43,024.20	34,803.83	27,524.14	609,427.98	16,922.77
Cayuga	163,720.82	362.15	145,546.77	13,760.86	11,147.64	16,964.91	351,503.15	8,672.52
Chautauqua	450,916.60	2,919.06	282,072.51	78,949.30	22,338.44	25,277.60	862,473.51	18,638.61
Chemung	547,240.52	2,340.44	250,858.41	24,237.13	54,564.13	26,539.82	905,780.45	27,711.10
Chenango	92,000.18	1,007.81	132,212.05	20,560.91	15,059.61	16,998.67	277,839.23	4,787.55
Clinton	142,321.11	386.32	137,025.07	33,343.13	11,610.07	24,676.59	349,362.29	4,807.80
Columbia	96,768.73	422.73	168,381.17	30,653.47	25,737.07	24,566.66	346,529.83	1,978.52
Cortland	77,366.10	550.78	85,857.03	24,590.93	12,402.60	13,279.60	214,047.04	2,172.01
Delaware	188,367.41	3,258.95	130,913.06	20,986.28	19,171.50	18,224.02	380,921.22	9,903.09
Dutchess	541,333.79	1,397.01	327,937.19	53,938.45	72,685.18	45,559.43	1,042,851.05	15,880.14
Erie	5,025,113.33	19,349.04	4,179,628.50	378,997.46	547,818.62	49,533.17	10,200,440.12	244,785.46
Essex	499,824.87	3,326.01	441,145.01	65,817.45	38,802.47	26,429.80	1,075,345.61	23,023.58
Franklin	706,294.38	4,751.12	382,208.83	36,951.12	54,233.49	44,648.40	1,229,182.34	23,053.40
Fulton	116,463.02	727.17	84,817.87	269.99	22,086.42	11,846.18	236,210.65	6,215.93
Genesee	241,602.85	807.22	108,367.49	18,134.48	8,492.57	6,281.98	383,686.59	8,769.12
Greene	112,338.52	1,312.79	59,597.59	17,598.56	16,093.66	16,061.88	223,000.00	2,609.42
Hamilton	27,187.87	483.60	48,920.42	9,794.13	4,909.31	5,684.65	96,979.98	624.28
Herkimer	687,132.95	5,216.26	395,115.76	108,312.29	68,774.51	49,599.77	1,314,151.54	22,077.93
Jefferson	728,253.80	3,000.56	270,093.75	21,711.54	39,277.90	28,996.19	1,091,333.74	24,422.10
Lewis	138,025.34	1,058.34	167,784.56	6,065.09	2,624.11	13,081.40	328,638.84	7,811.62
Livingston	350,460.24	29.60	169,101.00	87,729.49	25,960.37	42,358.44	675,639.14	13,627.27
Madison	132,076.91	957.00	107,092.92	8,857.65	12,915.80	10,834.75	272,735.03	6,577.51
Monroe	2,246,741.65	18,892.24	3,051,235.04	453,700.04	278,776.06	136,850.93	6,186,195.96	85,447.79
Montgomery	177,256.61	854.43	173,284.08	8,885.20	45,849.42	26,043.05	432,172.79	6,755.85
Nassau	6,281,710.80	49,540.23	8,429,243.40	498,935.96	814,040.58	121,350.68	16,194,821.65	180,532.46
Niagara	133,818.02	1,288.01	164,016.78	19,133.53	9,330.97	7,408.87	334,996.18	2,976.00
Oneida	499,296.56	4,308.24	253,974.91	2,489.39	49,359.78	39,237.98	848,666.86	10,925.96

Onondaga	1,208,225.10	10,781.02	1,562,425.29	146,883.32	134,022.51	45,728.77	3,108,066.01	75,646.08
Ontario	670,063.38	3,089.13	268,924.18	46,383.55	55,294.93	16,956.99	1,060,712.16	58,046.24
Orange	312,173.46	2,279.72	599,300.68	123,500.14	31,064.59	42,924.62	1,111,243.21	6,585.12
Orleans	137,193.85	1,037.49	207,501.93	40,268.52	9,717.94	19,486.51	415,206.24	6,025.84
Otsego	134,088.67	774.03	119,417.67	33,830.40	13,565.43	20,121.59	321,797.79	7,249.46
Putnam	120,034.94		108,742.21	6,441.59	18,446.55	15,876.04	269,541.33	5,094.69
Rensselaer	235,524.15	1,539.18	63,815.80	4,792.09	6,982.13	19,672.53	332,325.88	42,811.50
Rockland	486,869.56	4,862.27	350,547.52	71,258.40	58,297.02	12,101.71	983,936.48	13,495.05
St. Lawrence	708,857.70	5,401.73	593,983.37	98,966.04	50,336.34	49,758.10	1,507,303.28	31,269.62
Saratoga	317,839.46	985.52	473,563.92	5,798.83	18,247.58	26,889.11	843,324.42	21,534.01
Schenectady	835,179.20	4,755.03	656,419.67	94,541.55	86,364.36	94,723.99	1,771,983.80	26,021.95
Schohàrie	34,959.17	238.68	85,445.16	6,062.75	8,906.16	22,642.08	158,254.00	1,588.76
Schuyler	193,029.31	1,277.57	43,461.15	29,317.68	8,198.55	18,472.58	293,756.84	7,517.21
Seneca	225,652.14	783.78	130,037.42	24,500.09	11,180.74	20,430.45	412,584.62	7,369.50
Steuben	323,511.89	1,969.51	295,318.17	71,512.06	19,459.67	89,126.17	800,897.47	10,382.18
Suffolk	2,061,443.04	10,307.99	2,432,118.44	235,042.47	230,918.94	157,130.54	5,126,961.42	90,838.15
Sullivan	96,237.79	52.30	106,399.87	18,524.27	7,941.51	19,046.33	248,202.16	4,535.82
Tioga	236,236.08	706.08	85,787.18	16,042.67	22,024.12	13,300.93	373,929.22	8,982.32
Tompkins	118,288.26	301.59	130,958.49	42,419.66	10,053.69	38,753.71	340,775.40	2,974.54
Ulster	327,356.38	3,897.72	360,675.32	39,869.87	37,409.78	34,461.18	803,670.25	9,957.38
Warren	135,302.57	885.32	90,097.16	9,220.51	13,846.64	22,922.57	272,274.77	5,342.94
Washington	594,822.03	4,447.13	385,429.18	94,586.37	35,280.58	52,389.69	1,166,954.98	14,257.58
Wayne	368,255.47	3,001.64	191,229.18	46,632.91	16,140.79	39,664.37	664,924.36	15,864.94
Wester	3,898,772.50	25,257.23	4,818,415.58	155,406.36	301,173.88	131,941.72	9,330,967.27	276,305.44
Wyoming	217,759.99	2,065.31	161,562.71	32,812.93	11,783.89	19,795.35	445,780.18	3,582.11
Yates	125,207.99	1,060.92			10,580.93		136,849.84	3,243.35
Total Counties...	$35,778,260.19	$224,964.98	$35,604,570.70	$3,688,360.74	$3,666,695.74	$1,999,493.31	$80,962,345.66	$1,601,900.87
Grand Total..	$320,331,196.67	$1,388,748.17	$179,248,457.13	$25,225,849.76	$41,877,225.17	$18,331,854.22	$586,403,331.12	$9,195,479.64
N. Y. C. WPA Projects (Federal Funds only).			$2,554,644.41	$168,773.48	$16,353.33	$345,217.52	$3,084,988.74	

Publications of the Administration

Rules Concerning Home Relief. December, 1931 (8 pp.).
Rules Concerning Work Relief. December, 1931 (8 pp.).
Rules on Home Relief Relating to Records. December, 1931 (8 pp.).
Report of Temporary Emergency Relief Administration. January, 1932 (20 pp.).
Report of the Temporary Emergency Relief Administration. February, 1932 (16 pp.).
Explanations Governing Rules on Home Relief Relating to Records. May, 1932 (12 pp.).
Explanations Governing Rules on Work Relief Relating to Records. May, 1932 (8 pp.).
Methods of Reducing the Cost of Food Relief. June, 1932 (Mimeograph, 9 pp.).
Rules Governing Home Relief and Work Relief. June, 1932 (8 pp.).
Rules on Home Relief Relating to Records. June, 1932 (8 pp.).
Rules on Work Relief Relating to Records. June, 1932 (8 pp.).
Food Allowances. August, 1932 (30 pp.).
Emergency Unemployment Relief Laws in the State of New York: the Interpretation and Application of Emergency Relief Laws. October, 1932 (202 pp.).
Report of the New York State Temporary Emergency Relief Administration. October, 1932 (86 pp.).
Relief Needs in New York State, November 1, 1931–September 15, 1932. October, 1932 (15 pp.).
Summary of Relief Provided by State and Local Public Funds for the Year ending October 31, 1932. December, 1932 (Photo-offset, 21 pp.).
Subsistence Gardens in New York State in 1932. May, 1933 (22 pp.).
Reduction of Food Costs. May, 1933 (31 pp.).
Social Service in Local Public Relief Administration. May, 1933 (Mimeograph, 64 pp.).
Emergency Relief Act of the State of New York. July, 1933 (Mimeograph, 16 pp.).
Food Allowance Standards in the Up-State Welfare Districts. August, 1933 (Mimeograph, 65 pp.).
Local Administration of Public Relief: Personnel and Expenditures in Administration of Public Home and Work Relief. September, 1933 (Mimeograph, 72 pp.).
Relief Today in New York State, November 1, 1931–September 15, 1933. October, 1933 (17 pp.).
Relief Funds for Shelter: Policies and Practices. November, 1933 (Mimeograph, 70 pp.).
Report on Subsistence Gardens in New York State for 1933. April, 1934 (44 pp.).
Relief Activities of City and County Welfare Districts in Cooperation with the State Temporary Emergency Relief Administration. November 1, 1931–December 31, 1933 (135 pp.).
Standards of Home Relief Administration in 58 Cities and 56 Counties. May, 1934 (Mimeograph, 416 pp.).
The State in Public Unemployment Relief. March, 1934 (25 pp.).
Manual of Rules and Regulations Governing Medical Care. June, 1934 (50 pp.).
Emergency Relief Act in the State of New York and Related Statutes as Amended to July 1, 1934 (37 pp.).
Three Years of Public Unemployment Relief in New York State: The Need and How It Has Been Met. October, 1934 (29 pp.).
Rules Governing Home Relief and Work Relief. November, 1934 (8 pp.).
Emergency Relief in the State of New York: Statutes, Regulations, Opinions and Interpretation of Counsel. November, 1934 (240 pp.).
Home Relief Standards and Comparative Study of Home Relief and Work Relief in Nine Districts. December, 1934 (Photo-offset, 25 pp.).
Social Service Personnel in Local Public Relief Administration. February, 1935 (Photo-offset 30 pp.).
Comparative Summaries of Standards of Home Relief Administration in Up-State City Welfare Districts, November, 1931, May, 1933 and May, 1934. March, 1935 (Photo-offset, 119 pp.).
Social Service Exchanges and Central Indexes in New York State. March, 1935 (Photo-offset, 12 pp.).
Administration of Public Unemployment Relief in New York State. May, 1935 (37 pp.).
Aiding the Unemployed: Survey of Methods and Trends in 24 Foreign Countries. October, 1935 (104 pp.).
Public Unemployment Relief in New York State—Fourth Year. October, 1935 (37 pp.).
Budget Manual: The Family Budget as a Basis for Home Relief. November, 1935 (27 pp.).
Manual of Procedure for Local Relief Administrations. January, 1936.
A Manual on Legal Settlement for Public Welfare Agencies in New York State. February, 1936 (72 pp.).
Manual of Medical Care. March, 1936 (56 pp.).
Unemployment Relief in New York State, September 1, 1935–August 31, 1936. October, 1936 (26 pp.).
Five Million People—One Billion Dollars: Final Report of the Temporary Emergency Relief Administration. June, 1937 (67 pp.).
Monthly Bulletin on Public Relief Statistics. (Mimeograph, June–September, 1932, Photo-offset, October, 1932–June, 1937.)

Lightning Source UK Ltd.
Milton Keynes UK
UKHW021842271118
333060UK00011B/865/P